## DATE DUE

# Abe Fortas

*Abe Fortas* (1968) by Stanley Murphy. This painting hangs in the Yale Law School, where Fortas was student and professor.

LAURA   KALMAN

# Abe Fortas

A  BIOGRAPHY

Yale University Press    New Haven and London

Published with assistance from the
foundation established in memory of
Calvin Chapin of the Class of 1788,
Yale College.

Designed by James J. Johnson.
Set in Fairfield type by
The Composing Room of Michigan, Inc.
Printed in the United States of America by
Vail-Ballou Press, Binghamton, New York.

*Library of Congress Cataloging-in-Publication Data*

Kalman, Laura, 1955–
Abe Fortas : a biography / Laura Kalman.
p.   cm.
Includes bibliographical references.
ISBN 0-300-04669-3 (alk. paper)
1. Fortas, Abe.   2. Judges—United States—Biography.   I. Title.
KF8745.F65K35   1990
347.73'2634—dc20
[B]
[347.3073534]
[B]
90–31482
CIP

The paper in this book meets the guidelines for permanence and
durability of the Committee on Production Guidelines for Book Longevity of the
Council on Library Resources.

10 9 8 7 6 5 4 3 2 1

*For John Morton Blum*

# Contents

List of Illustrations     ix

Acknowledgments     xi

Prologue     1

## Part One. The New Dealer

ONE   Outsider     7

TWO   "The Greatest Law Firm in the Country"     27

THREE   Professor and Inquisitor     49

FOUR   The Lawyer as Bureaucrat     65

FIVE   Under Secretary     77

SIX   From Public Service to the Private Sector, 1     102

## Part Two. The Washington Lawyer

SEVEN   Cold War Distractions     125

EIGHT   The Washington Lawyer     152

NINE   The Actor     184

## Part Three. On and Off the Bench

TEN   The Adviser, 1     199

ELEVEN   New Roles     228

TWELVE  The Lawyer as Justice                                    249

THIRTEEN  Revolution                                             277

FOURTEEN  The Adviser, II                                        293

FIFTEEN  On the Defensive                                        319

SIXTEEN  From Public Service to the Private Sector, II           359

SEVENTEEN  "Suddenly Everything Seems Old-Fashioned"            379


Notes                                                           403

Index                                                           487

# Illustrations

*Frontispiece: Abe Fortas* by Stanley Murphy. *Courtesy Yale University Art Gallery. Gift of Arnold & Porter to the Law School.*

*Following page 76*

1. Fortas as a child. *Fortas Family Scrapbook; hereafter FFS.*
2. Young Fortas and friend. *FFS.*
3. High school graduation. *FFS.*
4. Blue Melody Boys. *FFS.*
5. Peach Case staff. *FFS.*
6. Abe Fortas and Carolyn Agger. *FFS.*
7. William O. Douglas named to Court. *Collection Supreme Court of the United States.*
8. General Counsel of the Public Works Administration. *Courtesy Carolyn Agger Fortas.*
9. Under Secretary, Department of the Interior. *FFS.*
10. With Harold Ickes. *Courtesy Carolyn Agger Fortas.*
11. Agger and Fortas with Jane and Harold Ickes. *Courtesy Carolyn Agger Fortas.*
12. Cabinet meeting, 1945. *Courtesy Carolyn Agger Fortas.*
13. Loyalty hearing for Owen Lattimore. *Michael Rougier,* Life *magazine, May 1, 1950,* © *Time, Inc.*
14. Bar association dinner. *Courtesy Arnold & Porter.*
15. At a Washington party. *Courtesy Carolyn Agger Fortas.*
16. Fortas as a Washington lawyer. *Courtesy Carolyn Agger Fortas.*

*Following page 248*

17. With Lyndon Johnson in the White House corridors. *Courtesy Lyndon Baines Johnson Library; hereafter LBJ Library.*

18. "I, Abe Fortas—." *Drawing © 1965 by Herblock in the* Washington Post.

19. "Not Yet." *Drawing by Alan Dunn, © 1965, The New Yorker Magazine, Inc.*

20. The Warren Court. *© National Geographic Society.*

21. Fortas arriving in Puerto Rico. *© 1966,* El Mundo.

22. With LBJ in the White House situation room. *LBJ Library.*

23. Cabinet meeting, 1965. *LBJ Library.*

24. White House discussion group. *LBJ Library.*

25. Drafting State of Union address. *LBJ Library.*

26. Announcement of Hirshhorn museum. *LBJ Library.*

27. 3025 N Street Quartet. *Courtesy Carolyn Agger Fortas.*

28. With Pablo Casals. *Courtesy Monique Lehner.*

29. Making music at the White House. *LBJ Library.*

30. With Lady Bird Johnson. *Collection Supreme Court of the United States.*

31. Hearing of the chief justice nomination. *Courtesy Monique Lehner.*

32. Fortas and Agger at their Westport home. *© 1968,* New York Times.

33. *Time* cover portrait. *Copyright 1968, Time, Inc. Reprinted by permission.*

34. Newspaper account of nomination hearing. *© 1968,* Washington Post.

35. Justices at Earl Warren's funeral. *Collection Supreme Court of the United States.*

# Acknowledgments

This book could not have been written without the help of three extraordinary women. Bella Linden chose me as the author. Mercedes Eichholz spent days talking with me about Abe Fortas and laboring over the photograph section. Carolyn Agger Fortas facilitated my work in every way, granting all of my requests for access, encouraging other people to speak with me, and always paying me the compliment of treating me as more than her husband's biographer.

The Fortas trail stretches from Berkeley to San Juan. I am obligated to the archivists at the Bancroft Library, the Columbia Oral History Project, the Franklin D. Roosevelt Library, the Gerald R. Ford Library, the Harry S. Truman Library, Haverford College, the John F. Kennedy Library, the Library of Congress, the University of Michigan, the National Archives, the Nixon Presidential Materials Project, the University of Oklahoma, the University of Oregon, the University of Puget Sound, Southwestern College, the University of Washington, the State Historical Society of Wisconsin, and the University of Wyoming, and especially to the archivists at Yale University. Claudia Anderson, Linda Hanson, Tina Houston, David Humphries, Robert Tissing, and Nancy Smith were gifted guides to the Lyndon B. Johnson Library.

In addition to Mrs. Fortas, I thank the firm of Fortas, Prokop & Hardman for granting me access to Fortas's personal papers, a portion of which will eventually be made available at Yale University to scholars. Fortas, Prokop & Hardman also provided me with a temporary office, and Abe Fortas's efficient former assistant, Inge Seckinger, made my stay there enjoyable. Fred Graham permitted me to quote from his papers deposited in the Library of Congress. I am grateful to the Fundación Luis Muñoz Marín for enabling me to see the Arnold, Fortas & Porter Office Files relating to Puerto Rico. Located on the grounds of Muñoz's summer house in Trujillo Alto, the Fundación proved a wonderful place to examine these materials. In Washington, the firm of Arnold & Porter made numerous non-privileged documents from the Fortas era available to me, and Katherine L. Q. Britton, Milton Freeman, Veronica Honsborough, Kim Marandino, Irvin Nathan, and G. Duane Vieth offered eleventh-hour assistance in readying the manuscript for publication. In Memphis, Fortas's sister, Esta Bloom, and the Gold family provided help and hospitality. In addition, I am very grateful to all the people who took the time to tell me about their particular Abe Fortas and give me a sense of his complexity.

A grant from the American Council of Learned Societies; a Faculty Career Development Award from the University of California, Santa Barbara; and a Regents' Junior Faculty Fellowship from the University of California enabled me to begin archival research. With the encouragement of Jeffrey Russell, the University of California, Santa Barbara, Academic Senate Committee on Research funded the work of Judith Parker, who ably transcribed hours of tapes. The American Bar Foundation twice subsidized this research, the first time through one of its legal history grants and the second by appointing me a Visiting Research Fellow in 1986–87. My research assistant at the bar foundation, Darren S. Weingard, combed the libraries of Chicago and proved an excellent critic. I am also indebted to two former students, Eric Hermann and Mark McGuire.

Many people generously read the book while it was still in manuscript. I thank Luis Agrait, William L. F. Felstiner, John Frank, Milton Freeman, Terence Halliday, Kenneth Karst, William E. Leuchtenburg, David Rabban, John Reid, Daniel Rezneck, James Simon, Rayman Solomon, and G. Duane Vieth for commenting on various chapters. Richard Abrams, John Morton Blum, Morton Borden, Robert Dallek, Mercedes Eichholz, Kermit Hall, Bella Linden, Charles Reich, and G. Edward White read the entire manuscript and made many helpful suggestions for revision. William E. Nelson read it twice, as did the members of the NYU Legal History Colloquium. Athan Theoharis kindly shared his FBI documents with me. It is a pleasure to acknowledge the sustained enthusiasm that Charles Grench, my editor at Yale University Press, has displayed for this book. I thank my talented manuscript editor at Yale Press, Cynthia Wells, for the painstaking attention she gave to the project in its final stages, and also thank Kathy Caruso, James Johnson, and Alexa Selph.

Writing a biography forced me to think about my own life and the many people who have contributed so much to it and to this book. Celeste Garr, Lee Kalman, and Newton Kalman furnished constant support. Gladys and Arthur Hirsch, and Nancy and R. Daniel Smith offered prolonged hospitality. I am also grateful to Penn Borden, Hope Firestone, Rena Fraden, Jamie Gracer, Tim Hanlon, W. D. King, Kate Saltzman-Li, David Marshall, Caroline and Clifford

Mass, Joan Murdoch, John Schweizer, Judy Shanks, Susan Smulyan, Candace Waid, and Rosemarie Zagarri. Above all, I thank W. Randall Garr.

Twelve years ago, John Blum introduced me to archival research and the New Deal. Since then, he has served as a model in three respects. He has been an engaging teacher, a scholar who combined intellectual integrity with civility, and an invaluable friend. It is to him that I dedicate this book.

# Prologue

ABE FORTAS WANTED TO BECOME A SUPREME COURT JUSTICE, PRE-
tended otherwise, was appointed anyway, nearly became Chief Justice,
and resigned in disgrace. Raised in modest circumstances, he became a
New Dealer, a subcabinet official, the founder of an eminent Washington law firm, a close adviser to Lyndon Johnson, and a member of the Warren
Court. He also brought the Hirshhorn Museum to Washington and ensured the
success of the Kennedy Center.

Few understood him. A private man, he did more for others than he allowed
them to do for him. He once remarked, "Friendship requires giving and taking;
and taking from others is the more difficult part."[1] Consequently descriptions of
Fortas varied dramatically. Some found him unspeakably tough; others, un-
abashedly affectionate. He seemed to want it that way. Above all, he was a
consummate actor. Because control mattered so much to him, he also wrote the
script. He could pretend anguish that was not there and adulation he did not feel.
Skeptical of biographies, toward the end of his life he tried to discourage the
writing of one by "proudly" telling a visitor, "I kept no copies of anything. I don't
even have copies of the speeches I gave."[2] Like others before him, the caller went
away convinced Fortas had retained nothing, when in fact his files bulged with
copies of his speeches, correspondence, and White House memoranda. No role
was too difficult for Fortas, and no two parts clashed, for he had an extraordinary
ability to compartmentalize his life.

The two most significant compartments were those of lawyer and musician.
Fortas himself perceived this primary duality. Asked for "a personal statement of
faith" by an artist who was painting his portrait, he wrote, "The law and music
are emotion and discipline. For me, the one without the other is barren."[3] Oddly,
Fortas inverted his words there. For him, law represented discipline; music,
emotion. Law was his life, music his love.

With his friends and clients, he was a lawyer. Throughout his life, Fortas

I

transmuted friends into clients and clients into friends. He designed ingenious strategies for protecting their interests. Though he was sometimes accused of cutting corners on their behalf, strictly speaking he did not. As a government lawyer, private practitioner, and Supreme Court justice, he did subordinate process to substance, for he believed that the ends justified the means. But the means had to be legal, and if they were not, he devised a way of bringing them within the law. Where his own affairs were concerned, however, the lawyer became more like a musician. Chamber music demands as much precision as law. But because Fortas pursued it as an avocation, music symbolized freedom to him. And he could be reckless in his personal affairs. He tolerated behavior in himself that he would not have accepted in a client or friend. As a public servant and officer of the court, he prescribed rules for society. As a private individual, he bent them.

In crises Fortas belatedly tried to become his own lawyer. He would describe his own behavior, which sometimes had been incautious, in terms framed to impress others in his profession with its legal correctness. Tragically, for himself, he rarely considered how journalists or politicians would judge his conduct. He viewed the world as a giant courtroom, and, though he thought he could take more liberties in it than he allowed his clients and friends, he never had as much freedom as he would have liked. The press and Congress, two institutions he profoundly distrusted throughout his life, frequently stymied him.

There were other contradictions. He was an outsider who played the consummate insider. His contemporaries viewed him as an elder, but he remained boyishly playful. He was relentlessly ambitious, but he was remarkably loyal to friends and clients. He seemed to think only of himself, but he often willingly sacrificed for others. He was a committed reformer, but he often seemed more a technocrat than an idealist. He wanted to do good, but he was equally interested in making good. He was an actor, lawyer, and musician; a devoted social reformer who reminded some of Sammy Glick and others of the prototypical bureaucrat.

Any biography of Abe Fortas necessarily must focus on his public life. The private man remains elusive. If Fortas did reflect upon his life, he left no record of his conclusions for posterity. His personal papers provide more insight into his activities than they do into his inner self.

Fortas's career mirrored the development of American political and legal liberalism. The liberalism that politicians such as Franklin Roosevelt and Lyndon Johnson espoused implied an instrumental view of social change and promised something to everyone from big businessmen to vagrants. The beginnings of this centrist liberalism first appeared in the Progressive Era, as individuals such as Charles Evans Hughes championed both big business and civil liberties.

Fortas's particular version of liberalism, which drew from his experience in the New Deal, had several facets. It demanded a strong executive branch of government, which Fortas advocated as a New Dealer and adviser to Lyndon Johnson. It meant intervention abroad, and at times Fortas seemed globalism's strongest advocate. Further, it entailed the preservation of capitalism, a goal Fortas advanced through his imaginative representation of corporations. Yet his liberalism also implied a commitment to civil liberties, civil rights, and the broader issues of social welfare. As New Dealer and Johnson intimate, Fortas was preoccupied with social justice.

The jurisprudential analogue of American political liberalism, legal liberalism, was also the product of the New Deal.[4] Fortas came of age at a time when ideas about law, public service, and government were dramatically changing. Proponents of the school of legal realism, with its emphasis on the role of idiosyncrasy in the judicial process, challenged the notion of enduring principles that determine the course of law. The New Deal's emphasis on meritocracy meant fresh opportunities for Jewish and Irish Catholic lawyers. Their intelligence won them access to new positions of power, and they tried to guarantee that only the intellectually qualified would serve the public interest by promoting the regulatory state, with its emphasis on the neutral expert who would possess wide-ranging discretion. As long as they were serving the public good, these lawyers believed they could manipulate or abandon the rules they themselves made. Their operating principles were therefore relativistic and particularistic. A faith that the state could resolve conflicts between competing interest groups by delegating its authority to regulators who would develop the right law for each situation became the foundation of their legal liberalism.

Government service during the New Deal enfranchised Fortas and other outsiders. It enabled them successfully to seek employment later in the private sector. There they retained faith in their own righteousness even as they turned their principal efforts to private pursuits in the aftermath of World War II and began representing the interests they had once attacked. Not until Lyndon Johnson became President and launched the Great Society were their goals again bruited around the corridors of power. And it was during the Great Society period that the tension between two fundamental liberal values—faith in positive action by government to protect the powerless and belief in the rights of dissident minorities against the state—became particularly acute. Yet although New Deal ideas were incorporated into American public philosophy during the 1960s, few veterans of the earlier program actually helped to implement Johnson's social agenda.[5] Fortas was a notable exception, a link between New Deal and Great Society. Few symbolized liberalism's promise and paradoxes as well as Abe Fortas.

PART I

*The New Dealer*

# CHAPTER 1

# Outsider

H E WAS AN OUTSIDER EVEN IN HIS OWN FAMILY. HE WAS THE ONLY one to attend college, the only one to become a professional, the only one to leave home before marriage. More than any of his siblings, he cut himself off from his childhood. He was the only one to become famous.

Abe Fortas's parents, Woolfe and Rachel Berzansky Fortas, were born in Eastern Europe; Woolfe in Russia in 1872, Rachel in Lithuania a year later. Rachel Fortas was remembered as a classic "Jewish mother" who cared about her husband and children to the exclusion of all else. Woolfe Fortas was multilingual, an amateur musician steeped in the culture of three continents. Before settling in the United States, he had lived in Russia, Africa, and England. He and Rachel decided to leave England, where they owned and managed a china store in Leeds, to join Woolfe's brother, Joe, in Memphis. They arrived in Tennessee with their children Nelle, Mary, and Meyer in 1905. Esta appeared three years later; Abe on June 19, 1910.[1]

In Memphis, the Fortas brothers ran a furniture factory until illness forced Woolfe to leave the business. He later owned a men's clothing and jewelry store. Though he was not a gifted businessman, Woolfe was able to provide his family with a life that was not uncomfortable. Her family was "ordinary," Esta Fortas Bloom recalled. It did not have a great deal of money, but it was not impoverished either. Her parents always owned an automobile and employed a domestic servant to help with household chores. Abe Fortas's life was no Horatio Alger story. As he became famous, reporters delighted in portraying him that way, and Fortas sometimes obliged by saying that his family had been "as poor as you can imagine."[2] But he put it more accurately when he wrote a great-nephew: "Your grandfather Fortas' generation (here, in South Africa and in England) struggled with adversity. My generation and that of your father's—both here and in South Africa—were more fortunate; but we had to make our way in circumstances of limited resources and opportunity."[3]

Abe Fortas had been born in a modest area of Memphis, but when he was a boy the family moved to larger and more comfortable houses, first on Linden Avenue, and then one street over to Pontotoc Avenue. Located in South Memphis, Linden and Pontotoc were across town from the Pinch, the twelve-block ghetto north of downtown where most of the city's poorer Jews lived and worked.[4] Still, Fortas was raised as an Orthodox Jew. His mother kept a kosher household. Both parents were members of the Baron Hirsch Synagogue, and his father belonged to the Workmen's Circle. Abe went to dances at the Menorah Institute and dated only Jewish girls until after he left college. Both he and Meyer learned Hebrew and had Bar Mitzvahs.

Being Jewish made Fortas an outsider in Protestant Memphis, but he was an outsider in Jewish society as well. His father, Woolfe, had changed his first name to William, and moved to an ethnically mixed neighborhood. Instead of associating with residents of the Pinch, Fortas spent his boyhood playing with the Italians and Jews who lived on his street and the blacks who lived in the alley behind it. "I played with Negro kids until I went to school," he later said. "Then the curtain fell."[5] Memphis's schools, of course, were segregated. His parents did not teach their children Yiddish but instead reserved the language for private adult conversations. For much of their youth, Fortas and his brother did not attend religious school, where they would have met frequently with other Jewish children. Instead they learned Hebrew from a tutor who came to the house. Perhaps partially in consequence, Judaism never had much spiritual meaning for Abe Fortas. He always identified himself as a Jew, but he viewed his religion as a handicap to disclose rather than as a heritage to claim. Even in the period of his life when he was most steeped in Judaism, he followed the other members of his family in viewing it primarily as a matter of ritual. The men in her family generally went to synagogue only on the High Holidays, Fortas's sister recalled: "They weren't that religious."

Music was more important to the young Abe Fortas than religion. Beale Street, "where the blues began," lay within easy walking distance of his house. "Owned largely by Jews, policed by the whites, and enjoyed by the negroes," as one description has it, it was the center of Dixieland jazz and a mecca for drug dealers, prostitutes, bartenders, and musicians.[6] Fortas's long tapering fingers made the violin, which he began to play at an early age, a good instrument for him. He took lessons from the nuns at St. Patrick's School, next door to his house, until he became too expert for them. Then he studied chamber music with the leader of a local trio.

The music helped when his father became ill. The Fortas males were frail. Abe was plagued by childhood diseases, and as a teenager he saw his father consumed by cancer. During the long months before his death in 1930, William Fortas often would call for Esta to play the piano and Abe, the violin. Even before the death of its breadwinner left the family in straitened circumstances, Abe Fortas sold that skill. As a young man he earned extra money by working as a shoe salesman and a violinist. "Fiddlin' Abe," as he was called, gave violin lessons to local children and played in bands at prep school and college dances. He directed the Dixie Peaches, an orchestra comprised of eleven young women, and he directed and played in the Blue Melody Boys, a band that performed two or three times a week at Edgewood Park, charging eight dollars per musician for an evening's work.[7] Fortas also played with the trumpeter Colie Stolz's band occasionally in high school and regularly through college, until Stolz let him go. Fortas "could read anything ever written," Stolz recalled, but he could not play by ear and the band required a "fakir." (Years later, when he was under secretary of the interior and Stolz was in Washington, Fortas invited the bandleader to his house for a party and introduced him as the "only man in the world who had the brazen effrontery to fire Abe Fortas. He fired me for crass incompetence." To Fortas's delight, the other guests gave Stolz a standing ovation.)[8]

## "A NATURAL BORN HUSTLER"

As his sister said, Fortas never got much time to play. When he was not selling shoes, playing band engagements, or giving violin lessons, Fortas worked in a plumbing store. A Memphis newspaper labeled him "a natural born hustler."[9] But much of his work—that involving music—was also fun. Fortas believed that only those from the West Coast "either worked or played," and he himself never treated work and play as two separate activities.[10] "Out there in the open-air grandstand, Abe would give a flourish with his bow, and we'd fill the air with 'Wabash Blues,' 'Dark Town Strutters' Ball,' or 'Blue Heaven,' " Fortas's drummer remembered. "We enjoyed playing."[11]

These jobs did not detract from his scholastic performance. Fortas completed grammar school in six years and secondary school in three, graduating at the age of sixteen. Yet he seemed neither precocious nor brilliant. He impressed contemporaries as a pleasant and well-adjusted young man. "Abe was never what you call a long-haired boy," one childhood friend remembered. "He liked to play with the rest of the kids." His eighth-grade teacher considered him "a darling boy, straight, honorable and smart."[12] To his speech and debate coach at South Side High School, he appeared a "very modest boy who didn't have anything aggressive in his makeup. . . . He was the type everybody wanted to see get ahead." But she emphasized that he did not graduate first in his class and that he was "no better in forensics than some of my other debaters."[13] Fortas succeeded academically through hard work. His family considered him smart and industrious but not exceptional. Returning home from work at midnight, he would turn on the radio and concentrate on his schoolwork. "With Abe, it was study, study, study," Meyer said later. "That is the thing I remember most."[14]

The wellspring of Fortas's unusually high motivation was not apparent. There is no evidence that his family pushed him; he prodded himself. To one journalist, it seemed obvious that Fortas studied so hard because he was determined to avoid his father's failure. According to this explanation, William Fortas died because he "found the hard competitive world too much for him," and "young Abe was determined it would be different with him."[15] Yet William Fortas died of a disease, and Abe Fortas never gave any sign that he viewed his father as a failure. Although as an adult, he said little about Rachel, he occasionally talked of William. He was especially proud of his father's expertise in cabinetmaking, a skill Abe acquired and made a lifelong hobby.[16] More likely, his father's illness and death deprived him of the sense of being protected. It may have made him more self-sufficient. He apparently viewed education as the most promising avenue of upward mobility.

Without financial aid, however, he would have been unable to go beyond secondary school. After he was graduated from South Side High School second in his class, Fortas was chosen as the first recipient of a new scholarship. A Memphis rabbi named Hardwig Peres had established the Israel Peres Scholarship in memory of his brother, a local judge, to pay the way of bright and needy students through Southwestern College in Memphis. Competition for the award was keen, and Fortas did not learn he had been selected over the other twelve applicants until September, just days before the fall term was to begin.[17]

Southwestern was a small Presbyterian college. His years there must have intensified Fortas's sense of Jewishness, because he was one of the college's few Jews, at the same time that they accelerated his assimilation by forcibly drawing him into the Protestant mainstream. Fortas continued to eat only kosher food throughout his college career and took a cheese sandwich to school every day. But chapel was compulsory at Southwestern, and every morning between 8:30 and 9, he would be found there in his assigned seat. Members of the faculty took turns conducting the services, which followed the basic Presbyterian format.[18] Bible class was also mandatory, although apparently not strict; in his senior year, Fortas composed a satire on Joseph's coat of many colors, which he read to the class.[19] Southwestern drew him away from his family intellectually as well as religiously. Although he continued to live at home while he was at college, his wife believed that once Fortas began at Southwestern he entered a different world from the one inhabited by his relatives. "He was thoughtful of them," she recalled, "but he wasn't terribly concerned with them, at least when he was young."[20]

Southwestern was scarcely a national institution in 1926. All of the fifty-seven men and women in Fortas's senior class were Southerners, and well over half of them had grown up in Memphis.[21] The professors were more worldly. Fortas's professors of political science and philosophy held advanced degrees from Oxford, and the four English teachers to whom he became close had studied at Harvard, McGill, Princeton, and North Carolina.[22]

Abe Fortas inspired his professors. "As far as scholastic records, there is no one better in the class," one of them noted. "But it is in the part that he has played in stimulating others to think that the extraordinary power of the man is seen."[23] When he was appointed to the Supreme Court, his teachers suggested that they had expected nothing less of him. His history teacher announced that Fortas had possessed one of the "most incisive" undergraduate minds he had ever encountered and that "everybody who taught him knew he would get somewhere."[24]

His contemporaries thought that Fortas was industrious and that he possessed extraordinary self-control. Legend had it that when a car door accidentally was slammed on his hand during a college celebration, he gave no indication of pain.[25] As an Orthodox Jew on a Presbyterian campus, he was predictably reserved. "As soon as classes were over, he took off," an acquaintance recalled.[26] He continued to work as a violinist and shoe salesman to supplement his scholarship award and also received assistance from the college president, a Presbyterian minister named Charles Diehl, who occasionally gave him money from his "oil can," a fund he established to help distressed students during the Depression.[27]

Yet Fortas was also popular. One classmate remembered him as "completely unassuming."[28] He apparently did have an active social life—in later years he joked about Southwestern's "secluded places . . . where, as I recall, I received and gave instruction"[29]—although he was sufficiently single-minded about his studies that one young woman who fell for him was told by her mother she was wasting her time.[30] He participated in such collegiate diversions as smearing his face with burnt cork and snake-dancing through the streets of Memphis, and devoted considerable energy to extracurricular activities.[31] Fortas joined several academic fraternities, presided over the drama club and two discussion clubs, directed the orchestra, debated, and contributed to the college literary magazine.

Of all these activities, those that seemed most important to him involved discussion and politics. At the age of eighteen, Fortas was urging his classmates to vote for the socialist Norman Thomas as President.[32] He was a member of the debating team for three years. In his freshman year, he debated Northwestern University students about whether the United States should regulate private capital invested in foreign countries. One teammate recalled that Fortas refuted his opponent's argument by taking from a book the quotation his adversary had used to prove one point and showing "that the exact reading of the quotation proved precisely the opposite."[33] Fortas won seventeen debates and lost only three times.[34] He also presided over the Nitist Club, an institution aimed at "the discussion of current problems of interest to the world today. Papers are read at regular meetings by the members and then gently, but nevertheless firmly, torn to pieces by the 'philosophers.' "[35] While others chose topics such as the history of humor, Fortas addressed the question "Is Life Worth Living?" and argued that it was not.[36]

That conclusion suggests the sort of self-consciously cynical pseudosophisticated attitude characteristic of both the jazz age and college students. Years later, when reminded he had described himself as a "pessimistic meliorist" when he was at Southwestern, he wryly commented: "It sounds like those days."[37] Elsewhere, he said he had been an existentialist "for a few growing up years, even before existentialism was conceived."[38] Perhaps being younger, he went out of his way to sound older. He was conscious enough of his youth to state on his law school application that he was "nineteen and ten-twelfths" years of age.[39]

There was nothing cynical about Fortas's commitment to social justice though. He identified instinctively with the have-nots. "As a Southerner—born and brought up in the Mississippi Delta—I recall the outrages of the Ku Klux Klan, directed against Jews, Catholics and Negroes," he later said.[40] For his generation, "the national goal of *E pluribus Unum* seemed to carry on its reverse side a qualification which darkly hinted that Jews, as well as Catholics and Negroes, might be excluded from its purview." He maintained that the threat to "meaningful survival" he and other Jewish contemporaries had faced made them "the shock troops in the war for humanity and social values."[41] As president of the Nitist Club, Fortas had been the first individual at Southwestern to invite a black to speak on campus.[42] He declined several invitations to join fraternities and instead organized the unorganized into the Non-Fraternity Club.[43]

Again, extracurricular activities did not divert Fortas from the pursuit of academic excellence. He was graduated first in his class, with first-class honors in English and second-class honors in political science. President Diehl reportedly kept Fortas's senior thesis on his desk for years as an exemplar of honors work.[44] Throughout his life Fortas placed great emphasis on writing well and liked to repeat a colleague's comment that Fortas's "only regret is that he never had a chance to rewrite the Lord's Prayer before it was published."[45]

Fortas appreciated Southwestern. When he became famous the school reached out to claim him. One of its later presidents recalled that "Fortas was highly revered in the college although not necessarily by some of the college's supporters who thought less of his politics."[46] He served as its official representative at several functions in Washington, donated money to the college, and hosted a fundraiser on its behalf. He once lodged an "urgent plea" with the Johnson administration for Hubert Humphrey to speak there.[47] He also valued Memphis. Yet as he became one of its most famous citizens, he went home less frequently— partially, relatives postulated, because he was always the center of attention. Fortas became closer to his family as he grew older, but even then he would return either before or after a relative's death rather than for the funeral itself, so as to ensure some attention for the deceased at the interment. When he did appear for a family gathering, he always proved the main attraction. Of the two hundred photographs taken at his niece's wedding in 1967, the bride and groom appeared in only eighty-eight. The remainder were pictures the guests had demanded of themselves with their "old friend Abe." Under those circumstances, he remained in touch with his relatives primarily by telephone and letter.[48] Yet throughout his life he maintained that he considered himself a Southerner.

Fortas was not destined to remain in Memphis, however, for as his sister said, "the future he wanted just wasn't here."[49] Although he had at times toyed with the idea of becoming a professional musician,[50] he had long wanted to be a lawyer. In his senior year at Southwestern, he applied to Harvard and Yale law schools and won scholarships to both institutions. Admission to either in 1930 was no great achievement. Harvard Law School in those days accepted three times as many students as it graduated and relied on the first year to weed out two-thirds of the group. Although Yale generally received three applications for each of about one hundred twenty places in its entering class, its admission process aimed only at eliminating those unlikely to attain a C average. "We do not, of course, get a group of geniuses," Professor Thurman Arnold reported.[51]

Scholarship requirements were more rigorous, and the Depression made competition for those awards intense. At Yale, they were given only to individuals believed eligible for law journal positions and enthusiastically supported by "people of responsibility" in their communities. Fortas might not have received a scholarship if the Peres family had not again intervened. Israel Peres had attended Yale, and Rabbi Hardwig Peres recommended Fortas to the law school's dean, Charles E. Clark. According to Arnold, Fortas was also admitted "because attorneys . . . in whom we had confidence practically underwrote him as to ability."[52] Fortas wavered, and the hometown newspaper reported that he was going to Harvard.[53] In the end he decided on Yale, partially, he said, because it offered slightly more generous financial aid and, "more important . . . [because] Peres had gone to Yale."[54]

## YALE

Fortas was even more of an outsider in New Haven than he had been at Southwestern. He stood out for his youth; a twenty-year-old law student attracts more notice than a nineteen-year-old college senior. At Yale he was also one of the few students from the South, one of the few who had not attended an elite college, and one of the few Jews.

His religion was less important to Fortas now. He no longer went to synagogue or restricted himself to kosher food. According to Arnold, Fortas was "not Jewish in appearance, and if his name were not *Abe* Fortas, I do not think anyone would know he was a Jew."[55] Nevertheless, his religion remained a handicap. Although fifty years later, Fortas recalled no anti-Semitism at Yale,[56] it pervaded the law school, at least in the form of social exclusion. Jews were not admitted to the Corbey Court eating club and pressure was placed on Gentiles who roomed with Jews to make other housing arrangements.[57] Arnold, who worked harder than any other faculty member at placing Jewish students and who later resigned from Washington's Cosmos Club over its failure to admit Fortas,[58] peppered his letters of recommendation with assurances that a particular candidate had "no traces of those characteristics which one associates with Hebrews."[59]

Few institutions hired Jews, regardless of how they looked or acted. When Arnold nominated a Jew for a position on the Northwestern Law School faculty, he was told that liberals at Northwestern had considered the employment of a law librarian with one Jewish parent a victory.[60] When Wall Street law firms wrote Arnold or anyone else to solicit recommendations, their letters commonly included a sentence along these lines: "We have no prejudices but have found from experience that Jews are so unlikely to click with our clients that we employ them only in very extraordinary circumstances."[61] Jewish law firms reported that when they advertised a position, they would receive at least a hundred applications and enjoyed "the pick of the Jewish students from the various Law Schools."[62] While the Depression only increased the opportunities for bright young Protestant law review men interested in corporate reorganization or bankruptcy, the options open to their Jewish counterparts were less impressive. The dean of Yale Law School periodically tried to bludgeon the university's president into increasing his budget by warning him that the low salaries they offered would force the law school to hire more of the "many brilliant Jewish boys, because these men like a life of teaching and because their opportunities outside are unfortunately more restricted than those of others."[63] It was an era of profound, if genteel, anti-Semitism, a time when a Jew's religiosity, or lack thereof, meant nothing. What mattered was that the world considered him a Jew.

Although advancement in the legal world outside was difficult for Jews, it was relatively easy inside Yale. The school that excluded Jews socially was one they frequently dominated academically, for Yale Law School was a meritocracy. Fortas did not immediately rise to its top. He later subscribed to the maxim that the first year of law school was "an ordeal."[64] He seemed to live at one particular table in the library: "You would see him there at all times of the day and night."[65] Even so, at the end of his first year, at least four students were ranked above him.[66]

Despite his relatively slow start, Fortas excelled at Yale. He became one of the two men in the class with an A average and won the second-year prize for law students. He did not graduate first in his class. That honor went to another Memphian, Luke Finlay, who completed law school in two years while moonlighting as an accountant, and whose final average of 82.7 exceeded Fortas's by almost two full points. Because of his accelerated status, Finlay did not compete for the law journal concurrently with Fortas, and Fortas proved the obvious choice as editor in chief of the journal. The outgoing board of editors ranked him first of the twelve students it endorsed as editor, and he received the school's most coveted position at the end of his second year.[67]

As a student and as a *Yale Law Journal* editor, Fortas came into contact with the dominant jurisprudence at the school, legal realism. This theory of law and of legal education reflected a rebellion against the traditional case method of teaching, which had dominated in law schools ever since Christopher Columbus Langdell had introduced it at Harvard in 1870. In keeping with the positivistic age in which he lived, Langdell had announced that law was "a science" which could best be learned through "printed books."[68] Specifically, students should master the appellate cases collected by Langdell and his colleagues in casebooks. As conceptualists, Langdell and his disciples preached that law could be reduced to a few fundamental rules and principles derived from this study of individual cases. A judge's decision, said these Harvard "conceptualists," did not reflect his own particular prejudices, the peculiar circumstances of the case, or social need. Instead of "making" law, the judge found concepts, rules, and principles that had been revealed in previous decisions and applied them. Conceptualists thus divorced law from life by treating law as if it were independent of social change.

In contrast, the functional approach was part of a "revolt against formalism" that swept the intellectual world in the first half of the twentieth century.[69] Philosophy, psychology, anthropology, linguistics, history, economics, and sociology all experienced a reaction against abstractions and concepts, a movement from the study of structure to a concern with operations. No longer was it possible to learn a discipline through the absorption of abstract doctrines; it had to be studied empirically, along with related disciplines and the culture in which they acted. Functionalism spurned notions of disciplinary autonomy, or formalism, and represented a particularistic attempt to achieve objectivity.

Legal functionalists, also called legal realists, challenged Langdell's notion that principles and concepts of law were the sole factors in a judge's decision. They tried to show that judicial decision making was idiosyncratic. While the realists did not wholly abandon legal concepts or principles and admitted that "law" often influenced judges, they argued that the Harvard conceptualists had misled their students by teaching them to expect each "correct" decision to be based upon the legal doctrine, rule, or concept laid down in the cases that preceded it. The realists warned that sometimes the legal rules cited by a judge to justify his result were simply camouflage with which to rationalize a decision grounded in private prejudice. Recognizing a judge's reaction to the facts of the case—facts which social and behavioral sciences such as psychology, economics, and history might illuminate—could prove as important as knowledge of legal concepts in enabling a lawyer to predict how this judge would resolve a particular dispute. If a judge's perception of business practices might influence his disposition of a case, it behooved a law student to learn economics. Appreciation of the particularities of the factual situation and the relevance of social sciences would clarify the policy issues legal problems raised. Unlike the conceptualists, the realists did not try to pretend that judges were not policy makers but worried instead about the intelligent formulation of policy. Realists thus believed that law schools had to devote greater attention to judicial behavior and to the social sciences if they were to produce lawyers who could more accurately predict and influence judicial decisions.[70]

Harvard was seen as the bastion of Langdellian conceptualism and thus as the enemy. "Harvard people tended to look upon us as unsound maniacs, and we in turn looked upon them as sort of antiques who time had passed by," Fortas said. "It was vastly exaggerated on both sides, but the Harvard attitude toward us was totally wanting in some respect, and our attitude toward Harvard was totally lacking in any semblance of veneration." He maintained that "the sort of extreme and somewhat distorted rivalry between the two was highly productive, at least so far as Yale was concerned," because it kept us "active and . . . in the frame of mind that competition always does, so that we were constantly pressing and improving our particular approach."[71] Perhaps so, but it was a contest that sometimes became nasty. When the realists declared that "no more time-wasting system of studying law" had ever been devised than Langdell's case method and turned the scholarly pages of the *Harvard Law Review,* the *Columbia Law Review,* and the *Yale Law Journal* into the battleground of their war against conceptualists, hackles rose.[72]

It was the great intellectual debate of Fortas's youth. Characteristically, he approached it with reserve. After he became editor in chief of the *Yale Law Journal* in 1932, a professor showed him one of Jerome Frank's vituperative attacks on Langdell. Frank, an attorney fond of describing the late professor as "a brilliant neurotic who had seduced American legal education," obviously wanted Fortas to publish the article and was using his Yale contact as a conduit.[73] Fortas, however, was of a different mind. He had found the piece "stimulating and . . . provocative of active and favorable criticism," he wrote Frank. "I might be tempted to ask for the privilege of publishing the *Comment,*" Fortas continued, "were it not for the fact that discussions of legal education in the Harvard, Columbia and Yale Reviews are likely to cause undesirable controversy if there is any ground for suspicion of a comparison of the pedagogic methods of the three schools. I feel as if your criticism of the 'Harvard' method and the commendation, here and there, of the methods employed in other schools makes it particularly undesirable for a publication of one of the other schools to print the *Comment.*" Fortas closed by saying how much he looked forward to meeting its author.[74] A disappointed Frank took his comment to the *University of Pennsylvania Law Review.*[75]

It was pure Fortas. Always a partisan, he never blanched at taking sides. Fifty years later, he still said Yale had made a mistake when it began hiring Harvard Law School graduates.[76] Yet except in the realm of civil liberties, where he never hesitated to speak out, he remained as circumspect as he had been as a youngster in Memphis. Though he enjoyed writing aggressive speeches and memoranda for others to deliver, he rarely ventured a provocative opinion publicly. It was not that he was a coward; the Yale professors he admired undoubtedly would have preferred him to publish Frank's article, but Fortas rejected it anyway. Typically, he was unwilling to throw the weight of the *Yale Law Journal* behind Frank in a debate Frank himself had made belligerent. Equally characteristically, he phrased his rejection to Frank in a manner at once deferential and authoritative.

Fortas did not throw himself into the Harvard–Yale debate with zeal, but legal realism deeply affected him. He attended law school when this movement was at its most vibrant, and Yale its center. For him, the school housed "a gallery of fantastic people" who would shape his life. Underhill Moore, a curmudgeon who delighted in throwing pieces of chalk and erasers at the errant, believed that the study of individuals' responses to traffic ordinances would enable him to understand the effectiveness of law as a form of social control. Moore, Fortas recalled, "had students counting the automobiles violating traffic laws." He was examining "the legal process in action and [making] quite a factual analysis of what went on in society." Wesley Sturges "was quite different," Fortas added. Sturges, who could spend weeks of classroom time analyzing a single case, employed a Socratic approach. Fortas's future law partner, Walton Hamilton, an economist who had been chairman of the Brookings Institution before he came to Yale, delighted in showing how judges judged according to their economic preferences and how they used history to hide those prejudices. Hamilton was, Fortas said simply, "fantastic."[77] Although he worked with many members of this faculty throughout his career, two individuals most influenced Fortas at the time. In spite of the fact that Yale was a meritocracy, a system of intellectual patronage existed in the academy. Advancement was determined not only by grades but by mentors who promoted particular students. William O. Douglas and Thurman Arnold became Fortas's mentors.

Students adored Arnold. His presence pervaded the law school and gave it much of its distinctiveness, just as it was responsible later for the uniqueness of the law firm he and Fortas founded. A paunchy man always covered with his own cigar ashes, Arnold reminded some of Rabelais.[78] Fortas probably loved him in a less ambivalent way than he loved anyone else, for Arnold was acerbic, irreverent, witty, and endearing. His tongue was glued to the inside of his cheek. Characteristically, he defended two Yale law students who swore that they were only playing cards and "listening to the *Nutcracker*" when they were found with chorus girls in their room by telling the law school faculty that if that was all they were doing, they should be dismissed for their "failure of initiative and imagination."[79] Whether he was screaming at his students that jurisdiction was "a horse" or bellowing to his colleagues about government policy, his presence commanded attention.[80]

While Fortas loved Arnold as a person and respected him as a jurisprudent, Douglas had a greater impact on his intellectual development and early career. Like other legal realists, Douglas treated law as an instrument of social policy, but another aspect of Douglas's scholarly work initially proved crucial to legal realism and always influenced Fortas: precision. The young Douglas railed against the plethora of sterile legal concepts used to describe his field of corporate law.[81] The importance of facts gleaned through empirical study and the social sciences lay at the core of Douglas's research. Nowhere did the fact-oriented and sociological-functional approach prove more fruitful than in the field of bankruptcy, and Douglas's study of bankrupts and their lawyers and creditors exemplified legal realism at its most empirical and reformist. Like Langdell, Douglas and his colleagues considered themselves scientists, but they believed in classification by facts and function instead of by principles and structure. Douglas hoped that their investigations of the social, economic, and legal phenomena surrounding bankruptcy would lay the basis for a social policy that would enable the entrepreneur to avoid dangerous business practices, ensure greater security for the consumer, lessen the chance of displacement for the worker, and furnish the legislator with a factual basis for new law.[82]

Douglas's faith in the neutral expert qua reformer was a legacy of the Progressive Era and a vital force behind the growth of the regulatory process to which Fortas, Douglas, and other New Dealers contributed so much. Such individuals generally ignored Woodrow Wilson's warning of a generation earlier, a warning Wilson himself ultimately forgot: "If the government is to tell big business men how to run their business, then don't you see that big business men have to get closer to the government even than they are now? Don't you see that they must capture the government, in order not to be restrained too much by it?"[83] Too frequently, the regulators became the captives of those they supervised or the bureaucracies they served. The concept of the "neutral expert" also bespoke the Progressives' elitism. There was a certain arrogance about their belief that only they possessed the requisite knowledge and objectivity to frame governmental policy.

Something of this arrogance was apparent in the young William O. Douglas. Considered "a mean son of a bitch" by students, he was an unpopular teacher when he began teaching corporate law and bankruptcy at Yale just before the Crash.[84] "The students didn't like him," a colleague remembered. "He didn't tell them much, he made them think, he'd ask them questions, make them work out the conclusions."[85] There were exceptions: Gerhard Gesell recalled that Douglas would come into seminars with the "horror stories as everything fell apart," and "you felt like you were in the middle of it."[86] Another exception was Fortas. Asked the identities of his best teachers at Yale fifty years later, he growled at the interviewer, "You know better than to ask a question like that," but as the discussion continued, it was clear that Fortas had prized Douglas most highly.[87]

Although Fortas regularly sought out individuals who could advance his career, he seemingly did not do so with Douglas. Rather, Carol Agger maintained, Douglas picked her husband.[88] Douglas's second wife agreed: "I think he thought Abe was one of the smartest men that crossed the horizon," Mercedes Eichholz said. Douglas once told her that Fortas had been his best student.[89] Perhaps in Fortas, too, Douglas saw something of himself. Douglas's childhood, unlike Fortas's, had been impoverished. Still, both men had been scholarship students at small local colleges before going east to elite law schools. Both had been sickly youths and had lost their fathers at an early age. Most important, both were bright and ambitious outsiders.[90]

Fortas admired his teacher's intellect. "Douglas had a very concise mind, and he worked out the techniques of the [functional] approach, and the broader sociological aspects of it," he recalled. "The thing that attracted me so much to Douglas was the incisiveness, the precision of that approach." Fortas compared Douglas's teaching to "playing scales on a violin. You don't mess around. You may have a great conception in your mind when you hear the music, but you . . . [must] get right the essential techniques and the essential harmonies for the purity of the approach. That was Douglas in the early years."[91] His influence on Fortas was most evident in the student's first published work, which grew out of a project Douglas had assigned him.

## "THE IDEALS OF SCHOLARSHIP"

In the spring of 1931 Douglas taught a seminar on consumer credit, an important topic to those who regarded the decline in mass purchasing power as one of the principal causes of the Depression.[92] Under his direction, students became "very much excited about wage assignments."[93] The Department of Justice was already studying the process by which wage earners bought products on credit and, as collateral for their purchases, assigned to their creditors the right to collect the debt from their salaries. Employers deplored the practice and sometimes fired those who engaged in it, not only because of their moral outrage that employees could not pay their debts in a timely fashion, but also because of the nuisance of having to hire personnel to make these deductions. Although employers strained to prevent workers from assigning their wages, in the 1931 case of *State Street Furniture* v. *Armour Company,* the Illinois Supreme Court ruled that it was illegal for Chicago's Armour Meat Packing House to restrict its employees from doing so.[94]

To prevent creditors from filing their wage assignment claims, some debtors paid companies such as the American Amortization Company in Chicago to cash their pay check, give them a subsistence portion, and divide the remainder among their creditors. American Amortization's president, Henry Coit, a kindly man descended from a long line of educators and clergymen, claimed as his motto "Most Men are Honest." The practices of the creditors he encountered, many of them loan sharks, horrified him. Coit wanted a study of Chicago loan practices, and Douglas, who was impressed by him, selected Fortas to undertake it.[95]

The study was intended to embody the functional approach. Conceptualists, the realists believed, had unthinkingly herded unlike facts together in categories and so treated all bankruptcies the same way. Douglas maintained, "Bankruptcy is not uniform. It never can be until the economic and social problems in various localities are uniform."[96] Wage assignments, for example, were rare in Boston but occurred frequently in Chicago. The study would be functional in its recognition of factual distinctions that the conceptualists ignored. The quantification of empirical research would yield the divergences. Fortas carried with him worksheets on which he gathered data about creditors, size of debt, and the debtors' income and payments. That information was put into an early computer, the Hollerith machine. But Douglas possessed a skepticism of quantification uncommon among the fact-oriented Progressive reformers. "When everything is reduced to numbers," he said, "the qualitative features tend to disappear. Thus often the essence is squeezed out." This vice he hoped Fortas would rectify through an "exhaustive descriptive study" that would "give a real picture of the operation of American Amortization Company."[97] It was here that the study became functional in the second sense of the word, for Douglas encouraged Fortas to employ the methods of other disciplines to obtain this picture. Fortas remembered seeing no lawyers in Chicago. His work was sociological, "a specific application of the functional approach," he explained. "What I did was go through the business enterprises and social agencies [which dealt] with the problems in life . . . that wage earners were facing."[98]

Fortas made his first research stop in New York, where he met with several social scientists. By this time he was thinking of devoting an entire issue of the *Yale Law Journal* to consumer credit. He intended to control it closely. He had already fended off a suggestion that one article be assigned to Leon Henderson, an economist. "I don't think H is the man to write for the Journal," Fortas told Douglas. "My conversation with him reminded me of talks with Democrats who were running for sheriff." Fortas did not think Henderson was "a scholar or interested in the ideals of scholarship: This is not merely a criticism . . . on the score that he is a propagandist, but essentially because he is by principle intellectually naif—you know, his not to ask why, his but to do or die."[99] Like his mentor, Fortas believed that the best reformer was a neutral expert.

Fortas's own work in Chicago, where he spent two hot months in the summer of 1932, revealed his ideals of scholarship. His research was exhaustive. He examined 658 cases to obtain data about individuals who used companies such as Coit's to prevent their creditors from filing wage assignments.[100] He analyzed the wage assignments filed against employees, obtained access to the records of the Better Business Bureau, pored through local newspapers, and spoke with professors, employers, and others in the city to determine the habits of local debtors and creditors. Coit was delighted with him. He reported that Fortas was making "splendid progress," was "very agreeable and certainly most diligent and intelligent in his method of assembling information."[101] Another student, dispatched by Douglas to study the Poor Debtor Court in Boston, which purported to perform the same function as Coit's company, quickly became cynical. He concluded that the Boston court was "merely a collection agency for the credit houses" and should have been named "court for the relief of poor creditors."[102]

Fortas, however, saw nothing disillusioning about the American Amortization Company and within a month was advising Coit how to attract a sufficient number of debtors so that the business could stay afloat.[103]

Years later Fortas complimented an article in one of the major law reviews, but noted that with the onset of age its author would be "sufficiently emancipated to avoid this kind of elaborate [doctrinal] analysis of a problem in which right and wrong are clearly apparent—happily in law as well as in conscience."[104] His own article in 1933 focused on how borrowers and their creditors could cope with debt. About the case which inspired it, *State Street Furniture Company*, with its holding that employers must permit wage assignments, he said little more than that it was wrong. He avoided examining every line in the court's opinion but made instead a more sweeping policy argument, based upon empirical and sociological data, that wage assignments themselves were ill-conceived.

His article revealed the intellectual foundations of a New Dealer, for Fortas based his argument upon a compassion for those in debt and a belief that the state should be permitted to intervene, even if intrusion lessened debtors' freedom. Why had so many impecunious individuals whose files he examined turned to companies such as Coit's, which charged at least 4.5 percent of the debt accrued to manage their finances? Fortas asked. "What brought these companies customers," he decided, "was not conscience but the desire to obtain relief from the harassment of creditors and in particular from the threat that their assignments would be enforced by filing them with the employer." Despite the fact that the wage assignments frequently proved invalid in court, his research demonstrated that employers treated them as a matter of routine and enforced them without establishing their validity. In such a situation, where no neutral party scrutinized the assignments for their soundness before they took effect and where even an employee's declaration of bankruptcy did not necessarily relieve him of his debts, Fortas contended that wage assignments were an inappropriate means of credit extension. They gave creditors too much power.[105]

Fortas's article also demonstrated the impact of the Progressive Era upon a young adult poised at the brink of the New Deal. Like the legal realists, the Progressive politicians during the early part of the century had treated the accumulation of facts as a prerequisite to reform.[106] Their empirical studies demonstrated the need for state action to protect the working class. Their moralism also distinguished Progressives, but Fortas did not share that characteristic. Some states, for instance, had enacted statutes authorizing an employee to assign his wages only with his wife's consent. Fortas suggested that this measure was insufficient: "Insisting upon the wife's consent may confine within reasonable limit the use of wage assignments for the benefit of mistresses, but beyond that its value depends upon an obsolescent conception of the wife's providence."[107]

The Progressives vacillated between two conflicting values, moralism and efficiency; they never fully realized either because the other stood in the way. The New Deal became Progressivism without moralism,[108] and Fortas possessed the qualifications to become one of its ablest lieutenants. Like his concept of family, his view of law proved less romantic and moralistic, and more pragmatic and efficient, than that of his intellectual forebears.

Efficiency characterized his activities as editor in chief of the *Yale Law Journal* upon his return from Chicago. He peppered the faculty with communications, asking whether a public affairs section would be desirable and urging professors to call to his attention cases which deserved comment.[109] He proved an unusually visible editor in chief,[110] and the 1932–33 journal testified to his skill. With articles on society's need for law enforcement by Thurman Arnold, on an "institutional approach" to banking by Underhill Moore, on wage-earner bankruptcies by William O. Douglas, on the small debtor by Walton Hamilton, and on the Supreme Court and American capitalism by Max Lerner, it was a manifesto for legal realism and among the most stimulating volumes of the *Yale Law Journal* ever published.[111]

This success was not achieved easily. Fortas had been a popular young man until he went to Yale. Now his personality seemed to change. His chameleonlike qualities, which made him deferential to superiors and stern with those in his power, were becoming apparent. Professors such as Douglas, who liked him so much, would have been surprised to know what Fortas's fellow students thought of him. From their perspective, he seemed an impoverished loner. Most of them had grown up in families which were at least upper middle-class. In the aftermath of the Crash, Yale law students saved money by sending their laundry home. Invariably, the box in which Ernest Meyers's mother returned the laundry also contained fried chicken and gruyere cheese. "Abe could never wait," Meyers said. "He got to that laundry box before I did." Meyers, who liked the young Abe Fortas and who used to sit up at night talking with him, never felt he knew him well. "On the law side, we were both full of expression, but when it came on the social side, I found him to be very tightlipped, very quiet."[112] Fortas obviously was more interested in the faculty than he was in his fellow students. "He seemed to hobnob with the faculty more than the guys," one classmate said.[113] Douglas and Arnold regularly ate Sunday brunch at Yale Commons, another remembered. If any student was part of their group, it would be Fortas. "He was always toadying up to the professor who was in the best possible spot for Abe."[114]

Where his fellow students were concerned, Fortas seemed calculating. As Christmas approached one year, a local Jewish social group invited Yale's Jewish graduate students to a dance. Fortas "caught me in the library," one of his Jewish classmates said. "We stepped out of the library to get some fresh air, and he said to me, he was fencing—see, he didn't know that I was Jewish and he wasn't sure that I knew he was Jewish . . . 'What are you doing Friday night?'" The classmate, who did not want to reveal that he was Jewish before he was sure Fortas was Jewish, vaguely replied that he was going to a party in town. Fortas asked whether by any chance it was a dance, and the classmate said it was. At this point, each man had made a preliminary determination that the other was Jewish, a subject discussed in the most circuitous way, and when Fortas asked if the Harmonie Club was hosting the party, the classmate replied affirmatively. Fortas then wondered whether they would be trapped with someone unattractive. "Let's have a signal," the classmate remembered telling Fortas. "'If you really get stuck with a dog, and want someone to break in, hold your hand that way instead of that way on her back . . . have your palm out—and, I'll cut in and your do the same for me.' Well, he didn't. He left me standing there with a dog, and he went off with someone that was rather cute." The man he left stranded was convinced that Fortas "had an edge on all of us. We thought we were so clever coming from the big city and being sophisticated and all, and here was this little country boy outsmarting us at every turn." Another recalled that whereas Yale law students tended to be "young kids," Fortas was "a full-blown adult conniver."[115]

As editor in chief, he was a clever administrator who knew tricks that had never occurred to his fellow students. When a contributor said his piece for the journal would be late, one staff member readily extended the deadline. Fortas said his colleague had been too accommodating. Why miss the opportunity to put the tardy individual in his debt? "'You make them think you're going through hell to take care of this,'" Fortas advised.[116] Co-workers at the journal found him dictatorial. The autocracy of the young man who rejected Jerome Frank's contribution to the journal even before Frank had a chance formally to submit it was evident in Fortas's stewardship. When one subordinate told him thirty years after their graduation that he remembered Fortas as "severe and demanding," according to others he was understating the case.[117] "Abe was a great guy to some people on the outside and a son of a bitch to those on the inside," one journal colleague said more bluntly. The twenty-two-year-old editor permanently embittered one friend on the staff when he ordered him to stay in New Haven over Christmas to do journal work. He angered another by overriding his objections to publishing a criticism of Dean Clark's scholarship. Fortas contended that inclusion would show the journal's evenhandedness. Soon after it appeared, Clark summoned both men to his office. "He laced into me about publishing it, . . . our own journal publishing against the dean," the beleaguered individual remembered. "And Abe sat there, never opened his mouth in defense, not a word. I took the whole beating from the dean." Fortas annoyed a third colleague by signing his wage assignment article. Traditionally student contributions to the law journal remained anonymous, and although Fortas's article entailed far more work than the average student comment, staff members remained irked.[118] They thought he devoted too much energy to the consumer credit issue of the volume and left the other seven or eight issues for them to handle, and their resentment only increased when they learned that he was telling the faculty that he was having difficulty in securing written work senior editors owed him.[119] "In my entire life," one of his co-workers on the journal said over half a century later, "I don't recall hating anyone except Fortas. I hated him because he was a monster."[120] In later years Fortas extended himself for his former staff. He found a job for one person when no one else would and telephoned another from Europe because the man had left a message that he needed help.[121] But Fortas never stopped insisting upon complete control.

By the middle of his third year of law school Fortas was beginning to think about career opportunities, and Douglas wrote New York lawyers about his prize student. To Emory Buckner of Elihu Root's prestigious Wall Street firm, Douglas commended Fortas as "not quite as old" as some recent graduates but "in every respect as mature and able. . . . There have been very few men graduating from here since I have known the place who would receive such wholehearted support and recommendations as Mr. Fortas."[122] To Wall Street's Colonel William J. Donovan, Douglas reported that Fortas was "not merely a good man, but an outstanding man in every respect. In my seven or eight years of teaching I have seen but few men equal to him. He is an extraordinary person." In the classroom and on his own, Fortas had shown "great independence of thought and an unusual amount of imagination and resourcefulness." Fortas was "not anxious to get into a big firm in New York [doubtless at least partially because Fortas knew that his religion precluded it]," Douglas continued, "but would prefer to work for men whom at a distance he has come to respect and admire."[123] To Walter Pollak, whose firm of Engelhard, Pollak, Pitcher and Stern combined civil rights advocacy with corporate practice, Douglas wrote: "I hate to see him not go into teaching, but if he goes into practice, I would rather have him under your tutelage than under any other person I know of."[124] Fortas accepted an offer from Pollak, whose small but prestigious law firm another recent editor in chief of the *Yale Law Journal* had joined.[125] At this stage Yale intervened. Douglas had sent Fortas to Chicago on the consumer credit investigation with the hope that he would win an invitation to the University of Chicago Law School's faculty.[126] By January 1933, Yale wanted to hire Fortas. At a faculty meeting that month, after extended discussion of his scholastic record and his work on the journal, his professors voted to offer him a teaching fellowship for 1933–34.[127]

"I talked with the people at the New York law firm and they were kind enough to release me from my commitment to them," Fortas recalled. During the summer of 1933, he added, "I stayed in New Haven and prepared myself to teach some courses." But Jerome Frank, as general counsel to the New Deal's Agricultural Adjustment Administration, had recruited Professor Wesley Sturges to help in Washington, and Sturges soon requested assistance from Fortas. Though Fortas earlier had rejected his article, Frank offered him a job. "I remember my reluctance," Fortas said. "I thought I would stay and work on my courses, but he and various other people on the faculty told me it would do me more good to go down there and come on back, and I [had] prepared my courses adequately, and this was a new and complicated form of experience."[128] For the next five years, Fortas commuted between New Haven and Washington. Yale had provided him with a jurisprudence to guide him and with mentors who would propel him to power.

# CHAPTER 2

# "The Greatest Law Firm in the Country"

THE SEVEN-HOUR TRAIN RIDE FROM NEW HAVEN TO WASHINGTON CARried its passengers into a different world. Yet New Deal Washington, like Yale Law School, venerated the bright youngsters whom Fortas, still only twenty-three years old, personified. Asked about youth in government in 1933, one New Dealer replied that "the symbol of the whole thing is Abe Fortas."[1] A contemporary article spotlighting Fortas was entitled "Uncle Sam Grows Younger."[2]

## SAINT JEROME'S HOLY CRUSADE

Washington placed lawyers at the top of its hierarchy. As the crisis generated by the Depression worsened and the excitement created by the New Deal rose, the nation had elevated its legal minds to positions of new importance. Franklin Roosevelt needed lawyers, and he attracted them in droves. Professor Felix Frankfurter's "Happy Hotdogs" from Harvard Law School and their Yale counterparts, the "Young Hotdogs," poured into the nation's capital along with other recent law school graduates.[3] "A plague of young lawyers settled on Washington," one administrator grumbled. "They all claimed to be friends of somebody or other and mostly of Felix Frankfurter and Jerome Frank."[4]

Fortas moved into a house on 34th Street, which he shared with several friends of Frank and Frankfurter: Justice Harlan Stone's clerk, Howard Westwood; Senator Robert Wagner's legislative assistant, Leon Keyserling; Justice Benjamin Cardozo's clerk, Ambrose Doskow; Thomas Emerson, from the Na-

tional Recovery Administration; and a journalist, James Allen. The residence on
34th Street, like that of most New Deal lawyers, was "a run-of-the-mill" three-
story house. The six men shared expenses and hired a cook who prepared breakfast in the mornings and made dinner for those with time to come home to eat.
There were sporadic parties, whose hallmark was "high conversation" and some
drinking.[5]

Like Fortas, some of his housemates were Jews and recent law school graduates. New Deal legal culture did not rely only on such inexperienced youths. The
most celebrated New Dealers, among them Jerome Frank and Thomas Corcoran, generally had come to Washington from corporate practice on Wall Street.
Nor was Washington unprejudiced. To cite but one example, Jerome Frank,
himself a Jew, said he worried about the number of "Palestinian wetbacks" he
hired at the Agricultural Adjustment Administration because his superiors were
watching him for signs of favoritism.[6] But the New Deal did create an opportunity for young outsiders. Jewish law review editors who had pounded the
pavements of Wall Street could find challenging positions in Washington, and as
the capital accepted them, they became more assimilated. There was an atmosphere of secular humanism in New Deal Washington and a commitment to
meritocracy that made religion less important. "We never knew who was Jewish
and who was Christian," one of Fortas's Protestant friends said. "It absolutely
made no impression. We would find out somebody was Jewish because their
parents would come and all of a sudden they'd be setting up a kosher kitchen."[7]

For young Jews and Irish Catholics, the New Deal was a fortuitous event, as
it created a demand for their services in Washington. In another era, they might
have had the option of becoming corporate lawyers, and they might have taken it.
Certainly many, including Fortas, later chose that path. The New Deal offered
them the chance to pit themselves against corporate attorneys with years of
experience at a time when other areas of law were closed to them. They went to
Washington out of opportunism as much as out of idealism.[8] Still, the idealism
was there. Like his housemates, Fortas was a committed liberal who was sure
that "people ought not to starve" and who insisted that "government has responsibility."[9] In a sense, as Fortas acknowledged, New Deal liberalism was conservative,
as it sought to avoid the revolution the Depression might have occasioned by
introducing reforms that would make capitalism more efficient.[10] Yet liberals
who pressed to expand the power of the state and address the most glaring
problems of poverty were also progressive. They were reconstructing the world
"from the chaos left by President Hoover's Administration," Fortas remembered.
"[We] could see the new world and feel it taking form under our hands. It was
one of those periods of flux when there was practically no obstacle between
thinking up an idea and putting it into effect."[10] During his first three days in

Washington, Fortas did not even unpack his suitcase. Though he did not yet have an office, or even a desk, he was putting in twenty-hour days. Fully dressed, he slept on a couch in an office at the Agricultural Adjustment Administration for a few hours each night. There was nothing unusual about his schedule, Fortas emphasized shortly before his death. "Mostly as you go through life you see giants become men but in the New Deal days men became giants."[11]

For Fortas, New Deal liberalism was the political analogue of legal realism.[12] Many legal realists became New Dealers, and they also perceived a strong bond between legal realism and the New Deal. In a speech entitled "Experimental Jurisprudence and the New Deal," for example, Jerome Frank contended that legal realism made New Deal liberalism possible.[13] The liberal atmosphere existed compatibly with legal realism because it too subordinated rules to results. But since most conservatives, and perhaps all politicians, also cared more about substance than process, that alone was hardly sufficient to establish an affinity between liberalism and legal realism. Nor were the legal realists the first to claim that enduring legal principles did not determine the course of law. Jurispruden- tially, there was little new in legal realism. It was because the realists were the first to apply these jurisprudential insights to legal education that the generation of which Fortas was a part was the first to learn in large numbers in elite law schools about the role of idiosyncrasy in the formation of private and public law, the importance of focusing on the particular context of a factual situation, and the utility of social sciences such as economics in illuminating legal issues. By the time they entered the New Deal, such lawyers were trained to adopt the same imaginative and modern approach to problem solving that liberal politicians were embracing. Further, since legal realism openly legitimated the use of law as a tool of social change, legal realists who became New Dealers differed from conser- vatives in that they felt no compulsion to hide their commitment to results over process.[14] They happily treated law as the great engine of social change. "I want to assure you," one New Deal official told his aides, "that we are not afraid of exploring anything within the law and we have a lawyer who will declare any- thing you want to do legal."[15]

At least in the beginning, the atmosphere also proved congenial to those who shared a vision of planning the economy in cooperation with big business and agriculture. Those who had Roosevelt's ear during the First Hundred Days reflected Theodore Roosevelt's strand of Progressive thought when they formed the National Recovery Administration (NRA) and the Agricultural Adjustment Administration (AAA). Those agencies suspended antitrust laws to allow busi- nessmen and farmers to set production quotas and minimum prices and to develop marketing agreements that might raise prices, stimulate business to invest in the economy, and end the Depression. Woodrow Wilson's conflicting

Progressive ideology, espoused in the New Deal by Louis Brandeis and by Felix Frankfurter and his protégés, would have constrained big business through antitrust litigation and restored competitive markets. The planners, in contrast, accepted large firms and farms on the grounds that they were more efficient than their smaller counterparts. They sought to make them more efficient still and to harness them to the public interest. Together, the NRA and AAA became the nation's most ambitious experiment in national planning.[16]

Fortas threw in his lot with the more visionary planners. His identification was apparent during the New Deal. Especially at the AAA and at the NRA's descendant, the Bituminous Coal Division, and even at the Securities and Exchange Commission, Fortas worked to develop a partnership between the government and the private sector that would make the economy function more smoothly. He was a reformer who demanded the upper hand for government in this partnership, but he looked forward, instead of seeking through the use of antitrust to turn the clock back to the distant nineteenth-century world of smaller economic units.

Jerome Frank, the general counsel to the AAA, symbolized the planners' imaginativeness much in the way that Fortas exemplified the New Dealers' youth. Frank's partners thought him insane to forgo a profitable private practice for government service, but he left anyway and gave young government lawyers the training they would have received in corporate firms.[17] The sixty-odd lawyers Frank eventually assembled included some of the best and brightest New Deal minds. One recruit boasted that Frank's staff was "the greatest law firm in the country."[18] In Fortas's words, Frank became "the spark plug and the genius of practically every important gathering of Government officials in those days." Asked to describe Frank, Fortas confessed that he was "somewhat appalled" at having to set down his impressions of a person so "vibrant, complex and colorful." According to Fortas, Frank never stopped talking, not even when he was galloping on a horse or applying the nose drops a sinus condition required him to take every two hours. "A customary Washington sight was Jerry continuing to talk, lying on the floor and medicating himself."[19]

Frank was charged with controlling the flow of farmers' output in order to increase demand. In many cases that meant reducing, and in some instances curtailing, the production of staple crops and other agricultural commodities. Though as under secretary of agriculture Rex Tugwell supported Frank's vision of a planned society, the AAA's mission still scandalized old hands in the Department of Agriculture who believed in the American farmer's right to produce as much as possible. They were convinced that, more disturbing still, none of Frank's young lawyers knew anything about farming. Like other New Dealers, Fortas enjoyed telling the story of his fellow AAA lawyer Lee Pressman, who thought farmers grew macaroni.[20] Yet when Frank had to single out someone on his staff who was unfamiliar with farmers' work he chose not Pressman but Fortas, whose performance, he said, illustrated "that a man need not have known anything about agriculture to have been competent in his work."[21]

Arguments over what was in the public interest rippled through the AAA almost from the beginning, dividing Frank's reformers from the traditionalists. The AAA administrator George Peek had no interest in promoting a planned economy. He cared exclusively about raising farm prices. He did not favor limiting production but placed his faith in marketing agreements that would regulate distribution. Peek favored large farmers, whereas Frank supported "the small farmer," Fortas explained.[22] Indeed Tugwell, Frank, Fortas, and others at the AAA hoped to redistribute income within the agricultural community. They promoted production control and maintained that when marketing agreements were employed to govern flow, the processors and farmers who benefited from the agreements' suspension of the antitrust laws should open their books and records to the government to show that the consumer was not being bilked. Secretary of Agriculture Henry Wallace, who was aware he had "two ill-matched horses in harness together" vacillated between the two groups.[23] Disagreements were made fiercer by the traditionalists' allegations that Frank and the Tugwell sympathizers on his staff were formulating policy when they should be worrying about law.[24] The friction gave young lawyers such as Fortas their first exposure to bureaucratic infighting. One veteran of the AAA recalled, "Both sides . . . learned to do good, as each side saw it, on the sly."[25]

Frank held his lawyers together through his unique ability to inspire loyalty. As a colleague said, because his "unceasing reach for affection from those around him" made Frank "quick to extend his own affection to others," he proved one of the best administrators in Washington. "He set up a bond between himself and the scores of young lawyers working for him that was unequalled . . . in any other branch of the Roosevelt Administration." Neither a systematic bureaucrat nor the British-style civil servant Frankfurter extolled, Frank nevertheless inspired his young to engage in "a holy crusade, with Saint Jerome setting the pace in his avid pursuit of salvation."[26] Fortas doubted "if there was ever a more vigorous, devoted and effective rescue squad than the group collected by him . . . [and] inspired by Jerry's fantastic ingenuity and boundless energy."[27]

Fortas's friendship with the AAA attorney never meant as much to him as did the three most significant relationships in his life—those with his wife, with Thurman Arnold, and with William O. Douglas—but Frank was one of the few persons to whom Fortas became close. They liked each other's company. They took long horseback rides together on weekends, and they were "always laughing and talking and making jokes." Fortas's wife later said that Fortas "loved Jerome

Frank through to the very end." She emphasized, however, that the bond between the two men was one of time and place.[28] As Fortas's first real boss, Frank
became another mentor. He demanded devotion from Fortas and relentlessly
fended off efforts by other government departments to raid Fortas for as long as he
was able.[29]

Jerome Frank taught Fortas the importance of loyalty and gave him his first
taste of real power. With major farmers and growers waiting for government
officials to tell them how much they could produce, Frank's New Dealers received authority rapidly and came quickly to enjoy it. The power that made
generations of government servants arrogant came to them when they were
unusually young and made them more so than most, as Fortas hinted in a later
description of his early days at the AAA. One of his most vivid memories, he said,
was "a recollection of people who were sitting in the anteroom waiting for one of
us young New Dealers to give them some time. These people sitting in the
anteroom were executives of large agricultural businesses who wanted the help
they thought they could get from these marketing agreements."[30]

They had to be patient. When Fortas arrived at the AAA, Frank's staff included only a few lawyers.[31] Three of his co-workers in the Legal Division had
been working without salary for more than two months.[32] Politics was the
culprit. Postmaster General Jim Farley, the godfather of FDR's political mafia,
had announced that he would withhold approval of all appointments to Frank's
staff until nominees had received "necessary political endorsements."[33] Indeed
he threatened that he would not approve Fortas until Frank sanctioned seven
patronage appointments Farley wanted to make.[34]

The planners' chosen method for making private interests accountable, the
regulatory process, made them distrust patronage. Regulation, they saw, had the
potential to reduce the power of the judges the legal realists had taught them to
suspect. Instead of allowing courts, which venerated individual rights, to decide
issues, they hoped to increase the authority of administrative agencies whose
officials would make hard choices on an ad hoc, continuing basis to promote the
common good.[35] The discretion the administrative process gave regulators meant
they had to be intelligent. They should be bright youngsters, like Fortas, not
political hacks. "Good men can make poor laws workable," the New Dealer James
Landis once said. "Poor men will wreak havoc with good laws."[36] The sort of
people who had the right political connections might well prove unable to do the
AAA's work, Rex Tugwell explained to the President. The Agricultural Adjustment Act authorized the AAA to help the farmer by negotiating with the industrial
groups which processed his goods—the packers, millers, canners, and tobacco
companies. The processors' groups could afford the best legal talent. "To cope
with these lawyers," Tugwell admonished FDR, "the Administration should

have, as nearly as may be, equally and, if possible, more able lawyers" who knew corporate law, commercial law, and business practices. "More than that, they must be extremely ingenious and alert to detect subterfuges, evasions, and artful devices designed to frustrate the purposes of the Administration."[37]

Tugwell also maintained that the regulatory process demanded honest administrators who would not become prisoners of those they governed. Fortas and other lawyers Frank had selected agonized over whether Fortas should keep a crate of oranges a grower sent him,[38] and Tugwell believed that the AAA required more attorneys of such moral rectitude. They "must be men of the highest integrity who cannot be deflected from their objectives by flattery, implied promises of future work, or the desire to obtain prestige. They must be hard working and devoted to the enterprise and not merely good technicians but men whose sympathies are completely—and intelligently rather than prejudicially— in accord with the ideals of the 'new deal.' "[39]

But in a depression hacks need jobs too.[40] Roosevelt encouraged compromise.[41] In this particular case, the settlement gave Tugwell the upper hand. Julien Friant, the special assistant to the secretary of agriculture for personnel, supported Tugwell's idea of recruiting the best applicants. Friant would assemble the dossier of one of Frank's choices, contact the member of Congress from whose district the hopeful came, tell the representative about the "fine young fellow from your district" and ask for a political endorsement, which almost always followed.[42]

Still, the issue of political patronage never entirely disappeared. Even Friant, who took pride in hiring the "cream of the crop" and boasted of the number of Ph.Ds the AAA employed,[43] was occasionally frustrated by the extent of Frank's enthusiasm for alumni of elite law schools who had never seen a farm.[44] Politicians were even less sympathetic. The Vice-President, John Garner, complained that "all this handing the top cards to boys who had never worked a precinct" was new to him.[45] "The issue was Ivy League or non–Ivy League," Fortas's housemate explained. "Not among us, but among the politicians and people who wanted patronage on the Hill, who were complaining that nobody who wasn't an Ivy League lawyer could get an important job."[46]

Thirty years earlier, Henry Stimson, as United States Attorney for the Southern District of New York under President Theodore Roosevelt, had rejected the suggestions of members of Congress and had made up his own staff of recent graduates at the top of their Ivy League law school classes. Most of his choices, with the notable exception of Felix Frankfurter, shared his Protestant elite background and could manage to live on the small government salaries he paid. In the intervening years, Frankfurter, who had become a Harvard Law School professor, had concentrated on placing his protégés in corporate law firms. Frankfurter, Frank, and some government officials were emphasizing the importance of intellect in government service once again, and they were expanding their pool to include outsiders such as Fortas. They were trying to replace the political patronage that had determined government advancement with the intellectual patronage of the academy. Though both processes were inherently undemocratic, the ideal of an intellectual meritocracy represented an attempt to bring about a more intelligent formulation of public policy.[47]

Frank hoped to pay his lawyers in accordance with their brains too. Within a month of his arrival, Fortas had made himself so essential that Frank, hoping to keep him in Washington instead of losing him to Yale in the fall, offered him a salary of $4000. After agreeing to take a leave from Yale for the fall term, Fortas learned that his pay would be $2600, based on the amount of time that he had been out of law school. The sum exceeded the average salary for most young New Deal lawyers, but Frank still became furious. The AAA and the Department of Agriculture had made "the strongest kind of moral commitment" to Fortas that his salary would be in accordance with his ability rather than his experience, Frank claimed.[48] Fortas stayed on anyway. Though he must have understood that the New Deal was not as much of a meritocracy as his boss tried to make it, he shared Frank's dedication.

### THE PEACH CASE

By the fall of 1933, Fortas had become the AAA's expert on peaches. During Fortas's first week in Washington that summer, Thomas Austern of the NRA was assigned to deal with a crisis regarding cling peaches raised and canned in California. Austern's boss, Judge J. Harry Covington, and a representative of the peach canning industry, Preston McKinney, explained that there were too many peaches on the market, and neither farmers nor peach canners were receiving an adequate price for their product. Fortas was the AAA's representative on the case, and, Austern recalled, they "talked to McKinney because both of us [being] city boys, we didn't know an awful lot about peaches."[49]

Nobody could tell them whether peaches fell within the purview of the National Industrial Recovery Act or the Agricultural Adjustment Act. "Neither of us had seen either statute or knew a damned thing about it," Austern said, "but we went to work, and we concluded that what we should do is write it in parallel." They would compose an AAA marketing agreement setting out the quotas producers could grow or can and an NRA code for peaches. Fortas and Austern worked quickly. Around midnight, McKinney got them a room at the Mayflower Hotel. At 5:30 the next morning, he awakened them, took them out to breakfast, and told them they were overexerting themselves. By nightfall, McKinney had become agitated and had begun ripping their work apart—literally. "McKinney was hysterical," Austern said. "I got the hotel doctor to give him a shot of morphine and then put the stuff back together again."[50] Shortly before midnight it was ready for delivery to the Department of Agriculture, which stamped it and set a hearing date. Only one marketing agreement of any kind antedated theirs, and Fortas and Austern's policy for peaches became, in the words of one contemporary economist, "something of a model for the form of agreement to be used."[51] Once Agriculture had accepted the marketing agreement, the NRA excluded peaches from its jurisdiction and the responsibility for regulating the California peach industry fell chiefly to Fortas.

From the beginning, Fortas and other government lawyers worried about the constitutionality of the Agricultural Adjustment Act. Several questions particularly puzzled those who worked with marketing agreements. The three most basic concerned delegation of legislative power, the commerce clause, and the due process clause.[52] Had Congress delegated its legislative functions to the secretary of agriculture without sufficiently clear guidelines and standards? Did the authority that the Agricultural Adjustment Act gave the secretary of agriculture to regulate goods "in the current of interstate . . . commerce" enable the department to control intrastate transactions? Fortas and Austern claimed that the peaches in question, for example, although grown and canned in California, were in the current of interstate commerce because they were shipped outside the state. It was unclear whether the Supreme Court would approve that interpretation.[53]

The act also empowered the secretary, "after due notice and the opportunity for a hearing," to enter into marketing agreements with producers, processors, and others who handled an agricultural commodity in the current of interstate commerce. A majority of the affected parties in a locality had to vote for a marketing agreement before it became enforceable via a license.[54] The small producers the AAA lawyers hoped to help sometimes opposed the marketing agreements because they thought they could do better by exceeding the suggested production quotas and undercutting their larger counterparts. Once a majority had accepted a voluntary marketing agreement, however, the license enforcing it became mandatory and bound everyone in the area. A committee composed of various individuals associated with the production of the commodity enforced the quotas and acted as the producers' representative to the AAA. Unlike the marketing agreement section of the act, the licensing section did not require a notice and hearing, and AAA lawyers agonized over whether it violated the due process clause of the Fifth Amendment.[55] They also fretted about the extent of their power over the licensee. They were uncertain whether licenses that fixed prices and production quotas, as well as each licensee's share of the market, did so legally. For all their insistence on the propriety of granting the AAA access to the licensee's books and records, AAA lawyers also wondered whether they legitimately could insert a "books and record clause" in the license.[56]

"The most important things that happened in Washington those days were over cocktails," Frank later recalled. "Martinis did an awful lot to stimulate thinking."[57] To some, the Agricultural Adjustment Act must have sounded as if it had been drafted after one drink too many. The lawyers who inherited the statute were bound to disagree over the strategy they should use to sustain it. Should they rush it to friendly judges who would uphold its constitutionality and increase its credibility, or should they try to keep it away from the courts for as long as possible?

Felix Frankfurter counseled caution. During the early days of the New Deal, Frank attended a luncheon where Frankfurter gave a speech "on how important it was not to go too fast." He was acting, some thought, as the mouthpiece of Justice Louis Brandeis, who not only distrusted the collectivism of early New Deal legislation, but also believed that it was so sloppily drafted that the Court would hold it unconstitutional, thereby damaging the credibility of Roosevelt's program. Frank wanted to go faster than Frankfurter.[58] Thurman Arnold, who had taken a leave from Yale to join Fortas at the AAA, wanted to go faster still. Like other administrative agencies, the AAA could not conduct its own litigation and had to work through the Department of Justice. When the first challenge to the AAA licenses arose, Arnold met Frank for lunch at the Cosmos Club and said that he had arranged a deal with Justice allowing him to rush the case to the Supreme Court. When Frank demurred, Arnold became indignant. He accused Frank of cowardice, comparing him to Frankfurter. "I'm perfectly willing to go up, but goddamn it we're in [the] wrong in these cases," Frank countered. "We can't win." Arnold and Fortas soon found a new case which they convinced Frank the AAA would not lose.[59]

The lawsuit involved Fortas's peach marketing agreement. One corporation, Calistan Packers, was ignoring production quotas and canning more cling peaches than its license permitted. "Ninety-five percent of all the processors of peaches in California were complying with the license," Thurman Arnold explained to a budget-minded bureaucrat who ordered him to explain why he and Fortas, instead of taking a train, had flown to California in what Fortas described as "a horrible journey" in a trimotor plane.[60] "It had required months of effort to build up this [peach processors'] organization," Arnold continued, "and members of the organization were complaining that inasmuch as Calistan Packers were not being immediately restrained from exceeding their allotment they would have to act in a similar manner to protect themselves." By the time that the Department of Justice and the AAA decided to file suit, Calistan was glutting the market and the situation was at a crisis point.[61]

The case raised all of the troubling questions about the marketing agreements. Was Calistan truly in interstate commerce given that almost all cling peaches were produced and canned in California? Could Calistan and others who had refused to sign the marketing agreement claim that the license did not bind them? Had Calistan implicitly acknowledged the validity of the marketing agreement by its application to the AAA for an allotment that would give it a share of the canning market? Could Calistan prevent the Department of Agriculture from examining its books and records? Was there any quicker remedy available to the AAA than setting a hearing to assess fines or revoke Calistan's license? The future of a vital New Deal agency was in the hands of Fortas, an inexperienced youth who had never tried a case. Frank had arranged a semester's leave of absence from Yale for Fortas, and had notified the university that Arnold would arrive a week late. Frank set up a team: Fortas, Arnold, and Special Assistant to the Attorney General James Lawrence Fly would go to San Francisco, where a U.S. attorney would aide them in arguing the peach case.[62]

The question of a remedy had not been settled before the lawyers flew to California. Realizing that Calistan would be undeterred by the prospect of a fine, Fortas and Arnold pressed for equitable relief in the form of a temporary injunction that would prohibit Calistan Packers from exceeding its quota.[63] The law did not appear to be on Fortas and Arnold's side. Since the Agricultural Adjustment Act did not specifically give federal district courts the jurisdiction to enforce the act, it seemed unlikely that they would grant an injunction against infringers. Justice Department lawyers searched vainly for a case that would support their plea. Returning from dinner one evening, Fortas and Arnold joined them. "That's nonsense," Arnold said when he was told that the lawyers could not find a precedent on point. "There's a case on every point." He went to a bookshelf and returned with exactly the right case. Fortas asked him how he had done it. "It was very simple," Arnold replied. "This involves canned peaches, can, can, can reminded me of sardines. I looked under sardines in [an index of cases by key] Words and Phrases and I found the case." To Fortas, the incident demonstrated his friend's genius.[64] The case, *People v. Stafford Packing Company,* became the cornerstone of the AAA's plea for injunctive relief.[65]

Their litigation strategy reflected the pragmatism of legal realism. Before raising those constitutional questions which Frankfurter feared the courts would decide negatively, Fortas and Arnold located compliant defendants and a friendly judge. Once they had prepared the case and arrived in California, Washington reconsidered the wisdom of bringing suit. Arnold convinced Frank to allow the team to try the case if Arnold could persuade Calistan to default. Arnold then went to Calistan and made an offer the packer could not refuse: "We'll waive all fines in this case, and in consideration of waiving all fines, will you agree not to present any opposition?"[66] Calistan, which was already teetering on the brink of financial insolvency, agreed to default.[67] As most judges would claim that the issue of constitutionality should be avoided as long as Calistan was not challenging the act, the next step was to find the right judge. Judge Adolphus St. Sure, a liberal Republican district judge, seemed tailor-made for an *ex parte* argument on the Act's constitutionality. Asked later how he had won the ruling that the act was constitutional in California, Arnold blithely replied that he had "a sympathetic judge" and that the atmosphere of national emergency so pervaded the country in 1933 that even the Supreme Court might have upheld the act.[68] At the time, however, the New Deal lawyers considered the participation of Judge St. Sure and Calistan's cooperativeness crucial prerequisites to the presentation of the case's constitutional issues.[69]

The strategy worked beautifully. St. Sure granted the temporary injunction, supported the government on all issues, and squarely addressed the constitutional questions about the Agricultural Adjustment Act that a judge in another case had evaded. Congress had "the power to regulate any and all commerce which may seriously affect the interstate trade," and it had not improperly delegated its legislative power to the AAA. Nor did the act, the marketing agreement, and the license before the court violate due process. Courts, St. Sure said, should not hastily invalidate such important legislation when Congress had made a legislative finding that a national emergency existed and farmers were in distress. Echoing Fortas and Arnold's brief, the judge observed: "To adopt the view that the Constitution is static and that it does not permit Congress from time to time to take such steps as may reasonably be deemed appropriate to the economic preservation of the country, is to insist that the constitution was created containing the seeds of its own destruction."[70]

Fortas and Arnold had been working until 3 A.M. each morning on the case. Arnold had visited only one San Francisco night club and had attended only one "wild party" sponsored by the Bohemian Club. (He had nevertheless formed an opinion about California: "I had never been in a place where the general artistic appreciation was so high and the general economic outlook was so bigoted and narrow. It made Connecticut look like a very liberal state. I have a theory that the reason that intelligent men cannot be elected to office in Connecticut is that people don't want to vote for them. The reason that intelligent people cannot be elected to office in California is entirely different. There doesn't appear to be any."[71]) Victory must have elated them.

It did not, however, make them overbold. Although invigorated by their victory in the peach case and by the Supreme Court's subsequent opinion upholding a state milk-pricing plan,[72] they realized that a decision by someone to the ideological right of St. Sure could jeopardize the Agricultural Adjustment Act. Frankfurter's advice to proceed cautiously influenced them far more than the Harvard professor assumed. At the same time, Frankfurter incorrectly regarded his protégés in the Justice Department as the voices of reason when in fact they had determined to test the constitutionality of the Agricultural Adjustment Act.

## STRATEGIC RETREAT

Fortas represented the Department of Agriculture in the case that brought the conflict between the AAA and the Department of Justice into the open and that exemplified the obstacles conservative judges posed for New Deal lawyers. *Hillsborough Packing Company v. Henry Wallace* involved the AAA as defendant rather than plaintiff. Two grapefruit packers had challenged the pro rata quotas in the Florida citrus marketing agreement and license. They filed for a temporary injunction to prevent the AAA and the citrus committee—which represented the citrus industry to the AAA and enforced the quotas—from restricting their production and share of the market. Both the Agricultural Adjustment Act and the citrus fruit license, they alleged, were unconstitutional.

The citrus commission retained as its attorney Francis P. Whitehair, a leading trial lawyer in Florida. A self-important man, Whitehair ultimately installed himself in the Francis P. Whitehair Building, which could be reached by two bridges, each named after him. "The slightest slight on Whitehair caused him to bridle and get red," one AAA lawyer said. "He was a very vain person with an exalted ego but smart as hell."[73] Whitehair's temperament posed an obstacle for Fortas. The case would be tried by a friend of Whitehair's, Judge Alexander Akerman, who vehemently opposed the New Deal and who had been the first federal judge to hold the National Industrial Recovery Act unconstitutional.[74] "Francis, although extremely able, was fairly emotional about the case, and it involved problems which were somewhat outside of his professional experience," Fortas recalled. Whitehair's emotionalism and egotism predisposed him to develop the constitutional issue. "From the point of view of the AAA, a cardinal element was to restrict damage that would be the foreseeable result of a decision by Judge Akerman, and at the same time to avoid mortal offense to Whitehair and the local Citrus Commission." Still, Fortas believed that the AAA and Whitehair shared the same objective, "to avoid damage to the citrus program, so far as possible."[75]

On that basis the two men worked out a strategy aimed at restricting Judge Akerman to the case's jurisdictional and procedural aspects and, they hoped, diverting him from the issue of constitutionality. Fortas and Whitehair agreed to argue for dismissal on three grounds: First, the secretary of agriculture was an indispensable party to the suit and, since the packers had not served him, the Florida court lacked jurisdiction over him. Second, the citrus commission's recall just one day before Akerman heard the case, of the pro rata quotas the packers were challenging, and the AAA's recent administrative changes in its license system made the case moot. Third, the suit was premature because the packers had not exhausted the administrative remedies the statute granted them in the form of appeals to the AAA.[76]

The packers filed suit on January 14th. Agriculture did not notify Justice of the pending suit until a week later, just five days before the date set for the hearing. At that point, problems arose. James Fly reported that the government considered the case "ideal for the purposes of litigation." The marketing agreement and license, which were supported by most citrus growers, involved an important industry indisputably engaged in interstate commerce. Fly argued for Justice that the risk of skirting constitutional questions and limiting the defense to procedural and jurisdictional issues was "a great one considering the importance of the case from a political and economic standpoint and that such a course of action would give the Court opportunity to criticize the Administration in general and the Department of Agriculture especially."[77] Unimpressed, lawyers from Agriculture responded that they had taken those factors into consideration and determined to take the risk anyway. Given the time constraints, Justice agreed to follow Agriculture's lead.[78] That decision left Fortas in the middle. Though he had formulated the strategy, Whitehair acted as if it were his own and engaged in acrimonious disputes with Fly throughout the case. Fortas shuttled between the two camps. Whenever friction arose between Whitehair and Fly, he tried "to calm ruffled feathers and smooth them down." Fortas considered tactful mediation his appropriate role. "I was a young man. I was the junior," he emphasized. Whitehair and Fly were "the two great impresarios, the two great opera stars."[79] But it was the twenty-three-year-old Fortas who, while maintaining a characteristically deferential demeanor, was really managing the team.

The impresarios argued their case in front of a judge who was himself a prima donna. One attorney from Justice said he had "never observed a more prejudiced Court."[80] During a trial that at times seemed straight from *Alice in Wonderland*,[81] Judge Akerman reluctantly acceded to Fortas's contention that his court had no jurisdiction over the secretary of agriculture. He then declared that the case could proceed without the secretary and, on the basis of a convoluted theory of agency, substituted the chair of the Florida citrus commission in Wallace's stead. Nor would he hold the case moot, as even one of the plaintiff's attorneys agreed was appropriate,[82] since Akerman suspected that the AAA had lifted the pro rata provisions the day before he heard the case only to influence him and might reimpose them "the day after" the hearing. Further, the judge refused to refer the plaintiffs back to the AAA. "If this Agricultural Act, A. A. A. or Q. Y. Z. or whatever it is, I cannot remember these names, is constitutional," he said, the AAA had the right to continue its operations. Although even the plaintiff's chief attorney had not argued that the Agricultural Adjustment Act was unconstitutional, Akerman continued that unless he were a coward, which he most emphatically denied he was, he had to pass upon the constitutionality of the act. So much for exhaustion of administrative remedies. Akerman went on to issue a temporary injunction and to declare the act unconstitutional. According to him, "eight yokes of oxen" could be driven through the holes Congress had left in it. [83]

Fortas's plan had backfired. He had sought to limit the case to its procedural and jurisdictional aspects, failed to consult the Department of Justice on trial tactics until the last minute, convinced Justice to ignore the constitutional dimensions of the case, and it had all been for naught. Justice Department lawyers naturally complained that they had been overridden. [84] Now the case was about to be appealed, as both Justice and Agriculture agreed was necessary, [85] and because Agriculture and the citrus commission had limited their defense to jurisdictional caviling, the lower court record to which the court of appeals was restricted contained no evidence demonstrating the economic justification for the Agricultural Adjustment Act and the grapefruit license. The court of appeals might well agree with Akerman that the act was unconstitutional. It was all Fortas's fault.

The appellate court, however, proved more satisfied with Fortas's approach than had the Justice Department. When the case came before the Fifth Circuit, the three-judge panel ignored Fly's arguments for the statute's constitutionality. It agreed with Judge Akerman that the secretary of agriculture was not an indispensable party to the suit and that the case was not moot. Nevertheless, the court held that Akerman had erred in reaching the issue of constitutionality and in issuing the injunction because the packers had not exhausted their administrative remedies. [86]

The case and its disposition on appeal reflected Fortas's style as a lawyer. Throughout his life, he proved exceedingly careful in his selection of test cases. When a situation demanded it, as in the peach case, he could invoke the special policy arguments associated with the most visionary legal realist. When he faced an unreceptive judge or when he considered a test of constitutionality otherwise inappropriate, as in the grapefruit case, he stood on the law with determination. That combination of precision, sensitivity to facts and context, receptiveness to social policy, and care in planning strategy made him, even at twenty-three, a brilliant attorney. The AAA experience defined and sharpened the lawyering skills that served him throughout his life. There were many people who came to Washington with Fortas's credentials, one of his housemates recalled, but it was in his months at the AAA that he emerged as "a superstar."[87]

During that period he also displayed an understanding of business practices and the ability to use the appropriate vernacular. When congressmen relayed complaints about the overly "professorial" fashion in which the Agricultural Adjustment Act was administered,[88] their accusations did not apply to Fortas. The young man who could reason with both Whitehair and Fly could communicate with anyone. He spoke easily with growers and processors, farmers and businessmen. Even in the strife-ridden AAA, he was widely admired. When Frank delegated the tobacco growers' problems to him, one colleague recalled, "Fortas's capacity as a negotiator with dirt farmers just became a fabulously recognized thing around the department, as did his composure and understanding. They all liked him."[89]

That capacity for brokering proved equally evident in Fortas's negotiations with the citrus growers in Florida. In the hyperbolic tones common to Depression-era magazines, Beverly Smith described Fortas's impact at the hearing on the marketing agreements for the citrus industry: "Assembled there you would have seen this country's leading orange executives, lemon barons and grapefruit magnates—men whose products are on your table every day. Grave and reverend seigneurs, these—many thatched with gray." As they expressed their objections to the hearing officer, "sometimes acrimonious quarrels flared, but these were always stilled when the gentleman presiding, quietly and courteously, clarified and restated the issues involved. The code went through as he proposed." The presiding officer, Smith dramatically informed his readers, "was Abe Fortas, age 23, of Memphis, Tenn." Fortas, Smith continued, would be indistinguishable in a crowd, for he was "short, lightly built, disarmingly modest in manner. He has a natural quiet politeness, made more attractive by the pleasant accent of Tennessee in his voice." It was "only his eyes" which suggested "that the mind back of them is taking in a lot of territory." Smith quoted one of Fortas's professors at Yale on "this child": " 'Fortas can talk law in terms that the farmer and business man can understand. Why, that boy can pick peaches or irrigate a field with the Due Process clause of the Constitution.' "[90]

## FORTAS AT HOME

Smith overlooked a quality in Fortas that other contemporaries noticed. Fortas the New Dealer, like Fortas the *Yale Law Journal* editor in chief, proved unusually ambitious. One housemate found him "not as engaging as the other men in the house. He was introspective and evidently his mind was so constantly churning on his own future and what to do about it, that he didn't give much to people." Fortas was "a young man on the make, on the go, no question about that," said another. "Very ambitious." As at law school, he sought few confidants.[91]

He was self-absorbed. Though there were Communists in the AAA, Fortas seemed never to have known it. "Once in a while it's occurred to me to wonder . . . why there was never any attempt to recruit me," he said years later. "I hope it wasn't because I was regarded as a reactionary."[92] It was probably because Fortas gave the impression that he had little time for long conversations about ideas or ideologies. That was the sense of his housemates on the rare occasions they saw Fortas at home. During the time they lived together, Leon Keyserling was drafting the Wagner Act. Surely Fortas might have been expected to be curious about that historic piece of legislation which threw the government's weight on the side of labor and against management for the first time. But according to Keyserling, unlike the other members of the house, Fortas "just didn't manifest an interest."[93] In his own way, Fortas was an idealist, but his idealism remained largely unarticulated.

Yet his housemates also found him likeable. "He was sort of elfin," observed Thomas Emerson. "He was in no sense an extrovert or a domineering person. But he was very bright and sort of sly and cute in a way. . . . He was a delightful companion." Ambrose Doskow described Fortas as "a very earnest and serious guy, but very playful. . . . There was something always puckish about the way he talked about things." That trait could be frustrating. "He was elfin in the sense that if you tried to talk to him about something serious, a matter of public affairs or something you were engaged in, he always made sort of a whimsical joke of it. You could never really engage him on anything," Keyserling said.[94] When Beverly Smith asked how young New Dealers achieved such impressive results, Fortas answered, "Only young men are willing to take the risk of being ridiculous." Smith noted, "This remark contains much nourishment, but there is more to it than that."[95] The straight answer was never Fortas's forte.

Carol Agger liked his puckishness. The daughter of Eugene Agger, an economist at Rutgers University, she was a Protestant from a privileged background. Hers was the sort of childhood that included a Grand Tour of Europe. Through her father, she was acquainted with many New Dealers and well-known professors.[96] She was Fortas's intellectual match. After prep school, she had enrolled in Barnard, where she worked hard but maintained an active social life. "She used to go out with people her mother didn't approve of, and I must say her mother was right," one close friend remembered many years later.[97] The Aggers did, however, like her first husband, a Dartmouth man Agger married upon graduation. The couple moved to Wisconsin, and she first obtained a master's degree in economics at the University of Wisconsin, and then attended Marquette Law School for two years, where she served as associate editor of the school's law review. Predisposed toward the integration of law and social sciences that legal realism stressed, she found that the school had little to offer a person who hoped "to correlate" law and economics. Nor was its faculty broad-minded: "Any institution conducted by the Jesuits has a pall of narrowness cast over it that . . . [one who has been] in our so-called liberal institutions for so long would find it difficult to credit."[98]

Meanwhile the marriage was not going well. Agger's first husband was a pleasant man who sold insurance, wrote fiction, and played the piano. "You couldn't help but like him," his college roommate stressed. He was "a charming fellow, always glad to help anyone." But he lacked drive. "She was ambitious, hardworking, dedicated," whereas at this stage in his life her husband was "none of those things."[99] The marriage, although amiable, petered out and ended in divorce. "He was a very nice man," Carol Agger later said of her first husband. "It just wasn't anything I wanted to continue that way."[100] On her own after her second year of law school, Agger went to Washington in 1934. "She walked the streets looking for a job," a friend remembered. She really had nothing, and [this was] a very brave thing to do."[101] She found a position in the Marketing Agreement Section at the AAA, where her work won the "strong commendation" of her superiors.[102]

Fortas liked her instantly. "He came in, and he talked to me and he started to make a pest of himself," she said fondly years later.[103] But Agger, who had another beau, was not interested. That did not stop Fortas. Even when they began dating, "she was holding Abe off a little bit," Emerson commented. "He was really pushing hard to get her into the marriage." Ambrose Doskow remembered a significant dinner: "There were just a couple of us there and Abe very enthusiastically picked up a wine glass and smashed it on the fireplace and this was a tribute to Carol." It was, Doskow said, "a great romance," and during it Fortas was "the most ebullient person in the house." Another friend from the early days put it simply: "He worshipped Carol."[104]

Perhaps Fortas sensed in Agger temperamental compatibility. He could not have differed more from her first husband. The two men shared only a love of music. Like Agger, Fortas was hard-working, dedicated, and ambitious. Perhaps, too, he sensed in her qualities he lacked. At this stage in his life, he was a man on the make. He was trying to transform himself. He might have considered himself a Southerner, but he did not want others to think of him that way. Agger remembered him trying to make his speech sound more Northern. He knew little of the social amenities and could not eat a meal "properly" when she met him. He learned by watching her. He talked little of his family, and Agger met his mother only once after they were married. She thought that he was closer to her own parents, "who were more like what he wanted to be."[105] After two years in Washington, Fortas had seen that anti-Semitism survived even in the new meritocracy, but it had become equally apparent that "if non-WASP lawyers were professionally qualified and properly 'WASP' in their behavior, they could achieve prominent positions hitherto reserved for WASPs."[106] Agger was the closest he could get to the Protestant elite. When she agreed to marry him in 1935 in a small ceremony at which William O. Douglas served as best man, Fortas thought he was moving up in the world. In a telephone call relaying the news to his mother, he told her not to be upset, because if anyone had reason for concern it was Carol Agger's family rather than his own. His mother did not seem unhappy. She confided to his sister that she was glad her son had found someone as intelligent as he was.[107]

Though Fortas often acted as if his wife was made of china, he was extremely proud of her. Later, he would often introduce her as his lawyer,[108] and William O. Douglas would write that Carol Agger and Abe Fortas "had the best legal minds of any couple I ever knew."[109] For the present, however, Agger needed to complete law school and Fortas, too, had to spend more time at Yale.

## "CHILDREN WHO WISH TO MARRY"

Frank's repeated calls for assistance at first kept Fortas from full membership in the Yale community. The only way he could serve the law school from the AAA, he joked, was "by advising my prospective colleagues to go long on grapefruit and roosters." Indeed Frank had drafted so many Yale Law School professors that Fortas thought Yale would "have to fight hard to prevent a liaison with Keokuk Agricultural College."[110] But Frank relied most on Fortas. He allowed him to return to New Haven for the 1934 spring term but brought him back to Washington that summer and wanted him to remain at the AAA permanently.

Fortas hesitated. He could not continue to take leaves from Yale forever. Frank was promoting him rapidly. In the summer of 1934 the AAA increased his salary from $4600 to $5600. Compared to the $2500 Yale offered, even $4600 seemed princely, and Fortas told Douglas that the AAA raise made "the Law School offer seem more like an offer made by a man who is not anxious to secure my services." But he was getting bored. "I find," he said "that the A.A.A. is still using forms which I drafted as a model for the marketing agreements and licenses and that I can do . . . very interesting work there in my sleep. This is a sad state of affairs for a young man who must 'get along little doggie.'"[111]

Since Fortas had been interested in corporate law since working with Douglas on bankruptcy in law school, he decided that he wanted to work for the newly formed Securities and Exchange Commission (SEC), which had been established as an independent administrative agency charged with regulating the stock exchanges and the sale of securities. When Douglas became director of a study of protective and reorganization committees initiated by the commission, he recruited Fortas. For his part, Fortas told Douglas that "there is nothing that I would like to do more than that sort of job with you." But Douglas's attempts to gain access for Fortas to the SEC official who could put him on the payroll proved unavailing.[112] With no offer from the commission in hand, but with a new job at the AAA and invitations from the Tennessee Valley Authority (TVA) and the NRA, Fortas had to decide at the end of the summer whether he would return to Yale.[113] Dean Clark had already begun worrying that "unfortunately" Fortas "still has his eyes somewhat turned to Washington."[114] The dean did not think that the university administration, which was becoming angry about the leaves its law professors were taking for government service, would renew Fortas's leave, and, in any event, Yale could not match his government salary "without raising a tumult throughout all our younger faculty."[115]

In fact, Fortas was not particularly interested either in returning to Yale or remaining at the AAA. He wanted to work with Douglas in Washington, and he wired Douglas to ask what he should tell Yale, but, since Douglas had influenza, he was no help.[116] Fortas now told Yale that he would not return to the university that fall. He asked for a leave of absence, and if that could not be granted, he offered to resign. Ever solicitous of Douglas, he subsequently wrote his mentor: "I realized that I was putting you in an intolerable situation by asking you virtually to decide whether I should return. For this reason I phrased my wire as a decision on my part not to return, subject to change if you should advise me that this decision would embarrass you." Fortas would remain at the AAA while Douglas continued to try to place him. Fortas must have realized that he was beginning to sound importunate, for he closed this last in his long series of letters about job possibilities by assuring Douglas that he was "*most* anxious to work with you on anything at all," that he knew Douglas's arrangements were uncertain, "and I am merely trying to keep you informed from time to time of my plans."[117]

When Douglas's future became more certain, however, and he was finally able to offer the commission position that Fortas so wanted, unforeseen complications developed. Jerome Frank informed Douglas he would not let Fortas go.[118] Although Frank subsequently released Fortas from the AAA, Fortas knew Frank still wanted him to stay. Indeed he described Frank's agreement to release him as "a grand tactical pyrotechnic." But while Fortas knew Frank had been manipulating him and was "somewhat taken aback by the realization," he added, "I am very, very fond of Jerome and it is true, as he stated, that he has taken the risk of promoting me among other youngsters, and that he may properly expect loyalty in return—particularly when, as in my case, he has put one of us in charge of important work and this person's leaving will seriously disrupt his work."[119] Trapped between Frank's pull on his allegiance and his wish to work with Douglas, Fortas wired Douglas that he was staying at the AAA "because [of] Jerome's very strong feeling. God knows how miserable I am at inconvenience to you and how deeply I regret inability to work with you and how sad I am that minimum loyalty and affection require me to acquiesce in Jerome's wishes."[120]

Yet loyalty also pulled Fortas toward Douglas. He "could not possibly be any more aware" of his debt to Douglas "and that you are again willing to place a bet heavier than ever upon me. More than this, I realize that my interests lie predominantly in your work, and that there also is promise of development and of a future just as bright as I can make it." Ultimately he had determined to remain at the AAA, Fortas told Douglas, not because of Frank's persuasiveness, "or oral magic, or even my affection and gratitude but the realization that Jerome's work is really in something of a crisis due to certain personnel problems—though it is probably a continuing crisis, and that my pulling out might cause positive injury."[121]

Douglas was not daunted. He had come to rely on Fortas at least as much as Fortas had come to depend on him and refused to consider going ahead with the study without his protégé's help. Douglas turned to his Yale colleague Wesley Sturges, who agreed to intercede with Frank. The situation of Fortas and Douglas, Sturges wrote Frank, was comparable to "that of the children who wish to marry but are afraid of what the old man will say and do; not that they do not have affection for the old man but because they want to do what they want to do and make him like that."[122] That apt analogy tickled Frank, who had cooled down. He responded that apparently Douglas and Fortas felt that Frank was "like old man Barrett in the Barretts of Wimpole Street. Nonsense! Bless you my children. You needn't elope. You can be married at the old homestead." He had told Fortas "to prepare his trousseau but to stay with papa for a brief time until I get a hired girl to take his place."[123]

The decision to leave the AAA for the SEC did not, as some have argued, represent a "turning point" in Fortas's life.[124] It is true that Frank's work was at a crisis point and Fortas undoubtedly would have been forced to leave the AAA within three months when Frank and the other reformers were fired. But those who were "purged" soon found jobs with other prestigious New Deal agencies. Frank himself immediately became special counsel to the Reconstruction Finance Corporation and then returned briefly to private practice before Douglas

successfully recommended him to the President for an sec commissionership in
1937. Had Fortas remained at the aaa, Frank and Douglas would have continued
to look after him, just as they did when he went to the sec.

The real significance of the episode was that though it seemed to represent an
unusual moment in the life of a person as ambitious as Abe Fortas, it was part of a
pattern. Offered the chance to work with his first mentor on an investigation
which would surely receive widespread attention, he had chosen to remain in a
job he considered dull largely because of loyalty to the aaa and Frank. In fact,
Fortas would again turn job offers down because of loyalty to a current position
and the sense that he was needed more where he was. To avoid alienating
anyone, he worded his declination in the most emotional terms, so the individual
he rejected would believe that the decision had been difficult. Carol Agger
thought that in this particular instance, Fortas "was torn because he liked both
men, and it would be hard to choose between them." But, as she said, the letters
described an anguish that was not there: "He made it up a little for each of
them."[125] Things tended to turn out well for Fortas that way. The new job meant
that he could return to Yale and Agger could finish law school. The university
reappointed Fortas in 1935. The Securities and Exchange Commission position
required that he spend less time in Washington than the aaa had demanded.
While Douglas headed the Protective Committee Study he commuted between
New Haven and Washington, and there was no reason, Fortas thought, why he
too could not couple teaching with his sec duties as the study's assistant director.
Further, Douglas's work for the sec meant that he could teach fewer courses.
Someone had to take over some of them, and as usual, Fortas stepped in willingly.

# CHAPTER 3

# Professor and Inquisitor

BE FORTAS'S LATER REPUTATION AS A TOUGH INFIGHTER DID NOT STEM from the AAA, where his tact and negotiating skills made him popular, or from Yale, where the young professor depended on Douglas to protect him. He acquired it at the Securities and Exchange Commission, where he counted on himself. His style at the SEC suggested that in some ways his edges had softened since his days as the editor in chief of the *Yale Law Journal*. The SEC marked the emergence of the adult Abe Fortas, who treated his mentors as equals. Taken together, the years at Yale and the SEC and the variations in his relationship with Douglas at both institutions showed Fortas's passage into maturity.

## YALE PROFESSOR

The faculty Fortas rejoined in 1935 was not the happy little band of legal realists he had known as a student. Institutional problems plagued Yale Law School. The coming of the Depression had meant a reduced budget for the school and lower salaries for junior faculty members. The Depression also led to the New Deal, and an alarming number of law professors, from the university's point of view, joined Fortas in taking leaves to toil in the exciting pastures of government service. More important, jurisprudential differences now divided the faculty. Cracks in the edifice had appeared earlier, but by 1935 the façade of a united group had nearly crumbled. Although all agreed that the Harvardians had overemphasized legal principles, older realists believed that their younger counter-

49

parts had abandoned principles altogether. The seniors also contended that their juniors had become too intent on integrating law and the social sciences. While they tolerated the presence of the economist Walton Hamilton, traditionalists were sure that the faculty did not require additional nonlawyers.[1]

Fortas allied himself with the more radical group of realists that Arnold, Douglas, and Hamilton led, and the circumstances of his appointment revealed the tension within the school. Dean Clark had coupled his request to the university administration for an assistant professorship for Fortas with the suggestion that Luke Finlay be hired as well. As Finlay had graduated at the top of Fortas's class, Dean Clark knew both men were able. "They are different types of minds and therefore make a desirable team," he wrote Yale's president. He and others preferred Finlay, "while Messrs. Arnold, Douglas, Hamilton and Sturges are most enthusiastic for Mr. Fortas. In view of the balance which both together give, it is perhaps unfortunate to lose one of them."[2] Both were appointed, but Finlay's decision to leave New Haven for Wall Street in 1934 soon upset the equilibrium. Hamilton and Arnold tried to appropriate his slot for the political scientist Max Lerner, but Clark and the traditionalists successfully blocked that appointment. By the time the Lerner episode had ended, the faculty had become more bitterly divided than ever, and rumors were circulating that Clark might resign as dean.[3]

Fortas sympathized with Clark's determination to retain a balanced faculty. "Thurman was very interested in other disciplines," he said, "and there were other people on the faculty who were dubious about all this. Charlie Clark's great contribution was to keep those two things running in their different cranks." Clark, Fortas emphasized, "had a hell of a time as dean because he had a bunch of . . . lions and tigers and jungle animals to deal with in this little group: Wesley Sturges, Douglas, [Walton Hamilton] and Arnold, and myself as the very junior man, on the one hand, and on the other hand, the right wing." Fortas was convinced that "it was right to have both conventional people and people that were interested in blazing new trails, so to speak. For example, I think [Arthur] Corbin was extremely valuable in running a conventional, solid casebook approach to law."[4]

Although Fortas appreciated the middleman's position, he nevertheless insisted on his own point of view. He did so firmly but politely. At one of the first faculty meetings he attended, he took on Corbin, the grand old man of the Yale Law School, the father of realism now disturbed by its excesses. "Corbin was the oldest member of the faculty, the most respected member of the faculty, and had run the school since 1910," explained Professor Myres McDougal. "He took some sort of position and toward the end of his talk, Fortas just spoke up and said:

'Arthur, that's nonsense!' in so many words and then proceeded to prove it was nonsense." According to McDougal: "There was just no question of Abe's brilliance. Everybody at the table listened very respectfully." McDougal thought Corbin might have been "just a little shocked at the violence of his language." But Fortas did it with "style. He had such a manner that people took him seriously." Nor did Fortas seem arrogant: "It was done aggressively, but in terms of the common interest." In part because of his tact, the friction which divided progressive members of the faculty from their conservative counterparts did not scar Fortas. "Even Corbin didn't bridle when Abe called his remarks nonsense," McDougal emphasized. "He was a great favorite of everybody's."[5]

It was not just his tact that explained Fortas's preferred position. His relationship with Douglas also helped. The most powerful member of the Yale Law School faculty and its choice as dean in 1939, Douglas possessed great authority. Where Yale was concerned, Fortas admitted that he was still playing "son" to Douglas's "father."[6] Together, Douglas and Fortas offered an array of business law courses relating to securities regulation that drew upon their work at the SEC. When either had to travel to Washington, the other conveniently took his classes. The situation proved especially advantageous for Fortas. Unlike most beginning law professors, he was permitted to teach his specialty. When Douglas became an SEC commissioner in January 1936 and could spend less time at the school, he put Fortas in charge of his courses for the rest of the year. Though the dean "worried lest this is too much of a load for a young man and somewhat as to the effect of giving these important courses to so new a man," he acceded because "Mr. Douglas seems quite confident of this arrangement."[7]

For a short while, that arrangement included taking the heat for Douglas. Someone needed to look after his creation, the Law-Business program. Begun in 1933, it brought together the best of Harvard and Yale's professional training by combining attendance at Yale Law School with study at Harvard Business School. Participating students spent their first year learning law at Yale, their second studying business at Harvard, and their third and fourth back in New Haven, where they took courses in law and business taught by both Yale Law School and Harvard Business School professors. To Fortas, the program exemplified legal realism at its finest.[8] Aimed at the cross-fertilization of two disciplines, it was also empirical. "The idea was to start and end with factual situations," Fortas said. "It was really a training for real life as well as a testing of the social and ethical impact of the law in real fact situations."[9] But the program encountered problems from the beginning. One colleague summed up the situation when he wrote Douglas: "Charles [Clark] has no real interest. [Yale President] Angell is O.K. Governing Board [Yale Law School's tenured faculty] dumb and uninterested."[10] Fortas was soon warning Douglas that "the business-law project is in considerable danger, first, from the Law School faculty itself and second, from the [Yale] Corporation."[11] Nor did Yale law students flock to it.[12]

Though anxious about the program's fate,[13] Fortas characteristically worried more about self-preservation. When he became concerned in the spring of 1936 that the dean would force him to teach a heavy load or make him responsible for courses unrelated to business law Fortas told Douglas that he did not relish the prospect of being forced to "undertake work in other fields or supervision of penmanship courses."[14] Douglas obligingly intervened on his behalf. Pretending that he had not spoken with Fortas, Douglas asked the dean to assign his protégé business law courses the following year and to make him adviser to the law-business program.[15] Though Fortas was ultimately given a slightly heavier teaching load than Douglas requested, it was not onerous and was restricted to the business law field. To an unusual extent, Fortas taught what he wanted. His mentor's stature and intervention shielded him. At Yale his colleagues continued to regard him as "Douglas's man."[16]

He was a more popular teacher than Douglas. Though he was neither dramatic nor inspiring in the classroom, Fortas was solid. He was "a young teacher," Eugene Rostow said. Another student found him "very businesslike, matter of fact." He did not use the Socratic method so dear to William O. Douglas and most law professors, which entailed tormenting students with questions. "Fortas was more expository," Rostow recalled. "In fact I think we felt that Fortas sometimes led you too much. But we liked him as a teacher." Some considered Fortas a "dull lecturer," Lloyd Cutler remembered, but overall he possessed "an excellent reputation as a teacher, as a securities specialist."[17] Teaching came easily to him, and he publicly admitted that it left him with plenty of free time.[18] Most junior faculty members spent the hours before class assembling full sets of teaching notes. Even William O. Douglas had a bulky volume of them. Fortas, on the other hand, needed no life preserver. Compared to Douglas, Fortas was extemporaneous and self-confident.[19] When Fortas's SEC duties became burdensome, the school hired Allen Throop to teach one of his courses. Throop asked Fortas for his notes, and Fortas agreed to send them. Throop waited expectantly until a disappointingly slim package of twenty or twenty-five pages arrived. "Abstract of this case or that case, maybe a comment or two, period. And these were his lectures," Throop recalled. "That was all he had, he didn't need any [more]. He was that brilliant."[20]

The years at Yale were pleasant ones for Fortas. He and his wife lived a comfortable life in New Haven. They had a house and servants. To his colleagues, Fortas seemed to live "very well from the time he was a very young man."[21] Typically, Fortas expressed his situation in different terms. "We located a Swedish girl, age twenty-one, who doesn't know how to cook but who is willing to learn," he wrote Douglas in 1936. "We hired her because she seems to be a nice girl who is afraid of the dark and who is trying to work her way through college. I shall probably have to do the cooking."[22] Yale Law School proved more agreeable to Carol Agger than had Marquette. Although she was generally talkative in class, she remained silent in her husband's classes.[23] Fortas found the law school environment challenging and shared good times with Douglas, Arnold, and others. To be sure, Fortas occasionally found Yale, the most progressive of contemporary prestigious law schools, overly conservative and spoke of leaving.[24] Years later, however, he dismissed the suggestion that he had not enjoyed his years in New Haven. "I had my very close friends there and I was working hard and doing very fast-lane work and very happy."[25]

Nevertheless, Carol Agger believed that her husband preferred Washington and government service to New Haven and Yale.[26] And it was a strenuous existence, for Fortas had to be at the SEC much of the time. When Agger graduated from law school in 1938, he therefore resigned from Yale. In later years Fortas liked to tell a story about why he had decided to leave when he did, and when his old friend Katie Louchheim interviewed him, he related it to her. "I had two dachshunds, one of whom got carsick. I had to drive from Washington to New Haven on U.S. 1 with the Sunday *Times* piled in the back of the car. The dog would get sick; I'd get out, take away a couple of layers of the *Times* and leave the dog on the other layers. And pretty soon that got kind of boring so I decided I had to quit." As Louchheim said, the story "was typical Abe, . . . his making a sort of travesty of what was obviously an important journey."[27] The story contained an element of truth—"really the reason that I left," he told another interviewer to whom he also described his dogs' carsickness, "was it got physically too difficult, and I had to make a choice"[28]—but his puckishness led him to the light touch.

## THE PROTECTIVE COMMITTEE STUDY

The study that Fortas and Douglas conducted for the SEC while they were teaching at Yale proved more important to each of them than their professorial incarnations. Indeed Fortas maintained that Douglas's accomplishments at the SEC, including the study and other activities, were among the most significant of his career. He credited Douglas with domesticating the New York Stock Exchange.[29] For his part, Douglas attributed much of his SEC success to Fortas.[30] The SEC, often labeled "the most successful of all federal regulatory agencies,"[31] increased Fortas's faith in the administrative process. It also reinforced his fundamental conservatism. He later claimed that "the country would have sup-

ported practically any measure that seemed directed against the money merchants of Wall Street" and expressed pride in New Dealers who sought a partnership between Wall Street and Washington that would tame the stock exchanges without bringing them under government control.[32]

Fortas and Douglas believed in cooperation with capitalists, but they still
possessed a healthy skepticism of big business. The Protective Committee Study
spotlighted the unethical and illegal activities of "protective" and reorganization
committees appointed to defend the interests of investors by corporations undergoing bankruptcy or the reorganization process that often accompanied and
followed bankruptcy. It demonstrated that the same corporate lawyers, officers,
managers, and investment bankers who had presided over a company's declining
financial situation generally preserved their control by placing themselves in
charge of the committees, or of newly organized corporations, to perpetuate their
profits and stifle customer complaints about their past misjudgments.[33]

Though Fortas later claimed that Protective Committee Study staff members
never intended for their report to lay the groundwork for "major legislation,"[34] he
and Douglas originally did have such high hopes. But they encountered problems
in Congress from the beginning. Congressman Adolf Sabath of Illinois, who was
also inspecting protective committees with a view to introducing his own bill,
posed the most significant of many obstacles. Despite his reformist image, Sabath
was part of the problem. His law firm was affiliated with the notorious S & W
Straus, a real estate bond house which, after persuading thousands of small
investors to put their money in "safe" real estate bonds, had used the money for
such speculative ventures that it had been forced to default. At that point, its
officers moved to dominate the reorganization process and to uphold their own
interests rather than those of the defrauded bondholders.[35] Sabath's firm allegedly
received $6400 in fees for legal services in connection with the reorganization.[36]
"You may want to check on Sabath's connection with the Chicago-based real estate
firms which were investigated during the Protective Committee Study (for example, S & W Straus)," Fortas advised a historian of the SEC later. "To state it mildly,
Douglas did not respect Sabath's objectivity and he found it impossible to work with
him—Further affiant sayeth not!"[37]

At first, Fortas and Douglas did try to cooperate with the Sabath committee
"as a happy family." The Sabath committee had even sent over to the Protective
Committee Study an employee who would work with Fortas and Douglas to
produce a bill satisfactory to both groups.[38] But it became clear that the two
committees could not coordinate their activities. "We have arrived at a stage with
these guys when we cannot much longer be cagey," Douglas soon told Fortas. "We
will have our own bill. It will compete with theirs and we will have to fight like
hell against their monstrous proposals."[39]

Congressman Clarence Lea introduced the SEC's bill in 1937. Drafted by Fortas and Douglas, the Lea Bill called for a uniform regulatory process for a variety of debtors undergoing the reorganization process. Among other things, it required the reorganized entity to disclose the fees paid to protective committee members, prohibited incumbent corporate managers and other interested parties from serving on reorganization committees, authorized the SEC to comment on the fairness of a reorganization plan at the request of the supervising court when the amount involved was less than $5 million, and, where the stakes were higher, empowered the commission to intervene in the court proceeding. Wall Street, the press reported, "greeted the Lea Bill with outspoken resentment mixed with no little ridicule" and condemned it as needlessly paternalistic.[40]

The House blocked the commission's bill. Sabath and other members of Congress testified against it, and the Lea Bill "quietly disappeared." The Protective Committee Study resulted in two pieces of less significant legislation, both drafted by Douglas and Fortas: chapter 10 of the Chandler Act of 1938, which made SEC assistance available to federal courts to analyze the fairness of reorganization plans, and the Trust Indenture Act of 1939, which added slightly to the fiduciary duties of trustees appointed to protect the interests of bondholders. Neither of those measures matched the breadth of the Lea Bill, which failed in large part because its authors did not acquire the political support they needed.[41] Therein lay a problem for Fortas. He could draft a bill, but he could not always persuade Congress to enact it. The meritocracy that had propelled him upward did not demand the knowledge of the legislative process that would likely have characterized a government servant chosen through political patronage. Fortas never understood how Congress operated. The early defeat on the Lea Bill apparently strengthened his faith in a strong executive branch even more. Increasingly, Fortas thought in terms of circumventing Congress rather than cooperating with it.

Once the possibility of significant legislation had been foreclosed, Douglas and Fortas cast themselves in the role of publicists. They sought, Fortas said, to develop "a series of case studies which essentially documented a wide range of reprehensible practices."[42] Even here, they were thwarted. Although Douglas wanted the final report to read more like the *Yale Review* than the dry *Yale Law Journal*, and although Fortas tried to carry out his wishes by urging the report's many authors to consider its "literary and dramatic effect" and to make "liberal use of quotations" so as to qualify it for "light reading for the Commission or as a basis for newspaper stories," only Douglas and Fortas seemed to understand the sort of engrossing reporting needed to draw the public's attention.[43] The Study's report to Congress was a ponderous, disjointed eight-volume document that Douglas believed only his friend Vern Countryman read from cover to cover.[44]

As Fortas saw it, the hearings that formed the basis for the report proved far more important than the report itself. The journalists who covered the hearings provided the publicity he craved. His years at the SEC taught Fortas the importance of courting the media.[45] The newspapermen Robert Kintner and Joseph Alsop wrote a series of articles on the hearings that Douglas's staff had conducted.[46] Those hearings, Fortas later noted, "were important in Douglas' own development; they were a bomb explosion in Wall Street generally (note the reportage of Alsop-Kintner in the *New York Herald-Tribune*); they added greatly to the fear-of-Douglas which was an important factor in inducing the financial community to participate in the reforms."[47]

Both in the hearings and the negotiations that preceded them, Fortas acted like a crusader. Contempt pervaded his letters to Douglas describing his dealings with corporate attorneys, officials, and investment bankers. "These guys are a lot dumber than I can ever comprehend," he wrote Douglas after receiving a reply to a questionnaire from Guaranty Trust, which had taken advantage of its insider's knowledge of one company's financial difficulties to ensure that the company paid off its debts to Guaranty.[48] "Their reply is wonderful—publicity for our Report." All Guaranty had done, Fortas said, was "to summarize and repeat our charges and respond *technically*. The most stupid of politicians whom they affect to despise could tell them that is a blunder."[49] As Fortas had learned at the AAA, it was crucial to use terms that the public could understand and that were persuasive.

Fortas was particularly inclined to play hardball in dealing with Wall Street lawyers. "You know I dislike giving any of these fellows a clean bill of health," he told Douglas.[50] In 1937, when Fortas and Douglas were investigating the collapse of the Kreuger and Toll Company holdings, they examined the two committees formed to represent the interests of buyers and sellers of Kreuger and Toll securities. The protective committee formed by bankers in the house of Lee, Higginson hired John Foster Dulles, an attorney at the Wall Street firm of Sullivan & Cromwell, as counsel. Another committee formed to oppose the bankers, and with an eye to suing them for fraud, retained Sigfried Hartman and the Untermeyer brothers as counsel. As Samuel Untermeyer had represented the public interest in the Pujo committee hearings on Wall Street investment bankers in 1911, he presumably would fiercely guard the rights of the defrauded buyers. Yet Douglas and Fortas learned, and Hartman confirmed in a letter to Douglas, that Dulles and Untermeyer had made an informal "treaty" to collaborate and divide legal fees. They also determined that the Untermeyers and Hartman had made a deal with Lee, Higginson's attorneys whereby Lee, Higginson agreed to buy back $24,000 in certificates of deposit held by seven individuals whom the Untermeyers and Hartman represented.[51] None of the parties had even informed the SEC of this transaction, as Lee, Higginson was obliged to do in the registration statement it filed with the SEC. The Untermeyers and Hartman, Fortas said, "were giving the Commission the run-around on the registration statement" until Hartman cracked and notified Douglas of the arrangement. "This was a secret settlement and they protected its secrecy in the face of a direct mandate of the law," Fortas protested. "They should certainly be called to task for this sort of business."[52]

Fortas himself called them to task before and during the hearing, and his manner in the prehearing negotiations revealed his developing style. Having made the rounds of New York law firms, he sardonically reported on the results to Douglas. He had found Eugene Untermeyer "by turns indignant and wheedling." Untermeyer insisted that his role had been minimal and that he had no relevant documents. He produced only his formal correspondence with Lee, Higginson's attorney. "You understand that my conversation with him was entirely amicable and that I did not push him in any way or ask any direct questions," Fortas told Douglas. "I merely led him on and statements that he made were for the most part untrue or half true as I then suspected and ultimately discovered." Fortas subsequently found a revealing letter from Untermeyer in Lee, Higginson's files. If Untermeyer did not come forward with the letter he had withheld, Fortas looked forward to introducing it himself at the hearing and "shoot[ing] a fast one down the middle of his [Utermeyer's] gizzard as an indication of the esteem in which I hold him. Not only was he stupid and secretive in his conversation with me, but he also, during the time I was there, raised hell with four law clerks and two young ladies who were his file clerks." Fortas particularly relished the lawyer's request that the hearing, then scheduled for Washington's Birthday, be postponed. He playfully hypothesized that Untermeyer "does not wish the hearing to come so close to the day which, above all others, stands as a symbol for the virtue of telling the truth, the whole truth and nothing but the truth."[53]

After serving Untermeyer with a subpoena, Fortas appeared at the office of Untermeyer's co-counsel, Sigfried Hartman. Hartman was worried that Fortas would introduce his letter to Douglas acknowledging the deal between Lee, Higginson and the Untermeyers. "Sigfried told me that he was principally concerned lest the bankers consider him a Judas. . . . According to him, lawyers do not ordinarily disclose that a settlement has been made; and although there was no agreement to this effect, it was implicit in the situation. Tearfully he beseeched me to refrain from making him appear as a Judas."[54] (When Hartman forcefully testified about the purchase of the certificates of deposit at the hearing, Fortas attributed his honesty "to the deal I made with him." But Fortas had not relied only on the deal. Throughout his examination of the witness, he held

the letter Hartman had written Douglas in his hand and "fingered" it mean-
ingfully to remind Hartman that if he did not "come clean," Fortas would introduce the letter that would brand him as the traitor.)[55]

Next, Fortas went to the "beautiful offices of Lee, Higginson Corporation"
and "after telling a couple of employees that they would not do for my purposes,"
he was ushered into the offices of a powerful former partner in the firm, who
"was in a rather whimsical mood. He told me all about himself and advised me
that he was spending every day winding up the affairs of Lee, Higginson," with
which he insisted he was no longer associated. Nor did he know anything about
the $24,000 settlement. "I subsequently had reason to believe that this was a lie."
After serving him with a subpoena, Fortas "strolled over" to see Lee, Higginson's
attorney, whom he described as "a very aristocratic gentleman of the old school,
the typical senior partner who is not accustomed to rough stuff. . . . He was
terribly distressed when, after we had conversed for a while, I advised him that
he would be subjected to the annoyance of a subpoena."[56]

John Foster Dulles, whom Douglas had found "pontifical" and arrogant when
he searched for work in the 1920s,[57] also received his share of criticism from
Fortas. Fortas earlier had sought a waiver of the attorney-client privilege from a
client of the firm, National Investors Company, to enable the SEC to examine
Sullivan & Cromwell's files. Dulles stood on ceremony and demanded a formal
waiver. Fortas admitted to Douglas that he was not even interested in the National Investors Company. It was "a beautiful case from the point of view of a
student of legal technics and problems; but it is not much of the dirt we so dearly
love." The idea of bothering Dulles, however, whom he hoped could "be had,"
delighted him. When Dulles's "smoothie" partner said that he had obtained an
informal waiver and the firm would surrender the files, Fortas gleefully observed
to another colleague that "we gained a point or two on Mr. Dulles."[58] Everyone at
the Protective Committee Study proved skeptical of corporate lawyers and investment bankers and described them equally disparagingly. Everyone enjoyed,
too, the prestige and power that affiliation with the study carried. "If I walked
into Cook, Nathan & Lehman, one of the great law firms, and said 'I'm from the
SEC,' Mr. Cook would interview me," a friend of Fortas's from law school recalled.
"I was treated as an equal. I was a little boy."[59] Beneath the surface there lay a
devotion to the project that led them to act as if the ends justified the means.

However acerbic and arrogant they became, most of the Protective Committee Study staff members still deferred to Douglas, who did not consider them
peers. There was one exception. "Douglas had great respect for Abe," one veteran of the study recalled. "He treated him as an equal."[60] Though Fortas was
very much the junior colleague in New Haven, his relationship with Douglas vis-
à-vis the SEC was different. Fortas was more dedicated to the SEC than he had

ever been to Yale, and although he treated Douglas as his leader, he relied on himself more and on Douglas less.

The plaintive and martyred tone that often crept into Fortas's letters to Douglas about Yale appeared less frequently in communications about SEC matters. Nevertheless, sometimes it was there. "Bill, the volume of work down here is perfectly staggering," he complained on one occasion. "There's nothing to be done about it, because we certainly can't afford a man to help me, but I wanted to let you know."[61] When Douglas tried to prevent Fortas from publishing an article in *Law and Contemporary Problems* because it gave away the commission's future plans,[62] Fortas appealed his case to Douglas, but only because he worried that his fellow Yale professors would not find his publication record sufficient. "Please don't be troubled in the slightest about my own feelings in this matter," Fortas wrote Douglas from New Haven. "If there are whisperers hereabouts who will look at the . . . issue and whisper about my absence and suggest that [Yale Law School Librarian Fred] Hicks and I are in the same class, they can whisper to their heart's content."[63] Douglas promptly approved an arrangement that would permit the article to be published.[64] Such broad hints, relatively frequent when Fortas was speaking of Yale, proved rare with respect to the SEC.

When he was not intimidating Wall Street lawyers, Fortas was managing the staff of the study. He had been advising Douglas about prospective employees from the time he was at the AAA, and he continued doing so after he moved to the SEC. Douglas generally refused to hire people before Fortas had interviewed them, and the letters between the two men indicate that Fortas served as the project's personnel director.[65] It was a delicate job. First, it required maneuvering around the commission's hierarchy. The first SEC chairman, Joseph P. Kennedy, had a special personal relationship with Douglas, which made Fortas's task easier. But Kennedy left in 1935.[66] His replacement, James M. Landis, from the Harvard law school, was a different sort of person—more cautious, less secure, more legalistic, more tense—and Fortas and Douglas approached him warily. He was more difficult to manipulate.

As a Frankfurter protégé, Landis might have been expected to sympathize with Fortas and Douglas's commitment to meritocracy, but other considerations moved the new chair. Fortas and Douglas ranked everyone on their committee according to intelligence and contributions made to the study.[67] Landis proved more political. Early on, he warned Fortas not to hire too many Jews.[68] When Fortas tried to employ two Illinois residents suggested by a respected law professor, Landis put him off. Fortas tried the old AAA tactic of calling the office of an Illinois senator to arrange an endorsement, "but the Senator's secretary did not seem to be at all cordial." The authorities obviously had been warned, he speculated, that Douglas "had been attempting to get men from universities instead of from the proper source of all good men and true—senators and congressmen."[69] But Fortas kept on fighting for well-qualified employees. "I have had considerable experience at knifing and I don't really mind playing the game," he said.[70]

Fortas's authority, which included the power to set salaries, set him apart from his contemporaries. "There were people almost as bright as he was, but frankly nobody had the assurance of manner that this fellow had," recalled Milton Freeman, who had graduated from law school only a year after Fortas but was making only a third of his salary at the sec. "He understood people exceptionally well: how you act to be taken seriously. The rest of us were learning how to do that."[71] Since Fortas could be more tactful than Douglas, he struck some as an easier boss. Douglas could be "nasty" to anyone in the sec days, but above all, "he was a good actor," Allen Throop said. "He could be almost anything he wanted." In contrast, Throop thought Fortas was "always a gracious gentleman. I don't mean he wasn't firm, but he could tell you you were dead wrong in a nice way probably, and Douglas would just say you were crazy."[72]

Therein lay a crucial difference between Douglas and Fortas. As one of Douglas's friends pointed out, Douglas was usually the same person at work or play, with notables or with family. "When you went for a walk with him, he was impatient; he was thoughtless of persons walking with him." This was true whether his companion was his sister or a famous judge. "You had to learn to put up with it. He could behave in a ridiculously awful way."[73] Even Fortas did not always like Douglas. He acknowledged the frailties of character that made Douglas such a miserable husband,[74] and when James Simon's biography of his friend appeared, Fortas said he liked it because it showed Douglas as a great man and a son-of-a-bitch.[75] But, though Douglas proved a good actor when he had to be, Fortas was an even better one. Indeed, Fortas was such a good actor that it was impossible to tell when he was on stage. He was more of a chameleon than Douglas. Critics might even have called Fortas phony. Even as a young man, he could scrutinize his audience, calculate the appropriate emotion, and call it forth.

Fortas and Douglas diverged, too, in their senses of humor. Fortas giggled; Douglas guffawed. Fortas was more a wit in the Thurman Arnold tradition than a practical joker of the sort Douglas became. To be sure, Fortas enjoyed Douglas's jokes. He loved to tell the story of Douglas's decision to subpoena their friend Wesley Sturges from New Haven to Washington to testify at a hearing. "He wanted to know what he was supposed to testify about. We just told him all that would become clear but that he had to stay around, he was under subpoena. And we kept him around and enjoyed his company for about a week and then told him he was excused."[76] Fortas's own style, however, was different. "Will you please send me ten or fifteen additional copies of the report," he once asked Douglas's secretary. "I received only two copies and the result is that I have been unable to send a copy to my Mother, my Aunt Katherine, my Uncle Louis, and Miss Catt, my first grade teacher. This is a hell of a situation."[77]

Both Fortas and Douglas inspired their associates. As the Protective Committee Study was scheduled to last only until 1936, its staff had to cram investigations, hearings, and report writing into less than two years. "Abe in commenting on our hard work schedule at the sec, would say 'We can at least outwork the opposition,'" Douglas remembered. "And we all did, for the opposition was made up of middle-aged lawyers who got sleepy and tired come ten o'clock."[78] In contrast, by ten o'clock, Fortas, Douglas, and their minions were just about to break for dinner at the Powhatan Hotel across the street from the sec building, "before we went back and worked a few more hours."[79]

After funding for the study ended, most of their colleagues had to go, while Fortas and Douglas worked on until 1937. Fortas tried to "sell" as many of the more talented staff members as he could to the sec and discharged the rest. "I have been able to do little except personnel work for some time," he reported to Douglas. "I suppose you can imagine the scenes I have been through. Everybody who is being let out is taking it on the chin in the bravest and most uncompromising way. But it is most distressing to have brought home in this manner the difficult situation in which people find themselves who have worked so loyally for us." Douglas replied: "I think we may be congratulated on the extremely high morale which we succeeded in creating in the staff. It was an extremely loyal gang."[80]

With the conclusion of the study, Fortas returned to Yale, but he remained involved in public policy. He developed a new interest in tax reform,[81] and he publicly supported Roosevelt's efforts to pack the Supreme Court with additional justices in 1937.[82] Such endeavors suggest that his eyes remained fixed on Washington. He and his wife moved there permanently the following year.

## THE PUBLIC UTILITIES DIVISION

When Douglas became the sec's chair in the fall of 1937, he asked Fortas to become assistant director of the Public Utilities Division. Fortas had enjoyed the Protective Committee Study's work and had been able to combine it with teaching. As he anticipated, the new job proved far less pleasant than either teaching or his prior sec experience. His willingness to join the Public Utilities Division indicated the depth of his devotion to Douglas.

Because the division was charged with administering the Public Utilities Holding Company Act of 1935, its workload promised to be enormous. "In the broadest sense," one historian notes, "the Holding Company Act gave the sec power to refashion the structure and business practices of an entire industry."[83] The act required holding companies to register with the SEC. Section 11, its celebrated "death sentence" provision, empowered the commission to simplify utilities' corporate structure and to destroy those empires that could not justify their existence. Historians have treated the act as a symbol of Roosevelt's shift away from the planners and toward the followers of Brandeis, who sought to restore competition,[84] but FDR's contemporaries regarded the holding companies as so predatory that such planners as Fortas and Jerome Frank could unite with the antitrusters in support of the legislation. Roy Smith, appointed director of the division by Douglas, favored the utilities, however, and lacked the predisposition to interpret the act in its broadest sense. Douglas had given Smith the job as a way of thanking a friend of Smith, SEC commissioner George Mathews, for support on other fronts. The appointment also pleased commissioner Robert Healy.[85] Staff attorneys had a different view. Smith was "a very pleasant, delightful person, good-looking but not the mental heavyweight Fortas was and not as liberal," one recalled.[86] Once he had appointed Smith, Douglas needed to place a trustworthy individual in the division so that he could bypass Smith and enforce the act.

"When Douglas telephoned me about taking on this task, he indicated the basic problem," Fortas said. "He felt that the utilities had Roy Smith in their pocket and that Roy Smith had strong personal support from Commissioners Mathews and Healy. The task, simply stated, was effectively to implement the regulatory and disclosure provisions of the Act, to prepare for implementation of the 'divestiture' or 'death sentence' provision, making whatever progress was possible and—above all—to resist sabotage of that provision."[87] The administrative complications made the job "mighty uncomfortable." Fortas admitted he would have refused to undertake it for anyone except Douglas.[88]

Fortas and Smith differed over policy. Frank credited Fortas with saving the Public Utilities Holding Company Act "from destruction."[89] Nevertheless, as director of the division, Smith retained some power, which he used to frustrate vigorous enforcement of the act.[90] Thus, for example, Smith overrode Fortas's objections and persuaded the commission to relax its rules by backing the election of Victor Emanuel, a major shareholder in Standard Gas and Electric, as that company's chair. Emanuel reportedly had promised Smith that in return for SEC support, Standard Gas and Electric would voluntarily comply with key portions of the act. Kintner and Alsop thought it "a fascinating fact . . . that a man openly backed by the New Dealer administering the hated Holding Company Act has been elected chairman of the second biggest holding company in the country" and applauded the harmony between government and business that Emanuel's election suggested.[91] But to Fortas and Frank, Smith's deed only proved he was no New Dealer. They considered Smith's willingness to bend the rules symptomatic of an inclination to foil administration of the act. And since Emanuel was being sued for having mismanaged Standard Gas and Electric's affairs as a member of its board of directors at the time of his election as chairman of the board, they viewed Smith's goal of electing Emanuel as an end that hardly justified questionable means.[92]

Meanwhile, as Frank said, "the tussle" for control between Fortas and Smith was becoming "nasty."[93] Frank complained on Fortas's behalf that Smith often disregarded the lawyers in the division.[94] For his part, like the traditionalists in the AAA, Smith distinguished between law and policy and claimed that Fortas and his lawyers were trying to formulate policy. According to Smith, they had "injected themselves much further than they should have into a great number of matters." Indeed Smith insisted that "if there is any friction at all within the Division, it is due almost exclusively to the aggressiveness of the lawyers."[95]

Though Douglas had protected his protégé at Yale, he did little to help Fortas now. "Again and again I urged Bill that we should demand Smith's resignation and vote him out if necessary," Frank wrote.[96] Douglas refused. He did not want to alienate Mathews. Power had made Douglas less committed to meritocracy and more politically sensitive. While Healy and Mathews continued to support Smith, and Frank loyally championed Fortas in customarily voluminous memoranda, Douglas kept silent.[97] Perhaps he reasoned that Fortas could take care of himself. Fortas was "hooksliding" around Smith, remembered one of his colleagues. "It was nothing in violation of the Boy Scout Code, but what I saw was the No. 3 man working directly with the No. 1 man and going through the legs of the No. 2 man."[98] "Roy Smith didn't have a chance," said another.[99]

Douglas finally came publicly to Fortas's aid. After the newspapers had a field day describing the tension in the division, the Administration demanded its immediate reorganization. Further, Douglas's own Supreme Court appointment in March 1939 meant that he no longer had to worry about conciliating Mathews. He finally fired Smith.[100] There is no evidence that Douglas's slowness alienated Fortas. He had understood that the job would be difficult when he accepted it, and his loyalty to Douglas remained undiminished. Indeed Fortas campaigned hard for Douglas's appointment to the Court, though it left him isolated in the utilities division.[101] Jerome Frank insisted that it was "*highly important that Abe Fortas stay on the job*. If he does so, Mathews—and perhaps Healy—will make life miserable for him. For that reason *Bill wants to get him another job.*" Fortas would remain, however, "if he's backed up" and if promised a chance at a commissionership when Frank left the commission.[102] At the time he wrote those lines, Frank did not know he would be the commission's next chair and would himself be in a position to "back up" Fortas. He thought he would be denied that prize because he had angered Mathews and Healy by supporting Fortas against Smith. No promise of a commissionership was forthcoming, however, and Fortas listened to Douglas. "The opposition to our reforms was so powerful that I thought Abe would be the first target and might even be destroyed in his lonely position," Douglas said later. "So I went to Harold Ickes, put the problem to him and asked him to put Abe on his staff."[103] Ickes agreed, and Fortas acquired a boss very different from William O. Douglas.

CHAPTER 4

# The Lawyer as Bureaucrat

B

Y THE TIME FORTAS ARRIVED AT INTERIOR IN 1939, ROOSEVELT WAS seeking a "Third New Deal" in the form of a changed political economy. It was becoming increasingly clear that members of Congress possessed their own agendas and would not hesitate to oppose the President. In the end, "the administrative state came into being, but the question of who would administer it remained unresolved."[1] In the meantime, Fortas continued to share other New Dealers' faith in a strong executive branch, as his suspicion of Congress grew. He was employed in one of the diminishing number of bastions of reform and social planning.

## "HUFFY HAROLD"

No one considered himself a more dedicated reformer than Fortas's new superior, Secretary of the Interior Harold Ickes. Nor did any Washington official feel more passionately about his work. "I love Interior," Ickes admitted. "I have built it up into a great, respected Department."[2] Though he professed to dislike the word *czar*,[3] few more eagerly sought to widen their fields of power or were more scornful of those who got in their way. Fortas aptly classified the Department of the Interior's approach under Ickes as based on "a dog's philosophy: anything you can't chew or screw, you pee on."[4]

A crusty and humorless man, Ickes was a self-described curmudgeon who delighted in fighting critics. "Although I . . . have never met you, I feel that I know you very well as a cowardly, skulking cur," he once wrote a publisher whose newspaper had printed an unflattering editorial. "I can see you in my mind's eye eating your own vomit with relish but enjoying even more the savor of the excrement in the pigsty in which you root for choice morsels."[5]

Ickes reserved his greatest passions for his diary into which he poured his feelings about the President and his "official family." He was dependent emotionally on Roosevelt. "I have never been given to hero worship, but I have a feeling of loyalty and real affection for the President that I have never felt for any other man," he wrote in 1933.[6] Yet by the time Fortas went to work for the secretary, Ickes believed he had fallen out of the President's favor. FDR had escaped the cares of office through poker parties at Ickes's farm during the early days of his presidency, but, as time went on, the secretary sadly noted that Roosevelt took his pleasure elsewhere. Ickes became increasingly frustrated. "I don't know anything harder than trying to do a job for a man whom you think does not want you about," he grumbled when he was deciding whether to make one of his periodic threats to resign.[7]

The men who surrounded Roosevelt irritated the secretary even more than the President himself. The White House treated Harry Hopkins as "near-royalty," Ickes fumed. "Usually Henry goes transcendental after thirty or forty minutes and only pretends to keep track of the conversation," he wrote of Henry Wallace. Leon Henderson was always "sobbing about what I was doing to him," and as far as Ickes was concerned he "could go to hell." Henry Stimson droned on forever in Cabinet meetings, Henry Morgenthau was "somewhat stupid," Samuel Rosenman gave Ickes "a squirmy feeling." As for the secretary's nemesis, Jesse Jones: "When he goes to Heaven his first effort will be to organize a kindergarten so that he can instruct God in some of the fundamentals." Even Ickes's friend William O. Douglas surrounded himself with "people of a rather low and insignificant type" and in his native state of Washington wore clothes "so old and foul-smelling that one can hardly go near him."[8]

As might be imagined, Ickes was a difficult boss. He never let his staff forget that he retained the upper hand. He liked to line up his highest officials in his waiting room and keep them sitting there a long time before summoning them for a word or two.[9] He removed the doors from the stalls in the men's lavatories in the Interior Department to prevent employees from reading newspapers while they sat on toilets.[10] Fearing that many division heads too blithely signed interoffice memoranda, Ickes circulated one that incorporated large pieces of *Alice in Wonderland*. (Everyone initialed it.)[11] His sobriquet, Honest Harold, reflected his own misplaced pride in his truthfulness. One observer more accurately nicknamed him Huffy Harold.[12]

Nevertheless, the secretary proved a vital icon of the New Deal. "In the liberal community he was something of a hero because he always took the right positions on the big things like race, civil liberties, and the coming war in Europe," a colleague emphasized. He provided a forum for the black contralto Marian Anderson when the Daughters of American Revolution would not. He likewise had a reputation for supporting the rights of Jews. "Ickes was very, very good on all the big things, and one was very proud of him for that. On the other hand, on all the little things he wasn't very good at all." Further, the secretary, who sometimes taped conversations with subordinates without their knowledge, "never made the connection between the means he frequently used and the ends that he felt strongly about."[13]

Tactful, thorough, liberal, and loyal, Fortas seemed the ideal subordinate for this irascible man. Harold Ickes made him general counsel of the Public Works Administration (PWA) in 1939. Intended to be the agent of a recovery measure that would put the unemployed back to work, the PWA had received nearly $6 billion in appropriations during the 1930s, which it used to build roads, bridges, hydroelectric power projects, public buildings, and other long-term projects.[14] Ickes had confidence in Fortas, who had been highly recommended to him. Nor did Fortas's religion bother the secretary, who noted, "While he is a Jew, he is of the quiet type and gives the impression of efficiency as well as legal ability."[15] The PWA position demanded both a good lawyer and a skilled administrator, for Fortas's predecessor had left the office in bad shape. The new job included a five-hundred-dollar raise; Fortas was now making nine thousand dollars a year.[16]

But only two months after Fortas moved to the PWA, Roosevelt launched one of his celebrated bombshells. He transferred the PWA's functions to the new Federal Works Administration and passed over Ickes to name John Carmody administrator of the new agency. "He gave Carmody my PWA and the other building activities of the Government," Ickes expostulated. "He did this although he knew that I wanted to carry on this work and despite the fact that labor leaders, contractors, Congressmen and Senators in great numbers urged him to appoint me."[17] Parting with his PWA staff, was for Ickes "one of the trying experiences of my life. I built that staff myself and I do not believe that a better organization exists in Washington or ever has existed."[18]

Ickes did not say good-bye to all his colleagues, for he invited those he valued most to continue on with him at Interior. The small number included Fortas, whom Ickes called in on the day Roosevelt sent Carmody's name to the Senate. Fortas believed that FDR "had made a great mistake," a satisfied Ickes reported. "I asked him whether he would care to come over in the Coal Commission and he said that he would like to be with me. I told him that this might mean a smaller salary, but this didn't matter."[19] Ickes treasured those who so willingly pledged their allegiance, and Fortas began moving up through the ranks of the Interior Department. He had a new mentor.

## THE MERITOCRAT

When Harold Ickes lost the PWA, he acquired power over coal, a crucial resource because of the impending war. Even contemporary journalists had seen that the seven-member Bituminous Coal Commission, which controlled the industry until 1939, was weak, ineffective, and easily dominated by the United Mine Workers' head, John L. Lewis.[20] Ickes considered the staff of the commission's legal division incompetent.[21] The Reorganization Act of 1939 changed the name of the commission to the Bituminous Coal Division. More important, it abolished the seven-man board and transferred its functions to the secretary of the interior.[22] Ickes named Howard Gray director of the division, but in appointing Fortas its chief counsel he delegated the real power to him. "The theoretical head" a colleague recalled, "was Howard Gray, but the real head of it was Abe Fortas."[23] Fortas commanded a staff of more than a thousand employees that operated on an annual budget of at least $3 million.[24] The house cleaning he began proved painful. Members of Congress protested strenuously against the loss of patronage, but Fortas remained committed to the meritocracy that had brought him to power.[25] He recruited an extraordinary group of lawyers, including a future law partner, Norman Diamond; Arnold Levy, a Frankfurter protégé who had worked on the Protective Committee Study; David Lloyd Kreeger, who became one of Washington's most generous philanthropists; and the brilliant Harold Leventhal, who became a distinguished appellate judge.

The perennial problem soon arose: the most qualified individuals, for the most part, were Jews. Ickes maintained that Jews did not predominate in the entire Bituminous Coal Division, but only on its legal staff, and he defended their presence there. His "principal difficulty," the secretary said, was finding good Gentile lawyers to carry on the legal work of a division that addressed a greater variety of legal issues than any other sphere of government except the Department of Justice. "What can one do if he wants legal ability and those who possess it and who offer themselves are preponderatingly Jewish?" Ickes replied to someone who had asked him how many Jews the Coal Division employed. "Even so, I try to keep a good balance and I don't even have to worry about balance except among my legal staff."[26]

Fortas worried about balance, too. After Kreeger hired a group of Jewish law review men from Ivy League schools, Fortas asked to see him. "This doesn't matter to me, [and] it probably doesn't matter to the Secretary of Interior, but could you hire some Gentiles?" Fortas requested. Kreeger promised to do his best. He soon found a blue-eyed, blonde Bostonian named Joseph Dunn. Though Dunn had not excelled at Harvard, Kreeger decided to lower his standards for an Irish Catholic. Fortas, he recalled, was "so pleased" by the news of the appointment. Then came the Jewish holidays. When Dunn asked whether he would have to work on Rosh Hashanah and Yom Kippur, his colleagues learned for the first time that Dunn was Jewish.[27]

Emphasis on a meritocracy remained essential because the work of the division was proving so taxing. Unless Congress renewed the Bituminous Coal Act, it would expire in 1941, only two years after Fortas took over the division. "We had to get the job done before the statute ran out, and every year at appropriations time, the question would come up as to whether the job was ever going to get done," Diamond said.[28] Bituminous Coal Division staff members also wondered whether they would ever complete their work. The Bituminous Coal Act continued the work of the defunct National Recovery Administration. It sought to eliminate competition and price cutting by directing the act's administrators to set a minimum price for every different size, quality, and type of coal in every one of the country's twenty-three coal producing districts.[29] "There were hundreds and hundreds of categories for coal," Kreeger recalled.[30] The process of price setting, which Eugene Rostow aptly described as an "extraordinary farrago," involved numerous stages and substages.[31] Although the Bituminous Coal Act aimed primarily at the establishment of minimum prices, when price schedules took effect in 1940, the Bituminous Coal Division was inundated with petitions from operators, consumers, and the Consumers' Counsel Division seeking relief from specific provisions. During the last three months of 1940 alone, the coal division received 536 petitions for relief.[32]

Fortas ingeniously reconciled the meritocratic ideal that the workload demanded with the need for patronage. The coal operators filed so many petitions that Director Gray could not hear all of them, and he created a staff of a few dozen hearing examiners. When members of Congress clamored for appointments based on patronage instead of intellectual ability, Fortas established an opinion-writing section, directed by Kreeger. It took its place alongside the division's findings of fact section, which set prices, and the compliance section. When the hearings were over, a bright young lawyer in the opinion-writing section would draft an opinion for the more pedestrian hearing examiner that would be released over the examiner's signature. Inevitably, irregularities arose. Fortas's successor, Arnold Levy, was embarrassed by one member of Congress who pointed out that opinions were being issued in the names of hearing examiners who had not heard the cases.[33] At the time, however, the distressed state of the coal industry seemed to justify procedural irregularities.

Fortas won from his subordinates the loyalty and commitment that Jerome Frank had received from his underlings at the AAA. Morale in the division was extraordinarily high. "Fortas certainly instilled a sense of industry on the part of the guys," Norman Diamond observed. Harold Leventhal thought Fortas "a peerless leader." David Lloyd Kreeger could never reconcile the stories that later circulated in Washington about Fortas as a private practitioner with the Fortas he knew at the Bituminous Coal Division. "He would come in, and he'd put his arm around you, and he'd say, 'Dave, how are we doing on that,' because I tended to be a last minute worker under pressure," Kreeger remembered. "Never a cruel boss, never a sharp tongue. He was very nice to work with."[34]

Unlike Frank, Fortas maintained of necessity an air of reserve. "The coal people were in and out of that place like kids in and out of a candy store," Diamond said. "You got to know them pretty well, and pretty soon you're on a first-name basis with everybody in the industry. But everybody always called Fortas 'Mr. Fortas.'" If Fortas knew people well, the veneer might temporarily disappear. Diamond recalled times when Fortas would relax with lawyers in the division and use the Yiddish phrases of his childhood.[35] But such occasions arose seldom. His staff lawyers noticed that Fortas responded warmly to their children but remained aloof with them. He had been "my great friend, he'd made my career for me," Arnold Levy said, but Levy saw a relaxed and chatty Abe Fortas so rarely at the Bituminous Coal Division that he vividly remembered two such instances—the first came after Levy's wife, Kreeger, and Fortas had been playing chamber music when Fortas began talking about the traditional Jewish dishes his mother had cooked, and the other when Roosevelt had just won a third term, and a jubilant Fortas asked Levy out for coffee.[36]

Fortas's days in the coal division remained special to him, as they did to those who worked with him. "I have never felt more keenly the happiness which comes only through feeling that one's close associates and fellow workers are friends and companions," he told Howard Gray when he left the division.[37] Although he easily slipped into flattery, Fortas was probably speaking truthfully here. The Bituminous Coal Division had provided his first opportunity since the *Yale Law Journal* to serve as absolute boss, and he had exercised his authority without arrogance.

## THE FIGHT FOR PUBLIC POWER

As Ickes increasingly relied on Fortas, he thought of him for other duties. Roosevelt's commitment to the production of cheap electricity had greatly changed the lives of millions of Americans who had previously been deprived of electricity and had brought New Dealers into conflict with the private utilities, which had long functioned without competition from or regulation by government. Since public power was a cornerstone of the government's program, Ickes naturally wanted exclusive control of it. Others frustrated him. Because of the number of agencies that had jurisdiction over some aspect of public power—the Public Works Administration, the Tennessee Valley Authority, the Bureau of Reclamation, the Federal Power Commission, and the Federal Trade Commission—Roosevelt had created the National Power Policy Committee (NPPC) to oversee power matters in 1934. Though Ickes chaired the commission, he had long been at odds with other NPPC members, such as the Federal Power Commission's Leland Olds and the Tennessee Valley Administration's David Lilienthal.[38] Ickes soon came to think that Fortas could help him acquire the exclusive authority over power that he sought. Recognizing that many in Washington believed that Assistant Secretary of the Interior E. K. Burlew in the Bureau of Reclamation was a conservative who hoped to "sabotage" public power, the secretary took jurisdiction over public power within the department from the Bureau of Reclamation. In the spring of 1941 Ickes created the Division of Power to represent Interior on public power matters. William O. Douglas suggested to Ickes appointing Fortas director of the division. Even before Douglas recommended him, Fortas had been in to tell the secretary that, "in his opinion, power matters were in a critical condition and that those who were trying to sabotage Interior on power matters were becoming very active and were gathering strength." Ickes decided to follow Douglas's advice, and Fortas quickly accepted the offer of a new job, much to the secretary's "relief and satisfaction."[39]

Fortas was leaving the Bituminous Coal Division to preside over a much smaller staff—fewer than twenty in the Washington office—but the Division of Power's work was inviting. The division was established to centralize control over power policy within the Department of the Interior and to establish procedures that would enable power units to sell and distribute hydroelectric power equitably. The job offered Fortas the chance to continue the fight against the private utilities he had begun at the SEC. He believed in public power. It seemed obvious to him that "electricity must be produced and distributed to the people without private profit."[40]

Almost everyone—from Burlew within Interior to the National Power Policy Committee outside—resisted Fortas's Division of Power from its inception.[41] Fortas tried to run interference for the secretary. In what Ickes considered a "brilliant" maneuver, Fortas designed a strategy to enable Roosevelt to appoint the secretary power coordinator. The President had hesitated to give Ickes that authority in 1941 out of fear of inflaming Olds and other NPPC rivals who also sought the mantle of champion of public power. Fortas simply suggested that the President name Ickes power coordinator in his capacity as NPPC chair rather than in his capacity as secretary of the interior.[42] But Olds successfully opposed Fortas's proposal in a bitter battle in which he alleged that a report Fortas had prepared was replete with "errors, misinterpretations and false innuendos, due to ignorance, combined with malicious intent," and exemplified "what may be expected from a Power Policy Committee Secretariat if it is constituted in the Department of Interior."[43]

Once again Congress also stymied Fortas. Some of its members agreed with Interior that private utilities should be brought to task but differed with Ickes over how to accomplish the goal. The dispute over means led to what *Time* magazine described as "one of the fiercest and most important struggles for power in the history of the New Deal" in the fall of 1941.[44] As director of the Division of Power, Fortas was involved in launching hydroelectric projects, at Bonneville and Grand Coulee Dam. As they had at the Public Utilities Division, the privately owned utilities opposed him. They "liked the idea of the government building those vast hydroelectric facilities, but they wanted the government to build it, generate the power, and then turn it over to them," Fortas said. "And some of us wanted some assurance, reasonable assurance, that the power would be distributed at lower rates to people to aid the economic development of the area."[45] Many in Congress shared Interior's view, but the Northwestern delegation proved particularly supportive. "I know that bunch," Congressman Walter Pierce of Oregon wrote of the utilities in tones echoed by his colleagues, "the cutest, smartest, ablest, oh well, I better not use any more adjectives, I might get into some that are bad."[46]

In the hope of domesticating the utilities, Senator Homer Bone of Washington introduced a bill in 1941 to create the Columbia Power Authority, which would replace the government agency temporarily operating the Bonneville and Grand Coulee electric systems. It would establish a procedure by which the authority could acquire privately owned electric utilities and resell them to cities and public utility districts.[47] Bone wanted the Columbia Power Authority to be modeled after the Tennessee Valley Authority and governed by a three-person independent board located in the Northwest. At the same time, Fortas and Ickes's allies in Congress called for a bill that would lodge the Columbia Power Authority in Interior and authorize Ickes to appoint one administrator.[48] The Bone and Interior bills shared the objectives of wresting power away from private utilities. The bills differed, however, over the issues of centralization and independence. Strongly influenced by his suspicion of TVA's Lilienthal, "that master propagandist," who, with Olds, prevented him from completely dominating public power, Ickes opposed the idea of an autonomous three-person board.[49] He argued that it gave private utilities a greater chance of finding a conspirator who would hamstring the board's honest members. "The trouble with the TVAers is that they aren't interested merely in getting into heaven; the means by which they get there is of paramount importance," he groused to the President. "The TVAers will not concede that a one-man administrator could possibly produce beneficial results even if he were God, Himself. They would not consider for a minute giving you the job."[50] The secretary's experience with the seven-person Bituminous Coal Commission had led him to the conclusion that "an executive job is a one man job."[51] Supporting the TVA was the greatest concession Lilienthal and other antitrusters would make to the goal of centralized economic development, but Ickes wanted more. For his part Senator Bone, who dated his interest in public power back to 1908,[52] agreed with the father of TVA, Senator George Norris, that a corrupt administrator or secretary of the interior would find it more difficult to dominate an autonomous board of several individuals.[53] According to Bone, "Ickes wanted to run the whole show and he got mad as hell when I suggested that he would not last forever."[54]

Personal differences also separated Bone and Ickes. They disliked each other, in part because they were so much alike. "I never got along too well with this peppery old boy who appeared to be on the warpath most of the time," Bone later told his intimate, Saul Haas.[55] Ickes found the senator equally difficult and completely mistrusted Haas. Nor did Ickes hide his feelings. He denounced Bone and his bill in the senator's home town of Tacoma.[56] As warfare between Ickes and Bone escalated, it became clear that they needed a mediator. Fortas may have been more sympathetic to an autonomous regional authority than his boss[57]— anyone would have been more receptive to the idea than Ickes—but Fortas tried to achieve the secretary's aims by pouring oil on the troubled waters. He wooed Bone's ally Walter Pierce. "It means a great deal to a youngster like me to feel that he is working for a common cause with you," he told the congressman.[58] Fortas also courted Haas. On one occasion Fortas participated in "the longest drinking bout he had ever sat through," consuming whiskey with Haas for some ten hours.[59] On another occasion in Washington, D.C., when Haas "actually looked as if he had been sober for a day or two," Haas prevailed upon the secretary to call Fortas back from Portland to negotiate a compromise between the Bone and Ickes forces. Fortas and Haas spent half the night and all of the following day trying to resolve the impasse between the senator and the secretary. But Ickes would have none of it. "At five thirty, Abe came into my office with more than two pages of language which was nothing but circumlocution," he griped. "This was proposed as a 'declaration of principles' as between Bone and me. I told Abe that we were wasting our time; to say to Haas that I would not go along on his suggestion, and that if we were to fight it out, we might as well go about it."[60]

Fortas kept trying. He and his colleague Tex Goldschmidt wrote a conciliatory speech for Ickes meant to take the sting out of the secretary's slap at the senator in Tacoma. When Ickes read the draft with its compliments to Bone, Goldschmidt remembered, he summoned his two speechwriters, and asked: " 'What are you two characters trying to make out of me, a love bird?' He was sticking out his jaw, very cross about it, because we'd said some nice things."[61] No one could make Ickes a lovebird, and the bill died in the 1941 session because no compromise ensued between the two camps.

Eventually Fortas wore Ickes and Bone down. By early 1942 Fortas could report that "Senator Bone and Secretary Ickes are in complete accord that it is particularly urgent on account of national defense situation to press for legislation authorizing the Bonneville Administration to proceed with full speed to accomplish acquisition of private utilities in the Northwest." Although the details of the legislation had not been completely settled, the discussions were proceeding, he said, "on an extremely cooperative basis."[62] Bone introduced the compromise bill in April. Both Interior and the senator backed down, but Bone surrendered more: the new bill provided for one administrator of what was now called the Columbia Power Administration and placed the agency in Interior. Bone had, however, ensured that the administrator would be appointed by the President and confirmed by the Senate. Though Bone forfeited localization and autonomy, he now maintained that it was "stupid to talk of sacrificing through a compromise when the bill itself achieves what the power folks in the Northwest want, viz., the acquisition of private systems."[63]

Credit for the settlement went to Fortas. "If Senator Bone is introducing amendments in the Senate and if Congressmen Smith and Hill are doing the same in the House, and the amendments are satisfactory to you, it looks as though someone has done a job," Roosevelt's administrative assistant wrote to Fortas. "Congratulations!"[64] Ickes told the President that the compromise, which was "entirely satisfactory" to him, had been effected by Bone, Fortas, and Goldschmidt and applauded "the final, happy ending of this chapter."[65]

But the ending was not to be so joyous, as Fortas soon foresaw. Ever cautious, he advised Haas to press Bone to arrange a prompt hearing for the bill. Fortas apparently realized that progressives would be trounced in the November 1942 elections and wanted to bring the bill to a vote before the liberals' loss of clout became apparent.[66] He could not hasten the process enough, and two months later he admitted that the bill was stalled. It was never enacted. "Had we been successful with this bill it would have created the greatest electric grid system in the world," Bone mourned.[67]

The defeat of the bill must have been especially difficult for Fortas. Had the compromise bill been introduced in 1941 with equal support from the Department of the Interior and Senator Bone, it might have pased. As it was, all of 1941 had been wasted in endless bureaucratic infighting over the means by which to assure a common goal, and "the final New Deal proposal to promote the planned promised land" was lost.[68] Abe Fortas had seen the Lea Bill die in his Securities and Exchange Commission days because of a similar jurisdictional squabble between the commission and Congress. By the early 1940s, a pattern of weak congressional support for executive initiatives was becoming increasingly evident.

## "ONE OF THE ABLEST LAWYERS IN WASHINGTON"

Though he was a skillful bureaucrat who generally smoothed Ickes's way unusually effectively, Fortas was acquiring almost as many detractors as fans on his ascent. Even before he came to Interior he acknowledged that "in my brief career I had acquired a remarkable number of enemies."[69] That became apparent in the spring of 1941. At a conference between Ickes and the President about the proposed Columbia Power Authority, Roosevelt spoke "in high terms of Abe Fortas' qualities" and said he was thinking of naming him an SEC commissioner. Ickes objected that "Fortas was very important to me, especially at this time." But when the secretary returned to the Interior Department and related the conversation to Fortas, he learned that his associate wanted to join the SEC. "Accordingly, I told him that I would not stand in his way and subsequently I wrote the President telling him that he could not find a better man than Fortas and that if he wanted Fortas he might have him, although it would be a great loss to me."[70]

By the end of the year, Roosevelt was canvassing his advisers for their opinions of both Fortas and Director of the Public Utilities Division Robert O'Brien, the two rivals for the open SEC commissionership. Jerome Frank unqualifiedly recommended Fortas as "one of the ablest youngsters the New Deal had developed."[71] William O. Douglas agreed that Fortas was "absolutely top-flight" and noted that he had done "yeoman service" in the SEC's early days but worried that Fortas was not sufficiently Western, warned that Ickes considered him "absolutely indispensable in the working out of plans for the Columbia River Authority," and thought that some who remembered the conflict between Fortas and Healy would be unhappy at Fortas's return.[72] While the outgoing chair of the Securities and Exchange Commission, Edward Eicher, credited both candidates with "tough minds" and "hearts in the right place," he too feared renewed tension between Fortas and Healy.[73] But James Landis doubted Fortas's heart was where it should be. "Abe Fortas has ability," he conceded, "but he failed to inspire in me . . . that sense of trust that was always reposed in O'Brien. Many others like myself thought Fortas personally too ambitious and that his judgment and his actions were not infrequently colored by this rather than being dominated by the public interest."[74] Even had Landis effused, Fortas's strained relationship with

Healy surely would have disqualified him. Fortas soon told Ickes that he would not receive an SEC commissionership, and, according to the secretary, "he did not seem to be distressed" about it.[75]

Perhaps Fortas was not concerned because he knew that Douglas was promoting him to Ickes for a bigger job. The secretary was unhappy with his under secretary, Jack Dempsey. In fact, none of his under secretaries had pleased Ickes. He complained of having had such "a bad break" with them that "I almost wish there was no such office."[76] First he had contended with Charles West, who had told reporters that Ickes was tapping his telephone.[77] West was followed by Harry Slattery, who lasted only a year before Alvin Wirtz of Texas succeeded him. "Wirtz was by far the best of the lot but I could not get much service out of a man who spent three-quarters of his time in Texas," Ickes lamented.[78] Wirtz left after a year and a half to manage Lyndon Johnson's senatorial campaign. "And now Dempsey," Ickes wrote, "—and I must say that I am greatly shocked and disappointed because I counted so heavily on him and believed that he would fit in as none of his predecessors had." Ickes suspected that Dempsey would be satisfied only if he could "step into my shoes."[79] By January 1942 rumors were circulating that Dempsey would resign and Douglas was hinting that Fortas should be appointed under secretary.[80]

When Dempsey finally quit in June, Ickes asked Roosevelt to name Fortas under secretary. Ickes recorded his conversation with the President in his diary. "I said, 'You know him, don't you?' and his reply was, 'Yes. He is a Hebrew, isn't he?' I acknowledged that he was but said that he was one of the quiet, unobtrusive types and pointed out that he was one of the ablest lawyers in Washington." Roosevelt showed "no evidence of resistance," Ickes noted, and Fortas "was very much pleased" when he received the appointment.[81] Ickes now looked enthusiastically ahead to the future: "I am certain that I will be getting a good man this time."[82]

Fortas as a child in Memphis

Fortas, *right,* with his best
childhood friend, Will O'Mell

South Side High School graduation, Memphis, 1926.
Fortas is in the center of the second row.

The Blue Melody Boys. As a teenager "Fiddlin' Abe," *second from left,* directed and played with this band.

Preparing for the Peach Case, one of the first cases to test the constitutionality of the Agricultural Adjustment Administration Act. *Left to right:* Thurman Arnold, Abe Fortas, H. H. McPike, James L. Fly.

Abe Fortas and Carol Agger shortly after their marriage in 1935. While Fortas taught at Yale Law School in the mid 1930s, Agger completed her law degree there.

William O. Douglas was appointed to the Supreme Court on March 20, 1939. Here he is being congratulated by his fellow commissioners at the Securities and Exchange Commission. *Left to right:* Robert Healy, Jerome Frank, Edward Eicher, George Mathews.

Fortas became general counsel of the Public Works Administration in 1939 on the recommendation of William O. Douglas.

At the age of thirty-two Fortas became Under Secretary of the Department of the Interior. Asked about the youth of the New Dealers, one government official replied, "The symbol of the whole thing is Abe Fortas."

Secretary of the Interior Harold Ickes, *right,* called Abe Fortas the best under secretary in the history of the department. Few employees managed to stay on good working terms with Ickes as long as Fortas did.

Carol Agger and Abe Fortas with Jane and Harold Ickes at Franklin Roosevelt's last inaugural, 1945.

Sitting in for Ickes at a cabinet meeting on the day of Japan's surrender, August 10, 1945. *Clockwise from left:* Clinton Anderson, secretary of agriculture; Lewis Schwellenbach, secretary of labor; John F. Blandford, national housing administrator; J. A. Krug, War Production Board head; John Snyder, war mobilization director; William Davis, director of economic stabilization; Leo T. Crowley, foreign economics administrator; Henry Wallace, secretary of commerce; Fortas; Robert Hannegan, postmaster general; Henry Stimson, secretary of war; James Byrnes, secretary of state; President Harry Truman.

Fortas defending Owen Lattimore against charges of communism before a Senate subcommittee, 1950. Arnold, Fortas & Porter was one of the few law firms to accept "loyalty" cases. (The unidentified young man next to Paul Porter is G. Duane Vieth, then an associate in the firm.)

Members of Fortas's firm at a bar association dinner. *Clockwise from the man in light suit, center,* Milton Freeman, Hermione McGovern, Norman Diamond, Phyllis Freeman, William McGovern, Bess Porter, Abe Fortas, Luna Diamond, Paul Porter, Carol Agger.

Fortas socializing with Washington lawyer Harold Leventhal,
Senator Mike Monroney, and Senator Lister Hill

Fortas the Washington lawyer in the salad days of Arnold, Fortas & Porter

# CHAPTER 5

# Under Secretary

JAIME BENÍTEZ, THE YOUNG CHANCELLOR OF THE UNIVERSITY OF PUERTO Rico, never forgot his first meeting with under secretary of the interior Abe Fortas. "When I went into the Department of Interior and walked into this enormous office, there was a babier face than mine," Benitez recalled. "We looked at each other and started laughing. He had heard about this child chancellor, I about this child under secretary."[1] Fortas's past as Jerome Frank's protégé at the AAA, financiers' watchdog at the SEC, and director of the Division of Power at Interior also made his elevation surprising. "It was almost impossible to believe that one who had had these successive posts, to whose controls the business interests now so powerful in Washington must have been actively hostile, could still be *persona grata* in the atmosphere of 1942," Rex Tugwell wrote. "Yet he had been confirmed as Under Secretary without protest. How he did it none of us knew."[2]

War had dramatically changed the atmosphere in the nation's capital. "Not merely conservatives, but Republicans, have frequently displaced liberals," Fortas complained.[3] Ickes groused that businessmen drafted into government service, rather than New Dealers, were "running the war."[4] The need to organize the war effort forced Roosevelt to turn to those he had once spurned. His appeals to noblesse oblige and patriotism brought Henry Stimson, John McCloy, James Forrestal, and many others to Washington. Although such individuals did not conspire to create a military-industrial complex, they promoted "policies that successively mobilized big business, aggrandized it, and linked it to the military establishment."[5] They coupled their arguments against reform at home with pleas for expansion abroad. A mutually perceived ideological chasm separated the old New Dealers from the new recruits. Assistant Secretary of War McCloy explained the difference between himself and Fortas simply: "I was a conservative, but he was a liberal."[6]

Progressive journals urged liberals to fight back. "The battle between progress and reaction is a never ending one and . . . war conditions in many ways favor reaction," the *New Republic* editorialized three weeks before Pearl Harbor. "American progressives should recognize now that they are in for a difficult time and that they will need to use all possible diligence both to prevent the loss of recent gains for liberalism at home and to make sure that the outcome of the war will not be another tragic folly like that of 1919 which made the present struggle inevitable."[7] Embattled liberals closed ranks to press for the domestic reform and internationalism the *New Republic* urged. They remained committed to the social reform that the President and his new appointees were rejecting and became more concerned about persecuted minorities. At the same time, their liberalism acquired global dimensions it had not previously possessed. As under secretary of the interior, Fortas participated in this transformation of New Deal liberalism.

### SOCIAL REFORMER

Fortas remained dedicated to domestic reform. His support of land reform bespoke his continuing interest in a planned society. His stance on martial law in Hawaii revealed his commitment to civil liberties. His opposition to the Japanese internment reflected his concern with minorities.

The under secretary became involved in "one of the bitterest controversies in California's recent history" when he began working with the economist Paul Taylor and the Division of Power director Arthur "Tex" Goldschmidt to preserve the claims of small farmers in California to water. The Reclamation Act of 1902, which authorized the federal government to build dams in the arid West, prohibited federally financed water projects from providing water to irrigate farms that exceeded 160 acres.[8] This limitation, which was intended to promote Jeffersonian ideals by giving an advantage to small landowners, had largely been ignored. When the federal government took over California's Central Valley Water Project, owners of large farms became concerned that the 160-acre limitation might be enforced. In a surprise maneuver, Congressman Alfred Elliot introduced a rider to a wartime rivers and harbors bill that was intended to alleviate their concerns. Also supported by Senator Sheridan Downey of California, the Elliot Amendment would have removed the Central Valley area from the 160-acre limitation.[9] To agribusiness-oriented Californians, Interior's formal opposition to the Elliot Amendment reflected a desire to "set up a communistic-socialistic agricultural program in the whole Central Valley basin."[10]

In contrast, others contended that conservatives in Interior were only too eager to accept the Elliot Amendment. The department's Bureau of Reclamation displayed little interest in the 160-acre limitation because its leaders needed large farmers' support in wresting appropriations from Congress for further development of the water and power project in the Central Valley. "Internally we had a Bureau of Reclamation that was disposed to cave in and yield," and "we wanted them to stand on principle," Taylor remembered.[11]

Goldschmidt and Taylor turned to Fortas, who took the matter to Ickes. The Bureau of Reclamation possessed "neither the desire nor the background to do the economic and social planning which are necessary," the under secretary charged.[12] "I am afraid that the Bureau is still seeking a formula which will in effect carry out the purpose of the Elliot Amendment," he advised Ickes in the midst of the battle. Later he warned that "some of our people" showed a "panicked desire . . . to settle with Senator Downey."[13] Taylor applauded Fortas for persuading Ickes to stand firm in resisting Downey and saving the 160-acre limitation: "Fortas was very solid on this issue. He convinced Ickes."[14] Historians might credit the Bureau of Reclamation with modernizing the West by developing an effective policy for water resources that minimized "monopolization of these resources for the benefits of large landowners, private utilities, and powerful corporate interests."[15] But, though his "socialized thinking" so irritated the bureau's leaders, Fortas fought more decisively than they against corporate hegemony.[16]

Because he cared about civil liberties in the territories over which Interior possessed jurisdiction, Fortas also opposed the governor of Hawaii's declaration of martial law the day after Pearl Harbor.[17] Ickes thought the governor of Hawaii was "a bunch of wet spaghetti" because he relinquished control of the island to the military. Even after February 1943, when a new civilian governor issued a proclamation restoring habeas corpus and some authority to his government, the War Department insisted that martial law remained in effect.

Fortas's unhappiness with martial law grew out of his distrust of Army control over civilian life. "The Declaration of Independence cites as one of the counts against King George that he had attempted to make the military superior to the civilian authorities," he noted to the president of the American Bar Association, Walter Armstrong. (Fortas was leaking information about his negotiations with the War Department to Armstrong, who was preparing an article condemning martial law.[18]) Fortas also shared his department's belief that martial law in Hawaii enabled the War Department and Hawaii's five largest companies to persecute labor unions.[19] Finally, the under secretary worried about political repercussions. When even the notoriously conservative *Chicago Tribune* challenged the constitutionality of continued martial law in 1944, Fortas sent copies of the editorial to McCloy and to Secretary of the Navy James Forrestal. "Certainly, neither you nor I should tolerate the continuation of a situation which permits that great liberal journal, the *Chicago Tribune*, to attack us as violating a fundamental principle of our constitutional government," Fortas joked to McCloy.[20] To Forrestal, Fortas took a more serious tone, emphasizing that neither the military nor American government would benefit if the issue of martial law reached the Supreme Court. He warned that the Court would hold it unconstitutional. The under secretary was sure, too, "that none of us wants to see this issue involved" in Roosevelt's reelection campaign.[21] When the military still did nothing, Fortas directed the solicitor of the Interior Department, Warner Gardner, to prepare a letter to the President requesting an executive order terminating martial law.[22]

By the fall of 1944, the Interior Department and Army and Navy had negotiated an executive order and were urging its approval.[23] But a new obstacle arose when Justice Department attorneys raised doubts about the legality of certain provisions in the executive order. Fortas maintained that the attorneys were overly legalistic. Those sections would never be litigated, he pointed out to them and to War Department officials. Why did they have to be legally correct?[24] Amid the exigencies of war, such reasoning prevailed. Martial law ended, and Roosevelt was reelected. As the solicitor of the Interior Department said, Fortas had proved "very discerning, very hardnosed, and exceedingly useful" in the process.[25]

Fortas helped to bring the internment of Japanese-Americans to an end, too. Ickes originally considered relocation "both stupid and cruel."[26] When the administration insisted in 1942 on sending the Japanese-Americans to concentration camps, however, Ickes believed that his department should administer the camps, but he acquiesced in the President's decision to make the War Relocation Authority (WRA) an independent agency and to appoint Dillon Myer its director.[27] After a congressional committee attacked the WRA in 1944, Fortas was told that Roosevelt was considering transferring the agency to Interior. The administration believed, Fortas wrote to Ickes, that as a champion of minorities, Ickes "would be able to provide a fighting defense of the WRA, and that . . . [he] would be able to resist those people who believed that the Japanese should be eliminated."[28]

By this time, neither Fortas nor Ickes wanted the WRA. They blamed the hysteria that led to the executive order excluding Japanese from the West Coast on Commander John De Witt and on racial prejudice,[29] and they thought that after having decided against placing the agency in Interior originally, Roosevelt should not expect Interior to bail out the WRA now.[30] "We were most reluctant to assume the role of guardian and foster parent," Fortas told Professor Eugene Rostow of Yale Law School. The under secretary, who was leaking information on relocation that Rostow used to write one of the earliest and most compelling indictments of the program, explained, "Both Secretary Ickes and I felt that the original evacuation order was a terrific mistake and we knew that the most we could do was to ameliorate the evils resulting from it."[31] Other members of the administration prevailed, however, and Interior received the WRA.[32]

Fortas now became responsible for administering the WRA. He addressed internment in his usual meticulous matter. He toured the camps, where, he recalled nearly forty years later, "the resignation and the apparent hopelessness of the Japanese" imprisoned in the "dismal, abnormal environment" appalled him. "But perhaps the primary reason why my visit made such a vivid impression upon me" he added, "was that I was taken to a schoolroom in the center, probably for children of kindergarten age. As I entered the room as the representative of the Department of Interior, the children, who were all neatly dressed and scrubbed . . . rose to their feet and sang 'America the Beautiful.' I am sure you will realize how profoundly affecting this was."[33] Ever conscious of publicity, Fortas argued that the WRA should not present "an excessively rosy view of the situation" but should emphasize "the real hardship to which these people have been subjected."[34] He also stressed the importance of publicizing the heroism of Japanese-American soldiers fighting in the armed services.[35]

Most of all, Fortas worked to secure the freedom of loyal Japanese-Americans. Mitsuye Endo, a Japanese-American Methodist who spoke only English, and who had been interned for two years despite government certification that she was a loyal American citizen, seemed the ideal plaintiff for testing the government's evacuation order.[36] Indeed her case appeared so strong that by the time it reached the Supreme Court in 1944, the Army wanted to make it moot by declaring its own willingness to release her from the camps. According to Fortas, Solicitor General Charles Fahy of the Justice Department, "facing the practically certain prospect of defeat, was inclined to agree. As a matter of fact, this desire to avoid defeat in the Endo case was so strong that, in the argument, the Solicitor General raised a small but troublesome question of jurisdiction." In claiming that the Court lacked jurisdiction because the WRA had moved Endo to a camp outside of the jurisdiction of the court where her writ of habeas corpus was filed, Fahy was trying to force the Supreme Court to dismiss the case on a technicality. "I heard Fahy's argument and returned to my office and did the unprecedented—and probably the most irregular—thing of writing a letter to the Supreme Court in which I assured the Court that its order or any order of the

District Court would be obeyed," Fortas said. Fortas believed that the quibbling over jurisdiction and mootness "illustrates the fact that the actual administration—on the firing line—of this program has been a constant struggle, particularly with the Army. On the whole, the Department of Justice has behaved quite decently and has been on the side of the angels. From time to time, however, their lawyers' approach has created real difficulties."[37] The Justice Department did behave decently, though legalistically. Fahy offered to waive the mootness issue during oral argument, and it was he who submitted Fortas's letter disposing of the jurisdictional issue to the Court.[38] Realizing that there was no military necessity to justify internment, Fahy sought to uphold the government's argument for detention in a fashion that one historian has described as "half-hearted at best."[39]

Had Fortas represented the government, he would not have opted for Fahy's ambivalent legalism. For Fortas, the results justified the methods. Since he opposed internment, he took steps that he admitted were irregular to ensure that the Court would hold, as it ultimately did in *Ex Parte Endo*, that loyal Japanese-Americans could not be indefinitely detained in concentration camps.[40] Thus one War Department attorney later remembered Under Secretary Fortas as "a very strong force for the good" but one who "also cut a few close corners."[41]

Fortas rarely cut corners without first evaluating the political consequences. In the spring of 1944 he drafted a statement for Ickes pledging that when internment ended, the WRA would return Japanese-Americans "as rapidly as possible to private life." Fortas warned the secretary, however, that although the pronouncement did not say that the WRA planned to reopen the West Coast to Japanese-Americans before war's end, it would "probably be so construed. . . . The California primary elections take place on May 16, and you will want to consider the possibility that your statement on this highly controversial subject may affect the outcome of the primaries."[42]

By the time Roosevelt finally lifted the executive order excluding the Japanese-Americans from the West Coast in December 1944, the President had been elected to a fourth term and circumstances had changed. At this point, Dillon Myer wanted to focus on the "benefit" of relocation to both the nation and the evacuees and to promise there would be no "hasty mass movement of all evacuees back into the coastal area."[43] Fortas could now make his own feelings clear. He reworked Myer's draft so that it strongly asserted the evacuees' right to return to the West Coast and made no pretense that they had received any advantages. "In a real sense, these people, too, were drafted by their country," Fortas's version said. "They were uprooted from their homes and substantially deprived of an opportunity to lead a normal life. They are casualties of war."[44]

Where Jews were concerned, Fortas's interest in persecuted minorities was less apparent. He seemed to feel that he could oppose Hitler only covertly. In 1942 he helped the United Palestine Appeal procure Ickes as a dinner speaker.[45] Yet when Fortas was invited to become an honorary member of the committee staging a "Rally of Hope and Courage" with 10,000 Jewish children in 1943, he declined. "I need not tell you that I am in complete sympathy with your splendid efforts to relieve the terrible plight of Jews throughout the world," he told the rally's chair. Fortas nevertheless insisted that it was "necessary in my present position to refuse to join or accept honorary membership in any organization however commendable may be their objectives."[46] Perhaps his caution reflected his own sense of vulnerability as a Jew in Washington, but others in the administration worked more aggressively to help their fellow Jews. The intercession of Secretary of the Treasury Henry Morgenthau and his general counsel, Randolph Paul, for instance, ultimately compelled Roosevelt to establish the War Refugee Board, which relaxed the quotas that had kept so many Jews from entering the United States.[47]

Once the War Refugee Board had been created, the War Relocation Authority worked closely with it, and Fortas did alert Dillon Myer to the importance of obtaining kosher food for the Jewish refugees lodged in the board's shelters.[48] He also objected when the Army, the Department of Justice, and the War Refugee Board tried to block Interior's program of restricted leave for those refugees. Fortas pointed out that Justice had paroled Latin American enemy aliens brought to the United States: "It seems to me obvious that if the Department of Justice is willing to permit persons of this character to leave a concentration camp, it should be willing to grant the same privilege to persons who are in this country as refugees from our enemies."[49] Nevertheless, Fortas, generally such an aggressive and politic defender of outsiders, had done little for European Jewry.

### THE INTERNATIONALIST

As they generally blamed World War II on the isolationism of the 1930s, liberals advocated internationalism in addition to domestic reform. Their commitment to globalism reflected their belated return to Wilsonian ideals that had withered in the aftermath of World War I. Their globalism exceeded in its ambitiousness even Woodrow Wilson's. First, they sought to ensure democracy abroad by preserving America's position as a world power. They were not the only ones to pursue this goal. The military and the State Department shared their preoccupation with American security. Indeed some government officials joined others outside the Roosevelt administration, such as *Time*'s conservative editor, Henry Luce, to ask for more. Luce maintained that war's end should signal the beginning of an "American Century," in which the imperialism that had fallen into disrepute would again be treated as a positive virtue. A second objective was uniquely the liberals' own. They wanted to export the reforms designed to save American capitalism that Franklin Roosevelt had implemented at home.[50]

Because as under secretary Fortas was the head of the Division of Territories, he represented Interior in negotiations with the State Department to develop a program for the ravaged Philippines. Fearful that Japan would issue a decree purporting to give the occupied Philippines independence but in fact legitimating the continuation of a puppet government there, the president of the Philippines, Manuel Quezon, proposed that the United States give the Philippines independence.[51] When Senator Tydings introduced a resolution providing for Philippine independence in 1943, Fortas opposed it and turned Quezon's attention away from independence and toward the more immediate problem of rehabilitation.

He did so for two reasons. First and foremost, the under secretary wanted military bases for the United States in the Philippines "which will make it possible effectively to defend the Philippines and effectively to participate in the establishment of a stable political arrangement in the Pacific." Fortas argued that freedom should be granted only after the Japanese had been expelled and the United States had taken what it needed. "The time to secure those bases is before the Philippines become independent," Fortas claimed. "Our negotiating position and our moral and legal right to bases in the Philippines after Philippine independence will not be nearly as good as they are at the present time." Yet Fortas's motivation was not wholly nationalistic. He also fought the Tydings resolution because he feared that a declaration of independence for the Philippines would make Congress less willing to authorize a generous economic rehabilitation program for the island. "While it is believed that—perhaps with some difficulty—Congress may be persuaded to appropriate the rather substantial funds [required for rehabilitation] while the Philippines are still a part of the United States, it is considered rather doubtful that either Congress or the public would endorse as costly a program for the benefit of a foreign nation, irrespective of historical affinities," Fortas observed.[52] He was right. After the United States acquired the bases and the Filipinos received independence, Congress gave the Philippines relatively little help with economic rehabilitation.[53]

Fortas had more latitude for maneuvering with respect to Puerto Rico than he had with the Philippines. Puerto Rico's proximity to the Panama canal made it as strategically important as the Philippines, and it too was underdeveloped. Still, the differences proved more significant than the similarities. The Japanese did not occupy Puerto Rico. With three hundred thousand Puerto Ricans in New York, many of whom voted, the Democrats were aware that they had to be sensitive to the island's problems.[54] When Fortas said that Puerto Rico "interested and challenged" him, he referred to problems that would have intrigued any liberal.[55] Puerto Rico was a poverty-stricken territory that produced only one export crop, sugar. It depended on outside sources for virtually all its food and industrial products. A few elite families and wealthy American and Spanish absentee corporate landowners dominated its politics. The *Coalicionistas* who made up the conservative ruling party between 1900 and 1940 generally found the governors sent by the United States highly sympathetic.

Hope for reform lay in three places. The progressive *Populares*, led by Luis Muñoz Marín, a Puerto Rican who had lived much of his life in New York, had won a bare majority in the Senate on a platform of "bread, land, and liberty" in 1940 and were now agitating for land reform. Fortas's old AAA colleague Rex Tugwell, who had become governor of Puerto Rico in 1941, sought a New Deal for the island.[56] At Interior, where the under secretary functioned as the colonial secretary to whom Puerto Rico reported, Fortas also hoped to improve the lot of the island's poor. Reform would not come easily, however. The small island housed many great egos. Puerto Rico's resident commissioner to Washington, a *Coalicionista*, was "an ardent enemy of Muñoz and an equally ardent ally of the sugar corporation."[57] Nor had Muñoz fully emerged as the charismatic and dynamic leader he was to become. Tugwell described him as "a sodden drinker," and Harold Ickes told the President that Muñoz was "too sleek."[58] Further, Puerto Ricans had not yet decided whether they wanted independence, statehood, or some other relationship with the United States, and if Muñoz appeared too supportive of the governor, he risked alienating the *Independistas* as well as Tugwell's enemies in Washington.

For his part, Tugwell, a cool intellectual, was not always as tactful as he should have been and sometimes seemed insensitive to local custom.[59] An enigma to the Puerto Ricans, Tugwell was anathema in wartime Washington, where Republicans in Congress regarded him as a reminder of the most idealistic days of the New Deal. Republican newspapers spoke of impeaching him.[60] A committee in the House of Representatives once approved a $15 million appropriation for Puerto Rico provided that none of it was spent while Tugwell was governor.[61] Tugwell's position in Washington, the ambivalence with which both he and the federal government regarded Muñoz, and the ever-present fear that the *Coalicionistas* would return to power because the reformers had destroyed each other made the situation in Puerto Rico volatile. Wartime food shortages only aggravated the situation.

Of all the problems concerning the island that plagued Fortas and Tugwell, its political future proved the most vexing. Although Puerto Ricans were American citizens, they could not elect their own governor, attorney general, Supreme Court justices, auditor, or commissioner of education, and they debated the island's status endlessly among themselves and with Washington. After discussing the matter with the under secretary, Tugwell noted, "In general Fortas and I hold what may be described as a liberal view that there must be progress and that the elective governor is the next step—he because it is a liberal view and because it is, as he says, a good gambit in the game of Congress vs. Tugwell, and I because it seems to me pretty silly to withhold a status from Puerto Rico which is conceded, for instance to Mississippi where illiteracy, poverty, etc. are just as prevalent." The "liberal view" was not universally popular. The Army opposed even an elective governorship, while Muñoz, Tugwell believed, pulled as he was by the *Independistas* in his party, secretly wanted independence, combined with American financial support.[62]

Roosevelt, who had decided on an elective governorship, appointed a committee in 1943 comprising four Puerto Ricans of divergent ideologies and four "Continentals" from the mainland United States.[63] The duty of chairing committee meetings fell to Fortas, who approached Puerto Rico's future in a more domineering fashion than that with which he had addressed the Philippines' status. Tugwell recalled that Fortas quickly and "firmly" set "arbitrary limitations on discussion" by directing the committee to ignore the question of Puerto Rico's "ultimate status" and to concentrate on the elective governorship.[64] "The United States Government will continue to be supreme in Puerto Rico, and that is flat," Fortas informed the committee. "There just is not any question about it. We might just as well quit if we are not going to proceed on that basis."[65] Although the President's directive had seemed to empower the committee to consider the island's status, Fortas redefined the committee's discretion more narrowly so that its deliberations would lead to a politically acceptable solution, instead of to a recommendation which, he repeatedly warned the committee, Congress would veto as too radical.[66] Fortas also did not think independence would help the island because it would mean an end to trade advantages and American aid.[67]

At first, all went smoothly, according to Tugwell, "since we were giving the Puerto Ricans everything." The committee agreed to suggest that Puerto Ricans be allowed to elect a governor, who would be empowered to appoint a cabinet and a Supreme Court.[68] But a crisis soon developed. Muñoz wanted the committee to recommend that a constitutional convention be held in Puerto Rico to determine the island's status and declare a preference to Congress as soon as the war ended.[69] "We could not have passed to the President an independence measure—which this would have amounted to—and he knew it," Tugwell complained. Indeed the governor thought that Muñoz merely was engaging in a grandstand play designed to please "his independista gang" and to force the Continentals to withdraw from the committee meetings. Tugwell suspected that

Muñoz would prefer seeing the sessions break up to telling his followers that he had been able to obtain only an elective governorship. [70]

Faced with the situation he had tried to avoid, Fortas acted decisively. He reminded the committee that the achievement of an elective governorship for the island would represent a significant accomplishment. Viewed "in terms of a world-wide situation . . . this is a great, startling, and in a sense a revolutionary step that we are taking to provide for an elected Governor, and we are more or less considering it as a bird in hand," he lectured the committee. "It is not very much of a bird, but when it was not a bird in hand it was a hell of a bird, and I suggest to you that this is a precious thing we are now considering." Nor was it in hand yet: "We have got to get this through the Congress." When Muñoz retorted that "it is no solitary bird"[71] and stood his ground, the under secretary abandoned all pretense that the committee operated democratically. Tugwell reported that Fortas was inclined "to use strong-arm methods to rule out consideration" of Muñoz's proposal and was even ready to bring Ickes to the committee's conferences. [72] Tugwell persuaded him against calling in the secretary but also asked Fortas "to work on" one Continental, Father R. A. McGowan, who had followed Muñoz in a straw vote. Exactly what Fortas told McGowan is unclear, but at the formal vote McGowan sided with Tugwell, making it four to three against Muñoz's motion. When Fortas "rather irregularly" asked to be allowed to vote, the count was five to three against Muñoz. [73] The bill the committee submitted called for an elective governor who would possess broad appointive powers. [74] Even that modest objective, which had taken all of Fortas's skill to acquire, proved too much for Congress. Puerto Rico did not acquire an elective governor until 1947. [75] The issue of the island's status preoccupied Fortas until the end of his life. One "good dividend" of the committee's wartime work, Puerto Rican's leading constitutional historian maintained later, was "the education of Abe Fortas on the Puerto Rican problem."[76]

Fortas's desire to increase American security and promote social reform through the encouragement of controlled democracy abroad grew during the war. He placed his hopes for the postwar United States in a strong United Nations, American security, and commitment to financial aid. He predicted destruction of the world unless the United States undertook a "whole-hearted, generous effort to provide the people of the various nations with economic assistance and a feeling of security against aggression. We must realize that the best assurance of our own wealth and possessions is the well-being of the world."[77] Thus he was interested in the problem of non-self-governing people, who constituted a quarter of the world's population at the end of World War II. Having fought to protect civilian interests in American territories during the war, Interior favored what Fortas described as a "liberal approach to the dependent peoples problem."[78] Its position brought it into conflict with the more conservative Army and Navy and with the State Department.

Government officials particularly disagreed over whether the islands won from the Japanese should be placed under American sovereignty or under trusteeships. That Army and Navy would seek sovereignty was clear before war's end. Fortas thought they were "obsessed with the objective of annexing the Pacific Islands."[79] State's position, while less clear, reflected a zeal to conciliate the military. Speaking for Interior, the under secretary maintained that a United Nations system of trusteeship provided all the advantages of sovereignty. "We can get everything we really want—perhaps more than we ought to have—under trusteeship and no phase of our national interest will be prejudiced," Fortas contended.[80] Further, trusteeships would bolster the authority of the new United Nations, provide civilian administration of the dependent territories, and offer the moral gratification of rehabilitating their occupants. If dependent peoples "are subjected to years of military administration and are not properly encouraged to develop their own economy," one of the under secretary's colleagues warned, "then the task of later civilian administrators will be truly Herculean."[81]

Government officials particularly disagreed over whether islands won from the Japanese should be placed under American sovereignty or under a United Nations system of trusteeship, which could be applied to areas captured from the enemy, old mandates, or territories whose administrators agreed to trusteeship. As designated trustee, the United States would possess civil and military responsibility for the dependent peoples on the Pacific islands until they were ready for self-government. Thus the American government could establish its desired strategic bases and appease internationalists by holding out the promise of eventual self-determination. That Army and Navy wanted more was clear before war's end.

Fortas fought the military's demands for American sovereignty. To Assistant Secretary of War McCloy, he was wryly sarcastic. "We have carefully, but surreptitiously, studied the records of the Navy's administration of American Samoa, Guam, and the American Virgin Islands prior to their liberation by transfer to this Department," Fortas said. Lest McCloy think Interior overly critical, the under secretary hastened to add that his department had discovered one "entirely commendable" aspect of Navy rule. "That is the elaborate set of rules, regulations and prohibitions governing the custody and use of four-legged bitches in American Samoa."[82] To Secretary of the Navy Forrestal, Fortas reiterated his goal of trusteeship for the Pacific islands, his conviction that it possessed the benefits of sovereignty, and his hope that "we will not in these islands repeat the basic mistake that was made in the case of the American Indians. That mistake was a failure to define and adhere to a consistent policy directed to a feasible type of development." Further, it was America's duty and "to our own advantage in the interests of eventual economy and good will, to assist the natives toward a better way of life within the limits of their capabilities and the potentialities of their environment."[83]

At the United Nations conference in San Francisco, Fortas continued the battle for trusteeships. He was not wholly successful. "What was finally reflected in the American proposal," he told Ickes, "was an ingenious and convoluted attempt to have our cake and eat it, too: to have a system of trusteeship but to have, in effect, a United States veto right with respect to all of the trusteeship agreements—and particularly the Pacific Islands." Chapter 12 of the UN Charter provided that territories could be placed under trusteeship only if all "states directly concerned" agreed. It also denoted two types of trusteeships, "strategic" and "nonstrategic." Strategic trusteeships lay in the jurisdiction of the Security Council, where the United States could exercise its veto, while nonstrategic ones would be handled by the General Assembly. For Fortas, Chapter 12 was "a 100% made-in-America product" that created two "monstrosities."[84] It placated the military by placing the future of the Pacific islands in the Security Council so that the United States could veto any unsatisfactory arrangement, and it avoided revealing how it would be determined which states were "directly concerned."

Fortas attended the first session of the United Nations General Assembly in London as an adviser on trusteeship. He boarded the Queen Elizabeth with the other members of the delegation headed by Eleanor Roosevelt on New Year's Eve of 1945 with the hope of selling the idea of trusteeships and of guaranteeing that trusteeship agreements had suitable contents. In his first walk around the deck with Eleanor Roosevelt and John Foster Dulles, Fortas, who was, he said, "trotting most of the time to keep up with Mrs. Roosevelt," directed the conversation to trusteeships because "in view of the short time that I have to spend on this mission I must put in as many blows as possible." Eleanor Roosevelt possessed a "splendid grasp" of the problem. His old nemesis, Dulles, "as usual, is timid and wants to proceed slowly." Fortas explained that it was imperative that other nations submit trusteeship agreements for mandated territories and captured nations and that they would be more likely to do so if the United States quickly submitted trusteeship agreements for the captured Pacific islands. By endorsing trusteeships, he argued, the United States would show humanitarianism and would win the good will of dependent people while surrendering no real authority over them. Dulles argued that "the time was not ripe." Fortas was more pleased by Mrs. Roosevelt, who agreed with him in principle and "made quite a speech to

the effect that we could not expect other nations to do what we ourselves were
unwilling to do (these fervent comments being delivered while we were all
galloping around the deck)."[85] But in subsequent meetings aboard ship and in
London, Fortas found the delegates and other key Americans only moderately
responsive at best.[86] And when Dulles returned to the United States, he and
other prominent conservatives effectively nullified the San Francisco Charter.
They maintained that the United States need not consult states "directly concerned" about trusteeship arrangements and that no member of the Security
Council except the United States could veto a Pacific Island strategic trusteeship.

Fortas disdained America's posturing before the United Nations. As a liberal,
he genuinely believed in providing dependent peoples with relatively beneficent
mechanisms for rehabilitation and self-government. He also claimed that those
who insisted on annexation instead of trusteeship, or who refused to honor the
"American-made" provisions for trusteeship developed at San Francisco, were
politically short-sighted, as trusteeship provided Americans with the same protection as sovereignty. "Given the present Wall Street lawyerish effort to make
black look white and vice versa, I can see only a precipitation of needless and
useless conflict in which we will assume a pious attitude but in which, in fact,
our hands will be extremely unclean," Fortas predicted.[87] Ultimately the Pacific
islands became a strategic trusteeship, but the larger implications of Fortas's
advice proved correct. American behavior regarding the United Nations hurt the
United States by contributing to the decay of its relationship with the Soviet
Union.[88]

Fortas deplored that deterioration. In the fall of 1945 he announced that the
United States should share information about the atomic bomb with the Soviet
Union.[89] He was ignored. By the following summer, Fortas was telling a gathering of Southwestern College alumni that "our bitter, acrimonious conflict [with
the Soviets] has reached the point where the United Nations is becoming little
more than a Madison Square Garden in which the people of the various nations
can watch the desperate fight for the championship of the world." Meanwhile
both the United States and the Soviet Union had "in fact if not in form, withdrawn from the United Nations." The United States had to stop insisting on "the
preservation of familiar boundary lines upon the map," and commit itself to
economic aid and coexistence. "There is no time to waste in arriving at an
agreement with Russia."[90] But few listened.

Though Fortas subordinated third world nationalism and indigenous culture
to American security, his position was progressive for its time in its emphasis on
peaceful coexistence with the Soviets and its recognition of the economic support
needed by dependent peoples. For Fortas, globalism represented the logical

culmination of the New Deal's attempt to preserve capitalism through social reform. "In this country, we have learned the hard lesson that it is impossible for half of us to be gloriously rich and the other half abjectly poor," he said. "We now have to learn the equally difficult lesson that we as a nation cannot long prosper while the rest of the world is in despair."[91] Further, though skeptics might jibe that there was no difference between the two political parties, in Fortas's mind benevolent internationalism was linked with the Democrats.[92]

### THE FORTAS STYLE

For a time, Fortas essentially ran Interior. That required political expertise. Wartime conditions moved the President to create new agencies with overlapping jurisdictions. Roosevelt had always loved to pit government departments against each other, but government by friction became less effective once so many new forces joined the fray.[93] Fortas displayed a bureaucrat's solicitude for his department's turf.

As under secretary, Fortas concerned himself with many different matters. "He was ubiquitous; he was all over town," recalled the equally ubiquitous McCloy.[94] A typical memorandum from Fortas to Ickes ranged over martial law in Hawaii, Japanese relocation, oil, Alaska, and the proposed Potomac River Bridge.[95] Fortas also could perform a variety of tasks at once. One candidate for a position in the territories recalled his job interview in the under secretary's office. Fortas was eating lunch, writing a speech, and answering his correspondence, and "rather than allow me to cool my heels out there," called in the applicant, Stanley Schroetel, to discuss the job. The under secretary proceeded to describe the position in "very inviting" terms. Schroetel was awed. "I've been back to the bureaucratic culture on many occasions," he said. "I have never seen that kind of dedication, I've never been greeted as warmly, I've never had such a genuine kind of communication."[96]

Fortas's perception of himself as a salesman lay at the core of his approach as under secretary. For him, competence was not enough. He once damned someone as "a good craftsman who is not yet reconciled to the fact that in Washington the doing of a good job is a sterile accomplishment unless it is accompanied by promotional work."[97] He succeeded as under secretary because he ably furthered himself, his boss, and his department. Sometimes he acted as if flattery were all-important. Fortas conceded, for example, that elder statesman Bernard Baruch was not "particularly adult." Nevertheless, as he was important to Ickes, Fortas advised "solicitous handling with complete awareness of the fact that Mr. Baruch is accustomed to homage."[98]

At other times, Fortas's tool was not flattery but an angry tone that still managed to deflect blame. When Dillon Myer announced at the beginning of 1945 that the WRA would close all concentration camps in January 1946, many internees said they would not want to leave if the war were still in progress because they feared retribution.[99] Troubled by complaints about the effects of closing the camps on the Japanese, Fortas invited John Burling of the Justice Department to join Assistant Secretary of the Interior Oscar Chapman, in reporting on the advisability of rescinding the closing order. After he and Burling had toured the camps, Chapman recommended that the closing order remain in effect. In contrast, Burling and his Justice Department colleague Herbert Wechsler argued that it would be "tragically wrong" to insist that the evacuees leave the camps by January if they were not ready to do so.[100]

Fortas took issue with Wechsler's letter setting out Justice's position. "Because of my respect, admiration and friendship for you and Burling, I dislike getting into a controversy with you, and I particularly dislike the necessity of record-making," he wrote Wechsler. "But your letter of May 16 forces my hand." He had always been eager to consult Justice on WRA matters "even though they may have been completely outside of your jurisdiction. It is for this reason that I made what appears to be the error of consulting you concerning the policy of closing the centers." Fortas admitted that his department had asked Burling to visit the centers with Chapman. "But I did not suppose that Burling construed the invitation as a commitment on my part that this Department would accept his recommendations regardless of what they were." Nevertheless, Fortas went out of his way to absolve Wechsler of responsibility. "When you sent me a formal letter which, I suspect, was drafted by John Burling, stating your firm conviction that our policy 'is tragically wrong,' I respectfully suggest that you have overstepped the bounds of propriety."[101] The letter reflected one strand of the Fortas style: firmly assert Interior's jurisdiction and mollify challengers by attributing their errors to someone else.[102]

In the case of coal regulation, Fortas sought to preserve Interior's position not through flattery or anger but through a sarcasm which revealed both his sensitivity toward turf and his orientation toward results. When bituminous coal miners under the direction of the United Mine Workers' head, John L. Lewis, threatened to strike in 1943, coal became one of the most crucial domestic issues. With the exception of Harold Ickes, who conceded that Lewis might be "relentless and unprincipled" but who could nevertheless work with him, most Washington officials despised Lewis, and he reciprocated their sentiments.[103] The academics and old New Dealers who resolved wartime disputes between labor and management at the National War Labor Board considered Lewis a threat to the no-strike pledge they had obtained from labor unions to prevent them from striking for higher wages during the cause of the war, and to their

Little Steel formula, which denied workers a wage increase except in the most exigent of circumstances.[104] Franklin Roosevelt, who never forgave Lewis for endorsing Wendell Willkie in the presidential campaign of 1940, found him equally difficult. In May 1943, after the Secretary of Labor had submitted the dispute between the miners and operators to the War Labor Board for settlement, Ickes assessed the situation: "Lewis hates the President and I think that either would like to destroy the other. He hates the War Labor Board, and it hates him, especially the labor members on that board. Notwithstanding, I wish that the Board were more interested in digging coal than destroying Lewis. It is unnecessarily foolish and priggish about its own authority and jurisdiction."[105]

The War Labor Board soon showed exactly how priggish it could be. After Ickes took over the mines for the government because of the threatened strike, the miners promised to walk out when their contract expired on June 1. Ickes tried to prevent a walkout by negotiating a contract between Lewis and the operators that would raise the miners' wages. He was unsuccessful, and the miners did strike. Still, a resolution seemed within reach. The operators, worried that government might nationalize the mines permanently, knew that only an agreement sanctioned by Lewis would prevent further stoppages, and they now began to negotiate in good faith.[106] But when it appeared that operators and miners would reach an agreement on June 2, the War Labor Board intervened to prevent a settlement by prohibiting further bargaining until the miners returned to work and by remanding the dispute to the President.[107]

The board forestalled negotiations for two reasons. It feared the loss of its authority over American workers, who would move to resolve disputes through strikes rather than by appeal to the board if Lewis successfully bypassed it. Further, if the board did not act before an agreement was actually signed, it would only be able to preserve its power by rejecting an agreement between labor and management, a step which would alienate workers throughout the country.[108]

Harold Ickes had no sympathy for the board's position. He justifiably thought that it cared more about preserving its own jurisdictional preserve and prestige than about settling the war's most serious strike.[109] He was sure also that it was unfairly prejudiced against Lewis.[110] On the afternoon of June 2, after Fortas had dissuaded Ickes from resigning, the secretary, Fortas, and members of the War Labor Board, including Wayne Morse, marched into Roosevelt's office, where Ickes engaged in his most "peppery argument" in Roosevelt's presence yet. "It was clear that the President was not pleased with the hot brick that had been handed to him" by the board, Ickes later noted in his diary. Roosevelt "had to do a lot of questioning and there had to be some prodding by Fortas and me before Wayne Morse finally said that the Board would neither receive nor consider such an agreement because it would have been arrived at under the duress that the strike constituted." Even when Interior's representatives pointed out that management and labor "might reach an agreement that would be highly favorable from the public point of view," the board was unmoved.[111]

Fortas had devised a solution that Ickes presented to the President. It gave the secretary of the interior, as the operator of the mines, the authority to make an interim settlement with the miners. Ickes told those gathered in the President's office that there were precedents. Executive orders had granted Joseph Eastman, director of the office of defense transportation, power to make labor agreements when he took over the Toledo, Peoria and Western Railroad and the Puerto Rican Railroad. "Wayne Morse strenuously denied this," Ickes recorded. "He insisted that he ought to know because he had drawn the [two executive] orders in question. Later, Fortas looked at the Puerto Rican order draft which he himself had helped to draft and it was plain that the power to negotiate wages had been given to Eastman. Fortas recalled that Eastman had refused to act in that instance unless he were given such powers."[112]

In fact, it was not quite as plain as Ickes and Fortas claimed. Both executive orders granted Eastman broad discretion, on the one hand, and implicitly retained a strong role for the War Labor Board during the takeover period, on the other. Though neither executive order expressly prohibited Eastman from altering the wage structure during the interim period of disputes, Fortas was reading them both—particularly the more restrictive Toledo, Peoria and Western executive order—rather legalistically.[113] What language conceivably stretched to permit, policy militated against. The government could not have intended to hold out the possibility of executive orders promulgating government takeovers to angry workers desiring to circumvent the War Labor Board and obtain higher wages.

Roosevelt refused to accept Fortas's formula for just that reason. He told Ickes that if he approved the order automobile workers would go on strike in the hope that the government would assume control of their plants and prove more generous than the War Labor Board. Ickes knew that this "was not an illogical position and my feelings were in no wise hurt by the President's decision . . . to stick to the War Labor Board although that outfit had distinctly put him on the spot." The secretary remained convinced, however, that the War Labor Board's actions reflected its desire for revenge against Lewis rather than the country's need for coal: "I remarked that when I was seeking to get a result I was not so much concerned about methods."[114]

Nor was Fortas. Returning to the Department of the Interior, the under secretary sent a memorandum to Roosevelt about the validity of the Eastman precedents. Wayne Morse answered for the board on the following day. Morse, who loved a fight, defended the board's exclusive jurisdiction over labor disputes, claiming that in the Toledo, Peoria and Western case it had been understood that the War Labor Board would be consulted about wages and work conditions during the takeover period. Morse insisted that neither Eastman, as director of the office of defense transportation, nor the War Labor Board "adopted [the] technical, literal, or legalistic interpretations of the Executive Order . . . such as Mr. Fortas had sought to apply throughout the handling of the coal case."[115]

Always one to rise to a challenge, Fortas replied to Morse: "I had not expected . . . to cause you or the National War Labor Board so much concern. After all, I considered your erroneous statement at the White House to be merely a lapse of memory." The under secretary had "only one answer" to Morse's "triumphant discovery" that Fortas sought authorization for Ickes to fix wages while government operated the coal mines: "I would like to have this coal controversy handled so that it will be terminated as soon as possible, and stable conditions restored to the mines. You might think about that for awhile."[116]

Though Fortas had assured Morse that he was not discussing the incident with the press or "bothering the President with a copy of this comment upon your trivial letter," Morse sent a copy of Fortas's missive to the White House along with his rejoinder, which alleged that Fortas and the secretary of the interior had "written a disgraceful page of American Industrial History by adopting the methods which you have followed in handling the Coal Case. . . . To my way of thinking, expediency is never a justification for sacrificing basic principles." Morse reiterated that the under secretary's interpretation of the Toledo, Peoria and Western executive order was wrongheaded. "Without knowing the history of the case and without being at all familiar with the procedures which were followed or with the understanding which existed at the time the President signed the Executive Order, you seized upon certain language in that order in an endeavor to justify what you and the Secretary of the Interior would like to have done in the Coal Case." The War Labor Board considered Fortas's tactics to be "of the trickster type."[117]

The situation deteriorated. Fortas replied that "it is completely useless to argue with a man who conducts himself as if he were bereft of his senses" and said that his "only remaining hope for the War Labor Board is that your splendid colleagues will be able to restrain your unscrupulous, undignified and irrational conduct." Morse countered that Fortas's letter was "most amusing, and it displays your own weaknesses in an unmistakable manner." The under secretary answered that he had not opened Morse's latest condemnation. He knew, he said, if he did so, "I would find that you excoriated me, my motives, intelligence, character and habits of life. Perhaps there are a few additional categories that would have occurred to you; and I am willing to concede that you would have done just as thorough a job of excoriation and vituperation as I did in my letter to you." Even Ickes got into the act, writing Morse that "you admit, which is all that Mr. Fortas argued, that 'technically, literally and legalistically,' Mr. Fortas' interpretation of the executive orders in the two cases was correct. But you didn't admit this to the President. You argued flatly to the contrary." As Ickes pointed out, "it isn't a question of whether Mr. Eastman exercised his powers technically or not. The question is whether he had such powers, and it was on this point that you deliberately undertook to deceive the President." Morse accused Ickes of "emotional instability."[118] Then the letters ceased. Meanwhile, the War Labor Board seemed to prevail. Roosevelt announced its exclusive jurisdiction to settle labor disputes.

The coal crisis gave Fortas a reputation for being legalistic in the name of expediency. Ickes thought "somebody on the War Labor Board has been arousing suspicions with respect to Abe" at the White House,[119] and the President's skepticism increased when the War Labor Board handed down its decision denying the demand of Lewis's miners for a wage hike in the form of "portal-to-portal" pay compensating them for travel time within the mine.[120] The board, claiming it lacked jurisdiction to decide the issue, suggested appropriate forums where the miners could press their claims but added that any settlement they achieved elsewhere would be subject to the approval of the board. After Lewis heard the decision, his miners walked out. Fortas wrote a bitter memorandum excoriating the board for passing the buck and condemning its order as "inconsistent, evasive and illogical."[121] But he said nothing about whether the miners deserved portal-to-portal pay, and when Ickes sent his under secretary's memorandum to the White House, Roosevelt was unimpressed. "I think you will like to see this screed of Abe Fortas," the President told the director of the Office of Economic Stabilization. "Of course, he entirely begs the main issue."[122]

In the end, Fortas and Ickes got what they had sought all along. The miners returned to work. Wayne Morse had considered the confrontation in Roosevelt's office that resulted in affirmation of the board's exclusive authority a great victory. But when the War Labor Board used that power principally to reject proposals Lewis submitted and another strike occurred later in June 1943, Roosevelt had had enough. After the government again seized the mines, the President asked Ickes to negotiate an interim wage agreement Lewis would find acceptable, even though that meant bargaining with a striking union. The secretary arranged a contract with Lewis giving the miners a wage increase of about 25 percent in the form of portal-to-portal pay, which the War Labor Board reluctantly approved. Lewis "had won the epic battle of his career." The coal miners began digging coal again, and Wayne Morse's achievement was transformed into a Pyrrhic victory.[123] The coal crisis had shown that Fortas could skillfully assume the role of bureaucratic infighter.

At times, he seemed interested only in grabbing the limelight for Interior and himself. Fortas justifiably complained that a Navy Department contract permitting Standard Oil to take oil from Elk Hills, California, was so favorable to the oil company that it represented a violation of the public interest. Roosevelt referred the dispute between Interior and the Navy to the Justice Department, directing it to determine who was right. When Assistant Attorney General Norman Littell sided with Fortas, Secretary of the Navy Frank Knox withdrew the contract from the Naval Appropriations Committee, where the Navy had a request pending for the funds necessary to put the contract into effect. Fortas received favorable publicity for his role. An article entitled "Inside Story of the Elk Hills Oil Scandal: How New Dealers Exposed Standard Grab" treated him as one of the heroes of the story. [124] But Fortas apparently wanted all the glory. At a subsequent conference with representatives of the Department of Justice and the Navy, Fortas seemed "a little supercilious because he, after all, felt himself to be the daddy of the whole matter," Norman Littell noted. When Littell, who knew he "had to put Abe Fortas in his place," pointed out errors Fortas had made, the under secretary seemed surprised and apologetic. But he was not embarrassed. That night, he telephoned Littell to ask whether he could borrow a copy of the assistant attorney general's report on the contract, which had taken Littell days to prepare. "The sheer, unadulterated nerve of the question after the superficial job he had done and the supercilious attitude he had at first taken in our conference struck me with considerable force," Littell admitted. Further, Littell knew Fortas hoped to precede him before a congressional committee investigating the contract and steal Justice's thunder "in accordance with Secretary Ickes' very definite wishes in the matter." It did not take Littell long to refuse Fortas. "Once in a while, in the course of life, there is a time to be ungenerous. This was one of those times." [125]

Even his most devoted subordinates found Fortas's behavior contradictory. Asked for his autograph by a youngster with rheumatic fever, Fortas sent along with his signature, some books about the American Indians. [126] He frequently extended himself for others as well. "He was a very gentle, soft-spoken person, the kind of person people could go to with problems," Tex Goldschmidt recalled. "But he could also get . . . very tough with the opposition," whether the antagonist was his own, as in the case of Wayne Morse, or that of someone he represented. In such circumstances, he sought "the last ounce of blood" and often proved "very mean and rough," Goldschmidt said. [127]

In defending Goldschmidt and Robert Morss Lovett—another Interior Department official accused of "un-American" activities—during the war, Fortas experienced his first brush with red-baiting tactics. Like Ickes, whose defense of civil liberties he had long admired, [128] the under secretary supported the two men.[129] An Appropriations subcommittee hearing was set to inquire into the subversive activities of government employees. Fortas called Goldschmidt, then Power Division director, to his office for a briefing before the hearing. Both Fortas and Goldschmidt had heard that committee member Albert Gore of Tennessee always asked a suspect if he believed in God on the grounds that if he answered affirmatively he could not be a Communist. "My trouble was that I don't," Goldschmidt said. "And everybody knew I didn't." Fortas and the others there "put terrific pressure on me about it," Goldschmidt recalled, telling him that the fate of the public power program and the Department of the Interior rested on his answer. They made Jesuitical arguments for an evasive reply. They asked him if he believed that the committee had the right to query him about his religion, for example. When he said that it did not, they demanded to know whether the committee therefore deserved an honest response. "It wasn't that they were asking me to lie," Goldschmidt said. "They were trying to find a way in which I could with my conscience . . . answer that thing." Ultimately Goldschmidt was saved. Someone—perhaps, he thought, his friend Lyndon Johnson—arranged for Gore to be absent from the hearing. Yet the episode had shown Goldschmidt a great deal about Fortas. "I hate to put it quite as bluntly as [that] the ends justify the means," he said, but "if Abe represented you, you knew you were being represented, and . . . no holds would be barred."[130]

Fortas could be extremely bossy. On another occasion, a congressional committee violated a prior understanding by asking Goldschmidt about his alleged subversive activities. "I answered lightly but earnestly," Goldschmidt remembered. He rode back to Interior with Fortas and another colleague, Michael Straus. Goldschmidt's jokes delighted Straus, who repeatedly told the director of the Division of Power how well he had handled the committee. But, Goldschmidt said, "Abe was strangely silent." As a lawyer, Fortas was thinking about the record. In the privacy of his own office, he berated Goldschmidt. The under secretary knew he had to worry not only about the audience at the hearing and the mood of the hour but also about how his client's statements would look on paper. "We've got to get a hold of that record and straighten it out," Fortas said. Goldschmidt replied that nothing need be done because he had been telling the truth. Yes, the under secretary responded, but Goldschmidt had been hesitant. "That's no way to answer questions," Fortas explained. "You [should] give them an answer and then qualify it afterward." He then lectured his friend on how to behave as a witness.[131]

The under secretary displayed no hesitancy about telling his elders how to act either. His relationship with Tugwell during Tugwell's tenure as governor of Puerto Rico got off to a bad start when, during a food shortage, Puerto Rico became the subject of a jurisdictional dispute between the Office of Price Administration and the conservative Agricultural Marketing Administration. Each agency insisted that it should head the distribution of food and supplies in Puerto Rico, and neither saw a role for the governor in the operation.[132] Both also complained about Tugwell to Fortas, who sent Tugwell a sharp reminder that the food supply program "must be run on a non-political and an efficient basis."[133] Tugwell was angry. "Young Abe Fortas is showing a tendency to run this Government from Washington, which is helpful in some instances and a hindrance in others," he confided to his diary. "He is a real help in trying to get authorization for local projects, but I had a letter from him yesterday which was amazing."[134]

The governor was even more surprised when Fortas summoned him to Washington. As Tugwell flew from Miami to the capital, he reflected that he was "being subjected again to the old squeeze play which federal officials in Puerto Rico always put on the Governor. This time O.P.A. and especially A.M.A. . . . have convinced Fortas—and it didn't take much convincing—that the Insular organization is political and inefficient." The governor concluded that the under secretary "had a trial in Washington and we were condemned. Of course Fortas is young and inexperienced and has never been in Puerto Rico." Nevertheless, Tugwell still did not believe that "a Governor should be treated this way by his home office."[135] The disagreement was settled. "Abe, as I have said, may have been young and may have had a policy of appeasement, but he also had humor, perspective, loyalty and generosity," Tugwell said publicly.[136] Soon, however, Tugwell was seething again when a messenger from Washington "brought confidential 'orders' from Fortas to back-slap the Chavez committee," a senatorial group investigating economic and social conditions in Puerto Rico. "Fortas is very young and very presumptuous," Tugwell noted in his diary. "Also he has little knowledge of the conditions he is trying to influence. There have been many instances of his trying to govern Puerto Rico *in absentia*. I ignore them when I can. He has a good heart and will learn."[137]

Fortas did learn, and he became invaluable to Tugwell. The governor wrote to Ickes so frequently that the secretary despaired of reading all his letters,[138] and the burden of running interference for Tugwell within the administration and in Congress fell on Fortas. "I just don't know what we shall do without you," Tugwell lamented when Fortas briefly left Interior in 1943. "So many pending things are dependent on the cooperation of informed, sympathetic people like yourself that I fear for the future of Puerto Rico."[139] Tugwell recognized how much he depended on Fortas, whom Ickes also found indispensable. When the governor pleaded with the secretary to send Fortas to Puerto Rico on a later occasion, Ickes tartly replied that it was "like asking the mountain to visit Mohammed."[140]

Like Tugwell, most of Fortas's colleagues tolerated his sometimes autocratic personality because they sympathized with his goals and considered him extraordinarily efficient in achieving them. They liked and respected him too. While Fortas was under secretary at Interior, for instance, he worked closely with Clifford Durr at the Reconstruction Finance Corporation. Durr recalled, "Abe when he was in the government was as honest and meticulous as any government official I ever dealt with."[141] Although publicly, Goldschmidt remembered, the under secretary was "extremely stuffy," in private "he could be awfully funny."[142] Sometimes he was playful. During the Hawaiian martial law controversy with the Army, he sent McCloy a set of lead soldiers with the message that the assistant secretary of war would have fun ordering them around.[143]

The under secretary who had no hesitation about rebuking subordinates such as Goldschmidt or overriding former bosses such as Governor Tugwell became a different person with helpful outsiders. While Ickes disappeared to his farm in the country after work, Fortas and Carol Agger hosted frequent dinner parties, their friend Elliot Janeway recalled. "They ran the New Deal salon."[144] Frequent guests included Bill and Mildred Douglas, Tom and Peggy Corcoran, Benjamin Cohen, Speaker of the House Sam Rayburn, and Lyndon and Lady Bird Johnson. That began a pattern for Fortas. He made business associates friends, for he reasoned that friends made better business associates.

He courted those who could help him or his department, making himself invaluable to them. Robert Caro has detailed Fortas's successful efforts at the SEC to help Lyndon Johnson get a dam built for his constituents.[145] As under secretary, Fortas continued to work for Congressman Johnson on oil matters,[146] all the while telling Johnson how much their friendship meant to him. "I think that you know that I treasure my association with you," Fortas once said. "You have certainly been a true and loyal friend to me—and for no particular reason."[147] Other members of Congress received the same assistance and declarations of friendship. "My warmest regards to you and to your wife, whom Carol and I like very much," he wrote Howard McMurray. "We had a grand time at your house. Dr. and Mrs. Agger, who are staunch New Dealers, expressed their great pleasure at having an opportunity to talk with 'liberal and intelligent Congressmen,' for a change."[148] Those flattering tones also resonated in his correspondence with supportive members of the press. Because he understood the importance of marketing himself, Fortas was quick to thank those who did his work for him. "Your piece in *Newsweek* about me was grand," he wrote the author of "Ickes' Field Marshall." "It helped me get over my cold."[149]

Fortas was generally pleasant with colleagues as long as they subordinated themselves to him. Puckish with a representative of a competing interest, such as McCloy, he became arrogant and sarcastic when a Wayne Morse made humor worthless. Warm, eager to assist, deferential, and sometimes wry, he made himself indispensable to the press or other influential individuals whose help he required. While he was never overly idealistic, he distrusted pragmatists. "A lot of people think they're being realistic when they're merely being ineffective," he said.[150]

In one important respect his emerging style of leadership contrasted sharply with that of Jerome Frank, his own first boss in government. Frank was genuinely outraged when he wrote someone a thirty-page letter of complaint. Fortas might well be posturing when he protested. He rarely took matters as seriously as he pretended. For example, he had known J. Howard Marshall since his student days at Yale. When the war began, Marshall came to Interior to work in the Petroleum Administration for War (PAW). When Marshall learned that Fortas was trying to take over oil fields PAW had pledged to keep in private hands, he persuaded Ickes that PAW could not break its promise. Marshall then went to his old friend's office and complained bitterly about what Fortas had attempted. The under secretary shrugged it off, replying that he should not be blamed for having tried. Marshall wanted a fight, but as he dryly recalled, Fortas would not oblige.[151] Fortas fought only when it suited him. He was rarely spontaneous. Rather, as his departure from Interior suggested, he was a superb actor.

CHAPTER 6

# From Public Service to
# The Private Sector, 1

T IME MAGAZINE HERALDED THE APPOINTMENT OF ABE FORTAS AS under secretary of the Department of the Interior. "Mr. Ickes will not find any difficulty in snuggling black-haired, esthetic-looking Mr. Fortas under his wing," the editors predicted. "How long Mr. Fortas will stay snuggled down was something for time, the terrible-tempered Mr. Ickes, and quiet, studious Mr. Fortas to decide."[1]

Ickes proved to be the most difficult boss Fortas had served. He demanded complete subordination. "When the old son of a bitch rings once, it's for ice water; when he rings twice it's for the under secretary," Fortas said.[2] Yet as Carol Agger observed, "Abe could manage him pretty well."[3] At first, the reserved young under secretary who fought so skillfully for Interior delighted Ickes. Fortas could do no wrong. Ickes considered him completely loyal and extraordinarily able.[4] In short order, Fortas made himself indispensable to the secretary. Ickes sent Fortas to the cabinet meetings he despised and began to relax. In the summer of 1942, as the secretary enjoyed a long Northwestern vacation nearly uninterrupted by calls from Interior, he recorded that "it was a matter of great comfort to me that Abe Fortas was on the job to keep things steady and going."[5]

## APPRENTICE SEAMAN

Naturally Ickes did not want to lose Fortas to the military. The secretary opposed the conscription of high-level government officials in general.[6] He felt even more strongly about the members of his own staff, particularly the lawyers. When one draft board announced that it would not grant deferments to government attorneys, Ickes became apoplectic. "Heaven knows that I have never felt like going overboard for the members of my profession, but this is so god-damned foolish as to be almost unbelievable," he protested. He maintained that the government contracts necessitated by the war required the scrutiny of good lawyers.[7]

Attorney General Francis Biddle agreed with Ickes on the importance of granting deferments to key civilians. The secretary of the interior could not attend the cabinet meeting in 1942 at which Biddle was to make his case, but he sent Fortas in his stead with instructions to support Biddle.[8] The attorney general told the President that "in all departments our best people are going, most of them going over to sit in unimportant War Department desks, doing trivial matters." Biddle agreed that no one should be retained "who really should be fighting but that the Government employees should be kept where they are if they are doing more important work." Afterward Biddle thought that "practically everybody" at the meeting had sided with him, and that Roosevelt, who worried about the political repercussions of keeping officials out of the military, could be persuaded.[9] Fortas's account was more pessimistic. He reported to Ickes that "Biddle had put up the matter strongly to the President and found him and the majority of the Cabinet totally unsympathetic."[10]

Ickes was more upset by Fortas's admission that he had said nothing on Biddle's behalf during the cabinet meeting and by the possibility that the attorney general might feel betrayed by Interior. "Perhaps Fortas has the common failing of his people," Ickes hypothesized. He defined this weakness as "a disinclination to engage in a rough and tumble, especially if he finds that sentiment is against him. I hope that I am not judging him unfairly."[11] The secretary was being unjust. Doubtless Fortas kept silent because he realized how self-serving he would seem if he openly favored deferrals for a group to which he belonged. Then thirty-two years old, without any children, Fortas was on the old side for military service, but he was still draftable.

It was a puzzling dilemma for him. On the one hand, speculated his friend Walter Gellhorn, Fortas "wanted to go into military service early in the game because he knew that as one of the young men, as a liberal, as a Jew, he would be subjected to particular political attack if he were outside of the military service in time of war." Other New Dealers had been attacked on just such grounds, and Gellhorn was sure that Fortas had quickly seen "the necessity of going into the military service in terms of his own peace of mind."[12] In that case, he could be replaced as under secretary by an older man. Fortas also may have possessed political ambitions that made him concerned about a future without a war record. On the other hand, he was doing essential war work in Interior, and he frequently requested deferments for far less vital employees.[13] Most important,

Ickes did not want anyone but Fortas to be under secretary.[14] In January 1943 Ickes asked for an occupational deferment for Fortas.[15]

Soon afterward, the storm broke. "The yellow press" learned what the secretary had done and "had a hullabaloo about it," Warner Gardner remembered.[16] Gellhorn recalled that the opposition stressed everything Fortas had feared: "Here was man of military age, a Jew, which was always emphasized, a New Dealer, all the 'bad things.'"[17] By the end of April, Fortas had had enough. He submitted his resignation as under secretary to Roosevelt, saying that he wanted to enlist. "It has become apparent to me that my continuance in the post which I occupy in the civilian branch of the Government may subject your Administration to criticism which, however unjustified, will not promote the conduct of the war," he told the President. "I know that you will understand that I am not motivated by personal considerations. I have only one desire, and that is to do my utmost for my country in this time of peril."[18] Prompted by Ickes, who refused to "lose my most important lieutenant," Roosevelt would not accept the resignation.[19] "You can best serve your country by continuing to do your job as Under Secretary of the Interior, which is responsible for so many war activities, and as a member of the various committees to which you have been appointed," he replied.[20] But Fortas's religion was making the administration nervous. As the White House readied a press release on the need for deferments for key civilians, Francis Biddle prepared two drafts of a statement for Roosevelt. "One took Abe Fortas and his proffered resignation as the text and the other was a general statement," Ickes noted. "I had agreed with Francis in advance, after reading the two statements, that Fortas, since he is a Jew, should not be singled out for special treatment. The President agreed."[21]

Casting the need for deferrals in broad terms, however, did not take the heat off Fortas. The press trumpeted Roosevelt's rejection of the under secretary's resignation. "No Administration has ever talked as much as the New Deal about justice and equality and demonstrated more prejudice and favoritism between groups and individuals," one journalist claimed.[22] Congressman Fish said that Fortas "ought to have been in the service long before," while Senator Chavez charged that the under secretary exemplified the thousands of government employees who should be drafted before the government inducted "honest to goodness fathers with family responsibilities."[23] Congressman Harness, a member of the special subcommittee investigating draft practices, even maintained that Fortas's duties in the Department of Interior "are purely administrative, and innumerable men may be found beyond the draft age to fill that position."[24]

With his draft deferment due to expire on November 15, Fortas determined to enlist. At the end of the summer, he again asked Ickes to release him.[25] Fortas explained that he feared an attack from Congress if he were still in Washington when the members returned from the summer recess. "With so much opposition to drafting fathers with children he would expect to be made a special target on the Hill," the secretary recorded after his conversation with Fortas. Ickes believed that he had to grant the request, "although his loss would be a terrible one for me to have to bear," lest Fortas "break" under the "punishment that would be in store for him."[26]

The episode weakened Fortas's faith in Congress even more. During the early years of war, as Congress increasingly had blocked almost all proposals associated with reform, Fortas came to believe that it was crippling the executive branch. "One Congressman, sufficiently assertive and positive, can and does inspire terror, even though he may be a minority of one and may exercise no influence in the Congress," he said.[27] Fortas himself was far more effective at dealing with other individuals in the executive branch than he was in negotiating with members of Congress, although his flattery and usefulness endeared him to a few old New Dealers there. Now he opposed Congress for personal reasons as well as political ones, as pressure from that body had forced him to enlist. The legislative branch had committed "some unfortunate excesses, particularly in personal attacks upon individual members of the executive agencies," Fortas later charged.[28] "He was petrified about anti-Semitism in Congress," Elliot Janeway recalled. "Really very much against Congress."[29]

It was not that Fortas did not want to join the military. His wife maintained that he would have left Interior when the war worsened even if he had not been forced to do so. Had there been no pressure, however, she thought he might have done "something more useful to the military, like an office job."[30] But under the circumstances Fortas would not take such a position. He considered it "a moral challenge to go in as an enlisted man."[31] Agger suspected that Fortas believed he could prove himself only by enlisting.

He applied for voluntary induction in the armed forces in October 1943 and was sworn into the Navy. "As you know, Sir, I am an Apprentice Seaman, Sir," Fortas wrote Saul Haas at the end of the month. "I suppose that just as soon as I can force my way through the assignments that are still here, I shall be sent to boot school where they will make the vain effort of trying to make a seaman out of me."[32] His Navy duties were to include a trip abroad. At Ickes's recommendation, Fortas had been placed on inactive status for a month so that he could head the Petroleum Reserve Corporation's mission to survey petroleum supplies in the Middle East.[33] In November, however, the President prohibited Fortas from joining the mission because King Ibn Saud of Saudi Arabia wanted no Jews present. "He was, of course, terribly disappointed," Ickes said of Fortas's reaction. Fortas blamed Roosevelt's change of heart on Under Secretary of State Edward Stettinius. "He was pretty sore about Stettinius and said that he would look for a chance to 'get' him."[34] Fortas quieted his critics by resigning from Interior. "If I stayed, my usefulness would soon be ended by the attacks I know would come," he maintained. Besides, I'd like to see a little of this fighting."[35] His friend Congressman Howard McMurray told Congress: "I should like to suggest that there are Members of this House who owe this great American an apology for the words that have been spoken on this floor about him."[36]

An exchange of admiring letters accompanied Fortas's departure. "I have heard many people speak of you in glowing terms—of your courage and integrity," Fortas wrote Ickes. "It has always seemed to me that everything that I have heard has been understatement and has somewhat missed the mark. It has missed the quality of the man, a quality which I cannot put in words but which has induced me to offer to you all the loyalty and devotion of which I am capable."[37] Ickes replied that Fortas was the best under secretary in the history of the department.[38] Roosevelt, who had apparently forgotten his impatience with Fortas during the coal crisis and who was relieved to have another potential embarrassment out of the way, told him: "I am sorry indeed that you are resigning as Under Secretary of the Interior. But you are right to go in to the Navy, and I want you to know that all of us will miss you. All the good luck in the world!"[39]

Fortas was "not ordinarily a man who [did] things out of spontaneous abandon," Warner Gardner remembered. He thought that Fortas might have possessed "a rather shrewd well-thought out plan to get the whole business behind him."[40] It is possible that that was Fortas's strategy. When he had told Ickes not to request another deferment, he had disclosed to him that he had ocular tuberculosis, which meant that upon physical examination he might be disqualified from active service.[41] "Tuberculosis of the eye seems scarcely credible, does it?" asked Fortas's friend Walter Gellhorn,[42] and even Carol Agger thought it sounded bizarre.[43] Skeptics jokingly defined ocular tuberculosis as "a yellow streak down the back."[44] Yet the condition had given Fortas trouble in 1940,[45] and if it recurred, as it might if he spent too much time in the sun or exerting himself physically, he had been told he might become blind.[46] Thus Fortas might have thought that having volunteered and been inducted, and then having been rejected after a physical examination, he could resume his position as under secretary with the stigma of "slacker" removed.

But it is more likely that he planned to spend the duration of the war in the military. He and his wife leased their home in Georgetown for two years. Carol Agger, who had been working in the Department of Justice, accepted a position at Lord, Day and Lord—the law firm of her mentor, Randolph Paul—and moved to New York to live with her brother. Fortas told a reporter that if the military rejected him, he would seek a commission in a noncombat unit.[47] Had Fortas suspected that his health would bar him from service, he would have arranged to have a house and spouse awaiting his return. Further, once he had been discharged, his thoughts did not turn immediately to Interior. Even if Fortas himself did not intend a short stint in the Navy followed by a return to Interior, that was the secretary's plan for him. When Ickes met with Walter Gellhorn, whom Fortas had suggested as a replacement, the secretary warned Gellhorn "that I did not believe that Fortas would really find himself in the Navy and that I had given no thought to anyone else for that position."[48]

Fortas did find himself in the Navy, but not for very long. With the Navy wallet his friend Congressman Lyndon Johnson had given him in his pocket, he arrived at New York's Camp Sampson for "boot school."[49] He had received only a cursory medical examination at the induction center, and he could not pass the more rigorous examination the Navy subsequently administered. The doctors who examined him at Camp Sampson therefore recommended a discharge. "Most of the Medical Officers who examined me had no idea that I was in any way different from Joe Doaks, so far as I can detect," he wrote Ickes. "I'm convinced—which is important to me—that the survey has been objective and the decision impartial."[50]

Fortas remained in the medical barracks with others the Navy had deemed unfit until he received his discharge. "I'm rather glad that I've gone through this," he said to Ickes. "I badly needed the change and rest, and I have a better idea of what this is all about." He could now see that enlisting had been a mistake. The average intelligence and training of his new companions was "so low" that Fortas no longer thought he belonged with them.[51] Other enlisted men were "illiterate and badly nourished, as I had never imagined," he told Jane Ickes.[52] "This nation has a long ways to go in providing education, medical care and nourishment for its young people," he reported to Douglas. "No one living here as I have with several hundred of them can fail to be impressed with this."[53] His days were boring, but Fortas tried to appear good-humored about his activities. "Our life is the same as that of the men in active training, except that we don't do the drills and physical exercises. We march here, march back, and march there; go on details (mine this afternoon was office boy to Officer of the Day—which was good fun); police the barracks; keep our clothes as clean as possible and [perform] like duties which are not exciting." He joked: "I have a great advantage here because I can read and write moderately well. In fact, I've been graduated to charge of the gear locker (brooms, swabs, towels, linen)."[54]

Fortas expected an honorable discharge. Instead he was handed an order to leave the medical barracks and report for active duty. Ickes promptly complained to Secretary of the Navy Knox, who learned that the Navy medical board's recommendation of an honorable discharge to Washington had been overruled by a junior officer. Knox, who suspected "other cases of this sort existed," was upset. "It may be the case of some upstart trying to get at Abe because he is a Jew or because he was Under Secretary of the Interior," Ickes noted after speaking with the Secretary of the Navy. Knox intervened, and Fortas received his honorable discharge in December, just a month after he had reported for duty.[55] By now he was ill, but he went straight to Manhattan, where Carol Agger, who had not known when her husband would be released, was surprised to find him in a sailor suit at her door.[56] After stopping in New Brunswick to pick up the civilian clothes he had stored with his in-laws, he made his way down to Washington.

## AN UNSETTLED MIND

Once he had been discharged, Fortas did not know what to do. He had been offered "a profitable and pleasant connection" as a lawyer in Manhattan.[57] He worried that "if I return to Washington, my draft board, which may not be entirely objective about New Dealers, will reclassify me 1-A at the end of the month and I may have to go through this bloody procedure with the Army.[58] But Ickes was "taking it for granted that you are coming back to Interior as Under Secretary. . . . Your country needs you and so do I."[59]

Fortas's morale was low, and he remained undecided. Elliot Janeway told Ickes that Fortas was on the verge of a mental or physical breakdown.[60] "He probably was pretty depressed," Agger said. "He had no house and he had a wife in New York."[61] Though he told Ickes that Agger was willing to return to Washington, Fortas may have doubted the sincerity of her offer.[62] It was virtually impossible for a female attorney to obtain a position in a prestigious law firm at that time, and Agger was finally getting some experience in private practice.[63] But she was earning more money than her husband, which may have galled Fortas. He may also have thought, or so friends believed, that his wife was happier sharing an apartment with her brother than she had ever been when she was living with him. If so, that meant he felt he had been rejected, not only by the Navy and by the power structure he had served which forced him into the Navy, but by his wife as well. And as one friend said, it was difficult for Fortas to cope with rejection.[64]

Nevertheless, the secretary continued to urge him to return to Interior, although even at their first meeting Ickes "could see at once how unsettled his mind was" and that Fortas "looked terrible. He had the appearance of an anxious ill man." Fortas explained he had been warned that his return "would be murder" for both of them. And he wondered aloud whether he shouldn't make some money. "He said that he owed no loyalty to the President, but that he did feel loyal to me." The secretary recorded that he had told Fortas that he wanted him back but that he should not return unless he really wanted to do so.[65] Perhaps Ickes understated the pressure he was applying, for Carol Agger suggested that her husband was inclined to become under secretary again only because Ickes professed to need him so much.[66]

Others advised Fortas to do something else. Janeway counseled him to head for California, where his understanding of environmental issues, his wife's expertise as a tax attorney, and the relative lack of anti-Semitism would enable the couple to establish a thriving practice.[67] Coincidentally, William O. Douglas was thinking along the same lines. He told Attorney General Robert Kenny of California that Fortas and his wife should not "get lost in the catacombs of New York," leading Kenny to hint to Fortas that Kenny's former law firm in California would like to hire both Fortas and Agger.[68] But Fortas had never worked in the private sector. He was not yet ready to make the break from government service, and entering private practice anywhere other than in Washington would have been foolish. Years later, Janeway said that he had recommended that Fortas go West only because he was "so beat up" at that particular point: "Given his connections, he would have been a nut to leave."[69]

In part, the anti-Semitism Fortas had suffered was taking its toll. Oddly, he had not even told Douglas that Roosevelt had barred him from the Saudi Arabian mission at the last minute because of Ibn Saud's hostility to Jews. When Ickes saw Douglas after Fortas returned from the Navy, he mentioned what the President had done. "That explains everything," Douglas exclaimed.[70] Douglas told Ickes he had advised Fortas against returning to Interior "unless he was prepared to slug, blow for blow, with anyone who attacked him, whether in or out of Congress," although he also claimed that Fortas was "devoted" to Ickes. "He stated further," Ickes wrote in his diary, "that it would mean a lot for Fortas's morale if I could arrange for the President to see him for a few minutes, just to pat him on the back and tell him he was all right."[71]

Just after his meeting with Douglas, Ickes received a letter from Fortas reporting that he had tried "a few days of doing nothing in New York," but that he did not "vacation very well." He had decided, "and this is final," to return as under secretary if Roosevelt would ask him in person to come back: "If the President should talk with me directly, it might help to minimize sniping around election time." Though that request was presumptuous, Fortas actually was worrying not about the President but about Ickes. He told the secretary that he could "readily understand it if you're annoyed with me about the whole business. It seems to me that I was never really in doubt as to what I should do; but the violently contrary opinions of devoted friends have made it difficult for me." There would be time enough to make money later, he added. "If I can't make a living when I get out after another year of service with you, I probably wouldn't have held on to the $40 to $75,000 which is being talked about now. And any punishment that I take during the next year will be taken in a fight that is more important to me than the pain which it may cause."[72]

Illness forced the President to cancel a planned appointment with Fortas, but Roosevelt did write to ask Fortas to return.[73] Since Congress was not in session, the President agreed to a recess appointment after Ickes prodded him.[74] The pressure on Fortas continued. His draft board, which consisted of "conservative Republicans—Roosevelt haters" required that Fortas undergo another examination.[75] "This persecution is a terrible thing for a man of his sensibilities to have to endure," Ickes observed.[76] Fortas bore it, however, and when he returned to work, the secretary thought "he looked well and his attitude seemed much more normal than it had been from the day that he became all hot and bothered about going into the Navy with the resultant public attacks on him. I was glad to see him back."[77]

## SHAKEN CONFIDENCE

After Fortas returned in 1944, however, his relationship with Ickes deteriorated. Fortas had stayed in the secretary's good graces longer than any of his predecessors, but Ickes could not allow the same person close to the throne for long. Fortas had changed too. In his first eleven years in government service, he had been autocratic, but he had also been a supportive and kind boss. Now, perhaps because of the rejection he had suffered, he reverted to the same nasty style of administration he had exercised as editor in chief of the *Yale Law Journal*.

When he learned, for instance, that Fowler Harper, the Interior Department's solicitor, was in direct communication with Muñoz Marín in Puerto Rico, Fortas sent a sharp memorandum of protest. "You are not in charge of policy with respect to the Territories or any aspect of territorial administration," Fortas admonished. "I hope that you will find it possible to confine yourself to legal matters, except when your advice on policy is requested, and to relinquish your assumed jurisdiction of policy in this field to the officials to whom it properly belongs."[78] The memorandum was puzzling, for Fortas usually behaved as if law and policy were inseparable. Similarly, though he correctly contended that, as a former executive of Standard Oil, Ralph Davies should not represent the Department of Interior on committees considering Middle Eastern oil problems, Fortas presented his views in a maddeningly self-righteous fashion.[79]

Ickes watched the new Fortas with some amazement. "The memorandum was little short of insulting," he noted of Fortas's communication to Harper. "I would never think of talking to anyone on my staff the way Fortas expressed himself."[80] As the disagreement between Fortas and Davies degenerated into an endless exchange of memoranda in the spring of 1944, the secretary concluded

Fortas was "deliberately making a record."[81] When Ickes threw his weight on Davies's side in April, Fortas sent him a memorandum that Ickes described as "the most extraordinary that I have ever received from anyone on my staff. It was controversial and arrogant and almost insulting."[82]

Ickes became even more annoyed with Fortas later that month. The secretary had read only as far as the first paragraph of a statement Fortas had drafted for him about the United Mine Workers for a planned meeting with John L. Lewis. On that basis, Ickes had approved the statement. At his meeting with Lewis, Ickes began reading it aloud. When his breath became short he handed it to Fortas. The under secretary continued reading and announced that the statement would be released to the press. "I had not been consulted about that," Ickes recounted, "but I was not concerned because the rule is that no release, except on routine matters, may go to the press without my prior written consent." Then Fortas finished the statement. To Ickes's surprise, the last paragraph included some "really offensive" remarks about John L. Lewis.[83] Lewis jumped to his feet and denounced Fortas. He said that the United Mine Workers had long known of the "retromingent" attitude of Mr. Fortas, which he pronounced *Fort-ass*. All those in the room waited eagerly until the moment when they could race to their dictionaries to learn the meaning of the adjective. When the meeting ended, they learned that it was a zoological term used to describe animals who urinate backwards.[84]

Ickes assumed at first that Lewis was simply on "a rhetorical holiday."[85] The secretary of the interior only began worrying after he left the conference. At that point, he learned that Fortas had authorized release of the statement and that it could not be recalled. When Lewis asked Ickes if he really intended to give it to the press, the secretary took Lewis up to his office. "I told him that I had not written the statement and that it was the first time in my life that I had ever read a statement that I had not gone over first carefully. He said: 'I knew that you had not written it and I know who did it. It was Fortas. Fortas hates the United Mine Workers.'" Ickes apologized to Lewis, he said, "because I owed him an apology."[86]

Harold Ickes never liked apologizing, and by the time he saw Fortas the following day he was angry. "Quietly, but with no smile on my face or expression of friendliness, I asked him if he had authorized the release the day before," Ickes related. Fortas said he had. The secretary reminded him of the departmental rule concerning press releases and repeated Lewis's accusation that the under secretary hated the United Mine Workers. "Fortas said that he did not hate the United Mine Workers but that he hated John L. Lewis. I told him that this was about the same thing and observed that this was not a very helpful spirit in which to negotiate matters."[87] "I cannot quite make Abe out," a puzzled Ickes wrote of the incident. Given the time constraints, Fortas should have known that the secretary would not be able to peruse the entire statement and should have called his attention to the last paragraph. "The truth is that I am not unsure that Fortas was not unwilling to use me, if he could, and by accident he was able to get away with it. This has shaken my confidence in Fortas considerably. I suppose that I am not unaffected by his expressions with reference to Davies."[88]

Actually, it was not difficult to make out Fortas. By 1944, as Lewis's biographers pointed out, many workers and liberals who had earlier supported him had become critical of the UMW leader. They believed that the coal strikes of 1943 had encouraged antiunion sentiment and that Lewis's subsequent threats to strike were "provoking a new wave of anti-unionism."[89] Fortas had tried to talk at least one friend in Congress out of voting for the antistrike Smith-Connally Act.[90] He undoubtedly joined other liberals in blaming the introduction of that legislation on the UMW chief. Nor was he as personally taken by Lewis as was his boss. Carol Agger thought that Lewis found the secretary easier to manipulate than the under secretary.[91] Indeed Lewis had charmed Ickes "out of his guts," one Interior Department official recalled.[92] Fortas respected Lewis, because, as Elliot Janeway said, Fortas "admired anybody who would stand up and call you a son of a bitch."[93] Nevertheless, Lewis had not charmed him. A telegram from the UMW to Ickes in 1944 referred to Fortas as "our cold and calculating enemy."[94] Fortas was always willing to cut off those to whom he felt no personal loyalty, and Lewis was no exception.[95]

After the Lewis incident, Ickes became disenchanted. "I have reluctantly come to the conclusion that Fortas is too much disposed to take from my shoulders the running of the Department . . . and that when it comes to selecting personnel he plays favorites," Ickes confided to his diary.[96] The secretary now began telling subordinates that "Fortas sometimes assumed powers that were not his."[97] He suspected that Fortas was feeding information to columnists.[98] He resented the weekends Fortas, who was living with friends, spent in New York with his wife, and he grumbled that the under secretary was too "ambitious." According to Ickes, "Fortas is always seeing the worst in things and he likes to think of himself as always saving a situation after 'working hard' on it. He does not let his light shine under a bushel and he is never reluctant to give himself credit."[99] Of course Ickes himself never hid from the limelight. He too leaked to the press. His massive diary attests to his obsession with leaving a record of his own rescue of innumerable situations. John McCloy once observed how alike Ickes and Fortas were.[100] Ickes never noticed the similarity.

Nevertheless, Ickes was right in one respect: Fortas was different in his second stint as under secretary. Once, for example, Fortas had been a good friend to Michael Straus. He had even offered to resign so that Straus, also a Jew, could receive a promotion without prompting criticism of Ickes's hiring practices.[101] Now, according to Ickes, Straus found his former ally "arrogant" and could "no longer . . . discuss matters with Fortas amicably."[102] Ickes reported other nega‑ tive views: Another Interior Department official considered Fortas "dictatorial, insolent and hard to get along with." A third colleague thought Fortas was "a sadist." Before he left for the Navy, Fortas had been popular in Interior, as he had been at the AAA, Yale, and the Protective Committee Study. Now he was no longer well liked.[103]

Some of those spreading stories about Fortas were disgruntled conservatives in the Bureau of Reclamation who had disapproved of his opposition to the Elliot Amendment.[104] But the new Fortas was not apparent only in professional dis‑ agreements. During the summer of 1945 a Washington columnist wrote that a high official in Interior had tried to discipline a black elevator attendant who had carried him past his floor because she did not recognize him. When he investigat‑ ed the incident, Ickes learned that Fortas had been the disgruntled official and that the under secretary had indeed tried to deny the attendant a promotion. Ickes was "astounded that Fortas should have done what he did."[105] Rumors now began circulating that Fortas had "a strong anti-Negro prejudice," and one friend who spoke with him about the episode said the under secretary "seemed sort of defenseless."[106]

As at the *Yale Law Journal,* Fortas could be helpful to those who were not in his power. He and Ickes still shared many liberal goals and worked harmoniously together for them. For the most part, Fortas continued to conciliate Ickes. In one instance, for example, the secretary charged that the governor of the Virgin Islands had tried to violate Interior policy by asking permission to accompany Fortas to a congressional hearing. Fortas did not think the governor had done so, but Ickes insisted that he "distinctly" remembered the request. "I am sorry that I still don't recall the incident as you have described it," Fortas told Ickes. "How‑ ever, since your recollection is distinct, I am willing to accept it. If you decide to send the letter as drafted, I shall be prepared to support the statements made therein."[107] Later, on a crucial issue, Fortas was unprepared to substantiate Ickes's recollection as fully as the secretary desired.

## "SYMBOL OF LIBERALISM"

By the time Fortas began thinking of resigning in the summer of 1945, many New Dealers had left government service. Roosevelt's death in April 1945 and Truman's ascension to the presidency had deprived them of power. "We fellows have to stick together," Tom Corcoran told Fortas.[108] The New Dealers now were political refugees. The glitter was gone, too. As President, Roosevelt had embodied their dedication. Truman did not. Further, the New Dealers needed money. Bureau of the Budget director Harold Smith's departure from a position in government service paying $10,000 for a $22,500 tax-free salary as vice-president of the International Bank for Reconstruction and Development inspired a flood of magazine stories that detailed the struggle of government officials like Fortas to cope with the high cost of living. [109] When Thurman Arnold was offered the position of assistant secretary of commerce, he refused it. "I cannot afford to go back to $8,600 a year," he said. [110] His thoughts turned to private practice. "It's this old curse of our crowd,"[111] Corcoran told Elliot Janeway. Jerome Frank originally objected to Cabell Phillips's generalization in the fall of 1946 that the "bright young men" of the New Deal had "moved into greener economic pastures,"[112] but when Phillips replied that he possessed a list of at least twenty individuals who had done so, Frank had to concede that the newspaperman was correct. [113]

The war against Hitler had not eliminated anti-Semitism at home, but it had brought many public servants to power, and power mitigated persecution. Businessmen's need for their expertise enabled New Dealers to contemplate starting their own law firms, an idea that would have seemed presumptuous twelve years earlier. "The Nation's business was struggling under the mass of rules, regulations and restrictions which World War II had spawned," Fortas said later. The government lawyers who drafted them and who knew their loopholes could guide corporate clients "through the maze."[114]

Oddly, entering private practice still seemed daunting to Fortas, though he did take and pass the District of Columbia bar examination in the summer of 1945. To the dismay of its conservative alumni, Yale Law School wanted to offer him a full professorship. Though Fortas flirted with Yale and other institutions, he was not interested. [115] His wife had opened a law firm in Washington with Randolph Paul, and both she and Fortas enjoyed living in the nation's capital. But Fortas wondered where he would find clients if he entered practice. [116] "He was really worried about the future," Carol Agger remembered. [117] Under the circumstances, he initially wanted to stay in government, albeit in a different and more highly paid capacity. His thoughts may have turned to the post of secretary of the interior. In June 1945 Washington gossip had it that Truman hoped to oust Treasury secretary Henry Morgenthau. Democratic party boss Robert Hannegan had reportedly said that the administration "was looking for a high-class Jew to put in the Cabinet before they can give him the bum's rush." Most politicians would have agreed with the current comment that "the trouble is that getting a high-class Jew is no easy job."[118] Fortas may have thought he could be it. Tom Corcoran, who remained close to both Ickes and Fortas, confirmed that once Morgenthau had left office and Ickes began hinting of his own impending resignation, "Fortas was playing to be the Jewish member of the Cabinet."[119]

Another prospect for Fortas on which Corcoran—who considered himself the head of a government in exile—was working seemed more likely. "How about Abe Fortas for the Circuit Court of Appeals down here?" Corcoran casually asked Edward Prichard, a New Dealer with close ties to the Truman administration. Corcoran thought government officials "figure they must put a Jewish boy in on the [District of Columbia] court set up. Instead of Alexander Holtzoff for District Judge, how about Abe Fortas for Circuit Court of Appeals judge?"[120] Corcoran pointed out that Fortas's administrative experience made him an ideal candidate for the D.C. circuit, the court of appeals for all administrative agencies. Fortas's political qualifications were good, too. The slate Truman reportedly was considering included Republicans and would be "a debased court from our point of view," Corcoran told Prichard. "Republicans don't appoint Democrats," he expostulated. "Why Democrats have to show they've got a fundamental inferiority complex so they have to appoint Republicans is . . . nuts!" Corcoran suggested Prichard contact Lyndon Johnson, who possessed "a great deal" of influence and would "be for Abe." He then spoke with Thurman Arnold, who indicated that Hugo Black favored Fortas. Even Harold Ickes was enthusiastic.[121]

Corcoran then telephoned Fortas, who was delighted by his friend's progress. "I really put your name in the pot hard for the Circuit Court of Appeals thing today," he reported. "Oh, fine," Fortas replied. "Now if you could get that, boy, you ought to take it," Corcoran continued. "You think it's possible, Tom?" Fortas asked. "Yeah, better, I think it's probable," Corcoran answered.[122] The effort foundered, however. Labor's drive to place William Hastie on the bench meant the promotion of other judges to make room for Hastie.[123] When it became clear that Fortas would not receive the D.C. circuit appointment, he was willing to settle for a district court appointment as long as it was understood he would move into any vacancy on the circuit court. Corcoran promoted Fortas for the district court as a "symbol of liberalism" whose selection would appease those concerned about the Truman administration's conservative appointments.[124] He told Attorney General Clark that the choice of Fortas over Alexander Holtzoff, a man known chiefly for his work on federal procedure,[125] might signify a "rapprochement" between the Truman and Roosevelt administrations and would please William O. Douglas. Corcoran also predicted that Fortas's appointment would "liberalize what you and I know is otherwise going to be a very much criticized conservative court."[126] He then recounted his conversation with Tom Clark to Fortas: "I said when you ski, fellow, they teach you to lean forward and not fall on your face, and that maybe that one of the smart things to do since it is a political matter is to advertise an alliance to the world rather than a disagreement. . . .

He said that he hadn't thought of that." Corcoran was convinced that "the Lyndon stuff has done its work with Clark" and that the attorney general might speak with Ickes about Fortas's appointment at the cabinet meeting that afternoon. Fortas said that the news was "wonderful" and asked what he should be doing.[127] As usual, Corcoran was overly optimistic.[128] The district court appointment went to Holtzoff, and Fortas's judicial ambitions were delayed for twenty years.

William O. Douglas now played father to Fortas for the last time. He wanted his protégé to enter private practice with Thurman Arnold, and Corcoran arranged the partnership.[129] When Ickes complained to Douglas in December that Fortas had not yet quit, the under secretary's resignation quickly appeared.[130] For the first time in his adult life, Fortas was self-employed. Even as he condemned Fortas, Ickes found him too useful to relinquish him. He readily accepted the under secretary's offer to go to London as an adviser on U.N. trusteeship matters until January 15, 1946, the effective date of his resignation.[131] Others remembered even more clearly than Ickes how much Fortas had done for Interior. Truman, for example, looked at the letter Ickes had drafted for the President to use in accepting Fortas's resignation and told a staff member, "I think Abe deserves a better letter. Honest Harold suggested this one."[132]

## "BOY, I WAS SCARED"

Truman was having his own troubles with Ickes by this time, and Fortas helped the President resolve them. Like Roosevelt, the new President had to maintain ties with both the Democratic machine and the liberals who admired Ickes. Truman's decision to name the conservative California oil magnate and former treasurer of the Democratic National Committee Edwin Pauley as under secretary of the Navy made Ickes angry. The secretary of the interior argued against placing an oil man in charge of oil. Indeed, he claimed that after Roosevelt's funeral and on another occasion, Pauley had tried to warn him off asserting federal title to the oil in the California tidelands, where Pauley and others had arranged profitable leases with the state. According to Ickes, Pauley had threatened that the secretary's proposed law suit would cost the Democratic party several hundred thousand dollars in contributions.

Truman forwarded Pauley's nomination to the Senate on January 18, 1946, the same day that he nominated the backslapping George Allen as a member of the Reconstruction Finance Corporation. Ickes had expected the Pauley appointment for at least a month and had been planning his course. He had decided that he could not oppose Pauley "of my own motion either directly or indirectly . . . so long as I am a member of the Cabinet." But if the Naval Affairs

Committee called him as a witness, he would answer its questions even though his replies might embarrass both Pauley and Truman.[133] Meanwhile Edwin Harris, a reporter who was writing a series of articles on Pauley, had uncovered the Ickes-Pauley connection.[134] Senate Republicans on the Naval Affairs Committee who were evaluating the Pauley nomination now realized Honest Harold could enable them to destroy the Democrats' credibility. When Ickes showed Truman the telegram he had received summoning him as a witness, the President "told me that I must tell the truth but he hoped that I would be as gentle with Pauley as possible. I told him that this was my intention."[135]

Ickes was rarely gentle. At the committee hearing, he surmised that Harris had drafted the questions Republican senator Charles Tobey was asking. The crowded room became quiet when Tobey inquired whether Pauley had ever warned Ickes that "filing of the government suit would be bad politically and that several hundred thousand dollars could be raised from California oil men if they could be promised that the suit would not be filed." Ickes responded, "This line of inquiry is embarrassing to me, but you are entitled to an answer—my answer is yes."[136] He smugly noted in his diary: "I did Pauley a great deal of damage. I think that the general impression was that I was not happy at doing this although I was telling the truth."[137] Ickes also revealed that Fortas had been with him when Pauley proposed the deal. Pauley, who testified later that day, declared that he had never taken "contingent contributions" and accused the secretary of misinterpreting the conversation.[138]

The Republicans had found the wedge they needed to divide the old New Dealers Ickes exemplified from the Truman Democrats Pauley represented. "I'm all right, but the Democratic party ain't," Tom Corcoran told Lyndon Johnson.[139] "The Democratic party is split, seriously split over the nomination," one Senate member confirmed.[140] All possibility of arranging a compromise with Ickes that would heal the breach soon evaporated. Truman, who took the secretary's attacks on Pauley personally, announced to the press that Ickes's recollection of his conversation with Pauley might "very well be mistaken."[141] Ickes now delivered his final, real resignation, a six-page opus, and tipped off Washington newsmen that his last press conference as secretary would include fireworks.[142] The Truman administration had lost one of its most important liberals, and Ickes was screaming to the press that Attorney General Tom Clark should prosecute Pauley for perjury. "It means a licking in November, boy, sure as hell," Corcoran lamented.[143]

Ickes was gone, but Pauley remained. If Fortas, as the sole witness to the conversation, forthrightly corroborated the former secretary of the interior's story, Pauley's nomination could not survive. Ickes became increasingly worried as to how forcefully Fortas would support him. At first, Ickes had every reason to believe that Fortas would verify his story. After testifying before Congress, he telephoned his former under secretary in Puerto Rico. "He told me that he remembered the occasion in my office at which time Pauley discussed the possible campaign contributions from oil interests in California and urged that I give certain assurances that the Government would not proceed with claims to title on offshore oil lands," Ickes noted. "He said that he would testify to that effect."[144]

Upon his return to Washington, Fortas reported to Corcoran that the telephone had been "a buzzing away," with calls from every side about the Pauley affair. "And, er, I told all these guys, including an emissary from Mr. Big, just what I would have to say if I were called." Fortas himself had telephoned Truman's secretary and explained what he would testify, "just to make doubly sure." "Maybe you'd better go to Puerto Rico again," Corcoran joked. "Well, hell, if they've got any sense, they won't call me," Fortas replied.[145] The Republicans, however, thought otherwise, and Tobey asked Fortas to appear before the committee. Corcoran now apprised his friend that he had no alternative but to tell the truth, "and since you're going to be goddamned for telling the truth, tell the whole truth."[146]

Once again, Fortas reassured Ickes. The truth, as he remembered it this time, lay between the Ickes version and the Pauley account, which the White House wanted him to corroborate. "The only respect in which his memory was not in full accord with mine was as to the word 'if,' " Ickes said after Fortas had privately explained his recollection. "As Abe put it, Pauley made two statements unconnected by a conjunction: (1) that he could collect 3 or 4 hundred thousand dollars from the oil interests and (2) that the government should not bring any suit for Federal claim to the tidelands. He remarked that the proposition was the same as if the two statements had been tied together by the word 'if.' " Ickes did not try to convince Fortas "that he might have forgotten this little word."[147] Fortas also identified "Mr. Big's emissary" for Ickes. His future partner, Paul Porter, had telephoned to ask whether he was present at the conversation between Pauley and Ickes. Fortas had confirmed that he was and had told Porter that he could so inform Pauley. Fortas assured Ickes "that even if we had become estranged, which we had not, he would tell the truth." Ickes found Fortas "very friendly indeed and he left me no doubt that on the basis of his own recollection he would support what I had already testified to except as to the one word 'if' which, after all, did not seem to me to be significant."[148]

Fortas was walking a tightrope. There were several reasons to support Ickes. First, as Fortas acknowledged, even if Pauley did not use the word *if,* he surely meant to convey to the secretary that the contributions were contingent upon the government's position regarding the tidelands. Second, the Pauley nomination repudiated the meritocracy Fortas had advocated his entire adult life. Arthur Krock referred to Ickes's opposition to Pauley as a "Hiroshima mission against the patronage policies and politics of the administration."[149] Democratic National Committee Chairman Robert Hannegan conceded that Ickes's attitude toward patronage bothered him: "When I send anyone over to Ickes for a job, you might think they had a recommendation from Hitler."[150] Fortas agreed that "the issue, as a political matter, has become one of good government (represented by Ickes) and bad government (represented by President Truman, Pauley . . . and Allen)."[151] Finally, Fortas valued loyalty, and Ickes needed him. He did not want it to appear "as if I'm walking out on Ickes."[152]

There were equally good reasons to desert his former boss. Fortas believed that Ickes's manner had needlessly inflamed the situation. "If I'd been over there with the Old Man, I wouldn't have let him do it this way," he told Corcoran. Fortas did not want to hurt the Democratic party. Most important, he did not want to hurt himself. At thirty-five years of age, just beginning a career in private practice that he had hesitated to undertake, he could not afford to alienate the Truman administration. By advising "the principals on both sides" of what he remembered, he hoped "to avoid any personal antagonism."[153] Fortas naturally confided in Corcoran, who was similarly torn. As a liberal, Corcoran wanted to placate Ickes, who helped to invest the teetering Truman administration with the aura of Roosevelt. As a former fundraiser for the Democrats, however, Corcoran wanted to avoid splitting the party or alienating generous contributors. And as a Washington lawyer, Corcoran knew that if he could satisfy Hannegan by arranging a compromise with Ickes and securing "two votes on the Naval Affairs Committee for Pauley," his client, the soap manufacturer Lever Brothers (which would later become one of Fortas's best clients), might receive its desired quota of fats and oils.[154]

Fortas decided upon a convenient lapse of memory. He did generally corroborate Ickes's story in his testimony before the Naval Affairs Committee. "Mr. Pauley mentioned contributions to the Democratic campaign by oil interests; and . . . he also mentioned the tidelands suit," he said. Although both subjects were raised, "I did not remember the contingent." Fortas added that his statement represented only "his best recollection" and that there was "the possibility of error."[155] "Fortas Memory Is Vague," the *New York Times* reported. Similarly, the *Chicago Tribune* noted "Fortas Can't Remember."[156]

He was evasive and oblique, at times curt and at other times unduly garrulous. Asked by Senator Tobey if Paul Porter had telephoned him, Fortas replied, "Now, Senator, this is a celebrated matter which your committee is considering. I don't think I have been anywhere where people haven't discussed it. People have discussed it constantly. But I want to say, with all the emphasis of which I am capable, that nobody has attempted in any way to refresh or to influence my testimony. I am sure—I hope so, at any rate—that if anybody had been so moved—and I don't think any of the people whom you have in mind would be so moved, but if anybody had been so moved, that they would have had a greater regard for me than to attempt anything of that sort."[157] As Fortas summed it up for Corcoran: "I didn't reply, but made a very curt statement about how nobody would try to refresh my memory or influence my testimony, and by the time I got through with that oration, they had forgotten what they asked me." He continued, "Boy, I was scared," but added, "it worked out very well. . . . I wasn't called on to state my impression, and I merely narrated the fact that the conversation had occurred." According to Fortas, Ickes was "pleased," and Paul Porter had indicated that Hannegan "says this fellow Fortas is high in his books and he'll do anything for him, anytime."[158]

Hannegan had reason to be pleased. As Corcoran said, Pauley appeared "at his very best after that Fortas testimony."[159] If the Truman administration still wanted Pauley, "the best chance of winning is to take advantage of the fuzziness of the Fortas testimony," which had provided "a loophole," Corcoran counseled. "Walk through that before the old man [Ickes] hits you again. Now, walk through it while it's fuzzy, fellow. Line your crowd up; and if you have the votes do it."[160] The Truman Democrats in fact did not have the votes to confirm the nomination, but Truman and Pauley could save face. The nomination was withdrawn only after a majority of the Naval Affairs Committee expressed its faith in Pauley's integrity. Although the Democrats took a beating in the November 1946 congressional elections, the Fortas testimony enabled the Truman administration to avoid a scandal.

Ickes knew it, and he was not nearly as satisfied as Fortas believed. "It is only fair to say that a careful study of the record would lead a lawyer to the conclusion that, on the whole, he had supported my position," Ickes conceded. "But he was lacking in forthrightness and vigor when he really had a chance to make headlines all over the country." Fortas had done Ickes "no harm," but he had done him no "particular good" either. "He was evasive and weak," Ickes justifiably concluded. "He gave an exhibition of a man balancing himself carefully on the edge of a sharp razor." The former secretary confessed that he was "disappointed" but that he had not expected much. "I have been the champion of the civil rights and human rights of the Jews all of my life, but I have always known that they would not fight and that in a pinch they would either equivocate or run." Fortas, he remarked, "could not slough off the racial habits of 2000 years."[161] Others in Washington had expected more of Fortas. "I was surprised that Abe didn't swing a little harder for Ickes," one friend acknowledged. "He kind of ducked."[162]

It was not surprising. There were three significant differences between

Fortas and Ickes. One related to style. A future secretary of the interior who worked with both men observed, "Fortas played a shrewd, carefully planned fight all the time, regardless of who it was that he was fighting about or who he was fighting for, but he would do this in a natural sense. Ickes on the other hand worked like a meat axe on you and he didn't try to be the world's champion diplomat."[163] The second related to independence. Having begun his political career as a Bull Moose Progressive, Ickes could disengage himself from the Democrats in the executive branch more easily than Fortas. The third related to loyalty. Ickes's first allegiance was to the liberal issues he promoted. Thus he publicly championed Jews, though he privately disliked them. Fortas was loyal to his own interests and to a few close friends, whom he supported even when he considered them wrong on the issues. Fortas dedicated himself to Ickes for longer than most people could. In a pinch, however, he decided against offering his former boss, as he had pledged, "all the loyalty and devotion of which I am capable."[164] As a colleague said, Ickes "inspired tremendous loyalty from his employees because he backed them on the issues," but their allegiance was "untouched by affection."[165] Fortuitously for Fortas, his partners for the next twenty years were people he both believed in and liked.

PART II

# The Washington Lawyer

CHAPTER 7

# Cold War Distractions

THURMAN ARNOLD WAS THE ONLY WASHINGTON LAWYER TO HAVE A building named after him. Like Abe Fortas, however, he originally worried about striking out on his own. Boredom drove Arnold to private practice. As the assistant attorney general in charge of antitrust during the war, he had protested the government's policy of suspending antitrust actions against certain monopolies and cartels to which it had awarded defense contracts. To get rid of him, President Roosevelt promoted him to a judgeship on the D.C. Circuit Court of Appeals.[1] Arnold described his two years on the bench as "a real rest," but he knew his temperament was "too active" to spend his life writing judicial opinions. Never an organization man, he chafed at the possibility of joining a large firm as partner. When he was approached separately by Coca-Cola, the Chesapeake and Ohio Railway, and Otis and Company and offered a total of fifty thousand dollars annually in retainers for legal representation, Arnold jumped at the opportunity to establish his own practice. He resigned from the bench in the summer of 1945 and established an office in Washington's Bowen Building with a colleague from the Antitrust Division of the Department of Justice, Arne Wiprud. Though he was happy to leave the bench, Arnold found the partnership unsatisfying; Wiprud was "quiet and very serious," and the two men lost a major antitrust case. At that point, Arnold dropped Wiprud and formed the firm of Arnold & Fortas.[2]

## "ARNOLD, INTEGRITY, INDIGNATION, FORTITUDE AND FORTAS"

The firm was small at first. Its associates generally arrived through personal ties to Arnold or Fortas, primarily through Yale or the New Deal. Milton Freeman had been a colleague of Fortas's at the SEC. In addition to studying with both Arnold and Fortas at Yale, Norman Diamond had worked for Fortas at the Bituminous Coal Division of the Interior Department. Walton Hamilton had been on the Yale Law School faculty when Arnold taught there. The firm soon acquired Paul Porter, whom Fortas described as "a good liberal," as the third name partner. Porter had worked briefly at the AAA before chairing the Federal Communications Commission, heading the Office of Price Administration, and serving as ambassador to Greece.

"I certainly hope we're going to be very rich," Frances Arnold said.[3] Representing the business interests he had attacked during wartime seemed one obvious way for her husband to accumulate wealth. "What a marvelous place Washington is," a former Yale colleague wrote Arnold, "and how the professors of the New Deal have become the most sought after persons to carry on the practical business aspects of the future!"[4] Money poured in. "Ever since the new firm of Arnold & Fortas was formed we have been going around like tops," Arnold reported. By the spring of 1946 the firm was grossing twenty thousand dollars each month. Arnold observed its success with some bemusement. "The name of our firm on the letterhead is going to be changed," he told a friend. "For the future it is going to be Arnold, Integrity, Indignation, Fortitude and Fortas. We are having a great deal of difficulty with this fellow Integrity," Arnold joked. "He doesn't seem to bring in any money and he has already driven away quite a little profitable business."[5]

Initially, Arnold and Fortas concentrated chiefly on building up their corporate and regulatory practice. But they also taught a seminar on antitrust together at Yale. There was time, too, for Fortas to become involved in the issue of Palestine and to consider arguing a test case for the American Civil Liberties Union.[6] Unlike such contemporaries as Joe Rauh and Clifford Durr, who made social causes their lives, Fortas regarded causes as diversions. "There was no suggestion that lawyers were not justified in conducting a purely commercial practice," he later said. If other avenues tempted the busy lawyer, "such as serving the poor or oppressed, those interests were part of his personal life, not integrated with his work with the law firm."[7] Truman's loyalty program, however, moved Fortas to integrate his own concern for the oppressed with his law practice.

A red scare had followed World War I, and, as World War II drew to a close, the deterioration of American-Soviet relations nurtured the development of a second one. The second red scare lasted almost ten times as long as the first, scarred nearly ten times as many people, and touched American culture in general more deeply.[8] While Republicans prolonged and exploited it for partisan reasons, there were some real grounds for fear in the late 1940s and early 1950s. The discovery of classified government documents in the office of *Amerasia* magazine; Elizabeth Bentley's charge that numerous government employees had been involved in a Soviet spy ring for which she had been courier; Whittaker Chambers's allegation that Alger Hiss, a former State Department employee, had passed secrets to the Russian government during the 1930s; the trials of Judith Coplon and of Julius and Ethel Rosenberg for conspiracy to commit espionage; Klaus Fuchs's confession that he had passed atomic energy secrets to the Soviets; the Soviets' explosion of a nuclear bomb years before the United States had expected them to master the necessary technology; the fall of mainland China to the Communists; and North Korea's invasion of South Korea understandably alarmed the American people.

Few remained above suspicion. The Army's pamphlet, "How To Spot a Communist" suggested the use of clues to recognize fellow travelers. For instance, if their vocabulary included the words *hootenanny* or *chauvinism,* or if they focused on the issues of peace or civil rights, they might well be Communists.[9] The Army thought its approach enlightened, and for its time it was. If radio broadcasters could verify the alleged popularity of Communism at Harvard and the University of Chicago by pointing to the apathy toward football on the campuses of those universities, almost any other method of detecting Communists could seem rational in comparison.[10]

Certainly, to many people, President Truman's did. As the cold war raised fears of domestic subversion to new heights, and he saw how the issue of "Communists in government" had aided the Republicans in the congressional elections of 1946, Truman formed a commission on employee loyalty, which proceeded to find existing security procedures for government employees wholly inadequate. In announcing Executive Order 9835, Truman initiated the broadest inquiry into employee loyalty in history. The order directed the head of each department and agency in the executive branch to establish at least one loyalty board to investigate the loyalty of its employees. An employee charged with disloyalty would have the right to appear before a board for an administrative hearing, but the board's determination that there were reasonable grounds for belief in an employee's disloyalty would justify a recommendation to dismiss. If the board did counsel dismissal, the employee could appeal the recommendation to the responsible authorities within the department or agency (that is, to the head of the department or agency or to persons designated by the head to hear appeals). If a decision to dismiss was made, the employee could appeal his case to the central Loyalty Review Board in the Civil Service Commission, but its recommendation would only be advisory and would not bind the department or agency. The language of Truman's order, however, did place the burden of proof on the boards to show disloyalty, and the President did veto the McCarran Internal Security Act, which proposed barring anyone who had ever belonged to a totalitarian organization from entering the United States. Congress passed the act over his veto, showing the depth of anticommunist sentiment. On its face, and in the context of the period, Truman's loyalty program was not radical.[11]

Nevertheless, it did not work well. As one of Fortas's colleagues observed, "If the objective was to discover spies or people who had engaged in illegal activities, it was most inefficient to canvas millions of employees instead of using the narrowly targeted enforcement powers of the Department of Justice."[12] And if there were any Communists in government, the loyalty program hardly ferreted them out. Of the 3,000,000 government employees the loyalty boards had screened by 1950, only 468 had been declared ineligible for employment. A mere 1068 resigned before completion of the investigation.[13] Nor had the boards uncovered a single case of espionage. Further, despite the language in the executive order the burden of proof always lay where Truman formally placed it in 1950—on the accused, to prove loyalty.

Decisions were made on the basis of secret "evidence," and frequently charges were so vague they lacked meaning. If the accused was "alleged to have associated with persons of Communistic sympathies," for example, the board might not specify the person with whom the alleged association occurred or the reason that the connection was undesirable. Nor did it reveal the context of the association. An individual might be placed under suspicion because he had been seen at a dance that "a subversive" also attended. Bert Andrews reported the case of a Mr. X against whom a characteristically unclear accusation was lodged. Unable to prepare a defense because he lacked any knowledge of exactly what he allegedly had done, he asked the board for particulars. The chair of the board replied: "We recognize the difficulty you are in, in this position; on the other hand, I'd suggest that you might think back over your own career and perhaps in your mind might delve into some of the factors that have gone into your career which you think might have been subject to question, and see what they are and see whether you would like to explain or make a statement with regard to any of them—that is about the best I can do so far as helping you along that line." Still clueless, X could not defend himself. He was dismissed from government service.[14]

Even had X seen the evidence, he could not have been sure of its source, for Truman's loyalty program denied suspects the right, traditional in Anglo-American law, to confront and cross-examine their accusers. A lawyer in Fortas's office once represented a bureaucrat whose colleagues had charged he was an "out and out Communist." The suspect's attorney asked the board which one of his client's co-workers lodged the accusation. When the board refused to answer, the lawyer inquired whether his client could guess the informant's identify. "There is no objection to guessing," the chair answered. "I recommend he guess in his own mind and not put it on the record, except his reason for the statement being made." As the attorney rejoined, that was "like trying to pin a custard pie to the wall, Mr. Chairman. I mean I am trying to get something in the record to rebut this statement." Ultimately a more generous board member prevailed and allowed the suspect to guess for the record. He then identified the informant and explained to the board that her allegations reflected her desire to "do me dirt" because they had a poor working relationship. [15]

The specter of loyalty boards dismissing people on the basis of information gathered from anonymous, and frequently malicious, informants would have frightened more liberals had they not shared Truman's goal of proving their anticommunism. The Republicans sought to return to power by linking New Deal reforms to Communism, thus putting liberals on the defensive. The most enduring postwar liberal organization, the Americans for Democratic Action (ADA), reacted to redbaiters' charges that liberalism was "soft on Communism" by embracing anticommunism and selling itself as the answer for those who disliked both McCarthyism and Communism. Indeed the ADA's hostility to Communism was so great that at times it seemed unconcerned about the loyalty program's abrogation of civil liberties. [16]

Lawyers as a group generally did not oppose the loyalty program any more strenuously than did liberals. The program's rejection of due process represented a derogation of the rule of law that should have provoked the most apolitical of attorneys, and in some cases it did. [17] But most lawyers remained silent. Moved in part by Attorney General Tom Clark's warning that they should be discriminating about representing those who "act like Communists" and by the criminal contempt convictions levied on the six attorneys who represented Communists accused of violating the Smith Act (a 1940 statute prohibiting the teaching or advocacy of the overthrow of the government of the United States by force or membership in a group supporting the overthrow of the U.S. government), the organized bar's reaction to the loyalty program was one of paralysis instead of protest. [18] "It is now almost impossible to obtain 'respectable counsel' in political cases," a friend of Fortas's observed in print. "Public opinion has risen to such a point that many lawyers believe they will be professionally ruined if they take such cases." [19] Not all liberals or lawyers were quiet, however. Fortas and his firm fought the loyalty program.

Though Fortas and his colleagues agreed that Communists should not hold high government positions, they displayed a willingness to assist noncommunist victims of the loyalty program.[20] "They got very quickly a reputation for being quite willing to defend the unpopular causes," Eric Sevareid said.[21] Several factors explained their involvement. First, they believed that courts should protect individual rights. As Fortas pointed out, during the 1930s liberals had believed that the national emergency justified downplaying due process in the administrative agencies and reducing the authority of courts over those agencies. But conservatives had prevailed, "and the result was clearly beneficial." The incursion of administrative agencies and the legislature into the sphere of the courts grieved him and his associates. "I believe that this is a startling and fundamental fact of our time: that the reality of power over the freedom of individuals has shifted from the courts and judges and lawyers to committees of Congress and bureaucratic boards—to committees and boards of men who frequently have had no training in the law or familiarity with its principles," Fortas claimed.[22] Spies were better tried by judges, but the loyalty program reduced the courts to tribunals of the last resort capable of intervention only after all administrative remedies had been exhausted and much damage done.[23] Fortas also resented the program's denial of due process, the lawyer's means of control. At least alleged spies—such as Hiss and the Rosenbergs, who were tried in the courts—had the chance to confront the witnesses against them. But the loyalty boards were different. "There are no issues—no specific points to be determined—except that everything that the accused has thought, done or read, and everybody with whom he has ever seen or with whom he has ever talked, are within the scope of inquiry. There are no standards of judgment, no rules, no traditions of procedure or judicial demeanor, no statute of limitations, no appeals, no boundaries of relevance and no finality. In short, anything goes; and everything frequently does."[24] Fortas considered the proceedings lawless.

Those reasons for attacking the loyalty program aimed at preserving the role of law in society by maintaining law's autonomy from politics. So too Fortas and his partners battled for the release of the poet Ezra Pound, who languished in Saint Elizabeths Hospital for fourteen years while awaiting a decision that he was sufficiently sane to stand trial for treason for his wartime broadcasts promoting fascist Italy. Though he disapproved of what Pound had said, Fortas insisted that his constitutional right to a speedy trial had been violated.[25] What mattered most, as Fortas said of the Sacco and Vanzetti case, was not the defendant's guilt or innocence: "the significant question is the integrity, fairness, decency and humanity of the processes of the state."[26] Many conservatives also disapproved of the loyalty program because it threatened an independent legal process. But to dislike was not necessarily to challenge. Even while they criticized loyalty boards and congressional committees, elite lawyers often declined to represent those called before them. His partners, who considered Fortas the driving force behind the firm's decision to accept loyalty cases, liked to quote his answer when he was asked why the firm took so many. "We have to do it," Fortas replied. "Nobody else will."[27]

Liberal lawyers knew that their conservative counterparts were best placed to defend those accused of disloyalty.[28] Yet liberal outsiders such as Fortas had an even greater stake in preserving the purity of the legal process than conservative attorneys, who more frequently came from privileged backgrounds and could fall back upon familial wealth if they lost clients. Thurman Arnold's, Abe Fortas's, and Paul Porter's financial success rested almost solely on the legal expertness which had gained them fame during the New Deal. That sense of their own ability may have left them particularly incensed about proceedings which gave them so little power and may have led them to believe that they had to preserve the integrity of the legal process to retain their influence.

Politics proved as important as law in explaining why Fortas urged his partners to take the cases. The loyalty program aimed at Communists but targeted liberals. The accused often had engaged in behavior once considered acceptable. "Everybody, I assume, now knows that in the thirties and part of the forties, thousands of fine, thoroughly non-Communist people contributed to Spanish relief organizations, attended anti-Fascist meetings, participated in rallies against Hitler, joined in organizations to promote friendship with the Soviet Union when it was our wartime ally, and even took out memberships in book clubs to get books and phonograph records at a discount," Fortas observed.[29] Nevertheless, previous affiliation with such organizations sparked loyalty proceedings "with monotonous regularity."[30] And with monotonous regularity, the victims were New Deal veterans. Fortas later explained his and his partners' involvement as a product "of the ideological identification of the members of the firm. We were 'liberals.' We were New Dealers."[31] In fact, Fortas and his partners were bitter about the general liberal abandonment of those charged with disloyalty.[32] But they thought liberals should fight the program.

Arnold, Fortas, and Porter undoubtedly recognized that they might have been victims themselves. Fortas admitted to having belonged in the 1930s to the National Lawyers Guild, which the House Committee on Un-American Activities subsequently declared a Communist front. Had he remained in government service after war's end, he might have been called before a loyalty board. Alternatively, like many of those he defended, he might have been charged falsely with having been a member of a suspect organization. Fortas knew how that felt. In the early 1940s the government had investigated whether he had joined the Washington Committee for Democratic Action and the American Peace Mobili-

zation. In fact he had never belonged to either group.[33] In what he described as
the "serio-comic atmosphere" of the late 1940s and 1950s, that might have been
difficult to prove.[34] Even in the 1960s, Fortas was still dogged by allegations that
in the 1930s he had been a member of two organizations that appeared on the
attorney general's list of Communist fronts, the International Judicial Association and the Southern Conference for Human Welfare.[35] Certainly, too, Fortas
had made enemies. Malice might have turned one of them into the sort of
anonymous informant upon whom loyalty boards doted. He had reason to empa-
thize with those summoned before loyalty boards.

Many of them were not only fellow liberals and New Dealers but his friends
or the friends of friends. If Congresswoman Helen Gahagan Douglas, who had
helped him in Interior days, referred someone to Fortas, he naturally accepted
the client. Similarly, he defended a Berkeley engineer whom he had known as
under secretary, the child of an old friend, and the wife of one of his housemates
on 34th Street.[36] Ideology and friendship moved Fortas, and he tried to be
cheerful about it. Writing to an individual who feared charges about her past
might endanger her husband's promotion, he joked, "If his own associations have
not been such as to invite the fishy eye of those who believe that Americanism
must include repudiation of all liberalism, it's a good thing that he is currently
associated with a good liberal like you."[37]

Though Fortas preserved his sense of humor, the Kafkaesque plight of those
suspected of disloyalty touched him. The secretary of one Washington attorney
recognized prospective clients immediately: "They never telephoned and they
always showed up about lunch hour. Their shrunken, shriveled look betrayed
them more than anything else."[38] After appearing before his first few loyalty
boards, another attorney invariably became physically ill: "The degradation of
the individuals involved disgusted him."[39] Asked what happened to those discharged from government service, one of Fortas's associates replied, "The people
cannot find jobs; the FBI hounds them; their social standing in the community is
ruined; they receive crank mail; their friends desert them."[40] Even when an
individual was cleared, Fortas observed that "heartaches and personal disasters"
invariably accompanied a loyalty case.[41]

In the world he occupied, anti-Semitism was never absent, and Fortas must
have recognized that suspects disproportionately were Jewish. One of his acquaintances liked to ask attorneys how he would advise an individual in government whose brother first had been responsible for Alger Hiss obtaining his job at
the Carnegie Endowment, and then had ignored a warning that Hiss was a
Communist and served as a witness for Hiss at the trial and publicly asserted
Hiss's innocence. The answer was always the same: in view of his brother's
activities, the individual should resign before he was charged with disloyalty. But

since the individual in question was CIA director Allen Dulles, and his brother was Secretary of State John Foster Dulles, that course of action was unnecessary. A New York Jew, on the other hand, was *"prima facie* under suspicion."[42]

Soon loyalty cases were consuming between 20 and 50 percent of Arnold, Fortas & Porter's working hours.[43] A minimum reasonable fee for these cases in the usual circumstances would have been about five hundred dollars, but except in the rare instance where the accused was wealthy, the firm charged only for expenses incurred during preparation of the case. A corporate client in the early 1950s, in contrast, might have been billed up to sixty-five dollars for an hour of Fortas's time.[44]

### THE LOYALTY BOARDS

The lawyers at Arnold, Fortas & Porter developed a strategy for handling loyalty cases. Like other attorneys who took these cases,[45] members of the firm departed from the usual practice of limiting a client to what seemed relevant and elicited instead a wide-ranging autobiography that would form the basis for a thirty- to seventy-page affidavit to be submitted at the hearing. Although the affidavit was broad, it responded explicitly to the charges. Arnold, Fortas, and Porter publicly attacked the vagueness of loyalty board charges as an indication of rejection of due process. They found, however, that at least by 1950 Washington loyalty boards would informally advise lawyers which Communist-front organizations their clients were said to have joined and, in some instances, would name the Communists with whom they allegedly had associated.[46] A good affidavit provided the fullest rebuttal. Thus an individual charged with joining the American Peace Mobilization in 1941 provided an extensive account of his involvement with that organization, the location of its meetings, the subject matter of its discussions, and the reason he did not know it was a "front organization." He named prominent people above suspicion who were then connected with the organization and explained his resignation from the group.[47]

Since the firm agreed with other attorneys who did loyalty work that the accused could best give the board a sense of his or her own personality by personally drafting the affidavit, Fortas's duty at this stage consisted largely of inserting lawyers' cautionary language and preventing his clients from making excessively broad statements. If a client stated that he had never belonged to an organization that advocated the overthrow of the government, for example, Fortas would object. It would do his client no good to appear to be disagreeing with the attorney general's characterization of an organization. Fortas would insist that the individual alter the statement to say he had never *knowingly* belonged to an organization advocating the overthrow of the government.[48]

Fortas counseled taking the offensive. The firm regularly sought character affidavits from at least one person involved in every phase of the accused's life since secondary school, and from several people who had known the suspect during the period in which he or she allegedly was disloyal. An affidavit should do more than discuss the accused's loyalty; it should reveal his or her hostility to Communism. "Persons supplying affidavits are asked to particularize them as much as possible: To state whether the expressed opinion as to the person's loyalty is based upon business, professional or social acquaintance and to describe that acquaintance as specifically as possible; to state specifically any anti-Communist statements that he recalls hearing the accused make; to state any anti-Communist activity that he knows the person has engaged in; to describe, if known to him, the accused's attitude during the time of the Nazi-Soviet pact (1939–1941); to describe the person's attitude, if known, towards Russia's invasion of Finland; and similar matters."[49] The firm then customarily selected four or five affiants who would make good witnesses and persuaded them to appear.[50]

In the context of his pro bono work in loyalty cases, Fortas advocated the use of influential witnesses and made use of his own contacts. "He would do anything that would help them," one colleague said of Fortas's attitude toward suspects.[51] Since Fortas quite reasonably assumed that statements from prominent citizens would be given more credit by decision makers than testimony from persons whose credibility was not established, he regularly sought affidavits from powerful individuals on behalf of the accused. Thus when he represented one former colleague, he obtained letters and affidavits from Congresswoman Helen Gahagan Douglas, from the under secretary of the Department of the Interior, and from an assistant secretary of commerce. It made for a stronger case. So, too, did knowing the appropriate official to contact. As old government hands, Fortas and his partners had no hesitation in approaching important people in government on behalf of their clients. Indeed they considered it their duty: "A lawyer would be delinquent in his responsibilities if he did not bring the matter to the highest level at which he believed it would be useful to protect the interests of his client."[52]

He and his partners were keenly aware, too, of the value of publicity. Few lawyers used the media more effectively than Fortas and his colleagues. They won their first loyalty case, which involved ten state department employees fired even before the Truman loyalty program began, by arranging for an attack on the department's "police state" tactics by Bert Andrews of the *New York Herald Tribune*. "We were getting absolutely no place until we got the front page of the *Herald Tribune*," a colleague recalled.[53] Fortas and his partners needed the affiliations with reporters for their clients, because sometimes an individual's only effective means of counterattack was to make the facts known to the public.

The partners' attention to contacts and to publicity were aspects of their meticulousness. Fortas, in particular, demonstrated the same concern with detail he had displayed at Interior. Returning a transcript of a hearing to one loyalty board, he observed that he had not eliminated the dashes the stenographer had included in the transcript. He then launched into a discourse on their impropriety. "I believe that these dashes may give the reader an unwarranted impression of hesitations in the statements of the witnesses. I trust that the members of the panel will agree with me that the dashes should not be so construed in this case."[54] When he represented one actor accused of left-wing tendencies, he drafted the actor's Academy Award speech.[55] It was part of the totality of his approach.

So was politeness. When Fortas obtained clearance for a client, he regularly drafted thank-you notes to all who had appeared or submitted evidence and suggested that the client do so as well.[56] Another attorney justifiably might have permitted himself to display hostility toward the boards, but Fortas treated members of loyalty boards with the same courtesy he reserved for judges. "We're all in this distasteful proceeding together," his demeanor inferred. "Let's get it over with as painlessly as possible." On one occasion, a member of the Commerce Department board thanked Fortas for "the frank and generous manner in which your client, our employee, has presented his case." The attorney replied, "I merely want to express my appreciation to all of you gentlemen for the courtesies that you have extended to us, and for the patient and thoughtful consideration which you have obviously given to this case." The chair of the loyalty board thanked Fortas, whereupon Fortas's client thanked the chair.[57] Unlike some radical lawyers who accepted loyalty cases, Fortas worked within the system and treated his clients' persecutors courteously.[58]

Fortas differed from radical lawyers, too, in a more fundamental respect. Though Thurman Arnold and Abe Fortas would not join in the Americans for Democratic Action because it excluded Communists,[59] they refused to represent Communists or former Communists before loyalty boards or the House Committee on Un-American Activities (HUAC). That decision caused Fortas anguish. His old friend Clifford Durr received a telephone call asking him to drop by Arnold, Fortas & Porter to discuss the situation of a scientist HUAC had subpoenaed. "They had the reputation of being a liberal firm, daring to take on these cases." When Durr appeared, Fortas told him that the scientist was as good as Einstein. Durr recalled Fortas's next words: "'We've thought about how far we can actually go, and we have decided that we don't think we can ever afford to represent anybody that had ever been a Communist, and he was briefly a Communist way back—and won't you please take his case?' And that was the great liberal firm of Arnold, Fortas & Porter." What struck Durr was that "Abe was so emotional.

He's generally a pretty cold blooded guy, but he's almost crying about this."[60] Fortas's old housemate, Thomas Emerson, who did defend Communists, did not share Durr's sense that the firm's rejection of Communists was hypocritical but noted the cautiousness with which Arnold, Fortas & Porter staked out its position on the loyalty program. "They did put in an awful lot of time and energy for it . . . but they were careful about the cases," Emerson said. Ideologically, the firm was "sort of in the center."[61]

After the red scare had ended, the firm's refusal to defend Communists before loyalty boards seemed to some disturbing and inconsistent,[62] as Fortas so frequently had insisted on any accused's right to counsel. At the time, however, the partners' willingness to go as far as they did was remarkable. In their minds, there were several reasons which militated against the representation of Communists or former Communists in loyalty proceedings. As long as the firm had the reputation of defending only noncommunists, the clients they accepted had a better chance of clearance. Fortas's associate G. Duane Vieth said that the firm would readily have represented a Communist charged with committing a federal crime. "We're not talking about that," he emphasized. "We're talking about this loyalty program, and this was a different kind of thing. You were pretty much at the mercy of a system that didn't have much due process involved." The partners thought they could do "the most people the most good" if they only represented noncommunists.[63] They rejected utilitarian arguments in their own private practice and even in other pro bono work. But as they assumed that the loyalty program was targeting a disproportionate number of innocent people, they believed that they should concentrate on the innocent. Strategically, they also recognized that Communists and former Communists had no chance before the loyalty boards. Often just the charge of once having associated with Communists was enough to force an individual out of office. A member of the firm said succinctly, "If you're a member of the Communist party, you're dead."[64]

There was a third reason for their decision. "There was one principle this firm has always stood by: it's that if we take on a case, we're in control of the case," Vieth stressed. "We're not going to let some other organization or individual take charge. We're going to be in charge. And there was a feeling that . . . the Communist Party would try to manipulate these cases for their own ends, and would try to take control."[65] Though playwright Lillian Hellman credited Fortas with devising the strategy by which she would take a "moral position" and discuss her own past as a Communist while not naming other party members, Fortas referred her to another attorney, Joe Rauh. He told one friend that Hellman had insisted on remaining in control and that he had gotten rid of her as soon as he could.[66] "Lawyers do not customarily undertake a case unless they have reasonable assurance that full disclosure of the relevant facts has been made to them and that they will have complete control of the case," Arnold, Fortas, and Porter told the *Washington Post*. Some members of their profession, they said, refused to represent Communists because of "a reasonable belief . . . that the Communists would not permit them to discharge the obligation of their profession in a creditable manner."[67] However, this rationale did not justify the firm's refusal to represent former Communists, who presumably were no longer susceptible to manipulation by the party.

Control always preoccupied Fortas, and he believed it especially important in loyalty proceedings. Perhaps he worried that his clients might unwittingly fall into a trap that would make them vulnerable to a perjury charge if he permitted them to speak much. Because he considered actors "flamboyant," he was particularly relieved when one actor he represented gave him "complete control" in a loyalty case.[68] But when Fortas represented a quiet woman accused only of being "interested in serious things happening in the economy," he proved equally insistent. "This was the most terrible experience of my life," his old friend Mary Keyserling recalled, and "Abe was so kind." He accompanied her to several hearings at the Department of Commerce. "Abe did the talking. That, if I may say so, troubled me. I would rather have done the talking, but he thought it was better that he did it." She allowed him to take charge because "I felt it was so generous of him to do this."[69]

Those ingredients—meticulousness, the sense for the offensive, the use of every means at every level to protect clients' rights, the sensitivity to publicity, the deference to opponents, and the insistence on control—became the cornerstone of the firm's approach to the loyalty cases. By the late 1940s word of its generosity and success in clearing clients had spread, and requests for assistance from government employees had multiplied. In 1948 the firm began to respond that it "could not assume additional cases except for impelling personal reasons."[70] Too many reasons impelled, and loyalty cases continued to threaten to overwhelm Arnold, Fortas & Porter's practice. Since clearance of clients on the facts only meant that their places would be taken by others, the partners searched for a case to take to the Supreme Court that would enable them to challenge the loyalty program's constitutionality.

## THE LOYALTY PROGRAM IN THE COURTS

The firm began its search for such a case early. In 1946, before Truman's loyalty program took effect, the Civil Service Commission dismissed a friend of Milton Freeman's from government service because of "a reasonable doubt as to his loyalty." Freeman, then an associate in Arnold, Fortas & Porter, unsuccessfully petitioned the Supreme Court to hear the case. After Truman's loyalty program adopting the same standard took effect, Fortas submitted a brief to the Supreme Court requesting a reconsideration of its denial of certiorari. He knew it was unusual for the Supreme Court to reverse such an order, the former under secretary of interior admitted. "But this, we respectfully submit, is an unusual situation; an emergency as great in our political and spiritual life as was the coal miners' [1943] strike in our economic affairs. A denial of certiorari in this case is a decision that the executive branch of this Government may, unbridled and unguided, launch this country upon a course of action which threatens to destroy our form of Government and our basic civil liberties." Unless the Court intervened, Fortas predicted that "a drive to eliminate Communism from our national life will itself become a more imminent threat to our democracy than is Communism itself."[71] The Court ignored his warning.

The partners remained on alert for a test case, but finding one was difficult. They required an irreproachable plaintiff who did not mind publicity, and the stigma of disloyalty so embarrassed most government employees that they would not fight.[72] Dorothy Bailey fulfilled Arnold, Fortas & Porter's qualifications. An expert on personnel and a former president of her local union, Bailey had worked for the United States Employment Service in the Federal Security Agency since 1933. She was a supervisor of its training section when her loyalty board charged in 1948 that she was currently or once had been a member of the Communist Party.[73] Bailey admitted to having attended one party meeting as part of an assignment for a social economy seminar she had taken at Bryn Mawr. But she denied ever having been a party member, and at her hearing she produced some seventy affidavits swearing she had never been a Communist. Although no hostile witnesses appeared and no affidavits against her were introduced, the loyalty board remained unconvinced. Although the executive order only authorized the board to make a recommendation, the board directed the Federal Security Agency to dismiss Bailey, declared her ineligible for federal employment, and prohibited her from competing in civil service examinations for three years. Arnold and his partners took the case.

In appealing the decision to the U.S. Civil Service Commission loyalty review board, Paul Porter claimed that the charges against Bailey represented "malicious, irresponsible, reckless gossip which . . . stems from an internecine union controversy."[74] The Board's chairman, Seth Richardson, countered that "five or six of the reports come from informants certified to us by the Federal Bureau of Investigation as experienced and entirely reliable." Porter asked for the names of the informants and whether they had been active in Bailey's union. "I haven't the slightest knowledge as to who they were or how active they have been in anything," Richardson replied. "Is it under oath?" Porter asked. "I don't think so," Richardson replied.[75] The loyalty review board upheld the decision to fire Bailey and bar her from government service. Her case was an ideal vehicle with which to ask the Supreme Court to examine whether a loyalty board could judge a person ineligible for government service and dismiss her from a non-security-sensitive post "(1) where there is no evidence against her, whatever, (2) where the only evidence presented consists of a conclusive showing in her favor, and (3) where the only basis for the determination against her is secret information obtained from confidential informants whose identities are unknown to the court, the employee or the loyalty board making the decision."[76]

All administrative remedies had to be exhausted first. After the three-judge panel of the loyalty review board had decided against Bailey, Fortas's firm lodged the first request ever for a review by the full loyalty review board. When the government decided that a review by the full board would be "cumbersome and unworkable," the case went to the courts. Had Fortas received the district court appointment that had gone instead to Alexander Holtzoff, or had Arnold remained on the D.C. Circuit Court of Appeals, the case might have developed differently. As it was, although Judge Holtzoff conceded that the procedure by which the loyalty review board had decided Miss Bailey guilty was "unusual," he upheld the constitutionality of the program. The court of appeals invalidated the loyalty board's decree prohibiting Bailey from seeking government employment for three years. But—despite a powerful dissent from Henry Edgerton, asserting that her dismissal violated due process—the court upheld the decision to remove her from her position.[77]

The firm approached the case in characteristic fashion. As the loyalty review board had done Arnold, Fortas & Porter carried the battle to the press. At an early stage Arnold and Fortas courted the columnist Richard Rovere. The upshot, after Holtzoff's verdict, was a "Letter from Washington" feature in the *New Yorker* comparing the Bailey case to the Dreyfus case and the loyalty review board's behavior to that of the Gestapo judges condemned at Nuremberg for relying on secret information to convict.[78] Arnold underscored Rovere's message for Attorney General J. Howard McGrath. Two weeks before *Bailey* was argued before the court of appeals, Arnold brought the suit to McGrath's "personal attention" in a letter complimenting the attorney general's "recent statements which clearly indicate your desire to keep the loyalty program from becoming an oppressive injustice." Arnold could not imagine that his friend would "want to exercise the weight of your great office in urging in effect that what was wrong for German judges to consider as evidence was nevertheless intended to be included by the President in the administrative hearings."[79] When the court of appeals upheld the trial court, Arnold swung his attention toward persuading the Supreme Court to grant certiorari. Despite Paul Porter's fear "that this is the kind of issue the majority may want to duck,"[80] the Court decided to hear the case.

"The Dorothy Bailey argument went very well," Porter reported after presenting the case to the Supreme Court. "What the press refers to as 'veteran court observers' told me privately that they had never seen a Solicitor General take the pummelling which Perlman got from Felix [Frankfurter], Jackson and Black. . . . When Perlman arose to argue it was a question of who was going to get him first."[81] When Solicitor General Perlman maintained that the loyalty boards had not forever barred Bailey from federal employment, because she could take the competitive examinations for a government position again, Justice Jackson interrupted. He did not mind being amused, Jackson said, but he did not want to be made a laughing stock. Did Perlman mean that Bailey could ever again get a federal job? As a practical matter she could not, the solicitor general conceded, but in theory she remained eligible. Did the government really wish to win the case on that point, Jackson asked? Perlman replied that the government had other points.[82]

But the Court received the solicitor general's other points equally unenthusiastically. Perlman contended, for example, that the character of loyalty board members ensured any accused of a fair hearing. Justice Frankfurter replied that, although he appreciated the board members' high character, they had exercised no judgment of their own in this particular case. Hugo Black then intervened. He forced the solicitor general to admit that since loyalty board members had not seen the unknown informant against Bailey, the FBI agent who interviewed the informant, or the FBI agent who certified the informant's reliability, they were in no position to evaluate the evidence.[83] "It was really quite a clam bake," Porter concluded.[84] He was cautiously optimistic after the argument. Douglas, Frankfurter, Black, and Jackson seemed sympathetic. Porter believed that the outcome depended largely on Justice Reed and thought "that the triumvirate of Frankfurter, Black and Jackson was needling Perlman primarily for the purpose of educating their brethren on the bench. I am optimistically placing great hope on Reed's innate sense of fairness." Nor had Porter given up on Fred Vinson, though he did not think that the chief justice "would be too upset if an affirmance resulted."[85]

Porter's hoped-for majority did not materialize. Only four justices voted to reverse. As Justice Tom Clark had disqualified himself because he had been attorney general when the loyalty program took effect, a Court equally divided upheld the government's decision to fire Bailey without giving her the right to confront her accusers.[86] Because it was tied, the Court issued no opinion in *Bailey.* On the same day, the Court released its opinion in *Joint Anti-Fascist Refugee Committee* v. *McGrath.*[87] There Justice Burton, who had never figured in Porter's calculations, joined Douglas, Black, Jackson, and Frankfurter in extending due process rights to organizations. The Court ruled that the attorney general could not label an organization subversive without first giving it the opportunity to prove the falseness of such a classification at a hearing. Since membership in an organization on the attorney general's subversive list often proved the basis for a loyalty board investigation, the two cases were linked. "So far as I recall, this is the first time this Court has held the rights of individuals subordinate and inferior to organized groups," Justice Jackson said in his *Joint Anti-Fascist Refugee Committee* concurrence. "It is justice turned bottom-side up." Douglas used his concurrence to attack *Bailey.* "I do not see how the constitutionality of this dragnet system of loyalty trials which has been entrusted to the administrative agencies of government can be sustained."[88] Still, his outrage did little to help Dorothy Bailey. Since she could not find a job, Arnold, Fortas & Porter hired her as office manager.[89]

The firm also continued the fight. It took another tilt at the loyalty program when it acquired John Peters as a client. A Yale Medical School professor who specialized in nutrition and metabolism, Peters served in a nonsensitive capacity as a special consultant to the surgeon general for less than two weeks each year. A loyalty board acquired information against Peters in 1949, but when he answered its written questions to its satisfaction, it cleared him without even holding a hearing. In 1952 the case was reopened. This time sixteen charges, including one of membership in the Communist Party, were filed against Peters. At the hearing, Peters testified that he had never been a Communist. He called eighteen individuals on his behalf, including the president of Yale, and submitted forty affidavits. Despite secret, and presumably damaging, evidence from informants, the board cleared him again. Although the loyalty board had twice dismissed the case, the loyalty review board targeted it for a "post audit" in 1953, a procedure by which it reviewed and sometimes reversed the decisions of lower loyalty boards. Once again, Peters appeared with his roster of powerful witnesses and affiants. Once again, the board reviewed secret information against Peters. This time, however, it determined that there was "reasonable doubt" as to his loyalty. He was dismissed and barred from government service for three years. "Thus the Department of Health, Education and Welfare was saved in the nick of time from a danger that had existed, apparently, since 1949," Arnold sarcastically observed in his oral argument before the Supreme Court. "They were saved by a secret informant or secret informants, some of whom were unknown even to the Board. It was apparent that Dr. Peters had the ability to fool the eminent people he had known all his life, and without this secret informant, he might still be pouring Soviet theory on metabolism and nutrition into the attentive and gullible ear of the Surgeon General of the United States."[90]

As in *Bailey,* all the evidence on record indicated Peters's loyalty, and his conviction stemmed from secret information he had not seen. Since the Court's decision in *Bailey* apparently applied to his situation, most attorneys would have advised Peters against taking the trouble to file suit. But the Supreme Court's membership had changed by 1954, and Arnold wanted to reargue *Bailey* before the altered body in the hope that it would reach a different conclusion. One change was that Fred Vinson had died, and Earl Warren had replaced him as chief justice. "It is a great pleasure to represent you," Arnold told Peters. "Your case is exactly like the Dorothy Bailey case which we lost in the Supreme Court four-to-four. I am hopeful that, now that Vinson who voted against us is gone and Warren takes his place, we can get them to reverse the outrageous notion that a man may be penalized in America without even knowing what the evidence against him is."[91]

Arnold realized that Warren's ascension did not necessarily mean victory. In *Bailey,* he had been able to count on Jackson, Frankfurter, Black, and Douglas to give him the four votes necessary for certiorari. Jackson died soon after Warren arrived, however, and though it looked as if Warren would become a fourth for certiorari, Arnold needed a fifth vote to win. He knew he would not get it from Sherman Minton, Harold Burton, or Stanley Reed, all of whom had opposed Porter in *Bailey.* Tom Clark would not recuse himself from passing on the validity of Eisenhower's security program, but since he had championed Truman's loyalty program as attorney general, he would probably support Eisenhower's. Victory required winning the support of Jackson's successor, John Marshall Harlan, whom Eisenhower had appointed to the Court. "They tell me he is a pretty good man," Arnold wrote to his client. "On the other hand, he will be indebted to Eisenhower and winning your case would make a big dent in Eisenhower's present loyalty program."[92]

Intent on winning Harlan, the firm began preparing the case. Arnold and his colleagues stressed the number of influential people who supported Peters. They insisted on control of the case. When Peters arranged to do a television interview, Arnold killed it, telling his client, "your case hangs in a very delicate balance," and the broadcast might offend Harlan.[93] Nonetheless, both the firm of Arnold, Fortas & Porter and the government engaged in so many off-the-record discussions with reporters about the suit that one columnist justifiably claimed that "we have seen the Peters case argued as much in the press as in the courtroom."[94] Fortas took the offensive when he added a passage in the brief designed to appeal to conservatives by pointing out that Peters's struggle to confront his accusers was traditionally American. "I especially like the suggestion in the conclusion that I am fighting a conservative fight," Peters said. "No one has ever accused me of any such thing before, although I have felt quite strongly that I had conservative instincts. It is all a matter of what you are conserving."[95] Everything seemed to be going well, and Arnold could not "escape a feeling of optimism about this case."[96]

But when the case reached the Supreme Court in 1955, Harlan helped undo the firm's strategy. So baseless were the charges against Peters that Solicitor General Simon Soboloff refused to sign the government's brief.[97] Although Assistant Attorney General Warren Burger, who ultimately argued the case, irked Frankfurter, Warren, and other members of the Court by arguing that he was entitled to see the secret evidence against Peters but that they could not,[98] they were not kindly disposed toward Arnold either. "What authority does the Review Board therefore have, this having been dismissed, to conduct a post-audit reinvestigation?" Harlan asked Arnold. "I think they have every authority, Your Honor," a surprised Arnold replied.[99] Indeed both Arnold and Burger maintained that the loyalty review board possessed jurisdiction to conduct a post-audit, and, in a rare show of unity, both sides filed supplemental briefs urging the Court to address the constitutional issue. Arnold told the Court that he wanted to raise the issue of the right to confront one's accusers and "would prefer not to argue on that particular narrow ground" of jurisdiction. "The question is not what you would like to whittle it down to," Frankfurter barked. "The problem before this Court is to decide all legal questions that arise on this record and to reach the Constitutional questions last, not first."[100] Despite stinging concurrences by Douglas and Black protesting the evasion of the constitutional question, Warren based the majority's decision that Peters should neither have been removed from office nor barred from government employment on the ground that the loyalty review board lacked the jurisdiction to conduct a post-audit after the lower agency board had twice cleared Peters and dismissed charges against him.[101]

Though the Court often declined to reach constitutional grounds during that period, Arnold was appalled by its failure to do so in *Peters*. "You are completely vindicated . . . [but] I think that the Supreme Court hit a new moral low when it dodged the question and it certainly will not look very good when the history of the times is written," he told Peters.[102] Fortas, however, believed that with newspapers everywhere condemning the Court for cowardice, the firm had won in the press a finding that the loyalty program was unconstitutional. "Although the initial shock of the decision was unpleasant," he wrote, "we are at the turning point in the loyalty program and some important changes will be made."[103]

Even though no significant changes in the program ensued after *Peters*, Fortas was right. The loyalty program was at a turning point. He and his partners challenged it one last time when ten scientists at Fort Monmouth were dismissed. "The process of appeal in the Fort Monmouth case was adorned with a new gimmick," Arnold recalled, when the accuseds' conviction was upheld by a loyalty review board whose membership was kept secret. Ultimately, perhaps having realized that it had gone too far, the government dropped the case when it reached the Court of Appeals.[104] Arnold, Fortas & Porter never succeeded in persuading the Supreme Court to declare the loyalty program unconstitutional, but the program gradually faded away.

## ANTICOMMUNISM IN CONGRESS

For some Republicans in Congress, including Senator Joseph McCarthy, who viewed the issue of Communism in government as a way of regaining the presidency, Truman's loyalty program never went far enough. Thus while Truman's program was in existence, congressional committees were also investigating loyalty in government. It was even more difficult to represent someone before such a committee than before a loyalty board. And that became Fortas's job. He specialized in congressional committees investigating "un-American" activities.

He established his expertness in this area when he undertook the representation of Edward Condon. An eminent physicist, Condon was director of the National Bureau of Standards at the Department of Commerce when in 1947 rumors that he was a security risk led him to request the departmental loyalty board to investigate him. On March 1, 1948, three days after the Commerce Department loyalty board had cleared Condon, a report of the Special Subcommittee on National Security of the House Committee on Un-American Activities branded him "one of the weakest links in our atomic security." Condon was notified that HUAC would hold hearings on his loyalty the following month. He went to Fortas.[105]

"We need publicity," Fortas told the staff counsel of the American Civil Liberties Union, and he devised a novel way of getting it.[106] Fortas seized the offensive. Attacks on scientists like Condon by HUAC, he charged, damaged national security by interfering with their work. "Nothing could be more effective for the Communist cause than false documents planted with the Committee by Communist agents in the hope that their publication will impair the reputation of some indispensable scientist and make his services unavailable to this country," he warned. "We respectfully suggest that the practices of your Committee may be retarding the scientific research which is the most vital part of our defense program."[107] Fortas planned to try HUAC along with Condon. In practice his strategy worked so well in putting HUAC on the defensive that a member of its subcommittee protested the "continuous vicious attacks."[108] Fortas considered HUAC's subsequent postponement on the Condon hearings "an indication of weakness."[109] The committee rumbled on about Condon to no avail. He remained director of the Bureau of Standards, and the hearings were never held.

Fortas again proved a match for congressional redbaiters in the case of Owen Lattimore. A sinologist who headed the Page School of International Relations at Johns Hopkins, Lattimore was in Afghanistan on a United Nations mission in 1950 when he received word that Senator McCarthy had denounced him as a "top Russian espionage agent." The senator had promised his charges of Communism in government would stand or fall on the credibility of his case against Lattimore. The accusations were not new. In the previous year Congressman John F. Kennedy had blamed Lattimore for America's "loss" of China.[110] But as Lattimore had consistently taken an anti-Communist line in his numerous books and articles on the Far East, he was not alarmed. He cabled that he was "delighted" McCarthy's "whole case rested on me as this means that he will fall flat on his face."[111] Meanwhile, others in Washington were taking McCarthy's claims more seriously. A Senate resolution spurred a subcommittee of the Senate Committee on Foreign Relations chaired by Maryland's Joseph Tydings to announce it would conduct hearings on the loyalty of State Department employees and would question Lattimore.

Realizing how much was at stake, Eleanor Lattimore went to see Fortas before her husband returned from Afghanistan. She had met him at a dinner party, and his discussion there of the strategy behind Condon's defense had impressed her. Lattimore, however, worried that the attorney might be a "fixer" instead of a "fighter" who would engage in the "slugging match" both he and McCarthy planned.[112] For his part, Fortas doubted Lattimore's courage. The only question he and his partners asked Eleanor Lattimore was whether her husband would fight. She assured Fortas he would, and Lattimore was comforted by a letter from Fortas announcing that Drew Pearson had broadcast a story on Lattimore's hostility to Communism. "A certain amount of drama is not only desirable, but also completely unavoidable," Fortas advised his client. "It may be necessary that you get down in the gutter in which we are now operating as a result of Senator McCarthy's personal attack upon you." With "immense relief," Lattimore realized that "my lawyers were not going to rely on passive defense."[113] Although Fortas would work more closely with Eleanor Lattimore than with her husband in devising a course of action, it was clear that all three players were committed to mounting an offensive.[114]

Fortas arranged a public relations blitz. An observer noted, "This was not exactly an unequal struggle."[115] When one columnist wrote that Lattimore would have made an excellent district attorney or prosecutor because "nobody comes close to him as a master of excoriation, searing adjectives and colorful denunciation," Mrs. Lattimore penciled in the margin "except A.F.P.!"[116] Because the Tydings committee did not permit him to cross-examine witnesses and because its proceedings received so much more attention than ordinary loyalty cases, Fortas relied chiefly on the media to air Lattimore's side. Years later, Owen Lattimore remembered "a saying in Washington that when Arnold, Fortas and Porter took on a case that everybody knew would get a lot of publicity, Thurman would ask 'How do we stand on the law?' Abe would say, 'We're all right on the law, but how do we present it to the public?' And Paul would add, 'Whom do we know?'"[117]

Thus Fortas saw that Drew Pearson, whose daughter had married Thurman Arnold's son, acquired the appropriate information. Fortas released a "fact sheet" rife with anti-Communist quotations from Lattimore's work. He also arranged for a press conference when Lattimore returned from Afghanistan and drafted a statement his client could give there. As it was pointless to try to win over McCarthy, Fortas's draft attacked him as "little Joe McCarthy," running "wild with a machine gun in his adolescent hands" in accusing the State Department of harboring fifty-seven Communists, Owen Lattimore included.[118] Fortas also sought to use whatever connections he could muster. "One of the first things he asked Eleanor to do was draw up a list of influential people," who might be able to help, Lattimore recalled. "When he looked at it, he said, 'Good Lord! Don't you know *anybody* important?'"[119]

Initially it seemed as if Fortas was taking needless precautions for it looked as if the Tydings committee would present no problem for his client. Tydings sympathized with Lattimore and opposed McCarthy. But the committee was not wholly friendly. Realizing that the failure of McCarthy's charges would embarrass the Republicans, Senator Bourke Hickenlooper tried to hurt Lattimore. McCarthy had claimed that, as a government official during the war, Lattimore wrote a classified letter to a subordinate directing him to fire those who sympathized with Chiang Kai-shek and hire Communists in their stead. In an attempt to destroy Lattimore at the hearings, Hickenlooper produced the document and asked Lattimore to identify it. Thanks to Fortas, Hickenlooper's effort backfired. Knowing that the letter indicated only that the Office of War Information should follow American policy by keeping out of domestic politics in foreign countries, Fortas arranged, over Hickenlooper's objections, for the committee to declassify it so that it could be publicly released.[120] Since McCarthy had torn his quotation out of context, Hickenlooper tried to scare Tydings out of declassifying it by piously protesting that he would "not want to violate an existing legal secret classification." Fortas agreed to read it aloud as the agent of the Senate Foreign Relations Committee.[121] By the time he had finished, "the steam had gone out of" Hickenlooper.[122] Tydings announced that he had heard no convincing evidence that the suspect had been a Communist or a spy, and the Lattimores and their attorney celebrated at one of Fortas's favorite restaurants.[123]

Lattimore thought the battle had been won, but it was just beginning. McCarthy soon launched a new assault by persuading the committee to subpoena the notorious Louis Budenz. Fortas dismissed Budenz, a former Communist, as "a bandwagon informer; that is, after people have been dramatically accused he joins in the attack."[124] Nevertheless, in Drew Pearson's words, McCarthy had "renewed public faith by calling Louis Budenz as a witness," and Budenz worried Fortas.[125] Calling Lattimore into his office, he explained that McCarthy was under great political pressure. "The report that Budenz will testify against you has shaken everyone in Washington," Fortas said. "It is my duty as your lawyer to warn you that the danger you face cannot possibly be exaggerated. It does not exclude the possibility of a straight frame-up, with perjured witnesses and perhaps even forged documents." Lattimore had two options, and he alone had to choose between them. "You can either take it head on, and expose yourself to this danger; or you can make a qualified and carefully guarded statement which will reduce the chance of entrapment by fake evidence." When Lattimore once again chose to take the offensive and "slug it out . . . Abe said nothing, but I could see from his face that I now had more than a lawyer. I had a friend and we believed in each other."[126] Indeed Fortas used to hold dinner parties for the Lattimores to boost their spirits.[127]

Fortas could do little to help his client before the committee. He prepared eleven and a half pages of questions for Budenz,[128] and he told Lattimore that if he and his partners had "been able to cross-examine him in a court of law, they could have torn to pieces the thin case he had tried to build against me."[129] But the committee did not allow Fortas to question the witness, and though Tydings agreed to direct the committee's counsel to use Fortas's questions, in fact almost none of them were asked.[130] Fortas proved more effective behind the scenes, where his attempts to discredit Budenz reflected his toughness. Having obtained from a Washington lawyer information, Fortas said, about "matters relating to Mr. Budenz's private life which I found to be quite distasteful, but also quite relevant to Mr. Budenz's credibility," he submitted it to the Tydings committee.[131] Fortas could indeed get into the gutter with McCarthy.

Further, the attorney and Lattimore arranged to have Brigadier General Elliot Thorpe, who had headed General MacArthur's counterintelligence service during the war, appear on Lattimore's behalf. Fortas surprised Hickenlooper by producing the general at the end of the first day of Budenz's appearance and asking permission for him to testify that day so he could catch an 11 P.M. train. Hickenlooper promptly objected to "the technique of interfering with the continuity of this [Budenz's] testimony until it is completed." Fortas replied that

Thorpe was "here as a volunteer, out of a sense of public duty, and I ask that this committee extend to him the courtesy of hearing his testimony this afternoon." Both Fortas and Hickenlooper were disingenuous. The Republicans wanted to adjourn so that the next day's newspaper coverage would focus on Budenz. Fortas was equally concerned with deflecting attention from Budenz by ending the day with a witness who would swear Lattimore was loyal. In this instance, he won and Thorpe testified.[132]

Having produced Thorpe in time for the evening newspapers' deadline, Fortas also tried to inject the affidavit of Bella Dodd. He had learned that Dodd, a lawyer who had reached the high echelons of the Communist Party before she was expelled, had never heard of Lattimore during her years in the party. But Dodd did not want to become involved in the case. Technically, Fortas told the committee, he could not subpoena her. In actuality, as the committee replied, it would call anyone he wished and it did in fact subpoena another witness at his request. Fortas, however, knew that a short affidavit indicating Dodd had never heard of Lattimore during her years as a Communist represented the better strategy. Since Dodd freely admitted that, despite her break with the Communists, she still believed "in the things that drove me to the Communist party," she would not be a good witness for his client. Were she to testify, Republicans would question her roughly and attack her credibility.[133] Fortas went to New York to persuade her to submit an affidavit. "You are going to find it hard to live with yourself if Lattimore is successfully framed," he said.[134] Besides, he warned Dodd, although he would not ask the committee to question her, the committee might do so of its own accord. She could give him the affidavit and hope that she would not be subpoenaed, or she could remain silent and greatly increase the risk of a subpoena. He returned to Washington with the affidavit. When the committee refused to accept the affidavit and announced it might prefer to subpoena Dodd, Fortas released the affidavit to the press. Fortas easily outmaneuvered Lattimore's accusers. Even McCarthy admitted that he was no longer certain that Lattimore had committed espionage. As Lattimore said, his "unbelievably generous and public-spirited lawyers," who charged only their expenses, had cleared him by refuting Budenz and taking the case to the press. The Tydings committee exonerated Lattimore.

Tydings, however, was a Democrat, and after McCarthy ensured his defeat in the 1950 elections, McCarthyism still held sway. Just a year and a half after Lattimore's ordeal before the Tydings committee, the Internal Security Subcommittee headed by Pat McCarran, a McCarthy acolyte, decided to recall Budenz, comb through Lattimore's writings, and reopen the investigation. Lattimore turned to Fortas. Once again, they took the offensive. One senator complained that Lattimore's statement to the committee kept "attacking and attacking."[135]

Lattimore and his attorney also continued to work hard for favorable publicity. They outraged the McCarran committee by releasing Lattimore's fifty-page statement before his first day of testimony.

Lattimore found the politeness Fortas generally urged more difficult before the hostile McCarran committee. The committee repeatedly interrupted him as he tried to read his statement, and as Lattimore became less and less deferential, Fortas tried the same approach he had used before loyalty boards: "I know many of you gentlemen; I have the greatest respect for all of you, and I am sure that it is merely because you do not realize, as I keenly do, the strain under which this man is and has been for many days and weeks that causes this," the attorney told the senators. Fortas apologized "for getting emotional about this, but I do believe it should be said."[136] But his remarks did not make the committee any more sympathetic.

Nor could Fortas much aid his client at other times. The McCarran committee restricted counsel more than most congressional committees. It did not allow the accused's attorney to cross-examine witnesses, to call witnesses on his client's behalf, to object to questions—regardless of how loaded and leading—or to question the accused in order to bring out facts that might prove relevant to his defense. The suspect's attorney could only advise him of his constitutional privilege against self-incrimination.[137] McCarran did permit Fortas to respond to any requests for advice. But Lattimore did not know when to confer with Fortas and feared he would fail to do so when he most needed help. "As a human matter, . . . that strain of having questions shot at him by a number of very skillful lawyers is very great indeed, and it is so great as to preclude his use with ordinary intelligence of the availability of counsel," Fortas told the committee.[138] It was no use. When Fortas requested a point of order, McCarran countered that he had no right to do so and threatened to exclude him from the hearings. When Fortas shook his head in reply to a question asked of Lattimore, the interrogator protested that he did not expect criticism from counsel. When a senator suggested that Lattimore could answer yes or no to an inquiry along the lines of "When did you stop beating your wife?" and Fortas tried to rephrase the question, he was rebuked. The committee had said it would conclude the hearings on Friday, and when it become apparent they would continue into the following week, Fortas, who had arranged to be out of town, objected. "You have other members of your firm," McCarran answered.[139] The committee's attitude made the accused's counsel irrelevant.

Its emphasis actually made Communism and espionage unimportant, too. The committee delighted in entrapment. Arnold explained: "The policy of the McCarran Committee is fir ' to have the witness in secret session, get him to testify to the best of his recollection as to events from five to ten years ago, then

bring him on at a public hearing, ask him if he did not so testify at the secret
session and then give him some letter to which he has not previously been given
access which shows that he is wrong. This then is branded as an untruth."
According to Arnold, the committee "long ago gave up all idea of proving Lattimore was a Communist. Instead they spend weeks of time in trying to catch him
up in contradictions and give the impression that he is an evasive and untruthful
witness."[140] Predictably, after the McCarran committee had concluded its hearings by condemning Lattimore's "contumacy," Lattimore was indicted for perjury.[141] Arnold took over Lattimore's defense from Fortas, and after two years of
frequently bizarre courtroom proceedings, the case against Lattimore was dismissed in 1955.[142]

By that time, the Senate had censured McCarthy, McCarran had died, and the
hysteria was subsiding. In 1950 dollars, the firm's legal fees for Lattimore's
defense—had they billed him—were estimated at $2.5 million.[143] "We of course
take his and all other cases for nothing and, if necessary, put up expenses, but the
burden of an individual firm is very great," Arnold said. "There are very few
lawyers of standing willing to take these cases."[144] Even Joe Rauh, who frequently
criticized Arnold, Fortas & Porter for its defense of wealthy corporations, conceded the firm did "wonderful, wonderful work" in the loyalty cases.[145] Other law
firms had done some loyalty work, as had some Washington solo practitioners,
tenured law professors, and Communist members of the bar, but Arnold, Fortas &
Porter had done a disproportionate amount.

The decision to represent those charged with disloyalty may have hurt the
firm's business. Milton Freeman remembered one occasion after the firm had
begun defending Lattimore when an important client told the partners that they
could not represent both him and an alleged Communist. "Abe made a big show
of it. He invited everybody in, and he said . . . 'What do we do?' So we all said,
'Don't let anybody run our firm. Say good-bye to this guy.' So instead of the
regular monthly retainer, we had . . . Lattimore."[146] Many who might otherwise have turned to the firm probably took their business elsewhere. One contemporary magazine article made it clear that the partners thought their stance
would lose them business but went ahead "because as Fortas quietly explains,
'There are some things you have to do in order to live with yourself.'"[147]

Although the dangers justifiably seemed real to them, they received favorable
publicity from Lattimore's book *Ordeal by Slander* and from the many newspapers
which praised them. One corporate client told Fortas that he was "proud to be
represented by lawyers with that kind of courage."[148] An article written about
Arnold, Fortas & Porter in 1951 joked that other lawyers in their building had
stopped practicing law in order to devote their time to "chasing down the thou-
sand-dollar bills, which flutter, unnoticed, out of the door of the Arnold, Fortas

& Porter suite."[149] Fortas earned over $80,000 the following year. The time the firm spent on loyalty cases did not prevent the partners from making an excellent living and ultimately may have increased business. Their actions during the McCarthy era gave the partners a reputation for combativeness, which they considered a positive attribute. "In the end after the hysteria was gone," Freeman noted, "people said: 'Well, these guys stood during tough times. Maybe it's all right to hire them now.'"[150] Still, whatever their reward for fighting McCarthyism, their position required courage.

# CHAPTER 8

# The Washington Lawyer

I VENTURE TO SUGGEST," CHARLES HORSKY WROTE IN A PATHBREAKING study, "that many people may not appreciate the extent to which the Washington lawyer did *not* exist before 1933, despite the temporary effects of World War I."[1] The regulatory process that reached an apex during the New Deal and World War II created a need for a new breed of attorney who understood the effect of government regulations on business. Corporations throughout the country clamored for that service. Within five years of its founding, Arnold, Fortas & Porter included among its clients Lever Brothers, Federated Department Stores, the American Broadcasting Company, Pan American Airways, and Coca-Cola. "Most firms would be delighted to build up such a well-heeled clientele over a period of two or three decades," one contemporary noted.[2] The firm did not restrict itself to problems with administrative agencies. Its members' skill in litigation and their "aggressive personalities" made them well-suited for the courtroom, and they developed a reputation as lawyers who could argue the hardest cases.[3] They also became excellent business advisors. Yet even their litigation and advisory work tended to revolve around governmental problems, for, as Fortas said in his review of Horsky's book, Washington lawyers were "specialists in the dynamics, the policies and practices of the Federal Government. Their work is distinctive primarily because of the limitations of their practice."[4] In his defense of big business and pursuit of good works, Fortas exemplified the "Washington lawyer" of the postwar era.

## CORPORATE ATTORNEY

Arnold, Fortas, and Porter's enthusiasm for big business put them in the mainstream of postwar Washington lawyers. "It was almost a common thing in Washington after the New Deal to cash in on your New Deal thing by representing the people that you had tried to reform," Joe Rauh said. Of those attorneys who went "to the other side," Rauh considered Arnold and his colleagues the ablest. "You had to go a hell of a distance to find three lawyers as good as those three guys. But then their talents were available to things they would have said ten years earlier: 'Oh, I wouldn't represent that bunch of hogbinders.' "[5]

Everyone deserved representation, Fortas typically replied to such criticisms, be he a "corporate malefactor or a presumably saintly civil libertarian."[6] Like many New Deal lawyers, Fortas became, to use William Simon's phrase, a "purposivist" who believed in distinct roles and jurisdictions for all the legal system's players.[7] The lawyer should dedicate himself to his client. It was for the legal system to determine the outcome. Public-interest and private-sector lawyers had their own places. For example, as under secretary of the Department of the Interior, Fortas was critical when Governor Tugwell tried to employ a private attorney to handle the island's legal work. "In my opinion, it is neither seemly nor appropriate for governmental agencies to be represented by counsel who are not regularly constituted government officials," Fortas contended. Any relationship between the department and private attorneys was "apt to lead to embarrassment, regardless of the unimpeachable character of the private attorneys who might be concerned."[8] Within a year after Fortas had resigned from the government and entered private practice, however, he had taken on Puerto Rico as a client.[9] For some, that was troublesome.[10] Yet Fortas would have said that when he was at Interior, he had been expressing the viewpoint of a public servant. What he could obtain from less scrupulous government officials as a private citizen was not for him to decide. And he might have pointed out that few governments ever received more competent or less expensive representation than Puerto Rico did for the next nineteen years.

Simon maintained that the purposivist scheme of the separation of powers enabled lawyers to "rationalize abandonment of the public interest by associating it with a role they no longer occupied." That would be a harsh judgment in Fortas's case, for he had not wholly forsaken the public interest. Nevertheless, as a corporate lawyer he was often representing former opponents, and a purposivist viewpoint did enable him to overlook the ethical and political responsibilities he had assumed as a government attorney. As Simon writes, "The contradictions persist, but it becomes easier to ignore them."[11] Some contemporaries, such as

Rauh, found the contradictions harder to overlook. They believed that Arnold, Fortas, and Porter had experienced a striking change of heart as they began building one of the town's most successful practices.

Those detractors overlooked continuities. Although Arnold, Fortas and Porter did "go over to the other side" to a certain extent, the New Deal itself had rested in part on coexistence with big business. Fortas had labored to establish a partnership between government and big business at the AAA and the Bituminous Coal Division. Thurman Arnold had once been an ambitious antitruster, but even then he had tried to use antitrust in a regulatory fashion by relying in large part on the consent decree, which enabled business and government to negotiate permissible behavior. [12] When he turned against big business during the war, he directed his fire at those corporations which trafficked with America's enemies. [13] Arnold himself saw nothing contradictory about the progress of his career. In the 1950s, he pointed out that as head of the Justice Department's Antitrust Division he had always answered entrepreneurs' challenge "to name one big American business that violated neither the letter nor the spirit of our antitrust laws . . . by describing The Coca-Cola Company," later one of his first clients. [14] Further, lawyers such as Arnold and Fortas proved comfortable with the tension inherent in working to preserve capitalism while promoting social justice because that tension had been inherent in the New Deal, which sought to reform in order to conserve.

Rauh and other critics also did not recognize that some liberals believed it was time for a new agenda. Big business now seemed less threatening than it had earlier. Whereas they had been frightened by the political power of business earlier, liberals thought they had established government and organized labor as countervailing forces during the 1930s. In the late 1940s and the 1950s they worried about "the economic power of business in particular markets rather than some general power position in society as a whole," the *New Republic* maintained. Liberals now focused on civil liberties and foreign policy rather than on domestic economics. [15]

The lawyering skills Fortas had developed during the New Deal and used to fight McCarthyism served him well with his corporate clients. He was meticulous. More than most senior partners, he situated himself in the law library and insisted that his colleagues get into the dark corners of legal problems. [16] Having researched all aspects of a case, Fortas did not hesitate to restate key points many times in the documents he drafted. In writing briefs, he used what he called "the art of subtle repetition." [17] Sometimes it did not seem that subtle. "Buyer wished to tie-up the Seller on the specific terms of this contract for *twenty years*," he said in a brief for the seller in one antitrust case. "*For 20 years*, competing purchasers cannot solicit the Seller to sell them any of the coal committed by this contract;

and *for 20 years,* competitors of the Seller cannot solicit the coal business of the Buyer." The phrase *"for 20 years"* appeared at least twelve times in the brief, in addition to repeated references to the "20-year exclusionary contract."[18]

He skillfully argued the cases he briefed. His colleagues claimed that by the time Fortas had presented a case, the judge thought that only two people in the courtroom understood it—himself and Abe Fortas.[19] "He was a fantastic advocate," one associate recalled. "He had just the right tone . . . and respectful manner." Milton Freeman saw "drama" even in the way Fortas argued motions before the SEC. "That didn't mean he screamed and tore his hair," Freeman cautioned. As always, Fortas remained "absolutely in control. There was passion in it, [but] he was restraining himself. Somebody else would stomp on the law, not Abe."[20]

Fortas would stomp on his opponent. He employed the same combative approach on behalf of big business that he had used in loyalty cases. He had a gift for turning things on their ear. For instance, if the government accused Federated Department Stores of monopolistic practices, Fortas would compare Federated's share of the market against that of other companies, such as Sears.[21] So, too, when the government charged that Lever Brothers, Procter and Gamble, and Colgate-Palmolive monopolized the American soap and detergent business in 1956, Fortas distinguished himself as "a superlative tactician" who positioned his client, Lever Brothers, effectively in the litigation. Part of his strategy entailed trying Procter and Gamble instead of Lever Brothers.[22] Eight years later, when the government alleged that Lever Brothers' purchase of the trademark for All detergent from Monsanto Chemical Company violated section 7 of the Clayton Act by decreasing competition, Fortas and his colleagues successfully countered that the transaction actually "preserved and enhanced competition." They pointed out that Monsanto would have discontinued the product if Lever had not bought it. There would have been one less detergent on the market, and Lever would have ceased being a competitor in the heavy-duty sudsing field. "Procter and Gamble's position would be made impregnable; Section 7 would have been employed, paradoxically, to smother competition."[23]

Fortas's aggressiveness proved especially effective when he defended Otis and Company. In 1948 Otis contracted to purchase a large block of stock from Kaiser-Frazer Corporation, which it envisioned selling to the public. In its contract with Otis, Kaiser-Frazer agreed to file a registration statement and prospectus that contained no material misstatements with the Securities and Exchange Commission. After Kaiser-Frazer filed the materials, Otis reneged. When Kaiser-Frazer sued, Otis claimed that Kaiser-Frazer's prospectus had overstated its earnings for 1947 by over $3 million. In fact, there was evidence that Otis had full knowledge of all the information concerning 1947 earnings at the time the contract was

signed and had even participated in preparing Kaiser-Frazer's prospectus and
registration statement. "If there ever was a case where it looked as if the plaintiffs
had the defendant, Otis and Company, dead to rights, this was it," Fortas's
colleague, G. Duane Vieth, recalled thirty-five years later.[24] Lloyd Cutler, an
attorney for Kaiser-Frazer, maintained that Otis had "welched on the entire
agreement."[25] The district court agreed and entered judgment for Kaiser-Frazer.

But Fortas transformed the argument on appeal with a principle that first-
year law students learned in their contracts course: a buyer who agreed to
purchase diamonds from a seller and then breached his contract would not be
held liable if the diamonds were paste. As long as the seller had misrepresented
any facts, regardless of how immaterial, the buyer could renege on the deal.
Fortas admitted that Otis had not performed its obligations but contended that it
should not be held liable because of Kaiser-Frazer's "extraordinary misrepresen-
tation."[26] "It really had nothing to do with the rightness or wrongness of
what . . . Otis and Company had done," Vieth emphasized. "It was a question of
showing that Kaiser-Frazer had not acted properly."[27] Fortas's presentation of his
theory so entranced the Second Circuit Court of Appeals that at oral argument
Judge Augustus Hand urged Fortas to proceed far beyond his allotted time.[28] The
court of appeals reversed the district court and entered judgment for Otis.[29]
"That was one of the best jobs of lawyering I've ever seen," Vieth said.[30] Even
Cutler conceded that Fortas's strategy in that case showed unquestionably that
"he was a brilliant lawyer."[31]

Fortas's briefs bristled with statements designed to put his opponents on the
defensive. "We do not propose . . . to discuss the many errors of fact and law in
the Solicitor General's brief," his supplemental statement in one case began.[32] In
another brief, he suggested that the Securities and Exchange Commission was
anti-Semitic. "We hope the Court will inquire of Counsel as to the reason why
Mr. Sherwood is referred to as 'alias Schlien,'" he said. "Is it to create the false
impression that he has a criminal record? Or is it for some equally base—or
perhaps baser—reason?"[33]

Fortas also knew when to back down. His associates described him as a
consummate strategist. Whereas some lawyers "just can't look at any challenge
without responding aggressively, Abe wasn't instinctively aggressive," William
Rogers explained. "He didn't go on the offensive just for the hell of it. He was
extremely calculating." Fortas would say, "The capacity of the lawyer is to
become angry at the right moment."[34] Edward Howrey provided an example of
Fortas's willingness to retreat. When Howrey became chair of the Federal Trade
Commission (FTC), Fortas argued a case for Lever Brothers before him. Fortas
began by saying that the FTC attorney for the case had misstated the facts.
Howrey stopped him and told him that when the hearing resumed after lunch-

eon, Fortas should be prepared to provide a detailed analysis of his adversary's alleged misrepresentations. As the attorney had not misstated the facts, Fortas had no alternative but to back down gracefully. That afternoon, Fortas apologized to FTC counsel. Howrey recounted the incident: "Upon reviewing the facts during the lunch hour he had decided that opposing counsel had . . . simply failed to emphasize certain points that he, Fortas, thought should be stressed. This cleared the air . . . Fortas went on to make a splendid argument on behalf of his client."[35]

Fortas was sensitive to all problems his clients faced. His colleagues agreed that he would have said that judgment is more important than intellect to the practice of law. Clients valued his counsel with respect to business as well as legal problems. He once reproved a colleague for giving a client technical advice without telling him how to use it.[36] His greatest talent as a lawyer, another associate thought, "was his ability to listen to a conversation of experts talking with multiple people present, and then summarize and synthesize the discussion, and to appear, at least, to extrapolate from the discussion the essential essence of it and the question that had to be answered before one could achieve the goal of the conversation."[37] That quality made him invaluable in boardrooms. Although the twenty-seven briefs he submitted to the Supreme Court and the seven cases he argued before it during his nineteen years of practice qualified him as a "lawyer's lawyer,"[38] one of his partners estimated that only 10 percent of the work he produced resulted in a brief.[39] Like Paul Cravath and other "prototypical law firm entrepreneur[s]," Fortas spent more time advising businesses than representing them before courts and administrative agencies.[40]

Lawyers outside the firm marveled at the ease with which Fortas moved in the business world. Asked to explain Fortas's relationship with the founder of Federated Department Stores, Fred Lazarus, the company's general counsel said, "The old man felt that this was the guy who, if he had grown up in the department store, would have been another Fred Lazarus. . . . Abe was capable of looking ahead four or five [or] ten steps . . . and also Abe had business judgment."[41] Paul Warnke, another Washington lawyer, agreed that Fortas "thought like a businessman, so it wasn't just consulting with someone who was going to tell you what . . . provision of the code . . . might be applicable."[42] Further, Fortas followed the New Deal pattern of considering policy before legality. Maurice Lazarus subscribed to the old saying that "most lawyers that you deal with tend to tell you why you can't do certain things," but Fortas, he said, asked clients what they wanted to do, advised them how to do it, then told them how to do it legally.[43] When Federated decided to acquire Bullock's Department Stores, Fortas correctly predicted that the Federal Trade Commission would consent to the acquisition only if Federated pledged to make no others in the immediate future. He therefore counseled Ralph Lazarus to make this merger "a big one."[44] In this instance, as in others, Maurice Lazarus stressed, "Abe was not only our lawyer, he was fundamentally a major adviser."[45] Indeed, though Federated employed its own house counsel and originally hired Fortas only to represent it before the FTC, it ultimately asked him to join its board of directors.

Clients frequently asked him to join their boards. By 1965 he had served as a director of Federated, Braniff Airlines, Franklin Life Insurance Company, and Madison National Bank. "I accepted directorship on these, and perhaps a few other boards," Fortas later remarked, "because of an illusion that in this way I could acquire a deeper insight into the operations of a variety of businesses for which I was performing legal services."[46] His position as Washington lawyer and director was anomalous. Law firms expanded in two ways: growth by general service and growth by special representation. The typical corporate law firm was a general service firm that prospered by serving its clients' routine needs. The specialty firm focused on meeting specific requirements. That distinction explained not only patterns of growth but lawyer-client relationships as well. In the general service firm, the client and attorney enjoyed a fiduciary relationship characterized, one observer wrote, "by continuity, mutual trust, an ongoing flow of information, an identification with the interests of the party and mutual dependencies." In contrast, special representatives were "the hired guns of the profession," retained for particular occasions.[47] As a law firm that touted its knowledge of federal government, Arnold, Fortas & Porter was a specialty firm. By its own account, it attacked "unique problems as opposed to routine retainer matters: 60 percent of the work is trouble-shooting concerning a single problem for a client. The firm is considered to be expert at handling difficult problems with the federal government that are beyond the expertise of corporate lawyers."[48] Two of Fortas's most valuable clients in the 1950s—Federated, and Unilever's Lever Brothers—possessed in-house legal departments that served their general needs. Unilever's Patrick Macrory characterized Fortas as a person the company turned to as a last resort because, as he said, "Abe didn't come cheap."[49] Yet Fortas's clients still treated him as a fiduciary as well as special agent, or so the invitations to join their boards suggested.[50]

## AUTONOMY AND INFLUENCE IN FORTAS'S PRACTICE

He did not preach reform there. Fortas generally accepted his clients' assumptions of what was right. He did not view himself as society's gatekeeper or tell clients that their proposed course of action was morally reprehensible. "The social implications of the position to be taken on the client's behalf were submerged by the lawyer's dedication to the value of the legal and constitutional system . . . to the duty of the advocate, and to the obligations of advocacy in an adversary system," Fortas maintained.[51] His concept of professionalism led him to identify with his client and to argue that everyone deserved the most energetic representation possible. An associate who had come to Arnold, Fortas & Porter from the New York firm of Cravath, Swaine & Moore immediately noticed a difference between the two firms. Documents emanating from Arnold, Fortas & Porter favored the client more than those produced by Cravath. In Washington the attorney frequently heard that his attempts too closely resembled law review articles.[52] "We always felt that we were advocates," Vieth underscored. "That's the role of the lawyer." Recent law school graduates sometimes took "an academic approach" to legal matters until the firm retrained them, Vieth recalled. "We're not doing a piece that's designed to show both sides of an issue. We're arguing one side, the other side can argue theirs."[53]

Most litigating firms identified with their clients, but after working at Arnold, Fortas & Porter for five years, Charles Reich concluded that this firm did so to an unusual extent. "You didn't stop short of 110 percent loyalty to the client," he remembered. The atmosphere was "righteous. The other sides were sons of bitches." To him, Fortas seemed "particularly aggressive in siding with clients. There was no middle ground." When Lyndon Johnson's crony George Parr was convicted of fraud, "we got him off on a technicality." Reich, who thought Parr was guilty, understood the lawyer's professional duty to seek acquittal, but marveled that "we were all gung ho."[54] In the business sphere, Fortas did not maintain autonomy from his clients. Neither did most other corporate lawyers. At the turn of the century, Louis Brandeis had urged attorneys to moderate corporate excesses both to avoid losing their professional status by becoming pawns of business and to stop "a revolt of the people" against business. In contending that lawyers should remain independent for professional and ideological reasons, Brandeis pointed to the existence of two different types of autonomy.[55] Few lawyers ever conformed to Brandeis's Progressive ideal. Corporate lawyers rarely changed the goals of their clients, and though Fortas's business judgment gave him more influence over clients in formulating strategies and refining objectives than most lawyers, he still lacked professional autonomy.[56]

Though Fortas, like most lawyers, did not challenge his clients' corporate objectives, he did retain ideological autonomy. Most corporate lawyers apparently followed their clients not only in the boardroom but in the polling booth as well. "Lawyers typically pursue their *long-range* interests," Stewart Macaulay explained. "This means positioning themselves to serve those clients they are likely to see and those who occasionally bring them cases they prize." Macaulay cited the example of the corporate attorney who decided against managing a Democrat's campaign for fear of alienating one of his firm's conservative clients.[57] John Heinz noted that if this practice is typical, "the political views and interests of lawyers' clients may have a substantial chilling or channeling effect on lawyers' political activity (or lack thereof)."[58] But his clients' politics did not intimidate Fortas. His involvement in the loyalty cases and other public interest work suggested he still carried some of the intellectual baggage of the New Deal.

The paradox of the lawyer-reformer had haunted elite members of the American bar at least since the nineteenth century when individuals such as David Dudley Field engaged in skulduggery for the robber barons while inveighing against corruption. One historian has aptly described this pattern as one of "institutionalized schizophrenia."[59] Yet purposivists who neatly carved their lives into separate spheres did not feel divided. His models, Fortas said, were his wife's two partners, Randolph Paul and Parker McCollester. "They were both experts in the art and science of the practice of law, and they were also outstanding persons and citizens. Particularly Randolph also maintained the independence and integrity of his personal views on the tax policy, politics, etc., although he had undoubtedly the largest corporate tax practice in the country."[60] Fortas also quoted Erwin Griswold: "Lawyers should sell their services but not their souls."[61] Fortas freely admitted that he practiced law to make money but contended that his ideological identification with liberalism remained strong.[62]

His liberal activism did not trouble his conservative clients. The Lazarus family was composed of ardent Republicans. "Abe was a rabid Democrat," Ralph Lazarus recalled, "and I disagree[d] with Abe on the extent of Social Security and Medicare." Asked whether Fortas's political work proved bothersome, Lazarus answered: "As long as he . . . [was] a good lawyer for the corporation, and as long as he was the kind of person that I could trust . . . I would applaud it."[63] Though Fortas did not significantly change his clients' grand corporate designs, in some cases he did influence their politics. He involved them in Muñoz Marín's Puerto Rico and in Lyndon Johnson's social programs.[64] His preservation of ideological autonomy constituted one aspect of his power as a lawyer.

The second aspect of his power as a lawyer—government influence—enabled Fortas to insulate himself from the clients whose causes he advocated so aggressively at the same time that it increased his control over them. Whereas most lawyers relied on their clients for legitimation, Fortas received validation from government officials, and his clients knew it. Indeed that was one of the reasons they hired him. To be sure, the firm refused to take clients who expected them to use influence to obtain results. "Like all good influential firms," Arnold, Fortas & Porter believed that "influence is the most over-sold commodity in Washington," a journalist observed.[65] In the 1960s Fortas once informed three colleagues that a large company under investigation by the Department of Justice had offered the firm a large retainer. Everyone was delighted until Fortas said another law firm would handle the grand jury work. "Do you think we should take it?" he asked. Recognizing that the company would be hiring them only so that Fortas would use his influence on its behalf, each said no. "That's the way I feel about it," Fortas responded.[66] Paul Porter more vehemently described the firm's attitude to a reporter in 1952: "'We are *not* five percenters and we are *not* fixers,' Porter will say, pounding on his desk with his fist. 'We don't pretend to have any influence and we don't try to get contracts for anybody.'"[67] That was disingenuous. The partners made their familiarity with many influential people clear. Though Porter might have had the reputation outside the firm for being the "front man" who drew clients, the lawyers at Arnold, Fortas & Porter agreed that Fortas originated the bulk of the business. A cultured individual who was equally comfortable in the drawing room, music room, boardroom, and courtroom, he possessed immense appeal for clients. Further, he courted them. "Much more than anyone I've ever known . . . he just brought his clients into his social life," a colleague said. "His whole life was devoted to that."[68] Since his social life involved so many well-known individuals, clients or potential clients quickly became aware of his proximity to power.

Fortas nurtured that awareness. Clients received inscribed copies of William O. Douglas's latest book.[69] When Stanley Marcus of Neiman-Marcus came to Washington, Fortas arranged a dinner for him with William Brennan, David Bazelon, Paul Porter, and their wives.[70] In the 1960s Fortas once told the investment banker John Loeb that he had invited "some of your friends" to dinner. The Loebs arrived and were sitting around the pool with Fortas and Carol Agger when Lynda Bird Johnson and Chuck Robb arrived, followed by Robert and Margy McNamara. A few minutes later President and Mrs. Johnson appeared, and the four couples settled in for the evening. It showed Loeb, who later became a client, how intimate Fortas and Johnson were, "because after all," he emphasized, "you can't deliver the President unless you're very close to him."[71] Fortas could always deliver someone for clients. In time, the three partners developed a star appeal of their own. As Lyndon Johnson's star rose, Fortas became a celebrity in his own right. By the 1960s he brought in perhaps three-quarters of the firm's work.[72] "There was a substantial increase in business when Lyndon Johnson became President because it was widely known that Fortas was his friend and adviser," one lawyer in the firm acknowledged. "People liked to be able to say in the country club: 'I was talking to my lawyer, Abe Fortas.'"[73]

Though Johnson's presidency helped the firm's image, it did not necessarily aid clients. One contemporary article on the Washington legal establishment reported that "it is generally, if cautiously, agreed that Fortas was always very careful not to trade on his relationship with the President. The fact that such a friendship is known is usually enough."[74] Vieth noted that "we would try to tell people that they should not think of getting any special arrangements." But as he conceded, the more people were warned not to expect favors, the more they anticipated them.[75] They got some, if not always the ones they hoped. In addition to a lawyer who advised Presidents, they acquired lawyers who were acquainted with everyone else in Washington. As the partners knew Democrats more intimately than Republicans, they felt their success was linked to that of the Democratic party. When his old friend Adlai Stevenson lost to Eisenhower in 1952, Fortas saw hard times ahead for the firm. He called his lawyers together and tried to boost their spirits. During 1953 and 1954, the firm's earnings briefly declined, though unpaid work for John Peters and Owen Lattimore kept the attorneys as busy as ever. Then, a colleague recalled, "things just took off again."[76] Fortas worried about losing business, so he must have thought, at the very least, that his clients' perception of the firm's influence was helpful. But, considering that the firm was as successful during the Eisenhower years as it had been during Democratic administrations, it was obviously selling something other than influence.

Influence in Washington, in any event, existed on a continuum ranging from knowing whom to telephone to being able to make backroom deals. At one level, it simply entailed what Charles Horsky termed "reputation." The true Washington lawyer had "undoubted advantages," Horsky admitted. It was "easier for him to arrange a conference, or to obtain a hearing for his client, or to discuss and discover the agency's position on particular matters that may come up."[77] A journalist put it more succinctly: "Faced with two minutes and a dozen phone messages to return, a Congressional aide will dial Arnold & Porter."[78] Thus when a wealthy Russian stockbroker feared an indictment for perjury in connection with draft evasion, he consulted Fortas, who arranged for Tom Corcoran to call the director of the Selective Service.[79] When a potential client wanted to begin exporting coal, Fortas made inquiries. "I don't know whether it can be done or not," he asked, "but I talked with my man over at Solid Fuels . . . who's the guy in charge of all that, and he thought there was a chance of doing it."[80] The relevant government official might be an old friend, colleague, or student. In 1963 a motorist in Puerto Rico became involved in a dispute with a police lieutenant. The driver alleged a breach of a civil rights statute, an indictment was returned, and it seemed as if the Justice Department would prosecute the police officer in federal court. Ever sensitive to situations in which it appeared that the federal government was intervening in Puerto Rico's local affairs, Fortas telephoned a former student, Deputy Attorney General Nicholas Katzenbach, to persuade him to allow the island to take responsibility for disciplining the policeman. Katzenbach initially "expressed profound doubt" as to whether he could intervene at this late stage. But, "after considerable discussion . . . he indicated that he might be able to reconsider the matter if the Puerto Rican authorities took some action."[81]

Influence might also facilitate the acquisition of advance information. "There are no secrets in Washington but there is such a thing as three hours head start," Corcoran once said.[82] When Fortas represented the defendant in an antitrust case during the Eisenhower years, for example, an attorney outside the firm suggested that he rush to obtain a consent decree because the current assistant attorney general in charge of antitrust, who was so generously handing them out, was about to resign. But Fortas had learned that some congressional committees that the Democrats controlled unofficially had expressed concern about the terms of those consent decrees, so that even the current assistant attorney general might soon become less willing to consider issuing them.[83] Indeed, members of Congress themselves came to him for help on a variety of matters when he did not approach them first to offer it. The Washington lawyer was also a lobbyist.[84] In 1961 Fortas and his partners worked with members of Congress to modify President Kennedy's minimum-wage bill so that their retailer clients could apply it more easily and practically.[85] Such aid was included by Washington law firms under the category of technical assistance and was frequently proffered and taken.[86] It was not necessarily antithetical to the public interest and sometimes advanced it by resulting in the development of clearer and more informed legislation.[87]

At another level, influence might have facilitated the sort of sinister deals that some suspected but never proved existed between Fortas and his partners, on one hand, and government officials, on the other. It was titillating to hint that Lyndon Johnson did not discuss cigarette smoking in his public health proposals to Congress because Fortas was the attorney for the Philip Morris Company, but as one responsible journalist noted: "It is more likely, of course, that this omission was due to understandable reluctance on the part of the President to take on a bruising fight that would pit him against many members of his own party."[87] Fortas might think of diverting discussion of the issue from the Federal Trade Commission to Congress, where the tobacco industry possessed greater influence, and he might lobby members of Congress for votes,[88] but that was part of his job. He had been adroit at maneuvering cases into the best forum for his client since his days at the AAA.

Skeptics made more of Fortas's behavior in the Federated-Bullock's merger, where he obtained an ex parte hearing for Federated before the Federal Trade Commission.[89] One FTC commissioner publicly complained that "the crucial decisions" were made during Federated's appearance before the commission and suggested that the commission might have reached a different decision had it given Bullock's chief executive officer the same opportunity to make an "informal presentation."[90] When the Federal Trade Commission decided to allow Federated to acquire Bullock's, although it had forced Procter and Gamble to get rid of Clorox in a similar fact situation, "a political deal was suspected by many agency staff and Washington lawyers."[91] According to Federated's Ralph Lazarus, however, Procter and Gamble's head "came to me and said: 'You guys just had the right lawyer and we didn't.' "[92] In this instance, the less conspiratorial explanation was more accurate. No rules barred ex parte hearings, and, as he had always done, Fortas simply directed the case to the decision maker before whom he had the greatest chance of success.

In retrospect, what is surprising is not the influence that powerful lawyers went to such great lengths to deny but the friendship they made no attempt to conceal. When a majority of the Supreme Court refused to restrict the power of HUAC in *Barenblatt* v. *United States,*[93] Thurman Arnold wrote his friend Hugo Black to congratulate him on his "magnificent" dissent.[94] "Your own opinions in the field of antitrust are glorious," Fortas told William O. Douglas in 1948. "You are very kind to treat me so gently on my comment on the Transparent Wrap case. I have been worried lest I was rash in writing you as I did."[95] But Fortas kept writing. Couldn't the justice write a paper tracing the different forms in which civil liberties issues had appeared before the Court, he asked on another occasion?[96] Justice Tom Clark and his wife received "a fan letter" from Fortas about their son Ramsey, who "has just about bowled me over. I was as proud of him as if he had been my own son."[97] Such letters indicated an intimacy between lawyers and the decision makers who judged them.

Friendship did not only permit the expression of opinion. It also required the performance of duties, and Fortas undertook many jobs for William O. Douglas. In 1947 and 1948 he kept Douglas advised about the maneuvering aimed at placing the justice's name on the Democratic ticket.[98] In 1949 he negotiated a book contract for Douglas with a publisher.[99] "He did legal stuff for Douglas all the time," a colleague remembered.[100] In 1959 Fortas organized a group to purchase Douglas a horse as a gift.[101] Should a Supreme Court justice have recused himself when the lawyer arguing a case before him had given him political counsel, acted as his personal attorney, and presented him with a large gift? If the relationship did not concern the justice, should it have bothered the lawyer? Such questions did not trouble Fortas or other elite lawyers, for they were living in a different world. Like all moral values, legal and judicial ethics were relativistic. In the nineteenth century Justice Stephen Field had not thought it necessary to recuse himself when his brother, David Dudley Field, argued a case before the Supreme Court.[102] By the middle of the twentieth century Justice Field's decision would have seemed inappropriate, but another pattern of behavior had replaced it which seemed equally questionable to subsequent generations. When Harold Medina went to Washington during World War II to argue a case before the Supreme Court, he called upon his former teacher Harlan Fiske Stone, then chief justice.[103] Powerful lawyers frequently remained close to decision makers before whom they appeared.[104]

There were practical reasons for this interaction. Many Washington lawyers and judges had worked in government. During the New Deal lawyers changed jobs frequently; they moved from agency to agency. Sometimes, as in the case of Thurman Arnold, they became judges. When Arnold entered private practice, he continued to address judges as if he remained their equal, just as a former SEC attorney who developed a private practice in securities regulation approached the commission differently from the attorney who had never been in government. Boundaries were crossed so frequently they blurred. Further, Washington was still a relatively closed society. The Supreme Court bar remained small. Lawyers throughout the country tended to recommend the hiring of "lawyers' lawyers" in the nation's capital or New York to argue cases before the Supreme Court and regulatory agencies until the advent of more widespread regulatory expertise and air travel in the 1960s.[105] Lawyers and judges might have labored together in government at a time when professional proximity had bred close friendships. Why should asking Fortas for legal aid prove an occasion for recusal, William O. Douglas might have reasoned, when he did not disqualify himself despite their close association as mentor and student and as colleagues in the 1930s?

While practical considerations made association between bench and bar inevitable, mid-century lawyers and decision makers would have argued that professional values made friendship irrelevant. Faith in the neutral expert and in meritocracy were intellectual cornerstones of the New Deal. The Washington lawyer who emerged from government service placed his faith in the use of intelligence to solve problems. Intelligence might be a matter of maneuvering a case into a forum where it would be decided by individuals whose political and social beliefs most closely matched those of his clients. It did not mean taking a judge or regulator to lunch. William Rogers remembered an ex parte case in the mid-1950s for which Fortas needed Hugo Black's intercession. He and Fortas drove out to Black's house, where the justice had just finished a game of tennis. "We sat on his couch and discussed the case. A wonderful way to get the Supreme Court to intervene." But Rogers emphasized that Fortas was "colossally fastidious in maintaining the proprieties. It's inconceivable that he would ever have taken advantage or allowed any justice to be put in a position of seeming to expose himself."[106]

Fortas knew that the appearance of impropriety could ruin careers. He told a friend that public administrators in the capital should be wary of situations which merely *seemed* questionable: "It might be unimportant that the suspicion were totally unfounded. The appearance of the situation might be undesirable."[107] But, at the time, Fortas and other elite lawyers did not see that friendship could ruin the appearance of justice, too. Friends had influence no stranger could buy. Professionalism might mute, but could not negate, friendship. However strenuously he denied it, influence did figure in Fortas's practice, though there was no evidence he used it in an unethical way. And when convinced his cause was in the public interest, he exerted influence more vigorously still.

## "THE GOOD EARTH"

One associate estimated that Fortas devoted a quarter of his time to Puerto Rico during the 1950s.[108] His friendship with powerful members of Congress during this period ensured the passage of significant legislation affecting the island. Yet Congress as a body continued to frustrate Fortas. Because of its recalcitrance he often had to dilute legislation he had helped to draft. He considered Congress "a retarded body, politically underdeveloped," one of the Puerto Ricans who worked with him recalled. "Abe suffered a lot during that period because he was a very liberal man. He was ashamed at the way his country was acting."[109] Fortas's work for the island also suggested the evolving liberal position toward dependent peoples. Convinced that independence was politically and economically unfeasible, he searched for a middle ground between freedom and colonialism which would inspire the world and save Puerto Rico from the underside of the American century.

Fortas's hopes for Puerto Rico rested in large part on his faith in the island's governor, Luis Muñoz Marín. Muñoz took office when the United States finally granted Puerto Ricans the elective governorship for which Fortas had lobbied as under secretary of the Department of the Interior. Between the period of his tense wartime conferences with Fortas and his first election in 1948, Muñoz had developed into a charismatic leader: a romantic who stopped conferences to see the sun set, a poet as comfortable with peasants as with heads of state.[110] By 1946 Fortas had come to view Muñoz as "a spectacularly great figure." Indeed he claimed that "Muñoz in his restricted sphere has no less greatness than Roosevelt; and that, as a matter of fact, he has some qualities of greatness which Roosevelt lacked."[111] The work he did for Muñoz also appealed to Fortas's idealism. The mood on the island reminded him of the heady atmosphere in Washington at the beginning of the New Deal. "Whenever I visit the Island, I feel as if

I have touched the good earth which we cultivated in the earliest days of Roosevelt," he said.[112]

But idealism in itself is insufficient to explain the depth of Fortas's attachment to Muñoz and Puerto Rico. Though he supported individuals and causes zealously, he generally maintained his distance from them. He appeared to worship Lyndon Johnson, but he did not; he appeared to worship Muñoz, and he did. Puerto Rico engaged Fortas. It became the one cause to which he was unconditionally committed. Indeed his attitude toward the island provided some clues about the kind of father he might have been. It was proprietary, protective, and loving. Muñoz once asked Fortas and José Ferrer to screen a film in progress about a Puerto Rican youth who migrated to New York, where he met a Puerto Rican woman. Hume Cronyn played an immoral character who exposed the young man to temptation, which he somehow resisted. "All the evil people in the picture are native Americans," Ferrer concluded. "I do not see how this picture can reflect discredit on the Puerto Ricans."[113] That was not enough for Fortas, who thought the film should celebrate Puerto Ricans. He suggested the final version of the film include a reminder that Puerto Ricans had "served conspicuously" for their country in the armed services and that many had died on Korean battlefields. He objected that the film did not acknowledge "the deeply religious" aspect of Puerto Rican life. Nor did it portray "the gentleness and beauty" which characterized the Puerto Ricans as a people. In real life, Puerto Ricans would have been "warm and affectionate" to Hume Cronyn's blind wife, and so they should be in the film. And couldn't the marriage ceremony and dance scene be more breathtaking? "Why not the dansa instead of the rhumba? Why not one of the lovely Puerto Rican songs?"[114]

Something about Puerto Rico obviously touched Abe Fortas on an intensely personal level. Muñoz's wife thought that, because Fortas was Jewish, he sympathized with persecuted outsiders. And, though Fortas had not been deprived of life's essentials as a child, he indicated to her and to another Puerto Rican friend that the island's poverty struck a responsive chord.[115] Fortas also appreciated the power he had in formulating policy and the relative speed with which it would be implemented in Puerto Rico as compared to Washington. He became one of Muñoz's most important advisers and the only one based in the nation's capital. Muñoz's secretary of state, Roberto Sánchez Vilella, could "not think of any important question that was discussed in Puerto Rico from 1943 to 1970 that he was not helpful in. He was in the very first line."[116] Fortas and Muñoz also became personally extremely close. Muñoz trusted Fortas "very profoundly," Inés Muñoz Marín recalled. For Muñoz, seeing Fortas was "like a holiday."[117] Muñoz's attorney general, José Trías Monge, also emphasized that the governor's association with Fortas "transcended any professional relationship." Whenever Fortas went to Puerto Rico, he spent hours in the evenings discussing literature, music, and wine with Muñoz, Trías, and Sánchez. Fortas was more than Muñoz's lawyer. He acted as friend and adviser as well.

Although he served in that treble capacity to others, he treasured this client most. "He was always available," Sánchez remembered, and regularly appeared on the island "within hours" of receiving a cry for help.[118] Nor was he well paid. Fortas's work for the island was "a work of love," Trías maintained.[119] Puerto Rico paid his firm a retainer of only ten thousand dollars a year—"a ridiculous sum," Trías said. Annual fees in addition to the retainer might amount to as much as one hundred thousand dollars, but even those were considered low.[120] "We knew, and Abe knew, and we discussed it, that his work for Puerto Rico was subsidized by private clients," Sánchez said. In the early 1950s Fortas received a per diem of fifteen dollars from the island whenever he went there on business. Since a room at his favorite hotel, the Caribe Hilton, cost twelve dollars a night, he paid for most of his expenses out of his own pocket. "Abe never showed any avariciousness in any way as far as Puerto Rico was concerned," Sánchez said. "On the contrary, he was just giving."[121]

Party leadership meant more in Congress in the 1950s than it did later, and the successes Puerto Rico scored there generally were partially attributable to Fortas's relationship with the most powerful Democrat in the Senate, the majority leader, Lyndon Johnson. Once Fortas made it clear that by helping Puerto Rico, Johnson would be aiding Abe Fortas, Johnson could not do enough for Puerto Rico. When a bill circumscribing the jurisdiction of federal courts over the island was introduced in 1956, for example, Fortas asked a Johnson staffer, James Rowe, to speak with the majority leader about it. The senator told Rowe that he would do "anything he can to help on it." Johnson instructed Rowe to talk with Senator O'Mahoney, in whose committee the bill had stalled, and promised to speak with O'Mahoney himself. Rowe joked in a message to Fortas, "I hope that when I return to the private practice and Mr. Fortas becomes a public servant, that he will take care of my clients as well as I take care of his."[122]

Johnson proved even more useful in 1958 when, at Muñoz's request, Congress considered a bill transferring the power to appoint adjutant generals of the National Guard for Puerto Rico from the President to the Puerto Rican government.[123] As state governors named adjutants general, the bill was symbolically important. Within two weeks after Muñoz had advised Johnson that his help was "greatly needed" to ensure its passage, Fortas could tell the governor: "Report on Adjutant General bill just sent by Pentagon to Budget Bureau, thanks to Lyndon."[124] Johnson then arranged to substitute the more favorable House version for the Senate version at Arnold, Fortas & Porter's request, and Congress enacted it.[125]

Stuart Symington also helped. "Abe," the senator jocularly said, after meeting Muñoz at a party Fortas hosted, "you are my leader."[126] When it came to Puerto Rico, Symington did follow Fortas. Thus when a member of Congress from Symington's state of Missouri introduced a bill granting the island independence, Symington immediately wrote Fortas for instructions. "Is this what you all want? . . . Can't be, can it?"[127] "You were absolutely wonderful on the Puerto Rican bill," Fortas wrote him after Congress had passed the adjutant general bill. "It was a great service and Muñoz and all of us Puerto Ricans are extremely grateful."[128]

Most Puerto Ricans acknowledged that Fortas's influence in Washington, which they viewed as a fortuitous by-product of his professional skill, helped the island. Muñoz's widow emphasized the access her husband gained to the Washington elite through Fortas's parties.[129] Yet Puerto Rican officials argued convincingly that they did not employ Fortas for his influence. Fortas "was more of a legal scholar and not so much of a lobbyist," Sánchez contended. The commonwealth valued his knowledge of the island's goals and his legal talent. "We could have been discussing a problem for six months. Abe would come in, someone would outline it for him in fifteen minutes, and Abe would have a draft the next morning."[130]

The most perplexing problem related to the island's status. The issue dated back to the *Insular Cases* of 1901, in which the Supreme Court had developed the doctrine of "territorial incorporation" stating that the territories of Puerto Rico and the Philippines, which the United States had recently won from Spain, "could *belong* to the United States without necessarily being *a part* of the United States for all purposes."[131] The Puerto Ricans discovered after World War II that being of the United States but not part of it had its advantages. Puerto Rico's ambitious wartime program of state-sponsored industrialization had had little success.[132] By 1946 Puerto Ricans knew they needed to attract capital from the continental United States. A United States Tariff Commission report issued that year strongly influenced Muñoz. It concluded that independence would raise a tariff wall between the island and mainland that would preclude free trade and make access to mainland markets more difficult. Economic realities thus demanded that Puerto Rico both turn away from its experiment with socialism and avoid independence. At the same time, economic and political factors militated against statehood. In 1948 Puerto Rico exempted American industry on the island from most federal taxes. "Operation Bootstrap" aimed at attracting industrial capital from the continental United States. Within the next decade, that money "quadrupled the island's income and transformed it from a pesthole to a shiny exhibit of democracy and free enterprise in action," *Life* magazine reported.[133] Statehood, which Congress in any event would have refused to grant, would have subjected investors to the same tax burden they faced at home. To Muñoz and Fortas equally, statehood was inconceivable.

With neither independence nor statehood feasible, Fortas's firm believed the task was to find "a way out of the dilemma . . . by resort to political invention."[134] In 1946 Muñoz began agitating for commonwealth status for the island, which would enable it to maintain a relationship with the United States comparable to that of New Zealand, Australia, or Canada with Great Britain. Puerto Rico's political status would be unique, however, for unlike these members of the British Commonwealth, it would not be an independent state. Fortas, Muñoz, Trías, and Puerto Rico's resident commissioner in Washington, Antonio Fernós Isern, were soon drafting Public Law 600 to set out the island's new status. Introduced in 1950, the act empowered Puerto Ricans to draft their own constitution. Its preamble stated: "Fully recognizing the principle of government by consent, this Act is now adopted in the nature of a compact so that the people of Puerto Rico may organize a government pursuant to a constitution of their own adoption."[135] The key phrase, "in the nature of a compact," implied to its authors that the United States could not unilaterally govern Puerto Rico. To them it seemed bold, so daring that Fernós, who was inclined toward cautiousness, feared using it. Fortas, however, considered the phrase "of paramount importance" and predicted Congress would accept it.[136] "Fortas and I fought for the language," Trías remembered. They finally convinced Fernós during a long luncheon at which "Fortas did most of the talking."[137]

The drafters agreed the law should be brief and that it should be introduced as an amendment to the Jones Act of 1917. Though that act had not extended to Puerto Ricans the constitutional guarantees of American citizens living in the continental United States and had even announced that Puerto Rico belonged to the United States, it had made Puerto Ricans American citizens.[138] Fortas's group believed that only a short amendment would survive Congressional scrutiny. Thus P. L. 600, the act on which the island's commonwealth status was to be based, was enacted as an amendment to an act declaring Puerto Rico belonged to the United States. Jaime Benítez, one of the island's leading constitutional scholars, recognized that P.L. 600 retained "the most offensive" aspect of the Jones Act.[139] But the strategy was successful. Congress paid little attention to P.L. 600 and speedily approved it.

What exactly had Puerto Rico obtained? Even on its face, the phrase "in the nature of a compact" was opaque. When read in conjunction with the Jones Act, its meaning became even murkier. Was Puerto Rico still a territory that could be unilaterally controlled by the United States? Many members of Congress thought so. They repeatedly said in 1950 that P.L. 600 did not alter Puerto Rico's political status.[140] Even its drafters seemed unsure of the significance of P.L. 600. "The authority of the Government of the United States, of the Congress, to legislate in case of need would always be there," Fernós told a congressional committee. Muñoz agreed.[141] Yet after the constitution adopted in 1952 gave the "Free Associated State" of Puerto Rico commonwealth status and declared the island a self-governing entity "within the terms of the compact agreed upon between the people of Puerto Rico and the United States of America," Muñoz maintained that commonwealth status removed "every trace of colonialism" as it was based on a "compact" and on the "principle of mutual consent."[142] As in 1950, however, members of Congress refused to concede that the compact language changed Puerto Rico's status.[143] In their eyes, it remained a territory.

Fortas summed up the constant uncertainty about the island's political status when he returned from a trip to San Juan during Puerto Rico's constitutional convention. "As soon as I recover, I am going to work on a successor to the Mambo which I propose to call the Constitutional Jerks," he told friends. "This will be a dance consisting entirely of whirling around, sometimes in alternate directions and sometimes in both directions simultaneously. It will also involve deep knee bends, hand stands and back flips. I have not perfected the details, but as you will observe, the dance is strenuous."[144] For the rest of his life, Fortas tried to persuade Washington officials that Puerto Rico had indeed entered into a compact with the United States and could not be governed unilaterally from the mainland. Puerto Rico was self-ruling, according to this formula, although the federal government retained the same power it would have over states in a union. The long battle demanded presentation of the "compact" idea on every front.

For example, the island decided in 1952 to discontinue the practice of submitting the periodic reports the United Nations required from the dependencies of member nations, and Muñoz drafted a letter that would accompany the State Department's transmittal of a memorandum to the United Nations explaining the decision. The United States liked the symbolic value of making the rest of the world think it had lost a colony. But as the state and interior departments still considered Puerto Rico a territory, they took offense at Muñoz's discussion in his draft letter of a compact between Puerto Rico and the United States and his insistence that Puerto Rico's association with the United States was voluntary.[145] For their part, Fortas and the government of Puerto Rico were offended by the State Department's draft memorandum. Fortas took over the negotiations with State. "We are still involved in great difficulty with the State Department on account of the interpretation of one member of its legal staff," Fortas wrote Trías in early 1953. "The issue is whether the Department will insist upon deleting the word 'compact' from its memorandum and substituting 'in the nature of a compact.' "[146] In the end, all references to any kind of a compact were deleted in the memorandum State sent to the United Nations. Puerto Rico had apparently lost.

A new development soon caused the American delegation to the United Nations to acknowledge the existence of a compact, however. In the interim between the transmittal of the state department's document and the presentation of the Puerto Rican matter to the United Nations, the commonwealth won what seemed a great triumph in Puerto Rico's federal district court. In *Mora v. Torres*, a case involving a Puerto Rican rice retailer, the court entered judgment for the commonwealth. The victory was less significant than the dicta. The presiding judge's sweeping decision concluded that Puerto Rico was no longer a territory because "a compact has been established between the people of Puerto Rico and the government of the United States, which precludes a unilateral amendment of the Puerto Rican Federal Relations Act by either party to the compact."[147] Puerto Ricans now convinced the United States to use the district court's opinion in its presentation to the United Nations. Although the state department omitted mention of the compact concept, the U.S. delegation to the United Nations spoke of the compact between the United States and the island.

Some other countries, hostile to American interests, wondered aloud in the United Nations how much autonomy Puerto Rico had received. "Puerto Rico's changed status became the center of a bitter parliamentary battle . . . [and] one of the two most significant issues of the eighth General Assembly," surprised American delegates recalled.[148] Soviet delegate Shtokalo protested that "the political farce of the adoption of the Constitution of Puerto Rico could not disguise the fact that it continued to be a United States colony."[149] Nevertheless, the United Nations approved the U.S. request to release Puerto Rico from the duty to submit reports in a resolution which explicitly indicated that a compact existed between Puerto Rico and the United Nations. But Shtokalo's skepticism also proved appropriate. The rice retailer appealed the *Mora* decision. Although Trías, as attorney general, and Fortas, as special assistant attorney general, persuaded Judge Calvert Magruder to affirm the lower court's decision, the judge ignored the district court's dicta. Magruder's opinion suggested that the implications of Puerto Rico's political status had yet to be determined.[150]

Writing to Trías six days after Magruder had decided the appeal, Fortas was glum. "I continue to feel that our logic is right, and I am somewhat comforted by the fact that Magruder does not even pretend his result is a logical one," he said. Nevertheless, Fortas did not think the commonwealth should request reconsideration of the opinion. That might insult Magruder, who "is of continuing importance to us." Instead Fortas recommended ex parte pressure. "I am attracted by the idea of your writing Magruder a letter in which you, in effect, tell Magruder that you and I both regretted that events worked out so that we had to throw at the court a brief which was hurriedly prepared with respect to the constitutional-jurisdictional issues . . . and that you would like to have an opportunity to talk to him at sometime either in San Juan or in Boston." After concluding this appeal to the judge's self-importance, Fortas thought Trías might go even further. The attorney general could inform Magruder that Puerto Rico was not filing a petition for reconsideration "because we are confident that he will approach the problems with an open mind when an opportunity presents itself for full-scale briefing and argument."[151]

Fortas did not rely only on letters to judges to secure a more favorable interpretation of Puerto Rico's status. Throughout the 1950s in characteristically aggressive fashion, his briefs emphasized that Puerto Rico was not a territory, that it had entered into a compact with the United States, that it was responsible for its internal affairs, and that any argument to the contrary played directly into the hands of Communist countries. Was it the commonwealth's, or rather the federal government's, right to determine the size of the container a corporation doing business on the island used to bottle wine? If the corporation bottled and sold its wine exclusively within any one state, the law of that state would govern. Therefore Fortas argued that the commonwealth should hold sway here.[152] When Treasury Department lawyers replied that Puerto Rico was a territory and that federal law should govern, Fortas pounced. "The grievous fact is that their position . . . echoes not the opinion of responsible American officials, but the views of spokesmen for Iron-curtain countries who challenge the good faith of American representations as to the meaning and effect of the Commonwealth. If the . . . lawyers are right, the compact was indeed a 'monumental hoax' perpetrated upon the people of Puerto Rico and a fraud perpetrated by the Government of the United States upon the people of the world as represented in the United Nations."[153] Although there were some victories, most courts agreed that Congress could intervene in Puerto Rico's internal affairs without the island's consent.[154]

Weary of this case-by-case battle, Muñoz, Fernós, and Fortas sought to validate the concept of the compact by again giving it explicit recognition in the Fernós-Murray Bill, which Fernós introduced in the House and James Murray of Montana proposed in the Senate in 1959. Fortas had been advocating such a step since 1954, and in 1958 he had counseled Muñoz to meet with members of Congress under the guise of "getting their advice" to "instill in them a desire to perfect the job that has been done to date by Congress."[155] Fortas drafted much of the Fernós-Murray bill and joined Fernós in recommending that it be presented as a clarification, rather than as a reclassification, of Puerto Rico's status.[156]

Muñoz followed their counsel. The governor explained to President Eisenhower that the bill's importance lay in its "restatement of the basic position of Puerto Rico: i.e., that there is a compact between the people of Puerto Rico and the United States; that this compact includes complete self-government for Puerto Rico and a statement of the terms of inter-relationship between Puerto Rico and the Federal Union."[157]

The Department of Justice posed one obstacle to the Puerto Ricans' version of the bill. Fortas reported to Muñoz that he had had "a very unhappy" telephone conversation with Harold Reis. The latter, a justice department attorney, contended that Congress had never entered into a compact. At that point, Fortas showed fury. What meaning did Reis attach to the words "in the nature of a compact" in P.L. 600? Reis replied that Congress had only intended the "compact" to apply to the new governmental structure anticipated for Puerto Rico in P.L. 600. When Puerto Ricans agreed to that structure and received Commonwealth status in 1952, "there was then instituted a 'government by consent,' but the compact ceased to be of any effect whatsoever." Congress retained "its full, undiluted powers" over Puerto Rico. "As my temperature soared while listening to this narration, I told him that this was a most extreme position and that I knew of no basis or authority for it," Fortas recounted. When Reis cited a professor at the University of Puerto Rico Law School (who later became its dean) as support, Fortas characteristically brushed him away as "no authority whatever."[158]

Despite Fortas's attempt to disarm the committee chairman, Henry Jackson,[159] at the hearings the senator took Reis's position and denied that the commonwealth status was based upon a compact. The senator insisted that the United States could unilaterally govern Puerto Rico.[160] As Jackson was a powerful figure, the bill was severely threatened. Enter Fortas with a new objective: circumventing Jackson. He believed that the key lay with one of Senator Lyndon Johnson's chief aides. "Robert G. Baker, known as Bobby, Secretary of Senate and extremely important is in San Juan," he wired the governor's mansion in Puerto Rico eleven days after the Senate hearing concluded. "Urgently suggest all attention and courtesies."[161] Baker, Fortas subsequently explained to Muñoz, "has always been an interesting personality to me because he is sort of the quintessence of homo politicus Texanisis."[162] Following his return from Puerto Rico, where Baker publicly stressed Johnson's commitment to the Fernós-Murray bill, Baker and Fortas conferred. Baker said that if Jackson continued to be obstreperous, he could see to it that someone else presided at the next round of hearings.[163]

It was no use. The bill languished in committee and was never reported out.[164] Fortas continued to maintain, through his last argument before the Supreme Court, that a compact existed preventing Puerto Rico from being governed unilaterally.[165] In the late 1980s the debate continued. Though Muñoz was still revered on the island, one leading Puerto Rican judge said that "colonialism with the consent of the governed is a painful fact of life for all politically conscious Puerto Ricans, including those who a generation ago hoped to establish the Commonwealth of Puerto Rico as a 'middle road to freedom.' "[166] That was partly Fortas's fault. He had long acted as if he could charm individuals such as Jackson or Magruder into acceding to his wishes, or as if appeals to someone like Baker would cause the less powerful to bend. He viewed the world as malleable, but it often was not. Not as many people responded to his one-on-one approach, his flattery, and his attempts to bring pressure to bear as he would have liked. Fortas and his fellow drafters had also been too clever by half. In presenting P.L. 600 as an amendment to the Jones Act, they made contradictory remarks about the meaning of the phrase "in the nature of a compact." Such tactics made the significance of victory unclear. Yet for its time, commonwealth status represented a distinct achievement. Had Fortas and his collaborators been more forthright, the conservative Congress would have given them nothing, and Puerto Rico would have remained a territory.

Other compromises made by Fortas and the island's representatives also proved questionable over time. Muñoz and Fortas advocated commonwealth status not only because this was the limit of autonomy that Congress would grant, but also because it offered tax advantages to doing business in Puerto Rico and thus could stimulate economic growth. In time, Fortas developed a stake in maintaining the political status quo. His was not an economic interest, for his firm had a rule preventing partners or associates from investing in any project on Puerto Rico.[167] But because Fortas justifiably believed that the island could only industrialize with the aid of American capital, he was as solicitous of potential investors as he was of congressional supporters of the island's interests.

Fortas scrupulously tried to avoid conflicts of interest. His firm refused to represent either private parties in Puerto Rico or new clients with problems involving the islands. In the case of retainer clients, "We reserve the right after consultation with you, to give them such guidance, if any, as may be appropriate," Fortas informed Puerto Rico's attorney general in 1959. He would do so, he explained, in order to help attract new capital to the island: "If, for example, I could fulfill a longstanding ambition to persuade Lever Brothers or the Kroger Co. to open a plant in Puerto Rico, they would probably expect me to talk with them about it." They would be referred, however, to another law firm for representation in obtaining the license and other legal accoutrements they would need to do business in Puerto Rico.[168]

Fortas sparked corporate clients' interest in Puerto Rico by including them in its economic affairs. When Teodoro Moscoso, as the administrator of the Operation Bootstrap industrialization program, spoke with Fortas about companies that might establish a chain of food stores on the island, the attorney was dismayed to find one of his firm's clients had been overlooked. "I told him that he had made a mistake in not including somebody from the best organization that I know: Kroger's," he subsequently wrote the head of the Kroger Company. "Moscoso then insisted that I communicate with you to solicit your views and to try to induce you to come to Puerto Rico to look over the situation."[169] Similarly, when Fortas decided that the island lacked sufficient financial institutions to supply capital for new projects, he contacted a financial officer at Lever Brothers, who agreed to discuss the situation with Moscoso.[170] A Commonwealth official expressed interest in talking with Stanley Marcus about the island's development as a fashion center, and Fortas was ready with an offer to make the opening telephone call: "Stanley Marcus is a friend and a client of mine, and I have talked with him many times about Puerto Rico."[171] When, "after trying for a good many years," Fortas succeeded in persuading Federated's Fred Lazarus to visit the island, he pulled out all the stops. "This is a visit to which I would ascribe a Triple 'A' rating," Fortas told the commonwealth's administrators. "If you have problems not only in retailing but also in distribution, finance, or any aspect of business which you would like to discuss with a really first rate businessman, I don't think you could find a better person."[172] The attorney even deferred a meeting with Muñoz so that he could accompany the Lazaruses on the first few days of their trip.[173] Fortas must have known that some of the excitement of the Puerto Rican adventure rubbed off on him. After observing the Puerto Rican government's veneration of their attorney, his clients undoubtedly prized him more than ever. But he was not just trying to promote himself; he genuinely wanted to help Puerto Rico.

In an effort to expose "the Puerto Rican people to the best culture that the world offers,"[174] Fortas convinced Muñoz that his government should subsidize culture along with industrialization. In 1957 the two men persuaded the renowned cellist Pablo Casals to hold the Casals festival previously held annually in Prades, France, on the island. Marta Casals Istomin recalled Fortas's emphasis on how much the festival could do for the people of Puerto Rico. When the cellist succumbed to the plea, Fortas made the legal arrangements.[175] After attending the first festival, Fortas told Muñoz that it was "a fulfillment—a kind of emotional representation of Puerto Rico, and of what you have done for Puerto Rico and its people; and for me, it is a symbolic representation of the wonderful opportunity that I have had to participate in the Puerto Rican unfolding."[176]

For Fortas, a happy by-product of the festival was the friendship which he developed with Casals, who began consulting him regularly on a variety of matters. "We trusted him," Marta Casals Istomin said.[177] No project was too small for Fortas where Casals and the festival were concerned. When the seam on Casals's cello broke at the last rehearsal before the 1958 festival opened, the maestro entrusted the instrument to Fortas, who flew it to New York, where an expert could repair it.[178] The attorney engineered the Casals concert at the White House in 1962, which came to symbolize the Kennedy administration's commitment to culture. The arrangements were so complex that Fortas swore to Isaac Stern he would not get involved in such an activity again even "if Jesus Christ were available for a Jew's Harp concert."[179] He negotiated the contract that authorized Columbia Records to record the Casals festival and persuaded the company to contribute five thousand dollars to it.[180] He arranged to have the Voice of America broadcast the festival performance in which Casals conducted Beethoven's Ninth Symphony.[181] Fortas also asked his friend Mortimer Caplin, the commissioner of the Internal Revenue Service, to expedite a decision that the festival constituted a charitable organization. He explained to Caplin that he felt free to contact him "because—and only because—this is solely a matter of public interest, in which I have no professional or pecuniary interest whatsoever."[182] For Fortas, any issue involving the island became a matter of public interest, and once he had reached that determination few boundaries mattered.

To his mind, his and his friends' creations—commonwealth status, the Bootstrap program, the Casals festival—enabled the island to retain and improve its political and cultural identity while simultaneously receiving American aid for social and economic reform. In fact, however, the American people never granted the island as much self-government as he had hoped. Fortas's attempt, pragmatic though it may have been, to seek both autonomy and improvement was politically and economically problematic. His definition of improvement was a mainland one, and when it required funding from mainland investors, autonomy was necessarily sacrificed. Yet in the 1950s and 1960s these pitfalls were not yet apparent. For its time, Fortas's vision of Puerto Rico was a brilliantly conceived experiment.

## COUNSEL FOR INSANE AND INDIGENT

Fortas's public-interest work was not confined to Puerto Rico and the loyalty cases. As counsel for the Animal Welfare Institute, he worked to obtain more humane slaughtering of animals by requiring butchers to anesthetize them or render them instantly unconscious before killing them. The *Washington Post* credited him with having played a major role in the enactment of the Humane Slaughter Bill.[183]

Even closer to his heart was the interest in psychiatry he expressed as vice-president of the Washington School of Psychiatry and as a member of the board of trustees of the William Alanson White Foundation. Fortas liked to point out the similarities between psychiatrists and lawyers. Both groups focused on troubled individuals, and both "must always be concerned about the recollection of past events that is induced by a desire for vindication or success, or by anxiety or fear." Indeed Fortas compared the lawyer to a therapist as he helped clients through crises and considered his meetings with clients as the occasions for transference. In his mind the lawyer—like the psychiatrist—assumed his clients' burdens. [184]

When the District of Columbia Circuit Court of Appeals appointed him counsel for Monte Durham, Fortas had the opportunity to fuse psychiatry with law. After a few drinks on a summer night in 1951, Durham had broken into the home of Alger Hiss's brother, just three blocks away from Fortas's own house in Georgetown. When apprehended, Durham was carrying an inexpensive suit that was far too large for him. The case went to the district court, where the historical quirk that had placed Holtzoff on the bench instead of Fortas in 1945 meant that an unsympathetic judge heard the case. Durham, who had suffered from hallucinations before he committed the crime, had been a patient in Saint Elizabeths Mental Hospital on three occasions prior to the breaking and entry and had twice been adjudicated insane. He pleaded not guilty by reason of insanity. At the trial Dr. Joseph Gilbert, a psychiatrist, testified that he was medically insane. But was he legally insane? Under the M'Naghten Rule devised in 1843 by England's House of Lords, which determined insanity in most American trial courts, he was legally insane only if he did not know his act was wrong or if he did not understand its nature and consequences. Accordingly, the prosecution asked Gilbert if Durham had known his act was wrong. Convinced that a finding of medical insanity should constitute grounds for acquittal, most psychiatrists would have prevaricated. Gilbert at first equivocated, but when Holtzoff pressed him, the psychiatrist admitted that he was uncertain whether Durham was legally insane. Holtzoff then ruled that there was insufficient evidence to rebut the presumption of sanity and sentenced Durham to three to ten years of imprisonment. [185]

A simple legal ground provided the basis for appeal. The D.C. Circuit Court of Appeals had held in *Tatum* v. *United States* that the defense need only show "some evidence of mental disorder" to rebut the presumption of sanity and shift the burden to the prosecution, which had to prove sanity beyond a reasonable doubt. [186] Though it was unclear Durham knew his act was wrong, his attorney in the district court had presented evidence he suffered from a mental disorder. Indeed Durham had more mental problems than Tatum, the appellant in the earlier case. [187] But Holtzoff had refused to apply *Tatum*. Thus the attorney who argued Durham's case on appeal need only show that Durham's prior history, as revealed in the trial court, included evidence of mental disorder.

But the signs were remarkably clear that the circuit court of appeals wanted Durham's attorney to go further. Fortas only became the appellant's attorney after a tax attorney in another firm had presented a technical argument on Durham's behalf before a three-judge appellate court. In an unusual move, the judges ordered Fortas to reargue it. [188] Abe Krash, then a young associate whom Fortas asked to work with him on *Durham,* put it simply: "It was a setup. . . . The Court obviously was primed to change the law. Fortas was appointed with a view that he would give him a brief that would give them a basis for changing the law."[189] Krash worked on a draft for weeks before leaving it for his boss. Fortas responded that it was worthy of one of the abler lawyers at Arnold, Fortas & Porter's rival, Covington & Burling. But it was not good enough for Abe Fortas. "Take it back and put some poetry into it," he concluded. Krash stared at Fortas. Poetry in a brief? Gradually his colleague's message became clear. "What he was really saying was [that] . . . he wanted me to range further afield in terms of nonlegal materials. . . . We then wrote one of the pioneering psychiatric briefs."[190]

It relied on both law and social policy. The brief used *Tatum* to maintain that Durham's prior history gave sufficient evidence of mental disorder to rebut the presumption of sanity.[191] But Fortas and Krash also contended that *Durham* should be used to overturn the M'Naghten rule. Dr. Gilbert had indicated that Durham was medically insane but refused to say whether he was legally insane in the sense of being unable to understand his act was wrong. That Durham could be insane and still might know that he was doing wrong suggested that the M'Naghten rule should no longer determine legal insanity: "The M'Naghten test reflected the morality and psychology of early Victorian England."[192] A psychologist friend of Fortas's had hosted a gathering for him and a number of psychiatrists while he was preparing the case, and his brief cited extensive material he had obtained from them indicating that psychiatrists considered the M'Naghten rule obsolete.[193] It also urged that the court adopt a new insanity test that followed England's Royal Commission on Capital Punishment and the state of New Hampshire by focusing on the defendant's "competence to regulate conduct" instead of his ability to comprehend the wrongness of his act. Substitution of such a test for the M'Naghten rule would improve cooperation between the fields of law and psychiatry, "would eliminate an area of controversy which has tended to discredit the criminal law in the minds of many thoughtful people," and would bring the criminal system closer to realizing its twin goals of rehabilitating the offender and protecting society.[194]

Fortas was successful. The circuit court of appeals ruled that Holtzoff's failure to find that the evidence of Durham's mental disorder rebutted the presumption of sanity justified remanding the case for a new trial. That was "the technical holding of the case," Fortas explained. "It is extremely difficult for a lawyer to argue that it was wrongly decided on the basis of technical legal principles." But as he acknowledged: "Obviously, that is not why the case is of interest."[195] In a rare public tribute to a lawyer's skill, the circuit court of appeals also said in its decision that Fortas had "ably argued" the M'Naghten rule should be abandoned. He had shown that it was inadequate, obsolete, and unresponsive to "psychic realities and scientific knowledge."[196] In its stead, the court adopted a new insanity test somewhat similar to the New Hampshire rule. The accused could not be held criminally liable "if his unlawful act was the product of a mental disease or mental defect."[197] Reaction to the case was mixed. One local newspaper ran a series of editorials claiming that application of what became known as the "product test" would cause a flood of criminals to be turned loose on the streets of Washington.[198] Judges on the D.C. circuit who had not sat on the case criticized the result their brethren had reached.[199] Fortas himself maintained that *Durham* freed psychiatrists from "the necessity of choosing between conscience and justice" and improved the collaboration between law and psychiatry.[200] William O. Douglas wrote an article applauding the decision, and Fortas correctly predicted that scholars and other knowledgeable individuals also would praise it.[201] Winfred Overholser, a leading psychiatrist, expressed his profession's satisfaction when he wrote to Fortas, "You were largely responsible for the Court's decision. . . . We can say, to paraphrase Galileo, 'The law *do* move!'"[202] Nevertheless, the District of Columbia found the product test difficult to apply and rejected it in 1972.[203]

Fortas again forced law to reflect social policy when the Supreme Court appointed him to represent Clarence Gideon in 1962. Accused of breaking and entering a pool hall in Florida with the intent to commit a crime, a felony in that state, Gideon asked the court to provide him with counsel. The trial judge denied his request, forcing Gideon to defend himself. On appeal, the Florida Supreme Court affirmed that he had no right to counsel. From prison, Gideon submitted on his own behalf an *in forma pauperis* petition for certiorari to the United States Supreme Court claiming that the denial of counsel constituted a denial of due process. Under existing law that was untrue. In the 1942 case of *Betts* v. *Brady,* the Supreme Court had rejected the argument that the due process clause of the Fourteenth Amendment guarantees the right to counsel in a state criminal trial for a noncapital offense.[204] The Court held in *Betts* that an indigent tried for a noncapital offense in a state court was entitled to free counsel only if there were "special circumstances," such as illiteracy or insanity, which would make him unable to obtain a fair trial without a lawyer. State courts were to determine the existence of special circumstances on a case-by-case basis. Gideon apparently was not aware of *Betts,* for he alleged no special circumstances. Nor could he know that Chief Justice Earl Warren had instructed his clerks to find a case that would permit the court to decide whether the long-criticized *Betts* v. *Brady* should be overruled.[205]

Fortas's interest in criminal law dated back at least to *Durham*. Since then, he had served as a member of the Advisory Committee on Criminal Rules, a special committee appointed by Warren to advise the Court on criminal rules, where he had distinguished himself as a vocal advocate of the rights of the accused.[206] Fortas believed it was a lawyer's duty to represent any indigent client the Court assigned him, but he was particularly happy to do so now. (Years later he objected to a film script about *Gideon* which portrayed him as "a rich lawyer who frequents posh restaurants and clubs." Though Fortas understood that the juxtaposition of the poor convict with the affluent lawyer made for a better story, he was still annoyed. "I gently suggest that your characterization fails to take into account . . . my own very deep feelings, which had been reflected in speeches, etc., on the constitutional and moral issues involved in the question of the right to counsel. If you feel that your dramatic purposes require that you portray my participation as that of a cool, cold professional, I won't complain; but it simply isn't true.")[207]

The Court's direction that counsel for both sides discuss whether *Betts* v. *Brady* should be "reconsidered" made Fortas's task easier.[208] It was clear that he was to address the issue of the accused's right to counsel. Civil liberties and civil rights lawyers before the Warren Court were not always so lucky. In another criminal procedure case before the Court, the accused's lawyer wrote a narrow, legalistic brief stressing the technical point on which reversal should be based. The Court went beyond the argument to the broad issue to reverse. "They very coyly hid it all from me," recounted the aggrieved, albeit victorious, attorney. "They didn't treat me like they did Abe Fortas, and say, 'Here's the question we want you to present.' Now, that would have been nice if they'd done that."[209]

Sometimes civil rights and civil liberties lawyers sacrificed their client for the policy issues. The attorney mentioned above said he "owed no loyalty" to his client and "corresponded with him as infrequently as I could get away with." He conceded that he "might not be the ideal lawyer for the defendant whose primary interest was in getting out of jail."[210] There was little doubt that the issue in the Gideon case interested Fortas more than his client. When his cousin asked Fortas if he had ever wanted to meet Gideon, Fortas replied: "Why the hell would I want to meet a son of a bitch like that? He's no good."[211] Nevertheless, Fortas believed that foremost he was representing Gideon, not the cause of right to counsel. Consequently the attorney sent for the transcript of Gideon's trial to determine whether the lower court had overlooked special circumstances that would justify the appointment of counsel. "If Gideon was 'incompetent,' it was my duty so as to advise the Court and to argue that his conviction should be overturned on the special circumstances doctrine—without the necessity of reconsidering the basic holding in *Betts*," Fortas said. "It would have been my duty to do this even though it would have made the case meaningless; even though it would have been frustrating to the Supreme Court, as well as annoying; and even though it would have meant that I was handling a more or less routine criminal case."[212] Fortunately, nothing in the trial transcript justified making a narrow argument that special circumstances existed. Gideon had done a good job of representing himself and had been treated gently by the judge. Another lawyer might have concluded at this point that a broad policy argument was justified. The meticulous Fortas asked Gideon for an autobiography, to make doubly certain no special circumstances existed. "On the basis of Gideon's reply to my letter, as well as the transcript, I was completely at ease in my mind and conscience that I could firmly state to the Court that there was no basis whatever for applying the special circumstances rule."[213]

Now Fortas could maintain that *Betts* v. *Brady* should be overruled because the due process clause of the Fourteenth Amendment required the appointment of counsel for a defendant in every criminal case involving a serious offense. His brief maintained that "the aid of counsel is indispensable to a fair hearing." Fortas quoted an old adage he would have done well to remember later: "'He that is his own lawyer has a fool for a client.' . . . Even a trained, experienced criminal lawyer cannot—and will not, if he is sensible—undertake his own defense."[214] Fortas cleverly seized the offensive. Thirty-seven states already had passed laws providing for the appointment of counsel in all felony cases, and twenty-two states joined in filing an amicus curiae brief asking the Supreme Court to overrule *Betts*. Abe Krash said, "I know of no parallel for this extraordinary action—a request by nearly half the states that the Supreme Court impose a constitutional requirement upon the states in the field of criminal justice."[215] Fortas still worried that some on the Court might protest that the federal government's assertion of the right to counsel in criminal trials represented an intolerable incursion on states' rights. He came to see, however, that he could argue that repeal of the special circumstances rule would actually place the states in a more favorable position vis-à-vis the federal system.[216] The holding in *Betts* "impairs the values of federalism," his brief claimed. Further, the case had caused "conflict between the federal and state courts because of the case by case review it entails and because it does not prescribe a clear-cut standard which the state courts can follow."[217] Fortas said on another occasion, "How corrosive it is for federal-state relations to have a federal court tell . . . [a state court] judge later that he did not do an adequate job."[218] When Justice Harlan claimed that "the fundamental principles of our constitutional system" were at stake on the day of oral argument, Fortas was ready with a variant of this argument, which emphasized that he had "the highest regard and concern" for federalism and that the result he advocated would advance its goals.[219]

"Probably no lawyer could have lost that case," Justice Potter Stewart said.[220] It is true that it was widely known that the justices hoped to overrule *Betts,* but Fortas made their work easier. "The Court just lapped it up," one observer recalled. "He did a brilliant, careful, polished job."[221] William O. Douglas considered Fortas's presentation "the best single legal argument" he heard in all his years on the Court.[222] Fortas's tact as an advocate impressed the journalist Anthony Lewis. The attorney could have claimed that Gideon deserved counsel because the Fourteenth Amendment incorporated the right to a fair trial guaranteed by the Sixth Amendment and made it applicable to the states. In reply to a question by Potter Stewart, during the last few minutes of Fortas's allotted time, the attorney announced that he was not making this argument. Hugo Black, who maintained that the Fourteenth Amendment incorporated the entire original Bill of Rights, asked for Fortas's reasons. Lewis recorded the interchange: "'Mr. Justice Black,'" Fortas replied, 'I like that argument that you have made so eloquently. But I cannot as an advocate make that argument because this Court has rejected it so many times. I hope you never cease making it.' Justice Black joined in the general laughter."[223] In a decision announced in the spring of 1963 the Court unanimously overruled *Betts* and held that the Fourteenth Amendment retroactively established the right to counsel in all state felony cases.[224]

Fortas's role in *Gideon* did not distract him from his corporate practice. He and Abe Krash worked simultaneously on *Gideon* and a Lever Brothers case until oral argument, and on the day Fortas went to the Supreme Court to argue *Gideon,* Krash appeared on behalf of Lever Brothers in the federal court for the Southern District of New York.[225] Fortas's representation of Gideon and Durham enhanced his reputation as a lawyer by increasing his already substantial professional prestige. The Court's request that he represent Gideon had been somewhat "like a Presidential invitation to dine. Few are turned down."[226] Two years later, Anthony Lewis wrote a popular book on the case with Fortas's cooperation. *Gideon's Trumpet* became the source for a movie of the same name in which a client of Fortas's from red scare days, José Ferrer, starred. Corporate lawyers in the early 1960s improved their image by doing pro bono work, and the publicity engendered by *Gideon* probably helped Fortas's firm. The public-interest work most important to Fortas—the less-publicized loyalty cases and his representation of Puerto Rico—went relatively unnoticed.

# CHAPTER 9

# The Actor

I HAVE NEVER MET ANYONE WHO WAS BRIGHTER THAN ABE FORTAS," Nicholas Katzenbach said in 1983. "I used to think if I ever got into serious, serious trouble, I would want Abe to represent me."[1] All those who knew Fortas professionally would have agreed he was among the most talented lawyers of his generation. Neither they nor any of his friends, however, ever claimed to understand him.

Even his choice of law partners seemed puzzling. Arnold, Fortas, and Porter shared a love of humor. Beyond that, they could not have been more different. One colleague compared Porter to a teddy bear, Arnold to a moose.[2] Fortas was more like a cat. By all accounts, Paul Porter was one of the greatest raconteurs of his time. His humor was infectious. When his listeners heard him chuckling before he began a favorite story, they would begin laughing too, no matter how many times they had heard the tale.[3] He could make anything funny. In 1944, while Porter was chairman of the Democratic National Committee, the Republicans scheduled a radio campaign speech by Thomas Dewey to begin immediately after a speech by the President. Porter countered by cutting Roosevelt's speech by five minutes and substituting an interim of somber organ music before the start of Dewey's talk.[4] His political experience put him on intimate terms with members of Congress. He gave the firm "a different dimension in terms of being comfortable in knowing political figures," one colleague explained. "He was a good outside man."[5]

Arnold and Fortas, however, constituted the core of the firm. "As partners should be, Howe and Hummel were opposites," Richard Rovere said of two turn-of-the-century "raffish" criminal lawyers to whom Fortas and Arnold delighted in comparing themselves.[6] Arnold was big, absent-minded, rumpled, loud, cynically humorous, spontaneous, expansive, and very human; Fortas slight, attentive, neat, quiet, witty, self-controlled, precise, and aloof. When Theodor Muller redesigned the firm's office in the 1950s, he asked Arnold for his ideas, only to be told that when clients hired Arnold to write a brief he did not ask them how they thought it should be done. Fortas, however, "would always want to see what you were doing," and Muller spent hours arguing with him about appropriate lighting fixtures.[7] Louis Pollak and Nicholas Katzenbach took a seminar on antitrust issues at Yale Law School in the late 1940s in which Arnold taught the first half of the course, Fortas the second. "I'd almost never seen such a sharp personality contrast," Pollak recalled. Arnold had been running a "gossip session about the New Deal," and "suddenly there was Fortas . . . slight, tense, dynamic, immense sense of energy [which] could scarcely be concealed. . . . The whole thing began to have an intellectual bite." Arnold was "bombast and funny," Katzenbach confirmed; Fortas more rigorous and so soft-spoken it was sometimes difficult to hear him.[8]

When Arnold had done his homework, he seemed as formidable as Fortas, and doubtless Fortas was drawn to Arnold's authentic genius, which enabled him to see connections invisible to anyone else. When William Rogers joined the firm, he was assigned to help Arnold with the Lattimore case as it worked its way through the courts. Arnold drove Lattimore and his wife "a little nutty," Rogers remembered. "I think in all the times he argued the case . . . he never quite got Manchuria and Mongolia straightened out, and they were a little impatient about that." Rogers too was nonplussed until Fortas called him in and explained, "Thurman is a genius, and you've got to let him be a genius in his own way and not tug on his sleeve and constantly try to keep him within the strict bounds of the truth and accuracy." For Rogers, that good advice reflected Fortas's respect for Arnold and his sense that "Thurman's idiosyncrasies were part of a great mind."[9] Another associate who worked with both men remembered that when Arnold noticed an issue he previously had overlooked, he never felt guilty because he did not see how he could have caught it, whereas an omission Fortas spotted was always something he should have considered.[10]

Yet odd as the threesome seemed superficially, their partnership made sense. Arnold was the lovable elder statesman, Fortas the craftsman, and Porter the backslapper. Neither Arnold nor Porter was a businessman. "To him, the law was kind of a social thing," one member of the firm said of Porter. "A client would get on the phone and ask him a question and the first thing you know, he'd be telling Paul a joke, and Paul would be telling him a joke, and in the meantime Paul would be . . . giving the store away."[11] Thurman Arnold, Jr., recalled that his father "was not a money-maker. He didn't even know how to charge a fee."[12] In contrast, Fortas always emphasized that people should be reminded that their questions took time and trouble to answer. Arnold and Porter needed him, and that suited Fortas. Asked why someone who worried as much about leaving government and making a go of it in private practice as Fortas did had not joined an established law firm, an old friend answered: "Abe always liked to run his own show." And what better way to do it, he continued, than with Arnold and Porter as partners?[13] Neither wanted nor knew how to exert control. Fortas's nearly congenital incapability of resisting cries for help, whether real or imagined, led another friend to believe he tried to play God to other people.[14] "He could make me feel so uncomfortable," a third person recalled, but Fortas still got out of bed in the middle of the night to rush to her aid when she became ill.[15] He performed herculean tasks for those he liked. Carol Agger said that Fortas was "very, very fond of Thurman" and wanted to smooth his and Porter's way.[16] What better partners for him than two men who aroused his protective instinct, of whom he was so fond, and who were so well known themselves? For Arnold and Porter were better known than Fortas. In the early years, they were responsible for the firm's image. New associates had invariably heard more about Arnold and Porter than Fortas. The firm was "legendary" at Yale in the 1950s because it was both successful and "deeply involved in major political issues of the day."[17]

The firm of Arnold, Fortas & Porter was considerably younger and smaller than most institutions of comparable prestige. With a total of nine lawyers in 1950, it was barely a sixth the size of the other prominent Washington firm, Covington & Burling, and was much smaller than the average Wall Street firms.[18] As late as 1960, there were only eighteen attorneys at the firm. In 1961 it doubled in size through a merger with the firm which employed Carol Agger. She had continued to work with Paul, Weiss, Rifkind, Wharton & Garrison throughout the 1950s, and that firm did the tax work of Arnold, Fortas & Porter's clients. When Randolph Paul died, Agger led her tax attorneys over to her husband's law firm.

Arnold, Fortas & Porter seemed superficially very different from the average conservative Wall Street firm. Outsiders saw it as a warm and convivial place, with weekly luncheons to which all associates and partners were invited and nightly cocktail hours in the firm's Garden Room, where Arnold and Porter held forth.[19] At first, the firm occupied quarters in office buildings, but it soon moved to a big old house where Theodore Roosevelt was said to have lived when he was Assistant Secretary of the Navy. ("We have never attempted to check it through any records," Arnold once said, "because if it isn't true we don't want to find out about it."[20]) Practicing law from a house instead of an office gave the firm an air of informality that more conservative firms lacked. The firm was also less bureaucratic than the Wall Street "law factories." Until the advent of Agger's tax group, Arnold, Fortas & Porter had no departments. To be sure, it possessed the three tiers of "finders, minders and grinders."[21] As entrepreneurs who attracted business, Arnold, Fortas, and Porter were "finders" and treated each other in a special fashion. At the next level were "minders," the managers who handled much of the business. Fortas believed in what he called the "lateral pass." He convinced the client he could not function without Abe Fortas, and then he persuaded him he could not live without G. Duane Vieth, Norman Diamond, or someone else who became the client's caretaker.[22] At the lowest level were "grinders," young associates who did the library work. Yet those tiers were not rigidly defined, and despite their existence, the firm seemed more democratic than most. Everyone in the office called everyone else by first name. Unlike many of its Wall Street counterparts, the firm listed associates as well as partners in the *Martindale-Hubbell Law Directory*. Nor did it differentiate between associates and partners on its letterhead.

Appearances, however, contrasted with reality. Fortas controlled the firm. Because he originated the most business, he might have assumed the leadership role anyway. But his administrative experience in the Department of Interior and the nonmanagerial temperaments of Arnold and Porter made it particularly appropriate for him. "I think that Arnold and Porter both made very great contributions to the firm," one colleague said. "But the kind of success that they were really looking for was in large measure due to Abe, and I think he felt a terrible responsibility, not only for them, but for those of us who were younger. That was why he was . . . a driven man and constantly working to develop the firm."[23] Every time another lawyer fathered a baby, Fortas and Arnold would joke about the new mouth to feed, but Fortas seemed to take such events seriously, to feel that the entire responsibility for the firm's future rested upon his shoulders. He had always seemed older than his contemporaries, but the firm made him older still. Although loyalty prompted him to reject the repeated offers of Arnold and Porter that his percentage of the profits should exceed theirs,[24] those offers in themselves acknowledged what every individual in the office agreed—it was Fortas's firm from the start. "He ran the place," one lawyer remembered. "It was Abe Fortas, and Abe Fortas alone. . . . He was managing partner, and he was senior partner, he was everything."[25]

When Paul Cravath had developed the prototypical Wall Street law firm, in which advancement was based on merit, he had made it a dictatorship.[26] Arnold, Fortas & Porter was a dictatorship too, and Fortas possessed even more power than most managing partners. Associates who joined the firm during his tenure all remembered that they could not be hired until Fortas had seen them, however briefly. He also decided who would become partner. Everyone recalled the one occasion on which a partnership was extended to someone against Fortas's wishes as the rare exception that proved the rule. Most frequently at the firm's partnership meetings, which began in the mid-1950s, "we would do what Abe wanted us to. That is what it amounted to." Everything passed through his hands. Fortas allegedly once reprimanded a junior partner who had ordered new bookshelves for not having consulted him first.[27]

Originally, nonfounding partners received short shrift. Until 1951 only Arnold, Fortas, and Porter were labeled *partners* in *Martindale-Hubbel*. Everyone else, including Walton Hamilton, who had held a chair at Yale Law School, was listed as an associate and received no share of the profits. In 1951 the firm began listing Hamilton and a few other veterans from the early days as partners, but, for some time after, associates who were promoted were partners in name only, for they were still paid a salary. In the mid-1950s the younger partners banded together at the end of one year and demanded to receive a percentage of the firm's earnings. "Abe didn't like that," one individual remarked. "He said we ruined his Christmas." The protesters now began to receive a small portion of the firm's earnings, but those who became partners after that incident continued to receive a salary. "I was one of the first guys elected after that, but I was not given a share," one lawyer remembered. "None of my generation were. . . . I didn't get a share in this firm until Fortas left. Immediately, then, I was given a share. . . . We were called 'the non-percentage partners.'" It "rankled."[28]

Fortas's relationship with associates was even more hierarchical. "In Russia in the 1920s, you used first names, but it wasn't democratic," one observed. "Every law firm has a taskmaster who's a son of a bitch," another said, and he thought Fortas took on this role. He "would gather all the young lawyers and hold little training sessions in which he'd read the riot act to us about being careful," a third recalled. "He'd lecture to us on how we had to do our work."[29] Fortas was more of a grinder than most senior partners, and he worked closely with the associates. He frequently rewrote their briefs. "In fact, it was always a question of whether he'd rewrite them 100 percent or 50 percent or 5 percent. . . . He was quite capable of scrapping everything."[30] When Fortas asked Abe Krash to work with him on *Gideon,* he told Krash to learn everything about the right to counsel "from the invention of money onward." Krash's first draft was just the beginning. "I'd give him a draft, and he'd give it back to me," Krash said. "The process was one of endless changing . . . even down to the proofs." During the process of preparation Fortas would listen to the associates' ideas. "You had to be goddamn sure . . . you had a point," Krash stressed, for Fortas did not tolerate fools lightly. But one of his skills was to absorb the arguments of the younger men and to weave together the points he liked.[31]

Once he had reached a final decision, he did not believe he owed subordinates an explanation. On one occasion, the firm was representing a publisher who wanted to file an amicus brief in an obscenity case. Fortas, Charles Reich, Abe Krash, and another lawyer drafted the brief. With Fortas's approval, they decided to include in it five photographs from the publisher's magazine, three of which had been ruled obscene. By challenging the Supreme Court to guess which pictures had been declared obscene and which had not, they hoped to reveal the arbitrariness of the obscenity standard. It was "good lawyering to do this," Reich explained, "because you couldn't tell what was obscene and what was not. . . . We talked about it so much." Reich filed forty copies of the brief at the Supreme Court on a Friday afternoon and went to New York for the weekend. On returning to work on Monday, he learned Fortas had sent another lawyer to retrieve the briefs, and had torn out the five pictures and refiled the briefs. Reich felt "undercut." The brief, he thought, had been "mutilated. Yet Abe would not say a word about it, didn't offer a word," and Reich did not feel he could ask.[32]

In many respects, Fortas was a great teacher. "It would be a rare week today," Krash said recently, "that I wouldn't sometime in my mind think of . . . how Fortas [would] say something or think."[33] All of the associates trained by Fortas were quick to concede how much they had learned from him. Some, however, thought Fortas exceeded the bounds of proper authority. The Cravath model was a benevolent dictatorship, and Fortas was rarely benevolent. Some managing partners had a twinkle in their eyes, but he did not. One associate who left Washington to see his family for the Christmas holiday was almost immediately summoned back by Fortas. His experience was not uncommon; those "who were associates with him in those days . . . all have their stories . . . about how he would interfere with their vacations."[34] As at the *Yale Law Journal,* Fortas seemed to disapprove of relaxation. Unlike Wall Street firms, where an associate's supervising partner had to approve his assignment to others, Arnold, Fortas & Porter thought an associate was fair game for any partner. Any lawyer could ask any associate if he had time for a job. "Who's to say what's very busy?" one attorney asked. "You knew if you said no that was a rebuff. . . . You didn't dare say no to Abe." His request was "a command," another confirmed.[35]

None of his associates who came to Arnold, Fortas & Porter was lazy or stupid. The firm placed even more emphasis on meritocracy than Jerome Frank had during the New Deal. Associates generally had attended prestigious law schools. Most had been law journal editors, and many had also clerked for important judges. They came to Washington expecting to work hard. Yet long hours devoted to law had left them unprepared for Fortas's ability to make them uncomfortable. Fortas lacked an inner compunction to treat people with civility. There was a "physicality of menace" about him as he sat isolated behind an enormous desk made from an antique piano, a former associate explained.

"When he criticized you it was a blow to your gut. . . . I didn't throw up, but I felt like it." It was said that one lawyer became severely nauseated whenever he left Fortas's office. "He was a very, very tough taskmaster," another remembered. "If the work wasn't good . . . you were told in no uncertain terms, very cold-ly. . . . It was very uncomfortable and very anxiety-provoking." A lawyer whom Fortas interviewed for a job was disconcerted when, while she was reading a sample of her work aloud to him at his suggestion, he paused, put his fingers in his ears, and stuck out his tongue at her. Fortas often deliberately threw subordi-nates off guard in an effort to learn whether they could maintain self-control. Indeed Fortas set such a store by self-control that he once reportedly rejected a lawyer he initially had decided to hire simply because he had learned that the individual was an epileptic who might suffer an uncontrollable seizure.[36]

Each young attorney had his or her own Abe Fortas, and experiences with him varied considerably. He would take one associate out to lunch with important clients on his second day at the firm and entertain another at his home, while a third would be kept away from all clients and would be treated like a Western Union messenger whenever he delivered a document to Fortas's house.[37] But even those young lawyers who liked him most agreed that he could easily humili-ate them. Though everyone admired him, he was not popular at the firm. "There were associates who worked with him who thoroughly didn't like him, there's no question about that," said one of his staunchest supporters.[38] Jerome Frank, William O. Douglas, and Thurman Arnold had advanced his career and had been involved in every aspect of his life, but, oddly, Fortas rarely played the mentor himself. "I think he took some pleasure in the fact that I was developing and that I was one of his bright young guys," one of his lawyers observed. "But you never had the sense that he was genuinely interested. . . . He didn't really know me or what I was concerned with except as a young employee, and I didn't know him." For instance, the individual continued, Fortas might have thought to invite his former colleague to the Supreme Court to see his chambers. "I was a young guy and here he was a Supreme Court justice, and it would have been just thrilling to me. . . . He never did."[39]

What had happened to Abe Fortas? As a young investigator for the SEC, Fortas had despised corporate attorneys who shamed associates. Degrading re-marks had forced him into the Navy, but he apparently forgot afterward how that sort of humiliation felt. Even if he had remembered, Fortas might have contend-ed that the firm required an iron hand. Arnold and Porter created an esprit de corps. Arnold, as one lawyer said, was "marvelously warm," the sort of person who would tell everyone that a document an associate had written for him was the best piece produced in the firm in the past five years. "Next week [Arnold would praise] something else," the underling recalled, but "you would go home and tell your wife because you would walk on air. You would glow . . . because he made you feel so good. He had a wonderful ability to encourage you and inspire you."[40] Porter too could inspire, with his oft-quoted dictum "When in doubt, do the right thing" or with the Kentucky rule he invoked, which provided that lawyers could cuss the court for twenty-four hours after an adverse decision.[41] As long as Arnold and Porter encouraged associates so frequently, Fortas might have reasoned, he did not need to do so and perhaps should be that much harder on them. "He felt that someone in a law firm had to be the mean guy, the tough guy, the heavy," a colleague recalled.[42]

Some still found him enigmatic. When Charles Reich wrote his memoirs, he named a character based on Abe Fortas "Mr. Henderson." "Mr. Henderson was a great liberal, a public-spirited lawyer, a man who had been a dedicated government official and now still helped in many progressive causes," Reich said. "He was a pragmatist, but also a man of taste and sophistication. He could not be written off as an organization man, a dull man, or a conformist. Why, then, the harsh cynicism, the toughness, the oppressive self-control, the approach to everything by strategy, the need for power over people?" Yet Reich thought that buried in Henderson lay something "that was in some way like me. . . . I am talking about the person who could not really want the unutterable isolation of having all other people at a distance. Very simply, I imagined that we were people who could have been friends."[43] Although the passage expressed "the other side" of Reich's feelings about his boss,[44] Fortas never permitted a friendship. "I'd be sitting there with a person scowling, angry," Reich remembered. "Then the phone would ring, and he'd be urbane and gracious with a client." As soon as he hung up, Fortas would begin glowering again. Only once during his five years with Fortas did Reich observe a different part of him. Fortas received a call from a client and was put on hold. "In that minute he said to me, 'This is my life, Charlie. This is my life.' " His tone was "weary and pensive. I never saw that person again."[45] That was not the real Abe Fortas. There was no single Abe Fortas. There were a variety of personae, and Fortas moved comfortably from one to another. With his clients, for instance, Fortas was suave, sophisticated, witty, sometimes so effusive he seemed like a courtier—and they adored him. He went out of his way to put them at ease. "You always felt as though you were in your carpet slippers," Patrick Macrory said of his conversations with Fortas. "Just say anything that comes into your mind." Yet Macrory knew from those at the firm that his lawyer "could be almost cruel." Despite his great affection for Fortas, whom he considered "one of the best men I have ever met," Macrory thought "there was something a little mysterious" about him."[46] Fortas built his firm around his knowledge of Washington and enjoyed showing off his understanding of the capital. When an elevator in the Export-Import Bank stalled, and those inside thought they were trapped, Fortas restarted the machine. "When his fellow passengers expressed their astonishment," the story goes, "Fortas replied with the mock innocence he occasionally affected, 'It's really quite simple, for an insider.' "[47] And yet even in his own firm he remained an outsider.

Fortas believed he needed to earn large sums of money, but no one was certain how much money mattered to him. It clearly mattered to his wife, and by the late 1950s she and Fortas possessed all the accoutrements of success—houses in Georgetown and in Westport, a stately Rolls-Royce Fortas had given to Agger as a present, a devoted housekeeper and other servants. "He'd fight like a tiger to get a client who would pay $5000, and then he wouldn't care much about the money," a colleague recalled.[48] Another agreed that while Fortas regarded the large fees he commanded as an index of his success as a lawyer and "liked being able to please Carol and being able to buy her all those jewels," he did not value money much.[49] He bought cheap suits for himself.[50] He and Carol Agger lived "in some fair style," Macrory remembered, "and yet although they plainly enjoyed the good life in a way, it always seemed to me that Abe really preferred the simple things." When Macrory brought him to London on business, he would offer Fortas a suite at the Savoy, but Fortas preferred to stay at Macrory's unpretentious home in the Surrey countryside.[51]

Others recalled that he loved Christmas and enjoyed elaborately wrapping up little gifts of no value—pliers, for instance—and giving them to friends.[52] He and Carol Agger held an annual Easter egg–dyeing party where they awarded prizes for "the most ridiculous egg," "the egg most likely to succeed," and "the most political egg." Prizes were returned so that they could be recycled.[53] As austere as he sometimes seemed to his associates, Fortas retained the playfulness that had characterized him as a young New Dealer. His jokes were strained, but Fortas never stopped trying to match the humorousness of Arnold and Porter. Tired of the constant flow of *in forma pauperis* petitions he received from prisoners after *Gideon,* he once wrote a mock reply that said he was leaving town indefinitely, "perhaps forever." He added, "There is no particular reason for this except I am damned tired of receiving and answering letters like yours." After having "reviewed the list of attorneys available to practice in the Supreme Court and not yet disbarred . . . I can and do recommend that you retain the services of Clark M. Clifford, certainly one of the nation's foremost experts on the Presidency—its cause and cure." He sent a copy of his letter and the prisoner's papers to Clifford.[54]

He particularly enjoyed bantering with musicians. Asked to persuade his friend Isaac Stern to speak at the Woman's National Democratic Club on what he would do for the field of music if he were President, he wrote the violinist: "Since I propose to run you for the presidency in 1968 . . . it seems to me that an announcement of your program would be strategically sound. I also think that five to ten minutes is about the right length of time since I want you to put your best foot forward." Stern was not to worry about "the rivals" the club was producing to speak on the same topic, who included "Cornelia Otis Skinner, some Russian named Balanchine, and a few other characters who will give us no serious trouble. In fact, I think it is well to have a backdrop of mediocrity against which your sparkling wit, matchless eloquence and irresistible logic can be projected to maximum advantage."[55] Fortas was at his most likeable with musicians. Carol Agger and her brother, a musicologist, had persuaded him to begin playing the violin again after the war, and he numbered Isaac Stern, Alexander Schneider, and Walter Trampler among his closest friends. "I remember seeing this urbane . . . gentleman have an entirely unurbane and unabashed enthusiasm for music," Stern recalled. "It was such a passionate and wholly unambiguous, unashamed love affair with music." Schneider thought that music meant more to Fortas than law. "His music making was as necessary an emotional and intellectual exercise as anything he ever did," Stern observed. Fortas formed what he called the "3025 N Street Strictly No Refund String Quartet," which performed on Sunday nights. Those evenings were "sacrosanct." He was a solid amateur. "He had wonderful rhythm," Stern said. "He never got lost. He was always there. . . . He knew the totality of the music he was performing, of the instruments that were playing, he knew where it was going. He knew the work."[56] Although he had an excellent command of the literature, Fortas was the first to admit that his sense of pitch was imperfect. He could have remedied it had he practiced more, but he never had enough time for his music. "I have a tin ear," he used to say when his playing was off.[57]

Generally Fortas's passion for success appeared in all he did. Helen Muller remembered playing ping-pong with him. "I was a better player than he was, but he beat me because he cared so much." Her husband recalled that during Fortas's first skiing trip, he broke two pairs of skis. "It's hard to break a ski," but Fortas was determined that the "damn thing was going to work. . . . He had to win."[58] But where music was concerned, Fortas tolerated imperfections in himself. Isaac Stern, who knew him as both lawyer and musician, said, "I've seen Abe operate in discussions of contracts . . . where without raising his voice and without changing his demeanor he would simply go absolutely cold and dissect the opposing counsel with a scalpel that would leave the man cowering in a corner." In the field of law, he added, Fortas was "authoritative, and in music he was always looking for the other authority."[59] The local professionals who played with him on Sundays for years were conscious of his strong streak of sentimentality. "The real pleasure was to see him light up and enjoy the music," one remembered. It was clear "his heart was opening up."[60] Stern thought that "when he would

smile, especially about music, or talking about music, or [while] listening or
playing, it was just sort of as [if] the sun was coming up."[61] When they performed
quartets, Fortas played the second violin, but in quintets he was able to play the
viola, which he found easier. His favorite piece was a slow movement from
Mozart in which he played the viola solo part. If he thought his group had
executed it well, there would be tears in his eyes.[62] Marta Casals Istomin
thought that music "was like a religion with him."[63]

More so than Judaism. Like many Jews of his generation, after the war he
continued to hate the Germans. "We had German clients that he would have
nothing to do with," recalled a colleague. "He was passionate about that." Jewish
lawyers in the firm believed he was harder on them than he was on their Gentile
counterparts because he identified with them and thought Jews had to do better
to be accepted. "I was the poor Jewish guy struggling to gain, and I think . . . he
had a kind of sense of good will or feeling about that," one remembered. "He
wanted to help me." Fortas even told him to wear longer socks. Once, letting
down his customary guard, Fortas bitterly complained that "he had suffered by
virtue of his Jewish background, suffered disadvantages and discrimination."[64]
Yet, at midlife, his religion held little appeal for him, though the culture of
Judaism sometimes engaged him. When his old friend Tex Goldschmidt sent him
a paper he had written for the United Nations referring to Jews as "cultural
outsiders," Fortas replied that Goldschmidt had "spent too much time with the
Arabs. . . . Sometimes Jews are cultural-insiders, sometimes they're cultural-
outsiders—and frequently they're cultural inside-outers. To put this proposition
in abstract terms which will be readily understandable to you: circumcision is
not always equivalent to circumspection."[65] Writing to one of the most culturally
Jewish people he knew, he might sign the letter "Yours in Christ." "He loved to
play like that," Carol Agger said.[66] Occasionally he would use a Yiddish phrase
"as an inside joke," one of the Jewish lawyers at Arnold, Fortas & Porter noted.
Martin Riger vividly remembered the one occasion on which Fortas used Yiddish
with him. Fortas said an individual who had pontificated too long at a Federated
Stores board meeting did not "'have much saychal,' and I said [to myself]: 'Gee
whiz, that was Yiddish.'"[67] Agger suggested that although Israel deeply interested Fortas, Judaism did not. Another friend thought that Fortas wanted to
be "perfectly honest about being Jewish" but that "it was very important to him
not to *feel* very Jewish at all."[68] He remained acutely conscious of his religion,
regardless of how ambivalent he felt about it.

In contrast, his feeling about children was clear. He became more interested
in his Memphis family once his siblings had children and then grandchildren.[69]
On meeting his great-nephew for the first time, Fortas brought out a bag of
marbles and got down on the floor and shot marbles with him.[70] Friends noted

that he would drop anything, no matter how important, to play with a child.[71] He spent hours reading teenagers' term papers and advising them about their futures. "Abe was always fond of children," Macrory recalled, "and children took to him, because he treated them as equals and never talked down to them. My own small sons looked forward to his visits, and not only because of the generous and imaginative presents he brought with him. One wonders what life would have been like if Abe had had children of his own."[72] As his wife said, Fortas adored women and babies.[73]

Friends knew, however, that Carol Agger had made it clear to Fortas at the time of their marriage that she wanted no children.[74] But though he was to have no babies of his own, he was not denied women. Perhaps it was his playfulness which drew them to him. Invariably male friends, partners, and business associates, some of whom found him cold and withdrawn, stressed his attractiveness to women. "He was one of the most charming men with women that ever lived," said one.[75] "He charmed women beyond belief," remembered another. "And we men were perhaps jealous, certainly envious, and never could understand why."[76] Although he "came from the same kind of background that I did—lower middle-class Jewish people," a third remarked, Fortas so enjoyed playing the "southern gentleman" with women that one began "looking for the plantation behind him."[77] One New Deal associate thought Fortas was more at ease with women than men.[78] It had long been clear women liked Fortas. One acquaintance recalled that groups of women surrounded him at parties even in the 1930s, before he had the added attraction of power.[79] As he grew older, the charm increased. Inevitably he was compared to his friend Adlai Stevenson. Lady Bird Johnson's press secretary, Liz Carpenter, fondly remembered the Fortas of the 1960s with "his cute little impish way, affection, kisses—nice juicy kisses— making you feel like you have all the wit and appeal in the world." To her, he seemed a more stately version of Stevenson. The two men, she said, shared a "gentleness," a "sophisticated sexiness," and a "twinkle in the eye."[80] In describing Fortas as elfin, Lady Bird Johnson also likened him to Stevenson. They differed in that "Abe had his hands, to my thinking, more on the world. He reached for the stars, but his head wasn't in the clouds." She saw in Fortas, however, what most women perceived in Stevenson: "the humor, the light touch, the exuberance."[81]

Fortas and Carol Agger were great friends and remained intensely loyal to each other, though even their lawyering styles differed. "Carol was totally down the channel of taxes and that's what one would talk to her about," recalled Lady Bird Johnson, who was a client of both. "[With] Abe, you just sort of ranged the whole world of philosophic relationships and everything. And yet they meshed wonderfully."[82] Friends thought theirs was a marriage of minds rather than one of passion. They had separate bedrooms, and Fortas had one serious affair in the late 1940s and a later, longer one. But even when he was involved in a serious relationship, he still pursued other women. He did not regard anyone, not even his wife's friends, as off limits.[83] One close friend was sure that if Carol Agger had ever told him to stop chasing women he would have done so.[84] Agger told another friend that she knew she had been the most important person in his life,[85] and it was clear to everyone that she was the only person to whom he really deferred. But she tolerated his behavior.[86] As long as Fortas could preserve the marriage he prized, he did not reproach himself for his extramarital activities. Indeed he sometimes bragged about them.[87] Such behavior might have seemed conventional to him. It was an era in which Washington valued conquest more than chastity, as a story Fortas told about Lyndon Johnson illustrated. The President could be most easily angered, he said, by mention of his predecessor's womanizing. Johnson would pound on the table and claim that he "had had more women by accident than Kennedy had on purpose."[88] Further, Fortas genuinely liked women. He found most of the women with whom he was involved interesting as people, but a relationship with one did not preclude others. The rest of his life was equally compartmentalized. There were many sides to Abe Fortas, and if no one else understood how he could live with all of them, he seemed to do so easily. His relationship with another actor, Lyndon Johnson, would change his life.

PART III

*On and Off the Bench*

# CHAPTER 10

# The Adviser, 1

A PHOTOGRAPH OF ABE FORTAS AND LYNDON JOHNSON TAKEN IN THE White House illuminates the perspectives of each on their relationship. A broadly smiling Johnson bends over his slightly built adviser. Fortas, grinning unusually widely himself, leans backward, away from the President. Fortas believed he looked "as if I am in mortal fear of being run over by a railroad train," whereas the President thought the attorney's pose connoted stubbornness. Indeed Johnson inscribed the photograph: "For Abe, who's resisting me with all the horsepower God gave him."[1] Although the President thought he saw resistance, Fortas rarely opposed Lyndon Johnson.

## "THE QUIET SORT OF APPROACH"

Even if Tex Goldschmidt had not introduced Congressman Lyndon Johnson to Abe Fortas, the two men undoubtedly would have met soon after Johnson's arrival in Washington in 1937.[2] For Johnson made it his business to seek out New Deal lawyers who could aid him in delivering cheap electric power to his constituents, while New Dealers such as Fortas always wanted to know members of Congress who might prove useful. Though the meeting was predictable, it was not immediately clear the friendship would prove important. At the time, Lady Bird Johnson said, it was Carol Agger, rather than her husband, who seemed special: she was a lawyer, an athlete, and "very liberal, very outspoken before practically all women were outspoken."[3] The Johnsons considered Fortas, Agger, and their friends "the workhorses of the New Deal," and soon they had become

part of a group which included Goldschmidt and his wife, Elizabeth Wickenden;
William O. Douglas; James and Elizabeth Rowe; Benjamin Cohen; and Thomas
Corcoran. "Evenings would always include dinner, but dinner was really the last
of our interests," Lady Bird Johnson recalled. "Talking was the interest: laying
out plans and shooting holes in them, and deciding whether so-and-so could be
done, and how it could be done. . . . Almost anything was possible."[4]

Among their more difficult challenges was making Johnson senator in 1948.
"It is unnecessary to emphasize the deep interest of your Washington friends in
your campaign," Paul Porter told Johnson. Every member of Arnold, Fortas &
Porter pledged a financial contribution to Johnson's battle against Coke Stevenson, a conservative former governor of Texas, for the Democratic nomination.
Further, Fortas planned to contact a wealthy friend in New York who frequently
raised funds in "campaigns where Liberals are involved."[5] Fortas and his partners helped even more with the legal side of the campaign. Both sides stole votes
in the primary, but Johnson stole enough to win. The charge of vote-stealing
made his "victory" by an eighty-seven-vote margin vulnerable. At 6:25 A.M. on
September 15, 1948, the morning after Johnson had been declared the Democratic candidate, Stevenson's attorney awakened federal district court judge T.
Whitfield Davidson and obtained a temporary restraining order forbidding the
Democratic Party from placing Johnson's name on the ballot as the Democratic
nominee. At a hearing a week later, Davidson announced that he suspected
fraud. He appointed two special masters to investigate charges that machine boss
George Parr had delivered illegitimate votes to Johnson. If they found that Parr
had indeed stolen the election, Davidson would invalidate the primary results.
Stevenson would surely become the Democratic nominee and, given the Democrats' primacy in Texas at the time, would be elected senator. In the meantime,
Davidson converted the restraining order into a temporary injunction that would
prevent the secretary of state from placing Johnson's name on the November ballot. Later Paul Porter claimed "it was perfectly obvious" why Stevenson had
asked a federal judge to interfere in a state primary. Davidson was a personal and
political ally.[6] Fortas agreed: "There really was no question about the merits of
the case. The injunction was improvidently entered; that is, the federal judge
enjoining the state election under these circumstances was just plain wrong.[7]
Though the law was on Johnson's side, since an unbiased judge would certainly
find that a federal court had no jurisdiction over a state primary, two factors made
his future bleak. One was time. Under state law, Johnson had less than a week to
prove he belonged in the race.[8] He had further jeopardized his position by summoning every important lawyer he knew to advise him. Arguments over appropriate strategy forestalled action.

Fortas was in Dallas working on an antitrust case when Johnson's mentor,

Alvin Wirtz, suggested consulting him. Fortas immediately traveled to a meeting of Johnson forces at a Forth Worth hotel, where he confronted "acres of lawyers" who "seemed to be having a great deal of controversy as to the next step."[9] There were "more lawyers than you could shake a stick at," Lady Bird Johnson confirmed. "Just lots of big name lawyers. And Lyndon was the only person in the room who wasn't excited. . . . In a time of extreme necessity, he would become very quiet." When Fortas spoke, his voice hardly rose above a whisper. "He certainly had no loud sense of command, he didn't stride in," Lady Bird Johnson emphasized. "It was the quiet sort of approach, and people finally found their heads turning toward him."[10] Fortas assumed leadership as he had done years earlier when internecine warfare between two prima donnas, Francis Whitehair and James Fly, threatened to paralyze the AAA's development of strategy in the grapefruit case, and he described his role in much the same terms. "I was an outsider and a youngster," he noted. In Texas, Wirtz was "in charge and with his usual kindness and graciousness, he deferred to me and let me take the lead, making sure to keep me on the straight and narrow path."[11]

Fortas turned the attorneys' attention away from politics and toward procedure. The problem as he defined it was not one of substantive law, since Johnson would surely win on appeal. It was only a question of determining where they could obtain a stay of Davidson's order pending an appeal, so that Johnson's name could be printed on the ballot. Although the Court of Appeals for the Fifth Circuit seemed the logical place, the three judges on that court who together would hear the appeal would not sit until the middle of October, and in that circuit, one judge acting alone could not grant a stay.[12] Success seemed more likely in the United States Supreme Court, but it was in recess. Still, since each Supreme Court justice also functioned as senior circuit justice for one of the circuits, there was the possibility that Hugo Black, as the senior justice for the fifth circuit, might consent to hear the case himself if Johnson's attorneys could convince him that the lack of time before the election demanded this extraordinary action. Fortas, an expert in Supreme Court procedure, believed that Black would not agree to do so unless Johnson's lawyers had first made an effort to obtain a hearing at the appellate level. "The important critical move in that litigation" he claimed later, "was the strategic decision to present this in a summary way to the Court of Appeals and then to go to the senior Circuit justice."[13] He so persuaded the lawyers in Fort Worth. Fortas drafted a petition one of them could present to the fifth circuit, and the appeal was docketed for a hearing on October 7. Predictably, the circuit court refused a stay in the interim. The case was now ready to be presented to Justice Black.

By the time Fortas returned to the capital, what Paul Porter described as "the greatest collegium of legal talent that Washington could supply" had convened.[14]

Porter, Thurman Arnold, Francis Biddle, Jim Rowe, Tom Corcoran, and Joe Rauh were among the former New Dealers already working on the brief for Black. Unlike their Texas counterparts, these Washington lawyers immediately deferred to Fortas. "Tommy was the leading personage and Abe was the leading lawyer," Rauh remembered.[15] Black agreed to hear the case, and Fortas presented it on September 29. The justice granted a stay prohibiting enforcement of the temporary injunction. A week later the fifth circuit set aside the injunction altogether. Joe Rauh, who accurately described the stay as "most unusual," always thought Corcoran had spoken privately with Black before the hearing.[16] Certainly, as a former senator with a New Deal past and populist tendencies, Black might have sympathized with Johnson. In his autobiography, William O. Douglas hypothesized that Black might have decided that, with vote fraud apparent on both sides of the campaign, he would help the better candidate.[17] Fortas tactfully suggested that his old friend's speculation about Black's personal feelings missed the main point. "Shouldn't you note—if you agree—that Hugo's decision was clearly right on the law—that the Federal District Judge had no legal right to enjoin the Texas Secretary of State on the law as it then was?[18] On another occasion, Fortas put it more strongly: "It made no difference who Lyndon Johnson was. The law is the law."[19] Yet if Lyndon Johnson had not possessed a devoted friend who was an expert at maneuvering cases into the most advantageous forum, the case would not have been heard in time and "justice" would not have triumphed. Johnson knew that Fortas's cleverness had saved him. "I wouldn't be in the running now except for you," he telegraphed Fortas two days after Black's ruling.[20] From the time Fortas guaranteed his Senate seat, Johnson regarded him as the best lawyer he had ever known.

## "ABE'S BOY"

Around this time, Johnson began routinely consulting Fortas and Clark Clifford on troublesome questions. If they disagreed, the two lawyers would argue the issue out in front of him. "Sometimes it kind of tickled him because each of us would rise to his forensic maximum in attempting to get his point over," Clifford recalled. By the time they finished the discussion, "Johnson said . . . he would feel that he had the matter about as thoroughly covered as if he had spent weeks on it."[21] With the exception of Clifford, who had begun his political career as an adviser to Harry Truman, Johnson's lawyer-advisers in the late 1940s and 1950s all had been New Dealers. Some of them worried that his responsiveness to Texas conservatives was preventing him from showing his true beliefs. "Decent disinterested Northerners" should not be blamed for distrusting him, Jim Rowe scolded. "It is the fault of Lyndon Johnson because he has consistently refused over the years to expose himself to these people so they can see what Johnson is like. These people are not as smart as Bill Douglas, Abe Fortas, Tommy Corcoran, Jim Rowe, Felix Frankfurter, Dean Acheson, Clark Clifford and other so-called 'liberals' but they are almost as smart!" Those aforementioned Washington lawyers and Supreme Court justices "are all Johnson men for only *one* reason. Johnson has exposed himself, his character, his ability, his intelligence, and— not the least—his charm to these people. If he can 'take' this tough crowd he can take the rest." Rowe was forever urging Johnson "to find a couple [of] bones to throw the liberals."[22]

But Fortas neither urged nor scolded. From the time he secured the Senate seat for Johnson, Fortas wholeheartedly supported him. Therein lay one of the secrets of his longevity as an adviser. He played, at least superficially, the role of Johnson's yes man. Fortas believed in Johnson's vision of himself as an embattled liberal who had to seem conservative. Rowe told Johnson why liberals disapproved of him;[23] Fortas reminded Johnson why they should applaud him. In the 1950s Fortas was always there with words of praise and encouragement. "You did a superb—and unparalleled—job during the last session of Congress," he complimented Johnson in 1956.[24] When the Civil Rights Bill of 1957 was introduced, it provided for trial by federal judge if violators were held in civil or criminal contempt. White Southerners were outraged. This provision would deprive them of a jury trial by peers who were likely to look favorably upon their offenses. As Senate majority leader, Johnson could not muster enough votes to enact the bill until he accepted an amendment guaranteeing the right to jury trial in cases involving criminal contempt. Liberals excoriated Johnson for diluting the bill, but Fortas maintained that the compromise of trial by jury in criminal contempt cases and trial by federal judge in civil contempt cases struck "an admirable balance between the competing values" of the historic right to trial by jury and effective enforcement of the statute. "You have made another magnificent contribution to the nation in your extraordinary management of the civil rights bill."[25] At the end of the year, he praised Johnson again: "It is so gratifying to me to encounter unanimous admiration for what you have done and are doing."[26] Although such letters seemed smarmy, there was more to them than that. Fortas recognized that Johnson "wanted to be accepted and *revered,* as he thought F.D.R. was."[27] Ever the skilled manipulator, Fortas apparently considered flattery and seeming reverence the best way to encourage Johnson to take a liberal stand. Since Fortas was also aware that Johnson "*was,* indeed, 'insecure,'" his letters also sounded a protective, proud and paternal note.[28] Indeed one mutual friend referred to Johnson as "Abe's boy."[29]

Fortas and Johnson seemed an odd couple. One was a larger-than-life Texas politician with a crude sense of humor; the other, an elegant, elfin lawyer whose love was chamber music. Johnson often seemed uncomfortable in the world of ideas, where Fortas felt very much at home. "We had to go through hell's fire . . . to try to get Johnson to conceptualize some of these wonderful things he stood for," Fortas recalled.[30] Fortas was controlled; Johnson, emotional. Once Johnson berated William O. Douglas. "'Liberty and justice,' he said, 'that's all you apparently think of. And when you pass over the last hill, I suppose you will be shouting 'Liberty and justice!' " When Douglas showed Fortas his account of the incident, Fortas wanted him to mute it. "This is a terrible reflection on L.B.J.," he observed. "I don't question that it happened; but certainly, he made a *major* contribution to liberty and justice, in various areas. Would you want to moderate the devastating impression that the incident will make on readers who will not take into account L.B.J.'s emotionalism?"[31] Johnson's emotions were real; Fortas tried to manage emotional reality.

Closer examination yielded similarities. Both were masters at manipulation. Both insisted upon secrecy and distrusted the media. Both coupled self-interest with the public interest. Having come to power during the New Deal, both continued to view themselves as liberals even when contemporaries charged they had abandoned reform. As unusual measures had saved the country from the Depression, both justified irregular actions that furthered noble ends. Something in their backgrounds had led both men to deviousness and dissembling.

Although both thought they were integral forces in Washington, each also considered himself an outsider. Fortas spoke frequently of Johnson's sense of exclusion from "the Charles River crowd," the Harvard emigrés who had settled in Georgetown.[32] Though Fortas himself felt at home with that group, he never felt entirely comfortable with social doyennes such as Cissy Patterson and Evalyn Walsh McLean, who ruled Washington before the influx from Cambridge. "You either belong or you don't," Thurman Arnold's wife said of Washington society in the 1940s and 1950s. She and her husband did; Fortas and his wife did not.[33] "I think it mattered to Lyndon that he came from the South," Lady Bird Johnson said of Fortas. She was sure that her husband would have liked Fortas regardless of his origin, but she thought a southern upbringing, which "stamps your character," gave them a special bond.[34] Each was also influenced by Washington political culture. Both Johnson and Fortas had spent most of their adult lives in Washington. As a Johnson aide, Harry McPherson, pointed out, Johnson was "a provincial, a very deep provincial, and this is one of his big problems." Skeptics dismissed Johnson as a Texas hick, but, on the contrary, he had lived in the nation's capital so long he assumed that "this orbit here is the dynamo on which the whole country runs."[35] Fortas, who lived in Washington even longer than Johnson did, was equally provincial.

The similarities in their backgrounds gave them a shared world view, but

Fortas's loyalty and intelligence attracted Johnson most. Fortas could summarize the positions of Johnson's advisers, write a speech, or draft a letter, and he did all of these willingly. "There was always a sense of comfort about Abe," Lady Bird Johnson recalled. "You were always glad of his presence. One, he had great competence, and it was reassuring. . . . And then he was also. . . kind and warm."[36] For his part, Fortas had always liked individuals who got things done, and he appreciated Johnson as a man of action. He also respected buccaneers, and the senator was a buccaneer. Further, Johnson possessed great power, which fascinated Fortas, and he used it brilliantly in Congress, where the attorney was deficient. Yet Johnson also needed Fortas, who loved to play mentor to his friends, if not to the associates at his firm. His relationship with Johnson enhanced his reputation as a lawyer and made him more effective at championing causes he had espoused since the New Deal. "I knew he had very good purposes," Carol Agger said in explaining Johnson's appeal, "and I think Abe was probably the same way."[37]

Johnson relied on New Deal and Fair Deal lawyers for advice more than did most contemporary politicians, but he called upon other lawyers for different reasons. Clark Clifford hypothesized that Johnson so frequently paired him with Fortas because the senator expected "greater objectivity" of Clifford. "He knew people pretty well," Clifford said of Johnson. "He very likely would turn to Abe but at the same time would have a tendency to be cautious because Abe might be so supportive. If Lyndon Johnson wanted something, Abe usually was all for it. . . . I might not be supportive at all."[38] According to Harry McPherson, Clifford was "a balance-wheel"; he was "the outside man" who provided the perspective of the business community, while Fortas was "the inside counsellor, the late-at night counsellor, the fellow who could help."[39]

In the 1940s and 1950s, Johnson also counted on Jim Rowe and Tom Corcoran. Whereas he viewed Fortas chiefly as a lawyer and Clifford as both lawyer and political strategist, he relied on Rowe and Corcoran primarily for their political acumen. Corcoran had "a marvelous sense of timing, which is probably the highest art of politics," Johnson's aide George Reedy recalled, while Rowe understood the political process.[40] Both devoted their efforts to positioning Johnson to the best advantage. As senator, Johnson paid a price for his dependence on them. Rowe apparently never requested anything for himself, but his law partner, Corcoran, asked for a great deal. During the late 1950s stories circulated in Washington that Corcoran was "seeking to create an illusion of behind-the-scenes power" by asserting he could forestall congressional hearings. He referred to his Texas speechwriting trip for Johnson, mentioned that his children had gone skiing with one of Johnson's daughters, and otherwise seemed to capitalize on his relationship with the senator.[41] When Corcoran came into disrepute for influence peddling in 1960, it was clear that Johnson would be tarnished as well.[42] Some believed that Fortas and other Washington lawyers were also exploiting their relationship with the senator. George Reedy maintained that Corcoran, Fortas, and Clifford all used their relationship with Johnson to help their clients but that only Corcoran was candid about doing so. "If Tommy was going to steal a hot stove, he'd tell you about it, and then when he went back for the ashes, he would also tell you he was going back for the ashes," Reedy explained. "Whereas Fortas, if he were going to steal a hot stove . . . would give you quite a story about how he was recovering an ancient relic from the infidel and restoring it to its rightful place." (He added that Clifford would tell a similar tale, but he would recount it so convincingly that when he finished, "you'd go and help him take it.")[43]

Joe Rauh, at that time a public-interest lawyer, was equally skeptical of Fortas. In 1949 Johnson successfully fought the reappointment of former New Dealer Leland Olds as chairman of the Federal Power Commission. Most liberals regarded Olds as public power's most dedicated champion.[44] To Lyndon Johnson, he seemed less attractive. Indeed the senator charged that Olds had "pursued a meandering but relentless course toward nationalization of the nation's fundamental power interests." Instead of possessing the judicial temperament that the position demanded, Olds was "a prejudiced crusader." Johnson made his charges even more potent by alleging that Olds, who had leaned toward the left in the 1920s, had once echoed "the party line."[45] It was rhetoric guaranteed to succeed in the Russophobic and anti–New Deal atmosphere of 1949, and it left many wondering how to explain Johnson's apparent apostasy over the cause of public power. To Fortas's chagrin, Rauh later told Merle Miller that he thought "the key" to understanding Johnson's position on Olds was "Abe Fortas. You have to know who Abe represented when he got Lyndon to fight Olds to really know the answer."[46] No evidence ever surfaced to support Rauh's charge, and Johnson's chief of staff at the time, Walter Jenkins, maintained it was false. According to Jenkins, the senator fought Olds because independent oil men in Texas did not like him.[47] Other sources reported that when they learned of Olds's defeat, "over 800 oilmen in attendance [at one meeting] voiced unanimous approval with loud whoopees and deafening applause."[48] If Fortas had joined the fight—and Jenkins, who emphasized that Johnson consulted Fortas "on anything that was controversial," was certain he did—Fortas's stance may not have derived from deference to oil and gas interests.[49] Fortas had distrusted Olds since the latter successfully had opposed the transfer of all public power matters to the Department of the Interior when Fortas was director of the Division of Power. He never had considered Olds a great advocate of public power.

Fortas did sometimes ask Johnson for help in the 1950s. "He has not talked to you because he says he has a rule that he does not talk to you about matters for which he is getting fees," Jim Rowe wrote Johnson while Fortas, as counsel for the Animal Welfare Institute, was steering the Humane Slaughter Bill through Congress.[50] That tenet meant little if Fortas circumvented it, as he did in this instance, by talking with one of Johnson's staff members. Although the government of Puerto Rico was a paying client, he frequently asked Jenkins for Johnson's aid in the Senate on Puerto Rican affairs. "You know how sorry I am to bother you; but this is a matter that I think is important to the nation and is very dear to my heart," Fortas said in one such plea.[51] Jenkins, who maintained that Fortas's interest in the island was a special case which did not derive from "the client-lawyer relationship," did not remember any requests from Fortas on behalf of other clients. In fact Senate diaries suggest Fortas spoke only infrequently with Johnson. "He was not like some of the others who called all the time on insignificant things," Jenkins observed. "The calls went the other way. Mr. Johnson would call him."[52]

Nor did Fortas seek to publicize his relationship with Johnson. Confidentiality was his watchword. Even when he served Johnson as adviser rather than lawyer, he continued to act as if the attorney-client privilege covered their communications. He enjoyed letting his clients and intimates know how indispensable Johnson found him, but he revealed nothing specific. He proved his allegiance anew in 1960.

## THE VICE-PRESIDENCY

Like other Democrats in the late 1950s, Fortas hoped that the Eisenhower presidency would represent a short interregnum of Republican leadership. "Carol and I really remain sort of fixed points in this changing scene," he said in a 1957 letter about New Dealers who had left Washington. "However, I expect that in 1960 a general call will be issued for all characters who were in Washington in 1933. That will really be something."[53] Fortas regarded the poor showing of the Republicans in the congressional elections the following year as cause for celebration but remained cautious. He was not yet certain the Democrats could regain the presidency: "The difficulty is that the level of [D]emocratic talent is sufficiently high so that it is extremely difficult for a single candidate to emerge"[54]—at least a candidate of whom he approved. Fortas had little enthusiasm for John Kennedy. "I am not persuaded that he would make a good enough president," he said in 1958.[55] "I do not endorse Jack Kennedy for the nomination," he told Stuart Symington. "I think he will have a difficult time against Nixon—but more than that, I am concerned about him as President for substantive reasons."[56] He probably saw Kennedy as a relatively inexperienced member of Congress who lacked the union card of New Deal employment. Although Kennedy was only seven years younger than he, Fortas identified with the generation of the candidate's father, with whom he had worked at the SEC. Indeed Fortas's correspondence reflected bemusement as to how "the young man" could have emerged as a front runner for the candidacy.[57] Nor could he have appreciated Kennedy's tolerance of McCarthyism and his criticism of Owen Lattimore's postwar attitude toward China. He was not alone. Even after the Americans for Democratic Action (ADA) came to favor Kennedy, some of its members still expressed doubts about the sincerity of his liberalism.[58]

A greater number of liberals, however, doubted Johnson was "a real liberal." According to the ADA, Johnson's voting record in Congress since 1940 placed him to the right of other Democratic presidential candidates.[59] Yet, as a Johnson intimate, Fortas was certain that the senator's apparent conservatism masked a genuine commitment to reform. His support of Johnson had "startled" his "liberal friends," Fortas acknowledged later, but Fortas told them that if they knew the man as he did, "people would be falling all over themselves to get behind him."[60] It was an uphill battle. "Lyndon Johnson has greatly gained in stature and acceptance, even among the liberal groups," Fortas claimed in 1958, "but it is still much too early to make any judgment as to feasible possibilities."[61]

Johnson seemed to share Fortas's doubts about his viability as a candidate. Indeed he dawdled about revealing his presidential aspirations for so long that his advisers began deserting him. Hubert Humphrey's staff members approached Jim Rowe in the spring of 1958 and invited him to join their campaign. Rowe, who believed a Johnson presidency would bind the North and the South together, replied that he would support Humphrey if he decided that Johnson would not run, and at the beginning of 1959 he made that determination.[62] "I think you are making a mistake not only for yourself but for your country," he informed Johnson. "But I will *not* press you again."[63] Clark Clifford had already taken charge of the candidacy of his fellow Missourian Stuart Symington. Corcoran's troubles at the time made him a political liability to avoid.[64]

Fortas remained in Johnson's camp until the end, even though he was pessimistic about the senator's chances. He asked Adolf Berle to endorse Johnson, for instance, but confided that he did not think his friend would win the nomination.[65] Nevertheless, in May 1960 Fortas signed an advertisement urging Johnson to run. Anxious not to alienate powerful friends, he carefully explained to Stuart Symington—who had been an ally in the Senate and whose son Fortas had brought into his law firm—that he had done so to encourage Johnson to become more involved in the race. "If he should, by whatever means, indicate that he has lost heart, prior to the Convention, I believe it might well cinch the nomination for Kennedy," Fortas said. "I want to see you or Lyndon get the nomination." He did not believe that "Lyndon has a chance," and he suspected Johnson might later support Symington. "In any event, it is imperative that he stay in the race." Fortas's name might not help Johnson, "but that doesn't matter. The important thing to me is that you know what I have done and why. Beyond this, I must rely upon your own realization of my deep affection, admiration and devotion."[66]

Once again, Fortas's political judgment was off. When Kennedy received the nomination at the Democratic convention in Los Angeles, the attorney was gloomy. "Looking back, the result was inevitable," he commented to William O. Douglas. "The plain fact of the matter is that Lyndon was unable to bring himself to do what was necessary months ago, when it might have been possible." To Fortas, "the Hell of it" was "that we must go on from where we are, and not from where we might have been. I think that the wreckage at this moment is fantastic and perhaps beyond repair."[67] Characteristically, however, Fortas assured Johnson that his acceptance of the vice-presidential nomination was "a noble act."[68] Thinking ahead to a possible Democratic loss at the top of the ticket, Fortas now took charge of litigation that would permit Johnson to run simultaneously for the vice-presidency and the Senate.

At the same time, Fortas was involved in protecting Johnson's reputation. The best indication that Johnson had known beforehand that George Parr would steal the votes he needed to have in the close Senate race in Texas in 1948, that he appreciated Parr's activities on his behalf, and that he wanted to keep Parr's name clean because he knew it was linked to his own lay in Abe Fortas's willingness to act as George Parr's attorney now that Lyndon Johnson was becoming a national figure. The Court of Appeals for the Fifth Circuit had affirmed the conviction of Parr for mail fraud in 1959, Fortas reported to Johnson, after "our offer to be of assistance without reference to fee was not utilized."[69] Parr reconsidered at the next level and Fortas won Parr's case in the Supreme Court, taking care to keep Johnson informed of all important steps along the way.[70] Fortas continued to help his friend's associates after Kennedy won and Johnson became Vice-President. Fred Korth ran afoul of the Kennedy administration soon after his appointment as secretary of the Navy. A former bank president, Korth had used Navy Department stationery to promote his bank, had entertained former associates and potential bank clients on the Defense Department's yacht, and was suspected of having intervened to ensure that the multi-billion-dollar TFX fighter-plane contract be awarded to General Dynamics, a client of his bank. Since Korth had long been Johnson's Fort Worth political manager, and Johnson had obtained his government position for him, his activities reflected badly on the Vice-President.[71] When Korth asked Johnson's office what he should do, he was advised to consult Fortas.[72] Once again Fortas helped Johnson's colleague, and once again Fortas passed along the relevant information to the Vice-President until, in this case, his client resigned. Although Fortas's disclosures to Johnson raise troubling questions about the attorney-client privilege, Lyndon Johnson could not have asked for a more dedicated lawyer-counselor.

Fortas, who deplored the powerlessness of vice-presidents, tried to make Johnson's position in the White House more tenable. "It would be a notable contribution to our Government if a pattern could be found within which Vice-Presidents can function," Fortas tartly observed to William O. Douglas. As for Johnson, he thought, "care should be taken that he is loaded with work—overloaded. This will serve his own peace of mind and it will also avoid the waste of his extraordinary talents."[73]

One assignment for Johnson resulted in new demands on the attorney's time. Soon after he entered the White House, President Kennedy asked Johnson to chair the President's Equal Employment Opportunity Commission (EEOC). In part to distract attention from his own failure to pursue vigorous civil rights legislation, Kennedy urged the committee to create a mechanism which would ensure that government contracts went only to those organizations that did not discriminate in hiring. "Johnson privately flinched," his friend William S. White recalled, because he wanted the program to work and feared that suspicion of him by blacks would jeopardize it.[74] More dispassionate observers traced Johnson's reluctance to his fear that this was a political firecracker that might explode his relationship with Southerners, were he too forceful, or his tenuous association with northern liberals, were he too weak.[75] Either eventuality might end whatever hopes he retained for the presidency in 1968. Yet when Kennedy insisted, the Vice-President had no choice but to accept. Richard Nixon had served as chair of the committee under Eisenhower, and had Johnson declined, he would have appeared softer on civil rights and more opportunistic than Nixon.

The Vice-President turned to Fortas. Johnson unofficially requested Fortas to improve upon the executive order by which Eisenhower had created the committee.[76] Kennedy's Special Assistant on Civil Rights, Harris Wofford, described the attorney as "a very key man," while Hobart Taylor, an EEOC member, considered Fortas "invaluable."[77] Fortas was committed to racial equality, and his experience as under secretary in the Interior Department had trained him to circumvent a conservative Congress by strengthening the executive branch. "We were able to find vast presidential powers for accomplishing the Committee's purposes, which were somewhat rusty because of disuse under the previous administration," he explained to Eleanor Roosevelt.[78] The executive order Fortas drafted shifted the burden of proof from minorities to businesses seeking government contracts. Blacks who believed businesses had discriminated against them would no longer be forced to lodge a complaint with federal agencies. Instead the order directed federal agencies to sign government contracts only with businesses which had pledged not to discriminate in hiring and authorized the committee to investigate those organizations it suspected of noncompliance. Violation of a pledge constituted a breach of contract and enabled the government to cancel its arrangement with the offending company. "The concept of the order was unique . . . because it moved responsibility from the individual to prove he had been discriminated against to the contractor to prove that he had not discriminated."[79]

Having written a strong order, guaranteed to win his friend praise from civil rights leaders, Fortas tried to insulate Johnson from responsibility for its enforcement. "I feel strongly on this point," he warned one of Johnson's staff members. "We should not involve the Vice President in the determination of individual cases, both as a matter of time and burden and for general strategic reasons."[80] The precise nature of these "strategic reasons" was not stated, but Fortas probably hoped to maintain Johnson's favorable position with Southerners by isolating him from a directive they would consider intrusive and divorcing him from controversy. Although the order granted broad powers to the committee and to Johnson as its chair, Fortas advised the committee to act as a board of directors and to limit itself "to matters of *general policy and general administrative policy surveillance.*" Johnson should "personally participate *only* in the 'educational' part of the work"—meeting with contractors and civic leaders, rebuking heads of government departments who were resisting the order, and praising individuals as appropriate. While Johnson would hold a ceremonial position, Fortas believed that the executive vice-chair of the committee should be responsible for directing the real work of the committee staff.[81] Indeed Fortas hoped to end Johnson's relationship with the committee altogether by the summer of 1961. As the committee had advanced from policy formulation to administration, the attorney thought a case could be made that the Vice-President had completed his job and should be permitted to resign as chair so that he would have time to undertake other assignments.[82]

But when Johnson continued on as chair, Fortas dropped talk of ceremony and strengthened the Vice-President's position. The attorney continued to advise the committee and in coordination with his client Fred Lazarus, whose appointment to the EEOC Fortas had recommended, ran interference for the Vice-President. Johnson early on concluded that a Kennedy devotee on the committee, Robert Troutman, wanted to usurp his power.[83] Fortas and Lazarus forced Troutman to resign as chair of a key subcommittee by denying him a separate staff, which might have allowed him to draw attention away from Johnson's work.[84] Eventually Robert Kennedy undermined Johnson's position on the committee by showing that he was an ineffective chair who was neither ensuring that contractors complied with the executive order nor increasing the number of jobs for Blacks. But during this period, as before, Fortas made Johnson's enemies his own and, for the most part, worked effectively against them.

### REPRISE FOR THE NEW DEAL

In a 1967 interview a prep school student asked Fortas whether Roosevelt's New Deal had confronted greater opposition than Kennedy's New Frontier. Perhaps because he was talking with a youngster, Fortas was unusually frank. Roosevelt had "definitely" faced greater resistance and had overcome it, he answered. "On the other hand, though, the Kennedy Administration toward the end was in a state of disrepair. Actually it was in shambles." (Fortas crossed out the last sentence of his answer when the transcript was sent to him for editing.) The student pressed on. Could Kennedy have persuaded Congress to enact Medicare or civil rights legislation? "Never," Fortas said. (This response he changed in the transcript to "I doubt it.") Fortas's replies reflected the dissatisfaction of Johnson and his advisers at the situation they inherited after Kennedy's assassination in Dallas.[86]

Fortas was working on a case involving one of Johnson's associates when Abe Krash called him to say Kennedy had been shot. The two men followed the news on television. When they learned that Kennedy had died, Krash predicted Fortas's life would greatly change.[87] Krash was right. Fortas was among the first people Johnson called upon for help. The attorney frequently met with a group of the new President's advisers, which convened "sort of day and night" after Johnson returned from Dallas.[88]

Fortas's primary concern was Johnson's first speech to Congress. As Fortas and other advisers sat around a table one night, one of Johnson's Texas friends warned the President against using his power to support Kennedy's program, which many believed would remain stalled in Congress. "I will never forget that, for perhaps thirty seconds—it seemed more like thirty minutes, the president didn't say anything," Fortas recalled. Finally, Johnson spoke. "'Well, what the hell is the presidency for?'" he asked. It was one of Fortas's favorite stories about the new President, for it showed Johnson's insistence upon a strong presidency committed to social justice. Fortas later admitted only to having added "some corn pone" to that first speech.[89] Working with Theodore Sorensen—who had composed an earlier draft—and Hubert Humphrey, he adapted the "ordered cadences" with which Sorensen had faithfully served Kennedy to the slower, more rolling gait of Johnson's Texas drawl, most frequently by inserting two words when one would do.[90] His contribution, however, went beyond developing the right language.

After ensuring that the speech, which in Sorensen's draft had focused almost exclusively on Kennedy, did not make Johnson sound too unworthy, Fortas turned to writing the section on the legislative program. As always, he worried about the reactions of Congress. Ironically, in view of the criticism he and Johnson would later receive for their consultations after Fortas had been appointed to the Supreme Court, among Fortas's contributions was a section in which the new President pledged to respect the constitutional doctrine of separation of powers. Fortas recommended that, because of his years of experience in Congress, Johnson should "go to unusual lengths" to emphasize the importance of congressional autonomy from the executive branch.[91] The pledge read: "As one who has long served in both Houses of the Congress, I deeply believe in the independence and integrity of the Legislative Branch. I promise you that I shall always respect this. It is deep in the marrow of my bones."[92]

Other portions of Fortas's draft that Johnson used emphasized the need for action, liberal programs, and unity. "I know we meet in grief; but let us also meet in renewed dedication and renewed vigor," Fortas wrote. "Let us meet in *action, in tolerance and vigor.*" Specifically, he vowed continuity for Kennedy's foreign policy and urged Congress to adopt Kennedy's civil rights bill and tax reduction plan. "I beseech you again, as I did in [1957] and again in 1960, to enact a civil rights law so that we can move forward to eliminate from this nation every trace of discrimination and oppression based upon race or color." Having reminded the nation of Johnson's longstanding dedication to civil rights, Fortas exploited the Kennedy mantle. "I ask that again, you demonstrate that the Congress of the United States can *act,* and act greatly. I ask that you do this by the enactment this *year* of the kind of Civil Rights Bill which President Kennedy recommended. There could be no more fitting memorial to him than enactment of the law."[93]

Though Roosevelt never had made civil rights a priority, the speech reflected the New Deal's emphasis on social reform. Some close to Johnson viewed Fortas as a vital link to that era. Before the President's first speech, an aide encouraged him to surround himself with friends such as Fortas who "might by their presence underscore the favorable factor of long experience in and around the Presidency. The 'New Deal' connotation would receive press attention, but at this moment, that would be more a plus than a minus."[94] Fortas himself also saw a relationship between the Johnson and Roosevelt agendas. He told one reporter that his friend's program shared with the New Deal a "concern for people" and a willingness to increase the role of government in order to help them.[95] Fortas also pointed to a "fundamental difference" between Roosevelt's New Deal and Johnson's Great Society, Johnson's "insistence on unity and consensus." During the New Deal "some segments of society had lagged so far behind that it was necessary to take measures for them alone," he explained. "The country's posture today is such that it can and should move as a whole to do the things that need to be done."[96]

Johnson's attitude toward the tax cut Kennedy had proposed dramatically illustrated the difference between the New Deal and the Great Society. When it confronted economic problems in 1937–38, the Roosevelt administration had divided into two camps. Some New Dealers had preached the appeasement of big business by cutting spending and avowing commitment to a balanced budget, while others had counseled Roosevelt to declare war on big business and engage in deficit spending designed to compensate for corporate unwillingness to invest in a Roosevelt-controlled economy.[97] The President had listened to the latter group, but neither he nor Congress countenanced enough spending to halt the Depression before World War II. In the end, his program only increased the antipathy between him and the business community by further unbalancing the budget. Nor did the government's relatively slight spending have a sufficient impact upon the economy to spur business to invest.[98]

In choosing to follow Kennedy, the first Keynesian President, in urging a tax cut, Johnson was trying to propitiate business. In a Keynesian world, the tax cut possessed the same validity as government spending, as it too represented an attempt to stimulate the economy by the creation of deficits. But as some observed, a reduction in taxes represented "reactionary Keynesianism."[99] Whereas a tax cut would aid the economy by encouraging private spending, deficit spending would have enabled the government to finance social welfare programs. Although Johnson professed to believe in such programs, he was wary of deficit spending. Fortas regretted that. Soon after the new President had delivered his first speech, Fortas sent Johnson a note citing the disproportionate number of blacks, women, and teenagers among the ranks of the unemployed.[100] He also urged Sorensen to write a speech for the President that would prepare the public and Congress "for a domestic program of considerable dimensions. We need this because of unemployment and many problems including youth, education, housing, women." It would prove essential if the tax cut did not stimulate the economy or if the business cycle brought economic problems, and it would promote national growth.[101] Fortas, then, sought to combine the advice of liberal and conservative Keynesians. His solution represented the logical conclusion of the consensus approach, for while the tax cut would aid the rich and the middle class, social welfare expenditures would help the poor.

Fortas appeared at other times to realize his own impracticality. A tax cut would affect the economy more quickly than government spending, and Congress certainly would refuse to increase spending for social welfare at the same time it cut taxes. Therefore Fortas more frequently contended that Congress would only approve the tax cut if the President simultaneously pledged frugality. Although some insisted that a tax cut would unbalance the budget, Fortas wrote in a draft of Johnson's first speech to Congress, "we need it as the cornerstone of a sound, progressive economic program." Yet a reduction in taxes should not diminish the government's commitment to social programs: "I do not believe that it is good economy to fail to provide our people with the facilities needed for their health, for the education of our children, for welfare, for the development of our national resources, or for our defense and the aid of those nations who are our loyal friends, who require assistance and put it to good use. But I firmly believe that these programs must be administered with *thrift and prudence.*"[102]

The "program for thrift and frugality" that Fortas developed for Johnson at the end of the first week of his presidency proposed that the President send a letter to each federal employee and defense contractor urging austerity, that he call a "publicized" cabinet meeting to emphasize his commitment to eliminating waste, and that he establish committees to study economizing in defense spending, government procurement, and government operations. Fortas also hoped the President would acknowledge that "there are unfulfilled needs for domestic programs." He predicted, however, that as long as the administration insisted upon tax reduction Congress would refuse to approve large appropriations. "We need a redirection of expenditures," Fortas reiterated. "Money saved by thrift, efficiency and economy is badly needed for urgent programs. We must find ways to do more with proportionately less money."[103] Johnson adopted the approach Fortas recommended, and the pairing of tax reduction with promises of economy in government allowed the tax cut to become reality.

The conciliatory approach toward business espoused by Fortas and Johnson seemed feasible in the 1960s. Economic upheaval and the hostility of business to the New Deal had led reformers such as Fortas to demand a strong hand for the government in the 1930s. But the early 1960s were relatively prosperous times, and Fortas apparently believed that Kennedy's antibusiness rhetoric had needlessly alienated entrepreneurs. The affluent society, along with the dependence on corporations some New Dealers such as Fortas had developed, pointed them toward a consensual approach to politics all interest groups could endorse. In particular, Fortas and Johnson hoped to convince business that only reform would preserve capitalism. There was nothing new in this. Roosevelt had unsuccessfully attempted to woo industrialists with the same song during the New Deal. But Fortas believed the White House should try again, and Johnson also thought the business community would respond.[104] "Our prosperity—our new plateau—must include all sectors of our society—not just some," Fortas wrote in a draft of the President's speech to a group of prominent businessmen. "Can't we really, and candidly, agree on this? And after all, isn't this common sense?" the attorney asked. "It would be a terrible mistake to seek to build a castle of luxury in a village of poverty.—It wouldn't work economically—it wouldn't work politically. One way or another, the castle would be destroyed."[105]

As Johnson's adviser, Fortas took pains to reach out to business. When Maurice Lazarus nominated someone for membership on the Federal Trade Commission, the attorney passed the recommendation along to the White House.[106] When Attorney General Nicholas Katzenbach requested names for an antitrust task force, Fortas solicited suggestions from Fred Lazarus.[107] When the chairman of the board of Federated's Boston store predicted that local businessmen would disapprove of the appointment of the economist Seymour Harris to the Federal Reserve Board, Fortas relayed the objection to a Johnson aide.[108] When Ralph Lazarus advised Fortas that failure to reappoint one National Labor Relations Board member would appear to confirm the "anti-management" bias the business community sensed in the NLRB,[109] the attorney drafted a letter to the President that Lazarus could send expressing that warning. Fortas passed along the recommendation of an airline executive that a man "not considered pro-union" should be reappointed to the National Mediation Board to balance the two board members who seemed to favor labor.[110] One of Fortas's law partners, Norman Diamond, had long represented the Kroger grocery company. Fortas asked Diamond to tell its chief executive "that I think the Food Commission is lining up all right and I should like to have his views."[111] Fortas thus began his tenure as a presidential adviser by building bridges between the White House and big business. As a corporate lawyer, he was well equipped to do so. "Don't you fellows have *any* Democrats for clients?" Johnson joked to Paul Porter.[112]

Some might view this effort as a conspiracy to further the aims of corporate capitalism. It was. But Fortas and the President wanted more from the business community in return than money for Johnson's 1964 campaign. They were trying to construct a system based on reciprocal favors that would harness the power of the state in favor of business and commit industrialists to supporting Lyndon Johnson and his social welfare programs. From the beginning, Fortas counseled the President to sponsor a liberal domestic program focusing on education, unemployment, urban redevelopment, health, and culture.[113] He strongly supported Johnson's War on Poverty, and the Office of Economic Opportunity's provision of legal services to the poor.[114] Fortas believed that the President's agenda required the aid of business. "Contributions from the Lazarus family [normally Republican supporters] are in hand," Fortas once teased the White House. "But I know that you are not interested."[115] More than monetary help was wanted. If Lyndon Johnson courted Fred Lazarus, for example, Fortas thought Lazarus would continue to be "a tower of strength in the Equal Opportunity Program."[116]

Few doubted the sincerity of Fortas's commitment to civil liberties and social justice. "On the great issues Abe Fortas is really just tremendous," Harry McPherson said. "The work of his life was in the social field," Lady Bird Johnson remembered. Asked what Fortas cared about most, Clark Clifford immediately answered: "The liberal cause. He was a deep-seated dyed-in-the-wool one-hundred-percent liberal. . . . He was a true-blue Roosevelt liberal." "He's really a *radical*, you know," one White House staff member said admiringly of Fortas. [117] Yet predictably Fortas sought to achieve his ends not by belaboring the Johnson administration's duty to the poor but by reassuring those who feared increased governmental involvement in social welfare. Remembering, as both he and Johnson did, the extent to which the New Deal had been condemned as "revolutionary," they tried even more explicitly than Roosevelt had done to remind the wealthy that reform carried its own reward.

## "GENERAL HANDY MAN"

Fortas liked to complain about how much time he was spending at the White House during the opening days of Johnson's Administration. "I have discovered that I am quite weary because of the tension of the last few weeks coupled with the effort to do my own work and also to act as general handy man to our friend," he told a client at the end of 1963. [118] He was indeed performing many odd jobs for the President.

Some were somber. Fortas originally joined Johnson in opposing the creation of a special presidential commission to investigate the circumstances of Kennedy's assassination. He tried to convince two supporters of the idea that it was untimely. "I am afraid they think they have a great idea though," the attorney reported. [119] Fortas explained to William O. Douglas that he had advised against a commission because people would assume that the government had a hidden motive in creating it and because the failure to follow normal procedures, such as an FBI investigation, would further shake the American people's confidence. Circumstances soon forced Johnson and Fortas to change their mind, and they turned to Chief Justice Earl Warren to chair a commission. The President had decided upon the chief justice, Fortas confided to Douglas, because "we thought that only a Warren investigation could head-off the Texas-legislative investigation which was in formation—and which would have proceeded upon the assumption that Kennedy's assassination was a communist plot." Fortas himself was "terribly afraid of the Texas circus that was about to be." [120] At Johnson's request, he was the first to speak with Warren about heading the commission. [121] Later, when Warren told Deputy Attorney General Nicholas Katzenbach that the results of the FBI investigation into Kennedy's death could not be revealed before the commission had completed its work, Fortas, Katzenbach, and Warren worked out a compromise by which the FBI would restrict itself to announcing its conclusions in cursory form and would turn over all its files to the Warren Commission. [122]

The power that came with Fortas's new responsibilities made them more attractive. He left some old causes by the wayside. Hoping that Fortas would intervene, Paul Taylor sent him word that Johnson's secretary of the interior supported permitting large farmers in California to circumvent the 160-acre limitation Fortas had fought to preserve as under secretary. "Isn't this where you and I came in, twenty-one years ago?" Taylor asked. "I have quite a problem with respect to my personal activity on the subject," Fortas circumspectly responded. [123] When Edward Condon suggested that Lyndon Johnson should ask a governmental committee to investigate the "unfair and exaggerated charges" of disloyalty that had been lodged against certain scientists during the redbaiting fifties, Fortas put him off. [124]

In other areas, Fortas pushed harder. At the end of 1963, Jack Valenti, a White House aide, suggested that the President establish "an organized recruiting committee" that would include Fortas and would begin functioning immediately. "We will be needing good men in all levels of government, and unless we begin NOW to organize a file of qualified men, we will be constantly delayed," Valenti told Johnson. [125] The assignment was bound to satisfy the meritocratic Fortas. He recommended scores of people for positions, ranging from membership on the Tariff Commission, to director of U.S. travel services, to the antitrust task force, to the under secretary of the Treasury, to regional director of the Peace Corps, to judgeships in the federal courts. [126] His personnel files were among the fullest folders in his White House records.

As was his way with outsiders, Fortas tried not to appear overbearing about his role as recruiter. "The Boss again nudged me to get together with you with respect to your new assignment, and he also asked me to call to your attention various names which I have in my custody," he wrote the new chair of the Civil Service Commission, John Macy, in 1964. "I told him that I was awaiting word from you, and this note is merely a reminder." [127] Yet, also as always, when Fortas wanted something, he pulled no punches. He viewed Johnson's presidency as an opportunity to help Puerto Rico and routinely drafted letters for the President and Muñoz to send each other which would promote greater amicability between them. [128] When he heard that Muñoz's former press secretary, Luis Laboy, wanted to become the Puerto Rican customs collector, Fortas strongly commended Laboy to Macy. Less than two weeks later he sent a reminder to Macy: "I certainly hope that the public interest can be served in the case of Luis Laboy." [129] Fortas also tried to enlist the support of others in the administration for Laboy. "I have done more in the case of Luis Laboy than I have ever done in this Administration with respect to a Federal appointment," he told Teodoro Moscoso.[130] It was no use.

Fortas took his loss well.[131] That too, was part of the attorney's pattern. Generally, he believed his job was over when he had sent a name to the White House with an enthusiastic recommendation. He involved himself in the decisional process itself, as in the case of Laboy, less frequently. But Fortas recognized that although the President always listened to him, he was only one of the voices which Johnson heard.[132] In rare instances, Fortas was unwilling to accept defeat gracefully. After he "urgently recommended" one friend from the New Deal for an appointment, all went well until an old charge that her mother-in-law had once rented a room to a Communist surfaced. At this point Fortas was asked to tell the candidate that Johnson wanted to "save" her for another position. "I blew my top," Fortas told her, because, although the White House denied it, he was sure the reason for her exclusion was the information about her husband's mother, "added to the usual anti-fascist stuff about you." Accordingly, he refused to make any alternative recommendations for the position. "I can't recall anything in the same category that disturbed and distressed me as much as this incident," he continued. "You know, from long and vivid experience, as I do, that the McCarthy type of damage is done not primarily by the ultimate result, but primarily, fundamentally and pervasively by the process—that is, by the nature of the issues raised and the kinds of questions presented for answer. I have no tolerance for this kind of thing—not the slightest; and if it occurred during the administration of a dear friend, that would not make me feel any more kindly toward it. On the contrary." He hoped he had not been "supersensitive to this issue," he concluded. "But I am so sensitive to it that I am . . . 'laying behind a log with my gun cocked.' "[133]

Fortas usually proved more ingratiating. After he had drafted the Animal Welfare Bill, had helped steer it through Congress, and had received the Albert Schweitzer medal as recognition for his efforts to obtain humane treatment for animals used in experiments, he became interested in a controversial bill that would make it more difficult for laboratories to acquire stolen pets. Fortas sent Johnson a photograph of beagles in a Texas dognappers' truck. "I find, to my horror, that beagles command premium prices from medical laboratories—apparently because they are among the few small dogs which are so constructed as to facilitate being cut up, etc., in experimental work," Fortas wrote the President, who owned a beagle named Him. "Congressman Pogue [sic] has introduced Bill No. 12488 to license dog dealers and laboratories which purchase dogs.—In any event, I am glad that Him is properly guarded." Though the Department of Health, Education, and Welfare advised Johnson against becoming involved with the bill, the President pleased Fortas by holding a signing ceremony to obtain maximum publicity for it. [134]

Fortas cared as much about culture as he did about civil liberties and social welfare. Shortly after Johnson became President, the director of the Smithsonian Institution, Dillon Ripley, warned Fortas that several foreign countries were courting the well-known art collector Joseph Hirshhorn. Fortas had known and liked Hirshhorn for some time. He agreed with Ripley that the United States should not lose the outstanding collection. The attorney enlisted the President, who invited the Hirshhorns, Fortas, and Ripley to lunch. Johnson persuaded Hirshhorn that the national interest demanded his art remain in the nation's capital, and the Hirshhorn Museum followed. [135]

Having engineered the Casals concert that won Kennedy his reputation as a patron of culture, Fortas hoped to increase his friend's stature in the same way. At one White House party early in Johnson's administration, Fortas was "startled and shocked" to find that the after-dinner entertainment coupled the violinist Mischa Elman with "some French singers who do a kind of third-rate boogie-woogie performance of Bach." Fortas asked Julius Bloom, of Carnegie Hall, to "do me, the nation, and the cause of culture a favor" by developing a list of musicians who might more appropriately entertain at such functions. This list Fortas forwarded to Lady Bird Johnson's social secretary. [136] In time many of the musicians named performed at the White House.

At Johnson's request, Fortas also began conferring with Lucius Battle, Isaac Stern, and Pierre Salinger about a new program for the arts in early 1964. [137] Kennedy had intended to appoint Richard Goodwin as Special Consultant to the Arts and had been in the process of establishing a large advisory council on the arts at the time of his death. "This was a bad plan," Fortas explained to Jack Valenti, "and President Johnson decided—on recommendation primarily of Isaac Stern and me—to junk the plan and not to appoint Dick Goodwin." [138] Meanwhile Fortas pretended to one of Goodwin's boosters that he would support the attorney for the position, although he did admit that he could not understand why Goodwin, an attorney, sought it. "However, I want to underline the fact that if Dick wants it, I am all for him, for whatever that may mean." [139] It did not mean much.

Fortas, Battle, Stern, and Salinger were about to create a new federal arts program to be supervised by the Assistant to the President on the Arts. This position would carry more authority than the Special Consultant job and would supplant it. They proposed that Fortas's friend and client Roger Stevens, chair of the planned Kennedy Center, be named the first presidential assistant, for they believed that Stevens, a well-known impresario, could win the respect of artists more easily than an outsider. They also recommended that Johnson replace

Kennedy's Advisory Council on the Arts with a body to be called the National Council on the Arts. These changes would "upgrade the program, giving it more substance," coordinate federal activity with respect to the arts, produce maximum use of the new Kennedy Center and, through the establishment of a nonprofit corporation that the Assistant to the President on the Arts would oversee, enable the government to attract private money to subsidize the arts.[140] Fortas was proud of his work. "Any congratulations on the matchless skill with which this was put together—the irresistible eloquence with which it is expressed . . . will be gratefully received," he joked to his collaborators.[141]

With the program's passage assured, Fortas renewed his pleas for the appointment of Roger Stevens as Johnson's assistant. The President was leery, particularly after information from a White House memorandum appeared in the press, but Fortas persisted. "Boss, there just isn't anybody available except Roger Stevens, who really fills the bill," he said to Johnson. "Neither you, nor Stevens, nor culture should be punished because somebody leaked—or which I think may have happened, somebody stole a reading of the memo from a desk in the White House."[142] "With fiddle in hand, I implore the President to appoint Roger," Fortas wrote Jack Valenti. "It is absolutely right that he should also be Chairman of the Trustees of the Kennedy Center so that there can be centralized loyal and dedicated direction of the two institutions—instead of conflict and difficulty."[143] Fortas's intervention secured a second job for Stevens. The President, who was obsessed with secrecy and paranoid about leaks,[144] might have declined to make the appointment. But when Fortas promised a candidate was "loyal," the President believed him. Johnson trusted that his valued adviser would always protect him.

## THE LAWYER AS ADVISER

Fortas had long served as attorney for Johnson's political associates with legal problems. In effect in such situations Fortas retained two clients: Johnson's colleagues and Johnson himself. That role came abruptly to an end when Johnson became President.

While Johnson was Vice-President, his former confidant Bobby Baker was accused of having used his influence as Secretary of the Senate for personal gain and was the subject of an investigation by the Senate Rules Committee. Harry McPherson, a Johnson aide, thought the Vice-President "felt defensive and protective about Bobby. He felt he had been a fool, but wanted to get good representation for him." McPherson was sure that Fortas's willingness to become Baker's attorney followed "some urging from Johnson."[145] As soon as Johnson became President, Fortas realized he could no longer act as both Baker's attorney and Johnson's adviser.[146] Citing the time-consuming duties he had assumed during the transition, Fortas turned the case over to the prominent Washington lawyer Edward Bennett Williams. The media was acutely aware of Fortas, and everything he did reflected on the President. He could no longer perform the same kind of damage control for Johnson he had before.

The President's need for such assistance again became apparent when Baker's business partner, Donald Reynolds, suggested Johnson had accepted a kickback. Reynolds alleged that after he had sold life insurance to Johnson in 1957, the senator's chief of staff, Walter Jenkins, had recommended he purchase $1200 worth of advertising on Lady Bird Johnson's television station and Baker had urged him to buy the Johnsons a stereo. Baker subsequently accused Fortas and Clark Clifford of concocting a false affidavit for Jenkins responding to Reynolds's charge.[147] That allegation was untrue, but Fortas did made a mistake in the Baker case. He thought in terms of law, not politics. He erred on the side of excessive technical accuracy, not illegality. According to Johnson's press secretary, George Reedy, Fortas urged the President to disavow Baker and devised a strategy by which Johnson could do so. When reporters asked Johnson about his protégé and friend, the President was to reply that Baker had not been a "protégé of anyone; he was there before I came to the Senate for ten years." Nor, Johnson should claim, had he made Baker secretary of the Senate when he was majority leader. Rather, the Democratic caucus, as the majority party, had elected Baker its secretary.[148] Johnson followed this scenario, but any Washington insider knew that although Johnson had described the literal procedure by which Baker was chosen, the Democratic caucus in fact had simply ratified Johnson's choice.

"The hoots of derision could be heard all the way to Mars, and if Abe had had any political sense he would have realized that," Reedy recalled. But Reedy thought Fortas lacked political sense. "Abe was accustomed to argumentation before a judge, and a judge will listen to points of law in a courtroom. The point that Bobby had been elected by the whole Senate Democratic caucus would have been a potent point, even if the judge had realized the emptiness of the argument. . . . But in the court of public opinion, that plus a nickel would not get you a telephone call." Reedy thought the incident typified Fortas's overly legalistic approach to politics.[149] Clark Clifford agreed that Fortas did not always "quite see the political factor." "I don't think his political judgment is very good," Harry McPherson said of Fortas.[150]

It never had been. Fortas did not understand how Congress and the public viewed events. And now that Johnson was President he could no longer act as lawyer for Johnson's associates. Why, then, did Johnson rely on him more than ever? "I would say that Lyndon Johnson valued Abe Fortas's advice more than he did any other individual'[s], with the possible exception of his wife," Clark Clifford flatly asserted.[151] Because Fortas understood Johnson so well and was so loyal to him, he could advise both the President and those who worked for him. His ability to protect the President from those who worked for him and interpret him for them made him indispensable.

Like everyone else in the Johnson circle, Fortas was aware of the strained relationship between Johnson and the Kennedys during his friend's first years in office. He did what he could to help Johnson pretend that it did not exist. When the Kennedy family selected William Manchester to write a book about the assassination, Fortas advised the President to plead lapses of memory or respond vaguely to those of Manchester's questions which highlighted the tension between Johnson and John Kennedy.[152] Even culture was politicized, and here Fortas's prediction that Roger Stevens would be loyal proved accurate. The attorney used Stevens to gauge the Kennedy family's plans for the Kennedy Center, which he relayed to the White House. When Stevens told Fortas that "Bobby K. had been overbearing at trustees' meetings," Fortas passed the report along to the President, along with the news that Kennedy's behavior had increased Stevens's "firmness" and moved some powerful trustees to transfer their allegiance from Kennedy to Stevens.[153]

At the same time that Fortas commended Stevens, he moved to distance the President from the friction surrounding the Kennedy Center. Anxious to prevent both "trouble or a public controversy" with the Kennedys, Fortas pledged "to do my best to keep things quiet and peaceful—and to avoid any events that would present a problem or an annoyance for the President." Fortas recommended "that Stevens (whose total dedication to the program and the President is beyond question) be allowed to bear this burden and that the President remain aloof."[154] Though Fortas prized both Stevens and the cultural program, he would not let either hurt the President. That was typical of him.

Johnson was not the only person Fortas guarded. He tried to mitigate the President's demands on his staff. When Johnson sought the attorney's aid in reorganizing the office of the presidency after his reelection in 1964, Fortas urged that "no member of the Office of the President should be allowed to work more than 8 or 9 hours a day . . . except in crisis (real crisis, created by external events!). . . . The President must discipline himself absolutely to refrain from asking, expecting or *permitting* any staff member to work overtime or to depart from the schedule except in crisis (real crisis, created by external events!)"[155]

Fortas also counseled Johnson's staff. When the President's Special Consultant, Eric Goldman, was considering writing a book on the Johnson administration in 1964, he turned to Fortas. Goldman, a historian at Princeton, was annoyed that intellectuals who had been so enamored of Kennedy were unfairly derogating Johnson. He believed that "an avowedly friendly volume, openly done in co-operation with the President and the White House, but one which rigidly preserved the right of independent judgment and critical statement," could help the President in the intellectual community. Yet Goldman was not sure whether Johnson would permit such a project. "I took the problem to a man I occasionally turned to for advice, a wise person, outside the White House, an intimate of the President for years, who had the same critical loyalty to him that . . . I did," he later said. Fortas agreed that such a book would help the President. "Then, tactfully, he gave me his opinion. We both knew the President's 'peculiarities'— he 'perhaps a little better' than I." Johnson's mind differed from theirs, Fortas continued; "'perhaps'—with a smile—'that is why he is President and we are not.'" Fortas explained that "the President has his own clear-cut picture of the world. It consists of two kinds of people, his friends and his enemies, and there are no in-betweens. The idea of a friendly but critical study makes little sense in that world." The attorney recommended Goldman think over the project "carefully, very carefully, *before*—he pronounced the word with special emphasis—I mentioned it to the President or anyone close to him."[156] The following day Goldman wrote Fortas: "I brooded over our conversation last night and decided to kill the book project without further discussion with anyone."[157] Goldman described a vintage Fortas performance. After professing admiration for the Goldman's idea, Fortas, in an unpatronizing manner had convinced the historian that undertaking it would destroy his standing in the White House.

The young attorneys in his own office whom Fortas treated so roughly would have been surprised to learn that Johnson's lieutenants trusted Fortas to shield them from their boss. They believed he would tell them what was in their own best interest vis-à-vis the President. Fortas's talent lay in thinking of them at the same time that he considered the President. Fortas was presumed to know the President so well and Johnson was believed to listen to the attorney so respectfully—Goldman considered Fortas "probably the single greatest influence on the President"[158]—that they believed trying an idea out on Fortas was tantamount to getting a preview of the President's reaction. He could persuade them that a policy he thought was in the President's best interest was also in their own. Jack Valenti told Fortas that he "chill[ed] at the thought of not having you near the President" and at the same time acknowledged that "you have been unfailingly kind to me."[159] So too when Johnson broke with Bill Moyers, it was Fortas in whom Moyers confided his frustration over the breach, and it was Fortas who gently warned Moyers that "it is always a mistake to think in terms of resuming a relationship, or any part of it, which has been characterized by such intimacy or interdependence."[160] Lady Bird Johnson liked Fortas in part because he was a "sympathetic person" who "followed a lot of his friends through divorces and helped both sides."[161]

Fortas put the President first, but his concern for Johnson's aides was real. In the autumn of 1964 Walter Jenkins was charged with disorderly conduct in the basement restroom of the Washington, D.C., YMCA, known as a gathering place for homosexuals. [162] Jenkins forfeited fifty dollars he had posted as bond and told his colleagues in the administration nothing about the incident. His silence seemed prudent, since few reporters read police blotters. But the story was leaked to a reporter at the *Washington Star*. On the morning of October 14, Charles Seib of the *Star* called Lady Bird Johnson's press secretary, Liz Carpenter, to warn her he was going to use the item. As Johnson and his press secretary were out of town, Seib asked Carpenter to comment: Had Jenkins been hospitalized for a nervous breakdown or was he undergoing medical treatment for emotional problems? Seib seemed sympathetic, and Carpenter appreciated the possible excuse he was devising for her. [163] She, however, did not consider an excuse necessary. Having known Jenkins, his wife, and their six children for years, she was so certain the charge was groundless that she telephoned Jenkins for a reply. Jenkins said he would telephone the *Star*. But Jenkins did not get in touch with Seib. Instead, Carpenter said, "He called Abe Fortas immediately, as anybody in a jam would do if they knew Abe Fortas." [164] Fortas and Jenkins met at the attorney's home. There, Johnson's aide told the attorney he had received a telephone call from the White House asking him how to respond to the report he had been arrested. Like Carpenter, Fortas assumed the charge lacked foundation. "Well, Walter, you have been in the kitchen before and no point in getting disturbed about this, what is it?" Fortas asked. "What is the charge specifically and is it true or is it not?" Jenkins, whose high blood pressure was soaring, could not answer. "The man could not at that moment put one word consecutively after the other," Fortas said. He installed the aide in a bedroom and telephoned Jenkins's doctor. After examining Jenkins, the doctor told Fortas "that this man was in the midst of a complete breakdown and that he wanted to take him to the hospital." Jenkins was hospitalized. [165]

Meanwhile Fortas, still unsure there was any truth to the story and concerned for Jenkins's family, was trying to reach Mrs. Jenkins. Unable to find her, he telephoned Clark Clifford and the two men went to the *Star*. After examining its data, Fortas admitted that the story appeared to be true but pleaded with the paper to delay releasing it. "In a low, exhausted voice he urged compassion— saying this was a sick man, a man who had been working day and night ever since Johnson assumed the presidency, a man so devoted to his boss and his job that his wife had to bring his dinner to his desk because he wouldn't take time out for meals," Seib later reported. Fortas reminded Seib and his publisher that Washington newspapers customarily did not carry such stories and asked them not to print this one until he could contact Mrs. Jenkins. Although he had not spoken with the President, who did not yet know anything about the incident, Fortas also assured Seib that Jenkins would resign his government position.

Seib was impressed. To him, the incident showed Fortas's "role in the official family," whose members turned to him instinctively when they needed help, and it also demonstrated Fortas's own "high status" at the White House. When Fortas promised the aide would resign, Seib knew that Jenkins's days in government were over. The newspaper decided to hold the news, and Fortas and Clifford then proceeded to the *Washington Post* and *Washington Daily News* to make similar pleas. They were successful in delaying publication of the story until that evening, when the United Press International wire service broke it. [166]

By that time, Fortas had finally gotten in touch with Johnson. At 3:57 that afternoon, Fortas and Clark Clifford telephoned Johnson in New York and discussed the situation with him. [167] The President refused to appear at an important Democratic Party event that evening until he learned that Fortas had obtained Jenkins's resignation. Time was of the essence. Fortas proceeded to the hospital, where he faced an obstacle for which he himself was responsible. He had made sure that no one except Jenkins's family or physicians would be admitted to see the shattered individual. Now he had to gain admission to notify his friend he was jobless. After evading security, he found himself in Jenkins's room. Fortas tried to soften the blow. Instead of informing him that the President had demanded his resignation, Fortas suggested that Jenkins should quit. Jenkins immediately resigned. [168]

Carpenter vividly remembered the damage control team—made up of herself, Lady Bird Johnson, Fortas, and Clifford—which gathered in the White House the following day. Clifford sat in a chair clasping and unclasping his hands. "Abe was concerned, . . . and I think this is what makes him the kind of lawyer you would always want to have. He was as interested in solving the human problem as the legal problem." She found both lawyers extraordinarily skillful, "but one was so much more full of heart and compassion, and it was not [just] another case to him. It was . . . a human tragedy."[169] Years later when asked why people in trouble turned to Fortas, Jenkins said that "it was because they thought he had more wisdom than most people." Fortas's wisdom differed from Clifford's, he continued, in that "it was certainly more personal. Clark Clifford was more business." Jenkins believed Fortas was "more interested in the person as a human, as opposed to [as] an issue."[170]

Fortas assumed he should try to obtain a delay in publication, both to help Jenkins and to enable the Johnson forces to prepare their side of the story. Had he decided that Johnson and the aide's interests did not coincide, Fortas doubtless would have regretfully sacrificed Jenkins. But in this case, as in other situations, he was able to help both the President and one of his aides. "I am very concerned about Jenkins who is one of the finest men I have ever known," Fortas told his cousin. "I hope that we have minimized the political damage—and I hope that Walter can be salvaged."[171]

The ethical implications of his actions in this case did not concern Fortas. Although the editors with whom he spoke agreed he had exerted no pressure and had simply requested compassion, the fact remained that as a quasi-official representative of the government, he had asked newspapers to censor themselves. When he had been accused earlier of asking the *Star* and the *Post* not to carry stories about Bobby Baker, Fortas had hotly denied the charge: "I have never in my entire career, in any context or for any purpose whatever, attempted to induce newspapers to suppress a story."[172] At the very least, he had now sullied his record by delaying one, but that did not bother him. "I am not ashamed of it at all," he said of his visit to the *Star* about the Jenkins case. "I am glad of it. I am proud of it."[173] Indeed he was so appreciative of the *Star's* cooperation that he gave Seib one of the most candid interviews about his relationship with the President that he granted during the 1960s.[174] Fortas reminded the editor of the *Washington Daily News* that "there is nothing in the Old Testament, the New Testament or the Koran that says the news media may *never* be decent and compassionate to a public official. I know that the general rule is kick the s——t out of them—but once in a long while maybe an exception is permissible."[175] Particularly, Fortas might have added, in cases where that exception would aid Lyndon Johnson.

To an unusual degree, twentieth-century presidents have chosen lawyers to be their political advisers. The case of Abe Fortas suggests why they have done so. Once Johnson became President, Fortas could no longer help him by planning courtroom strategy for his friends. But his protective instincts toward Johnson survived. He was still a lawyer, and he still treated Johnson as his client. Fortas did his job so well in part because of his professional negotiating skills, which enabled him to explain Johnson's position to others in terms they could understand. Realizing Fortas's value to him, the President sought to broaden his adviser's scope of operations.

# CHAPTER 11

# New Roles

I F YOU ONLY WORKED AS HARD FOR US AS YOU DO FOR CULTURE, JUST think where we might be!" one White House aide told Fortas.[1] While he was "glad to have the opportunity to be of service to . . . my lifelong friend," Fortas refused to take a job with the President.[2]

## GREY EMINENCE

Reports that Fortas would join the Johnson administration had begun circulating almost as soon as the new President took office. Newspapers highlighted Fortas's role as an adviser to Johnson and suggested that he would soon be leaving his law firm. But to all the friends who sent him copies of such stories, Fortas had only one reply: he was staying put. He confided to Simon Lazarus, "I am desperately trying to avoid a government post, and I hope and believe that I will be able to."[3] At the end of 1963, he told another friend he was trying "to cut the cord and to resume my full time practice of the law."[4]

Of course he was unable to do so. Even after the transition crisis ended, Johnson called upon him so often that Fortas's partners joked about it. Abe Fortas had more time to practice law "in the good old days of Eisenhower," Paul Porter teased the President. "So get up a little earlier in the morning," Johnson answered.[5] "He just wasn't around," another partner said of Fortas. The firm's business was increasing because so many people wanted to hire Lyndon Johnson's lawyer, but they rarely saw Fortas. Although he put in appearances at meetings with important clients whenever he could, he had no time to grapple with their

228

problems. When he did enter the office, a colleague who worked closely with him recalled, he would begin working his way through the sheaf of messages that had accumulated in his absence. "The President would call and that was the end of it."[6]

It was not just conversations with the President which disrupted his life, but the many requests from friends, clients, acquaintances, and even strangers he received for intercession with the White House on their behalf. Paul Porter's secretary, Dorothy Page, asked Fortas to block construction of a freeway in San Antonio that a group of nuns opposed.[7] Fortas's friend and client Troy Post hoped that the White House would arrange a tour of the premises for his daughter's class at which the President would appear and single out Miss Post.[8] Piute Pete, a square-dance caller, thought Fortas should plan a square dance at the White House.[9] Sister Mary James coveted an autographed official portrait of the President.[10] Mrs. Fred Lazarus sought a post on the National Council of Arts for one of her friends.[11] Tex Goldschmidt wanted Fortas to meet a promising young law professor.[12] And everyone seemed to want some position in the administration for themselves or a friend.

Fortas tried to handle "these somewhat embarrassing letters" with "reasonable tact and without passing the buck" to the President's staff.[13] He had kept her request on his desk for so long because he hated to refuse her anything, he explained to Page. "But the President would think I am out of my mind if I talked to him about a proposed freeway in San Antonio. . . . I am all for the Sisters and against the freeway. But this is sentiment, not knowledge." He hoped she would "understand and excuse me."[14] After he arranged for Judy Post's group to visit the White House, he told her father, "I know that the President will want to greet them if he possibly can—but you know how uncertain this must be."[15] He had sent her candidate's name to the White House, but "you must not feel chagrined if a place . . . is not available," he wrote to Irma Lazarus. If there was no vacancy, he added, he would recommend her friend for a position on the music committee.[16] "Et tu, Brute!" Fortas exclaimed to Goldschmidt. "Happily," he would be out of town during the visit of Goldschmidt's acquaintance. "Otherwise, I would see [him] . . . and curse you."[17]

Fortas frequently sent playful notes to the White House along with the requests he forwarded. "Here's the letter from your old friend, Piute Pete," Fortas wrote Bess Abel. "If you will look at the illustrations at the foot of the letter, you will see four suggestions for White House entertainments. Personally, I prefer to play post office."[18] "I realize that a man of your imagination and daring might want to take this letter and run with it," he wrote to Richard Nelson of Sister Mary James's request. "Perhaps you politicians and public relations men might think that this could be parlayed into a lot of votes—Catholic votes at that;

and everybody knows that Catholic votes are the best votes. So far as I am concerned I reject any political ideas and I am interested only in the fact that this dear lady receive the autographed portrait as she requests."[19] Efficient as his secretary was, Fortas had to compose all those sympathetic and self-consciously clever letters himself. That he took the time to do so suggested he was becoming conscious of himself as a public figure in his own right. He had long been important in the legal community. Now he was becoming known throughout the world as an *eminence grise* who counseled the President.

Fortas professed to hate publicity about his new role. "The only reason I don't like talking with these writers [about the President] is that they invariably mention me in their articles," he remarked to Jack Valenti. "You know that I don't like this worth a damn and I do everything that I can to discourage it."[20] But he did not succeed. In 1965 *Who's Who in the South and South West* listed Fortas's occupation as "Presidential adviser" and his address as "care of the White House, 1600 Pennsylvania Avenue." The accusation that he had composed the entry himself angered Fortas. "How in the world could you possibly have accepted the falsehood that I listed my address as 1600 Pennsylvania Avenue!" he reproved a former colleague. "It was an invention—and perhaps a malicious invention—of somebody or other. How could you think I would be guilty of this degree of bad taste."[21] While Fortas would not have admitted it publicly, he was in fact spending almost all his time at the White House.

That did not inconvenience his partners so much as embarrass them. "We used to have to cover for him," one remembered. Still, they recognized, as another put it, that when Fortas had to apologize for missing a meeting because the President needed him, "it's a tremendously attractive thing to say to clients." And he had trained the younger lawyers so well that they could assume his responsibilities. Any complaints they might have about his absence were muted by the growth of the firm's business, the increased power they gained in the office hierarchy with Fortas's absence, and their own commitment to the liberal legislation Johnson was promoting between 1963 and 1965.[22] Further, though many in the firm did not like Fortas, they admired him and did not begrudge him his fun. Of course he complained about the time he devoted to his White House duties. He had believed that one devalued a job by appearing to enjoy it ever since he had been editor in chief of the *Yale Law Journal*. One partner remembered, however, that "it was obvious that he just revelled" in his role as presidential adviser.[23] Given that the firm was managing without him and that he genuinely liked his work for Johnson, why did Fortas refuse Johnson's invitation to become attorney general?

He believed, reasonably, that he was indispensable to the firm's success. He worried about its future if he accepted a government post. "We've got a lot of fine young lawyers who marry fine young wives and have fine young babies," he told reporters in 1964. "I have my responsibilities here."[24] Further, it was one thing to advise the President, it was another to be in his employ. "You can admire him, and he was very good in some ways, but in others he was just appalling," Carol Agger said of Lyndon Johnson. "Other people who worked with Lyndon were often being kicked around by him."[25] Yet Johnson never kicked Fortas around. Agger "often wondered how remarkable it was" that the President treated her husband so respectfully in view of the way he derogated others. "Lyndon, who sometimes was demanding and called on people on Saturdays and Sundays and 6 o'clock in the morning and 12 o'clock at night," refused to telephone Fortas during his Sunday night chamber music sessions "unless the situation was desperate," Lady Bird Johnson recalled. "He had a sort of respect for that because he knew how it fed Abe's soul."[26] Indeed the Johnsons once invited themselves to such an evening at the last minute. Fortas and Agger had planned an informal supper for themselves and their musician friends because it was their cook's night off. Even after they learned of the Johnsons' plans and recalled their cook, they still had nothing unfrozen in the house and considered themselves lucky to cajole a local restaurant into parting with some raw steaks. "'We played for them while they had their steak supper,'" one of the musicians said, and when the performance ended Johnson buzzed the cook to tell her how good the dinner was. "Mr. President, I'm glad you liked it, but in the future if you could give me more notice, I could do much better,'" she tartly replied. No one found it "exactly pleasant" that the President dropped in for dinner and an evening of chamber music, although it testified to his respect for Fortas's interests.[27] Still, it also reflected Johnson's intrusiveness. If Fortas accepted a government position, he risked losing whatever autonomy he retained. Fortas believed as well that he had devoted adequate time to the government. "I do not want to accept a Government position, particularly in view of my long service in the years past," he explained to an associate.[28] He had imbued his own subcabinet position in the 1940s with as much authority as many cabinet posts carried. Government service represented no new challenge, and it paid substantially less than the $173,274 he reported as income from his partnership in 1964.[29]

Finally, Carol Agger did not want her husband to become attorney general. After Johnson offered Fortas the position, she and the President argued about it for well over an hour on the telephone. In the course of the discussion the President lamented that not even his dog would do anything for him. While similar bathos convinced Earl Warren to head the commission investigating the Kennedy assassination and other equally strong people to change their minds, it did not sway Carol Agger. "It's work to say to LBJ you can't have him," she remembered, but she succeeded.[30] For the time being, Fortas remained, at least in name, a Washington lawyer.

## "C.J. DAVIDSON"

The high profile he maintained as presidential adviser contrasted with Fortas's clandestine role in the Dominican Republic intervention. On April 24, 1965, rebels led by Colonel Francisco Caamaño Deñó staged a coup against the right-wing ruling junta, which they suspected would cancel or rig the upcoming elections. By the following day, the rebels described the coup as a "populist uprising." The "constitutionalist" troops handed out guns to their Dominican supporters and indicated that they would not hold new elections. Instead they would ask Juan Bosch, who had served as president for only seven months in 1963 before a right-wing counterrevolution forced him into exile in Puerto Rico, to finish his term. When Bosch publicly accepted the invitation to return to the Dominican Republic, a group of generals headed by Elias Wessin y Wessin took action. Within hours, civil war had erupted on the island between Caamaño's supporters and Wessin's right-wing forces.[31]

Those events placed the United States in a difficult position. On the one hand, Johnson opposed restoring Bosch to power, for he was sure Bosch had socialistic tendencies. Nor did Johnson think that Bosch possessed a stable power base. Most important, Johnson feared the island would go the way of Fidel Castro's Cuba. "What can we do in Vietnam if we can't clean up the Dominican Republic?" Johnson asked an adviser.[32] On the other hand, the President did not want to endorse a right-wing dictatorship hostile both to Bosch and to the forces of constitutionalism he represented. Indeed Johnson hoped for the establishment of a democratic government in the Dominican Republic.

That was not immediately evident. On April 28, without having consulted the Organization of American States (OAS), the President announced the first landing of American marines in a Latin American country in thirty-seven years. Four hundred Marines were preparing to evacuate U.S. residents stranded in the Dominican Republic. Two days later, Johnson declared he was sending in some 1200 more troops. On that date, April 30, the White House publicly revealed for the first time a primary reason for American intervention: avoiding the triumph of the constitutionalist movement, which the President wrongly believed was dominated by Castro supporters. Before the crisis ended, he had dispatched over 20,000 additional troops to the Dominican Republic. Johnson insisted that his ultimate aim was not to establish a right-wing dictatorship but "to encourage

Dominicans to find the men and the formula to lead them from stalemate to an interim government and elections."[33]

Fortas was committed to evacuating American nationals from the Dominican Republic, but he opposed intervention. Carol Agger cited the crisis as one instance in which Fortas resisted the President's decision.[34] Fortas later supplied some insight into the reason for his position. In 1969 he made an unusually frank statement to an interviewer. "I think that if I had been asked at the time 'Should we or should we not send troops in,' that my inclination would have been no," he remarked. His long involvement with Puerto Rico had made him sensitive to Latin Americans' fear of Washington's interference, and "on the basis of my limited knowledge I would have been very skeptical about the possibility of important Communist participation. And as matters turned out I think the Communist participation was quite slight." The major figures involved were "military people and not Communists."[35] Fortas believed, moreover, that there were no legal grounds for intervention by the United States in the Dominican Republic. Although international law gave some credence to the argument that a state could dispatch troops to another country to protect its nationals, that concept was no longer universally accepted and seemed contrary to the OAS Charter. If the United States now claimed intervention for that purpose as a matter of legal right, Communist nations might employ the same argument in the future to justify action the United States strongly opposed. Further, although the State Department maintained that the United States could legally remain on the island in order to preserve the capability of the OAS to function, Fortas knew of no legal basis for its contention. The OAS had not requested the marines, and, again, the State Department's position might provide a useful precedent for Communist governments.[36]

"I wouldn't be surprised if he opposed it," Johnson's national security adviser, McGeorge Bundy, said when asked about Fortas's reaction to large-scale American military intervention in the Dominican Republic. But, Bundy emphasized, Fortas was never one to dwell upon defeat. "Fortas was always talking about what came next," not criticizing what had been done. Though he had convictions of his own, "he was trying to do a job for the guy with constitutional responsibility."[37] Thus Fortas continued to advise the President throughout the Dominican Republican crisis. Johnson spoke with him by telephone more frequently than with anyone except Bundy.[38]

Fortas even had a suggestion of his own. Because the President had not consulted the OAS before sending in the Marines, that organization was understandably reluctant to bail out the United States by taking the lead in stabilizing the Dominican Republic. If the OAS stalled, Fortas asked the President, why not see that Romulo Betancourt of Venezuela, José Figueras of Costa Rica, and Luis Muñoz Marín of Puerto Rico were designated as trustees to supervise the restoration of order on the island? State Department officials considered Fortas's idea naive, impractical, and illegal and after fruitlessly pursuing it for a few days gave it up as unworkable.[39]

In the meantime, Fortas had established direct communication with Bosch. To Bosch and his supporters, who suspected that the United States was actively fomenting counterrevolution by aiding Wessin's men, Fortas would have seemed the obvious link between the constitutionalists and the White House. Flanked as he was in Puerto Rico by two of Fortas's admirers, Governor Luis Muñoz Marín and University of Puerto Rico Chancellor Jaime Benítez, Bosch would have regarded Fortas as one of the more progressive voices around the President.[40] On May 1 Fortas was informed that Caamaño's constitutionalist forces were not respecting the cease-fire agreement they had recently signed with Wessin's troops. That defiance was intolerable to the United States. Shortly after learning this news, Fortas telephoned Bosch in San Juan.[41]

From Fortas's notes, it would appear that the conversation did not go well. "I told him that his forces were continuing to fire—were violating the cease fire and were planning further violence for tonight," Fortas recorded. "I said that it was impossible to overstate the gravity and seriousness of my message to him." Unless Bosch and Camaaño's troops respected the cease-fire, United States marines "would be compelled to respond," presumably by firing on the constitutionalists. Bosch replied that the United States sympathized with Wessin's counterrevolutionaries and was ignoring him and his supporters. Fortas responded with a tough lawyer's argument: America's behavior did not matter. "The plain, critical issue was *whether the Bosch forces would cease fire.*" Fortas maintained that Bosch now backed down. He told Fortas he could not communicate with his troops from Puerto Rico. Fortas answered that he was "extremely sorry but he must realize that if his forces continued firing, he could not expect the US forces to remain inactive." Having delivered the message, Fortas ended the conversation. "May God help you," he told Bosch. According to Fortas, the exiled leader replied: "May God bless you for your efforts and may He have pity on the Dominican Republic."

The attorney then telephoned McGeorge Bundy and said that he had concluded "with the greatest regret" that Bosch no longer controlled his backers. Fortas begged the White House to make "every effort" to communicate with Caamaño's forces before firing on them. He then reported back to Bosch, who reiterated that he was out of touch with Caamaño's troops.[42] Bosch offered, however, to fly to Santo Domingo to ask his compatriots to stop fighting, after which he would return to San Juan. He would lodge his plea not in his capacity as president, but as a Dominican citizen. "I said I could not ask him to do that—and if I had further word I would communicate again," Fortas recorded. In fact, he and Bundy contemplated approving just such a move until Benítez called and said that, as conditions had become more peaceful, Bosch had decided against returning to the Dominican Republic. When Bosch entered, "he wanted to do so as President."[43]

That was exactly what Fortas and others in Washington wanted to avoid, but they did not want to break off their discussions with Bosch. Therefore Fortas persuaded Johnson to appoint John Bartlow Martin, who had served as ambassador to the Dominican Republic during Bosch's presidency, as his special envoy to the Dominican Republic. "The sending of John Bartlow Martin as the President's emissary to the Dominican Republic was an extraordinary effort on the part of the President and Fortas toward gathering as broad and sympathetic a picture as possible of the Bosch cause," Benítez subsequently explained to a *New York Times* reporter.[44] Unbeknownst to Fortas and Johnson, however, Martin had always been suspicious of Bosch and soon turned against him. After conferring with the former president in San Juan for ten hours on May 2 and 3, he wired Washington that Bosch was "completely unable [to] believe that what began as a PRD [democratic] rebellion has been taken over by Castro/ Communists, unscrupulous military men, and adventurers all merged into violent extremist leadership. Is completely out of touch with reality."[45] Martin proved even less sympathetic to Caamaño, whom he thought might well become "a Dominican Castro."[46]

At this point Fortas and Martin still hoped for the establishment of a constitutional government. But the democracy they worked for was to be constrained. They opposed a Caamaño presidency, for despite his constitutionalist pretensions, the colonel was a military man with an unsavory past who seemed to be growing increasingly sympathetic to Communists. If possible, they wanted also to avoid a Bosch presidency. Nor was the new government to be independent. Fortas demonstrated this attitude when he telephoned San Juan, where Martin was conferring with Bosch, with a new proposal on May 3. Fortas instructed Martin to explore with Bosch the possibility of a constitutionalist government headed by someone other than Caamaño. The United States might even tolerate a return to power by Bosch himself, though Fortas thought it would be in Bosch's "own long-range political interests . . . to withdraw from present political ambition and let an interim government be formed without him."[47] In exchange for these concessions, Fortas demanded cooperation. Bosch should legitimate the American intervention by announcing the possible presence of Communists in his own forces and asking American troops to remain on the island for at least six months. In short, the United States would consent to a constitutional government as long as it could ensure that government was sufficiently tame.[48]

Not surprisingly, Bosch refused the deal. When Martin returned from his telephone conversation and, without identifying the caller, began dictating Fortas's conditions, Bosch felt betrayed. "How . . . could one explain the . . . proposition that I declare the intervention legitimate, that I confirm the fantastic barrage of falsehood rained upon the Dominican constitutionalist revolution?"[49] Consequently Bosch drafted an excoriation of the United States which compared the intervention to the Wilson administration's ill-advised occupation of the island in 1916 and urged the Dominican people to rally behind the forces of constitutionalism. Since it was impossible to reconcile the statement Fortas had suggested Bosch make with the one the leader wanted to deliver, it was decided that Bosch would make no announcement for the present.[50]

Disgusted, Martin left San Juan after his final conversation with Bosch and returned to the Dominican Republic. On May 4, after he had been duly elected by the island's constitutional convention, Caamaño was sworn in as the Dominican Republic's president. In his inaugural address he proclaimed that American declarations that the Communists had captured control of the revolution were "lies."[51] Martin now turned his efforts in a new direction. Within two days, he had arranged for his country to recognize a five-man anti-Bosch junta headed by General Antonio Imbert Bareras. Bosch, who had endorsed Caamaño's government, justifiably charged to reporters that Imbert's "Government of National Reconstruction" was "a creation of the United States to prevent recognition of Col. Francisco Caamaño's constitutional government."[52] Even Martin later admitted Imbert was "an assassin" who lacked "a liberal coloration."[53] Had the United States intervened in the Dominican Republic simply to substitute one right-wing government for another?

Fortas would have said no. He would have maintained that some individuals in the administration remained committed to democracy and worked to achieve a solution of "constitutionalism-without-Bosch" that the former president himself would approve.[54] Fortas resumed communication with Bosch when the exiled leader telephoned several days after the *New York Times* had run a front-page story about Fortas's endorsement of Martin as an envoy to San Juan.[55] In the process of apologizing for having inadvertently mentioned the attorney's name to the press, Bosch explained to Fortas that he had been compelled to endorse Caamaño as President. He also enthusiastically told Fortas that General Wessin had just complied with an American request to resign. Bosch felt that President Johnson seemed better informed than he had been at the outset of the crisis. But Imbert, Bosch added, was unpopular in the Dominican Republic. When Fortas asked Bosch what should happen now, Bosch replied that the United States should recognize the constitutional government and enigmatically hinted that he might consider replacing Caamaño. Bosch concluded the conversation by confiding that he had declined an invitation to participate in a teach-in at Harvard about the war in Vietnam. He did not, he explained, want to join the liberals in the Democratic party in attacking Johnson. The President had been misinformed about the Dominican Republic, but he had acted honorably. Instead, Bosch said, he was contemplating holding a press conference in New York.[56]

Fortas's notes of his negotiations with Bosch, which provided the most detailed information available about their conversations in Puerto Rico, may simply have reflected an attempt to build a record to support Fortas and Johnson's version of events. But if the notes are accurate, they indicate that Bosch was coming around and may have been willing eventually to acknowledge that he had underestimated the number of Communists among his initial supporters.[57] Nevertheless, the United States could not risk allowing him to hold a press conference. Instead Johnson decided to send Fortas to San Juan to negotiate a coalition government. Accordingly, Fortas announced he would come to Puerto Rico and suggested that Bosch cancel his trip to New York.[58]

To keep the mission secret, Fortas abruptly vanished. "Abe disappeared suddenly and no one knew where he had gone," his wife later recalled. "I was quite uncomfortable."[59] The Macrorys arrived from England for a long-scheduled visit while Fortas was away, and he also was inexplicably absent from a dinner party honoring several Supreme Court justices and other Washington notables that he earlier had arranged in their honor.[60] After several days, Carol Agger received a mystifying telephone call from the White House indicating that "C. J. Davidson" would soon be returning on a military plane.[61] Fortas's choice of C. J. Davidson as an assumed name indicated his puckishness. "This was something of the man," Agger later said. "Making a joke when he was rather in danger."[62] He had been urging the appointment of C. Girard Davidson to some important post since Johnson had taken office.[63] Further, Davidson, an old friend from Interior days, had long been involved with Puerto Rico. Muñoz, Benítez, and Fortas's other Puerto Rican friends knew him well and were tickled by the allusion.[64] The choice of the letter *J* over *G* was one more inside joke, because Davidson's friends called him "Jebby."

Fortas must have taken an assumed name at the behest of the White House, for he thought such cloak-and-dagger arrangements were silly. When he arrived at Muñoz's summer house to meet with Bosch, a small group was standing outside. Benítez's chauffeur, Julio Caballero, announced, "There comes Mr. Fortas." A federal agent immediately contradicted Caballero: "No, that is Mr. Davidson." At that moment, Fortas saw Caballero, whom he had known for twenty years. He immediately walked over and embraced the chauffeur. "'How is my Puerto Rican family?'" Fortas asked, referring to the Benítezes. The chauffeur's "triumphant look defied the U.S. Secret Service."[65] The atmosphere inside proved more grave. Fortas's notes suggest that, at their first meeting on May 12, Bosch seemed wholly committed to constitutionalism. His position presented several problems for the United States. For example, under the Dominican Republic's constitution of 1963, which Bosch had pledged to restore, no Dominicans could be deported for political reasons. The United States wanted reactionaries and Communists off the island, but Bosch argued that deportation would make martyrs out of the Communists and encourage them to travel to Cuba for additional training. With time, Bosch bent. After a lengthy discussion, Benítez wrote out a statement for Bosch in which the former president agreed that some individuals would either be interned or forced to leave the island.[66] Historians who found Bosch's willingness to accommodate the United States on this point "surprising" ignored "Davidson's" persuasive abilities.[67]

Other obstacles seemed greater. The former president insisted upon a fully "constitutional" government headed by Caamaño " & no compromises." When Fortas suggested that a transitional period might be required before such a government could take office, Bosch balked.[68] Fortas was "helpful and understanding," Benítez recalled, but he "liked efficiency also and that was not what you had from Bosch."[69] By about 9:30 that evening, Fortas had decided a tantrum was in order. "I told J.B. [Juan Bosch] that he was presenting the alternative of Caamaño or no arrangement, that he must know that this left us with no alternative—that we could not accept Caamaño; and that his choice was flexibility or responsibility for the death of thousands of people which would result if there were no arrangement," he said. "I then walked out ostensibly to pee and came back in 15 minutes." Fortas found Bosch more acquiescent on his return. His display of toughness had impressed the Dominican. Fortas noted that "from this point until we parted for the night—and through the next day—our discussions proceeded with much greater flexibility and mutuality." But while Bosch was listing candidates for the presidency other than Caamaño, Benítez dropped a bombshell in the form of "an impassioned speech to the effect that there was only one possible and appropriate choice—that was Bosch himself." Why Benítez did this remained unclear for he subsequently compared Bosch—who was comfortably sitting out the revolution in San Juan—to Hamlet, and as he said, "you can't be a politician and Hamlet at the same time."[70] But according to Fortas, Bosch was no longer interested. "It was unnecessary for me to do anything beyond scowling, because J.B. said that he could not and would not—and he added that he would never run for the presidency," Fortas recalled. "He said, with much emotion, that this (the process in which we were engaged) was his last act for his people."[71]

Bosch did unsuccessfully run for president the following year, but at the time of the discussion with Fortas and Benítez he no longer seemed a threat. When negotiations resumed the following day, Fortas, Bosch, and Benítez drafted a statement for Johnson in which he would support the authority of the OAS to restore order in the Dominican Republic and promise economic assistance to the island.[72] More important, they agreed on a president—not Bosch, nor Caamaño, but someone who was connected with Bosch's earlier presidency. Fortas and Bosch's new choice was Silvestre Antonio Guzmán, who had once been Bosch's secretary of agriculture. Bosch also agreed to endorse a coalition government that would include individuals with "special appeal" to the right-wing. A solution seemed imminent.[73]

Johnson was holding a meeting on the Dominican Republic when Fortas called the White House to report on his progress. The discussion turned to which member of the administration should be dispatched to confer with Guzmán. "I would button this whole damn thing in 36 hours," Johnson told his advisers. "I could send anyone—no one is tougher than Abe Fortas." The President explained he had a "belly-to-belly deal" in mind.[74] Later that evening, Fortas telephoned again and refused "to take 1 oz. of responsibility for Guzmán." Ultimately the White House also decided he would not be a good candidate. When Fortas, Bundy, Benítez, Bosch, Guzmán, and several others met in San Juan the following day, they at first seemed on the verge of agreement. In the end, however, negotiations broke down, apparently because Guzmán refused to acquiesce in the removal of Communists and rejected a new American demand that leading constitutionalists be deported as well. Ambassador Ellsworth Bunker now went to the Dominican Republic. There, with the support of Under Secretary of State Tom Mann, one of the more conservative voices in the administration on Latin American affairs, Bunker negotiated a provisional government that would assume power until elections could be held.[75] That government eventually took office, but not before Fortas had objected to Bunker's and State's political orientation.

"Abe Fortas thinks less than nothing of the 'Bunker-Mann' plan," Bundy told Johnson. "He just does not think that a government of 'technicians' can do the job, and his belief is that this phrase covers an intent to have a hard-nosed right wing government. He believes that there is no real middle-of-the road here, and that we have to be for progress, or against it, right from the start." Fortas also observed that Bundy and the President had substantially rewritten a draft of a State Department document. "He thinks we are trying to get our principles with Tom Mann's practices and that it won't work." Bundy had replied that compromise was necessary. "I told Abe that we were trying to get agreement and not disagreement among the President's advisers, but he stood his ground."[76]

Fortas's enthusiasm for "progress"—although it stamped him as one of John-

son's more liberal advisers—was somewhat misleading, as he considered progress synonymous with democracy. His old boss Henry Wallace told him during
this time that democracy was unfeasible in underdeveloped countries, where the
economy depended on a few export crops that foreign corporations controlled and
where high birth, illiteracy, and malnutrition rates prevailed. "The alternatives
are totalitarian dictatorship more or less well run, colonialism, or communism. I
hate to say it but democracy . . . just will not work under the Dominican situation."[77] Fortas demurred. He maintained that democracy, "staffed by people who
understand its essential meaning and containing within itself the potential for
political and economic development," was the best option for the island. On the
basis of his "very restricted familiarity" with the Dominican crisis, Fortas declared himself "impressed by the need for firm direction—and at the same time,
a set of words and concepts which promise satisfaction of the aspirations of the
intellectuals and the masses of the people."[78]

Fortas's answer to Wallace ignored the frequent occasions on which the
United States had declared its commitment to "democracy" in a third-world
country, only to back a leader who was an American puppet. In the case of the
Dominican Republic, Johnson's decision to send in a large number of troops
reflected little sensitivity to self-determination or third-world nationalism. Fortas himself justifiably had resisted intervention, for this action represented one
of the most disgraceful episodes in the history of American foreign policy. Another individual who opposed the President under such circumstances might
have broken with him, but deserting Johnson was inconceivable for Fortas.
Instead he negotiated a tough deal with Bosch which, put most charitably,
enfeebled the concept of democracy. Just five days after labeling the United
States' action in the Dominican Republic illegal, he was in Puerto Rico searching
for a solution his boss could accept.

By entrusting his adviser with such a delicate mission, Johnson showed he
had no doubts about Fortas's devotion. Johnson knew that, though the attorney
might disagree with him, no one was tougher than Fortas in trying to get the
President what he wanted. Johnson intended to reward that loyalty by awarding
Fortas the most coveted position in the legal profession.


### JUSTICE FORTAS

Adlai Stevenson's death on July 13, 1965, began a sequence of events that
ultimately changed Fortas's life. Vietnam was becoming an increasingly important issue, and the President required an effective ambassador to the United
Nations to replace Stevenson. As Johnson told it, he was visiting with John
Kenneth Galbraith when the economist mentioned that Justice Arthur Goldberg

was restless at the Supreme Court. Goldberg confirmed Galbraith's report in a conversation with the President on the way back from Stevenson's funeral on July 19. When Johnson offered him a Cabinet position as Secretary of Health, Education, and Welfare, Goldberg replied that he was more interested in foreign affairs. On July 20 Goldberg informed the White House that he would accept the ambassadorship to the United Nations. Because Johnson knew that Goldberg, a former secretary of labor and skilled negotiator, would be "an outstanding representative of our nation in that crucial international organization," he appointed Goldberg as Stevenson's replacement. At least that was the President's story.[79]

Others recalled the incident differently. Arthur Goldberg later insisted he had not been bored with the Court. "I left because of vanity," he explained. "I thought I could influence the President to get out of Vietnam." He maintained that he would not have resigned if Johnson had not pressed him.[80] So eager was Johnson to make a place for Fortas on the Supreme Court that he was tempting Goldberg with the vice-presidency. "You're over there isolated from the action," he said, "and you can't get to the Vice-Presidency from the Court."[81] The President had offered the position at the Court to Fortas even before Goldberg had definitely decided to resign. According to Paul Porter, Johnson telephoned Fortas as he was flying back to Washington from Stevenson's funeral and informed the attorney he was about to be named to the Supreme Court.[82]

Johnson had thought hard about the appointment. When he began contemplating the "vacancy," he told Attorney General Nicholas Katzenbach that he could not choose Fortas because "'they're going to say I'm appointing a crony.' It made him very nervous." But his attorney general did not agree. He pointed out that Fortas possessed a national reputation as a brilliant attorney: "They're going to say you're lucky to have known him, not that he's a crony." Katzenbach added that Johnson need not worry about losing Fortas as an adviser. Supreme Court justices had always counseled presidents.[83] Johnson, then at the peak of his power, must have reasoned he could handle any criticism the appointment might cause. And there were few people to whom he owed more than his old friend. Lady Bird Johnson emphasized that her husband came to consider Fortas the most qualified individual for the job and to believe he must want it. What lawyer did not hope to join the Supreme Court?[84]

The lawyers in Fortas's firm did not think Fortas aspired to the job. Certainly he repeatedly told them he was uninterested.[85] Close friends knew better. He was "delighted" at the prospect of becoming a justice, Mercedes Eichholz recalled. He was "greatly touched and honored" by Johnson's offer.[86] Others confirmed Fortas's desire to become a Supreme Court justice. Fortas always thought about money, one maintained, except in this instance. Although justices earned less than a quarter of Fortas's income, "he was will ng to do it."[87] But Fortas turned Johnson down. On July 19, after receiving the President's telephone call, he sent a handwritten letter to the White House: "After painful searching, I've decided to decline—with a heart full of gratitude." He preferred "a few more years of activity" during which he could serve the Johnson family, a function, Fortas implied, that he could not fill from the Supreme Court. He owed it to the young attorneys at Arnold, Fortas & Porter to remain there. He had reached his decision over the opposition of his wife, he added. "Carol thinks I should accept this greatest honor that a lawyer could receive—this highest appointive post in the nation."[88]

"I did not keep a copy—I did not write it for the record," Fortas later insisted. "I wrote him because I didn't want to go on the Court and I wanted to tell him why."[89] If that was his motivation, Fortas's letter was preposterous, since he did not just omit the most important reason for his refusal but actually denied it. Like Fortas's other friends, Lyndon Johnson believed that Fortas had refused the job principally because his wife had serious objections. But Fortas declared otherwise. "That sure was a charade," one friend said of Fortas's declination letter.[90] "I don't know why he said that because I didn't think he should take it," Carol Agger observed. When Agger saw the letter she asked: "What the hell is that?" Fortas replied: "Oh, you know." Agger believed that, as he had done when deliberating between working for Jerome Frank at the AAA and enlisting with William O. Douglas at the SEC,[91] Fortas had inserted some extra verbiage into his correspondence in order to make his decision sound tougher.[92] Another friend suggested that Fortas's protestations about history to the contrary, he wrote the letter to protect his wife from charges she had prevented him from accepting the position.[93]

At one time, Carol Agger might have welcomed a Supreme Court appointment for her husband. In 1964 the President had tried to draft her for a judicial position, and Fortas had asked Mercedes Eichholz to persuade her to accept it. But Eichholz was unsuccessful. Carol Agger declined, she explained to Eichholz, because her acceptance could preclude Fortas from accepting a Supreme Court appointment, "which might come up within a year."[94] In the months between that conversation and Johnson's offer to her husband, however, Fortas and his wife had assumed new responsibilities. After living for over twenty years in a comfortable house on N Street in Georgetown, they had decided that they needed more land and had bought a handsome house on R Street with ample room for garden and swimming pool. As they planned extensive remodeling, the selling price, reportedly near $250,000, represented only the first of their expenditures.[95]

These facts led many, including Fortas, to presume that Agger did not want him to join the Supreme Court because of the pay cut entailed. Agger had commented to friends that the couple could not afford to permit Fortas to become a justice. The story circulated that someone had responded that the salary reduction could not make a significant difference: she was making a great deal of money as a tax attorney and taxes took a large portion of both their incomes already. Agger allegedly replied: "My friend, two big gross incomes equal two big net incomes." Others suggested her opposition stemmed from different factors. "I think it was rather that they had got their lives very well structured from her point of view, and she didn't want them to be thrown into a totally new situation," one friend said.[96]

Years later, although she admitted money had been a factor, Agger maintained that more important reasons had prompted her to oppose a Supreme Court position for Fortas. She told Johnson that her husband should join the Court in five or six years, she recalled. She considered Fortas, then fifty-five, too young for the position. He needed more experience and a wider field of vision. He had worked in government for years in the past, and she did not think he was ready to reenter it. Since leaving the Department of Interior, he had begun playing music seriously, had become involved with the Kennedy Center, and had launched an excellent firm for which he felt responsible. Those activities made him happy, she emphasized, and their lives were at a good point. She did not welcome change.[97]

In some ways, Fortas agreed that he was not yet ready. When rumors of his departure from Arnold, Fortas & Porter began to circulate, and some clients complained,[98] Fortas worried whether the firm would continue to prosper if he left. The sense of responsibility and the financial considerations that had led him to decline the attorney generalship made him hope that the Supreme Court appointment would come later rather than sooner. He hinted to one friend that he wanted to join the Court in two or three years, when he would have saved more money. After hearing him describe his situation another friend was equally convinced that Fortas hoped to wait. When Fortas asked Abe Krash whom he should recommend to the President as Goldberg's successor, Krash asked why Fortas himself did not take the job. Fortas answered that he could have it, but he did not want it at this point. Krash and another associate speculated that Fortas might have thought about Earl Warren's possible retirement while Johnson was still President, allowing for Fortas to be appointed directly to the chief justiceship. Yet Fortas was a pragmatist who knew that history could be managed only up to a point. The opportunity had arisen now, and it might not occur again. For that reason, he continued to contemplate becoming a justice. Although he had formally refused the position, he knew he could reconsider.[99]

He regarded few people more highly than his mentor, William O. Douglas, who was vacationing in Washington State and did not know that Fortas had been offered the position. Douglas wrote Fortas on July 20 to say he had heard in a radio report that Goldberg was going to the United Nations. "If that is true my hope is that you will be named at once—*and without delay*," Douglas stressed. "I have talked with Lyndon several times about naming you to the Court on the first vacancy," he continued. "Last month he promised me he would!!"[100]

A letter of July 21 from Mercedes Eichholz to Douglas, which crossed his letter to his protégé in the mail, indicated that Fortas remained uncertain. Eichholz had spoken with Carol Agger the previous evening and had just completed a long talk with Fortas. "I am sorry to intrude on your seclusion, but he more or less asked me to see if he could talk with you," she wrote. Since her former husband had no telephone in Goose Prairie, she advised him to make the hour's drive to Yakima to call Fortas. "For his own future and the future of your august body I think it is worth your effort to go and persuade him this is the thing he should do. The only objection that I have gleaned is 'not being able to give to Carol all the worldly goods he is killing himself working for now.'" Fortas never blinked at playing the martyr, but Eichholz's letter suggested that he was not yet ready to do so. He retained judicial aspirations.[101]

Realizing that, Johnson kept pressing. "I think he was overweening in that instance," Lady Bird Johnson subsequently reflected.[102] The President was about to announce a dramatic escalation of the American effort in Vietnam. As he and Fortas related it, on July 28 Johnson telephoned Fortas and asked him to come to the White House. When Fortas arrived, the President said he was preparing to announce the commitment of fifty thousand men to Vietnam and the attorney's appointment to the Supreme Court. If those fifty thousand individuals could sacrifice for their country, Fortas could too. Fortas could remain in the Oval Office if he wished, but since Johnson was revealing his appointment, he thought Fortas should go with him to the press conference. "He looked at me in silence for a moment," Johnson wrote. "I waited. Then he said, 'I'll accompany you.' That was the only way I managed to get him on the Court."[103] As Fortas told the story, Johnson did not notify him of the appointment until "we were half way down the hall to the press conference. To the best of my knowledge, and belief, I never said yes. . . . I so strongly felt that I did not want to do it."[104] When Herblock drew a cartoon of Fortas's investiture, the new justice's right arm was twisted.[105]

The story ranked with Felix Frankfurter's tale about his own surprise news from Franklin Roosevelt nearly thirty years earlier. The President, who had earlier said he could not appoint another Jew to sit alongside Brandeis on the Supreme Court, telephoned to say that he was choosing Frankfurter after all. "This image of Frankfurter, clad only in undershorts, struck dumb by Roosevelt's change in heart, has a certain romantic appeal—but it is wholly false," his leading biographer has pointed out. In fact, Frankfurter had been lobbying for the job for weeks.[106]

The Johnson-Fortas version of Fortas's appointment proved equally engaging. It was a good story, which illustrated how Lyndon Johnson always got his man and how reluctantly Fortas became a Supreme Court justice. It implied that Fortas had not thought of joining the Court since declining the position on July 19, when, in fact, he had probably thought of little else. It suggested that Fortas did not want the appointment, when in fact he wanted it very much, though he had reservations about its timing. Finally, it indicated that he had no time between Johnson's disclosure and the press conference to reflect. Surely there was some element of surprise—how else could Johnson circumvent Carol Agger? Still, the shock was exaggerated. Isaac Stern retained a vivid recollection of hearing a pajama-clad Fortas predict that Johnson would appoint him, and Fortas was sufficiently collected to telephone Mercedes Eichholz from the White House and ask her to call his wife that evening.[107] But as a good actor, Fortas always recounted the story of his surprise appointment convincingly.

The news astonished Carol Agger, who heard it while in a meeting with a client and government officials at the Internal Revenue Service. "You don't treat friends that way," a partner overheard her say when Johnson telephoned her at her office later. She hung up on him.[108] When Eichholz spoke with her that night, she thought that Agger "sounded as if she had been in an automobile accident and was in a state of shock."[109] But Johnson found that Agger had sufficient strength to resist him. He called to ask the couple and some of their friends to dinner on his yacht, but she refused to go, and as she said, no one else went either.[110] Fortas later confided to Paul Porter that he had "never heard anybody talk to the President like Carol did."[111] She would not talk to Johnson for the next two months, and her relationship with her husband during that period was also tense. Eventually, however, she forgave Fortas.[112]

Others were cheering. Arthur Goldberg, who viewed Fortas and himself as jurisprudential "clones," wired that "the President could not have made a better choice."[113] Everyone from Elvis Presley's manager to FBI officials sent congratulatory messages.[114] News of the appointment delighted old New Dealers. Florence Frank kept thinking "of how gratified Jerome would be if he were here. You were one of his most treasured persons."[115] When Benjamin Cohen congratulated Fortas on "the opportunity to apply the great talents of your mind and heart in meeting the critical and significant problems which challenge the powerful development of the Great Society," Fortas replied, "The only man I know of who is supremely qualified for the Court is you."[116] That graciousness characterized as well his exchanges with members of the Johnson administration who wrote to express their pleasure. He responded by telling them what a good job they were doing.

With others, Fortas was more humorous. "I have to tell you—to warn you—

that this is merely a half-way point in my career," Fortas told Alexander Schneider. He had accepted the appointment "only as a stepping stone to something
greater. My service on the Court will permit me to practice scales every morning,
and in two or three weeks I expect to apply for the position of second violinist with
the Budapest Quartet—Assistant Director of the Casals Festival—friend of
innumerable women—and whatever other positions you hold which require
great training and much concentration. In short, I warn you that my musical
activities will increase and not diminish. So maybe you had better start practicing."[117] To another group Fortas expressed humility. He had tried unsuccessfully
to understand his own original refusal to serve and his "present ambivalence," he
told Adolf Berle. "Apart from the objective—and publicized—facts, I have, I
think, an apprehension of inadequacy."[118] That was also the tone he sounded in
responding to notes from members of the Court.[119]

While his new brethren on the Court looked forward to the future, the
feelings of the colleagues Fortas was leaving behind were mixed. Even those who
had found him difficult expressed pride in his appointment and a sense of loss.
"Sure you chewed us out from time to time," one partner admitted. "But you
never asked as much of us as you gave of yourself."[120] Many feared for the future
of the firm. Paul Porter and Thurman Arnold tried to put a good face on it, but
one senator who saw them after Fortas's nomination had been announced
thought they looked as if they were "in mourning."[121]

They need not have worried. Fortas was seeking out his clients to prevent
defections. "I am so pleased to know that Unilever will continue to sends its
problems to this institution in which I have so much of my life and blood," he said
to Patrick Macrory.[122] Fortas assured Fred Lazarus, whose company would also
continue to employ his firm, "how deeply devoted I am—and how grateful I am
for the opportunity to have shared in the wonderful blessing of your friendship
and esteem. Nothing in my adult life has given me so much profound joy and
satisfaction."[123] Fortas's old friend Ernest Meyers, who had retained the firm to
represent the recording industry, voiced the attitude of many when he saw Fortas
after the nomination. "Abe, we hired you, not your law firm," he observed. Fortas
promised that Arnold would represent them well. Although Meyers subsequently came to agree with Fortas, at the time he was skeptical. But, he said
later, "I felt loyalty to Abe and his recommendation."[124] By the time Fortas left
for the Court, he had made sure that his clients would stay.[125] Fortas's care
suggested the depth of his feelings for Arnold, Fortas & Porter.

No one who wrote him was quite sure how his appointment would affect his
relationship with the President, but most assumed that he would have more
leisure and that Johnson would call upon him less frequently. "We were all so fed
up with the way the President was monopolizing his time," Eichholz remem-

bered. When Fortas telephoned her from the White House to say he was joining the Court, Eichholz told him how happy she was. "It's so wonderful because now you will be independent of this man."[126] Indeed Fortas's old friend Elizabeth Wickenden speculated that might be the reason the President had insisted upon the appointment. "Once Johnson became President you were willy-nilly a public person," she observed. "Even an 'eminence grise'—or even the denied appearance of being one—is an institution," though a "shadowy" one. "And, moreover, considering the peculiar symbiosis of temperament and need between you and the President, it seems to me that—in effect—there was no other escape except into a greater and obviously independent institutional role. I wonder if Lyndon in his own curiously intuitive way did not understand this, that he was sacrificing his own interest in setting you free—the way ancient conquerors used to free their enslaved counsellors in gratitude."[127] Or, at least, so many of Fortas's friends hoped.

For his part, Fortas downplayed his relationship with Johnson at his confirmation hearings. "There are two things that have been vastly exaggerated with respect to me," he disingenuously volunteered when asked if his relationship with the President might compromise his judicial independence. "One is the extent to which I am a Presidential adviser, and the other is the extent to which I am a proficient violinist. I am a very poor violinist but very enthusiastic, and my relationship with the President has been exaggerated out of all connection with reality."[128] The puckish and misleading answer distracted the Senate Judiciary Committee.

He had more trouble diverting the committee's attention from his position on jurisprudential issues. Senator Hiram Fong of Hawaii proved most insistent. Would the principle of reapportionment according to "one man–one vote" recently upheld by the Supreme Court lead Fortas to rule all states did not deserve equal representation in the Senate?[129] How would he reconcile the Court's action with the constitutional language that guaranteed each state two senators? Although Fortas repeatedly and politely refused to answer on the grounds that he should not address a legal issue he had not yet studied, Fong pressed him. "Do you think these words [in the Constitution] are clear enough?" he asked Fortas. "My profession is words," the attorney replied. "And I have the greatest, greatest respect for them, and there are very few words that are simple. I don't want to answer your question, Senator." Ultimately, however, Fong won, when Fortas admitted he found reapportionment of the Senate "inconceivable."[130]

Another opinion he tried harder to restrain himself from voicing was more controversial. Attorney General Nicholas Katzenbach and Judge David Bazelon had recently exchanged letters concerning an accused's right to counsel. Bazelon maintained that the poor were entitled to appointed counsel at any stage at which the rich could summon their attorneys. Fortas believed that Katzenbach had contended that, as the poor were more likely to commit crimes, a different standard should be applied to rich and poor. He had recently drafted a long letter to Bazelon condemning Katzenbach's position as "morally offensive and constitutionally invalid."[131] Asked what he thought of the controversy at the hearings, however, Fortas did not refer to his letter but attempted to obfuscate his thoughts on the issue in a long, rambling reply reminiscent of his performance before the congressional committee that had asked him whether Edwin Pauley had tried to bribe Harold Ickes. At last, however, Fortas advanced an opinion "because I am interested in your committee getting as much of an impression of me . . . as possible." The "scales of justice" should not be weighted in favor of either the poor or the rich. "But I do profoundly believe and I want to make this clear that I believe that because a man is poor he should not be deprived of the representation of counsel and of the wherewithal, the facilities to make his defense in our courts of law."[132] Though Fortas's confirmation hearings for the chief justiceship three years later became a forum for alleging that the Supreme Court's opinions favored the poor and criminals, in 1965 the Judiciary Committee reacted to this statement complacently.[133]

Indeed, viewed from the perspective of the 1968 confirmation hearings, the committee's enthusiastic response to Fortas in 1965 seemed odd. Here was a close friend of Lyndon Johnson's, a man who had championed domestic reform and civil liberties his entire adult life. Yet no one on the committee objected to him. When redbaiters alleged that Fortas had long shown un-American tendencies, they found senators singularly unsympathetic. James Eastland, chairman of the committee and one of the more conservative members of Congress, interrupted a witness's remark that Communists had served with Fortas in the AAA to ask: "What has that got to do with the nominee?"[134] In the halcyon days of 1965, Fortas rightly could reprimand the progressive journalist I. F. Stone for complaining that Eastland had treated Fortas harshly. Fortas could legitimately claim that "Senator Eastland conducted the proceedings with the utmost fairness and friendliness" and invite Eastland to his swearing-in as an associate justice without seeming hypocritical.[135]

Times had changed since the 1950s. "It is almost unbelievable that the lawyer for Dorothy Bailey and Owen Lattimore is now one of us," William O. Douglas told Fortas on his first day as a justice. "Twenty years ago the odds would have been 1000 to 1 against it."[136] The year 1965 represented a unique moment when Johnson and the Warren Court could envision completion of the liberal agenda. Appearances were deceiving.

Lyndon Johnson inscribed this photo: "For Abe, who's resisting me with all the horsepower that God gave him!"

"I, Abe Fortas — "

Many believed that Johnson spent days twisting his friend's arm before Fortas reluctantly agreed to become a Supreme Court justice on July 28, 1965.

IMPEACH ABE FORTAS

"*Not yet!*"

The "Impeach Earl Warren" movement anticipated a new target in 1965.

The Warren Court as Fortas entered it. *Left to right:* Justices William Brennan, Potter Stewart, Byron White, Hugo Black, Abe Fortas, William O. Douglas, John Harlan, (Chief Justice) Earl Warren, Tom Clark.

Fortas addressing a Puerto Rican audience at a celebration of Commonwealth Day. He had helped fight for commonwealth status for the island.

Fortas and Johnson in the White House situation room

Making a point to President Johnson during the Dominican crisis, 1965. *Clockwise from left:* Fortas; John Bartlow Martin, former ambassador to the Dominican Republic; Vice-President Hubert Humphrey; Admiral William Raborn; Thomas Mann, assistant secretary of state; Jack Vaughn, assistant secretary of state for inter-American affairs; Kennedy Crockett, director of the Office of Caribbean Affairs; George Ball, under secretary of state; Dean Rusk, secretary of state; President Lyndon Johnson; Robert McNamara, secretary of defense; Jack Valenti, special assistant to the President.

A session of the Tuesday Luncheon Group meeting to discuss Vietnam, January 4, 1966. Fortas was later roundly criticized for sitting in on such meetings. *Clockwise from left:* Fortas; George Ball; Dean Rusk; President Johnson; Arthur Goldberg, ambassador to the United Nations; Bill Moyers, special assistant to the President; McGeorge Bundy, national security adviser.

Clark Clifford and Fortas help the President draft his State of the Union address, 1966

Fortas played a prominent role in persuading Joseph Hirshhorn to give his art collection to the nation. At the announcement of the projected Hirshhorn Museum, *left to right:* Smithsonian director Dillon Ripley, Joseph Hirshhorn, President Johnson, Olga Hirshhorn, Lady Bird Johnson, Vice-President Hubert Humphrey, Justice Fortas, Secretary of the Interior Stewart Udall.

The "3025 N Street Strictly No Refund String Quartet" played regularly on Sunday evenings. Even Lyndon Johnson tried not to interrupt Fortas then.

Pablo Casals and Abe Fortas. Fortas was both friend and legal adviser to the eminent musician for many years.

Fortas and Alexander Schneider sit in with members of the Marine Corps Band, much to the President's delight. The audience includes Mr. and Mrs. George Meany and Congressman Gerald Ford.

Lady Bird Johnson and Fortas at the LBJ Ranch. "There was always a sense of comfort about Abe," Mrs. Johnson recalled.

Justice Fortas in his chambers getting word of his chief justice nomination from the President, June 26, 1968

Fortas and Carol Agger at their Westport home, July 1968

Fortas's nomination as chief justice was the cover story for *Time* magazine on July 5, 1968

# Fortas Concedes Move to Correct War-Cost Critic

## Won't Say If Johnson Was Involved

By John P. MacKenzie
Washington Post Staff Writer

Justice Abe Fortas acknowledged yesterday that he telephoned a former business associate last year to seek correction of his friend's "exaggerated" and widely publicized estimate of the cost of the Vietnam war.

But Fortas declined to tell the Senate Judiciary Committee whether he made the call at the request of the Johnson Administration, which was reported at the time to have been equally upset about the matter.

Fortas, longtime friend of President Johnson, who nominated him to be Chief Justice, asked to be excused from either affirming or denying "any conversation" he may have had "with the President of the United States."

Fortas was already a member of the Court at the time of the phone call. The call was one of several made to Hot Springs, Va., by associates of the President in May, 1967, after news reports said that a member of the Business Council, which was meeting there, had indicated the Administra-

Associated Press

Fortas leaves Senate after second day of testimony.

The Senate hearings on Fortas's nomination as chief justice were front-page news for days. Justice Fortas was questioned—sometimes berated—not only about his own actions and opinions but also about controversial decisions made by the Warren Court long before he joined it.

Earl Warren's funeral, July 12, 1974. *Standing on the steps of the Supreme Court building, from top:* Chief Justice Warren Burger; justices William O. Douglas, William Brennan, Potter Stewart, Byron White, Thurgood Marshall, Harry Blackmun, Lewis Powell, William Rehnquist; former justices Tom Clark, Arthur Goldberg, and Abe Fortas.

# CHAPTER 12

# The Lawyer as Justice

I N 1930 KARL LLEWELLYN SHOCKED THE LEGAL WORLD WITH HIS DEFINI-
tion of law: "What these officials do about disputes is, to my mind, the law
itself." Subsequent remonstrances that those empowered to resolve disagreements might be Nazis forced Llewellyn to retreat.[1] Yet his comments,
or those of other legal realists, apparently affected Fortas. Years later his own
words on the subject reflected that influence. After having described himself as
"a man of law," Fortas defined the rule of law in this way: "The state, the courts
and the individual citizen are bound by a set of laws which have been adopted in a
prescribed manner, and the state and the individual must accept the courts'
determinations of what those rules are and mean in specific instances. *This is the
rule of law,* even if the ultimate judicial decision is by the narrow margin of five to
four!"[2] Fortas did not address how judges were to determine what "the rule of
law" was.

As a Supreme Court justice, Fortas confronted legal realism's most troubling
question. The realists had shown that legal rules did not always determine judicial
results. Once he had participated in a revolution questioning the existence of
principled decision making, how would Fortas himself reach decisions? Ultimately
Fortas judged according to his own concept of fairness. He and the eight justices he
joined—Chief Justice Earl Warren, William J. Brennan, William O. Douglas,
Hugo Black, John Harlan, Byron White, Potter Stewart, and Tom Clark and
his replacement in 1967, Thurgood Marshall—made landmark decisions that
hastened the pace of social change. Though Fortas frequently sided with the
Warren Court's "liberal" majority, he developed his own set of guiding principles.

Since he recognized no distinction between Fortas the person and Fortas the judge, he became an advocate of the outsiders with whom he identified himself.[3] His opinions showed greatest concern with empowering the underprivileged and protecting the right to privacy. To promote these and other ends, he used whatever means he had at hand.

## ENFRANCHISING OUTSIDERS

Fortas's law clerk Daniel Levitt stressed the justice's "determination to reduce the number of 'non-persons' in our society—people who are left out of due process and equal protection because of some exclusionary formula."[4] Fortas worked to increase equity among voters. He sought to exclude alcoholics from the category of criminals, and he maintained that criminals must receive a fair trial. He also insisted that children were entitled to at least the same protection the legal system gave adults.

Of all his opinions, *In re Gault,* which extended to juvenile offenders many of the rights of adults, best illustrates Fortas's personal approach to judging and his identification with those left out of society. "When we talk about juvenile offenders . . . and what's done to or about those offenders, we're talking about '*us,*' not '*them,*'" he emphasized in a discussion of that case. "We're talking about what is happening and what's going to happen to '*us,*'" as juvenile delinquents become seasoned adult criminals. "And we're talking about *all* children: our children, White as well as Black, Middle class as well as poor—not just *theirs.* Because juvenile offenders include children of all classes; and children of all classes are growing up to be adults in a world inhabited by the criminals who are graduates of today's juvenile offender system."[5]

At the turn of the century, reformers had created juvenile courts to obtain more sympathetic treatment for children. As proceedings in these courts were classified as civil rather than criminal, they saw no reason to grant to juveniles the due process rights accorded adult criminal defendants. What is more, the state aimed to rehabilitate, not to punish, the juvenile and acted in *parens patriae,* in place of the authority of the parents rather than as the children's adversary. But by the 1960s, Fortas had come to believe that the Progressives' solution was only breeding criminals. He considered the juvenile offender system "the most appalling and dangerous part of the bankrupt estate of our national services" and regretfully admitted that "due process won't cure this situation. Something is wrong—drastically wrong with the system, with the handling of the children and juveniles who enter this never-never land."[6]

Introducing due process was still the largest contribution to improving the juvenile courts Fortas believed he could make as a judge. One of his early opinions, *Kent* v. *United States,* had hinted that the Court might grant juvenile offenders the due process rights of adult criminals in the future. Sixteen-year-old Morris Kent, a resident of the District of Columbia, had been on probation for two years when he was charged in juvenile court with housebreaking and rape. The judge denied the motion of Kent's counsel for a hearing and refused him access to the file on his client that had accumulated during Kent's probationary period. The judge then relinquished jurisdiction in accordance with a local statute which authorized him, "after full investigation," to decide that such cases were better tried in the adult criminal courts. When the case reached the Supreme Court, Fortas's majority opinion ruled that the judge had not in fact made a full investigation before he surrendered jurisdiction and that such an inquiry must be completed before Kent's case could be transferred to the adult criminal court. Although his opinion rested on statutory rather than constitutional grounds, Fortas already was considering the constitutional standards appropriate for juvenile court trials. In an early draft of the opinion, Fortas observed that Kent's case suggested "basic issues as to the justifiability of denying to a juvenile less protection than is accorded to adults suspected of criminal offenses." He questioned whether juvenile courts were doing their job: "While there can be no doubt of the original laudable purpose of juvenile courts, studies and critiques in recent years raise serious questions as to whether actual performance measures well enough against theoretical purpose to make tolerable the immunity of the process from the reach of constitutional guarantees applicable to adults. . . . There is evidence, in fact, that there may be grounds for concern that the child receives the worst of both worlds: that he gets neither the protections accorded to adults nor the solicitous care and regenerative treatment postulated for children."[7] According to Fortas, "the admonition to function in a 'parental' relationship is not an invitation to despotism." Although he substituted "procedural arbitrariness" for "despotism" in the final version of *Kent,* he retained the implication that juvenile courts were not protecting their charges adequately and held that "the [surrender of jurisdiction] hearing must measure up to the essentials of due process and fair treatment."[8]

The Gault case involved a less serious offense than Kent's and a disproportionately long incarceration. A neighbor complained that Gerald Gault, a fifteen-year-old probationer together with a friend had made an obscene telephone call to her. Without informing Gault's parents, the police picked up the two boys and took them to the Children's Detention Home, where probation officers interrogated them and kept Gault in custody for several days without any explanation. Before the hearing authorities filed a petition formally stating that Gault was a "delinquent" that included no grounds for their determination. No transcript was made of the hearing, and participants subsequently disagreed about what had been said there. The juvenile court judge claimed that Gault had admitted making some lewd statements, while Gault's parents and the probation officer maintained that the boy had not conceded any wrongdoing. All agreed that, although the boy's mother had requested that the complaining neighbor be asked to appear, the judge had ruled her presence unnecessary. At the end of the hearing, Gault was committed to the state industrial school until his twenty-first birthday. The case went to the Supreme Court on appeal.[9]

To Gault's lawyers, the boy's plight raised major constitutional issues. Did due process require that a juvenile receive written notice of the charges against him, be permitted to confront his accusers, be advised of his right to counsel and his privilege against self-incrimination? Was a juvenile entitled to a written transcript of the proceedings, and did he have a right to appellate review? Nevertheless, Fortas's clerk John Griffiths was unenthusiastic. His memorandum about *Gault* suggested that the justice may have been searching for a case that would enable him to translate into law his implication in *Kent* that juvenile offenders deserved due process. If *Gault* had come to the Court on a writ of certiorari, Griffiths would have wanted to deny review: "This is too murky a case to take as the first one in which to extend Kent to the states." Because *Gault* came on appeal, however, he thought the Court should hear it. Griffiths acknowledged that "as an appeal, it seems to me absolutely impossible to deny that substantial federal questions are presented as to the applicability of the due process clause, and more specific constitutional requirements, to the states."[10]

Fortas made *Gault* a good case by emphasizing the facts. "I had written a draft of an opinion . . . with a typical sort of wooden law-student-type statement of facts with absolutely no pizazz," Griffiths remembered. The justice told the clerk his work was "rubbish" and rewrote it. Griffiths did not consider the new version an improvement, except for the statement of facts, which was "fabulous."[11] Fortas used every detail that suited his presentation of Gault as a victim of injustice. Another justice might have said that Gault was on probation because he had accompanied a friend on a purse-snatching mission. Fortas isolated his subject from the thief and implied that Gault had not participated in the crime. He wrote that Gault had been placed on probation "for having been in the company of another boy who had stolen a wallet from a lady's purse."[12] Like most of his statements of fact, it was longer, more richly detailed, and more repetitive than those of his colleagues. "He would have said that if you're arguing a case, the most important thing is to state the facts in your way," Griffiths recalled.[13] Although Fortas was now a justice, he still considered himself an advocate.

In this instance, he had few legal precedents to help him make his case. The best was his own opinion in *Kent,* which he highlighted: "Although our decision turned upon the language of the statute, we emphasized the necessity that 'the

basic requirements of due process and fairness' be satisfied in such proceedings."
He relied on two other precedents, neither precisely on point. "While these cases
relate only to restricted aspects of the subject, they unmistakably indicate that,
whatever may be their precise impact, neither the Fourteenth Amendment nor
the Bill of Rights is for adults alone."[14] Fortas then called forth the notion that
the due process clause guarantees "fairness, impartiality and orderliness" and
noted that "the procedural rules which have been fashioned from the generality
of due process" had long guaranteed individual freedom.[15] Add a brief attack on
the doctrine of *parens patriae* as constitutionally "debatable," and Fortas's legal
argument was complete. He could now announce that "under our Constitution,
the condition of being a boy does not justify a kangaroo court"[16] and conclude
that a juvenile proceeding must feature notice of charges, notice of the right to be
represented by counsel and to have the court appoint an attorney if the parent
cannot afford to hire one, notice of the right to confront and cross-examine
witnesses, and notice of the privilege against self-incrimination. Since the realities preoccupied him more than the legalities, Fortas also challenged the *parens
patriae* doctrine on sociological grounds. To Fortas, research in the social sciences
suggested that "the appearance as well as the actuality of fairness, impartiality
and orderliness—in short, the essentials of due process—may be a more impressive and more therapeutic attitude so far as the juvenile is concerned."[17] The
studies he cited indicated that juvenile courts' performance might be improved
by the addition of some due process safeguards.

Why some, rather than all? If, as Fortas said, the Bill of Rights and the due
process clause of the Fourteenth Amendment were not intended for adults alone,
to what extent were they meant to apply to children? *Gault* raised more questions
than it answered.[18] The decision did not indicate whether all the protections
available to adult criminal defendants should be awarded to children. Were they
entitled, for example, to a public trial, trial by jury, and grand jury indictments?
Practical reasons prevented Fortas from resolving those issues. According to his
conference notes, Warren, Brennan, and Harlan initially did not even favor
extending the privilege against self-incrimination to juveniles.[19] Fortas himself
might have been willing to grant juveniles all the rights of adult criminal defendants, and perhaps some additional ones, but he did not want to lose his majority.[20]

One member of the Court thought Fortas should have written a more sweeping opinion nonetheless. Hugo Black joined the majority but issued a concurring
opinion reiterating his longstanding conviction that the Fourteenth Amendment
incorporated the entire Bill of Rights and challenging Fortas's contention that the
due process clause contained a guarantee of fairness. "Appellants are entitled to
these rights, not because 'fairness, impartiality and orderliness—in short, the
essentials of due process'—require them and not because they are 'the pro-

cedural rules which have been fashioned from the generality of due process,' "
Black sardonically observed, "but because they are specifically and unequivocally
granted by provisions of the Fifth and Sixth Amendments which the Fourteenth
Amendment makes applicable to the States."[21] Though Black's reasoning provided a neat way of extending to juveniles rights that Fortas wanted to give them,
neither Fortas nor his colleagues were ready to agree that the Fourteenth Amendment "incorporated" all the rights granted in the first ten amendments.

Just as Fortas's opinion did not give juveniles all the protection adults received, so too it did not say whether they possessed any rights not currently
available to adults. In noting that "the features of the juvenile system which its
proponents have asserted are of unique benefit will not be impaired by constitutional domestication," Fortas seemed to leave open the possibility that the Court
might award juveniles unique rights if subsequent cases showed they would
profit from protections adults lacked, or that states could constitutionally do so if
they desired.[22] In indicating that juveniles' rights would be determined on a case-
by-case basis, *Gault* guaranteed much further litigation.

The decision still deservedly received much praise. Earl Warren predicted it
would be known "as the Magna Carta for juveniles." Gault's attorney, Norman
Dorsen, wrote Fortas that "the 'thanks' you so generously gave me is much
appreciated, but it is really I and my colleagues who owe thanks to you for laying
the groundwork in the Kent case as well as for your opinion in Gault." The
Committee on Social Welfare of the National Council of the Churches of Christ
expressed appreciation for Fortas's "scholarly and humane opinion." For Inés
Muñoz Marín, the decision reflected "all the tenderness, kindness and fairness
of true love, that I have known in your eyes when you met children." The *New
York Times* praised the Court for "forcing needed and long overdue reforms,"
while the *Washington Post* editorialized that "children were surely meant to be
included within the promise of equal justice for all."[23]

Others questioned Fortas's opinion. Even his clerk admitted that "the sociological and psychological research in this area is distressingly thin."[24] Some
did not believe that the social sciences justified Fortas's decree that juvenile
proceedings should resemble criminal trials. "To impose the Court's long catalog
of requirements upon juvenile proceedings in every area of the country is to
invite a long step backwards into the nineteenth century," Stewart said in his
dissent. He argued that the majority opinion undid the work of "dedicated men
and women" who had devoted themselves "to the enlightened task of bringing us
out of the dark world of Charles Dickens in meeting our responsibilities to the
child in our society." Stewart admitted possessing "neither the specialized experience nor the expert knowledge to predict with any certainty where may lie the
brightest hope for progress in dealing with the serious problems of juvenile

delinquency. But I am certain that the answer does not lie in the Court's opinion." To him, Fortas's solution seemed an unjustifiable and unwise intervention into a sphere in which the Court did not belong.[25]

Right-wing opponents of the Warren Court proved even more harsh. They complained that Fortas would promote crime by granting to juveniles the rights the Court too generously had given adult criminal defendants. "The Supreme Court is the criminal's best friend," a cartoon mailed to Fortas charged. "Why not . . . follow the Constitution?" an angry citizen asked. "One of many disgusted Americans" said: "By all means, give them all the constitutional rights now extended to ADULT offenders. Of course, we the public assume, by the same token, as they get ADULT RIGHTS for breaking the law, they naturally will also get ADULT PUNISHMENT when appearing in the courts of law. Or is that too much to expect from the law?"[26]

Fortas's willingness to expand the rights of alleged adult criminals also alienated critics on the right. To him, safeguarding constitutional integrity was paramount. In one concurring opinion Fortas maintained that the guarantee of a fair trial required the prosecution in a rape case to disclose evidence about a victim's sexual conduct with others and about her state of mind that might enable the defense to prove she had consented to intercourse. "Our total lack of sympathy for the kind of physical assault which is involved here may not lead us to condone state suppression of information which might be useful to the defense," Fortas lectured his colleagues. "A criminal trial is not a game in which the State's function is to outwit and entrap its quarry."[27] Sometimes Fortas was vague about the constitutional basis for such decisions. In *Johnson* v. *Avery,* he wrote the majority opinion invalidating a Tennessee regulation that punished prisoners who helped fellow inmates prepare habeas corpus petitions. To hold otherwise, Fortas reasoned, would effectively prevent illiterate and indigent prisoners from filing such petitions. Thus where the state provided no alternative means of legal assistance, it had to tolerate jailhouse lawyers. Since it was unclear, though, whether he rested his opinion on the due process clause or the equal protection clause, and whether he would eventually find that the state must permit jailhouse lawyers in other postconviction actions besides habeas corpus proceedings,[28] he was preserving maximum flexibility for the Court in the future.

Where the privilege against self-incrimination was concerned, Fortas's opinions were never murky. He was an absolutist who insisted that accused criminals should never be forced to implicate themselves. One law clerk considered the justice the "greatest champion" of the Fifth Amendment of his era.[29] In *Miranda* v. *Arizona,* Fortas joined Black, Douglas, Warren, and Brennan in what has been called the Court's "most controversial" decision in the realm of criminal law.[30] With them, he voted that the Fifth Amendment privilege against self-incrimination required police to warn a person who had been arrested of his right to remain silent and his right to counsel and that anything he said might be used against him. But although most of his colleagues were content to stop at *Miranda*, Fortas was not. As his clerk said, "He believed passionately in freedom from compelled self-incrimination, and he defined that in a way which went far beyond how other Justices defined it."[31]

In *Schmerber* v. *California* a majority ruled that the Fifth Amendment notwithstanding, the state could forcibly perform a blood test on an individual suspected of intoxication because the evidence would disappear unless the test was performed immediately. That rationale did not persuade Fortas. "I'm clear. I vote this is unconst[itutiona]l," his notes indicated.[32] "In my view, petitioner's privilege against self-incrimination applies," he said in his four-sentence dissent.[33] When the Court relied upon *Schmerber* in *U.S.* v. *Wade* to hold that an accused could be compelled in a police lineup to speak words said to have been uttered by the perpetrator at the time of committing the crime, Fortas was furious. The Court's reasoning was ill-founded, he charged, because "*Schmerber*, which authorized the forced extraction of blood from the veins of an unwilling human being did not compel the person actively to cooperate—to accuse himself by a volitional act which differs only in degree from compelling him to act out the crime, which, I assume, would be rebuffed by the Court." For Fortas, the volitional element in *Wade* placed "the compelled utterance of the accused squarely within the history and noble purpose of the Fifth Amendment's commandment." Further, he maintained that doctrine enunciated in *Schmerber* should be limited to the facts in that case. "To permit its insidious doctrine to extend beyond the invasion of the body, which it permits, to compulsion of the will of a man, is to deny and defy a precious part of our historical faith and to discard one of the most profoundly cherished instruments by which we have established the freedom and dignity of the individual."[34]

Fortas was nearly as passionate about the prohibition against unlawful searches and seizures in the Fourth Amendment. In *Alderman* v. *United States*, he was not satisfied with the Court's decision that a defendant could challenge the introduction of evidence gained from the government's illegal electronic wiretapping only if the wiretapping took place on premises he owned or if he participated in the overheard conversations. Fortas would give anyone against whom an illegal search was directed standing to object to the introduction of evidence obtained from that search.[35] But the case also showed that the justice was more conservative than his brethren where national security was concerned. The majority voted to force the disclosure of all surveillance records to any defendant who possessed standing, while Fortas wanted to allow the trial judge to screen out any evidence involving national security that was irrelevant to the defendant's case.[36]

Some scholars have maintained that "there were limits to the protections for defendants that Fortas would enforce."[37] In *Bloom v. Illinois,* a decision cited as an example for that proposition, Fortas questioned the majority's insistence that state courts must try more criminal contempt cases by jury. "We should be ready to welcome state variations which do not impair—indeed, which may advance— the theory and purpose of trial by jury," he said.[38] But Fortas still joined the majority in *Bloom,* and his implied willingness to forgo a jury trial in certain circumstances hid an ulterior motive. Earlier, when the Court was deciding one in a line of cases culminating in *Bloom,* Fortas had confided to Brennan that he was "worried about the situation in the South if we insist on jury trials in all criminal contempts."[39] As an adviser to Lyndon Johnson, Fortas had endorsed jury trial for those held in criminal contempt for violation of the 1957 Civil Rights Act. To guarantee the act's passage, he was willing to allow bigots the cushion of a white jury that likely would free them. But Fortas's comment to Brennan indicated that he was more reluctant to risk depriving black criminal defendants of their freedom by exposing them to an all-white jury.

No case better exemplified Fortas's willingness to adopt unusual measures to protect defendants' rights than his unsuccessful attempt to promote a constitutional insanity defense in *Powell v. Texas.* Powell, a chronic alcoholic, had been convicted of violating a Texas statue that made it a crime to be intoxicated in a public place. His attorneys argued that penalizing him for public intoxication violated the Eighth Amendment prohibition against cruel and unusual punishment, which the Fourteenth Amendment made applicable to the states. The trial court agreed that chronic alcoholism was a disease and that the chronic alcoholic who was intoxicated in public acted under a compulsion. It also conceded that Powell was a chronic alcoholic. But it rejected his constitutional defense and found him guilty of violating the statute. At the conference held after oral argument of the case before the Supreme Court, Fortas, Brennan, Douglas, Stewart, and White agreed with Powell's attorneys that the case was controlled by *Robinson v. California,* a decision holding unconstitutional a California law that made it illegal to be addicted to narcotics.[40] According to the Court in *Robinson,* penalization for the status or condition of being a narcotics addict was "cruel and unusual punishment" in violation of the Eighth and Fourteenth Amendments. Fortas and his colleagues reasoned that as addiction to alcohol resembled addiction to drugs, *Robinson* provided grounds for reversal of Powell's conviction. Fortas was assigned the majority opinion. "*Powell v. Texas* is the one thing I can remember that he really cared about," David Rosenbloom recalled.

Rosenbloom, one of his clerks at the time, thought that Fortas's position proved his sympathy for the underprivileged "sprang from the gut. . . . In terms of the downtrodden and the poor, Fortas had a real feeling."[41]

Early drafts of Fortas's majority opinion made that feeling apparent. In a lengthy discussion of whether alcoholism was a disease, Fortas again took an interdisciplinary approach and cited the work of numerous scholars and medical doctors who agreed it was. But after concluding alcoholism was a disease, Fortas retreated to the more acceptable confines of law and based his decision on the Constitution. "These data provide a context for our consideration of the instant case," he noted. "They do not dictate our conclusion. The questions for us are not settled by reference to medicine and therapy, but just as we must turn to medical science for answer to basic legal issues raised, for example, by the defense of insanity, so here we must approach our problem in the light of medical data." Fortas then turned to a legal analysis of Powell's case, in which he relied almost exclusively on *Robinson* v. *California*. "*Robinson* stands upon a principle which, despite its subtlety, must be simply stated and respectfully applied because it is the foundation of individual liberty and the cornerstone of the relations of a civilized state and its citizens," his draft said. "Criminal penalties may be inflicted only if the accused has in fact elected to engage in the activities defined as an offense." Under *Robinson,* and "read against the background of the medical and sociological data to which we have referred," the Texas statute at issue in *Powell* therefore violated the Eighth and Fourteenth Amendments.[42]

By the time Fortas's draft in *Powell* was printed and circulated, he had broadened it in one important respect. In *Durham* v. *United States,* he had urged the District of Columbia to abandon the old M'Naghten test for insanity. As a result of Fortas's presentation, the court held that an accused could be judged not guilty by reason of insanity even if he realized his act was wrong. As long as "his unlawful act was the product of a mental disease or mental defect," he was not criminally liable. The crucial sentence that Fortas added to his draft in *Powell* stated that "the findings of the trial judge call into play the ancient principle of our law that *a person may not be punished if the acts essential to constitute the defined crime are not voluntary but are part of the pattern of a disease.*"[43] In essence, he was broadening the *Durham* test by requiring the accused only to show that the act was part of the "pattern" rather than the "product" of the disease and by eliminating the requirement that psychiatrists prove the disease was "mental." He then applied the new insanity test to the entire country.

Hugo Black found Fortas's position untenable. In his draft dissent, he argued that the majority had exceeded the limits of judicial power. Black accused the majority of basing its decision on medical data about alcoholism instead of on law and castigated Fortas for producing a document that "reads more like a highly technical medical critique than a Court opinion deciding a question of constitutional law." Black thought *Robinson* inapplicable, because the Texas statute challenged in *Powell* made public intoxication, not chronic alcoholism, a crime. He twice charged that Fortas had manipulated the findings of fact to hold that Powell had been penalized for his condition rather than his acts and therefore bring his behavior within the purview of *Robinson*. "By this verbal twist, the Court replaces any attempt to understand what happened here with a play on words." But Fortas's declaration that there could be no criminal liability for an act that was part of the pattern of a disease infuriated Black most. It represented "a revolutionary doctrine of constitutional law that tightly restricts state power to deal with a wide variety of other harmful conduct . . . [and indicates] that it is cruel and unusual to punish a person who is not morally blameworthy." Black warned that the Court's opinion would wreak havoc in the thirty-odd states which still employed the M'Naghten test and in the states "which had recognized insanity defenses similar to the Court's [proposed] new constitutional rule" as well. In a final jibe, Black predicted that "the resulting confusion and uncertainty will make us envy the experience of the District of Columbia Circuit," which had encountered "enormous difficulties" in applying the rule Fortas had persuaded it to accept in *Durham*.[44]

While Black tried to undermine Fortas's majority, Fortas was struggling to preserve it. Though Fortas initially worked hard to win votes for his positions,[45] Potter Stewart recalled that for most of his tenure, Fortas generally was "not a lobbyist."[46] The Powell case was so important to Fortas, however, that he lobbied White to maintain his majority. White made numerous suggestions for change as the majority opinion went through various drafts, and Fortas incorporated them all. In the end, however, White changed his mind, and Fortas lost his majority.[47] "I think it was a big disappointment to him," one of his clerks recalled.[48]

Fortas now filed a dissent that reiterated the points he had made in his earlier draft opinion for the Court.[49] Both White and Black concurred with Marshall's majority opinion distinguishing the case from *Robinson* and claiming that "nothing could be less fruitful than for this Court to be impelled into defining some sort of insanity test in constitutional terms."[50] Black's concurring opinion, which remained critical of Fortas's arguments, elicited one word from Fortas: "Yech!"[51] In retrospect, it seems more surprising that Fortas briefly had gained majority support in *Powell* than that he lost it. William O. Douglas had labeled Fortas's opinion for the majority "great and outstanding."[52] It was, however, revolutionary. Fortas's draft majority opinion would have upset the balance of power between the federal government and the states in the realm of criminal law and proposed a constitutional standard of criminal liability that most states would have been unwilling to accept even when a defendant pleaded insanity. *Powell* suggested the depth of Fortas's commitment to the disenfranchised.

He proved equally protective of their entitlement to the franchise itself. In *Harper* v. *Virginia Board of Elections,* he joined Douglas's opinion invalidating a state poll tax. Fortas's draft concurrence emphasized that "the Virginia poll tax is an impermissible attempt to impose a charge or penalty on the exercise of a 'fundamental right.' "[53] According to Fortas, even illiteracy was not a legitimate basis for denying the right to vote. *Cardona* v. *Power* involved a Spanish-speaking woman raised in Puerto Rico who moved to New York and challenged the state's requirement that voters be literate in English. When the case reached the Supreme Court, the majority sent it back to the appellate court with directions to determine the level of the woman's education, for under the Voting Rights Act, which the Court upheld in a companion case,[54] anyone who had successfully completed the sixth grade in an American [including Puerto Rican] school where Spanish was the primary language of instruction could not be prevented from voting because of inability to read or write English. Douglas's draft dissent in *Cardona* urged the Court to consider the constitutionality of New York's literacy requirement. He argued that it violated the equal protection clause, as it discriminated against voters literate in other languages. Still, Douglas granted that "a state has sufficient interest in the intelligent use of the ballot to justify conditioning it upon ability to read and write."[55] After reading Douglas's draft, Fortas told his friend that the literacy requirement should eventually be abolished altogether. "I would extend Thurman Arnold's remark generally: that there is no evidence whatever that reading and writing have been of any assistance to the people in Virginia. In my opinion, this is universal truth. In Puerto Rico, it was the illiterate people who were responsible for the election of Muñoz Marín."[56]

Fortas ultimately joined Douglas's dissent after his friend inserted language expressing doubt as to whether literacy was a "wise prerequisite for exercise of the franchise" and deleted a reference to Puerto Rico as a nation of illiterates. In fact, by the time Fortas had finished with Douglas's dissent, it championed the Puerto Rican electorate. Douglas included a footnote written by Fortas maintaining that while Puerto Rico was "fast overcoming its illiteracy problem," even when it had housed a large proportion of illiterates, they had elected "highly progressive and able officials."[57]

Though Fortas believed in every American's right to vote, he was sometimes frustrated by his colleagues' insistence that every vote count equally. He came to the Court too late to participate in *Reynolds* v. *Sims,* which held that the equal protection clause demanded the extension of the principle of "one man–one vote" to election of members of the state legislature.[58] He was, however, involved in the reapportionment decisions determining whether *Reynolds* should be applied to other governmental units, and he found his colleagues overly rigid in those instances. In *Kirkpatrick* v. *Preisler,* the Court announced that in redistricting for congressional elections, states had to make a good-faith effort to achieve mathematical equality between districts and to justify any disparities, however small. [59] Though he joined the opinion, Fortas's concurrence observed that "no purpose is served by an insistence on precision which is unattainable because of the inherent imprecisions in the population data on which districting must be based." The majority's exactitude reflected a "search for the will-o'-the-wisp." [60]

Fortas broke with the Court when it applied *Reynolds* to city and county governments in *Avery* v. *Midland County.* [61] His dissent contended that although the principle of "one man–one vote" was appropriate for a state legislature because each person stood in the same relation to that body, the individual special-purpose units of local government generally had a greater impact on some citizens than others. In the instant case, as the Midland County Commissioners Court handled mostly rural matters, Fortas concluded that the Court's decision would actually violate the equal protection rights of country residents by increasing the voice of those in the city. "Constitutional commandments are not surgical instruments," Fortas reminded the majority. "They have a tendency to hack deeply—to amputate." Here the Court was applying "the hatchet of one man–one vote" to the wrong thicket. [62] Even so, Fortas maintained in *Avery* that the one man, one vote principle should be applied whenever a local governing unit's work affected all citizens equally, and he affirmed his faith in *Reynolds* itself. [63] Indeed, he praised the Court's action in that case so highly that Stewart issued a separate opinion expressing his agreement with most of Fortas's reasoning and explaining that he would have joined his dissent were it not for his colleague's "unquestioning endorsement of the doctrine of *Reynolds* v. *Sims.*" [64]

Where outsiders were concerned, Fortas often positioned himself to the left of a majority the Warren Court's critics on the right thought radical. Even his dissent in *Avery* can be interpreted as an attempt to protect increasingly marginal inhabitants of the countryside from being overwhelmed by an urban society. Fortas also went further than the Warren Court's liberal bloc in asserting the right to privacy.

## THE RIGHT TO PRIVACY

In 1965 the Court made privacy a constitutional entitlement when it held in *Griswold* v. *Connecticut* that a state statute prohibiting the use of contraceptive devices violated the right to privacy. Unable to agree upon that right's origin, the justices evaded the problem by declaring that "specific guarantees in the Bill of

Rights have penumbras, formed by enumerations from those guarantees that
help give them life and substance" and that those penumbras included a right to
privacy in certain situations, here a married couple's right to privacy within the
home.[65] For Fortas, who came to the Court after *Griswold* had been decided,
privacy was crucial. His belief in it ran through his Fourth and Fifth Amendment decisions and was especially evident in some of his First Amendment
decisions.[66] Like Brandeis, who railed against newspaper reporters who pan-
dered to "idle or prurient [public] curiosity," Fortas was skeptical of the press.[67]
Indeed one of his clerks believed that Fortas loathed and feared the press.[68] The
Walter Jenkins incident deepened his conviction that the press was overly intrusive. He could not understand the insistence of justices Douglas and Black upon
its First Amendment rights. Indeed he regarded their protection of the media
with the same bemusement with which another individual would have contemplated a defender of the rattlesnake's right to strike. It was therefore "no secret"
to Fortas's clerks that one of their boss's ambitions "was somehow to narrow the
scope of *New York Times Company* v. *Sullivan.*"[69] Traditionally truth had constituted the only defense in a defamation suit. But in 1964 the Court expanded
the defenses available to the press. In *New York Times* v. *Sullivan*, the Court said
that public officials would win a defamation action only if they could prove that
the press had acted with "actual malice," defined as either knowledge or falsity or
reckless disregard for the truth.[70] The case of *Time* v. *Hill* "involved a first look
by the Supreme Court at competing claims of individual privacy and institutional
press freedom" in the post–*New York Times* and post-*Griswold* context.[71]

After fugitives held the Hill family hostage for nineteen hours, the Hills
turned down lucrative offers to tell their story and accelerated their plans to move
to another state in an effort to avoid publicity. Media attention had diminished by
the time Joseph Hayes wrote *The Desperate Hours*, a novel about a family held
hostage by fugitives. When *Life* magazine was preparing a review of the stage
adaptation of *The Desperate Hours*, it received a tip that the Hills' experience had
inspired the book. The magazine arranged for actors in the play to be pho-
tographed in the house where the hostage episode had occurred. Although their
captors had in fact not physically mistreated the family, the photographs followed
the play in suggesting that the fugitives had behaved violently toward the son and
daughter. The magazine never asked Hayes about the link between the family's
experience and his novel, and it did not contact the Hills for comment.[72] The
first draft of the review did not mention the Hills by name, although it stated that
the play was "a somewhat fictionalized" version of an incident which had actually happened. But a senior editor dropped that colorless language and revised the
draft to indicate that the play was a reenactment of the "desperate ordeal of the

James Hill family."[73] Mrs. Hill became seriously ill after she read the review in *Life,* and Mr. Hill sued the magazine's owner, Time, Inc.

Hill based the lawsuit upon a New York right of privacy statute that prevented the use of a name, portrait, or picture "for advertising purposes or for the purpose of trade" without written permission from the individual involved. The New York courts decided in favor of Hill, and *Time,* Inc., appealed to the Supreme Court. At issue was whether the "actual malice" standard should be applied to immunize the press from breach of privacy suits filed by public figures. Though Fortas rarely had been on the same side as the Hills' chief attorney, Richard Nixon, he shared that Republican's belief that, when freedom of the press was weighed against the right to privacy, the scales tipped toward the latter. Indeed, according to another one of James Hill's lawyers, at oral argument Fortas and Chief Justice Earl Warren, another old enemy of Nixon's, "almost outspokenly" sided with him: "Nixon later commented that these were two political men and so knew firsthand how fierce and lacerating the press could be when it fastened on a target." Their encouragement left Nixon confident he had won a narrow majority.[74] He had done even better than that. The story in *Life* was "a fictionalization of these people's experience and false and, in that circumstance, there's no First Amendment problem," Warren announced at the conference after Nixon's presentation. "In this limited application, I see no threat to a free press." Six members of the Court decided to affirm the judgment in favor of Hill, and Fortas was assigned the opinion.[75]

Fortas's draft included a detailed statement of facts, which emphasized the mistreatment *Life* alleged the fugitives had inflicted on the Hill children and the effect of the review upon Mrs. Hill. Fortas observed that "Mr. Hill resisted his impulse to resort to the direct remedy of a simpler age—physical violence upon those whom he considered had perpetrated an outrage upon his family." The effect conveyed by his statement of facts was that this impulse must have been resisted only with the greatest difficulty.[76] Since Hill had reacted in a civilized manner, Fortas could come to his aid only by condemning the press and asserting Hill's right to privacy. Those were the two noteworthy aspects of Fortas's draft opinion. The "art of subtle repetition" was nowhere evident in his attack upon the press. According to Fortas: "The facts of this case are unavoidably distressing. Needless, heedless, wanton and deliberate injury of the sort inflicted by Life's picture story is not an essential instrument of responsible journalism. Magazine writers and editors are not, by reason of their high office, relieved of the common obligation to avoid deliberately inflicting wanton and unnecessary injury. The prerogatives of the press—essential to our liberty—do not . . . confer a license for pointless assault."[77]

As Fortas acknowledged, *Life's* unjust behavior did not necessarily make it liable for the damages Hill sought: "We are dealing with a problem of law, and not merely a question of civilized standards." If the article on the family deserved First Amendment protection, its "offensiveness" was irrelevant. In a singularly ungracious assertion of First Amendment guarantees, Fortas noted that "this Nation is prepared to pay a heavy price for the immunity of the press in terms of national discomfort and danger and in the tolerance of a measure of individual assault."[78] Fortas continued however, that in the incident under consideration, the magazine had violated the right to privacy established by the New York statute. He then startled his colleagues by claiming that the statute was based upon a constitutional right to privacy. While *Griswold* had suggested that a right to privacy existed in limited circumstances, Fortas now described its existence in broader terms than any member of the Court had ever used:

> There is . . . no doubt that a fundamental right of privacy exists, and that it is of constitutional stature. It is not just the right to remedy against false accusation, provided, within limits, by the law of defamation; it is not only the right to be secure in one's person, house, papers and effects, except as permitted by law; it embraces the right to be free from coercion to incriminate oneself, however subtle; it is different from, but akin to the right to select and freely to practice one's religion and the right to freedom of speech; it is more than the specific right to be secure against the Peeping Tom or the intrusion of electronic devices and wire-tapping. All of these are aspects of the right to privacy; but the right to privacy reaches beyond any of its specifics. It is, simply stated, the right to be let alone.[79]

Fortas concluded that in asserting the right of privacy the New York statute did not conflict with the First Amendment, which gave rise to a cause of action only in the case of fictional accounts that were commercially exploited. "The deliberate callous invasion of the Hills' right to be let alone . . . cannot be defended on the ground that it is within the purview of a constitutional guarantee designed to protect the free exchange of ideas and opinions," he maintained. "This is exploitation undertaken to titillate and excite, for commercial purposes. It was not a retelling of a newsworthy incident or of an event relating to a public figure. . . . It was fiction: an invention, distorted and put to the uses of the promotion of Life magazine and of a play."[80]

Fortas's attempt to support his far-fetched statement that "the right to privacy reaches beyond any of its specifics" proved a fundamental problem with his draft. As Fortas said, the Court had vindicated certain rights that might be classified under the heading of *privacy,* though it had not always described them in those terms. But that gave him no basis for claiming that the Court's action in those specific instances had the synergistic effect of creating a general right to privacy grounded in the Constitution. Indeed Fortas acknowledged that he did not know the right's constitutional origins. He followed his paean to privacy with a citation to *Griswold* v. *Connecticut*. According to Fortas, *Griswold* stood for the proposition that "privacy is a basic right," and it followed that "the States may, by appropriate legislation and within proper bounds, enact laws to vindicate that right."[81] But as Douglas—the author of the majority opinion in *Griswold*—said in the draft dissent he filed after reading Fortas's document, *Griswold* rested on the Court's belief in the importance of preserving "barricades to the sanctuaries of our homes." *Griswold* granted a specific right to privacy in a private place.[82]

But it was White rather than Douglas who was jeopardizing Fortas's majority. White believed that the New York Court of Appeals had suggested that the state's invasion of privacy statute might "permit civil and criminal liability for publishing a truthful account of a newsworthy event, whether current or past, as long as the jury finds that the publication was solely for the purposes of trade."[83] If the statute did make such material actionable, it would indeed have been overbroad and unconstitutional. Fortas revised his draft majority opinion to insist that the New York statute required "deliberate, intentional, pervasive fictionalization." As he recognized, however, he was not sufficiently persuasive in making the argument to lay to rest the doubts White's draft had created among some of his colleagues. In the end, Fortas called for reargument to determine the meaning of the New York statute and the "fictionalization" standard in the following Court term. Reargument vindicated Fortas's understanding of New York law, but it was too late.[84] By the time Nixon had returned to the Court in 1967, Fortas had lost his majority.

On the day before Nixon reargued the case, Hugo Black circulated a memorandum that ridiculed Fortas's draft. Black repeated his understanding that the First Amendment promised "unequivocal press freedom" and his conviction that any attempt to "balance" other interests, such as those of reputation or privacy, against it was ill-founded. Black believed that any argument to the contrary by Fortas and other justices involved substituting their perceptions of fairness for the Founding Fathers' wisdom. "We, the judiciary, are no longer to be crippled and hobbled by the old admonition that 'We must always remember it is a Constitution we are *expounding*,' but we are to work under the exhilarating new slogan that 'We must always remember it is a Constitution we are *rewriting* to fit the times," he sarcastically said.[85]

While Black tolerated no attempt to weigh constitutional rights against the First Amendment, he became scathing when his colleagues "balanced" a right he charged the Constitution did not recognize. Fortas's "rhapsodical descriptions of the great value of 'right to privacy'" had not convinced him that such a right existed. Although he acknowledged that the Constitution protected certain rights of privacy, Black reiterated his dissenting argument in *Griswold* that "it approaches the fantastic for judges to attempt to create from these a general, all-embracing constitutional provision guaranteeing a general right to privacy."[86] Even if he were to recognize, "which I do not," that judges should weigh the press's First Amendment rights "against a judge-made right of privacy," Black would hope, he continued, that "at the very least this weighing should be done with a clear and complete understanding of what is being weighed against freedom of the press." As in his *Powell* v. *Texas* opinion, he charged that Fortas had manipulated the facts in "an obvious and unjustified effort" to develop "invidious characterizations of Life" and to weight the scales against the publisher. "The Court's choice of inferences supposedly drawn from the evidence in the record and their staccato-like repetition could hardly be pointed to as models of understatement even in an advocate's brief." To Black, *Life* was guilty of what was "at most a mere understandable and incidental error of fact in reporting a newsworthy event." One did "not have to be a prophet" to foresee that the severe penalty Fortas hoped to inflict on the magazine would "frighten and punish the press so much that publishers will cease trying to report news in a lively and readable fashion." In sum, "after mature reflection," Black was "unable to recall any prior case in this Court that offers a greater threat to freedom of speech and press than this one does."[87]

After hearing the reargument and reading Black's memorandum, the justices voted to reverse the New York Court of Appeals and decided in favor of Time, Inc. As the senior justice in the majority, Black assigned the opinion to Brennan, who extended the *New York Times* standard to private citizens who sued the press for invading their privacy by presenting them "in false light" after they had become the object of public interest. Black issued a concurring opinion which, less stridently than his original memorandum, articulated his opposition to "weighing."[88]

Fortas's dissent was also more restrained in tone than his draft majority opinion. While he made it clear that he remained annoyed by the press's "reckless and heedless assaults," most of Fortas's invectives against the press had disappeared, and little of his paragraph detailing the right to privacy remained. He still maintained that privacy was "a basic right," but he no longer claimed that "the right of privacy reaches beyond any of its specifics."[89] The relative moderateness of Fortas's dissent was strange. Like most judges, Fortas generally sounded a different tone in his dissents than he did in his majority opinions. He tried to make his majority opinions judicious, but he usually allowed himself to express anger in dissents. When he cared enough about dissents to write them himself, Fortas composed them quickly.[90] In dissent written the year after the *Time* v. *Hill* decision, Fortas went out of his way to attack the press. "The First Amendment is not a shelter for the character assassinator, whether his action is heedless and reckless or deliberate," he said. "The occupation of public officeholder does not forfeit one's membership in the human race."[91] In *Time* v. *Hill*, on the other hand, Fortas's dissent had the tone of his majority opinions. In spite of its stateliness, it left no doubt that Fortas possessed an unusually deep belief in the right to be let alone by the press.

## TO THE RIGHT?

For some observers, Fortas's stance on big business also distinguished him from the Court's liberals, with whom he so frequently sided on individual rights, and gave his decisions a "schizophrenic" quality. Such commentators viewed him as "an almost certain conservative vote when it came to the practices of big business."[92] But Fortas's attitude reflected sensitivity, rather than solicitude.

His reputation as big business's champion stemmed largely from his dissent in *FTC* v. *Dean Foods*. The case arose during his first year on the Court when two competitors defied a Federal Trade Commission (FTC) warning that their proposed merger might violate antitrust laws. After filing a complaint that alleged that the merger agreement transgressed the Federal Trade Commission and Clayton Antitrust acts, the FTC applied to the Seventh Circuit Court of Appeals for a temporary restraining order and a preliminary injunction that would delay the merger until the commission had held a hearing on its legality. When the court of appeals ruled that the FTC lacked standing to initiate the judicial proceeding because that was the Department of Justice's job, the government rushed the case to the Supreme Court. The primary issue before the Supreme Court was whether the commission could obtain preliminary relief in the courts in such cases. The Clayton Act authorized the commission to issue cease-and-desist orders against mergers and empowered the Justice Department's Antitrust Division to obtain relief in district courts.[93] It remained silent about the commission's power to seek preliminary relief in either the district courts or courts of appeal.

A majority opinion written by Justice Clark reversed the appeals court decision. Clark concluded that the FTC could apply to the court of appeals for a preliminary injunction to prevent a merger pending a commission decision on its legality. Although Clark noted that five successive Congresses had not responded to the commission's request to allow it to issue preliminary injunctions itself or to authorize it to sue for relief in the district courts, he did not construe silence as denial: "Congress neither enacted nor rejected these proposals; it simply did not act on them."[94]

In his first months at the Court, Fortas frequently tried to influence his

colleagues through a practice he largely abandoned later because of its ineffec-
tiveness. "He bombarded his brethren with memos about argued cases," a clerk
remembered.[95] Fortas's memorandum disagreeing with Clark suggested a wariness about congressional intent concerning the Federal Trade Commission and
an unwillingness to disturb the balance of power existing between the commission and the Department of Justice. "Congress deliberately withheld provision
for the FTC to seek preliminary relief against unlawful mergers," he contended.
Members of the FTC, as well as Congress, had "repeatedly" indicated that the
commission had no power to seek preliminary relief in the courts under existing
law, and Fortas did not think it should be allowed to do so. It would be "at least an
anomaly" if in addition to adjudicating the legality of mergers, the commission
could also prosecute the participants in the courts. Fortas maintained that Congress had intended for the FTC to devote itself to "administrative" and "investigative" matters and had left "enforcement" to the Department of Justice: "The
relief here sought would intensify the FTC's tendency to ignore these functions
and to become a carbon copy of the Antitrust Division of the Department of
Justice." If Justice decided a preliminary injunction were appropriate, it could
seek one. "Bureaucratic rivalry should not induce us to engraft a major amendment to the statute and a major distortion in the scheme of antitrust division."[96]
But Fortas's plea won no additional votes.

The animating force behind Fortas's "blistering" dissent, the *Harvard Law
Review* observed, was "the unstated premise . . . that the FTC has a history of
irresponsibility in its enforcement of the antimerger law" and would too quickly
use its new weapon to block mergers. "Certainly there is widespread distrust of
the agency's fairness among members of the antitrust bar."[97] Whereas Clark's
majority opinion displayed a distrust of mergers, Fortas's dissent suggested that
"not every merger deserves sudden death." Permitting the FTC to obtain a preliminary injunction to prevent the merger "during the years required to complete the
Commission's proceedings, often—probably, usually—means that the plans to
merge will be abandoned." That was unwise, according to Fortas, because although some mergers "serve no purpose except the pursuit of bigness," others
were "distinctively beneficial to the achievement of a competitive economy. I
respectfully submit that this Court should not encourage the machinegun approach to the vastly important and difficult merger problem."[98] In his oral
announcement of his dissent, Fortas emphasized even more pointedly that "not
all mergers are bad."[99]

As a matter of policy, Fortas's position might be disputed. Forcing the commission to delay action until the Department of Justice had prosecuted a merger in
the courts could cause irreparable damage. "By the time illegality is established,
the merger often is a *fait accompli,* making restoration of competition virtually

impossible."[100] But from a legal perspective, Fortas's dissent was sound. In an appendix, he listed thirty-seven unsuccessful congressional bills proposing to grant the FTC the authority to seek preliminary relief in the courts.[101] Clearly Congress had never intended to grant the commission the power to seek injunctive review. Even the *Harvard Law Review*, which applauded Clark's majority opinion as a matter of policy, thought his assertion that legislative silence did not constitute denial was disingenuous.[102] Other commentators who also liked the result the majority had reached remained wary of the legal arguments it had used to get there.[103]

Although most of these commentators viewed Fortas's dissent in *Dean Foods* as an effort to promote big business, his argument is better interpreted as an attempt to preserve the delicate balance between the administrative process and the courts. Just as Fortas opposed expansion of the commission's jurisdiction, so he protested the broadening of the courts' jurisdiction. In a case decided the following year, courts were authorized to review regulations promulgated by the Food and Drug Administration before that commission enforced them. The opinion—which, according to the *Harvard Law Review*, which marked "a triumph for proponents of judicial review of administrative action,"—annoyed Fortas.[104] Charging that the Court's action authorized "federal injunctions [which] will now threaten programs of vast importance to the public welfare," his dissent in *Gardner v. Toilet Goods Association* condemned the majority for opening a "Pandora's box." For Fortas, "experience dictates . . . that it can hardly be hoped that some federal judge somewhere will not be moved as the Court is here, by the cries of anguish and distress of those regulated, to grant a disruptive injunction."[105] Fortas still thought the administrative process he had promoted should safeguard the public interest through a flexible ongoing system of control.[106]

That faith animated Fortas's concurrence in *Vaca v. Sipes*.[107] There, the Court decided that an employee need not rely on his union to pursue his grievance against an employer. The majority opinion permitted an employee to proceed directly against the employer and recover damages for breach of contract only when the union violated its duty to represent the employee fairly. The decision also granted courts concurrent jurisdiction with the National Labor Relations Board to enforce the union's duty of fair representation. In forcing the employee to demonstrate wrongdoing by the union as well as the employer, the Court's opinion reflected an explicit preference for industrial peace over individual rights,[108] which was roundly condemned by commentators.[109] Fortas, however, seemed more concerned about the expansion of the courts' authority. Though he expressed his "regret [at] the elaborate discussion in the Court's opinion of problems which are irrelevant," the nub of his concurrence bespoke his conviction that breach of the duty of fair representation was an unfair labor practice over which the National Labor Relations Board possessed exclusive jurisdiction.[110]

Although Fortas continued to believe in the administrative process, his trust was limited. His dissent in *Dean Foods* suggested that he did not always find an administrative agency with which he had had substantial experience to be an effective guardian of the public interest. Nevertheless, he counted on administrative agencies to resolve disputes in a way that would produce the greatest good for the greatest number, while reserving the courts for altercations involving individual rights. Thus he objected to expansion of an administrative agency's jurisdiction in *Dean Foods* and protested the expansion of the courts' authority in *Gardner* and *Vaca*. Fortas's dissent in *Dean Foods* indicated more about a liberal's approach to the administrative process than it did about his outlook on big business.

In fact, despite his position in *Dean Foods* and his insistence in another merger case that "we should be conservative and restrained, I think, when all we can say is *no*,"[111] he often did not favor big business. Even though many of his friends were captains of industry, Fortas had "a very low opinion of businessmen as businessmen," Griffiths recalled. "His opinion was that businessmen don't on the whole know how to run their business well and that lawyers can do it better." With his clerks, he took the attitude that "those people are trying to screw around, and I know they are trying to screw around because I've had so many of them as clients," Griffiths said.[112] "He knew all the tricks and he wasn't going to be soft on them . . . just because he was an antitrust lawyer," another clerk agreed.[113] But he attacked with care. Though he generally voted with the Court's liberal majority on issues relating to big business,[114] he sometimes issued narrow concurrences.[115] There was a unifying thread behind his business decisions. They resonated with his sense of legal authority and an assurance that he understood the practices of what he called "the real world."[116] His past made him more alert to technical aspects of antitrust cases, such as efficiency analysis and definition of the relevant market, than were justices such as Warren.[117] Where the chief justice showed a broad commitment to strict antitrust enforcement, Fortas was more legalistic.[118]

As the author of one of the Warren Court's most radical antitrust opinions, *U.S. v. Arnold, Schwinn and Company,* he declared that a manufacturer's imposition of territorial and customer resale restrictions on distributors was illegal per se and prohibited by law, regardless of the reasons for the limitations. Thus the Schwinn Company could not force distributors who bought its bicycles to resell them in particular market areas or present distributors from reselling bicycles to unenfranchised retailers, such as discount houses. But when Schwinn sent bicycles to distributors on an agency or consignment basis, it might lawfully fix reasonable territorial and customer restrictions. Fortas's opinion rested primarily on the legal concept of title. To allow the manufacturer who has parted "with title, dominion, or risk with respect to the article" to set territorial and customer restrictions "would violate the ancient rule against restrictions on alienation." Where a manufacturer retained ownership and the risk of liability, territorial and customer restrictions might prove "reasonable methods of meeting the competition of giants and of merchandising through independent dealers."[119]

The result Fortas reached in *Schwinn* was not strange, as he usually voted against big business, but the grounds for his decision were. At common law, "title" had been crucial. But when the legal realists attacked conceptualists in the 1920s and 1930s, they argued that in the modern law of sales, "most problems commonly dealt with under headings of 'title' are obscured rather than clarified by that dealing."[120] Fortas was here betraying legal realism by resting his decision on an outdated legal concept. "The state of the common law 400 or even 100 years ago is irrelevant to the issue before us: the effect of the antitrust laws upon vertical distributional restraints in the American economy today," Potter Stewart observed in his dissent. "The problems involved are difficult and complex, and our response should be more reasoned and sensible than the simple acceptance of a hoary formula."[121] One antitrust expert dismissed Fortas's opinion as "an exercise in barren formalism," and others also condemned it.[122] Ten years later, the Court overruled *Schwinn*'s holding that territorial and customer restrictions on sale transactions were illegal per se and stated that, as previously had been the case in agency and consignment arrangements, such restrictions would be judged on the basis of their reasonableness.[123] Where big business was concerned, Fortas sometimes seemed excessively legalistic.

## LEGAL STRATEGIST OR LEGAL REALIST?

Fortas treated legal realism's exposure of the role of idiosyncrasy in the judicial process as a license to be idiosyncratic. He consistently tried to legalize his personal prejudices. Did that make him a legal realist? Some of those who worked most closely with Fortas during his Court years doubted that he was moved "by anything that could be called a judicial philosophy." John Griffiths, who served as his clerk for two years, believed that Fortas's approach to a case instead reflected the opportunistic outlook of a good lawyer.[124] In general, legal principles seemed relatively unimportant to Fortas. Griffiths suggested that Fortas regarded them as "a necessary form of packaging that had to be provided for things he wanted to do." Griffiths remembered giving a draft of a particular memorandum to Fortas. After telling his clerk that the draft was unsatisfactory, Fortas "took it off and wrote it himself with the very strong emphasis on the factual part." On his return, Fortas threw the memorandum on Griffiths's desk. "Decorate it," he ordered. The "decorations" consisted of legal cases that would justify a decision Fortas had already reached.[125] The incident showed Fortas's skeptical approach to the "rule of law." Like the judges the legal realists had described, he reached decisions first and rationalized them later. Observers have commented that Fortas's opinions contained more than the requisite number of legal citations.[126] But they were there to a large extent because his clerks insisted upon them.[127]

The legal realism Fortas had studied at Yale in the 1920s and 1930s had been both policy-oriented and receptive to the social sciences. Most important, it showed a disdain for traditional legal concepts and a concern with functional context. In *Snyder* v. *Harris,* an opinion sharply at odds with his approach in *Schwinn,* Fortas seemed a legal realist in the tradition of his Yale mentors.

Federal courts had long required that the "matter in controversy" in diversity of citizenship cases brought by citizens of one state against another involve at least ten thousand dollars. Rule 23 of the Federal Rules of Civil Procedure (1938) said that parties to a suit who asserted "joint" rights possessed a "true" class action and could aggregate their claims to reach the ten-thousand-dollar minimum that would enable them to prove federal jurisdiction. When they claimed "common" or "several rights," however, they were engaged in a "hybrid" or "spurious" class action that affected only the parties named in the suit, and they could not aggregate their claims. As courts struggled to determine whether a class action fit into the *joint, common,* or *several* category, it became apparent that Rule 23 was not functioning efficiently. As amended in 1966, it abolished the old distinctions among the three categories. The new Rule 23 adopted a functional definition of a class action, which increased judicial discretion. Instead of focusing on whether the "character of the interest" involved was joint, common, or several, the judge would now decide upon the *suitability* of a class action in the particular circumstances.[128] Since the old rule permitted aggregation in the "true" class action where a "joint" interest was at stake, should aggregation now be permitted in all suits defined as a class action under the new rule?

Hugo Black thought not. In his majority opinion in *Snyder* v. *Harris,* a diversity of citizenship case brought under the new rule, Black acknowledged that some would claim that his decision undercut the amended version of Rule 23 and would force the courts to resort to the old categories. But that did not bother him: "The disadvantageous results are overemphasized, we think, since lower courts have developed largely workable standards for determining when claims are joint and common, and therefore entitled to be aggregated, and when they are separate and distinct and not aggregable."[129] In effect, Black had disregarded the amended version of Rule 23 and said that courts should return to considering whether the interests at stake were joint, common, or several.

Fortas dissented. "The artificial, awkward and unworkable distinctions between 'joint,' 'common,' and 'several' claims and between 'true,' 'hybrid,' and 'spurious' class actions which the amendment of Rule 23 sought to terminate is now re-established in federal procedural law. . . . Litigants, lawyers, and federal courts must now continue to be ensnared in their complexities and inanities in all cases where one or more of the co-plaintiffs has a claim of less than the jurisdictional amount." The amendment had tried to avoid that "morass" by replacing "the metaphysics of conceptual analysis . . . by a pragmatic, workable definition of when class actions might be maintained, that is, when claims of various claimants might be aggregated in a class action." Black's opinion defeated its purpose by insisting upon "a perpetuation of distinctions which the profession had hoped would become only curiosities of the past."[130]

Many applauded Fortas's dissent. Law reviews condemned Black's opinion.[131] Charles Alan Wright, an expert on the Federal Rules of Civil Procedure said in a letter to Fortas that the Court's decision provided "the worst of all possible worlds. A rule cast in functional terms but that must still be applied with an eye to the old conceptualism." Wright just wished that someone would show him those "largely workable standards" Black had said the lower courts had devised.[132] The *Snyder* v. *Harris* opinion exemplified the legal realism Fortas could employ on occasion.

In contrast, Fortas's opinion in *Epperson* v. *Arkansas* rested conventionally on the narrowest constitutional grounds. Epperson, a biology teacher in an Arkansas high school, had challenged a state law that made the teaching of evolution in the public schools a misdemeanor and grounds for dismissal. Although they had been repealed everywhere except in Arkansas and Mississippi, such statutes had long existed in the southern states where religious fundamentalists congregated. Indeed the Arkansas law was an adaptation of the antievolution statute that the Tennessee Supreme Court had reviewed in the celebrated Scopes "Monkey Trial" in 1925.[133] The Tennessee Supreme Court's dismissal of the case on a technicality at that time prevented the United States Supreme Court from deciding the constitutionality of antievolution statutes. The Arkansas Supreme Court proved no more helpful than its Tennessee counterpart. In a two-sentence *per curiam* opinion, it upheld the statute on the grounds that it represented a "valid exercise of the state's power to specify the curriculum in its public schools." But the majority specifically declined to say whether the state statute prohibited any explanation of the theory of evolution or, more narrowly, barred instructors from teaching that evolution definitely occurred. At the very least, as one member of the Arkansas Supreme Court noted, the court's evasiveness "beclouds the clear announcement made in the first sentence."[134]

"Unfortunately, this case is not the proper vehicle for the Court to elevate the monkey to his proper position," Fortas's clerk argued. He recommended dismissal of the appeal. It was not clear that Epperson would violate the statute by teaching the theory of evolution, and there was no evidence that school authorities were enforcing the statute. According to the clerk, the case was therefore "too unreal." Fortas thought otherwise. "Maybe you're right—but I'd rather see us knock this out—& [Arkansas] Sup[reme] Ct seems to be playing games," he replied.[135]

Although at oral argument Epperson's attorney conceded he knew of no prosecutions under the statute, he nevertheless painted a grim picture of its deterrent effect. Because dictionaries, considered textbooks, contained an explanation of the theory of evolution, "a teacher couldn't refer a student to the dictionary for fear that that student might turn to the page that had the explanation of the evolution on it." The statute might even be read as commanding that schools eliminate from their libraries every general reference book that mentioned evolution. "That is book burning at its worst," he contended.[136] Fortas underlined that statement in the transcript.

Fortas articulated his position on the day of oral argument when he suggested a *per curiam* reversal on the basis of *Meyer* v. *Nebraska*.[137] In that case, decided in 1923, Justice James McReynolds had written an opinion for the Court stating that a Nebraska statute that aimed at prohibiting the teaching of German in public grammar schools violated the due process clause of the Fourteenth Amendment because it was "unreasonable and arbitrary."[138] *Meyer* provided the broadest grounds for holding the antievolution statute unconstitutional.

Everyone on the Court agreed that the statute had to be reversed, but only Warren was willing to join Fortas in using *Meyer* to do so.[139] In implying that the Court could invalidate legislation it did not like simply by holding it "unreasonable" or "arbitrary," *Meyer* represented a bow to the principle of substantive due process, Black complained. "It was McReynolds' philosophy, which I utterly reject," he said, adding, "There's no case or controversy here." Douglas believed that *Epperson* should be reversed on the grounds of the statute's vagueness, while Stewart thought that the statute abridged the right to freedom of speech.[140] Harlan offered a solution to the disagreement. He argued that the Arkansas statute violated the prohibition against laws promoting the establishment of religion in the First Amendment.[141] The majority opinion was assigned to Fortas, who agreed to base his reversal "on what to me is the narrowest ground—establishment of religion. I don't have trouble getting to that."[142]

The case appealed to Fortas. As a teenager in Memphis, he had followed the Scopes case. "He had always admired John Scopes, and felt that striking down the Arkansas law would also erase the blot on Tennessee's history," one scholar noted.[143] Though he often asked his clerks to write the first drafts of his opinions, he did this one himself. He was sufficiently proud of the final version to send copies to friends.[144] The idea of invalidating the "monkey law" seemed to tickle him. Dean Louis Pollak of Yale Law School called on Fortas during that time and found the justice working on the case. The justice's portrait, which his former partners had commissioned as a gift for the law school, sat in a corner. Fortas was dubious about the painting, which was impressionistic. He told Pollak that while he worked on *Epperson* he looked at the painting occasionally and tried to decide whether it indicated mankind "ascended from or descended from apes."[145]

Fortas began his opinion by declining to hold the statute unconstitutional on the grounds of vagueness. Since both of its clauses violated the promise of religious freedom in the First Amendment, it did not matter that it was unclear whether the law targeted explanation or endorsement of evolution.[146] This section impressed neither Black nor Harlan, both of whom concurred in his opinion. Harlan charged that Fortas's discussion of vagueness obscured the majority's "otherwise straightforward holding."[147] Black noted that the Arkansas Supreme Court had "deliberately refused" to pronounce upon the statute's meaning: "It seems to me that in this situation the statute is too vague for us to strike it down on any ground but that: vagueness." In Black's view Fortas's reliance on the seemingly narrow grounds of the establishment clause really gave the Court a license to "supervise and censor the curriculum of every public school in every hamlet and city in the United States."[148]

That prospect did not alarm Fortas. He had championed a secular, national culture all his life. If public schools did not pursue religious neutrality, he believed the Court should intervene. Fortas warned that when a state possessed only a religious interest in passing a statute, the Court would presume the law invalid and scrutinize it carefully. In this case, he maintained, "the law's effort was confined to an attempt to blot out a particular theory because of its supposed conflict with the Biblical account, literally read." No information could be omitted from "the body of knowledge . . . for the sole reason that it is deemed to conflict with a particular religious doctrine." Nor could religious information be added as a counterweight against secular information.[149] Decisions rendered after Fortas's tenure on the Court used *Epperson* as grounds for invalidating Arkansas and Louisiana statutes providing that public schools need not instruct students on the origins of mankind, but that if they did teach evolution they were obliged to give creationism "balanced treatment" as well.[150]

Fortas's discussion of *Meyer* v. *Nebraska* in his *Epperson* opinion hinted that his holding might have been far more sweeping. The former case stood for the premise that the due process clause guarantees "the right to engage in any of the common occupations and to acquire useful knowledge," he claimed. But "we need not take advantage of the broad premise which the Court's decision in *Meyer* furnishes, nor need we explore the implications of that decision in terms of the . . . multitude of controversies that beset our campuses today. Today's problem is capable of resolution in . . . narrower terms."[151] His extensive comments about a case superfluous in the current instance demonstrated that he stood ready to affirm substantive due process. *Epperson* was a clever opinion. Fortas had followed traditional standards of adjudication by striking down the statute and striking out at a governmental embrace of the American evangelical tradition on narrow constitutional grounds. But he had made it clear that he was reserving *Meyer* and substantive due process for emergencies and that he believed in broad judicial discretion to invalidate legislation with which he disagreed.

In the 1930s legal realists had criticized conservative jurists such as McReynolds for translating their own opinions into law by ruling that some policies or statutes were fair, whereas others were not. But the realists also taught Fortas and other students to use law as a tool of social policy. They never resolved the contradiction between their attacks on judges for how they made law and their own incursions into making law. In the 1960s Fortas was considering the use of the tools conservatives had ably framed to further their own social visions. He never seemed to worry that the pendulum might swing, and conservatives would again predominate on the Court. Rather Fortas seemed determined to make the most of the time he had.

As a justice, he was a legal strategist. To Fortas the cases and materials he cited in his opinions were tools, not the building blocks of a legal philosophy. When he had to embrace legal realism, he did. Some of his opinions, such as *Gault* and *Powell*, relied on the social sciences. Others, such as *Snyder*, attacked traditional legal concepts. But *Schwinn* showed he was equally capable of conceptualism. He could use law as a tool of social policy, as he did in *Time* and threatened to do in *Epperson*, but in *Dean Foods* he reproved his brethren for that practice. As always, what mattered to him were results. Despite his attempt to present himself as "a man of law," Fortas rarely believed that law commanded him to act against his own wishes.

## CHAPTER 13

# Revolution

W E MAY BE THANKFUL THAT THIS INESCAPABLE CONFLICT HAS been brought to decision in the courts and not in the streets," Fortas declared in a speech in 1962 on "the social revolution."[1] Law remained the agency of social transformation. But changing times soon brought the revolution to the streets, forcing the courts to rule upon the lawfulness of dissenters' behavior. The first such cases before the Court involved civil rights activists who turned from litigation to direct action in their drive to desegregate the South. As the number of protesters swelled to include those who demanded an end to the war in Vietnam, the issue of First Amendment guarantees arose in increasingly difficult contexts. Deciding if and when violence or a challenge to authority justified curtailing freedom was always a difficult exercise. No group of cases more clearly suggested the societal tension of the mid to late 1960s.

### SPEAKING SHARPLY: THE SIT-IN CASES

In 1963 the Court had held that a state could not use a breach of peace statute to prohibit a civil rights demonstration at its capitol because the demonstrators were exercising their right to free speech in its "most pristine and classic form."[2] But by 1965, as Black demonstrators increasingly chose the tactics of civil disobedience espoused by Martin Luther King, some members of the Court had doubts about the legality of civil rights protests. Their opinions reflected their ambivalence about the appropriate range of permissible conduct in public facilities.[3] "What is needed in effect is a set of Robert's Rules of Order for the new uses of the public forum," the First Amendment scholar Harry Kalven suggested.[4]

Fortas treated one of his first cases, *Brown* v. *Louisiana,* as an opportunity to begin drafting those rules. It involved five Blacks convicted of violating Louisiana's breach of peace statute after they sat in at a public library to challenge its segregation policies. When the case reached the Supreme Court, five members voted to reverse the protesters' convictions, and the opinion was assigned to the Court's newest justice.

Fortas's draft noted that *Brown* represented the fourth time in slightly more than four years in which the Court had considered convictions under Louisiana's breach of peace statute. In each of the first three instances, the most recent of which had been *Cox* v. *Louisiana* in the previous term, a majority had reversed the convictions.[5] "After these decisions, it would hardly be fanciful to expect that Louisiana would no longer tolerate the use of its breach of peace statute to punish persons engaged in orderly, peaceful, controlled civil rights demonstrations," Fortas sarcastically remarked. He argued that Henry Brown and his friends had been denied due process, as there was no evidence they had disturbed the peace. Their defiance of an order to leave the library did not in itself suffice to uphold their conviction given that their presence in the library, a public facility, "was unquestionably lawful."[6]

But according to Fortas, "another and sharper answer" was in order. Even if Brown and others had breached the peace, a conviction would have violated their constitutional protections. "The barebones of the problem" was that they had been arrested for exercising their First Amendment rights of free speech and assembly. Those guarantees "embrace appropriate types of action which certainly include the right in a peaceable and orderly manner to protest by silent and reproachful presence, in a place where the protestant has every right to be, the unconstitutional segregation of public facilities. Accordingly, even if the accused action were within the scope of the statutory instrument, we would be required to assess the constitutional impact of its application, and we would have to hold that the statute cannot constitutionally be applied to punish petitioner's actions in the circumstances of this case."[7]

Fortas included with the draft he circulated among his colleagues a memorandum indicating he had become "concerned about the impact of language in the Court's opinion in *Cox* v. *Louisiana*" while he worked on the opinion. "Perhaps *Cox* should be read as holding that the Louisiana breach-of-the-peace statute is unconstitutional on its face," he proposed. In fact, Arthur Goldberg's majority opinion in *Cox* included ample evidence to support that interpretation.[8] Goldberg had said that the statute was "unconstitutionally vague in its overly broad scope," and he had cited *Stromberg* v. *California,* in which the Court had declared a statute unconstitutionally vague on its face. But Goldberg had also engaged in a detailed application of the statute to the facts in *Cox,* although a finding of vagueness or overbreadth generally made such an analysis unnecessary.[9] It seemed that Goldberg had struck down the statute on the basis of vagueness and overbreadth and that his examination of the statute's application to the facts had been superfluous. If so, Fortas feared that his approach in *Brown* was inappropriate: "If the Court is of the view that *Cox* held the Louisiana statute unconstitutional for all purposes, I think we should dispose of the present case on the basis of a short *per curiam.*" Such a reading of *Cox* would not be to his liking, Fortas added, "because I believe that there is a permissible and constitutional office for this kind of a breach-of-the-peace statute—and it would be difficult to distinguish the Louisiana statute from the statutes in a number of States." Therefore Fortas had drafted a footnote which "tactfully" expressed, he hoped, a more advantageous reading of *Cox,* that is, that the Court had held the Louisiana statute "unconstitutional for vagueness and overbreadth. The Court's opinion was confined to the unconstitutionality of the statute as applied." As Fortas explained, his footnote suggested that the Court had decided "that the Louisiana breach-of-the-peace statute was unconstitutional *as applied* to the facts in *Cox.* I recommend this formula."[10]

Fortas was capable of brilliant flashes of insight, but his footnote construing *Cox* was not one of his better efforts. From a technical perspective, it made no sense. If a statute was vague and overbroad, the Court need not consider its application to the facts.[11] Of course it was not Fortas's fault that Goldberg had left the basis of his decision in *Cox* ambiguous, but Fortas's footnote only drew attention to the problem of interpreting Goldberg's opinion. In the end, Fortas deleted it. From the perspective of policy, however, Fortas's footnote was sound. A holding that the breach of peace statute challenged in *Brown* was unconstitutional on its face would indeed threaten a number of statutes in other states that might be employed for legitimate purposes. Fortas did not want to jeopardize those statutes, but he would delineate some of their unreasonable applications. In a sentence omitted from later drafts, he claimed that "instead of summarily reversing so as to afford the Louisiana Supreme Court an opportunity to apply Cox to the present case . . . we have to consider this case in extenso because of the importance in light of the situation in Louisiana and perhaps elsewhere incident to the current process of racial adjustment, of unmistakable clarity and providing direction which should terminate the use of statutes of this sort for unlawful arrests and convictions."[12]

Had he retained that sentence and the footnote interpreting *Cox,* the opinion would have been confusing as a legal document, but his motivation would have been clearer. Fortas hoped to protect legitimate state interests while also promoting individual civil liberties.[13] He wanted to extend protection to the sit-ins and to emphasize that breach of peace statutes could not be used to abridge First Amendment rights. But he insisted that those rights be exercised peacefully. In his opinion, he repeatedly observed that Brown and the other protesters had not disrupted library activities and suggested that he might have reached a different result if other patrons had been present in the library when the sit-in began.[14] Earl Warren justifiably had suggested that Fortas's opinion in *Gault* would become a Magna Carta for juveniles, but the *Harvard Law Review* made a different and equally justifiable prediction about *Brown:* "If, as seems likely, the scope of first amendment protection would be narrowed whenever others are present, the theory developed by Mr. Justice Fortas will not prove a Magna Carta for civil rights demonstrators and other protest groups."[15]

Nevertheless, only Warren and Douglas agreed to go as far as Fortas in upholding the rights of Brown's group. Brennan's concurrence stressed that the Court need not decide whether the protesters' activity was constitutionally protected and implied that had the statute been more narrowly drafted, he would have held that it did not violate their First Amendment freedoms.[16] White's concurrence grounded reversal on his theory that the protesters were denied equal protection of the laws when they were denied access to the library on the same basis as whites.[17] Thus only a bare majority of the majority shared Fortas's views.

His opinion also provoked spirited opposition. Black's strong dissent in *Brown,* which Warren did not believe reflected "the better part of his nature,"[18] argued that "there simply was no racial discrimination practiced in this case." By remaining in the library after they had completed their business, the petitioners had indicated that they did not want to use it "for learning" but for an activity to which it was ill-suited. Nor did Black think that the protesters' activity represented a legitimate exercise of First Amendment rights. He maintained that the First Amendment "protects speech, writings and expression of views in any manner in which they can be legitimately and validly communicated," but "it does not guarantee to any person the right to use someone else's property, even that owned by government and dedicated to other purposes, as a stage to express dissident ideas."[19] Black thus distinguished between speech (which deserved protection) and conduct (which did not), an attempt at categorization that seemed particularly inappropriate in an era in which so much conduct constituted symbolic speech. He did not accept Fortas's willingness to balance the First Amendment right to engage in both speech and conduct against the state's interest in regulating expression. For Black, nothing could weigh against the right to speech, whereas control of conduct was almost always justified.[20]

Nor did the civil rights aspect of the demonstration affect him. Indeed he found it particularly unfortunate that the case involved Blacks: "It is an unhappy circumstance in my judgment that the group, which more than any other has needed a government of equal laws and equal justice, is now encouraged to believe that the best way for it to advance its cause, which is a worthy one, is by taking the law into its own hands from place to place and from time to time." Although their demonstration had been peaceful in the instant case, "I say once more that the crowd moved by noble ideals today can become the mob ruled by hate and passion and greed and violence tomorrow." To Black, "the holding in this case today makes it more necessary than ever that we stop and look more closely at where we are going."[21] William O. Douglas thought it was clear where the Court was going. "I can't understand why you did not get 5 for what you wrote," he told Fortas. "It's a mystery." When Black announced his dissent, Douglas sent Fortas another note: "You can now see what I meant last summer when I said the majority of the Court was moving toward the anti-Negro side."[22]

The majority might have been moving in that direction, but Fortas was not. He continued to insist that conduct protesting inequality represented a legitimate First Amendment activity. In 1966, in *Adderly* v. *Florida,* Black convinced four other justices that civil rights demonstrators on the grounds of a jailhouse had engaged in conduct unprotected by the First Amendment and therefore had been lawfully convicted of violating a Florida statute prohibiting trespass. Fortas joined Douglas's sharp dissent, which charged Black with ignoring the line of cases culminating in *Brown* v. *Louisiana* that "drastically limited the application of state statutes inhibiting the right to go peacefully on public property to exercise First Amendment rights."[23]

Fortas likewise disapproved of the Court's decision in the case of *Walker* v. *Birmingham.*[24] There Justice Stewart's majority opinion affirmed a contempt conviction against Martin Luther King for defying an injunction specifically prohibiting demonstrations he had organized at Easter of 1963. Fortas believed that the conviction should be reversed and agreed with his clerk's assessment that the Birmingham officials "resorted to the last legal refuge of an oppressor-scoundrel: the injunction."[25] He joined both Brennan's and Douglas's dissenting opinions. Nonetheless, when Stewart sanctimoniously counseled in an early draft that blacks exercise "a modicum of patience" and Brennan reacted angrily, Fortas did not side with either colleague. The opening sentence in Brennan's draft dissent charged that Stewart's opinion "reflects only sensitivity to today's transitory shift in political and social attitudes towards the civil rights movement." Fortas's clerk noted in the margin, "I think this statement is unfortunate, it's really an attack on the Court as an institution, not just the majority."[26] Fortas too must have been sensitive to any suggestions that politics influenced the thinking of the justices. He himself staunchly defended civil rights activists' challenges to segregation. Protest against the war in Vietnam raised similar First Amendment issues, but it proved a more problematic area for him.

## THE RETREAT: *O'BRIEN* AND *STREET*

As a liberal Southerner, Fortas felt strongly about civil rights. He was delighted that the 1960s marked the beginning of "one of the greatest, if not the greatest peaceful social revolutions in history," whose "beneficiaries were the poor and the Negroes."[27] On the Supreme Court he had helped to expand the power of the state to assist the outsiders with whom he identified. But in the late 1960s, the spotlight was shifting from civil rights to the war in Vietnam.

"For all his liberalism on other issues," one of Fortas's clerks recalled, whenever "anything that could be viewed as criticism of the Vietnam war, or Johnson in particular or even the Executive in general [arose] . . . , Fortas was probably the most conservative judge on the Court."[28] Fortas publicly distinguished the "Gandhi type of protest" in which Martin Luther King engaged "from the adolescent antics of kids who break into the Pentagon."[29] King and his colleagues expected arrest and viewed it as part of their witness against injustice. Many of the protesters against the war considered arrest unjustified and were engaging not in civil disobedience, but in criticism of the state. Personal convictions also explained why Fortas proved so much less tolerant of those who opposed the war or burned the flag than of those who challenged racial prejudice. He did not regard the young antiwar protesters as oppressed individuals who deserved special treatment, and he supported both the war in Vietnam and the President who fought it.

In the first case concerning protest against the war brought to the Court, *U.S. v. O'Brien,* David O'Brien had challenged conscription and the war by burning his draft card on the steps of a Boston courthouse. The district court ruled that he knowingly and willfully violated an amendment of 1965 to the Universal Military Training and Service Act (1948). The Rivers Amendment prohibited destruction of draft registration certificates; Congressman L. Mendel Rivers of South Carolina had introduced it as "an answer" to those who dramatized their antiwar opinions by destroying their draft cards. The circuit court of appeals reversed O'Brien's conviction on the grounds that the Rivers Amendment abridged First Amendment rights.[30]

When the case reached the Supreme Court in the 1967 October term, O'Brien's lawyer argued that his client had engaged in "symbolic speech" by burning his draft card and that the Rivers Amendment was "an act of hysteria" intended to suppress dissident views. Warren, who was troubled by both those assertions, told O'Brien's attorney that if draft-card burning were defined as symbolic speech, a soldier in Vietnam who deliberately broke his rifle could also say he had engaged in symbolic speech. The chief justice further suggested that congressional motives in passing the amendment did not provide a basis for overruling it. At conference the justices unanimously agreed to reverse the holding that the Rivers Amendment was unconstitutional. Warren announced that he would write the Court's opinion. [31]

When he received Warren's draft of *O'Brien*, which virtually repudiated the idea of symbolic speech, [32] Fortas scribbled a comment in the margin that hinted at a new position on First Amendment rights:

> I think I'll concur in the judgment. 1) The statute as a whole serves a legitimate Cong[ressional] purpose, and the emphasis on classification added by Congress is saved by this purpose. We don't inquire into intent in any case. If we did, I couldn't say intent was other than to punish burners of draft cards. 2) This *is speech*—but it is a form which constitutes violation of a valid law. . . . Petitioner is responsible for *means* he selects and if means he selects is not essential to the communication . . . and violates a valid const[itutional] law, he must suffer consequences. [33]

Though Fortas remained unwilling to renounce symbolic speech, his proposed grounds for concurrence in *O'Brien* were still at odds with his opinion in *Brown* v. *Louisiana.* He had balanced the right to free speech against the state's duty to regulate activity in *Brown,* but now he seemed predisposed toward the state. Suddenly he believed that the competing state interest need only be "valid," and he was concerned with how "essential" the means of communication employed were. But, to quote Fortas, there was "another and sharper" answer to his notes in *O'Brien.* He was contending here that "speech" might not receive protection if it violated a "valid constitutional law." In *Brown,* his opinion had specifically said that even if the demonstrators had broken the law, the Court would still be required to hold that the statute could not be applied constitutionally to the facts of the case. [34] He was less concerned in *O'Brien* about the state's intent in applying a statute and less tolerant of protest that violated valid statutes. Before he wrote his concurrence, however, Fortas received a new draft majority opinion from Warren that grudgingly left open the possibility that O'Brien's behavior might be categorized as symbolic speech, [35] but declared that nevertheless it was not constitutionally protected. [36] Fortas decided to join the majority.

By the time the Court announced its decision in *O'Brien* on May 27, 1968, a large group of antiwar demonstrators had closed down Columbia University. Fortas was completing his "broadside," *Concerning Dissent and Civil Disobedience,* which addressed the issues raised in *O'Brien* and at Columbia. His pamphlet placed most student behavior outside of the limits of permissible dissent. "Fortas' strong condemnation of some of the current student tactics has been noteworthy, not only because justices rarely speak out on events that could eventually reach the high court, but also because he has impeccable liberal credentials as one of the court's most consistent libertarians," a reporter who covered the Court noted.[37] Fortas now maintained that civil disobedience was morally, politically, and legally unacceptable when it involved violation of constitutional, valid laws merely to dramatize dissent.[38]

To illustrate his point, he compared the library sit-ins at issue in *Brown* with the draft-card burning involved in cases such as *O'Brien*. In doing so, he reinterpreted his opinion in *Brown* in a way that reflected his diminishing tolerance for dissent. "In the library sit-in case the protesters violated a segregation ordinance," he claimed. "This ordinance was unconstitutional and its violation could not be constitutionally punished." According to Fortas, draft-card burning was another matter entirely. "If the law forbidding the burning of a draft card is held to be constitutional and valid, the fact that the card is burned as a result of noble and constitutional motives is no help to the defender."[39] In fact, Fortas had exonerated the demonstrators in *Brown* of violating a breach of peace statute that he had gone out of his way to declare constitutional. He had also expressly said that even if the protesters had actually violated the statute, their conduct still would have represented a valid exercise of First Amendment rights.[40]

Though Fortas insisted in internal Court documents that he remained as committed to his original interpretation of *Brown* as ever,[41] he was obviously wavering. After the Court handed down its opinion in *O'Brien* and Fortas published *Concerning Dissent and Civil Disobedience,* another case involving dissent, *Street* v. *New York,* arose. Fortas's dissent there suggested his wariness of civil rights demonstrators who employed the methods of antiwar activists. By the late 1960s, flag burning was being practiced as frequently as draft-card burning to protest the war in Vietnam, and Fortas wrote "Hold for O'Brien" when he read his clerk's memorandum on *Street* v. *New York.* The Street case, however, involved a civil rights demonstration and also raised more complex issues.

Sidney Street, a World War II veteran who lived in Brooklyn, had been listening to the radio when he heard the news that racists had ambushed the civil rights worker James Meredith as he was marching from Memphis, Tennessee, to Jackson, Mississippi. Taking the American flag he displayed on national holidays, he carried it outside and began to burn it. He was found guilty of violating New York's flag desecration statute, which made it a misdemeanor "publicly [to] mutilate, deface, defile, or defy, trample upon, or cast contempt upon either by words or by act any flag of the United States." The indictment charged that Street had "willfully and unlawfully set fire to an American flag and [had] shout[ed], 'If they did that to Meredith, We don't need an American flag.'" The New York Court of Appeals affirmed his conviction. Street's appeal to the Supreme Court charged that the statute was overbroad on its face and as applied because it made desecration of the flag by "words" a crime. His lawyers also alleged that the statute was vague because it did not define the behavior it invalidated, and because his destruction of the flag constituted an act of expression protected by the First Amendment.[42]

"Today when a fellow burns a draft card in public, we very well know what he is doing, that he is communicating a protest against the Vietnam war," Street's attorney observed at oral argument. "Flag burning hasn't gotten that secondary meaning, but I submit it may very well get to that point." That line of reasoning did not appeal to Fortas. "We have to face here a situation which is not confined to burning or desecration of the American flag, but it is a situation which includes the very troublesome aspect of words, speech," he said. Though the state's attorney insisted that Street's words were "mere surplusage" and that the statute was "divisible, that it can be separated, that the appellant was convicted only for the act of desecration, notwithstanding the fact that the officer in his complaint set forth the words" Street used, Fortas seemed unconvinced. He asked whether under the statute, Street could be convicted for using "only words, words expressing the utmost contempt and hatred for the American flag." When the state's attorney answered affirmatively, Fortas replied: "Then that's the nub of the trouble here."[43]

Fortas's comments implied that he considered the statute overbroad on its face but by the time of the justices' conference he was willing to go along with others in ruling Street's conviction unconstitutional on more narrow grounds. A majority of justices decided to evade a decision on the constitutionality of the statute and flag burning and to hold the statute unconstitutional as applied. They agreed on an opinion which would reverse Street's conviction on the ground that the speech element had played a part in his conviction. In his opinion for the Court, Justice Harlan maintained that "careful examination of the comparatively brief trial record" suggested that Street's words "could have been an independent cause of his conviction." The Court had "resist[ed] the pulls to decide the constitutional issues involved in this case on a broader basis than the record before us imperatively requires."[44] Harlan's narrow opinion inspired a strong draft dissent from Warren. The chief justice charged that the trial record showed that Street had been convicted for conduct alone and argued that flag burning could constitutionally be prohibited.[45]

Perhaps because *Street* involved civil rights rather than the war, Fortas initially sided with the majority. In December 1968 he circulated a concurrence that responded to Warren's dissent. Fortas emphasized that the constitutionality of a flag desecration statute "would be clear, regardless of the defendant's motive and even if the prohibited act were accompanied by speech. But the present case raises the question whether the appellant may constitutionally be convicted for speech independently of burning the flag." According to Fortas, he could not. Since "the statute punishes, and the indictment charged, speech itself," Street's conviction had to be reversed.[46] Within three months, Fortas's resolve had crumbled. He now told his brethren that he planned to join the dissenters in arguing that Street deserved punishment. He no longer thought that speech played an important part in Street's conviction. "I have concluded that it is fair to say that the conviction was for the conduct of publicly burning the flag and not for the words used," he explained. "As my concurrence stated, I believe that the First Amendment does not preclude a State from enacting a statute making it a criminal offense publicly to mutilate, deface or defile the flag, and I have finally concluded that it is sensible to accept the realities of the facts: that appellant was arrested for publicly burning the flag and that the speech need not be considered part of the offense, but may be treated as merely part of the surrounding circumstances." Fortas apologized to Harlan "for [my] inconstancy!"[47]

Fortas apparently had come to believe that conduct violating a valid statute was impermissible, regardless of whether it constituted symbolic speech. In *Street*, he suggested why flag desecration could be prohibited. "The test that is applicable in every case where conduct is restricted or prohibited is whether [this] is reasonable, due account being taken of the paramountcy of First Amendment values. . . . . "If, as I submit, it is permissible to prohibit the burning of personal property on the public sidewalk, there is no basis for applying a different rule to flag burning."[48] Whether he still would tolerate the protest in *Brown* was unclear. The dissent also revealed Fortas's sensitivity to national symbols. Having cited *O'Brien* to support the proposition that the intent to protest a valid law did not legitimate violating it, Fortas continued, in words that more conservative justices would quote decades later: "Beyond this, however, the flag is a special kind of personalty. . . . A person may 'own' a flag, but ownership is subject to special burdens and responsibilities. A flag may be property in a sense; but it is property burdened with peculiar obligations and restrictions."[49] Read alongside his reinterpretation of *Brown* and his reflections on draft-card burning, Fortas's *Street* dissent suggested he was losing his enthusiasm for symbolic speech.

### A REASSERTION? *TINKER*

In another opinion in the same year, Fortas returned to the strong support of symbolic speech he had urged in 1965. The Court examined in *Tinker* v. *Des*

*Moines School District* whether students possessed a right to protest and, if so, what forms their dissent might legitimately assume. Fortas's opinion for the Court, along with his correspondence about both *Tinker* and *Concerning Dissent and Civil Disobedience,* suggested the factors which influenced his zigzagging position on symbolic speech.

The Tinker case involved students in Iowa who determined to express their objections to the Vietnam war and their enthusiasm for the Christmas truce called in 1965 by wearing black armbands. Upon learning of their plans, school administrators took action. Although they had tolerated the wearing of other political symbols, such as the Iron Cross, the officials now adopted a policy prohibiting students from wearing armbands to school, and they suspended those who refused to remove them. The students sought both an injunction against further discipline and nominal damages, but the district court dismissed their complaint. Although it recognized that the wearing of an armband constituted symbolic speech within the ambit of the First Amendment, it concluded that the policy prohibiting armbands represented a reasonable and constitutional effort to prevent disturbance. When the court of appeals affirmed the decision, the students petitioned the Supreme Court to grant certiorari.

Fortas did not want to hear the case. Despite his position in *Epperson,* he was not certain that the First Amendment "authorizes us to intervene in school discipline matters except where discrimination or clear abuse is involved." Nevertheless, he acknowledged that "this is a tough case & probably will be granted."[50] Although he voted to deny certiorari, five justices agreed to hear the case. At oral argument, Fortas was still worried about the implications of the Court's intervention. "This gets the Supreme Court of the United States pretty deep in the trenches of ordinary day to day discipline," he remarked to the students' attorney. "Suppose some child shows up in school wearing an outlandish costume . . . that is in violation of a regulation . . . and this child says I am wearing this outlandish costume because I want to express the very strong belief that I have in the utmost freedom of the individual."[51] Fortas's hypothetical example, however, raised a more difficult issue than that posed in *Tinker.* The district court had already conceded that the students had engaged in symbolic speech because they wore the armbands to protest the war.

That ultimately settled the matter for Fortas. "First Amendment rights, applied in light of the special characteristics of the school environment, are available to teachers and students," his opinion for the Court noted. He drew attention to the fact that the case did not involve a regulation describing appropriate skirt lengths, clothing, hair style, or conduct. "It does not concern aggressive, disruptive action or even group demonstrations. Our problem involves direct, primary First Amendment rights akin to 'pure speech.' "[52] He thus neatly

avoided the problem of defining the term *symbolic speech* and determining the
different types of conduct it included.[53] Having decided that the students' conduct resembled speech, he announced that authorities could proscribe it only if
they could show that "students' activities would materially and substantially
disrupt the work and discipline of the school."[54]

Tinker resembled *O'Brien* in that authorities had targeted one particular form
of expression. But Fortas's test in *Tinker* proved more protective of First Amendment rights than the one he had contemplated in *O'Brien*. Fortas inquired more
closely into the state's intent than he had done in *O'Brien*. There neither his
proposed concurrence nor Warren's final opinion publicly acknowledged that the
statute aimed only at suppressing draft-card burning. But in *Tinker,* Fortas
claimed the school's policy was suspect on its face because it prohibited only one
particular symbol of protest. Thus his opinion could be read narrowly to hold that
a school could not permit some such symbols while banning others. Nevertheless, influential commentators insisted on reading it broadly to require tolerance
of nondisruptive "speech."[55] After all, Fortas had noted that "in our system,
state-operated schools may not be enclaves of totalitarianism."[56]

Further, Fortas's opinion in *Tinker* shifted the burden of proof from where the
Court had placed it in *O'Brien*. In *O'Brien* the Court assumed that the state had
been engaged in reasonable activity and placed the burden on the individual to
prove that the state had engaged in more than "incidental" regulation of his First
Amendment rights. In *Tinker* the Court required the state to show that the
individual's exercise of First Amendment rights "materially and substantially"
interfered with the state's competing interest.[57] Yet Fortas did not even refer to
*O'Brien* in his opinion in *Tinker*. That was characteristic, for he cared little about
precedent. Although he included a celebration of the duty of authorities in a free
society to tolerate dissent[58] (a position at odds with his attitude toward treatment
of the press), one of his clerks remembered having to "sneak" a reference to the
leading case on point, *Terminiello v. Chicago,* into the opinion.[59] In fact, Fortas's
opinion in *Tinker* might be viewed as an attempt to translate into law the grounds
that would have been the basis for his concurrence in *O'Brien*. There, and in
*Concerning Dissent and Civil Disobedience,* he had stressed that the *means* of
speech was a crucial factor in determining whether it deserved First Amendment
protection. He repeatedly emphasized the nondisruptive nature of the student's
conduct in *Tinker,* as he did in his private correspondence.

Soon after the Court announced its decision in *Tinker,* Jaime Benítez sent
Fortas a copy of a letter he had written to another administrator justifying the
regulation of picketing on the University of Puerto Rico campus. Benítez's prediction "that within a few years the American climate of opinion will change and
that Courts will discover that the right to reflect is not excluded from the

Constitution" irked Fortas, who greatly respected his old friend.[60] "This amazes me, coming from you; because I am sure that you know that this Court—and all other courts so far as I know—have drawn a stern and sharp line between speech and disruptive conduct—whether or not the latter is accompanied by speech," he wrote Benítez. That was the point, he said, of *Concerning Dissent and Civil Disobedience* and of his opinion in *Tinker*. "The question is not just of primarily the rule of law," Fortas told Benítez. "The question is one of policy strategy and tactics for the governing authorities of schools when they are faced with protest or demands in their various forms." Fortas had tried publicly to indicate "the deep sympathy that I feel for school administrators confronted with this problem; and my profound belief that what is effective and rational for them to do in one situation may be extremely destructive in another. To put it specifically what may be an appropriate response in a situation confronting American University here in Washington may be entirely inappropriate or inadequate in Puerto Rico." Fortas concluded the letter to Benítez by specifying the extent of First Amendment protection:

> As the First Amendment cases of this Court amply establish (both as a matter of constitutional law and the democratic spirit), there is no reason why reasonable rules and regulations to authorize peaceful demonstrations cannot be adopted. They should be sensitive to the line that exists between suppressing the expression of views, on the one hand, and regulating the form of that expression so as to permit others to go about their work and their daily rounds without being subjected to interference or assault. With reference to what for a better term has been called 'pure speech,' as you know, our Constitution and democratic principles insist upon the utmost freedom.[61]

As the letter suggested, Fortas had come to his current reading of the First Amendment not because of the rule of law but because of his political intention to fashion a test that would protect both the right to dissent and the legal authority of public officials. He explained to another friend that he had written *Concerning Dissent and Civil Disobedience* after he had spent two years visiting the nation's college campuses and determined that "faculties in the besieged schools are very largely demoralized and at their wits ends. . . . My object really was to try to provide the balanced members of the faculties (not all of them are in this category by a long shot) with a constructive and reasoned theoretical basis upon which they could communicate with their students."[62] That also seemed to be his aim in *Tinker* and in a subsequent concurrence in which he upheld the suspension of college students who had been engaged in an "aggressive and violent demonstration and not in a peaceful, nondisruptive expression such as was involved in *Tinker*."[63]

Hugo Black was even more skeptical of Fortas's approach than were Fortas's friends. "The Court's holding in this case ushers in what I deem to be an entirely new era in which the power to control pupils by the elected 'officials of state supported schools . . .' in the United States is in ultimate effect transferred to the Supreme Court," Black's dissent in *Tinker* began. He also predicted it would mark "the beginning of a new revolutionary era of permissiveness in this country fostered by the judiciary." Indeed he was certain the opinion only encouraged "groups of students all over the land [who] are already running loose, conducting break-ins, sit-ins, lie-ins, and smash-ins" and subjected "all the public schools in the country to the whims and caprices of their loudest-mouthed, but maybe not their brightest students."[64]

Surprisingly, Black did not argue that the First Amendment did not protect symbolic speech. He implicitly conceded that the wearing of armbands might constitute speech but claimed that the armbands "took the students' minds off their classwork and diverted them to thoughts about the highly emotional subject of the Vietnam war."[65] In an apparent retreat from his traditional absolutist interpretation of the First Amendment, which had led him to urge its enforcement "without any ifs, ands, buts or whereases,"[66] he claimed: "The truth is that a teacher of kindergarten, grammar school, or high school pupils, no more carries into a school with him a complete right to freedom of speech and expression than an anti-Catholic or anti-Semite carries with him a complete right to freedom of speech and religion into a Catholic church or Jewish synagogue."[67] More explicitly than in *Epperson*, Black also warned that Fortas and other liberal justices on the Warren Court were involved in the same kind of usurpation of power that conservative justices, such as McReynolds, had engaged in during the New Deal. "If the majority of the Court today, by agreeing to the opinion of my Brother Fortas, is resurrecting that old reasonableness-due process test," Black considered it "a sad day for the country."[68]

Fortas placed exclamation marks in the margins throughout his copy of Black's polemic. "We're relying on *Black* not *McReynolds*," he remarked of Black's charge he had revived substantive due process. During World War II, Black had maintained that a state could not expel children who were Jehovah's Witnesses from schools if they refused to salute the flag. Black had written his concurrence in that case at a time when Americans were dying for that flag, but he had insisted on the First Amendment right to religious freedom.[69] Now, with the country in another war, Black was less certain of the Court's wisdom in intervening to protect students' First Amendment rights. Indeed he sounded like such a different person that Fortas scribbled "Hugo Black!!" next to Black's assertion in *Tinker* that "uncontrolled liberty is an enemy to domestic peace."[70] But Fortas, too, wanted to regulate dissent.

## THE LONELY CENTER

To his credit, Fortas expanded First Amendment protection of pure speech in an important draft opinion for the Court in 1969 which held that the state could punish speech only if it incited "imminent lawless action."[71] To his further credit, Fortas willingly extended First Amendment protection not only to words but also to certain forms of conduct as well. Even when students protested against a cause he championed, as did the antiwar youth in *Tinker,* or against a President he supported, as did a group at a speech given by Lyndon Johnson at the University of Texas,[72] Fortas still defended their right to engage in peaceful demonstrations.

Nevertheless, Fortas's solution was arcane. In the late 1960s Fortas's emphasis on nondisruptive conduct seemed as anachronistic as had his insistence in *Epperson* on invalidating an antievolution statute the state no longer enforced. Writing in the *Harvard Law Review* in 1968, Louis Henkin, no radical, maintained that in burning his draft card, O'Brien had made a speech and that he "deserved a better opinion." The opinions of Fortas and his colleagues increasingly resembled exercises in line-drawing, as they struggled to extend protection to one form of conduct and remove it from another. Although he acknowledged that virtually all judicial opinions involved exercises in drawing lines, Henkin reminded his audience that the lines must be "rational." If they were not, "the law and legal process become less rational and lose the confidence of those they serve."[73]

By 1969 Fortas's position on symbolic speech had helped to erode confidence in the Court. Few on the right seemed to realize that he agreed with them that in many situations state interests might outweigh First Amendment rights. One person displeased with *Tinker* informed Fortas that he was a "decadent, unethical, immoral, debased and odious practitioner of the Far Left" who represented "the permissive wing of permissive Jewry." Students would soon be wearing signs proclaiming "Join Abe Fortas and the S.D.S.," another predicted. A school superintendent warned Fortas that "you and your buddies on the court . . . have made . . . a burden on the enforcement of laws," while a high school dean of students warned that Fortas would "receive letters from all over this country, from school officials who know that the 'highest court' has once again poked its nose into a matter which is not its business at all." An envelope addressed to "Marxist Justice Fortas, Judicial Star Chamber, Legal Politburo, Division for Marxist Sociology," suggested where most of Fortas's critics believed he belonged.[74]

The left wanted no part of Fortas either. As he admitted, it had not welcomed his broadside setting out his views on dissent and civil disobedience. "Feeling on many campuses in this country is so strong that most of the letters that I have received from students and faculty of colleges and universities about my pamphlet . . . [are] critical of my position *because* it insists that disruption of classes, sit-ins, and, of course any form of violence or forceful interference with the rights of others, is lawlessness and is not protected by the purpose that the students may have—however noble they may consider that to be."[75] That was true. Howard Zinn's *Disobedience and Democracy,* for example, attacked Fortas's broadside, pointing to "nine fallacies" on law and order it expressed. "For the crisis of our time, the slow workings of American reform, the limitations on protest and disobedience set by liberals like Justice Fortas, are simply not adequate," Zinn argued.[76]

Fortas's difficulty with symbolic speech exemplified the problems many "liberals" faced by 1969. Reviled by the Right for going too far, they were condemned by radical students and faculty for refusing to go far enough. Much of the power of modern American liberalism derived from the hope that the reforms its proponents promised would deflect radicalism, but the changes Fortas and others had brought about instead seemed to have sparked radicalism. Perhaps they had been insufficient. Alternatively, perhaps their reforms had been so successful that they had stimulated the New Left with visions of what might be possible at the same time that they mobilized a new Right by threatening the traditional vision of the good society.[77] Whatever the reason, the revolution was occurring now, and it was directed against Fortas, Lyndon Johnson, and other reformers in the center.

# CHAPTER 14

# The Adviser, II

ORTAS RETAINED TWO CLIENTS WHEN HE JOINED THE SUPREME COURT. One was Pablo Casals, who, Fortas noted, was "obviously . . . not impressed by the fact that I am no longer in law practice. However, since he is 90 and a half years old, I don't want to disturb him by suggesting that it is impossible to continue our relationship."[1] Another younger and more demanding client also seemed unaware Fortas was no longer his attorney. As a colleague on the Court said, for most of his tenure as a justice, "Abe was sitting in Lyndon Johnson's lap."[2] Because Fortas proved unable to resist the President's pleas for assistance, he became embroiled in the issues that led to the downfall of Johnson's particular combination of globalism and domestic reform.

## ATTORNEY AND CLIENT: VIETNAM

Just before Johnson's landslide victory in 1964, National Security Adviser McGeorge Bundy counseled him to stop running the White House on a crisis basis and to organize it for "the long pull." Bundy recommended that Johnson consult "those who know you best and those who know the Presidency best."[3] Johnson took that advice. With Walter Jenkins gone, he relied increasingly upon Clark Clifford and Abe Fortas. The two men complemented each other. Clifford was more intimate with the presidency than with the President, Fortas knew more of Johnson than the office. Clifford's strength lay in foreign policy, Fortas's in domestic affairs.

It was unfortunate that the expertise of Johnson's closer adviser mirrored his own, for foreign policy became ever more important after 1964. The war in Vietnam dwarfed all other issues and left Johnson "a deeply frustrated man."[4] Yet neither Fortas nor the President possessed the background to resolve the war. Most of the President's other foreign policy advisers were older men who had served as policy makers during World War II. Although they were overly influenced by memories of Munich, they had nevertheless grappled with world affairs. Fortas had not. He understood the Caribbean, but not Southeast Asia. One of his friends said—and others agreed—"Abe didn't know a goddamn thing about foreign affairs."[5]

Near the end of his life, Fortas himself admitted that he and Johnson had been "unsophisticated" about the war. In retrospect, he maintained that the United States could not have won. "Our basic fault was a misunderstanding of the mind of the Communist leaders," he said. "We thought that, like us, they would be horrified by death and destruction." But according to Fortas, they were not. "You bomb the hell out of people and kill them off and despoil their country, and they're impervious to it. It's a very un-American attitude," he joked.[6]

Fortas claimed that Johnson might have recognized the futility of the struggle had he not felt obligated to continue the policies of Kennedy, from whom he had inherited the war. "If we had not been involved in Vietnam when he became President, I think it's by no means clear that he would have involved us in terms of armed forces."[7] Johnson, he contended, would have shunned a ground invasion in favor of other options that might have compelled the North Vietnamese to settle. But Fortas never specified those options, and, while Kennedy was a convenient scapegoat, it was Johnson who committed ground troops in Vietnam, an action Kennedy had declined to take. Fortas opposed that decision. "I always felt that we should not be in Vietnam with armed forces," he recalled. Fortas did not participate in the July 1965 meetings that preceded the President's promise of an additional fifty thousand ground troops, and he told his friend he thought that was "a bad call." Characteristically, however, Fortas supported Johnson when the President replied that there was no alternative. "I'm an operational person," Fortas explained, "and it was done and that was settled." McGeorge Bundy argued that "the country was in a mood to accept grim news," but the President wanted good news as well. Though he disapproved of the escalation, Fortas helped distract the country's attention from it by allowing Johnson to announce his appointment to the Court at the same time.[8]

Once on the bench, Fortas remained the President's lawyer, treating the war as if it were a problem that vexed his client. After listening to him hold forth at dinner one evening, Benjamin Cohen observed that his old colleague seemed intent on preserving a safe position to which the President could retreat at every stage of the war.[9] He made no value judgments in 1965 and 1966 and focused on strategy or implementation. Fortas saw his role as one of presenting ways in which to advance while preserving a way to retreat safely as well.

That led some to believe he never expressed a preference between options. When Robert F. Kennedy was deciding whether to seek the presidency, some of his advisers refused to push him. "Everybody was a junior Abe Fortas," a participant said of one meeting. "Nobody wanted to say what to do; everybody was just laying out the alternatives to be analyzed."[10] Fortas himself preferred that version of his role. "The President and I have been associated mostly as lawyer and client, for many years," the justice later told the Senate Judiciary Committee. "The President does me the honor of having confidence in my ability, apparently, to analyze a situation and to state the pros and cons." At White House conferences called to consider "the fantastically difficult decisions about the war in Vietnam," which Fortas said he attended "very seldom," Johnson "called on me last. And it is my function, then, to sum up the arguments on the one side, the considerations on the other."[11] That version underestimated both the number of such gatherings he attended and the role he played.

Fortas actively participated, for instance, in the conference Johnson called at the end of 1965 to consider ordering a pause in the bombing as a signal to Hanoi of his willingness to negotiate. Some of the President's counselors argued that such a halt was essential to satisfy public opinion. In the words of McGeorge Bundy, who joined Secretary of State Dean Rusk and Secretary of Defense Robert McNamara in advocating this course: "Any pause should be very hard-nosed, and we should expect that it will not lead to negotiations, but it will strengthen your hand both at home and abroad as a determined man of peace facing a very tough course in 1966. It is quite true . . . that the bombing is not what started the trouble, but it is also true that we have a great interest in proving our own good faith as peace lovers."[12] Toward the end of the session, the President called upon Fortas, who recapitulated the arguments in favor of a pause.

Fortas then dismissed them. As the United States did not plan to notify the Soviet Union of its plans, he argued, the Soviets would not be swayed by the pause to press Hanoi to negotiate. "It is too little to get the Soviets to do anything." Further, Fortas found the proposed pause "ambivalent and ambiguous." Clifford had maintained that staging the action during the Christmas season would make it look like "a gimmick," and Fortas agreed that the timing would "dilute . . . the effort in its hoped for psychological and political results." A pause would neither appease Hanoi nor satisfy the American public, who "really want-[ed] . . . cessation of hostilities." Fortas worried that Americans would perceive the pause as "evidence of lack of certainty" on their government's part and feared what might happen when, as was likely, the pause failed to produce substantive results. Rusk countered that "in carrying the political battle, I need something more than we have at the present time." The justice replied, "Perhaps it looks different on the inside than it does on the outside."[13] Contrary to his description of himself as one who merely summarized alternatives, Fortas made his doubts about a bombing pause clear.[14]

Fortas, naturally, placed his friend's decision to agree with the insiders and order a thirty-seven-day bombing halt in the most favorable light. He always insisted that the December pause, like others later, reflected Johnson's sincere desire for peace. Fortas characterized the allegation that they occurred for any other reason, such as politics, "utter nonsense." The President had been "an emotional man, and when you talk about war and killing people, it was very meaningful to Johnson," he emphasized. According to Fortas, Johnson was "desperately seeking negotiation, and he was listening to people whom I wouldn't have given the time of day. . . . He talked to so and so and he was a second cousin to the third secretary of the Vietnamese delegation in Paris, or so and so in Albania would talk to this guy and that guy and so on. It was all unbelievable; it was just fantasy."[15]

Fortas also claimed that Johnson welcomed disagreement. Subsequent disclosures that the President could not tolerate dissent and that he relegated those who differed with him about the war to "the doghouse" irritated Fortas. According to him, Johnson "always insisted upon getting a diversity of opinion, contrary to what you hear from some softheaded people."[16] That was untrue, and Fortas knew it. The President routinely did call upon selected staff members to express their opposition to the war, but their positions constrained such individuals. Uncontrolled dissent, however, bothered Lyndon Johnson. Mercedes and Robert Eichholz dined weekly with Fortas and Agger. After White House business had forced Fortas to cancel on several occasions, Carol Agger telephoned Mercedes Eichholz. "I've refused to break the date this time, so the Johnsons are coming here," she said. "But you have to promise not to bring up the war." The Eichholzes, who had stopped discussing the war with Fortas long ago to preserve friendship, promised they would not raise the issue unless Johnson did. The evening went smoothly until after dinner. While Fortas was in his study examining papers the President had brought for him, Johnson remarked on the tremendous pressures on him to withdraw from Vietnam. "If you do that, Mr. President, you'll go down as a national hero," Mercedes Eichholz responded. The First Lady warned against another Munich. At this point, Fortas, who had overheard the conversation and was aware that criticism from an old friend would bother Johnson more than he let on, rushed in "as if he had roller skates on," put his hands over Eichholz's mouth, and repeatedly hushed her. "That was real censorship," she said. But Eichholz understood it. Fortas was protecting the President once again.[17]

Fortas himself felt sufficiently comfortable with Johnson to advocate a radically different course of action in Southeast Asia. During the first week of 1966, he suggested to the President that the United States present in the United Nations an offer to leave Vietnam. As Fortas envisioned it, the formal note would state his country's willingness to accept a cease-fire "on terms acceptable to a representative group of states," its pledge to begin disengagement immediately after the signing of the cease-fire, its commitment to "complete withdrawal within the shortest reasonable time, not later than 3(?) years thereafter," and its lack of interest in acquiring or operating military bases in Southeast Asia.[18]

Fortas considered that course expedient for two reasons. First, "there persists widespread doubt as to the integrity of our intentions." Those who doubted American sincerity pointed to the ambiguous statements of the administration about when U.S. troops would be removed, arguing that the intention was not to leave until a stable, non-Communist government was installed in South Vietnam, and noted silence on the question of negotiating with the political arm of the South Vietnamese Communists. Second, Fortas anticipated an increased Soviet presence in North Vietnam: "This is a threat, but it may have advantages." It could reduce the risks associated with American withdrawal by intensifying tension between the Soviets and the Chinese, preventing the Chinese from dominating Southeast Asia, and placing "an additional and vexatious burden" upon the Soviets. Though Fortas realized his solution might ultimately result in Communist domination of Southeast Asia, "it is possible that we can deal with the long-range, with future problems, more advantageously if we are *out* of Viet Nam than if we are there, engaged in what appears to be a long war of dubious extent and debatable outcome."[19] But Johnson would not quit.

Therefore, toward the end of January 1966 Fortas advised the President to resume the bombing. If Johnson were not going to end the Vietnam involvement, he believed that the President should act forcefully. Fortas insisted that Communists all over the world were working to extend the pause.[20] When Ho Chi Minh's widely publicized letter describing the American search for peace as deceitful and hypocritical circulated later that month, an unsigned memorandum to the President apparently written by Fortas described the letter as "merely the latest in a series of cleverly devised moves by the Communist nations to prolong the suspension of bombing for their military, strategic and political benefit." According to Fortas, the letter was part of the Communist attempt to persuade the public that the North Vietnamese were continuing the war only because they doubted the intentions of the United States:

This is phony. The tactic is—or should be—transparent. The Communists know very well that the United States has no territorial, strategic or long-term military ambitions with respect to Vietnam or Southeast Asia. They know very well that they may completely rely upon our statements.

The plain fact is that the Communists do not want to discuss or negotiate. They want unconditional withdrawal. They do not want a peace based upon conciliation or negotiation. They want a total Communist victory.

To further their interests in total victory, they are playing upon American public opinion with the immediate purpose of substantially reducing the use of our most effective military weapon—our air power. Meanwhile, they are building up their own military effectiveness and intensifying the pressures upon us to effect total withdrawal.[21]

The memorandum was a lawyer's brief, not a summary. Fortas's success in private practice had derived in part from his conviction that the attorney was also an advocate. Because he not only laid out options for his clients but also helped them choose the best one, his clients emphasized he was "more than a lawyer." Where the war was concerned, Fortas in 1965 and 1966 listed the alternatives and spoke for those he preferred. Having done so, he accepted his client's decision and worked faithfully to execute it.

Fortas's skill in exposition proved useful when Johnson had to justify his actions in Vietnam to the American people. In later years, accusations that he had helped write the President's State of the Union address for 1966 jeopardized Fortas's claim that he had not been one of Johnson's most intimate advisers. "Saying that I worked on the draft was erroneous," Fortas insisted. If he had made any contribution, "it was certainly specific."[22] The President's files, however, indicated that his adviser made extensive suggestions for revisions.[23] That was appropriate, for the speech reflected Fortas's continuing concern with domestic social policy. Although it was the first such address during Johnson's presidency to subordinate domestic affairs to foreign policy, it included a ringing endorsement of the Great Society and a forceful warning that the American government's course of action in Vietnam must not endanger reform at home. If there were some who did not believe that the government could both fight in Vietnam and continue to pursue the Great Society, Johnson told the country, "then, in the name of justice, let them call for the contribution of those who live in the fullness of our blessing, rather than try to strip it from the hands of those that are most in need."[24]

While the President implied he preferred increasing taxes to sacrificing the Great Society, both he and his adviser proved reluctant to raise taxes. Fortas wrote Fred Lazarus at the end of 1966 that he "still" considered a tax increase "undesirable." On the same day he wrote that letter, Fortas confided to Maurice Lazarus his fear that "the inadequate supply of money is likely to result in lower receipts, while the demands of the Vietnam War continue to rise." Fortas thought the U.S. government should absorb at least $15 billion of its 1967 deficit. [25]

Fortas did not rely upon letters alone to convince the business community that the government could manage the budgetary deficit the war had created. Throughout Johnson's presidency, Ralph Lazarus served as vice-chair of the Business Council, a group of prominent businessmen. In May 1967 Lazarus informed the council that on the basis of his conversations with knowledgeable individuals in Washington, he believed the President had underestimated the cost of the war; he cautioned that the deficit would climb some $5 billion above Johnson's projected figures. Lazarus then left for a meeting of the Dartmouth Alumni Fund. Upon arriving in New Hampshire, he received a telephone call from Fortas on behalf of the President. The newspapers had not yet printed Lazarus's prediction, but the White House had learned of it. The justice said it "would do great harm to the country."[26] Would he retract it? Lazarus declined to do so. As in the Bobby Baker case, Fortas then resorted to pettifoggery. Apparently reasoning that the prognosis would carry less weight if the public perceived it as Lazarus's conclusion rather than as a statement of fact by a public official, Fortas asked whether Lazarus would tell the Business Council that the conclusion was his own, reached after talking with several people, and that he had not received the warning from any one person. Lazarus replied he already had done so. "Would you tell them again?" Fortas requested. "Well, I will, Abe, if you ask me," Lazarus answered. "Yes, the President would like you to do that," Fortas replied. Lazarus then telephoned the Business Council and reiterated that he had relied on no one source for his prediction. The episode left a bad taste in his mouth. He had always considered Fortas "one individual that I would go to for advice," and he thought his former attorney had taken advantage of their friendship. [27]

Fortas seemingly would do anything for Lyndon Johnson. Of all his corporate clients, Fortas had valued the Lazarus family most, and he had developed a close personal relationship with its members. What is more, he rarely requested favors from anyone, least of all prized clients. The incident testified not only to his loyalty to the President but also to his fear that pessimistic forecasts about the cost of the war would endanger the social welfare programs about which he and Johnson cared most. Whenever he could, Fortas tried to insulate domestic reform from the impact of war. [28]

But he was unsuccessful. When Johnson called key businessmen to the White House in the summer of 1967 to acknowledge that he had indeed underestimated the war's cost and would require a tax increase, he was informed that budgetary cuts must accompany it. "The people will buy this as a war tax. Couple the tax with some cuts and it will help psychologically.[29] Sustaining the war meant paring social reform; Fortas had used his business contacts to delay this sacrifice for as long as possible.

## "WE'RE GOING TO SEE THIS THROUGH"

Fortas's role as an adviser on Vietnam changed dramatically over time. During the first phase, he counseled the President as he would any client. During the second, which began around the time he telephoned Lazarus in May 1967, Fortas became shrill. He now saw only one alternative—escalation—and he pressed Johnson to adopt it. The beginning of the second phase coincided with the outbreak of the Six-Day War between Israel and Egypt, and that conflict may have increased Fortas's commitment to American perseverance in Vietnam.

Fortas's attitude toward Judaism changed when he became a Supreme Court justice. He now worried about the propriety of giving a speech on the first night of the Jewish New Year.[30] He passed messages from Jewish groups to the White House and spoke more frequently before Jewish groups.[31] He became friendly with the Chancellor of the Jewish Theological Seminary, Louis Finkelstein, who, Fortas explained to the White House, was regarded by American Jews as "the nearest thing to Jesus in the United States."[32] He maintained a warm correspondence with the mayor of Jerusalem, Teddy Kollek, who sent the Cuban cigars Carol Agger enjoyed by diplomatic pouch.[33] The sincerity of Fortas's spiritual involvement remained questionable. He stayed home on the most solemn day of the Jewish year, but he did so because his secretary insisted, not because of his own sense of its significance.[34] Since he was the only Jew on the Court, he tried to appear more publicly observant.

Fortas's concern about Israel was sincere, as he soon proved. In 1966 the new pro-Palestinian government in Syria concluded a mutual defense treaty with Egypt. Syrian–Israeli fire fights intensified in 1967. On May 14 President Gamal Abdel Nasser of Egypt began moving his army into the Sinai Peninsula, next to Israel's western frontier. Four days later, he successfully demanded the immediate withdrawal of the 3,378 troops in the United Nations Emergency Force, who had long patrolled the Israeli–Egyptian border. On May 22 Nasser closed the straits of Tiran to Israeli shipping. On May 30 King Ibn Talal Hussein of Jordan flew to Cairo to sign a mutual defense pact with Nasser, his former enemy. Clearly the Israelis were in danger of an immediate attack.

Fortas now became a "back channel" for communications between the Israeli Embassy and the White House.[35] Again, as during the Dominican Republic crisis, he negotiated for the President. He seemed an obvious choice for the role. Fortas had known the Israeli ambassador, Avraham Harman, since Harman's arrival in Washington in the fall of 1959. When Prime Minister David Ben Gurion came to the United States in the following year, Fortas arranged a breakfast meeting at his house between Ben-Gurion, Harman, and Lyndon Johnson.[36] Subsequently, Harman and Fortas saw a good deal of each other. "I made it my business to keep him informed of the situation in Israel and could always feel that . . . he would be frank and open in expressing his assessment of American reactions and attitudes," Harman recalled. By 1967 the Israeli ambassador had come to view Fortas as "a man of great wisdom and perceptive judgment."[37] For his part, one of his law clerks said, Fortas had become "a great admirer of Harman, and enormously respectful of his and Israel's intelligence and realism."[38] By keeping Fortas apprised of events, the ambassador could receive his counsel and make sure that the justice had the most recent information when he conferred with the President. "Of course I knew that he was close with Johnson," Harman noted years later.[39] For several weeks before the crisis erupted into war, the Israeli ambassador was "in very frequent contact" with Fortas and regularly visited the justice at his chambers or his house.[40]

As the tension between Israel and Egypt mounted, Fortas reportedly became increasingly upset with the State Department and with Secretary of State Rusk. The secretary, who was trying with little success in the United Nations to arrange a multilateral force to test Egypt's blockade, was not a warm enough supporter of Israel for the justice.[41] As he said goodbye at his office door to Harman, who was returning to Israel to report to the cabinet, Fortas made his feelings clear. "Rusk will fiddle while Israel burns," Fortas's clerk overheard the justice say to the ambassador. Fortas then warned Harman that Israel could not count for support on any other country, including the United States, and would have to help itself.[42] Whether Fortas was delivering his own evaluation of America's position or passing along the President's advice, if indeed he made such comments, was unclear.[43] But given his closeness to Johnson, the Israelis surely would have assumed he was speaking for the President. They viewed such statements as proof that the United States no longer expected them to show restraint.[44] "What is of course clear is that this judgment of Fortas was borne out by the actual events," Harman emphasized.[45]

By this time, Fortas seemed more knowledgeable about the Israeli situation than the White House. On June 4, while Rusk continued to fiddle, Johnson, Secretary of Defense Robert McNamara, and John Loeb attended a dinner party at Fortas's house.[46] As the men gathered in the study after dinner, Fortas warned the President that war might soon erupt in the Middle East. Johnson turned questioningly to McNamara, who answered that the Defense Department's intelligence indicated that there would be no war. The President said that his intelligence confirmed McNamara's.[47] Johnson left Fortas's house at 10:58 P.M.[48] At 4:30 A.M., a telephone call from his national security adviser awakened the President. Israel had attacked Egypt.[49]

A State Department definition of the United States' position as "neutral in thought, word, and deed" annoyed most American Jews,[50] including Fortas. He left a message for the President advising him to "refrain from getting into the 'neutrality issue' any more."[51] But when John Loeb asked him "why cannot we take a more positive stand for our friends and against our enemies?"[52] Fortas defended his President. "My impulse is to agree with you about the desirability of our being outspoken in the Middle East, but I think that unless we maintain as much room for negotiations as possible, the situation will be hopeless."[53]

Israel's success cheered Fortas. "When they get back from Egypt, I'm going to decorate my office with Arab foreskins," his clerk heard him say.[54] After Isaac Stern had toured the territories Israel had captured from Syria, Jordan, and Egypt, he wrote to Fortas, "Your inner self would smile." The justice agreed that everything had gone very well. He believed that it was now "critically important for the apparently solid Arab front to be broken, so that a community of interest can be developed between Israel and at least one of the Arab countries." Such an alliance would aid Israel were it attacked and would answer "charges of Israeli intransigence . . . which are being vigorously exploited and which may injure Israel's capacity to obtain the economic and military assistance that it will need." Fortas knew that goal seemed utopian. "Maybe this can be accomplished only if you become head of an Arab state," he joked to the violinist. "Why not? We are all brothers in circumcision, as I understand it."[55]

In some respects, Fortas's attitude toward the conflict proved more moderate than that of other American Jews. He told John Loeb he hoped the Israelis would reach an agreement with Jordan's King Hussein to internationalize Jerusalem and demilitarize the West Bank: "If Hussein does not agree, I should think that the best answer would again be apparently unilateral action by Israel to set up an Arab state on the western bank and to offer to internationalize Jerusalem."[56] Although he emphasized that those were his own views and he spoke for no one else, Fortas's position echoed that of Western diplomats. Most Israelis had no interest in internationalizing Jerusalem or countenancing an Arab state.

American Jews such as Loeb and Stern who insisted the United States should intervene aggressively on behalf of Israel in the summer of 1967 were beginning to doubt the wisdom of American intervention in Vietnam. To the bewilderment of Lyndon Johnson, some hawks on Israel were becoming doves on Vietnam.[57] Indeed a conversation with two key American Jews who "were personally distressed by the failure of the Jewish Community to recognize the similarities between the Middle East and Vietnam and the inconsistency between the position of many Jews" so cheered Joe Califano that he reported it to the President: "They both hoped that at least out of the Middle East would come stronger support from the Liberal Jewish Community for your policy in Vietnam and a greater understanding of it."[58]

That seemed to be the impact upon Fortas. After the Six-Day War he took a harder line with respect to Vietnam. In the letter to Isaac Stern in which he expressed his enthusiasm regarding developments in Israel, Fortas disparaged his friend's belief that the United States was courting disaster by bombing sites in North Vietnam close to the Chinese border. As Fortas explained it, the military had provided the impetus for bombing the supply routes connecting China and Hanoi. The President had resisted doing so as long as he could, and Fortas assumed he yielded only after assuring himself that the Chinese would not retaliate even if they were accidentally hit. He then responded to Stern's tacit suggestion that the United States stop bombing North Vietnam entirely: "I am still firmly of the opinion that the idea of terminating the bombing of North Vietnam is absurd. We could justify this only if there were some indication other than the mouthings of politicians and third parties that it would produce some positive results in terms of the institution of negotiations. There is nothing upon which to base a hope. Hanoi has never at any time so indicated. On the other hand, it is merely idle talk to suggest that the bombing of North Vietnam has no substantial military value. It is perfectly clear that it has had a very great military value and that cessation would inevitably result in a large scale increase of the Viet Cong-North Vietnamese military potential and effectiveness south of the border."[59]

To other friends who tried to persuade him that the United States should alter its course in Vietnam, Fortas had but one reply. If they saw the intelligence reports shown to him, if they knew the whole story, they would view the situation differently.[60] When a lawyer with whom he had played chamber music expressed his dissatisfaction with the war in October 1967, Fortas fairly bristled in reply. Lyndon Johnson was "pursuing a course of action which is right, and pursuing it without regard for domestic political consequences." That was a President's duty. Of course "the so-called intellectuals" did not support him. They had not stood by Truman during the Korean War, and, Fortas implied, they rarely remained loyal to leaders forced to make tough decisions. It was "utter nonsense for distinguished and presumably informed people to talk in any terms other than our continuation of our military program, on the one hand, or total withdrawal like the French at Dien Bien Phu, on the other. —That is the situation. I realize you won't get it by reading the press or by listening to the statements of some of our distinguished senators."[61]

Though he had considered withdrawal a feasible option in early 1966, Fortas no longer did so. "*We should take or make an early opportunity to state, emphatically, that we're going to see this through to a successful conclusion,*" he counseled Johnson in the autumn of 1967. "*Nothing,* I think is as destructive as the notion that we may quit." Predictably, Fortas the adviser, like Fortas the lawyer, believed that an aggressive sell provided the answer to negative public opinion. "We've got to go on the offensive in the propaganda war." The United States should spend less time contending that it was in Vietnam to aid the people of that country. Instead it should describe its perseverance as a way of "*helping ourselves and the free world* to combat the 'new' Communist technique of conquest by infiltration and subversion."[62]

When Johnson convened his advisers for a general examination of the war in November 1967, most of the Wise Men made numerous suggestions. Fortas made just one. A briefing by George Carver of the CIA had convinced him that the United States could triumph. The country should hear that report. Paradoxically, Fortas also implied at that meeting that propaganda was unnecessary, because the public already supported the war. "I believe there is a good deal of over-reaction to what appears to be the public attitude of the United States," the justice told the others. "This opposition exists in only a small group of the community, primarily the intellectuals or so-called intellectuals and the press." According to Fortas, "the public would be outraged if we withdrew."[63]

Did Fortas really care about public opinion? Probably not. When McNamara suggested that the public wanted a halt to the bombing that same month, Fortas hinted to Johnson that the public needed a new Secretary of Defense. In a memorandum to the President derogating McNamara's recommendations, the justice reiterated that "the 'American people' . . . do not want us to achieve less than *our objectives—namely, to prevent North Vietnamese domination of South Vietnam by military force or subversion; and to continue to exert such influence as we reasonably can in Asia to prevent an ultimate Communist take-over.*" But in the same paragraph, Fortas insisted: "*Our duty is to do what we consider right.*"[64] As during the New Deal, he remained indifferent to public opinion.

Indeed his political heritage explained in part why he gave the President such poor advice. Fortas had come of age in an era when it was easy to dismiss the public and those of its representatives who obstructed the presidency as conservative and to label the sage men and women in the executive branch liberal. But by the end of 1967, most "liberals" opposed the war, and many of those opponents were in Congress. Fortas could not adjust to the change. He continued to view Congress and the public from the perspective of the 1930s and 1940s. One should handle them as best one could, but if they could not be manipulated there was no cause for concern for they knew little. Given his own past, Fortas's inadaptability was not unreasonable. As a member of the executive branch during the New Deal and World War II, he had often found Congress unhelpful. His personal experience with public opinion, which had driven him into the Navy against his own better judgment, reinforced his dubiousness about "the people." It would have been strange if he had begun to trust Congress and the public now.

But it would have been preferable. In the wake of the Viet Cong's Tet offensive in January 1968, pollsters found that only 35 percent of the public approved of the way the President was managing the war.[65] Tet, however, only intensified Fortas's commitment to his country's persistence in Vietnam. He treated few individuals with the deference he accorded John Loeb. But when Loeb told him in February 1968 that the United States should suspend strategic bombing in North Vietnam, Fortas replied that "this is one of the few times when I have to differ with you." Suspending the bombing of Vietnam had never paid off. The Communists construed it "a sign of weakness and an invitation to increase their agitation for total and unconditional cessation of bombing," and "certain segments of our articulate population" had treated it as grounds for intensifying the pressure to stop all bombing. The justice concluded his letter on what he doubtless considered a pacifying note: "Like everybody else, I am unhappy with the war in Vietnam, but I think that it is now in a stage where there is absolutely no alternative except to proceed with it until a point is reached when North Vietnam is willing to call it a day. As far as I am concerned, this means only that we must go ahead until we are able to achieve a cessation of hostilities. In view of the totality of the difficulties that we face, to which you refer, I would strive for very little in terms of political arrangements; but I would absolutely insist upon a cessation of hostilities. It is this that the Communists are not ready to concede."[66]

During that month Fortas advised Johnson against another bombing pause. The President should not worry about public opinion, his adviser claimed again. *"The only thing that matters is how it all comes out!"* Fortas now believed success essential for domestic reasons as well as for deterrence of Communist aggression: Earlier he had tried to insulate social policy from the war. Now he argued that reform at home demanded perseverance abroad. "If we do not 'win' here, I think that a long period of national self doubt and timidity will be reflected in our economy, our social programs, etc; and our nation will be sufficiently shaken so as to be in real danger from a demagogue (who is not likely to have even the virtues of DeGaulle)."[67]

While he had told Loeb he would not challenge Communist governments in North or South Vietnam, Fortas said something else to the President. He warned Johnson in a long letter that the United States could not win in South Vietnam *"without changing the basic situation in North Vietnam."* Everything short of nuclear weapons and an American invasion must be attempted. In the immediate aftermath of the Tet offensive, the United States would have had an excuse for "escalation" or "retaliation," words Fortas advised his President to avoid. Since it had not seized that pretext, it should seek another. Lest the President have any doubts as to the course of action he had advised in the previous seven pages, Fortas summed it up in a sentence: "In brief, I am saying that not only domestic

considerations but our world posture will be served by *strength* now—by shelv-
ing, totally, for the time being, the 'what-can-we-do-to-get-them-to negotiate'
nonsense—regardless of provocation—and by carrying the war to North Vietnam—without explanation or apology."[68]

The proposal impressed Johnson, but not the President's advisers.[69] At a
meeting that Johnson convened shortly after he received Fortas's letter, the
justice claimed that conciliatory gestures would not satisfy the public. The
United States should reinforce the troops it sent to Vietnam and reconfirm its
commitment. Clark Clifford, who himself had recently turned against the war,
replied that Fortas was operating in the wrong context. In World War II, "'prevail we will' would work because conditions were right. Now they aren't."[70] At
the meeting of the Wise Men that Johnson called the following week, the justice
and the President were also outnumbered. An overwhelming majority believed
that the United States should reduce its involvement in Vietnam.[71] Five days
later, Johnson announced he would not seek reelection as President.

## "THE PRESIDENT DOES NOT ASK MY APPROVAL"

Johnson did not limit his conversations with Fortas to Vietnam. A Supreme
Court justice may have had more free time than a Washington lawyer, but Fortas
was spending it at the White House. While the bulk of his advice to the President
between 1963 and 1965 had concerned social policy, culture, and personnel, by
1966 he became involved in the tough domestic issues that were tearing the
United States apart.

Friends proved more reticent about asking Fortas for White House jobs once
he was on the Court, but he still supplied many names of qualified individuals to
the executive branch.[72] Although he later publicly maintained that "to the best
of my knowledge and belief, I have never, since I have been a Justice, recommended anybody for a U.S. judgeship," he engaged in active—and unsuccessful—campaigns to promote three friends as judges.[73] Additionally, he sometimes sounded out potential government appointees on their political views. Like
Johnson, Fortas hated Robert Kennedy. The justice believed that Kennedy had
compromised himself by working for Joseph McCarthy and was making Lyndon
Johnson's life miserable by presenting Americans with a vision of liberalism
without globalism.[74] Fortas queried one person he was interviewing for a government position about his attitude toward Robert Kennedy, and he probably never
knowingly recommended a Kennedy supporter to the President.[75] A candidate
who disagreed with Johnson's position on Vietnam received no backing from
Fortas either.[76] The justice also was sent scores of memoranda from the White
House. His opinions were solicited on matters ranging from campaign financing

to consumers' rights.[77] When the nation was threatened with a rail strike in 1967, Fortas met frequently with the White House team working to avert it.[78]

By the following year, he was helping the President cope with the Black unrest which, beginning in 1964, had exploded each summer into riots. The problem vexed the President for two reasons. He did not understand the cause for the violence. As the twentieth-century President who had supported the most civil rights legislation, Johnson believed that he understood and had helped Blacks. He felt personally betrayed by their increasing demands during his tenure. On the other hand, while he condemned violence, he also felt sympathy for the rioters. When Vice-President Hubert Humphrey announced in a speech before the NAACP that if he had seen rats gnawing at his children's feet, he too would riot, he was speaking in terms Johnson understood.[79] "It was that ambivalence of the liberal," White House staff member Harry McPherson remarked.[80]

The Detroit riots of July 1967 would "remain forever etched in my memory," Johnson recalled.[81] When the Governor of Michigan, George Romney, recommended that the President send federal troops, Johnson initially hesitated on political grounds. The Constitution did authorize the President to protect a state against domestic violence upon application of its governor. But, perhaps because Governor Romney harbored presidential aspirations, the initial pleas for help from Michigan were tentative and did not convincingly demonstrate that the situation required federal troops. Fortas believed that Romney wanted to avoid "the political fallout" a request for federal troops would cause and "was trying to force Lyndon to send the troops in without invitation."[82] Fortas refused to allow the President to fall into that trap. Once Johnson had rejected his attorney general's view that the violence was "substantially exaggerated" and followed the advice of Fortas and Secretary of Defense McNamara to send Cyrus Vance to Detroit as an observer, the President's course became clearer. Vance reported that the situation continued to deteriorate and that even Romney now had "no doubt" that state and local troops could not handle the rioters. Johnson decided that a constitutional basis for dispatching federal troops existed.[83] Having resolved to intervene, the President now faced an equally complex problem. He believed that in drafting the message that would accompany the executive order announcing troop deployment, he had to make a choice between emphasizing law and order, on the one hand, and sympathy for the rioters, on the other. He summoned Fortas and Special Counsel Harry McPherson to help him make the decision.

McPherson knew the sort of message Johnson and Fortas expected him to produce. "I guess they thought I would write the usual bleeding heart speech," he said. "Old soft McPherson is the guy that would always throw in: 'Of course, there are reasons why people are rioting.' "[84] After laboring over his draft for about an hour, McPherson took it to the President's office. Johnson was reviewing the justice's version.[85] It was tough. According to McPherson, the Fortas draft "was in effect saying, 'You folks up there in Detroit, if you think you're going to get the keys to the city by this, you're wrong. You're going to get a fistful of fingers.' " The speech reflected Fortas and the President's determination "to speak very forcefully and without the 'understanding.' " Asked what he thought of Fortas's effort, McPherson hesitated. Nevertheless, he endorsed it. The justice was surprised. "Are you really going to approve that?" Fortas asked. McPherson answered affirmatively.[86] "I was troubled by something in the statement, but I thought it was the absence of compassion for the Negroes of Detroit, and I was reluctant to start an argument about that when the cameras were waiting and the men around me wanted a decisive call for order," he said later.[87]

But McPherson would have voiced his views had Fortas been absent. "I was intimidated by the stature and the brains and the judgment and the reputation and my own relationship with Justice Fortas," he told oral historians from the Johnson Library in 1969. "I was very much the junior man and although I would have argued with the President alone about it, I didn't argue with Justice Fortas."[88] Asked about that statement years later, McPherson expressed surprise at his own candor and explained, "Johnson would bluster at you sometimes, and you could feel . . . that it was being done as a form of exercise. So I tended, as kids do with a blustering father, to just push it aside, and wait until you get to something really serious, at which point Johnson was far more intimidating than Abe." Since Fortas was "free of bluster," McPherson took him more seriously.[89] The President's special counsel also thought Fortas a voice of reason in the troubled 1960s. If someone who could speak so wisely to both dissenters and those who would lock them up believed the President should deliver a forceful message, perhaps he was right. As a young lawyer, McPherson felt sure enough of himself to disagree with the President of the United States but did not feel sufficiently confident to argue with a Supreme Court Justice "with an almost unparalleled record and standing."[90]

Like other Johnson intimates, however, McPherson never had been in awe of Fortas's political sense. In this instance, as the President was delivering the speech, McPherson belatedly realized where it erred. It was not that it was tough. It was that Fortas bluntly had said again and again that the President had agreed to the unusual step of troop deployment only because Romney could not control the situation. Johnson's words hinted strongly that the governor could not handle his own office and therefore would be incapable of managing the Oval Office. McPherson understood that the repeated argument represented an attempt to provide a legal basis for sending in the troops. But as McPherson noted, "law is based on politics." In the days that followed, it was difficult to persuade reporters that federal intervention in Detroit did not grow out of the President's desire to discredit Romney.[91] Fortas downplayed his role in the resolution of the Detroit riots. "I did not write that message," he lied to the Senate Judiciary Committee in 1968, though he acknowledged he had seen it before it was delivered. Asked whether he approved it, Fortas replied, "The President does not ask my approval."[92] Technically, that may have been correct. As Johnson had consulted him before any important decision, his answer was also legalistic and misleading.

Fortas's behavior during the Detroit riots indicated his own ambivalence about the racial violence of the 1960s. Just two days after drafting Johnson's message, Fortas advised the President to deliver a television address asking the country "to observe Sunday as a day of reflection on the racial torment our country is suffering." Fortas suggested that his friend ask churchgoers to pray the upheaval would soon end and call on Black organizations to oppose the rioting. "Abe feels that after the tough statement of Monday night, you should now speak as a teacher and moral leader, appealing for public order," McPherson told the President.[93] Of course the justice's recommendation, which Johnson adopted, may have been politically motivated and may have reflected a desire to improve the President's standing with the public. But McPherson saw it as "a change of view."[94] Like Lyndon Johnson, Fortas was torn about the course of action the country should take. Violence made them question the wisdom of a compassionate social policy, but they remained committed to the policy. Their wavering hurt them, however. One the one hand, the harshness of the President's Detroit message alienated the Left and Johnson's liberal constituency. On the other, the President's attempt to exercise moral leadership seemed to the Right symptomatic of his failure to address the real problems. Many critics who condemned the Warren Court for its "softness" on law and order were coming to consider the President part of the problem.

Crime raised some of the same issues as racial unrest, and Johnson and Fortas displayed equal uncertainty in coping with it. When Southern Democrats and Republicans combined in 1966 to introduce the District of Columbia Crime Bill, which allowed police to hold suspects for four hours prior to arrest and to question them without interruption for six hours prior to arraignment, liberals in the Democratic party opposed it.[95] Fortas condemned it as "an obscenity."[96] Other advisers maintained that aspects of the bill contained "serious constitutional problems" and advised Johnson not to approve it.[97] The justice joined in their recommendation and helped draft the President's veto message, which stressed that "fundamental constitutional questions pervade the bill."[98] Johnson's staff also knew, however, that "the majority of Americans who know of the bill no doubt regard it as good because it will 'Help stamp out crime and is tough on criminals.' "[99] Though the President's own position was more progressive than punitive, he too wanted police organizations to function more efficiently.[100] Therefore once he determined to veto the bill, he decided also to present Congress with an administration-supported crime bill for the District of Columbia.

Johnson's District of Columbia Crime Bill of 1967 did represent a substantial improvement over its predecessor. Nevertheless, Fortas recognized that it contained one substantial defect. It obviated the most serious constitutional problem with the 1966 bill because it did not permit police routinely to question suspects for hours before arrest. It still sanctioned questioning for three hours prior to arraignment and provided that any statements by the suspect during that time would be admissible at trial. A decision of the Warren Court, *Mallory* v. *U. S.* (1957), held that generally no delay should occur between arrest and arraignment. When there was a lag, a court properly might rule that a suspect's statements during that interval had been made under coercion and might exclude them at trial.[101] Fortas therefore counseled against inclusion of the section permitting three hours of questioning in the 1967 bill. He believed that such a provision "will put you in the middle of a fight that is nationwide and will not be resolved for some time."[102] Of course when Johnson decided to retain the section, Fortas helped to draft the President's message urging its passage.[103]

Once again, Johnson and Fortas were moderating their civil libertarian inclinations in an attempt to walk a middle line. But in the 1960s, it was as difficult to compromise on crime as it was to fluctuate on civil rights. By allowing the continued abridgement of civil liberties, the 1967 bill alarmed those on the left. By reducing the power its predecessor would have given police, it alienated those on the right. By 1968 congressional conservatives had more power than they had possessed two years earlier. They used it to enact the Omnibus Crime Control and Safe Streets Act of 1968. It empowered police to question a suspect for six hours prior to arraignment and authorized the federal government to engage in wiretapping. Both the Republicans and George Wallace's third party effectively capitalized on the law and order issue in the election campaign of 1968.

## TWO FRIENDS

During the Johnson years, Fortas was part of the judicial branch and, as well, an unofficial member of the executive branch. Supreme Court justices have always advised Presidents, and Fortas used his power as a presidential confidant to promote the values he advocated as a justice. His efforts resulted in the passage of a better crime bill in 1967. Yet even that bill proved imperfect.

That might have created a problem for Fortas. Although the President might advance measures which include seemingly unconstitutional provisions, Supreme Court justices were not expected to do the same. Johnson's job was to propose legislation, the Supreme Court's to decide whether that legislation was constitutional. The President had only one job. His adviser had two. When Fortas reluctantly accepted the White House position on the delay between arrest and arraignment in 1967, when he suggested the President consider "direct federal measures [against crime]—although they are necessarily drastic and constitutionally dubious," such as a federal gun registration act, he ran the risk of compromising his judicial integrity.[104]

Some hinted that his participation in decisions regarding the war also might have been inappropriate. "Abe—architect of our Vietnam policy—sat in the five cases raising the question of the constitutionality of the war—absent a declaration of war," William O. Douglas noted. "I could not tell . . . whether he was being hammered on that or not."[105] But Potter Stewart, who sometimes joined Douglas and Brennan in dissents insisting that the Court should rule on the war's constitutionality, saw nothing wrong about Fortas's refusal to side with them. No other member of the Court agreed with Stewart, Douglas, and Brennan either, and one person in Stewart's family acted as if he were "guilty of treason."[106] Fortas also advised the White House on how to manage the demonstrators who poured into Washington. In August 1967 Fortas sent a memorandum to Johnson's staff on White House picketing: "If anything is to be done, it should be done quietly. Publicity with respect to forceful action . . . would create unrest and uneasiness." Nor did he find any basis for preventing picketing in the park across the street from the White House. Fortas saw "much more justification for prohibiting picketing on all of the sidewalks adjacent to the White House. But I doubt the wisdom of doing this at the present time." He suggested that a permit could be required and that groups be limited to seventy-five participants. But the justice preferred another solution. "If the security officers are worried about the prospect of difficulties within the next few months, perhaps some basis can be found for closing off the sidewalk entirely," making them inaccessible to picketers and passersby alike.[107] Though Fortas could have foreseen that the Supreme Court would consider the constitutionality of ordinances regulating demonstrations against the war, he still advised the White House on drafting such an ordinance. He may have reasoned that advice he gave as counselor did not bind him to any decision as a justice. Yet his behavior was still questionable. Why was he willing to undertake such chores for the President?

No one knew exactly what he discussed with the President at the time, but many doubted the wisdom of their continued close relationship. Fortas boasted that he knew secret entrances to the White House and often traveled there through the tunnels connecting it to the Executive Office Building or the treasury building in order to minimize media attention.[108] His colleagues at the Court were aware of his closeness to the President. They knew he had a private line to the White House and that when the red light on his secretary's phone lit up, they could not interrupt him. "Everybody talked about it around town," one of his brethren said of Fortas and Johnson's closeness. It made some of the other justices "uncomfortable."[109] In part, his colleagues' discomfort derived from a sense the President was keeping the Court from receiving the full measure of Fortas's wisdom. Although he was a good judge, Fortas had been a better lawyer. His ardent defense of civil liberties and establishment of a flourishing corporate law practice in the 1950s were memorable achievements. Given the short amount of time he had been at the Court, Fortas was performing remarkably well. Nevertheless, either his temperament, more lawyerly than judicial, or his White House obligations were preventing him from growing into the job. Those at the Court blamed the White House. One colleague believed that Fortas was "distracted" as a justice. Others at the Court recalled he acted as if he could do the job "with the back of his hand. . . . He's going to take twenty minutes and he's going to sit down, and between appointments at the White House, he's going to write a few paragraphs that will put the apportionment decision in context." One clerk knew he could safely take naps in the justice's chambers because Fortas spent so little time there.[110]

The intimacy between Johnson and Fortas also made some in the White House uneasy. Secretary of State Dean Rusk considered Fortas "ill-informed" about foreign policy and thought a Supreme Court justice should not advise a President.[111] Assistant Secretary of State Eugene Rostow, who had known Fortas for years, was "absolutely shocked" when he arrived at a meeting about Israel and saw the justice there.[112] Johnson, who was in many respects historically oriented, generally collected every scrap of paper for his archives. Yet when Fortas spoke of taking steps to fight crime, even a White House secretary wondered whether the justice's comments should be destroyed.[113]

One White House staff member with a long historical memory tried to put the relationship between Fortas and Johnson in context. Asked whether the presence of a Supreme Court justice at White House meetings had made him ill-at-ease, McGeorge Bundy said no. Smiling, he added: "I had known Felix Frankfurter."[114] In fact, the Fortas-Frankfurter analogy was not very useful. The pulls toward the President were even stronger for Fortas. Unlike Frankfurter, Fortas has been the President's attorney before he reached the Court. While Frankfurter had peppered Roosevelt with unsolicited advice, Johnson asked Fortas for help.[115] And as William Brennan observed, there was a difference in degree.

"Fortas had a lot more influence with Johnson than Frankfurter with Franklin D. Roosevelt."[116] Further, as times had changed, so had views of propriety. Arthur Goldberg once warned his successor away from Johnson. "Abe, while Felix did it, according to present reactions, people do not like a Supreme Court justice being too close to a President," he remembered saying. "While Abe would listen, I could not judge his reaction."[117] But the relationship never seemed to bother the Johnsons. Lady Bird Johnson, who considered Fortas a special confidant, recalled that she and the President were untroubled by it. "We didn't discuss the Court's business," she emphasized.[118]

On at least one occasion, however, as Athan Theoharis has discovered, Fortas did talk with Johnson about a case that was pending before the Court. In 1966, after the Court had declined to review the Washington lobbyist Fred Black's conviction for tax evasion, the solicitor general sent a memorandum to the Court volunteering the information that in the course of an unrelated criminal investigation in 1963, FBI agents had bugged Black's hotel suite and had electronically recorded conversations between him and his attorney. According to the solicitor general, however, none of the information obtained from the recordings had been used in Black's prosecution for tax evasion. The Court now directed the Justice Department to file a supplemental memorandum stating the legal authority for the FBI's microphone surveillance of Black. The order alarmed the FBI's head, J. Edgar Hoover, because he had ordered the illegal bug installed without the authorization of then–attorney general Robert Kennedy. Realizing that his only hope for protecting himself and the FBI lay in claiming that Kennedy must have known of the bug and implicitly approved it, Hoover attempted to insert language in Justice's supplemental memorandum indicating that Kennedy had received information "which could only have come from a microphone and that Kennedy could well have inferred that this information did come from a microphone."[119] When the current attorney general, Nicholas Katzenbach, a close friend of Kennedy's, protested the proposed wording and said that the memorandum would indicate Hoover had authorized the installation of the listening device on his own, Hoover decided to go over Katzenbach's head. He had already sent his correspondence with Katzenbach to Marvin Watson at the White House, but he needed to be absolutely certain that the President was properly briefed.[120]

Fortas was the obvious intermediary. William Brennan had recently chosen Michael Tigar as his law clerk, and Fortas was helping the FBI torpedo the appointment. A brilliant young man, Tigar had graduated first in his law school class at Berkeley. Though law study had left him no time for politics, in his undergraduate days, "Tigar had been in the first generation of Berkeley political activists. He demonstrated against the House Un-American Activities Committee, went to a left-wing youth festival in Helsinki, protested ROTC and favored the Cuban revolution, and was president of SLATE, the student political organization at Cal." When Brennan's selection of Tigar became public knowledge in the spring of 1966, conservatives across the country protested.[121] "The right wing deliberately set up a program—a system of pressure—that involved Abe Fortas, who was on the Court then; J. Edgar Hoover; and, more particularly, Hoover's right-hand man, Clyde Tolson," Brennan recalled. "Clyde Tolson came over to see Fortas, and Fortas came in to see me to tell me that if I went through with this there might well be an inquiry [conducted by Congress], which would be most embarrassing to Tigar and to me—and to the Court." The pressure worked; Brennan informed Tigar the job was no longer his. Told that Fortas's role seemed inconsistent with his commitment to the First Amendment, Brennan was amused. "He was very supportive of the First Admendment, but he was also very close to Lyndon Johnson, and also to J. Edgar Hoover," he replied. "They used Fortas for a lot of things."[122] Now the FBI decided to use Fortas to take its story about Robert Kennedy's approval of illegal wiretapping to Johnson.

In June 1966, Assistant Director of the FBI Cartha DeLoach telephoned Fortas and asked to see him. In an informal memorandum to Deputy Chief Tolson, DeLoach said that he had warned Fortas that their discussion would involve "a matter which he might consider bordered on a violation of judicial ethics." Fortas responded that he would gladly discuss any matter with DeLoach "on a confidential basis" and invited the FBI official over for breakfast.

If DeLoach's memorandum describing their conversation is accurate, Fortas's behavior at the meeting the following morning was clearly improper. "He was told specifically of Katzenbach's evasive tactics in attempting to defend Bobby Kennedy," DeLoach recounted, and was informed "that while the Director planned to furnish the Attorney General specific honest, hardhitting answers to the Supreme Court's questions, we nevertheless knew that Katzenbach would throw our answers out the window and present his own slanted version to the Supreme Court." After agreeing with DeLoach's prognosis, "Justice Fortas stated that the entire matter boiled down to a continuing fight for the Presidency." Fortas remarked that Kennedy was trying to capture the "left-wing" voters who had once belonged to Vice-President Hubert Humphrey, adding that "if facts, as possessed by the FBI, concerning Kennedy's approval of wiretapping were made known to the general public it would serve to completely destroy Kennedy."

That prospect, of course, would have pleased Fortas, who reportedly then divulged that the Supreme Court had held a confidential meeting about the Black matter. Though Fortas and Justice White, who had worked in Robert Kennedy's Justice Department, had disqualified themselves from the case, they had nevertheless attended. There the justices had decided that "rather than remand the Black case to a lower court, the Supreme Court would set itself up as a tribunal to gather further information concerning the usage of electronic devices and afterwards make a decision." Fortas observed that some of the members of the Court were "somewhat belligerent in their attitude towards Kennedy and Katzenbach," but he was afraid that Katzenbach's distorted presentation in the supplemental memorandum would prevent the other justices from seeing what Fortas himself knew—that "the FBI had acted in a complete above-board and honest manner at the specific urging of Kennedy and the Department." The problem, as Fortas formulated it for DeLoach, was to determine how the FBI's "irrefutable evidence exposing Kennedy" could best be communicated "to the Supreme Court and the people."

According to DeLoach, Fortas proffered a solution. He would "slip in the back door" and tell the President how the situation appeared from the vantage point of the Supreme Court. "He then stated that his plan of action would serve to protect the President and the FBI and could spell 'back seat' for Katzenbach and Kennedy," DeLoach related to Tolson. Fortas's farfetched plan called for the appointment of an arbitrator who could examine all the evidence and report to the Court. "Justice Fortas added that naturally the arbitrator would be someone whom the President could trust to furnish the absolute true facts." The two men then discussed possible candidates.

By DeLoach's account, Fortas had seen their meeting as an opportunity to bring up some other matters as well. He had already taken steps to disqualify himself from the appeal of teamster Jimmy Hoffa's jury-tampering conviction, Fortas informed DeLoach, but now he wondered whether Robert Kennedy had known of any "irregularities" in the FBI's investigation of Hoffa. When DeLoach answered that Kennedy had specifically asked the bureau to bug an attorney against its will, "Justice Fortas replied that he had felt such might be the case and that under the circumstances he would sit with the rest of the Court on the Hoffa case and would make certain that Kennedy was exposed." After predicting that the Court would confirm Hoffa's conviction, Fortas moved on to the matter of Courtney Evans, a former FBI employee who had served as the bureau's liaison to Justice while Kennedy was attorney general and who had developed a close friendship with Kennedy. Told that Evans was now working for Katzenbach, "Justice Fortas replied that this was the worst news he had received since Bobby Kennedy's urging that the Viet Cong be allowed to sit down at the conference table." Fortas then promised he was protecting the FBI's reputation at the Court, ascertained that the bureau believed Assistant Attorney General Ramsey Clark (who, Fortas confided, was a "dreamer") to be a "Johnson man," and encourged DeLoach to contact him with any further problems.[123]

When DeLoach told Hoover that the meeting with Fortas had been "well worth it," Hoover agreed. "I was dubious as I don't know Fortas well myself, but I thought he would try to weasel out on the grounds it was improper for him as a member of the Court to even discuss the matter," Hoover observed in a memorandum for his personal and confidential files on his conversation with DeLoach. "He apparently is a more honest man than I gave him credit for. DeLoach stated that it boils down to the fact that he has to defend the President."[124]

In the short run, Fortas's intervention did little for the bureau. DeLoach's subsequent informal memoranda to Tolson indicate that Fortas found Johnson cool to the idea of appointing an arbitrator,[125] and the Justice Department's supplemental memorandum in the Black case said that Hoover had approved the installation of the bug on his own authority.[126] When Black's attorneys filed a petition for a rehearing, the Court vacated his conviction and ordered a new trial, at which Black was acquitted.[127] But the long-run results of Fortas's conversations with the President could only have pleased the FBI. When Fortas telephoned DeLoach to say the President would not intervene in the Black case, DeLoach took the news as a good sign. "I told him I hoped that this possibly meant that certain people were leaving the Government and therefore there would be no need for such action," DeLoach noted. According to DeLoach, Fortas replied that "he certainly hoped so too. He added that the man in question was certainly of no benefit to the President."[128] Within four months, Katzenbach had resigned, and Ramsey Clark had replaced him. His bitter exchange with Hoover over the Black case, Katzenbach later recalled, "persuaded me that I could no longer effectively serve as Attorney General because of Mr. Hoover's obvious resentment toward me."[129]

The memoranda describing DeLoach's conversations with Fortas, of course, may represent an attempt to establish a paper trail that would exonerate Hoover of responsibility for the bureau's illegal acts. Neither informal memoranda nor Hoover's memoranda for the personal and confidential files were serialized or indexed in the FBI's central record system, and both sets of documents were targeted for destruction. That the memoranda describing DeLoach's conversations with Fortas survived suggests that Hoover may have seen them as a way of implicating Attorney General Kennedy and protecting himself.[130] But the nature of the documents also suggests their authenticity, since the FBI generally reserved informal memoranda and memoranda for the personal and confidential files for information that might incriminate the bureau. And since Fortas's personal papers also include correspondence between Hoover and Marvin Watson about the disagreement between the FBI and the attorney general over the supplemental memorandum, it seems probable that Fortas did indeed discuss the Black case with both DeLoach and Johnson. All his past behavior suggests he would not pass up the opportunity to make Johnson's enemies his own, even if it meant undercutting a former student and friend such as Katzenbach and undermining the Court and his beloved Fourth Amendment.

Fortas had always proven adept at compartmentalizing the disparate segments of his life. Still, perhaps in part because of the Black case, even he had mixed feelings about his relationship with the President. Isaac Stern thought he did worry about the appearance of impropriety.[131] And he had no free time. The President regularly broke into Fortas's vacations in Westport or skiing holidays in Quebec with telephone calls or a summons to return to Washington. At home, calls or envelopes from the White House disrupted the justice's existence at all hours and with monotonous regularity. Johnson hounded Fortas. Yet Fortas would not relinquish his role as White House adviser. He clearly enjoyed his power. "I am sure that he liked advising the President," Nicholas Katzenbach emphasized.[132] Other friends and acquaintances agreed. One recalled a dinner party at Fortas's house that was interrupted by the arrival of a package from the White House. "He must have dropped his fork right on the spot and ran to the door," the guest said of Fortas. "It was . . . really strange behavior, almost like a kid at a birthday party."[133] Further, while everyone found it hard to refuse Lyndon Johnson, the task would have been especially difficult for Fortas. He hated to deny his friends. Most of them would have agreed with White House press secretary Liz Carpenter that the justice represented "the ultimate in friendship."[134]

As Johnson became increasingly beleaguered, he reached out to his adviser. During the White House years, the two men became even closer. The Supreme Court justice was among the few who could joke with the President. Fortas once sent Johnson a photograph of the President's adviser attorney Edwin Weisl with the actress Yvette Mimieux. "Since you left Uncle Eddie in private practice, he's able to do these things—I mean private practice," Fortas teased.[135] On another occasion, he read a mock press release at a party announcing that in retirement Johnson planned to "devote his major efforts to the attempt to up-grade the curriculum and faculty of Harvard and MIT so that they can be accredited for the Head-Start program."[136] The President reciprocated with equal warmth. David Lloyd Kreeger remembered Johnson's pride the night he persuaded his adviser to perform a work by Mozart at the White House with the Marine Corps Band and Alexander Schneider. "The President came over to the quartet beaming. . . . He would gather people around him and point out his protégé, Fortas, playing the violin."[137] Clark Clifford stressed that he himself had a "business relationship," with Johnson, while the President turned to Fortas as "a very old and valued friend."[138]

At times Fortas appeared to worship Johnson. But, though he seemed reverential, though he insisted on referring to the President as "the boss," though he allowed Johnson to treat him as a protégé, Fortas never stopped trying to protect and reassure the President. Lyndon Johnson remained "Abe's boy." Fortas had many reasons for risking accusations that he breached the doctrine of separation of powers by advising the President, but the most important undoubtedly was his perception that Johnson needed him. "My dear friend," he wrote after the President's birthday in 1967:

> You are entitled to a good feeling about yourself—the warm comfort of knowing that you have served others, unselfishly and greatly, and that you have fully—and marvelously—used the extraordinary talents of mind and heart that God has given you.
>
> Your administration, I am confident, will be viewed in history as characterized by the opening of a new chapter, comparable to Lincoln's. History, I believe will be wise enough to realize that the fulfillment of democracy . . . commenced in these years because of your courage and ability; and I think, too, that history will record that it was in your administration that resolute opposition and careful, discreet statesmanship began the process of eliminating communism as a threat to mankind and of converting it from a destroyer of man's aspirations to a competitive method of political organization.
>
> In brief, please feel good and happy and content about yourself! Greatness is not happiness. It is antithetical to happiness of the usual sort. But there is another kind of happiness, deeper and more intense which I hope is yours: the happiness of a job well done and a life well-lived. [139]

A decision by Johnson to stand for reelection in 1968 would have meant continued demands, but Fortas had hoped he would run. He believed the President's refusal to seek another term grew from the combination of the problems in Vietnam and his poor health. "My own conclusion—based on L. B. J.'s statement to me about his intention not to run, was that he knew he was a fatally afflicted man—indeed, at least in hindsight, perhaps he *overestimated* his illness and had done so for some time."[140] The justice wanted his friend to persevere, and Johnson's decision disappointed him.[141] For his part, the President determined to give Fortas one last reward.

# CHAPTER 15

# On the Defensive

ORTAS INSISTED THE SUPREME COURT HAD NO SPECIAL APPEAL FOR him. "I have wondered about this and I think that perhaps it is because neither Carol nor I have any interest in position or office," he confided to Luis Muñoz Marín.[1] Nevertheless, Fortas was also a proud man who had always relished seizing the offensive when attacked. Surely it must have galled him to watch from the sidelines as his enemies denied him the chief justiceship.

## RESTLESSNESS

While he may have found his role as presidential adviser more absorbing, Fortas seemed to like being a Supreme Court justice. He had always enjoyed writing, and his clerks considered him a good editor.[2] His rhetorical flourishes added flair to their products, as well as to his own. Fortas's opinions had style. Some of them rested on his own evaluation of social policy, but Fortas also proved an excellent legal craftsman on occasion. In time, he would have developed a more coherent jurisprudence.

At oral argument, Fortas seemed engaged. Sometimes he showed off his knowledge of arcane aspects of a case, as if he wanted to remind the audience that Attorney Fortas would have done a better job of arguing the case than the lawyer standing before Justice Fortas.[3] He retained a lawyer's perspective on oral argument. Fortas told Potter Stewart that Thurgood Marshall asked too many questions, and generally he was critical of those justices who frequently broke into lawyers' presentations.[4] He had been "so highly successful a practitioner and so imbued with a resentment [about interruptions] that he was not likely to ask as many questions as some of the rest," Brennan said.[5]

The pomp of the Court tickled Fortas, and sometimes the issues it considered spurred him to doggerel. When an interracial couple challenged a miscegenation statute in *Loving v. Virginia,* he wrote:

> For a Negro to marry a White
>     Results in serious Blight
> So argues the State of Virginia
>     But science is all agin 'ya . . .
>
> Loving may marry a Malay
>     A Greek or Turk or Indée,
> But not a Black, even one-third
>     With two-thirds blood of the [Va. Sen. Harry] Byrd . . .
>
> If the Lovings lie asleep all night
>     Fearful of the copper's light
> Instead of tasting true love's might
>     Why the hell did they get married in the first place?[6]

Though his colleagues worried about the time Fortas spent at the White House, most liked and respected him. Fortas likewise found them congenial. Colleagues believed William O. Douglas was his best friend on the Court. Even Douglas's hostility toward the war and increasing ambivalence toward Lyndon Johnson did not destroy his relationship with his former student. Next to Douglas, Fortas seemed closest to William Brennan, who occupied the chambers next to his, and to Chief Justice Earl Warren. "He loved Warren," Carol Agger recalled.[7] Fortas also developed a special intimacy with John Harlan and considered him "one of my dearest friends, although we usually are on the opposite sides of issues here."[8] Both men had been corporate lawyers, and both owned summer houses in Connecticut. Harlan's daughter, a pianist, became one of Fortas's chamber music companions during vacations, and Fortas sometimes consulted her husband, a restorer of keyboard instruments.[9]

Of all the justices, only Hugo Black seemed hostile to Fortas. Though Potter Stewart later said, Fortas and Black "didn't like each other, I think, beginning at the word go,"[10] that was untrue. News of Fortas's elevation to the Court delighted Black, who tried to reconcile Agger to the appointment, and at first all was well between the two men, who had been friends since the 1930s.[11] Initially, too, Fortas and Black had given every sign of agreeing on law. "I am happy to agree to your first Court opinion," Black wrote Fortas upon reading his draft of *United Steel Workers of America v. R. H. Bouligny.* "May you write many more like it in which you lead the Court in sticking to its own business of interpretation rather than yielding to the temptation to make laws either on a legislative or constitutional level."[12] Black began to be disenchanted when a draft dissent circulated by his new colleague in response to Black's draft opinion in an obscure case, *U. S. v. Yazell*, won sufficient support to convert Fortas's position into that of the majority, thereby transforming Black's opinion into a dissent.[13] Though his written dissent in *Yazell* was moderate, Black's oral characterization of Fortas's position proved so shrill that John Harlan wryly asked whether Fortas "realize[d] you were describing all that?"[14] Even so, when Fortas wrote his opinion for the Court in *Brown v. Louisiana* several months later, he and Black still maintained a cordial relationship. Indeed in view of the harshness of his dissent, Black refused to refer to Fortas's opinion as such. Instead he explained to Fortas that he would call it the "prevailing" opinion "because the use of your name would disturb me."[15]

That collegiality soon evaporated. By the 1968 term one of Warren's clerks considered the tension between Black and Fortas "one of the most basic animosities on the Court."[16] In every case Fortas cared about—*In re Gault, Powell v. Texas, Time v. Hill, Snyder v. Harris, Epperson v. Arkansas, Tinker v. Des Moines School District*—Black was on the other side. A man of firm jurisprudential principles, Black apparently considered Fortas's approach to decision making opportunistic. In part to lessen judicial discretion and encourage literal interpretation of the Constitution, Black long had contended that the due process clause of the Fourteenth Amendment incorporated the constitutional guarantees of the first ten amendments and applied them to the states. It followed that he would disagree with Fortas, who did not believe in full "incorporation" and who argued that the courts properly could interpret due process as a broad guarantee of fairness.

The feud between the two men also became personal, and one of their brethren said, "I blame that on Black."[17] Black, who probably was disturbed not only by Fortas's opinions but by his closeness to Lyndon Johnson as well,[18] could be jocular about his differences with Fortas. On one occasion, when Fortas's clerk Walter Slocombe was visiting a clerk in his chambers, Black jokingly remarked that he was surprised that Slocombe was twenty-seven. He had expected his colleague's clerks to be teenagers because *Tinker* and *Gault* showed that Fortas was "so fond of these young people."[19] More frequently, however, Black was unprofessionally venomous in his attacks on Fortas in internal court memoranda and in published opinions. Privately Fortas might contend that Black's position in a case constituted "a disgraceful subversive job of attempted sabotage of this Court" or joke of the elderly justice: "De seniliti, legis curat mucho."[20] But while the feud saddened Fortas,[21] he took it less seriously than Black did, placated Black whenever he could, and publicly expressed disagreement in more collegial terms. Fortas had been shrugging off office feuds since he worked with Harold Ickes and had rarely taken them personally.

Fortas remained ambivalent about his job not because he disliked any of his colleagues but because it represented such a dramatic change in his life. As he thought in terms of outcome instead of process, he found the Court overly deliberate about its work and told friends his brethren took too long to reach a consensus. [22] He confided to his cousin that he missed contact with the heads of corporations. He did not always agree with them, he added, but at least corporate leaders were purposeful. [23] The isolation from his life of the previous twenty years made him anxious. Most of all, he and his wife missed the money he had earned in private practice. At $39,500 until it was raised to $60,000 in 1969, a Supreme Court justice's salary constituted a small fraction of his annual income as a Washington lawyer. His wife still earned a handsome salary, but their combined income did not seem sufficient. Though Fortas joked about his new dependence on Agger's earnings, neither of them liked it. Perhaps irrationally, both felt strapped. When Stanley Marcus sent him a photograph of a six-hundred-dollar necklace he thought his wife might like, the justice turned it down. "Since I am now a government clerk, I can't reach this high."[24] Fortas and Agger had established the Forage Foundation to help unemployed artists and musicians, but now that he was on the Court, its work was discontinued. [25] He had to sell his Philip Morris stock in the summer of 1966 and his Greatamerica stock later that year. [26] When he thanked Gustave Levy, an investment banker, for his assistance with the latter transaction, Fortas added, "This means a great deal to me, because the financial circumstances of being a Government clerk are oppressive and depressing. This is a mild hint that if something comes your way by which I can, by small investment, reap a rich and steady income, I'll be glad if you would let me know!"[27]

By the time he wrote Levy, Fortas had accepted—and then rejected—one arrangement which promised a steady income with no financial investment whatsoever. A financier named Louis Wolfson had become a client of Fortas's firm in June 1965. Wolfson had begun having problems with the Securities and Exchange Commission in 1964, and at the time Fortas joined the Court, he was the subject of an SEC investigation to determine whether he had engaged in illegal stock manipulation. He was also a philanthropist who wanted to relieve Fortas's financial insecurity.

In the past, Wolfson often had offered public servants monetary assistance. When Arthur Goldberg left the Court for the United Nations, the financier wrote him a letter applauding the former justice for forfeiting more profitable opportunities. Wolfson volunteered a salary supplement. "I gave him the back of my hand right off," Goldberg said. Though Goldberg did not consider it appropriate to accept money from Wolfson, he did not think the investor was trying to influence him. "I think . . . he liked to be close to the celebrities, and maybe he really felt what he said in the letter," he recalled.[28] Others, who found Wolfson eager to hire individuals with government influence and gullible about those who had it, were less certain of the purity of his motives. Wolfson told one acquaintance that he had consulted a lawyer who had shown him his "direct line to the White House," a telephone in the bottom right-hand drawer of his desk. When the attorney asked for a $25,000 retainer, Wolfson paid it. "That's the kind of guy he was," the acquaintance said. "He'd pay someone $25,000 for having a phone in his bottom right-hand drawer." Some considered him an unscrupulous character who had long engaged in suspect dealings. "He wasn't really house-broken," one of Fortas's Wall Street friends recalled. "Common prudence tells you to stay the hell away from Wolfson types," a lawyer at Arnold & Porter added.[29]

The distinction between individuals whom lawyers could represent and those with whom they should associate made no sense to Fortas. In his mind, his clients could do no wrong. And he liked Wolfson. They both came from immigrant Jewish families and had made their own way in the world. They shared an interest in civil rights, juvenile delinquency, and broader issues of social welfare. At one of their first meetings, Wolfson spoke not only of his legal troubles but of the charitable work of his family foundation as well.[30]

When Wolfson heard rumors that Fortas might join the Court, he pleaded with his attorney to do so: "Our nation certainly needs all the great brains that are available today in order to cope with many of the dangers and problems existing not only nationally but internationally." Unlike other clients, who were reminding Fortas they had hired him rather than his partners, Wolfson was sure his corporation would "still be in good hands" at the firm. Since the new job might entail financial sacrifice, he continued, "if you accept this appointment, I would like to arrange for the Wolfson Family Foundation to assist you financially for as long as you are in public service. The Foundation is a non-profit corporation and does not have or expect to have any activities in business nor any relations to or in connection with the Supreme Court or any other affiliations that could cause you criticism or embarrassment in any way whatsoever."[31]

Wolfson's letter was timely. Four days later, Lyndon Johnson announced Fortas's judicial appointment. Fortas invited Wolfson to a reception at the Court that October, and while his former client was in Washington, the justice agreed to become a consultant to the foundation. Fortas even drafted a letter the foundation could send him setting out the terms of his employment. The letter spelled out the justice's obligation in very general terms but specifically addressed his salary: "We are aware that the amount of work that you will do will vary from year to year, and we hope it will be agreeable to you if, instead of attempting to fix varying payments to be made to you from time to time, we undertake to pay you

$20,000 per annum for your life, commencing January 1, 1966, with the under-standing that the payments would be continued to Mrs. Fortas for her life if she should survive you."[32] Wolfson agreed to the conditions, and Fortas received his first check from the foundation in January 1966.

Others on the Court had made similar arrangements. William O. Douglas had long been president of the Parvin Foundation, which he described as being "engaged in an educational program involving people in underdeveloped na-tions."[33] Many considered its head, a Las Vegas casino owner, as questionable a figure as Wolfson, but that did not bother Douglas. "Bill gets so much for this Parvin work," Mercedes Eichholz told Fortas. "You could do something like that too."[34] If Wolfson's legal troubles did bring him to the Supreme Court, Fortas reasoned, he would recuse himself anyway. "Wolfson had been a client of my office, and whether or not I had any arrangement with him or his Foundation, I would have disqualified myself merely because he had been a client."[35]

Meanwhile Wolfson's problems were increasing. In the spring of 1966 the SEC recommended criminal prosecution against Wolfson and an associate for failure to register their plans to sell stock in one of Wolfson's companies. Though Carol Agger was not aware of all of the details of her husband's lifetime agree-ment with the financier, as she thought more about what she did know, she "didn't like it."[36] But Fortas remained supportive of his embattled friend. In May he sent Wolfson a long letter. He had waited to write, he explained, until he could find "time and peace of mind to reflect" and until he saw two people—one a former law partner, the other a Wolfson Family Foundation trustee. Fortas had hoped they "might report something which would have a bearing on the [legal] problem." Whether they did so, he did not indicate. Instead he shifted into a discussion of Wolfson's efforts to combat discrimination, which Fortas found impressive and moving. "I hope that we can discuss this—and perhaps you will let me come down in June for a Foundation meeting and to begin a talk with you leading to the formulation of a specific program in which I hope you will agree to be the central and moving force—for without a dynamic and dedicated central figure programs of this sort end in sound and fury, but little accomplishment."[37]

Fortas nevertheless believed that Wolfson should not give up his business affiliations with various companies to devote himself to social welfare work. "I think it would be a serious mistake—and while I know how deeply you want to do so in order to free your time for the public cause, it would *not* be an act of friendship for me to be less than frank and blunt in stating my considered opinion." Fortas gave two reasons for this advice. First, such an act would diminish Wolfson's effectiveness as an opponent of discrimination. Crusaders for social justice needed the credibility that directing corporations could give them. Second, if Wolfson resigned, "the pack would be at your heels with intensified zeal and savagery; and the absence of official connection with or position in the companies would make you vulnerable and reduce your defensive capacity in critical respects."[38] Clearly Fortas considered the latter reason paramount and was trying to situate Wolfson to the best possible advantage vis-à-vis the SEC prosecution. Although the advice was the sort that a lawyer might impart to a client, it was the sort a friend might give as well, and the letter offered no substantive legal advice. During the following month, when he was supposed to be presenting the Court's budget to Congress, Fortas went to Florida to see Wolfson at his horse farm.[39]

At the time of Fortas's visit, his clerk Daniel Levitt knew Wolfson was a former client who had problems with the SEC. Levitt did not realize, however, that Fortas had become a consultant to the Wolfson Foundation. When Fortas's secretary mentioned that the justice had accepted money from the financier, Levitt became alarmed. Judges were prohibited from practicing law by federal statute, and Levitt worried that Fortas's arrangement with Wolfson might be considered illegal. A fellow clerk remembered that "Dan exploded."[40] Because Levitt so persuasively argued that his boss should not become involved with Wolfson, Fortas resigned from the foundation in June.[41] But he delayed returning the check from Wolfson that he had deposited in his bank account in January. Fortas waited until December 15 to write a reimbursement check for $20,000.[42] That enabled him to avoid reporting the income on his 1966 tax return.

Fortas now looked for funding to subsidize the social welfare research he had planned to undertake for Wolfson. In an earlier conversation with Sol Linowitz, a Washington lawyer, the justice had indicated that he was "intensely interested in doing a study of some of the hitherto unexplored implications and consequences of our poverty problems." Linowitz immediately wrote to August Heckscher, a director of the Twentieth Century Fund, to suggest that the fund sponsor the project.[43] When Hecksher consulted Adolf Berle, he found that old New Dealer equally enthusiastic. Berle thought that Fortas understood aspects of the problems of poverty others had not addressed and apparently believed his friend was restless on the Court, because he added, "It would be happy as well as useful to bring him into the picture, for I think he will not wish to limit his intellectual interests to the Supreme Court alone."[44] After he had terminated his arrangement with Wolfson, Fortas indicated his renewed interest in working with the Twentieth Century Fund.[45] The agreement was apparently never consummated, however, and Fortas was soon exploring an invitation he had received to join the board of trustees of the Russell Sage Foundation, which also supported research on social welfare issues. "I am intensely interested in the Russell Sage Foundation's program, and I'd really like to join your Board except that I continue to be worried about the question of time and expenses involved—which I don't think we talked about."[46] Though Fortas did become a trustee of the foundation in mid 1966, it never financed any of his own research.

Fortas began giving lectures at college campuses, synagogues, and other institutions. He generally spoke on the civil rights revolution or on the Warren Court and social justice. His agent, Harry Walker, arranged his schedule and compensation, which was generally at least $1750 and expenses per session.[47] The justice appeared to find lecturing pleasant and remunerative, but Paul Porter wanted more for Fortas. Though Arnold, Fortas & Porter had changed its name to Arnold & Porter when Fortas joined the court, Porter still treated Fortas with the same solicitude he would give to a name partner. Now he decided the justice might more advantageously spend his extra time teaching. Fortas expressed interest in returning to the classroom, and in the fall of 1967 Porter approached Dean B. J. Tennery of the Washington College of Law at American University with a proposition. Did the dean want Fortas to lead an interdisciplinary seminar on law and contemporary society the following summer? The justice would concentrate "on such acute problems as welfare housing, poverty and race relations. The idea . . . would be to cover problems of this sort in terms of the dynamics and techniques of the law, and to view the law from the perspective of these social problems."[48] The legal realists had invented that sort of course when he was at Yale, but Fortas's own teaching had been limited to corporate law. Porter envisioned the seminar, for which he promised to arrange financing, as the first step toward the creation of an institute for the study of law and the social environment, one with which Fortas might develop a permanent affiliation. Dean Tennery responded enthusiastically. The two men determined that such a seminar would cost twenty-five thousand dollars annually, half to be paid to the justice as salary, the remainder to be used for administrative costs, tuition grants, and other expenses.[49]

While Fortas began writing experts on social welfare law to ask for suggestions on how to organize the course, Porter began raising the necessary funds. He had no trouble; in fact, he quickly raised $30,000. Maurice Lazarus of Federated; Troy Post of Greatamerica; Gustave Levy of Goldman, Sachs; and John Loeb of Carl M. Loeb, Rhoades & Company each contributed $5000, while Paul Smith of Philip Morris donated $10,000. Smith, Lazarus, and Post had been Fortas's clients, and all those who contributed were good friends of Fortas's. To Levy, Benjamin Sonnenberg (of Loeb), and Lazarus, Porter explained his reason for establishing the seminar in this way: "Since Abe has been on the court, I have sensed a certain restlessness. While this great responsibility is sufficient to absorb the energies of an ordinary individual, Abe's energies and talents are so tremendous that he has engaged in unorganized outside activities including random speeches and lectures throughout the country which I have long felt lacked a central purpose and thus was a kind of waste of a great natural resource, viz. Abe's imaginative intellect and his capacity for creative innovation."[50] Porter's idea did promise to furnish Fortas with an intriguing outlet for his talents. Unbeknownst to Fortas, however, his life was about to change drastically. At the time he agreed to teach the seminar the justice was unaware that Johnson was about to nominate him for an even higher post.

## CRONIES

When Earl Warren told the President in June 1968 that he intended to resign as chief justice, Johnson faced an important decision. The President followed his usual pattern under those circumstances. He telephoned Clark Clifford and Abe Fortas and summoned them to the White House.

Johnson asked Clifford to come early so that they might have some time alone together. When the lawyer arrived, the pajama-clad President was still in his bedroom. "I want to talk to you about the Supreme Court," he told Clifford.[51] There would soon be one vacancy, and if he promoted from within the Court, there might be two. The President wanted to make Fortas chief justice "because he was the most experienced, compassionate, articulate, and intelligent lawyer I knew, and because I was certain that he would carry on in the Court's liberal tradition."[52] He hoped to elevate federal appellate judge Homer Thornberry, an old friend from Texas with whom he had served many years in Congress, to replace Fortas.

Clifford was alarmed. The President had become a lame duck when he made his announcement in March that he would not seek reelection, but Clifford had noticed "that he really was not conscious of how much his power had diminished." Now the lawyer tried to tell him. If Johnson had nominated Fortas and Thornberry before March, Clifford noted, he believed that the Senate would have approved the two men. He continued: "But you can't get it through now because the Republicans are planning on winning in November of '68. . . . One of the best things that could happen for this country would be for Abe Fortas to be chief justice, but you're never going to get it through." Mystified, Johnson asked why. The lawyer answered that Thornberry would be viewed as a crony of the President's and would detract from Fortas's appointment. Oddly, Clifford did not worry that Fortas also would be viewed as a Johnson intimate. He considered his friend's qualifications for the chief justiceship outstanding.[53]

Johnson, however, believed that the nomination of Thornberry would strengthen Fortas's chances of Senate confirmation. He knew that Senator Richard Russell of Georgia would applaud Thornberry's nomination, and he believed that the senator would support Fortas in order to get Thornberry. The President thought that enough of Russell's Southern colleagues would follow his lead to insure against a Senate filibuster directed at Fortas. Thus Johnson reasoned that although they might consider Fortas too liberal, Southern senators would approve him in order to clear a place for an old friend and colleague.[54] If conservative Southerners combined forces with the Northern liberals the President expected to hail the Fortas nomination, Johnson envisioned no problems in the Senate.

Clifford suggested an alternative strategy. He begged Johnson to couple the nomination of Fortas with that of a respected nonpolitical Republican lawyer to take Fortas's place. "The Senate will react well to that," Clifford argued. "They won't have anything against Abe particularly. He is liberal, but if they can [also] get a good . . . solid moderate Republican, they'd take it. They'd be delighted." Johnson was unenthusiastic. "There isn't any guy like that I could appoint," he said. Clifford offered the name of Albert Jenner, a prominent Chicago corporate lawyer who then served as chairman of the Committee on the Federal Judiciary of the American Bar Association. Johnson remained committed to Thornberry. "By the time Fortas arrived, the President and I had gotten into quite an argument." They looked to Fortas as an arbiter. Both men stated their positions. Fortas supported the President.

Years later, Clifford spoke with regret of the timing of the episode. Often he and Fortas would be called to the White House at the same time and would go there together. "If I had had a shot at it [explaining the situation to Fortas] first, you see, I could have said: 'Abe, listen, this is the way we ought to go.' " While Clifford disagreed with Fortas, he did not fault the justice for his position. "Here's Abe being offered in effect the chief justiceship of the United States, and it was . . . very difficult for him to say, 'Mr. President, you're wrong. You've just had this long argument with Clifford, and I'm now going to agree with Clifford.' It [would have] sounded terribly ungracious." Still, he thought Fortas's choice of sides unfortunate. "Well, I'm supported by Abe," Johnson could now say. "I just don't agree with Clifford."[55] On June 26 Johnson publicly declared that he was nominating Fortas as chief justice and Thornberry as Fortas's replacement.

To many outsiders, Johnson appeared to have made a sinister deal. The language of Earl Warren's resignation letter and Johnson's acceptance suggested that the President planned to retain a liberal at the helm even if the Senate did not approve Fortas's nomination. The chief justice had written Johnson that he intended to resign "effective at your pleasure." In a letter Fortas may have helped draft,[56] the President had replied: "With your agreement I will accept your decision to retire effective at such time as a successor is qualified."[57] Senator Sam Ervin of North Carolina wondered aloud whether vacancies on the Court for Fortas and Thornberry even existed.[58] The *Washington Post* called for Warren to submit a more definite resignation letter.[59]

Further, Thornberry's nomination seemed strange to some members of the Senate. While he possessed Fortas's handicap of closeness to Johnson, he did not share the advantage of a reputation as a great lawyer. Although one Republican senator told the White House that the Thornberry appointment was "cute on the President's part" and reported that it had "taken [the] edge off some Republicans who might otherwise have been opposed," Republicans undoubtedly would have greeted the nomination of one of their own even more warmly.[60] Following the President's announcement his aides spoke with twelve Democratic senators, most of whom were from the north and west. "All of these favor Fortas," they reported. The senators were less enthusiastic about Thornberry but would not oppose him: "Some wondered aloud whether Thornberry adds or detracts."[61] Russell Long of Louisiana, a conservative Southern Democrat, thought that while Johnson "might sell a Fortas-Fowler package," coupling the justice with Secretary of the Treasury Joe Fowler, "a Fortas-Thornberry package would be real trouble."[62]

Southern senators remained restive about Fortas because of his reputation as a judicial activist. Even some members of Lyndon Johnson's own family disapproved of the Warren Court. One of his cousins often used derogatory language about Blacks and attacked the Court for extending their rights.[63] Most Southern senators agreed and disparaged the Court's "softness" on criminals as well. The best Johnson could elicit from the chairman of the Senate Judiciary Committee, James Eastland, who had treated Fortas so warmly in 1965, was a pledge that he would not hold the nominations in committee indefinitely. Eastland, however, was vague as to when he would allow them to be reported out, saying only that he would do so "at my own time."[64] Further, he informed the President at the outset that Fortas could not be confirmed, and he predicted a Senate filibuster against the appointment. Indeed Eastland reported that he "had never seen so much feeling against a man as against Fortas."[65] Senate Judiciary Committee member Sam Ervin told the White House that "considering what the Supreme Court has done to the Constitution, I'll have to read Fortas' decisions before I can decide."[66] John McClellan of Arkansas considered Fortas "an SOB" and eagerly anticipated fighting his nomination on the Senate floor.[67] Although he later moderated his stance, Robert Byrd of West Virginia initially promised to do "everything in my power" to oppose that "leftist" member of the Court.[68] To Russell Long, Fortas was "'one of the dirty five' who sides with the criminal."[69]

The opposition concerned him, but the President thought the Senate would approve his nominations. His confidence derived from a sense that he had two allies in his counterattack. They were Senator Richard Russell and Senate Minority Leader Everett Dirksen. Since he left nothing to chance, Johnson had confirmed his understanding that Russell would stomach Fortas to obtain Thornberry by inviting the Georgia senator to the White House for dinner the night before he announced the nominations. It was a nostalgic evening. The President, his daughter Luci, and Russell reminisced about old times when the two men served in the Senate together. In those days, Russell had often dined at the Johnsons' house. In the Senate years, Johnson "would want to talk business and Sen. Russell would want to play with the children," whereas at the White House dinner both the President and Russell focused their attention on Johnson's young grandson.[70] Still, Johnson did not neglect business. The Georgian was crucial to the President's "Southern strategy." Russell indicated his enthusiasm for Thornberry and also said he would back Fortas. Southerners might despise Fortas, but as Russell controlled the votes of a minimum of a dozen Southern colleagues, at least that many would probably vote for him.[71] Though Eastland warned Johnson the following day that Russell would ultimately oppose Fortas, the President continued to believe his old friend would not disappoint him and would deliver the Southern delegation.[72]

Eastland was right. Russell soon began to suspect that Johnson was deliberately delaying the appointment of Alexander Lawrence, whom Russell very much wanted to see become a federal district judge in Georgia. In reality, the President, with Fortas's approval, was trying actively to persuade Attorney General Ramsey Clark to overlook segregationist speeches Lawrence had made as a younger man and approve the appointment.[73] Nevertheless, by July 1 the Senator had decided the President was holding Lawrence as a hostage to ensure his support of Fortas and Thornberry, and he determined to protest. In a blistering letter to Johnson that marked the end of a twenty-year friendship, Russell expressed his resentment at "being treated as a child or a patronage-seeking ward heeler. . . . The long delay in handling and juggling of this nomination . . . places me in a position where, if I support your nominees for the Supreme Court it will appear that I have done so out of my fears that you would not nominate Mr. Lawrence." Russell now released himself from the duty to honor "any statements" he had made to Johnson about Fortas and Thornberry and expressed his resolve "to deal objectively" with those nominations.[74] His defection even before the hearings began eliminated the White House's hope of an acquiescent contingent of Southern senators.

Johnson had not counted on the opposition of Republicans either. He believed Everett Dirksen could blunt any such efforts. The senator and Fortas were on good terms. When Fortas was sworn in as an associate justice, he had asked Dirksen to join Carol Agger, her parents, the Arnolds, the Porters, and other close friends in the special section at the Court reserved for the inductee's most valued guests. While Dirksen himself probably would not have selected Fortas for the chief justiceship, he considered him a brilliant attorney.[75] The senator soon became even more enthusiastic about Johnson's plans. Dirksen needed a favor. The Subversive Activities Control Board, whose existence he deemed crucial to maintaining his credibility among conservatives, would expire on June 30, 1968, unless Attorney General Clark agreed to refer cases to it. Clark had no intention of providing a stay. Like Fortas, he was a civil libertarian, and he could not justify the existence of a government board that would regulate the activities of "subversives." Thus, when Johnson asked Dirksen for his help two days before he announced the Fortas and Thornberry nominations, the senator began talking about the board's impending demise. The President ordered Clark to refer some cases to the board, and Dirksen promised to support Fortas and Thornberry.[76]

Like Russell, Dirksen once had been among the most powerful members of the Senate. In 1964, for instance, he had pressured many Republicans to vote for the Civil Rights Act. Accustomed to the mores of the Senate in his day, the President assumed that the support of both men guaranteed victory. And for a long time Dirksen courageously did remain with the administration on the Fortas nomination. When constituents inquired how he could endorse an individual with "the lets [sic] reinterpret the Constitution inclinations" of Fortas, Dirksen lectured them on the Senate's obligation to support all Supreme Court appointees who possessed the professional qualifications for the office.[77] But by 1968 Dirksen's power was waning. He could not even convince his son-in-law, Senator Howard Baker, to endorse Fortas, a fellow Tennesseean.[78] Ever the egotist, however, Dirksen believed he could block an organized campaign against the justice. He did not count on a freshman senator, Robert Griffin of Michigan.

Griffin opposed Johnson's nominees even before he knew their identities. Having heard a rumor that Earl Warren might resign, the senator announced that the President, as a "lame duck," should not be permitted to fill any vacancies on the Court. "I do not know whether Mr. Johnson in such an event, would appoint a Democrat, a Republican, a liberal, a conservative, or a moderate," he told his colleagues. "The point is that such an appointment should be made by the next President—whether he be a Democrat or a Republican—after the people have had an opportunity to speak in November."[79] Of course in reality Griffin hoped that Johnson's successor would be a Republican who would name a conservative individual as chief justice. The senator's sanctimonious façade proved attractive, however, to other colleagues in his party and to the Republican presidential candidate, Richard Nixon. Opposition to the Warren Court was one of Nixon's campaign themes, but he did not stress it when the Fortas and Thornberry nominations were announced. Instead on the evening news he suggested that Johnson's successor should name Warren's successor.[80] The following day seventeen senators joined Griffin in signing a petition declaring "that the next Chief Justice of the Supreme Court should be designated by the next President of the United States."[81]

Senate Majority Leader Mike Mansfield of Montana reacted by threatening to postpone the summer adjournment of Congress until the Senate had confirmed the nominees. To one of the President's aides, Harold (Barefoot) Sanders, it seemed clear that "Senator Mansfield is just inviting a successful filibuster on the Fortas-Thornberry nominations with his comments."[82] Dirksen treated the petition more sanguinely. "We will win this one," he told two of Johnson's emissaries several times in a meeting on July 2. There would be no filibuster, and the debate over Fortas would only consume two days of the Senate's time. Right now, according to Dirksen, the best strategy was "to let this simmer over the holiday weekend."[83] Dirksen had miscalculated. His colleagues were already boiling. Opposed to the Court and hopeful that a Republican would win in November, they refused to accept his direction. By the fourth of July weekend, they had obtained a pledge that seemed to promise victory: Richard Russell had decided that dealing "objectively" with the nominations meant fighting them. He told Griffin that his senators would silently support the Republican effort to deny Fortas the nomination.[84]

Had the White House known of this agreement between the Republicans and the Southern Democrats, it might have concluded that all was lost at the outset. The Russell-Griffin deal placed opponents of the Fortas nomination so close to victory that it virtually guaranteed they would launch a filibuster. In that event, Fortas's supporters would have to obtain the votes of a two-thirds majority of senators present to impose cloture and end the filibuster, a difficult task with at least three-tenths of the Senate already opposed to the nomination. But the President and his aides remained unaware of the secret alliance. Although Eastland predicted defeat for the nominations "unless conditions changed" on July 9,[85] and the White House had become sufficiently concerned about a filibuster to wonder whether it had the votes for cloture by July 15,[86] Johnson continued to assume his nominees could be confirmed. His staff and the Justice Department devoted their efforts to destroying the opposition.

The Justice Department approached the battle in a scholarly manner. It prepared and circulated widely a memorandum containing "some highlights of the judicial career of Mr. Justice Fortas" designed to "show that his judicial performance has been balanced and moderate."[87] Deputy Attorney General Warren Christopher asked Charles Fairman of Stanford Law School whether Senator Ervin was correct in arguing that the language of Warren's resignation letter precluded the existence of a vacancy. "The objection struck me as so unsubstantial and Ervinesque that, as Justice E. D. White once said, 'To state the proposition is to refute it,' " the constitutional law expert replied. Fairman provided evidence to disprove Ervin's contention, including the information that in resigning from the Court in 1902, Horace Gray had used similar language to that employed by Warren.[88] Anticipating that Fortas would be criticized for having advised Johnson from the bench, Christopher also collected examples of close relationships between Presidents and Supreme Court justices to demonstrate that the Fortas-Johnson relationship had numerous historical precedents.[89]

The White House concentrated on more direct methods. With the help of Paul Porter, it used the press and big business to influence members of Congress. Friendly reporters and publishers were funneled information that could be used in supportive editorials.[90] After discussions with Porter, who undoubtedly stressed Fortas's opinion in *FTC* v. *Dean Foods,* some corporate executives lauded Fortas for his sympathy to "business and the free enterprise system." Coca-Cola, a longtime Arnold & Porter client, went to work on Senator Harry Byrd. Fred Lazarus and his sons lobbied senators on Fortas's behalf, as did another Arnold & Porter client, American Airlines. Representatives of Eastern Airlines contacted at least ten senators.[91] Such pressure backfired. Fortas's opponents could use the media equally effectively. On July 2 Griffin held a press conference to announce that the White House was "pulling all the stops" and was asking executives from large corporations with government contracts to telephone senators and urge confirmation of Fortas and Thornberry. Three other Republican senators corroborated Griffin's charges the following day.[92] One of them telephoned Eastern's president to ask "why business was so active in fighting for these confirmations."[93]

Congress seemed unresponsive to White House coercion. Even more than had Woodrow Wilson, Lyndon Johnson functioned as a prime minister,[94] and for five years he had tightly controlled Congress. For the past two, however, it had chafed under his leadership. Now senators seemed to be going out of their way to show they feared the President no longer. Despite all the activity on Fortas's behalf, only Albert Gore of Tennessee, George Smathers of Florida, and Fortas's onetime enemy Wayne Morse of Oregon were vigorously endorsing the nominee on the Senate floor.[95] Indeed, the White House staff considered Morse "one of the few tough, stand-up fighters we have on the Fortas-Thornberry confirmation."[96] Old friends of Fortas's, such as Stuart Symington of Missouri, were proving strangely lackadaisical in their support.[97] At best, the Senate response to the appointments before the hearings on the nomination began seemed lukewarm.

## "A VERY TORMENTED MAN"

Meanwhile Fortas sat by the sidelines. Superficially, he seemed detached. He told Muñoz that news of his elevation "did not arouse great excitement or delight in the heart," and he seemed oddly placid on the day that Johnson announced his appointment.[98] On an impulse, Yale Law School dean Louis Pollak telephoned to ask whether he could visit the justice in his chambers. "I couldn't believe he would be available," Pollak recalled. "Surely if you'd just been nominated Chief Justice there were 89 things that you would be doing, and you probably wouldn't be at the Court at all." The dean was wrong. When Pollak arrived, the justice focused the entire conversation around Yale. To Pollak, it appeared that Fortas "was really single-mindedly interested in what was going on at the school." Becoming chief justice seemed unimportant to him.[99]

Nevertheless, colleagues thought Fortas was looking forward to the job. He soon began planning proposed changes in the Court's procedures.[100] Although he told one law clerk who had recently joined his staff that the chief justiceship entailed so many administrative chores that he would understand if she resigned, Fortas himself liked such work.[101] Having been managing partner of his law firm, he was eminently qualified to manage the Court. Johnson had every reason to believe his friend would make an outstanding chief justice. Scholars have focused on two kinds of leadership chief justices can provide. "Task leadership serves to complete the court's work in the most efficient manner, while process leadership provides a friendly environment to facilitate the conduct of judicial business. According to this model, Chief Justices are successful to the extent they are able to combine both functions, or recruit allies capable of playing the role they themselves reject."[102] In terms of task leadership, Fortas might have become the best chief justice in the Court's history. He was nothing if not efficient. But while he rarely personalized intellectual disagreement, he lacked Earl Warren's presence, and process leadership might have proven more difficult for him. In that event, if his past history was a reliable guide, he would have relied on someone such as William Brennan to provide the process leadership Thurman Arnold and Paul Porter had offered at his own firm.

At his law firm, however, Fortas had protected others ably. As the President's nominee for the chief justiceship, he could not defend himself without politicizing the Court. Fortas believed that decorum demanded he appear above the battle that the White House was waging with Congress. He kept informed about their efforts through Paul Porter, whom the justice had designated "the central clearing house in information and assignments."[103] But it was not the same as coordinating the effort himself. As Lady Bird Johnson said, "When Abe is the man who is being pilloried, where is there an Abe Fortas for him to turn to?" And as she noted, Paul Porter was "delightful, . . . smart and funny, but he was not an Abe Fortas."[104]

Fortas was unable to remain remote. His appointment had hardly been announced before the justice was writing a speech for Senator Abraham Ribicoff of Connecticut to deliver on the floor of the Senate. It was an attack. Was Griffin seriously claiming that the President should be deprived of his constitutional power to fill vacancies because he would no longer hold office after November? "I cannot believe that the Senate will seriously consider this novel and radical idea. It will mean a national receivership in the last year of the second term of every President. And what is sauce for one party will be sauce for the other!"[105] A delighted Johnson, apparently unaware who had written these words, instructed his staff to thank Ribicoff for his "fine statement" and help the senator in any way it could.[106] Fortas also began sending advice to Porter. He suggested, for example, that his former partner telephone George Smathers, a member of the Senate Judiciary Committee, to insist that the committee not request the justice to appear. Fortas pointed out that no sitting justice had ever testified before the committee. He also argued that "confirmation of Associate Justice to be Chief Justice is unnecessary in law." But even Fortas appeared uncertain about that implausible allegation, for he originally had written the word *probably* before *unnecessary*.[107] His efforts proved unavailing. Senator Eastland determined that his committee should question both Fortas and Thornberry.

Fortas could have declined to appear, and one colleague thought he should have done so.[108] He pointed out that when two other sitting justices, Edward White and Harlan Fiske Stone, had been nominated as chief justice, each had decided that it would be inappropriate to testify before the Judiciary Committee because senators would inevitably ask about their past decisions. White and Stone maintained that answering such inquiries would breach the Constitution's commitment to separation of powers. The Senate had nevertheless confirmed both men. The boundaries between the branches of government had never been as clear for Fortas, however, as they were for some justices. He had, after all, advised the President during his tenure on the Court. He was comfortable at congressional hearings, which he had attended frequently as a lawyer. By testifying he could alleviate the frustration that had characterized the previous weeks when he had felt compelled to remain silent. As Fortas had done "superbly well" before the Judiciary Committee in 1965, "he felt confident about appearing" in 1968, Deputy Attorney General Christopher recalled. If he were to decline, he would seem "timid." The White House agreed with Fortas's assessment. Indeed because of his prior experience with the committee and because "he was no stranger to the ways of Washington," Christopher's staff devoted less time to coaching him on appropriate responses than it normally spent with judicial nominees.[109] It had already become clear that his nomination was far more controversial then either White's or Stone's had been, and his remarks might broaden his base of support. Thus once "invited" to appear, he agreed to do so.

Fortas apparently intended to make a long opening statement to the committee, explaining the principles that would guide him when he answered its questions. In an early draft, he spoke of the tension that had frequently characterized interchanges between Supreme Court nominees and the Judiciary Committee. "The difficulty is inherent in the constitutional situation," he explained. Although the committee would have to explore the nominee's qualifications if it were to recommend appropriate action to the Senate, both the nominee and the committee had to contend with the constitutional principles of an independent judiciary and separation of powers. According to the draft statement, Fortas found his own case "particularly difficult" because he had served on the Court for three years and "I shall continue as an Associate Justice whether or not I am confirmed and appointed as Chief Justice." He argued persuasively that he could legitimately refuse to answer questions regarding his past votes and opinions but announced his intention to disregard that course of action: "I believe that each nominee, whether he is drawn from the ranks of the judiciary or otherwise, should and must make his own independent judgment as to the course of action that he considers appropriate and consistent with his constitutional responsibilities. So far as I am concerned, I have concluded that the proper course for me is to rely upon the Committee's own judgment as to the appropriate scope and nature of any interrogation that it may care to make, knowing as I do, that the Committee is sensitive, as I am, to the constitutional problem." He intended to answer questions about his past votes and opinions except in instances where his replies "would seem to me to involve a clear judicial impropriety, or would impinge upon the prerogatives of my colleagues or of the Court."[110]

The short opening statement he actually delivered in his first appearance before the committee on July 16 was quite different from his draft. "I want to say that I am very happy to be here," Fortas began. "And I am very happy to answer any and all questions that the committee may ask. I am not a novice in Washington. I am not a novice in Senate Hearings." Assuring the committee that "there is nothing I love better than a legal discussion or debate," Fortas declared his eagerness "to discuss all questions that anybody may have in mind about the work of the Court. I shall, however, . . . because that is the sort of person I am—I shall be and continue to be conscious of the constitutional limitations upon me." Nevertheless, he came before the committee "very willingly" and hoped that its questions and his replies "will serve to clear thoughts that are in your minds."[111] Fortas's opening remarks reflected a change in approach. The draft he discarded reflected the cooperativeness and deference he usually displayed under such circumstances. It pretended that he and the Senate Judiciary Committee were allies rather than opponents. But this pose was too farfetched for even Fortas the actor. His statement before the committee was more honest. It acknowledged that he anticipated discord, not harmony. It also gave him greater control in defining the scope of appropriate questions. Originally he had volunteered to depart from tradition in his responses. Now he was only promising to address "the work of the Court" in the context of "the constitutional limitations." He was reserving a right he ultimately exercised—the privilege to decline to answer questions about the Court's opinions and his votes.

On Fortas's first day, however, the Judiciary Committee did not seem interested in his work at the Court. Instead the senators wanted to know about his relationship with the President.[112] In an unusual move, Senator Griffin had appeared before the committee as its first witness on the opening day of hearings. After labeling the justice a presidential "crony" and detailing the instances reported by the media on which Fortas had counseled the President, Griffin asked, "If the doctrine of separate powers is important, what justification could be offered in the event a member of the judicial branch should actively participate on a regular, undisclosed basis in decisions of the executive branch while serving on the Bench?"[113] Griffin's opening salvo indicated that Fortas's opponents had devised a new strategy. Up until this point, they had condemned Fortas for his jurisprudence and had claimed that Johnson's lame-duck status disqualified him from appointing a new chief justice. Now they dropped the latter theme. Instead they would alternate caustic questions about the justice's closeness to the President with equally tough inquiries about his behavior on the Court.

That made Fortas's position even more difficult than it had been in 1946. Then the Senate had examined him on one subject, Edwin Pauley. Twenty-two years later it planned to test him on two, Lyndon Johnson and the Warren Court. The stakes were also higher. In 1946 Fortas had hoped to protect Harold Ickes, the Democratic Party, and himself. This time also he had three concerns: Lyndon Johnson, the Supreme Court, and himself. Without a doubt Fortas cared more about the President and maintaining respect for the integrity of the beleaguered Warren Court than he had cared about either Ickes or the Democratic Party. Further, in 1946 loyalty to Ickes had pulled him in one direction while self-interest and the welfare of the Democratic party drew him in another. In 1968, however, Fortas must have reasoned that he would best serve Johnson, the Court, and himself by downplaying his relationship with the President. Thus, whereas in 1946 he had resolved the competing demands upon him through legalistic obfuscation, in 1968 he simply lied.[114]

The pattern was set on the first day. Fortas denied ever having recommended candidates for a judgeship or a public position and said he had never "initiated" suggestions or proposals to the President. In fact, he had been among the White House's most fertile sources of recruitment advice and had pressed Johnson to move forward on cultural and other fronts. He described a limited role with respect to the war. According to him, he had attended just a few meetings on Vietnam and had only restated arguments others advanced. The committee proceeded to his role in the Detroit riots. Had he drafted the President's message ordering federal troops to Detroit? Fortas replied negatively.[115] When Eastland turned to Fortas's jurisprudence, the justice was equally untruthful. To what extent and under what circumstances did he believe that the Court should spearhead social, economic, or political change? "Zero, absolutely zero," Fortas answered. Asked such a question in a confirmation hearing by a senator openly hostile to judicial activism, perhaps most nominees would have replied the same way. But in the context of Fortas's other answers, this one seemed symptomatic of his dishonesty.[116]

Further, Fortas's inability to resist making debaters' points grated. On his first day before the committee, he attempted to prove that as a justice of his state supreme court Senator Ervin, a Judiciary Committee member, had been more of a judicial activist than Abe Fortas. He quoted from one of Ervin's opinions, which said that courts need not observe precedent when to do so would perpetuate wrongs. "Senator, I would not go that far myself," Fortas sanctimoniously noted.[117] When Senator Strom Thurmond cited the Court's opinion in "*Berger* v. *New York*, 280 U.S. 41," the justice felt impelled to tell him that he had the volume number wrong. "That is 388, isn't it?" Fortas interrupted.[118] Senator McClellan, reviewing the justice's prior testimony, read aloud the word *purpose*. Fortas once again broke in to inform him that the transcript was incorrect: "I believe I said 'purport.' . . . I was distressed when I saw the word 'purpose.' "[119] Correcting his opponents on technicalities may have provided Fortas some satisfaction, but it could not have increased his popularity.

At times on the first day, the justice volunteered untrue information. After Fortas had given his versions of his role in making policy on the Vietnam war and the Detroit riots, Senator McClellan asked whether there were "any other areas of consultation you would be willing to identify?" None existed, Fortas replied. Then the justice added: "I guess I have made a full disclosure now, because so far as I can recall those are the two things."[120] Despite Fortas's gratuitous remark, his questioners would not drop the subject. Earlier, when Griffin had raised the issue of Fortas's extrajudicial activities before the committee, Dirksen had disposed of it through mockery. He maintained that presidents had long named "cronies" to the Supreme Court. Lincoln had made his campaign manager, David Davis, a justice, and Kennedy had elevated one of his lieutenants, Byron White, to the Court. Fred Vinson had advised Harry Truman, but when the President appointed him chief justice "nobody got up on his hind legs and shouted cronyism." Did Griffin expect a President to appoint his enemies to the Court? The cronyism charge, Dirksen exploded, was "a frivolous, diaphanous—you know what that means, don't you—gossamer—you know what that means, don't you—argument that just does not hold water."[121] Dirksen, however, had avoided the issue of a crony counseling a president even after he had joined the Court. When Ervin returned to Fortas's role as a presidential adviser on the justice's second day of hearings, Fortas tried to dispel the issue by turning discussion to the numerous examples of Supreme Court justices from John Jay through James Byrnes who had acted as presidential advisers.[122] The Senate committee seemed uninterested in the history lesson.

Instead, Senator Ervin asked whether Fortas had telephoned a participant in the Business Council meeting in May 1967 to complain that he had exaggerated the cost of the Vietnam war. Since Ervin mistakenly had identified the individual in question as Albert Nickerson of Mobil Oil instead of Ralph Lazarus of Federated Department Stores, Fortas could have denied placing the call. That would have been risky, however, since some of the facts surrounding the incident had already come out and others were bound to follow.[123] Fortas confirmed that he had telephoned a businessman friend, whose identity he did not then disclose. The justice tried to put the best face upon his action. He had placed the call "as a citizen," he maintained. When Ervin pressed him on whether he had done so at the request of the President, Fortas refused to answer. "I have endeavored Senator, and Mr. Chairman, to err, if I erred, on the side of frankness and candor with this committee," he outrageously claimed. "But I think that it is my duty to observe certain limits, and one of those limits is any conversation, either affirmance or denial, that I may have had with the President of the United States."[124] Since Fortas had pledged earlier that he had recounted all occasions on which he had worked with Johnson, it now seemed as if he were hiding additional information from the committee.

Philip Hart tried to rescue Fortas. Earlier Hart had said little about the nomination on the floor of Congress, but once the hearings began he became the justice's most ardent supporter in the Senate. "He is just superb," Hart told the White House after the justice's first day of testimony. "He made me feel like a plumber listening to him."[125] The Senator commented that after having heard Fortas place "this adviser to the President business in historic perspective, I think most of us would agree that Justice Fortas is restrained." Even Hart, however, confessed that "I think all of us, as citizens, had the notion that the contact between Presidents and Justices of the Court would be social only." Fortas responded that, although precedents for a close relationship between a President and a Supreme Court justice existed, he worried that such a relationship could present "a problem." But, he added, "it is a problem that for me is very temporary" as Lyndon Johnson would be leaving office in January 1969, and Fortas was not an intimate of any of the men who hoped to succeed him.[126] Still, the damage had been done. "Fortas Concedes Move To Correct War-Cost Critic—Won't Say If Johnson Was Involved," the front page of the *Washington Post* announced the following day. [127] The *Post* editorialized that Fortas's disclosure of his continuing association with Lyndon Johnson was "welcome in the sense that it puts on the record what official Washington has long known privately. Nevertheless, neither the Justice's explanations of the situations in which he gave the President advice nor his historical citations showing that other Justices have advised other Presidents makes the relationship wise or proper." Though the *Post* considered Fortas's conduct "irrelevant" to his excellent qualifications for the chief justiceship, the justice's antagonists on the Senate Judiciary Committee did not agree. [128]

It was in pressing the issue of the Warren Court, not in questioning Fortas's relationship with the President, that his opponents on the committee finally destroyed the nominee's composure. By the end of the justice's third day of testimony, Ervin repeatedly had condemned the Warren Court for judicial legislation and had criticized some of its decisions at length. Now Strom Thurmond took over and berated Fortas about the Court for two hours, focusing attention on its criminal law decisions. He held the nominee responsible even for cases decided before Fortas's tenure as justice. Thurmond was particularly angry about the 1957 case of *Mallory* v. *United States,* in which the Court had freed a confessed rapist whom the police had held too long before arraignment. "Do you believe in that kind of justice?" the Senator bellowed. "Does not that decision, *Mallory*—I want that word to ring in your ears . . . shackle law enforcement? Mallory, a man who raped a woman, admitted his guilt, and the Supreme Court turned him loose on a technicality?" Was not that the sort of decision "calculated to encourage more people to commit rapes and serious crimes?" [129]

The reporters in the press section could see the shocked look on Fortas's normally enigmatic face. The nominee turned toward Eastland, apparently thinking that the committee chairman might intervene and call Thurmond to order. But Eastland, who appeared to be reading something, did not look up. Fortas said nothing for several minutes. He was pondering the best response. By this time, he had refused repeatedly to discuss the Court's opinions, saying that although he "should love to have that opportunity, . . . I believe the Constitution of [the] United States, which I am sworn to uphold says to me that I must not do it—that it is incompatible with a sitting Justice's obligation, and incompatible with the theory of the separation of powers that our Constitution embodies." [130] At various times in the hearings prior to Thurmond's interrogation, however, Fortas had demonstrated a willingness to volunteer certain information. For example, when Ervin had criticized the Court's criminal law decisions, Fortas had lectured the senator on the constitutional antecedents of the Warren Court's extension of the rights of criminals. "Now here I have done something I should not have done," he apologized. [131] But Fortas did it still again.[132] Now he decided not to answer Thurmond. Quite slowly but dramatically, Fortas said, "Senator, because of my respect for you and this body and my respect for the Constitution of the United States, and my position as Associate Justice of the Supreme Court of the United States, I will adhere to the limitations I believe the Constitution of the United States places upon me and will not reply to your question as you phrase it."[133]

Though Fortas's masterly display of self-control did not shame his critics, it increased sympathy for him. A friendly group had gathered to support him by the following day, his last before the committee. When Thurmond asked Fortas whether he agreed that the Court's decisions "make it terribly difficult to protect society from crime and criminals [and] are among the principal reasons for the turmoil and near-revolutionary conditions which prevail in our country," the justice simply replied, "No." His well-wishers applauded.[134] Perhaps fortified by his audience, Fortas apprised the committee of the difficulty of his position. To Thurmond's query about the Court's reapportionment decisions, the justice responded, "We are back where we were yesterday." Each morning, Fortas continued with some emotion, he told himself, "You are not participating in this hearing as Abe Fortas, you are participating in this hearing as an Associate Justice of the Supreme Court of the United States with responsibility solely to the Constitution of the United States." Although it pained him to deprive himself of the opportunity to explain his decisions as a justice, "I will not be an instrument by which the separation of powers specified in our Constitution is called into question."[135]

Senator McClellan wanted to make Fortas precisely such a tool. When he took over the attack from Thurmond, McClellan returned to the justice's relationship to the President. Specifically, he focused on Fortas's telephone conversation about the war's cost with the as-yet-unidentified businessman, which Ervin had raised the first day. In the interim, the press had correctly guessed its recipient was Ralph Lazarus.[136] Fortas confirmed that he had telephoned Lazarus. In the justice's mind, that made his behavior proper. Lazarus was "an extremely close friend of mine with whom I suppose I have discussed everything on earth from time to time—except, of course, Court business." Fortas took another opportunity to remind the committee that he was more than a Supreme Court justice: "I don't know how anybody can be a person and not discuss with his friends these days questions about the budget and about the Vietnam war. I'm a person, too. I am a Supreme Court justice, but I talk to people, and people talk to me."[137]

Unlike Fortas the Supreme Court justice, Fortas the person was an advocate, and his self-imposed restrictions on protecting himself bothered him. Instinct preached self-defense. If anyone could have convinced his adversaries of the propriety of his relationship with the President or the soundness of the Warren Court's decisions, it would have been Fortas. In this case, however, he was a witness rather than advocate, and taking the offensive was proscribed. When Ervin suggested that Fortas was guilty of a conflict of interest in advising the President, the justice would have liked to countercharge that Ervin supplemented his income as a senator by appearing before the Supreme Court on behalf of the North Carolina textile interests. The White House had mustered such facts and passed them along to Fortas, but he thought their use inappropriate. As a result, one White House aide recalled, he was "a very tormented man throughout this whole nomination process because he could not fight back."[138]

## THE CITIZENS FOR DECENT LITERATURE

The justice's completion of four days of testimony left the field to his enemies. If they voted down his nomination as chief justice, Johnson would certainly delay Warren's departure, and there would be no vacancy on the Court. They clearly intended to do so. The committee's indifference during his sole day of testimony convinced Thornberry that the Senate intended to deny Johnson the privilege of naming the next chief justice.[139] One of the next witnesses before the committee made the Senate's task easier. His name was James Clancy, and he appeared on behalf of a group called Citizens for Decent Literature. After examining fifty-two of the Court's recent decisions in the realm of obscenity law, he had concluded that Fortas had cast the deciding vote that the material was not obscene in forty-nine of them. "Notwithstanding the complete knowledge of every citizen that the moral standards are being eroded throughout the Nation," he argued, "we have a set of decisions by the U.S. Supreme Court which completely throws caution to the winds, and is an open invitation to every pornographer to come into the area and distribute millions of copies—and I am not exaggerating—millions and millions of copies of what historically had been regarded in France as hardcore pornography."[140]

To put Fortas's alleged deeds in graphic perspective, Clancy had brought along a thirty-minute slide show displaying the highlights of some pornographic films the Court's rulings had permitted to remain in circulation, which he suggested screening privately for the senators and the press. He also carried with him one pornographic film entitled *0-7*. Clancy was particularly annoyed by the Court's one-sentence opinion in *Schackman* v. *California* in 1967 overturning the lower courts' finding that *0-7* was ineligible for First Amendment protection because of its obscenity. Finally, Clancy submitted selected photographs from pornographic magazines. Prodded by Thurmond, who arranged for his colleagues and the press to see *0-7*, Clancy also postulated that pornography bred violence.[141]

"Mr. Clancy, I want to thank you for coming here, for the contribution you have made to these hearings," Thurmond gushed when the attorney had completed his testimony.[142] The senator had reason to be grateful, for Clancy had given Fortas's opponents new ammunition. To the handicaps of his relationship with the President and his seat on the Warren Court, they could now add his presumed position on obscenity. While Ervin spent the last day of the hearings denouncing all of the Warren Court opinions of which he disapproved, Thurmond showcased the Court's obscenity decisions. In fact, Clancy's charges were unfair. The Supreme Court's one-sentence reversal in *Schackman* had included no grounds for the decision. In fact, obscenity had played no part in it. The Court had overruled the lower courts in *Schackman* because the police who had confiscated the film lacked a valid search warrant.[143] The decision was grist for those who would attack the Court's work in criminal law, rather than for its opponents on obscenity.

Nor was it clear that Fortas had cast any deciding votes or that his views on obscenity had led to the breakdown of public standards. Since most of the Court's obscenity decisions in which he had participated were unsigned, even Senator Jack Miller of Iowa, who accused Fortas of destroying community morals, admitted that "we do not have his judicial philosophy on this subject."[144] Fortas's one signed dissent in the area, *Ginsberg* v. *United States,* argued that states constitutionally could enact laws protecting children from obscenity. Fortas even suggested that juveniles and children were entitled to protection from material which was not legally obscene but which they had bought from someone who exploited its prurient content. His pandering formula would have permitted states to prevent panderers from distributing offensive material to minors.[145]

Indeed at one point, Fortas had tried to prevent panderers from distributing offensive material to adults as well. In a case decided two years earlier than *Ginsberg, Ginzburg* v. *United States,* he joined an opinion written by William Brennan holding that the publisher Ralph Ginzburg had employed "the leer of the sensualist" in his marketing of three publications—*Eros, Liaison,* and the *Housewife's Handbook on Selective Promiscuity.*[146] The case had arisen at the same time that the Court was deciding whether a seller of John Cleland's *Fanny Hill* had purveyed obscene materials. At the conference on the two cases, a majority that included Brennan initially voted to affirm the lower court opinion judging *Fanny Hill* obscene. That alarmed Fortas, who worried about "a new wave of 'book burning.'" Consequently he said he would vote with the majority in *Ginzburg* and another obscenity case only if the Court overturned the obscenity finding with respect to *Fanny Hill.*[147] Fortas then persuaded Brennan, who had been assigned the majority opinion, to adopt the pandering formula that focused on the manner of distribution and to decide against Ginzburg.[148] By pressing that solution, Fortas actually made it easier to convict those accused of marketing obscenity. He had devised a way of legitimating state regulation of material not technically "obscene." At the time, he was so proud of developing a consensus that he deviated from his usual policy of silence regarding the Court. "This wouldn't have happened without me," he told friends. "I worked every one of those guys over."[149]

But he had compromised principle for tactics, and Fortas later regretted his position in *Ginzburg*. Thurman Arnold wrote him that the decision was "a bit rough on Ginzburg," and other civil libertarians agreed.[150] His clerk suspected that Fortas "got into terrible trouble in the Georgetown cocktail circuit because of that opinion."[151] To William O. Douglas, Fortas divulged that "subconsciously I was affected by G's slimy qualities."[152] He tried to resolve the problems created by the welter of the Court's decisions regarding obscenity by suggesting a new test. A showing of pandering alone would be insufficient. Instead, just as the prosecution was required to show that a criminal possessed the *mens rea*—or specific intent—to commit a crime, so it must prove that the seller possessed the *mens rea* to purvey obscene materials. The government could justify the prosecution only of those individuals responsible for "conscious and purposeful pandering." Fortas could not persuade a majority of the Court to go along with him.[153]

The veil of secrecy that Fortas had drawn over the Court's work at the hearings, however, meant that he could not tell the Citizens for Decent Literature or the Senate that the Court's decision in *Schackman* had nothing to do with obscenity, that Fortas was responsible for the Court's action in *Ginzburg,* or that he regretted his role in that case. Fortas did draft a letter for the Washington lawyer Edward Bennett Williams to send to the *Washington Evening Star* disclosing the truth about *Schackman* and using the justice's vote with the majority in *Ginzburg* as grounds for characterizing his position as "middle of the road," omitting any mention of Fortas's second thoughts about *Ginzburg.*[154] This effort to frame his attitude toward obscenity in terms the committee would find appealing foundered. Neither the Senate Judiciary Committee members nor others in Congress ever acquired any more concrete information than Clancy had provided.[155] To them, Fortas stood for obscenity.

For McClellan, who was already disturbed by the disclosures about Fortas's relationship with Lyndon Johnson and who was angry at the White House anyway about the remarks the President had made when he signed the Omnibus Crime Control Act of 1968, Clancy's presentation on Fortas and obscenity justified postponement.[156] Although he privately conceded to one White House official that Fortas was "probably the most able lawyer" he knew, McClellan did not give that impression publicly.[157] Immediately after the hearings ended, he moved that the committee delay reporting out the Fortas nomination for a week to give its members and their colleagues time to ponder the justice's approach to obscenity and to see 0-7. In ten days Congress would recess until September, and McClellan's motion ensured that senators would spend seven of them watching pornographic movies. Despite the White House's best efforts, it could not persuade the committee to report out the nomination prior to congressional adjournment for the presidential nominating conventions.[158]

## HOPELESSNESS AND PERSISTENCE

"I have masochistically spent the last two evenings watching the Republican convention," Carol Agger reported after the Republicans met in Miami at the beginning of August. "Ugh." Strom Thurmond had been "prominently on display" on the platform next to Richard Nixon. In his speech, Nixon criticized "some of the courts." Agger thought she understood the tableau. She believed that Nixon had been paying off Thurmond for preventing the Florida Republican delegates from shifting their support to Ronald Reagan.[159] Agger, who had lived in Washington for thirty years, understood politics better than some of her husband's more naive supporters. They hoped that Nixon would say something on Fortas's behalf that would reverse the tide flowing against the nomination. Of course they knew that Nixon had said publicly that the next President should name the next chief justice. But since Nixon was also sensitive to charges of anti-Semitism, they assumed that he would hesitate to oppose Fortas. And Nixon had told Gustave Levy that "he would surface more aggressively if the issue of bigotry was raised."[160]

An ardent Republican himself, Fortas's old friend Eugene Bogan had appointed himself the justice's liaison to the Republican party. In his extensive letter-writing campaign, Bogan repeatedly warned his fellow Republicans that "this weird war against the Fortas nomination" was weakening his party's chances of victory in November because "Dick Nixon is getting 100% tarred as being the schemer and plotter to block this nomination." According to Bogan, rumors were circulating that Nixon was anti-Semitic and that he had already made "a deal" to give the seat to someone else. At the very least, the possibility that Nixon might credit "phony arguments" about Johnson's status as a "lame duck," the absence of a vacancy on the Court, or cronyism was raising "questions respecting his intelligence."[161]

What frustrated Bogan was that he believed Nixon agreed with him. When he sent a message "topside" to the upper echelons of the Republican campaign asking Nixon "to call off his dogs," Bogan received a heartening reply, which he transmitted to Paul Porter on the first day of Fortas's appearance before the Senate Judiciary committee, and which Porter immediately passed along to the White House. Bogan had been told that the Republican nominee did "O.K."

the Fortas nomination and was "*not* a party to . . . Griffin's shenanigans—doesn't approve."[162] Bogan erred in accepting such statements at face value. Nixon played the situation with consummate political skill. He remained noncommittal about Fortas before the Republican convention, at the convention, and in the three weeks following the convention, and frequently said he would not interfere with the Senate's right to decide on the nomination. By attacking the Warren Court, however, Nixon implicitly challenged Fortas. Years later Bogan remained bitter about Nixon's role in the affair: "I didn't realize then, of course . . . what a crook he was." In retrospect, he believed that the Republican candidate "was running the campaign against Fortas all the time. . . . Nobody was doing this without direction. It was too well-organized."[163] John Ehrlichman later confirmed that Nixon had encouraged conservatives to oppose Fortas.[164] But no one could be certain that Nixon was working with Fortas's opponents in 1968, and given the assurances to the contrary that he was receiving, Bogan saw no reason to distrust the Republican presidential nominee.[165]

The challenge, as Fortas's proponents saw it, was to persuade Nixon that bigotry explained the opposition to their man. Indeed, even at the end of August Paul Porter retained the hope that the presence of anti-Semitism might move Nixon "quietly [to] use his influence and blow the whistle on a probable filibuster."[166] Anti-Semitism did in fact contribute to the reaction against Fortas. "In this nation of 150 million Aryans, it seems that Mr. Johnson couldn't find a single qualified person to fill that important post," the American Nazi Party declared in a taped telephone message. "Instead, he dug up this despicable Jew with a 'red' record that smells to high heaven."[167] The Nazis were not alone. Senator Eastland reportedly was worried that he "could not go back to Mississippi" if the Senate confirmed a Jewish chief justice.[168]

Potentially the justice's religion could help as much as it hurt. Fortas hoped that it might make Jacob Javits of New York, a Judiciary Committee member, a more enthusiastic supporter. A liberal Republican Jew who had mildly praised the nomination and who had promised Fortas "to help in any way he can,"[169] Javits nevertheless had classified the Fortas and Thornberry appointments as "old cronyism."[170] Members of Los Angeles's most elite Jewish country club were "going all out to support Fortas," one Democrat reported to the White House in June. "This group has . . . gotten to Javits. We have gotten the Jews wound up," a prominent Jewish lawyer in Los Angeles confirmed.[171] To date, however, Jewish pressure had not paid off. Nixon was quiet, and Javits was muted. While the Republicans were sufficiently concerned about anti-Semitism to discuss it at their policy breakfast at the beginning of July, Javits reassured his non-Jewish colleagues that he would defend them if they were accused of bigotry.[172]

Since Porter and the White House knew the danger of trivializing principled opposition to Fortas based on intellectual grounds by dismissing it as anti-Semitic, they initially approached the subject with caution. Before the hearings began, Fortas's friend Alan Barth at the *Washington Post* asked Harry McPherson "whether the issue of anti-Semitism should be openly raised, and by inference attributed to some of the opposition." The White House staff member replied, "If I were writing the editorial, I would warn the opponents that there *are* reactionary voices being raised over this nomination, and that those who have more acceptable purposes in opposing Fortas might find themselves in bed with anti-Semites."[173] In those early days, Fortas's chance to become the next chief justice had seemed good. Now raising the specter of anti-Semitism more loudly seemed one of the few options available.

Fortas and his advocates received some help from Javits's Democratic opponent in the upcoming Senate race. Soon after the hearings ended, Paul O'Dwyer charged that anti-Semitism explained the Senate's delay on Fortas and asked why Javits was tolerating it. Virtually everyone understood that O'Dwyer was trying to siphon off some Jewish votes by this ploy. Nevertheless, Javits refused the bait, replying only that he had no "solid evidence" that anti-Semitism was at issue.[174] Fortas sent Porter some evidence. He enclosed a copy of a statement opposing the nomination on the grounds of his religion that one group had released and suggested that a copy be forwarded to "our friend Javits who purports to think that there's nothing naughty here." Fortas also relayed a rumor that one congressman's mail on the nomination was 80 percent anti-Semitic. "Of course, I don't believe it exists either, except some," Fortas added sarcastically.[175] Although he knew that anti-Semitism was not the primary reason for opposition to his nomination, and he did turn to the issue in part because of its promise as a political weapon, Fortas genuinely believed it partially explained the hostility against him. But he never convinced Javits of that.[176] Nor did he persuade the Republican presidential candidate. When Nixon finally did protest feebly against a filibuster of the nomination in mid-September, he did so because the Democratic candidate, Hubert Humphrey, had goaded him into it, rather than because he worried about appearing anti-Semitic.[177]

Despite his implicit efforts to distance himself from his mentor's jurisprudence at the hearings, Fortas kept in contact with Douglas, who was vacationing in the West. In a letter he wrote to Douglas after the hearings ended, Fortas confided his own assessment of his adversaries' motivations:

> I don't know how much you have heard about the events relating to my nomination. It's been pretty bloody. All the accumulated venom about practically everything seems to have come to a focus. The principal mouthpieces of evil are Senators Thurmond and Ervin, but as you know, they merely reflect in an articulate way the feelings of others.

Primarily, the bitter response mirrors the opposition to what has happened with respect to the racial question and the general revolution of human dignity, reflected by our decisions in the field of criminal law, etc. Secondarily are the factors of resentment to the President and a small admixture of bigotry towards me. I think the last is quite small a factor, but it would be pointless to say that it doesn't play some part.

Every decent constitutional decision in the last three years, and for some years prior thereto, has been denounced. Now they have discovered that I was part of the majority which voted to clear a lot of 'filthy' movies. . . . The great Society for Decent Literature and its lawyers have taken their case to the Senate.[178]

Fortas stressed the theme that hostility to the Warren Court explained the Senate Judiciary Committee's behavior in a talk he gave before the American College of Trial Lawyers in Philadelphia at the beginning of August. His speech brilliantly defended the Court's criminal law decisions. "To set aside the conviction of a man who has been tried in violation of the standards of our constitution is *not* to set it aside on a mere technicality," he reminded his audience. "Constitutionalism is not a technicality."[179] Paul Porter, who was already worried about "the possible spiritual and psychological erosion which might result in the event—God forbid—Abe is not confirmed," sent the speech to the White House. He reported that the "tumultuous standing ovation" Fortas had received had given the justice "an enormous psychological boost."[180]

Like Porter, however, Fortas could read the writing on the wall. "As matters now stand, it is highly doubtful that the Administration forces could break the threatened filibuster," he had written to Douglas at the end of July. The only hope lay in an "unexpected development," such as an early statement by Nixon urging against a filibuster.[181] Realizing the likely outcome of his own situation, he sought to maintain the ideological balance of the Warren Court. He wanted Warren to continue as chief justice. "I think it very important that it work out this way, and I hope you agree," he said to Douglas in the same letter. "Any other resolution would hand the forces of evil a resounding victory." Fortas reiterated his concern to Warren in a letter describing the attitude in the Senate as a "combination of Nixon-Republican partisanship and non-partisan reaction on both sides of the aisle. The common element is bitter, corrosive opposition to all that has been happening in the Court and the country: the racial progress, and the insistence upon increased regard for human rights and dignity in the field of criminal law." After having appealed to the chief justice's well-known hatred of Richard Nixon and his protective instinct regarding the Court, Fortas suggested that it would be "imprudent" to expect his and Thornberry's confirmation before the beginning of October Term. Indeed if events worked out as Fortas thought they might, "it may be desirable to consider whether your notice of intention to retire should be withdrawn."[182]

At the same time that Fortas sought to ensure the continuation of a liberal Court, he tried to defend himself to his colleagues. It was pointless to do so with Hugo Black. At the time, Fortas did not know that Black had advised Senator Lister Hill of Alabama to vote against the nomination.[183] Nevertheless, the jurisprudential chasm that separated the two justices was so great that Fortas may have inferred Black's lack of enthusiasm. Other colleagues were more sympathetic, but they still required attention. John Harlan sent a warm letter but still posed a probing question: "To be sure we *are* citizens as well as judges, but am I wrong in believing that the former privilege is burdened by the need for detachment, in appearance as well as in fact?"[184] Harlan set the question in the context of discussing whether justices should try actively to increase the public's understanding of the Court's work, but he clearly was gently querying Fortas's role as a presidential adviser. At least, Fortas interpreted the comment as a criticism of his relationship with the President. "As to outside activities: dear John, all of my life, I have concentrated on the job in hand," he replied. It was true, he allowed, that he had counseled Johnson, but here again, Fortas gave his public version of his role, claiming that he had "never 'volunteered' suggestions" and had only summarized others' viewpoints for the President on occasion. He had done so "with uneasiness," he admitted, but he had acted out of patriotism, friendship, and sympathy for Johnson, and he did not regret it. Indeed he would do it "all over again because I believe I did bring him some comfort; because I cannot believe that I injured the Court as an institution; and because I really don't care if my response to the President's requests contributes to the withholding of my confirmation as Chief Justice."[185]

The loyalty that explained Fortas's defiant and bitter defensiveness in his letter to Harlan was also apparent at the White House. Even in June, Johnson had worried that the Senate might jeopardize the nomination by stalling. "We've got to get this thing through, and we've got to get it through early, because if it drags out we're going to get beat," Johnson had warned his liaison to the Justice Department at the outset. "Dirksen will leave us."[186] Now the delay the President feared had materialized, and Johnson's staff was already anticipating a filibuster of the nomination in September.[187] Sam Shaffer, a *Newsweek* correspondent, told one of the President's representatives on July 30 that Fortas's opponents had gained strength, that his supporters had nowhere near the votes they needed to end a filibuster, and that the obscenity issue had been "devastating."[188] Johnson's aides counted only fifty-seven senators pressing "hard for" Fortas. Of course if Johnson could persuade some of the justice's opponents to absent themselves from the Senate on the day of the vote on cloture, he might yet carry his friend to triumph. But with thirty-two Senators "hard against" the nomination and an additional two "leaning against" it, the President's chances of victory were slim.[189] At the beginning of August, Senator Eastland visited the President in Texas. "He told me flatly that Abe Fortas would not be confirmed as Chief Justice," Johnson recalled. "I realized after that August meeting that we probably could not muster the votes to put the Fortas nomination through."[190] But the President would not give up. He persisted in order to avoid hurting Fortas. Later, an adviser who knew the White House lacked the two-thirds majority necessary to impose cloture, recommended that the nomination be withdrawn before formal consideration by the Senate. Johnson refused. Although the President's inability to bend the Senate to his will would damage his prestige and end his tenure "on a note of defeat," Johnson believed that Fortas would be able to hold his head higher if he could say that a majority of the Senate had supported his nomination.[191]

With Johnson determined to fight on, the White House's chief concern lay with Fortas's advocates rather than his adversaries. "Griffin and the Southerners are knocking us around pretty hard every day now," Barefoot Sanders informed Johnson at the end of July. "The net effect of all that has happened to date is that our *Senate supporters are pretty discouraged. They need to be pepped up. The best— and perhaps the only—way that can be done is by the President.*" He suggested that Johnson hold a press conference to emphasize his continuing strong interest in the Fortas and Thornberry nominations.[192] The President did so the following day, but the continued apathy of Fortas's political friends was dismaying. One magazine reported a rumor that the justice was "hurt" because so few strongly defended him. "I'm getting a lot of people who know Abe only by reputation to 'change,'" Bogan said to Paul Porter. "*How* do we activate more of Abe's well placed friends?"[193] When Carol Agger heard that a friend's mother was lobbying her senator on Fortas's behalf, she had but one comment: "Too bad that there are not more like her."[194]

A sense of isolation engulfed Fortas's supporters. In September John Kenneth Galbraith wrote Porter to solicit a contribution for a former colleague who was having financial problems. "Where the hell are you and the rest of my liberal friends with respect to the confirmation of Abe Fortas as Chief Justice?" Porter asked when he sent in his check. "Is the bitter attitude toward LBJ so pervasive that a decent liberal with impeccable credentials [is] going to be sacrificed while the so-called liberal community stands mute? I think this silence and lack of involvement is disgraceful."[195] Porter sent a copy of the letter to Joe Rauh, Washington's keeper of the liberal flame, who accused him of being "paranoid! I have never seen an issue on which liberals are more united than they are on Abe Fortas."[196] But the battle was becoming ever more lonely. As it turned out, Fortas had more to fear from his friends than his enemies. It was Porter who inadvertently gave the nomination the death blow and permanently injured Fortas's reputation in the process.

## NAILS IN THE COFFIN

By the time Congress reconvened in September, still other allegations against Fortas had surfaced. A journalist had reported that the justice had worked with Clark Clifford on the President's State of the Union address for 1966.[197] Senator Gordon Allott, a Colorado Republican, told reporters that Fortas had participated in drafting the legislation providing Secret Service protection for presidential candidates that the White House introduced in 1968 in the aftermath of Robert Kennedy's assassination.[198] For Robert Griffin, these two accusations constituted evidence that Fortas had not made full disclosure to the Senate Judiciary Committee. He recommended that the justice be asked to reappear, and additional hearings were scheduled for September 13 and 16. Fortas, who rarely made the same error twice, declined to testify.[199]

Another gambit of Griffin's proved even more damning. Neither Fortas nor American University had ever hidden the fact that the justice was teaching a seminar there that summer. Observers had assumed that Fortas was compensated out of university funds. Griffin's office, however, had received an anonymous tip from an American University employee that the law school had raised an exorbitant sum from businessmen to pay Fortas's salary. Griffin passed the information along to Strom Thurmond, who telephoned B. J. Tennery of the Washington College of Law and suggested he avoid a subpoena by appearing voluntarily before the committee to discuss the seminar.[200] At the hearings, Tennery acknowledged that Gustave Levy, Troy Post, John Loeb, Maurice Lazarus, and Paul Smith had indeed underwritten Fortas's teaching salary.[201]

When Paul Porter heard that the Senate had discovered the source of Fortas's seminar salary and would be holding further hearings, he went to the White House. Neither the President nor his staff had known anything about Porter's fundraising before. "Tears were welling in the eyes of this singularly big-hearted and humane man" as Porter spoke, one White House aide recalled.[202] Porter assumed all responsibility. "Naturally this is a source of grievous personal distress to me because with the best of intentions I participated in the organization and funding of this project," he explained to Clark Clifford. He had arranged the seminar only because he had thought Fortas should not waste his talents by giving speeches. *"Abe did not know until these hearings the identity of any donors."*[203]

That was true. Funding for the seminar had made Fortas uneasy from the start. When he reluctantly consented to allow his former law firm to pay for a portrait of him that would hang in the Yale Law School, he wrote Porter: "There is one fundamental condition. If—as I fear may be the case—the firm contributed to the American University project, I want to cancel the whole business of the firm's financing a portrait of me." Porter replied that he was "happy to report that the firm did not contribute a wooden nickel to the American University and the budget which Tennery set has been oversubscribed—by whom you will never know."[204] While he prevented Fortas from compromising himself, however, Porter was also trying to salve the contributors' egos. He told them that he had reported their participation to Fortas, and the justice had been pleased and touched. That was unfortunate because Porter's blarney created the impression that the justice knew who had put up the money.[205]

No one could prove that Fortas had been aware of the donors' identities at the hearings, and no one attempted to do so. Nor did anyone deny it had been an excellent seminar. Both Tennery and the students who had enrolled in it spoke of it in glowing terms.[206] While it has been suggested that the incomplete state of his teaching notes indicated that the course did not engage Fortas,[207] his teaching notes had been sketchy at Yale and there is no reason to doubt his own comments that he worked hard at leading the seminar and enjoyed it.[208]

Still, the funding provided new justification for Fortas's detractors. Strom Thurmond maintained that the contributors' substantial business interests—in forty corporations, among the five of them—might well embroil them in litigation before the Court. If so, the justice would be placed "in a difficult position."[209] The point might as easily have been made in 1965, when Fortas's antagonists could have contended that his roster of friends and clients included many rich and powerful individuals who might well become involved in Supreme Court litigation. They had not done so then, and the objection was patently bogus now. Fortas routinely disqualified himself from any case involving a former client or personal friend. Other complaints about the fund seemed more valid. Since the fifteen thousand dollars he received for nine weeks of teaching represented over 40 percent of a Supreme Court justice's salary and more than seven times as much as Tennery could remember paying any other seminar leader, many considered Fortas's remuneration excessive. It did little good for the dean to argue that the justice was being paid not only to teach but also to prepare a syllabus and set of materials to turn over to American University. Nor did Tennery's observation that a popular folk singer had received ten thousand dollars for a single performance on the campus dilute the criticism.[210]

Porter's role also made many believe that the whole American University project was a front for subsidizing Fortas's income. That was only half true. Porter's primary motivation in arranging the course was to enable his friend to grapple with an intriguing subject. He was also aware, however, that Fortas believed he needed more money. Given that the justice had asked Levy for help in selling his stock in Post's company and had told Smith he needed to sell his Phillip Morris stock, at least some of those from whom Porter solicited funds for the seminar also may have surmised that Fortas was having trouble adjusting to his new salary. Perhaps that made them more willing to contribute. Nevertheless, Porter did not undertake the solicitation, and they did not respond to it, simply to supplement a friend's income. Had that been his and the contributors' only motivation, one of Fortas's clerks pointed out, Porter could have found another way of funneling much more money to the justice.[211] But since Fortas and Agger's dissatisfaction with the Supreme Court salary was well known in Washington, the whole arrangement seemed suspicious. Over and over again, hostile senators would point out that Fortas's former partner had raised the money by going to the justice's former clients.[212]

Fortas had made an error in judgment. Though he did not know who the donors were, he should have realized that Porter logically would have raised the money from clients and friends. Even the justice's most ardent supporters agreed that Fortas and Porter should have been more alert to the appearance of impropriety. It was "such a bad mistake to let Paul Porter solicit Abe's clients to provide that fund," one colleague on the Court mourned.[213] Eugene Bogan thought Porter had unwittingly put "a knife in Abe's back."[214] Other knives were being sharpened. The obscenity issue would not disappear. After Tennery had testified, Thurmond called a member of the Los Angeles Police Department's Antiobscenity Department to the stand. He had been the arresting officer in *Schackman* and he brought with him two pornographic films and 150 pornographic magazines for the committee to review. He testified that the Supreme Court's action in that case had opened the floodgates of obscenity in Los Angeles. Philip Hart tried to blunt the force of the officer's testimony by observing that Fortas might have voted with the majority to reverse for reasons having nothing to do with obscenity, but his efforts were ineffective. "It is pretty apparent that the smut factories and the filth merchants are having a field day under the present lack of law enforcement," McClellan said at the end of the day. He alleged that the Court's obscenity position aggravated the country's crime problem and expressed the hope that a way would be found to stamp out this "trash."[215] By this time, Senate Judiciary Committee members were becoming testy. Hart, about to leave the session to take his son—a high school senior bound for a year of study in Spain—to the airport, sarcastically predicted to his colleagues that the young man would soon be able to explain Spain's obscenity laws. "We are not sending him out because we think there is a collapse here at home," he added. "Maybe the laws in Spain can be enforced because the Supreme Court doesn't have jurisdiction there," Ervin retorted. Hart shot back, "If Franco is the Franco as we once knew him I am sure it is a great place."[216]

The last day of hearings was anticlimactic. Senator Allott testified that in

May 1968 he and other members of the Appropriations Committee had gathered with Under Secretary of the Treasury Joseph Barr to draft legislation that would authorize Secret Service protection for presidential candidates. In the midst of the meeting, Barr had received a telephone call that occupied him for perhaps half an hour. After the group had adjourned, the under secretary told Allott that he had been talking with the White House and said that the President's associate special counsel, DeVier Pierson, and Abe Fortas had approved the proposed language.[217] The story was untrue. Barr denied ever having made the comment about Fortas, although Pierson admitted Barr might have done so "as a flippant comment in jest." The White House also said that Fortas had never been involved with that particular legislation. If Barr accepted the committee's invitation to appear, however, the senators would have to choose between his word and Allott's, and Pierson feared that Allott's testimony would be persuasive. Barr refused the committee's invitation.[218] The accusation that Fortas had assisted in drafting the State of the Union address for 1966 was true, but the White House devised a convenient way of preventing the Senate Judiciary Committee from conclusively establishing that fact. When the committee invited Fortas's collaborator on the speech, Clark Clifford, to appear, the new secretary of defense responded that he had no "precise recollections" about White House meetings he had attended with Fortas and that the press of world affairs prevented him from testifying.

Neither of the two new charges was important in itself. Even Allott admitted that the Secret Service legislation was noncontroversial.[219] The article mentioning Fortas's work on the State of the Union speech had appeared while the July hearings were still in progress. No one had introduced it into the record then, and Fortas's opponents seemed to be grasping at straws in doing so now. Yet the new allegations came at an unfortunate moment. Senators who had listened to Fortas cite the doctrine of separation of powers as justification for his refusal to discuss Supreme Court decisions now seized upon the accusations as evidence that he had breached that very doctrine. Disclosures about the content of American University seminar strengthened their hand. They could now ask how the justice who had so sanctimoniously refused to tell members of Congress about Supreme Court decisions in which he participated could have discussed those decisions with law students. In fact, other Supreme Court justices had discussed the Court in law schools and refused to do so before the Senate Judiciary Committee, but their nominations had occasioned less disagreement.[220]

When the hearings ended, the President's Senate liaison met with Dirksen and Senate Majority Leader Mansfield. Dirksen reported that the senators were now less worried about Fortas's role as presidential adviser but that the obscenity issue had hurt the candidate. "The movies are what the opposition needed to make their position jell." Strom Thurmond "tastes blood." The aide reported that both Dirksen and Mansfield agreed that as "a secondary issue," Fortas's fifteen-thousand-dollar lecture fee for the American University seminar had been "hurtful, particularly since Paul Porter raised the money."[221] Though the Senate Judiciary Committee reported out the nomination by a vote of eleven to six the following day,[222] bad news continued to arrive at the White House. "My fourth cousin, Paul Porter, should have used better judgment," Senator John Cooper from Kentucky remarked to Harry McPherson.[223] According to one of the President's aides, Griffin's staff "claim[ed] three switches against Fortas because of the $15,000."[224] But once again the worst news came from Fortas's supporters. The previous week Barefoot Sanders had confided his doubts about the nomination to the President. "My own impression—and it is not based on anything anyone said, simply a feeling—is that Mansfield and Dirksen are going to do whatever they have promised to do in bringing the nomination out of the Committee and to the floor but that neither is approaching this fight with any enthusiasm or confidence, or sense of outrage at what [the] Senate Judiciary [Committee] is doing."[225] As it turned out, even that assessment was too optimistic.

When the Fortas nomination reached the Senate floor on September 25, Mansfield did not ask the Senate for approval. Instead he tried to head off a filibuster by moving that the Senate be allowed to debate the nomination, a strategy that Hart considered "the first encouraging thing that's happened in three months."[226] The majority leader's cleverness did not daunt his opponents, who still began a filibuster. At that point, Mansfield did not follow the example of Lyndon Johnson as majority leader, who would have broken the filibuster by keeping the Senate in session late into the night and wearing his enemies out. Mansfield sent Fortas's antagonists home for a good rest every evening. His halfhearted defense of the justice included a public characterization of the American University lecture fund as "unfortunate."[227]

For his part, Dirksen declared on September 26 that he would not vote for cloture. The senator's attempts to justify his switch on the basis of newly formed principled objections to Fortas were lame. In fact, as Johnson had predicted, the delay on the Fortas nomination had stymied Dirksen. He had to join Griffin's challengers or risk losing the remnants of his power.[228] A majority of Senators still wanted to end the filibuster by imposing cloture, but Dirksen's defection thinned their ranks. When Mansfield called for a vote on October 1, only forty-five of the eighty-eight Senators present voted for cloture. Fortas could have pressed for a second vote, but he was so far short of the two-thirds majority he needed that he asked Johnson to withdraw his nomination that night. Two days later Thornberry echoed that request, and on October 10 Johnson announced that he would not nominate anyone else as chief justice. For the present, Warren would continue to occupy the office.

"Win or lose the stain of this terrible ordeal will remain with Fortas on or off the Bench," Dirksen had told the White House.[229] For the present, that did not seem true. In the aftermath of his defeat, liberals made Fortas their darling. A note from Justice Thurgood Marshall was representative:

> You are still 'my man'!
> You are still 'my leader'!
> I still love you!
> OH what I could say about the opposition![230]

The day after Johnson had withdrawn his name, Fortas found himself on the same platform as Arthur Goldberg at New York University Law School on the occasion of the centenary of the Fourteenth Amendment. Goldberg took the opportunity to indicate his "profound regret" at the Senate's action and told the audience that his wife had recalled some appropriate words from Benjamin Franklin: "Do not in public life expect immediate approbation of one's services. One must persevere through insult and injury." Fortas, who followed, paused in the middle of his speech and emotionally promised, "I shall persevere." The standing ovation that followed that remark lasted for three minutes.[231]

Fortas tried to insulate himself from his defeat. "Here, of course, the phenomenon is the fragmentation of liberalism," he explained to Muñoz.[232] That was partially true, for the ideological reaction against the Warren Court was one important reason for his defeat; it gave his enemies the impetus to make an issue of his nomination. Indeed had Johnson appointed him in 1968 directly from private practice, his friend would have had a better chance. With Fortas's approval, the President had been too clever by half. "Johnson just outsmarted himself," Nicholas Katzenbach recalled. "He thought that Homer Thornberry was so much liked by the Congress . . . that in order to put him on the Supreme Court, they would let Fortas be Chief Justice, and he just miscalculated."[233] Even members of the President's staff thought that the appointment of his two dear friends to the Court resembled "old crony week."[234] Fortas might have become chief justice had the President followed Clifford's advice and nominated a highly qualified Republican as associate justice at the same time. Alternatively, had the President elevated Fortas before he announced his decision against standing for reelection, Fortas almost certainly would have been confirmed. In retrospect, Fortas surmised that the nomination failed partially because Johnson had lost his power. And he believed that the President agreed with him on that point.[235] His attempt to appoint both Fortas and Thornberry and his reliance on Dirksen and Russell suggested the President had lost his touch.[236]

Had Johnson appointed another individual closely associated with the Warren Court to become chief justice—even after March 31—the outcome might also have been different. Though his power was waning, the President might have been able to succeed in installing William Brennan or Arthur Goldberg. Even Robert Griffin declared himself ready to accept Arthur Goldberg,[237] and Goldberg regarded Fortas as a kindred spirit. That suggested that despite all fuss over obscenity and the state of criminal law, neither jurisprudence nor anti-Semitism wholly explained the outcome.

Neither Goldberg nor Brennan had counseled Johnson from the bench as frequently as Fortas had. Indeed, Justice Fortas's views on Vietnam carried greater weight with the President than those of Arthur Goldberg, who sacrificed his seat at the Court in the hope of bringing an end to the war in Vietnam. His close association with Johnson while he was at the Court contributed to Fortas's defeat. It was Fortas's misfortune to have his advisory role exposed at a time when there was increasing anxiety among both the public and members of Congress about the growth of presidential power. To senators, that fear made it more important than ever to maintain the sanctity of the separation of powers doctrine.

Fortas's relationship with the President also meant that Congress associated him not only with the liberalism of the Warren Court, but with the policies of Lyndon Johnson as well. Johnson had not done well, and Fortas was partly to blame. Generally Fortas's was a wise voice when it came to counseling the President on culture, social reform, and civil liberties, but he gave Johnson bad advice on Vietnam and in doing so, unwittingly helped to destroy his friend's presidency. Fortas and Johnson's position on Vietnam also hurt the cause of liberalism, by discrediting internationalism, diminishing the resources available for social reform and culture, and, in some instances, reducing enthusiasm for civil liberties. By 1968 the popularity of Johnson and his ideology had reached its nadir. When Lady Bird Johnson said that the reaction against Fortas represented "the rising anger against Lyndon and mostly the rising anger against liberalism," she wisely differentiated Johnsonian liberalism from that of the Warren Court.[238] Opponents held Johnson responsible for the actions of the Warren Court, but they did not blame the Warren Court for Johnson's actions. Like Johnson, Fortas had to answer for both the executive and judicial branches, for the consequences of domestic reform and of globalism. His roles as presidential counselor and Supreme Court justice—not the revelations about the lecture fund after the situation was already judged hopeless—destroyed Fortas. Had he been a better politician, Fortas might have realized that the twin handicaps of being a justice and presidential adviser would make it impossible for him to become chief justice.

Fortas's character was a factor in his defeat in only one respect. He should have declined to appear before the Judiciary Committee. Although his refusal to do so would not have guaranteed his confirmation, his testimony only gave his opponents new ammunition. His decision seemed reasonable at the time because testifying represented his only chance of fighting back and assuming control. But it was still a mistake. When he agreed to go before the committee Fortas did not sufficiently appreciate the extent to which the rules for judges diverged from those for lawyers. He originally intended explicitly to defend his votes and his and his colleagues' decisions, but instead he had to fall back on "separation of powers" as a justification for his refusal to discuss decisions or votes. He did so at enormous personal sacrifice. "The hard thing to take," he subsequently told Muñoz, "was the vileness and defamation of the process itself—particularly since I had committed myself to 'judicial aloofness.' This is a role to which I am not yet accustomed and which requires the most severe discipline!"[239] A test of his "judicial aloofness" that would prove even more difficult still lay in store for him.

# CHAPTER 16

# From Public Service to the Private Sector, II

I N THE AFTERMATH OF FORTAS'S FAILED NOMINATION, HUGO BLACK AND his wife talked late into the night about the Court's future. Black was worried. He was eighty-two and would not "last forever." William O. Douglas was wearing a pacemaker. John Harlan was nearly blind. Earl Warren's impending retirement meant he was "only sitting on half a chair."[1] As it turned out, however, Fortas became the first to go.

## "A QUESTION OF ETHICS"

Like Abe Fortas, Louis Wolfson had been having a rough time. After completing its investigations of him in 1966, the Securities and Exchange Commission refused to give him an opportunity to explain his actions. Instead the commission referred the matters to the Justice Department with a recommendation that Wolfson and his associate Elkin Gerbert be criminally prosecuted for activities with respect to two companies in which Wolfson held controlling interests, Continental Enterprises and Merritt-Chapman & Scott. After Wolfson and Gerbert were indicted, the Justice Department assigned both cases to United States Attorney Robert Morgenthau of New York, a man whose career had centered on fighting white-collar crime. Wolfson's financial adviser, Alexander Rittmaster, became the government's star witness. In September 1967 Wolfson and Gerbert were convicted of conspiracy to violate the securities laws and of selling unregistered stock in Continental Enterprises. Nine months later, they were found guilty of conspiring to violate the securities laws, of perjuring themselves before the SEC, and of filing misleading annual reports regarding Merritt-Chapman & Scott. Wolfson's wife was dying of cancer, he recently had suffered a heart attack, and he was about to begin serving a one-year prison term.[2]

Both Wolfson and Gerbert, who was being represented by Arnold & Porter, clung to the hope that Fortas would come to their rescue by using his influence with the Johnson administration on their behalf. Earlier Gerbert had tried to boost Rittmaster's spirits and to prevent him from aiding the prosecution by confiding that Fortas was "furious" that the SEC had not given Wolfson a hearing before referring the cases to the Justice Department. The justice had even come to Florida to discuss Wolfson's situation. As a witness for the prosecution, Rittmaster passed that information along to Morgenthau's office and also reported that Fortas had become a consultant to the Wolfson Family Foundation.

Part of this news had already reached Congress. The Senate Judiciary Committee had received an anonymous letter dated September 22, 1968, advising exploration of Fortas's association with Louis Wolfson.[3] On September 23, a representative from Senator Griffin's office called upon Cartha DeLoach of the FBI to report that "Senator Griffin has received considerable information which he feels represents conflict of interests and violation of the traditional separation of powers on the part of Justice Fortas but which he is having considerable difficulty in 'running out' because of a lack of trained investigative personnel." Could the Bureau provide some individuals who had the expertise to track down Griffin's leads? DeLoach explained that the FBI could do so only with the approval of Attorney General Ramsey Clark. Griffin's representative replied that the senator would not pursue the matter "because of the fact that the Attorney General had fully endorsed Fortas and would not authorize the FBI to conduct [an] investigation along lines which might seek to discredit him."[4]

William Lambert proved more persistent. This reporter for *Life* magazine had heard that Fortas had become a consultant to the Wolfson Family Foundation and, further, had not paid income tax on his honorarium from that institution. Lambert's source, whom he never identified, was probably someone in the Internal Revenue Service, as that agency was investigating the Wolfson Family Foundation. In November, Ramsey Clark received "a complete surprise" when Robert Morgenthau telephoned him one evening to warn that *Life* was about to print Lambert's accusation that the justice had not reported the income he had received from the Wolfson Family Foundation. Realizing that the allegation could damage Fortas, Clark went to his friend's house the following day. After hearing the charge, Fortas telephoned his secretary, and she reviewed the justice's financial records while the attorney general waited. The news was good. "I paid that money back," Fortas reported to Clark. "I decided that I couldn't do it." Relieved that he need not devote the waning days of the Johnson administration to the prosecution of the President's adviser and a man he admired, Clark nevertheless continued to wait anxiously for the appearance of Lambert's article. When it did not appear in either of the next two issues of the magazine, he forgot about it.[5]

Fortas did not. His telephone call to his secretary in the attorney general's presence had been another fine performance. Though he pretended to Clark that his relationship with the financier was so insignificant he could not remember it, the justice knew his files contained numerous communications from Wolfson and his family. And, although the letters and memoranda provided no hard evidence that Fortas had intervened to help Wolfson, their tone would arouse suspicions. In thanking the justice for a particular telephone call, for example, Wolfson had said that one of his associates would be sending Fortas "the documentation" and expressed his gratitude "for the swiftness with which you handled this serious matter."[6] Some months later Fortas wrote to Mrs. Wolfson to say that her husband would "need all of your strength, as well as his own, to survive the ordeal which he may face—but which we all hope will be avoided."[7] But although his letter was warm and sympathetic, it promised nothing. Indeed the justice replied to a plea from the wife of one of Wolfson's employees with this comment: "As you will readily understand—and I am sure Mr. Wolfson knows— I am bound by the rules and customs of this Court."[8] Nevertheless, Fortas's files also included myriad legal documents drafted by Wolfson's attorneys, as well as the financier's claims that both SEC chairman Manuel Cohen and the judge who had convicted Wolfson were unfairly prejudiced against him.[9] Fortas could not have forgotten about his association with Wolfson when he spoke with Ramsey Clark.

How could he prevent Lambert from learning more about it? At their meeting, the attorney general had recommended that Fortas might try to forestall damage by offering information and an explanation of his own. The justice turned to Paul Porter, who obligingly invited the reporter to visit his law firm a month from Nixon's election as President in 1968. During a long session filled with anecdotes about his former partner, Porter explained that Fortas had indeed accepted "fifteen or twenty thousand dollars" from the foundation. When he discovered he was too busy to act as a consultant later that year, he had returned the money. He had not reported it to the Internal Revenue Service because it had not been taxable income. Unfortunately for Fortas, Porter's disclosure only whetted Lambert's interest. For the present, however, *Life* concentrated on embarrassing Fortas rather than exposing him. In its first issue in 1969 it included the justice among its "Winners and Losers" for the year 1968. The caption's reference to the role of his obscenity decisions, his acceptance of lecture fees, and his relationship with Lyndon Johnson in explaining his abortive nomination as chief justice made it clear that *Life* numbered Fortas among the losers.

"This man, in the considered judgment of the U.S. Congress, condoned dirty movies, accepted extravagant fees and befriended you-know-who. Justice Fortas was fortunate not to have been arrested."[10] Fortas's angry response, which he did not mail, condemned the magazine for its "brutal and savage assault" against "a defenseless subject" and speculated that the magazine was acting "in retaliation for" his dissent in *Time* v. *Hill.*[11]

If revenge was *Life's* motivation, it was obtaining additional ammunition. Lambert continued digging. His government sources divulged that Fortas had not returned Wolfson's check until after the financier had twice been indicted. The reporter also began to hear that Wolfson had assured associates that Fortas would shield them from the government. Lambert did not know that Wolfson had agreed to pay Fortas $20,000 a year during his life and Carol Agger the same amount for the remainder of her life should she survive Fortas, but he was acquiring enough information to remain interested in the story.[12] When Lambert noticed that the justice recused himself from the Supreme Court's decision not to hear Wolfson and Gerbert's appeal on April 1, 1969, he decided to press forward. Because he needed corroborating evidence, he turned to the Department of Justice. Lambert met with Will Wilson, an attorney in charge of the Justice Department's criminal division. Lambert insisted to a reporter that he had already completed virtually all the work on his story and that he did not learn anything new from Wilson.[13] The meeting proved more fruitful for Wilson. An enemy of Lyndon Johnson's, Wilson was also no fan of the Warren Court. "In all candor, we wanted Fortas off the Court," he later said.[14] Wilson determined to launch his own investigation of the justice's activities and indicated his plans to Nixon's attorney general, John Mitchell, and to J. Edgar Hoover of the FBI. Mitchell passed the news along to Richard Nixon, with whom Hoover met on April 23.

Richard Nixon had been coy about his opinion of Fortas's qualifications for the chief justiceship before he became President, but he had never hidden his opinion of the Warren Court. Now that he had replaced Lyndon Johnson, he intended to appoint more conservative justices. He also apparently intended to tarnish Lyndon Johnson's legacy of reform. As an architect of both Johnson's and the Supreme Court's liberal proposals, Fortas could do double service as a target. Nixon told Hoover that he understood *Life* was publishing an article about Abe Fortas. The FBI director responded that the story must be "very strong" because its author had already informed Fortas about it in order to minimize the risk of a libel suit.[15] Lambert had sent a letter to the justice to ask for a meeting to review "information in my possession that might indicate an impropriety on your part," but Fortas had answered that since he had committed "no impropriety or anything approaching it, . . . no purpose would be served by any such meeting."[16]

Hoover remarked that if Lambert had the facts, "and I understand he does," it might "do something [to damage Fortas]." Nixon, himself the beneficiary of a slush fund in 1952, asked why Fortas, who did not need the money, would "do such a silly thing." Hoover commented that the justice was guilty of further transgressions. The FBI director had given Wilson evidence that Fortas had combined with other judges and prominent public figures to buy a building in Virginia, which was rented to the government. "While that is not a violation of law, it is a tax dodge because they can claim depreciation and I think people who have sat on a court ought to have enough sense not to do that," Hoover editorialized. Nixon replied that Fortas "ought to be off of there."[17]

Wilson was doing everything he could to see that the President's ambition was fulfilled. Two days after the meeting between Hoover and Nixon, Louis Wolfson entered prison. His last-minute plea that Fortas ask Lyndon Johnson to request a presidential pardon for him from Richard Nixon had gone nowhere.[18] Wolfson's sole hope now lay in arranging a deal with Nixon's Justice Department. His attorney, William Bittman, told Wilson and Mitchell that Wolfson would provide the FBI with a statement about his relationship with Fortas, but only after the article in *Life* appeared.[19] Whether Wolfson was promised anything in return is not completely clear. He served nine months of his sentence for misdeeds with respect to Continental Enterprises before he was released in 1970 for good behavior. But Wolfson had also been found guilty of illegal activities with respect to Merritt-Chapman & Scott, which called for a separate eighteen-month prison term. Though the U.S. Court of Appeals for the Second Circuit reversed his Merritt-Chapman & Scott conviction in 1970, the government retried the case. After two trials in 1972 had resulted in hung juries and the government had raised the specter of yet another trial, Wolfson had had enough. The U.S. Attorney's office in the Southern District of New York possessed a well-known hostility to plea-bargaining under such circumstances, but Wolfson may have had friends in high places. He now pleaded no contest to the charges, and in chambers the assistant U.S. attorney explained to the judge that "the U.S. Attorney General had directed his office to consent to the plea."[20] It is possible that after three trials and an appeal, the Justice Department had decided to cut its losses. But Justice also may have been rewarding Wolfson. John Mitchell had resigned as Attorney General in March 1972, but his successor, Richard Kleindienst, had begun working in the Justice Department in 1969 and surely knew about the earlier discussions with Wolfson. Significantly, though Edward Bennett Williams had replaced Bittman as Wolfson's attorney, Bittman was brought in to negotiate with the Department of Justice.[21] Thus, although the Nixon administration seems to have been reluctant to create the appearance of having struck a deal with Wolfson in 1969, it may have intervened on his behalf in 1972.

In 1969, however, without confirmation of Lambert's accusations, there could be no story in *Life* and the Nixon administration could not eliminate Fortas from the Court. Lambert therefore went once more to the Justice Department. J. Edgar Hoover later told Attorney General Mitchell a reliable source had confirmed that the Justice Department had furnished the reporter "with considerable information . . . which . . . enabled Lambert to expose the Fortas tie-in with the Wolfson Foundation." The fact that Hoover named no individual but spoke of the Justice Department in general terms "indicated that the leaks were official, perhaps authorized by Mitchell."[22] Hoover's observation was not wholly accurate, for at the time of Lambert's visit Wilson's investigation had turned up little, and the department did not yet possess "considerable information" on the link between Fortas and Wolfson. It still lacked their correspondence, which would provide the needed concrete evidence of their relationship. Nevertheless, the Justice Department so wanted to remove Fortas from the bench that one of its officials confirmed Lambert's facts anyway.[23]

Lambert's story appeared on the newsstands on Monday, May 5, 1969. Entitled "Fortas of the Supreme Court: A Question of Ethics," it was subtitled "The Justice . . . and the Stock Manipulator."[24] It featured two large pictures of Fortas and Wolfson above a caption asking: "Why would a man of his legal brilliance and high position do business with . . . Louis Wolfson, a well-known corporate stock manipulator known to be under federal investigation?" The article explained that Fortas had received a check for twenty thousand dollars from the Wolfson Family Foundation in January 1966 and had not returned it until December. "Ostensibly, Justice Fortas was being paid to advise the foundation on ways to use its funds for charitable, educational and civil rights projects. Whatever services he may or may not have rendered in this respect, Justice Fortas' name was being dropped in strategic places by Wolfson and Gerbert in their effort to stay out of prison."

Lambert considered the $20,000 payment troublesome for several reasons. First, that Wolfson and Gerbert mentioned Fortas "without his knowledge does not change the fact that his acceptance of the money . . . made the name-dropping effective." Second, as the foundation's gross income in 1966 amounted to only $115,200, Lambert found Fortas's fee "generous in the extreme." Third, in his letter to *Life* denying any impropriety, which Lambert quoted in full, Fortas had not acknowledged receiving any money from the foundation. He admitted only to having been present at a meeting centered on the foundation's charitable program during a "brief visit to Mr. Wolfson's famous horse farm" and added that he "did not, of course, participate in any of Mr. Wolfson's business or legal affairs during that visit, nor have I done so at any time since I retired from law practice." Finally, Lambert obviously suspected that Fortas returned the money only because Wolfson had been indicted. The reporter conceded that *Life* had not "uncovered evidence making possible a charge that Wolfson hired Fortas to fix his case." But by the time he finished setting out the facts, Fortas's association with Wolfson hardly seemed innocent. Lambert described the justice's visit to Wolfson's horse farm before the indictments, cited Rittmaster's accusation that Fortas had discussed Wolfson's legal problems, and spoke of the number of occasions on which Wolfson allegedly had used the justice's name. The article prominently displayed two sections from the American Bar Association's Canons of Judicial Ethics. One said that "a judge's official conduct should be free from impropriety and the appearance of impropriety." Another warned against conflicts of interest which might "interfere or appear to interfere" with the fulfillment of judicial obligations.

As Joe Rauh recalled, Fortas now "violated a cardinal rule of Washington: tell everything right away and make a clean breast of it."[25] He should have found a lawyer and held a press conference to disclose his original agreement with Wolfson instead of waiting for a reporter or the Justice Department to do it for him. But Fortas did not want to make an elaborate statement until he had talked with his Supreme Court colleagues, who were on a short recess. "Instead of being so damn duty-stricken," Fortas later told a reporter, "it would have been better to have quickly made a detailed public statement."[26] Believing he had to say something immediately, Fortas focused on Lambert's allegations and innuendoes in a brief statement released to the press. He unequivocally denied having provided the financier with legal advice or legal services while serving on the Court. In discussing his association with the Wolfson Family Foundation, Fortas engaged in the same kind of obfuscation he had employed decades earlier in the Pauley hearings. After denying he had accepted "any fee or emolument" from Wolfson or his foundation, the justice acknowledged that the foundation had "tendered a fee" to him to study "racial and religious relations" that he had given back when he concluded he was too busy to accept the assignment. He said nothing about his lifetime arrangement with Wolfson.[27] One observer labeled his statement "a triumph of lawyerlike craftsmanship over personal credibility."[28]

In legal terms, Fortas's statement was correct. He had not "accepted" the fee the foundation had offered him since he had returned it without performing the obligation that accompanied it. But this trial was taking place in the nation's press rather than its courtrooms, and the justice's defense seemed weak. The hoots of derision were deafening. They came from many who had previously been his supporters. Liberals deserted Fortas.[29] The normally sympathetic *Washington Post* editorialized that "unless Justice Fortas can provide a more compelling explanation, publicly and in some reasonable detail, he can best serve himself, the Court on which he sits and his country by stepping down."[30] Though Robert Griffin warned his staff that "we must be careful not to gloat,"[31] those who had denied Fortas the chief justiceship vociferously condemned him. Strom Thurmond, for one, lost no time in declaring that the disclosures about Fortas and Wolfson brought to mind "the questionable arrangement which Justice Fortas had with the American University Law School." He called for Fortas's resignation.[32] By this time, the justice's opponents knew their man. When Fortas finally asked Johnson to withdraw his nomination as chief justice, he had cited as his reason his desire to protect the Court. The task in 1969 was to strike out at individuals about whom Fortas cared even more than the Court, until he caved in.

## "ACTING RESPONSIBLY"

Fortas's wife, Carol Agger, and his mentor, William O. Douglas, became the first of those targets. On May 5, the same day the *Life* story appeared, Senator John Williams of Delaware introduced a bill that would penalize any judge or public official who accepted any payments from a tax-exempt foundation. While the revelations about Fortas provided the occasion for his action, Williams focused his attention on Douglas, who received an annual retainer of twelve thousand dollars from the tax-exempt Parvin Foundation, which, Williams charged, was "controlled by a group of Las Vegas gamblers, who likewise are in trouble with the Department of Justice."[33]

When the Parvin Foundation had come under fire in 1966, its officers had retained Carol Agger as an independent analyst to examine its tax returns. After she said they had done nothing wrong, the Internal Revenue Service dropped its investigation. In light of the charges about her husband, however, it seemed likely that her independence at that time would be challenged. "The next round of gossip, columnists' stuff—nothing serious, you know, but delicate questions of propriety—will be directed against Mrs. Fortas," Judge Charles Wyzanski told a reporter.[34] The Administration soon broadened its attack against Fortas to include Agger, one of the justice's closest friends, Paul Porter, and another former colleague. On Tuesday, May 6, reporters learned that the Justice Department had "quietly" begun a grand jury investigation to reopen the question of whether Arnold & Porter had withheld subpoenaed documents in a price-fixing case two years earlier. Some of the documents the firm earlier claimed to have misplaced had been found in Agger's office safe. Lyndon Johnson's Justice Department had investigated the charge that the firm had deliberately concealed the documents and found no criminal wrongdoing, but Richard Nixon's Justice Department thought it worth another look. Though the *New York Times* reported in a front-page article that "Attorney General John N. Mitchell is known to have been so eager to avoid any suggestion that the move was motivated by politics, that he obtained the opinions of career attorneys outside of the criminal division before he cleared it for presentation to the grand jury,"[35] Arnold & Porter lawyers were skeptical. They believed that in investigating Porter and Paul Berger, an attorney in the tax division Carol Agger headed, Mitchell was putting Fortas on notice that the Nixon administration could destroy both the firm he had founded and the professional reputation of his wife.[36]

This time there was no doubt that Nixon and his associates were working closely with Fortas's enemies. It was unclear, however, what the President and Mitchell wanted. Did they hope that Fortas would resign, or did they intend to have him impeached? The answer became apparent on May 6 when Patrick Buchanan, a White House staff member, informed the President that "the cloud gathering over Justice Fortas makes it a good probability that he will be forced to resign after 'a decent interval.'"[37] At a meeting with Mitchell and other key Republicans that day, Nixon dissuaded members of Congress from initiating proceedings to impeach Fortas. Impeachment would take too long and would divide the country. Nor was it necessary. Mitchell implied that the justice would resign.[38]

That evening, the attorney general finally received some hard evidence against Fortas. The Internal Revenue Service had subpoenaed the correspondence between the justice and Wolfson from the Wolfson Family Foundation as soon as Lambert's piece had appeared on the newsstands. At 1 A.M. Mitchell arrived back in Washington from a speaking engagement in New York. He was traveling with his press officer, Jack Landau, whose wife was an attorney at Arnold & Porter. Will Wilson and his assistant, Henry Petersen, were waiting for Mitchell and Landau at the airport. They were carrying Fortas's contract with the foundation, and they now knew that Wolfson had agreed to pay the justice twenty thousand dollars a year during his lifetime and the same amount to Carol Agger if she survived him.

Mitchell was shocked. Years later, Landau retained a vivid recollection of the attorney general's reaction: "He kept looking at Harry Petersen and saying: 'It can't be real!'"[39] The Justice Department had succeeded beyond all expectations. In attempting to corroborate the charge that Fortas had accepted a single payment from the Wolfson Foundation, it had learned of a much more sweeping financial arrangement. This news was too good for Mitchell to keep to himself. After speaking with Nixon the next morning, the Attorney General decided to share it with Earl Warren.

Why Warren? Wilson later said that Fortas had telephoned Mitchell to ask for an appointment and that he had warned the attorney general against developing a personal relationship with the justice. As he told it, Wilson conceded that it would be appropriate for Mitchell to communicate with Fortas's attorney and argued that as chief justice, Warren came closest to that role.[40] Henry Petersen's recollection differed from Wilson's. He claimed credit for himself for advising Mitchell to see Warren rather than Fortas. Petersen said his reasoning was that the Justice Department did not yet have an "airtight" case against the justice. After all, Fortas's public statement remained legally accurate even after the department's discovery of his contract with the foundation. Fortas "would have told us to go peddle our papers," Petersen explained to a reporter.[41] Though their accounts differed, Wilson's and Petersen's thoughts likely were running along the same lines. Both wanted to add Earl Warren's voice to those already raised for Fortas's resignation. Wilson's reasoning was byzantine. He obviously was not really thinking in terms of the person who most closely resembled the justice's attorney. If he had been, Wilson would have turned to Paul Porter, Clark Clifford, or William O. Douglas instead of Earl Warren. But Douglas was in South America, at any event, and both Porter and Clifford would have defended Fortas. The chief justice, who would want to avoid marring his own impending retirement with a scandal, might prove more responsive. Petersen was more direct. Instead of engaging in pettifoggery, he acknowledged that the Justice Department might more easily impress Warren than Fortas.

When Mitchell met with Warren on May 7, he brought the six documents he had acquired from the Wolfson Family Foundation. For the first time, Warren learned of the justice's lifetime arrangement with Wolfson. But the material the chief justice saw contained no evidence that the justice had ever contacted a government official on Wolfson's behalf, and it showed that Fortas had returned the first and only payment to the financier. The information Mitchell revealed did not incriminate Fortas legally. Still, the meeting between Mitchell and Warren hurt Fortas. "He can't stay," Warren remarked to his secretary at the time.[42] Warren himself had made that impossible. The chief justice may have had strict standards of judicial conduct and may have condemned Fortas for casting "a blot on the image of the Warren Court,"[43] but Warren's talk with Mitchell itself breached the doctrine of separation of powers. Warren's response to the affair was "tragically mistaken," one judge later admitted: "As a matter of hindsight, it is clear that the Chief Justice should have refused to discuss the matter, and told the Attorney General that if he had any evidence of crime he should present it to a Grand Jury."[44] By listening to Mitchell, Warren enabled the attorney general to receive maximum publicity for the fact that he had further information against Fortas without forcing Mitchell to disclose its nature publicly.

The next issue of *Newsweek* featured an article by the reporter Samuel Shaffer discussing Mitchell's "backstairs call on Chief Justice Earl Warren. The message: there was still more damaging material in the Fortas file—and it was sure to surface unless Fortas withdrew."[45] The veteran reporter Robert Shogan recalled that Shaffer's story "created a sensation comparable to the reaction to Lambert's initial article."[46] White House aide Bryce Harlow wanted the attorney general to disclose the evidence he had given Warren immediately, but Mitchell was too smart for that. Shaffer's article encouraged the nation to imagine the worst, and Mitchell fed its fantasies when he publicly acknowledged that he had visited Warren to give him "certain information."[47] The justice's lifetime contract with Wolfson would have seemed tame in comparison to what the nation was coming to believe Fortas had done.

Actually, by the time Shaffer's article appeared the Nixon administration had learned that the foundation contract was the most damaging evidence against the justice it could muster. Louis Wolfson had kept his promise to speak with Justice Department officials after the publication of Lambert's piece in *Life,* but when Will Wilson and two FBI agents talked with him on May 10, Wolfson informed them that Fortas had never helped him. This news must have disappointed the Justice Department. Two days earlier the department had let it be known that it was investigating Fortas's relation with the Wolfson Family Foundation to determine whether the justice had broken two laws. One prohibited federal officials from receiving compensation from private parties in connection with any private proceeding, while another prohibited federal officials from practicing law.[48] But none of the letters from Fortas that the financier turned over to the Justice Department was sufficiently explicit to make a charge of practicing law possible, and Wolfson swore that Fortas had "made no offer of assistance nor did he indicate he would do anything one way or the other in connection with this matter."[49]

Wolfson's claim that the justice never communicated with a government official on the financier's behalf was open to question but probably true. Henry Petersen told Lambert that Fortas had telephoned the SEC chairman, Manuel Cohen, around the time of Wolfson's legal problems.[50] However, Cohen and Fortas had known each other for many years, and a telephone conversation between them might have covered any number of topics. Presumably, Fortas would have wanted to receive credit from Wolfson had he spoken with the SEC chairman on the financier's behalf. But when Wolfson indignantly asked later why Fortas had reneged on a promise to contact Cohen, Fortas replied that it "would have been like lighting a fuse on our own dynamite."[51] The exact nature of the justice's assistance to Wolfson, if any, remains a mystery. It is clear that if Fortas gave Wolfson legal counsel or spoke to government officials about him, the Nixon administration was unaware of it. Indeed, Mitchell later admitted that Fortas had committed no crime.[52]

Those facts did not concern Mitchell and Nixon in May of 1969. Even though Wolfson had exonerated Fortas, he was enabling them to embarrass the justice. Regardless of whether they had legal grounds, they intended to force Fortas off the bench. The White House did its best to appear circumspect. The President's domestic affairs adviser, John Ehrlichman, had the job of showing "how responsible Mitchell's handling [of the Fortas case] was."[53] When Douglas Kiker reported on NBC that the Nixon administration had resorted to "intense private pressures" to prompt Fortas's resignation, the President ordered a White House staff member immediately to give the newsman an off-the-record briefing on "how responsibly the Administration has conducted itself vis-a-vis all aspects of the Fortas matter."[54]

The truth about the justice was proving far less important to Nixon's associates than what they could leak to the press about him. Shogan later said that the Administration "did far too much, and talked far too much about what it did."[55] At the time, the reporter Max Frankel similarly, but more temperately, had observed that the news media "have had to chase down the rumors, record the allegations and catch the insinuations in dark corners. They have felt compelled to convey the forebodings of 'more to come' without yet knowing the credentials of those who claim a deeper knowledge."[56] Frankel spoke from personal experience. When he talked with John Ehrlichman about the case, Nixon's adviser told him that Mitchell was the one who could direct him toward "more" on Fortas. Would the administration discourage reporters "from trying" to learn more? Frankel asked. Ehrlichman replied, "I never discourage you guys from trying to do better."[57]

RESIGNATION

Spurred by the Nixon Administration, the press hounded Fortas. On Thursday, May 8, the justice addressed an enthusiastic crowd of about 1300 people at Northeastern University on the subject of "the generations." The justice often delivered this conciliatory and uplifting speech on college campuses. "These days we hear so much about radicalism and riot on the campuses that we're all in danger of utter confusion," Fortas began. "Some people, indeed, regard a visit to a college like a safari to a land inhabited by long-haired, long-fanged, unkempt beasts who are ready to attack anybody wearing a blue suit and necktie. All of us know better." The justice said he understood why poverty, racism, and the war in Vietnam frustrated the nation's young. In fact, he and his contemporaries, whom college students now vilified as "the Establishment," had launched a social revolution to cope with those issues. "Most of the trouble you see boiling over now is visible because we—older generations—raised the lid on the pot. The trouble was there all along—boiling away." Fortas was sure that his listeners would not have wanted their elders to shut their eyes to those problems. The young were inheriting "a mess" and they had "a basis for complaining," but they should finish work on the "great, and may I say, heroic and idealistic things that have been started."[58] Though the justice's insistence that the younger generation had inherited a half-full cup rather than a half-empty one was couched in apology it represented the strongest defense of liberalism possible in the face of its repudiation, on the one hand, by the Nixon Administration and, on the other, by the nation's radical young. But as one reporter noted, "it detracted something from the inspiration of his message that when the Establishment's spokesman was finished, he had to be hustled from the auditorium into a waiting car, shouting over his shoulder to reporters: 'No, no, no.' "[59]

The media would not go away. Reporters followed him to speeches at the Richmond Public Forum and Memphis State University. Though Fortas tried to use the press to his best advantage, his efforts backfired. His office announced that he had turned down the $2000 fee he had been offered at Northeastern and was accepting only $675 to cover his travel expenses and his booking agent's fee. Fortas was donating the money he received in Richmond to the University of Virginia Law School. "For some time the Justice has either refused fees or has given them to charity," his spokesman declared.[60] At least one reporter seemed skeptical. Another, who was a friend of Fortas's asked: "What was an Associate Justice of the Supreme Court doing with a 'booking agent?' "[61]

Things were no better in Washington. The media had set up a command post in front of Fortas's house in Georgetown. When Eugene Bogan's wife dropped off some fresh eggs from her farm at the justice's house one day, her husband saw her on national news that evening. Barbara Winslow, Fortas's onetime music companion, had long planned to stay with Fortas and Agger during the week of May 12 when she returned to Washington to perform at the National Gallery. "It was just like a three-ring circus out there," she said. Whenever Winslow and her husband left Fortas's house they were besieged by inquiring journalists: "I remember looking out the window, and there was a reporter climbing over the wall of the garden." Since Carol Agger and her husband had only lived in the house for four years, the trees she had planted around the back of the property were still too short to provide any privacy. At first, Agger eluded the press by exiting through the alley behind the house. Robert Eichholz drove her to and from work each day. But reporters soon staked out their route. "It got so awful," Agger recalled. She told Helen Muller, "You certainly learn to know who your friends are."[62]

As always, Fortas was the consummate actor, showing different emotions to different people. He was tightlipped with the press, though occasionally mischievous. At Northeastern, he joked that he was "impressed by all of the cameramen here taking pictures of me about to deliver an ordinary speech."[63] At the

conclusion of his talk in Memphis, a reporter jumped on the dais and pretended
to be a well-wisher. While he was shaking the justice's hand, he asked whether
Fortas had anything to say. "Yes," the justice replied. "Let go of my hand."[64]
Barbara Winslow and her husband found Fortas the considerate host. Instead of
talking about his problems, Fortas wanted to know how their rehearsals were
going. Mercedes Eichholz had been a close friend for twenty years, and while she
saw Fortas every day during this time, she had no inkling of what he intended to
do. Even when Fortas asked his clerk Martha Field to write a memorandum on
whether he could be criminally prosecuted for nonjudicial conduct, Field
thought he "kept a stiff upper lip. He did a really good job of holding himself in."
But to Hugo Black and his wife, Fortas seemed "terribly down," his voice "hurt"
and "weak."[65]

Strangely, Fortas was telephoning to ask Black to meet with him. Why he
wanted to see someone with whom he so frequently disagreed was unclear.
Perhaps he called Black at Warren's urging.[66] Alternatively, Fortas may have
reasoned that if he could win over his most critical colleague, he could win over
all of them. Most probably, Fortas chose Black because of Black's background. As
a former county prosecutor and a senator, Black had good qualifications to
visualize the case against Fortas and predict how Congress would react to it.
Fortas had known Black longer than any of the other justices except Douglas,
who was still away. He had never taken their jurisprudential disagreements
personally. If Black had been in his position, Fortas would have wanted to help
him. He reached out to Black.

When Fortas consulted Black on Saturday, May 10, he continued his performance. His colleague counseled him to resign to protect the Court. Fortas
answered that if he did that they "would put him through hearings and it would
kill Carol." His statement must have reflected a desire to change Black's mind. If
so, it worked. Black, who prided himself on his gallantry, immediately said "if it
would kill Carol, he wouldn't resign." He now started to back his colleague. He
reminded Fortas that he had committed no criminal or impeachable offense and
urged him to make a clean breast.[67] In fact, though friends recalled that Agger
was "very supportive" throughout the crisis, she was urging Fortas to quit. "Abe,
it's too much," she told him. "The hell with it. It's not worth it to live this way."[68]

Fortas himself was coming to that conclusion. By Monday, May 12, the
*Newsweek* article detailing Mitchell's visit to Warren was on the stands. Everett
Dirksen had suggested that the Senate Judiciary Committee investigate the
twenty-thousand-dollar fee Wolfson had tendered the justice. Congressman H. R.
Gross of Iowa had prepared articles of impeachment. House Judiciary Committee
Chairman Emanuel Celler had expressed publicly his "hope" that the justice
would make a more complete explanation of the fee.[69] "To hell with it," Fortas told
Paul Porter.[70]

Before he told his brethren his decision, he conferred with Clark Clifford and with Douglas, who had finally returned to Washington. In his autobiography, Douglas said he had spent two successive nights pleading with Fortas to remain on the bench and that Clifford had advised resignation.[71] Neither Fortas nor Clifford recalled it that way. Ever Douglas's protector, Fortas for many years continued to corroborate his friend's account of having served as "a sounding board" for Fortas during those two evenings. Indeed one of Douglas's biographers seemed impressed by the description of "Douglas's loyalty during the crisis" that Fortas obligingly provided.[72] Toward the end of his life, however, Fortas told an interviewer that he had made up his mind to resign before he conferred with Douglas. He claimed that he had spoken with his colleague for only fifteen minutes and had replied to Douglas's plea against resignation by saying, "It's too late. You should've told me earlier. I might have acted differently."[73] Actually, he probably would have quit anyway. Clifford, who preceded Douglas, maintained that even before his "long, long talk" with Fortas began, the justice "had already unequivocally made up his mind to resign from the Court. And I couldn't understand why because it didn't seem to me that the offense warranted that action." But Fortas was insistent, and he appeared to be rational. "Here was his whole career, his whole life," Clifford pointed out. Nevertheless, he emphasized, Fortas spoke "very quietly" and approached the issue in the same "reflective and analytic" way in which he had grappled with every problem since Clifford had known him.[74]

On Tuesday, May 13, Fortas met with all his colleagues on the Court. Warren did most of the talking, and he concentrated on Fortas's lifetime arrangement with Wolfson. By this time, Hugo Black and Douglas both knew that *Life* had inaccurately portrayed it as a one-year arrangement, but their colleagues did not.[75] "We were obviously just stunned," William Brennan remembered. Fortas indicated he would resign but said little else. No one tried to talk him out of quitting. "The sentiment was that he should do . . . what he decided to do because that's the usual approach at the Court," Potter Stewart said. "You disqualify yourself from a case if you think it's right to disqualify yourself, and if you think it's right to resign, you resign."[76]

Fortas submitted his letter of resignation to Earl Warren the following day. It was the fullest public explanation he ever gave of his relationship with Wolfson. He insisted that the financier had called upon him because Wolfson knew that the foundation's "program—the improvement of community relations and the promotion of racial and religious cooperation—concerned matters to which I had devoted much attention." Fortas implied that the fee Wolfson had offered him had not been disproportionate to the foundation's projected outlays, since Wolfson pledged to increase the foundation's budget and expand its activities when he asked Fortas to become a consultant. Because Wolfson's "program was a long-range one," he and Fortas had decided upon the lifetime contract, with payments to Carol Agger should she survive her husband. After attending a trustees' meeting in June 1966, Fortas had decided to terminate his association with the foundation because he was so busy and because "I had also learned shortly before informing the Foundation of my decision to terminate the arrangement, that the SEC had referred Mr. Wolfson's file to the Department of Justice for consideration as to criminal prosecution." When he wrote Wolfson canceling the arrangement on June 21, 1966, however, he cited the "burden of Court work" as his only reason. Though Fortas told Barbara Winslow he had retained the check until December because he wanted to return it personally to Wolfson with his thanks,[77] his letter to Warren implied that he held on to the check for so long because he contemplated keeping it. After Wolfson's indictments in the autumn, he wrote, "I concluded that because of the developments which had taken place, the services which I had performed should be treated as a contribution to the Foundation."[78]

"There has been no wrongdoing on my part," Fortas insisted. Wolfson had sent him material relating to his problems on occasion, but the financier had sent material to "many other people" as well. "I have not interceded or taken part in any legal, administrative or judicial matter affecting Mr. Wolfson or anyone associated with him." Still, Fortas believed he had to resign. "So far as I am concerned, the welfare and maximum effectiveness of the Court to perform its critical role in our system of government are factors that are paramount to all others. It is this consideration that prompts my resignation which, I hope, by terminating the public controversy, will permit the Court to proceed with its work."[79] He observed to a reporter that "there wasn't any choice for a man of conscience."[80]

Although his desire to shield the Court partially explained his resolve, other reasons were probably more important. "I resigned to save Douglas," he explained later.[81] If that was Fortas's primary motivation, his act was wasted. "Douglas is next," Strom Thurmond announced the following month.[82] Congress dogged Douglas about his relationship with the Parvin Foundation for the rest of the year and concluded that no grounds for impeachment existed only after a House subcommittee had completed an extensive investigation in 1970. Fortas's protectiveness toward Carol Agger and the law firm he had so painstakingly built contributed to his decision. The grand jury did not indict Porter and Berger. There were no grounds. But that might not have dissuaded the Nixon administration from harassing the firm until Fortas submitted his resignation. Carol Agger, who considered her law practice her life,[83] might have been ruined in the process. There was also his own future to consider. Fortas told Clark Clifford he had received a message from the Nixon administration that if he did not resign, it would institute criminal proceedings against him, and Clifford thought "that concerned him quite deeply."[84] The precise content and source of this message remain unclear. Fortas may have been referring to a newspaper report that the Justice Department was investigating whether he had violated two statutes, or he may have been sent a more direct threat. In any case, resignation seemed preferable to criminal charges and possibly imprisonment.

The embarrassing rumors that the administration, Congress, and the media were circulating about Fortas may also have convinced him that self-preservation demanded resignation. As J. Edgar Hoover had anticipated, Congress had jumped on the justice's reported enthusiasm for tax shelters.[85] Fred Graham reported that while he was in private practice, Fortas once had contacted the chairman of the Securities and Exchange Commission on behalf of a client, Texas executive James P. Ling. By Graham's account, Fortas had performed the role of Edwin Pauley, advising that Ling be accorded better treatment because of his large contributions to the Democratic Party.[86] Fortas telephoned Graham to deny the story, but the reporter stood firm. The most Graham would concede was that he had incorrectly identified in print the SEC individual he alleged Fortas had approached.[87] Other gossip was more startling. No one who knew of Fortas's enthusiastic heterosexuality would ever have accused him of homosexuality, but Graham and Lambert were told, presumably by sources within the government who offered to "bootleg" the information "out of the FBI", that the FBI had a morals file on Fortas that included allegations he had once been involved in a sexual relationship with a teenage boy.[88] Regardless of their truth, such stories were damaging.

Ironically, the Nixon administration considered Fortas's resignation untimely. The President planned to give a speech to the nation on Vietnam that night and wanted nothing to distract attention from it. When Earl Warren telephoned Nixon on the afternoon of May 14 to say that the justice was quitting, the President informed him that he would not release the two-sentence resignation letter Fortas had sent to the White House and the copy of the letter to Warren the justice had enclosed until the following day. When Fortas heard that news, the chief justice told the President, he asked "if he may be advised shortly before the release in order that he might inform President Johnson before he hears it on the radio. I would appreciate it if this could be done."[89]

Johnson had remained in the background during the crisis. He had known nothing about Fortas's relationship with Wolfson, and Lady Bird Johnson described the news as "a painful surprise. Not that in my opinion he had done anything wrong, but just that he [Fortas] was going to be hurt more from another quarter." She did not think that Fortas spoke with her husband during this time, and the former President issued no declaration of support. Though her husband would not have believed a statement would do "any good," she said, ". . . he certainly would have expressed himself warmly and fondly" had he been asked to do so.[90]

Like others, then, Lyndon Johnson saw his friend's troubles unfold in the media. The justice's hope to warn him in advance of his resignation probably remained unrealized. When Fortas awakened on May 15, he learned that a story in the *Los Angeles Times* described his lifetime contract with Wolfson and noted that the Justice Department was interpreting documents in its possession "to mean that Fortas appeared to be willing to assist Wolfson in a Securities and Exchange Commission investigation of the financier."[91] Fortas telephoned the Court's press officer at 8:45 A.M. and precipitately ordered him to release the news of his resignation. As the President was supposed to acknowledge a resignation before the public learned of it elsewhere, Fortas's action was a breach of protocol.[92] Given the shabby way the Nixon administration had treated him, that must have seemed unimportant. At least this way he would have his statement on record before the Justice Department could leak any more information about him.

Lyndon Johnson did not take the news well. "I made him take the justiceship," he said. "In that way, I ruined his life."[93]

## "AS IF AN AUTOMOBILE HIT ME"

Even for those who saw Fortas as a victim of political circumstance, one question remained. Why had he negotiated a lifetime contract with Louis Wolfson? Fortas later said that he entered into the arrangement with Wolfson to prevent "dying on the bench, to get away from that isolation. . . . That's why I got involved with that board."[94] By itself, that seemed an unlikely explanation. At the time that Fortas agreed to become a consultant, he had been on the Court for less than three weeks. Carol Agger recalled that he found his new job difficult at the outset, and one of Fortas's cousins agreed that during this time he was "preoccupied with grappling with his new life as a member of the Court."[95] Indeed this may have been the period when he found the Court's work most challenging. Still, there was an element of truth to his statement. In part, his association with Wolfson reflected his desire to remain active in social welfare law in a nonjudicial capacity, just as his American University course did. Fortas considered Wolfson respectable, as he thought his clients were always right. He agreed to work with him chiefly because he wanted to supplement his income, and focusing on issues that continued to interest him seemed a good way of accomplishing that objective.

Why did he want to supplement his income? Many thought he was greedy.

Thus the standard explanation: obsessed with money, Fortas had been unable to adjust to a Supreme Court justice's salary.[96] His lifestyle gave that theory credibility. Although he did not live ostentatiously by the standards of New York or Los Angeles, he seemed to flaunt his wealth in a town where so many lived on government salaries. Fortas had given his wife a Rolls-Royce, and though he sat up front with his driver "because he detested the distinction" between passenger and chauffeur that riding in back would have symbolized,[97] many viewed the car as evidence of his imagined excesses. This interpretation particularly appealed to liberals who might otherwise have admired Fortas. "There is simply no blinking the fact that he deliberately chose to flout the principle, so crucial to the integrity of law, that a judge must avoid any entanglement, political or financial, that might render his decisions anything less than disinterested," Vincent Blasi of Columbia Law School wrote in the *New York Times* nearly twenty years after Fortas's resignation. "I still harbor anger for the man who squandered the opportunity to lead the Court in directions different from and better than those it has taken since he properly was forced to resign. Fortas paid a price for his greed, but so did the nation."[98]

Though there was reason for irritation with Fortas—for his agreement with Louis Wolfson, like his relationship with Lyndon Johnson, hurt the Court by tarnishing its image as an institution that provided "equal justice under law" and discredited the liberalism with which Fortas was identified as well—the explanation that avarice motivated him seems implausible. As one friend said, $20,000 a year was not "real money" to a person in Fortas's position.[99] Fortas's behavior more likely reflected his and his wife's fear of poverty. In the 1960s few lawyers had retirement plans, and a Supreme Court justice's pension was small. Fortas was accustomed to seeing big money, but he worried about steady money. His wife did, too. Though she was eminently capable of taking care of herself financially, neither of them seemed to realize it. Obviously, Fortas viewed his contract with Wolfson as an annuity for them both. One colleague thought he had always been "driven by his insecurity. That was the only flaw he had in my judgment."[100] It was one which many who had grown up during the Depression shared. The essential lesson of the Crash was the fragility of good fortune. Many worried about money ever after. Indeed one writer thought that the Depression had left an "invisible scar" on the American people.[101] Nevertheless, the reasonably prudent individual—the pillar of lawyers' hypotheticals about human behavior—would not have accepted a yearly retainer from Louis Wolfson for life under the circumstances that Fortas did.

Insecurity may have moved the justice, but his arrangement with Wolfson reflected insensitivity and arrogance. "When a man goes into the White House, he forgets who he is and feels he can do no wrong," Fortas once said of Richard

Nixon.[102] Without having become President, Fortas had come to share that assurance. On the night of his resignation, Eric Sevareid eulogized the former justice on the national news. Fortas, he pointed out, was "one of those rather few men who went to the high court directly from the top layer of the Washington legal governmental complex; there had been years of easy familiarity with powerful political leaders, the press, the country's biggest clients, the court justices themselves." He continued: "Clearly it never occurred to him that anyone could question his personal probity. Clearly, his habits and reflexes prevented him from immediately taking the veil upon entering the Court which the people think of as a kind of monastic order. This may help to explain, if not to justify." Fortas's behavior also reflected his rise to power at an early age. Sevareid was told that Lyndon Johnson thought his interpretation was exactly right, and it so moved Carol Agger that when she later tried to thank the newscaster for his statement, she began crying.[103]

Fortas, who had kept so many clients out of trouble, had not considered how his agreement with Wolfson would be perceived by the public. Even when it was all over, he still did not realize the impropriety of his behavior. "It's just as if an automobile hit me as I stepped off the curb," he told a journalist.[104] Fortas implied that anyone could have suffered his fate, but he would not have let it befall anyone he represented; he would never have permitted his clients to follow his example. Meticulous about the affairs of others, Fortas was reckless about his own.

In the end, his fall mirrored Lyndon Johnson's. There was a curious parallel: both wanted too much. In an effort to preserve domestic reform while persevering in Vietnam, Johnson lied to the American people about the war and consequently lost his power. In his attempt to combine doing good with making good, Fortas entered into a contractual arrangement that he unsuccessfully tried to keep secret and that in time forced his return to private life. It was almost as if neither man could accept being considered an insider; both were driven to destroy their own credibility. "The stakes were not as grand," Robert Burt reflected, "the stage was not the entire world for Fortas as it was for Johnson: but I would say that Wolfson was Fortas's Vietnam war."[105] Both Fortas and Johnson were scarred by the secretiveness that had helped them rise to power.

## CHAPTER 17

# "Suddenly Everything Seems Old-Fashioned"

D O YOU THINK ABE IS RUINED?," CAROL AGGER ASKED A FRIEND OF Lyndon Johnson's. "I don't think he's ruined," was the reply. "I think he's hurt."[1] That assessment proved correct. Public life had damaged Fortas, and the year following his resignation held an equally bad blow for him. Still, between 1970 and his death in 1982 he "came back."[2]

### EXILE

Though Fortas would not admit wrongdoing at the time of his resignation, in the days that followed he seemed to realize he had made a mistake. He was chastened. He reached out to people as he had rarely done in the past.[3] Few responded. Since no one knew of the role the Nixon administration had played in engineering his fall, Fortas seemed entirely to blame for his troubles. Washington treated Fortas "like a leper," one friend recalled. "Every group that treasured Abe felt they had been done in," another said. Fellow Jews, liberals, and lawyers shunned him.[4] Within a week of his resignation the American Bar Association announced that Fortas's relationship with Wolfson was contrary to the provision in the canons of judicial ethics that a judge's conduct must be free of the appearance of impropriety. Indeed his actions led the association to revamp its canon of judicial ethics in an attempt to deter judges from accepting outside income.[5]

A few people tried to help him. Musicians rallied. Isaac Stern, Walter Trampler, and Eugene Istomin showed their friendship by playing music with

379

Fortas as frequently as they could. "What can I do?" Joseph Hirshhorn asked
Mercedes Eichholz. She suggested that the art collector lend Fortas his home in
Cap d'Antibes, where he could obtain some relief from the press. Hirshhorn
enthusiastically agreed, but Carol Agger, who hated airplanes, initially resisted.
"You have to do this to save Abe," Eichholz told her closest friend. "He's just
about at the end of the road." Fortas, Agger, and the Paul Porters soon left for two
weeks in Europe.[6]

Fortas's fall left his other former partner "heartbroken." When Eugene Rostow dropped by to commiserate, Thurman Arnold acted as if he were in mourning. He believed Fortas had made an error in judgment, but Arnold remained
loyal to his friend.[7] In fact, while Fortas and Porter were in Europe, Arnold
worked on a project he had begun the day after his friend resigned: finding Fortas
a job. On May 16 Arnold wrote the former justice that "Paul has just left the
office to tell you of our irrevocable decision to welcome you back to the firm."
Intended "to celebrate that occasion," Arnold's letter lavished praise upon Fortas.
"I came down to the office this morning with all my worries and cares rolled away,
with a feeling of triumph. Never in my long experience with you have I ever been
so proud of being your friend and associate. Your support of the Court which was
under heavy artillery fire was magnificent." In his characteristically offbeat
manner, Arnold predicted that Fortas's resignation would actually increase his
historical stature: "You have been a great credit to the profession and the Court,
and your manner of leaving the Court will insure you recognition which you
might have missed if you had just kept on writing opinions." As he had read
Fortas's letter to Earl Warren and his interviews with reporters in the morning's
press, Arnold said, he had repeated to himself one of his favorite poems from
Kipling, "If," which he set forth in full in his letter to his friend. "This may
sound corny to people who understand why Ezra Pound gets a poetry prize
(which I don't)," he concluded. "Nevertheless, it fits my mood this morning. I
arrived at the office with a feeling of happiness, triumph and pride."[8]

Like his reference to Kipling, Arnold's letter evoked a lost world. When
Fortas ran the firm, Arnold and Porter were at its epicenter. But when he left
they lost power. The other partners were uniformly surprised to learn of Arnold's
letter, which implied that he and Porter could offer Fortas a job without consulting their colleagues. "Thurman must have misgauged something," one of Fortas's
supporters said.[9] Arnold had misjudged the reactions of the young men who had
been associates when Fortas was at the firm and who had become partners after
he left. Now in their late thirties and forties, they had become important members of Arnold & Porter. Two men led a faction opposing Fortas's return, each
with his own reason for doing so. The first, who acknowledged that Fortas had
built the firm, said that he would have supported making a place for Fortas had

he wanted to come back after he was denied the chief justiceship. But the resignation was too much. To Fortas's surprise, the firm had done better than ever after he joined the Court, but in 1969 it had temporarily fallen upon hard times.[10] The Justice Department's investigation of Berger and Porter had hardly helped business, and the partner thought that offering a job to the first Supreme Court justice ever to resign under a cloud would cause the firm to "sink like a stone." The other individual's resistance stemmed from his memory of Fortas as a colleague. "I felt that I couldn't get along with him," he said. "The notion of having a restoration of the old order was not something that I felt was acceptable. . . . I had changed too much, and I thought other people had changed too much."[11] Many others did not want Fortas back for just the same reason. The associates he had trained had eventually taken over representation of Fortas's former clients, who would doubtless opt to become Fortas's clients again if he returned, one partner explained. And the suggestion that Fortas would want it any other way would be farfetched. He had long held the leading role, and it seemed unlikely he would willingly become a supporting actor now.[12] The split over Fortas's return was generational. The people who had worked with him since the early days of the firm shared Arnold and Porter's belief he should be invited back, but they lacked the power to transform Arnold's written invitation to Fortas into reality. After numerous discussions about the subject, Arnold and Porter decided to let the matter drop for the time being in the hope that the younger partners would become more agreeable.[13]

Fortas was soon thrown into extensive contact with all members of the firm. When Frances Arnold found her husband dead of a heart attack at about 2 A.M. on November 7, Fortas was among the first people she telephoned. He immediately came to her house and remained there all the next day. Elizabeth Black thought Fortas and Porter were "magnificent. They would tell funny stories about Thurman and everybody laughed and cried." Fortas took charge of the services at the National Cathedral and in Laramie, Wyoming. He personally arranged for rental cars to transport everyone from the Denver airport to Laramie. "He was meticulous," Thurman Arnold, Jr., recalled.[14]

After the service in Laramie, which the entire firm attended, Porter apparently promised Fortas he would go to any length to bring him back to Arnold & Porter. Porter began playing "hardball." He threatened to reconstitute the firm without Fortas's opponents. Alternatively, he warned that the firm would lose its founders' names, as he would withdraw his and persuade Frances Arnold to retire her husband's. Other forms of pressure may also have been employed. Joe Califano, who had joined the firm after his stint at the White House, reportedly did not originally favor Fortas's return. When he changed his mind, some speculated that Lyndon Johnson had twisted his arm. But nothing swayed other young partners. At a final meeting on the subject in December, they prevailed. No formal vote was ever taken, but it was clear that a consensus in favor of Fortas's return did not exist and could not be produced.[15]

Though Fortas said publicly that he "never considered going back," Arnold & Porter's failure to recall him probably hurt more than his resignation from the Court.[16] For nearly twenty years he had been responsible for the firm's success. His ambivalence about joining the Court had derived in part from his fear about its future. Generally speaking, he bore no grudge against those who wronged him or disagreed with him. Jacob Javits had not given Fortas much help during the chief justice confirmation battle. Still, when Fortas learned that Ramsey Clark, who had always supported Fortas, planned to challenge Javits in the Senate race in New York in 1974 he immediately warned Clark, "If you run against Javits you will make it necessary for thousands of people, who otherwise would support you, to withhold their support." He also told Javits of his "consternation that Ramsey Clark is raising money to run against you."[17] After he left the Court, Fortas even remained on good terms with Richard Nixon.[18] But he took his firm's rejection personally. He refused to speak with the two leaders of the faction against him. "We once sat in a plane side by side, I in one seat and he in the other, and he didn't say hello to me," one recalled. The other ran into Fortas and Carol Agger at La Guardia Airport. After greeting Agger, he extended his hand to her husband. Fortas turned his back on him.[19] Though Fortas saw more of Paul Porter than he had when the two men practiced law together,[20] he rarely set foot inside the firm.

Some thought it strange that Agger remained at Arnold & Porter. Others guessed that Fortas, with his extraordinary ability to compartmentalize, would have urged her to do so. He knew how comfortable she was there, and since he had resigned from the Court in part to protect her position at the firm, it would be foolish to permit her to quit on his account. Then, too, it was difficult for senior partners to transfer from one firm to another, and they needed her income,[21] for in the year following his resignation Fortas did not have a steady job. After returning from Europe, he rejected a publisher's invitation to write his memoirs and secluded himself in his study.[22] He soon began lecturing on college campuses again, carrying the message "that dissent was an alternative to violence."[23] His activities came to the attention of J. Edgar Hoover, who wrote Fortas to express his resentment at the former justice's statement that "unless colleges and universities can operate without fear of police spies, freedom in this country is in mortal danger." The FBI director's remonstrances did not faze Fortas, who sternly replied that he had been vilified by the left for his admonitions against violence, that he carefully emphasized in lectures "my complete respect for the F.B.I. which, as you may recall, I have elsewhere demonstrated," and that he knew exceptional circumstances sometimes warranted the bureau's presence on campuses but that he believed university authorities should always be forewarned. "I have taken this position because I believe that if students and faculty are in fear of a police presence, the result will inevitably be an inhibition upon freedom of discussion and expression of views."[24]

When Fortas thought he was speaking directly to the young instead of to their opponents, he was allowing himself to be more openly critical than he had been in the past. In the aftermath of his resignation, he began writing a book about tyrannicide. As he had in *Concerning Dissent and Civil Disobedience,* in his Supreme Court opinions, and in his lectures, he planned to explore the limits of acceptable dissent against the state. "Suddenly everything seems old fashioned," his manuscript began. "Suddenly, people have changed." The old remained the same, but the young were different, and the change in them was not ordinary. The conciliatory tone he had taken toward young adults in his earlier lectures was gone. In its stead he used their own language to castigate them. At the beginning of the book, he contrasted his own generation's early social commitment with the anomie of contemporary youth:

> We danced together—with the Nation. When it was at war. With everybody else—when we were poor, poor, poor, and President Hoover let us be poor, poor, poor. With President Roosevelt and the Brains Trust and John Lewis and the unions and against McCarthy and against Hitler. We sweated and stank and flowered and swayed, together. . . .
>
> But this is incredible—preposterous. Look at what you have: a nice, exciting war—not too big; one-sixth of the population (35,000,000 people) officially classed as in the poverty group; 25,000,000 Negroes in a historic struggle for their rights; the Peace Corps; Vista; the astronauts; the moon shot; the depth of the ocean. There's plenty for you to embrace. Go to war; join the Peace Corps; enlist with the O.E.O.; go to Mississippi; march on the White House; become an astronaut. If you'll excuse my putting it this way, What's the matter? Why don't you quit dancing apart and grab 25,000,000 people or 35,000,000 or three and a half billion people or a couple of planets or a few thousand cubic miles of ocean—and go to it?
>
> Is it just too tough? Or too big? Or too too?—Or, not enough? Is that it, baby? It's so big that it's not enough? It's so big that only G\*O\*V\*E\*R\*N\*M\*E\*N\*T can do it? So big that it's cold, cold, cold. So big that it can't be You-ness? So big that you have to look for something So Small— that is, for you, yourself. Well, I weep for you, baby, because you won't find it.—It was lost before you were born.[25]

Of course some of the young were enthusiastically undertaking all of the activities Fortas accused them of ignoring. To cite but one example, they had been marching on the White House since 1967, when Fortas had tried to limit the impact of their demonstrations. Fortas's real problem with young adults in 1969 was that he disapproved of their activities. Publicly, he might urge protest as an alternative to violence, but privately he thought little of dissent as a means of reform. He remembered the days when young men and women who wanted to make the world a better place had gone to law school, taken jobs in government, and worked within its constraints to improve the world. But because he knew that many young adults did not share his nostalgia for those days, and many young lawyers no longer believed it necessary to accept corporate capitalism to tame it, he was coming to feel that he and all the liberals of his generation who had given part of their lives to the cause of reform were relics. Fortas never finished the manuscript. He completed two chapters on the propriety of tyrannicide in Greek and Roman times before turning to protest in his own day, and stopping abruptly. Perhaps he realized that his bias made the argument unpersuasive.

The tone of that manuscript contrasted sharply with Fortas's tribute to Thurman Arnold in the 1970 *Yale Law Journal*, one of his best pieces. Other authors in that issue described the new "public interest lawyers" who worked for the poor and for other politically correct clients. They singled out for praise Arnold & Porter's pro bono publico program, which enabled one partner to work full time and other lawyers to spend up to 15 percent of their time defending cases and clients for the advancement of social justice.[26] At the same time, however, they asked whether it was possible to combine traditional private practice with representation of the public interest.[27] That criticism was ironic, as the editors recognized, in light of the fact that the issue was dedicated to Thurman Arnold. The articles about the legal profession that appeared amid the memorial tributes to Arnold "at least implicitly, question his life as a model for the future."[28]

In his article, entitled "Thurman Arnold and the Theatre of the Law," Fortas defended the Arnold (and Fortas) model. Reviewing the history of his law firm, he acknowledged that he and Arnold had entered private practice to make money, admitted that they had only become involved in the loyalty programs by chance, and conceded that "to the new generation, . . . the defense of Dr. Peters' right to a job, threatened because he held and expressed modestly deviant political opinions, may seem like a production of *Lady Windemere's Fan;* it may be interesting and good theater, it may present a human problem, but it's not significantly 'relevant.'"[29] But Fortas was no less critical of the younger generation than it was of him and his former partner. He suggested that its lawyers were engaged in "project-lawyering, rather than client representation." Their devotion to social causes had led them to treat the client as "a technical necessity, not a person whose life or welfare is at stake" and had made them forget their obligation to the legal system.[30] "Lawyers are agents, not principals," Fortas said repeatedly.[31]

Young lawyers who asked whether law firms should represent the cigarette companies that had long supported Arnold and Fortas missed the point. Fortas made his familiar argument that everyone from rapists to cigarette manufacturers to napalm producers deserved counsel. He insisted that clients' conduct or social values should be irrelevant to the lawyer unless he found them so repugnant that he could not bring himself to provide adequate representation. In that case, the lawyer should decline the case, although Fortas implied that such an inability to achieve the requisite degree of detachment would make him professionally deficient.[32] The article was a forceful and engaging exposition of the lawyer as hired gun, the traditional view of the lawyer's role and one many young lawyers were rejecting.[33] But the piece was not shrill, and at its conclusion, Fortas even speculated that Arnold "was secretly delighted by the vitality reflected in the new activism of young lawyers and the new dimension of the theatre of the law."[34]

Though Arnold's colleagues refused to employ Fortas, one public-interest law firm was eager to do so. William O. Douglas was as anxious to help Fortas in 1969 as he had been when the attorney left government service the first time more than twenty years earlier. The justice asked his friend Charles Reich of Yale to offer Fortas a position as senior adviser to an environmental law firm the professor had helped establish. Reich was enthusiastic. Fortas's experience in the field dated from his years at Interior, and though he might not always have represented the "correct" side as a practitioner, he was still an expert. Further, while Reich had found working with Fortas exceptionally difficult when he was an associate at Arnold, Fortas & Porter, he sympathized with his former boss's current position. He believed that the firm's refusal to take Fortas back "went a little too far because he built the whole thing." Reich telephoned Fortas to ask for an appointment and was invited to breakfast, where he set forth the invitation to become a public-interest lawyer. It was the first time he had ever enjoyed Fortas's company. "He seemed interested," Reich remembered. "He was gracious. He appreciated my talking to him. . . . [Then] he never even wrote me." Reich thought Fortas might have been remembered differently had he taken the job.[35]

Fortas did not want to be remembered differently. He wanted to be old-fashioned. He treasured the memory of Thurman Arnold, and he could not tolerate criticism of the firm, though its younger members had rejected him. He told the reporter Victor Navasky that he did not appreciate the *Yale Law Journal* editors' intimation that Arnold's life might not provide the best model for the future. "I'm mostly sorry that these boys were caught in a moment of history where they felt it necessary to make a remark that was derogatory of a great man," Fortas said. Navasky's suggestion that the editors were not questioning Arnold's character, "but only his contemporary relevance," did not impress Fortas. "They could have made the point in a thousand different ways," he replied.[36] When Reich was quoted in the *New York Times* in 1970 as saying that he had left Arnold, Fortas & Porter because the lawyers there were "quite interested in money . . . [and] were not my kind of people," Fortas sent him a sharp letter asking how he could have made that "snide and insensitive comment." Fortas told Reich he resented the statement "because of Thurman Arnold." Reich immediately explained he had been misquoted, but that did not appease his former boss.[37]

While Fortas kept the flame, he looked around for other jobs. Because of his SEC experience, a cousin urged him to move to New York and make a fresh start in investment banking, but Fortas maintained that the law was his life.[38] A few individuals, including Arnold Bernhard of Value Line and John Loeb, had asked him to be their attorney immediately after his resignation.[39] But these gestures of personal support would mean little unless Fortas established a law practice. For Fortas a practice required partners, because he believed that like the Supreme Court, a law firm was a collegium.[40] He asked three old friends from the New Deal—C. Girard Davidson, Leon Keyserling, and Martin Riger—if they wanted to work with him, but they were either uninterested or unavailable.[41] Fortas spoke with Edward Bennett Williams about entering Williams's firm, but that did not work out either.[42] According to William O. Douglas, Fortas even invited Wayne Morse to become his partner but was turned down.[43] The period from spring 1969 to spring 1970 must have been the worst year of his life.

## THE RETURN OF THE NATIVE

In the spring of 1970 Fortas found a colleague unexpectedly. Howard Koven, a partner in the large Chicago firm of Friedman & Koven, had first met Fortas in the 1950s. Characteristically, Fortas was standing in front of a washroom at Arnold, Fortas & Porter arguing with a plumber about how to remodel it when he and Koven were introduced. Soon afterward Koven found himself with a difficult natural gas case and, remaining uncertain about his tactics even after he had conferred with another attorney, he consulted Fortas as a "lawyer's lawyer's lawyer." He spent several days with Fortas, who approved his strategy and made a few minor suggestions. The two men remained friendly over the years and saw each other occasionally. In 1970 Koven was embroiled in a "very messy" reorganization of a company owned by his firm's first and largest client. He needed an outside opinion, and he called on Fortas. The former justice flew to Chicago and for three days offered "meaningful, creative suggestions on how to steer the negotiations." When Koven was driving him to the airport to return home, Fortas casually mentioned he had noticed that the firm listed only one Washington lawyer's name on its letterhead. What was Friedman & Koven doing with its Washington office? "Very little," Koven replied. "I've been waiting for you."[44]

"I don't know what made me say what I did," Koven later recalled. But it was good news to Fortas, who grinned and offered to take a later flight. After several hours of conversation in Chicago, he asked Koven to fly to Washington with him, where they spent another day talking. Fortas wanted the Chicagoan to move to Washington, but family obligations prevented that. Instead they agreed to become partners in Washington, where they would form the firm of Fortas & Koven. Fortas would be of counsel to Friedman & Koven. Koven would come to Washington whenever Fortas needed him, and the Chicago office would provide the "backup" the Washington firm required. Koven was now a partner in two different firms, while Fortas was a partner in one and of counsel to another. Friedman & Koven paid his administrative expenses and sent him associates and partners whenever he wanted help. Koven rightly considered the arrangement "very uncommon."[45]

For Fortas, it was a second chance. "I am about to move into an office to resume the law practice which I love," he wrote Rex Tugwell in April 1970.[46] For his part, Koven "basked in reflected glory I hadn't planned." Hiring Fortas did not hurt his firm's reputation. Instead, the arrangement increased Friedman & Koven's stature.[47] The firm started out slowly, but by August Fortas could write Lyndon Johnson that he was "busy, interested and relative prosperity is beginning to appear."[48] From 1974 through 1981 Fortas's average annual income from practicing law exceeded $390,000.[49] In real dollars he may have earned less than he had made at Arnold, Fortas & Porter ten years earlier. "The fees didn't come in on the basis of $300,000 off the cuff from Philips Petroleum," Koven noted. Still, they were "quite respectable."[50]

As always, Fortas retained two nonpaying clients, Pablo Casals and Lyndon Johnson. Casals consumed more of his time than ever.[51] Johnson, whom Fortas insisted was "the last President we had," took somewhat less because others now handled his legal affairs.[52] Further, for the first time in all the years of their friendship, the two men no longer lived in the same city.[53] Nevertheless, they remained in close contact. Shortly after Fortas's resignation, he and his wife took "a very private trip to Texas," and Fortas continued to visit the former President at his ranch.[54] He and Johnson also saw each other regularly in Washington: on one occasion, Koven, Fortas, and Agger returned home after they had dined out to find Johnson waiting for them.[55]

Fortas was now trying to keep his good friend's spirits high and to protect his historical standing. The former task required the same notes of praise at Johnson's accomplishments it had always demanded.[56] The latter was more difficult, as the war still threatened to sink the former President's reputation. When *The Pentagon Papers*, a selection of government documents that detailed the history of American involvement in Vietnam, was published in 1971 Fortas perceived his job as one of controlling damage while keeping "a low profile."[57] He spoke with former secretary of defense Robert McNamara about the revelations, and he invited Johnson's national security adviser, Walt Rostow, to his house for dinner in the hope of persuading him "to formulate four or five sentences to be used" in a television interview. [58] David Wise, a journalist, wanted to know about Johnson's use of government files in writing his memoirs. Fortas responded with a bit of advice to Johnson's secretary: it would do "no good" for anyone close to Johnson to speak with Wise. [59] Of all the oral memoirs with the former President's associates the Johnson Library obtained, Fortas's was surely among the least revealing, but even then he worried about it. "I have tried to appraise it from President Johnson's viewpoint, but I see no reason why he would want it to be restricted," he said when he returned his transcript. "If you have a chance to check this with him, I should be grateful."[60] And at Johnson's death Fortas was there, adjuring the country to remember the President's greatness. [61] "There is no other friendship like Abe Fortas' and no one's is more appreciated," Johnson had written in his final letter to Fortas. [62]

Fortas continued to see himself as Johnson's lawyer, in death as in life. He responded to Lady Bird Johnson's request that he donate his personal papers to the Johnson Library by gently telling her what he repeated to everyone else. "As I think you know, I have not retained papers relating to my relationships with Lyndon—or for that matter with Harold Ickes, et al. Particularly with Lyndon, I have always felt that my relationship as counsel and friend is such as to impose upon me the strictest obligation of confidentiality."[63]

Fortas also had other clients he did not charge. He made a herculean effort to obtain parole for a convicted murderer because he was moved by the tears of the young man's mother, an immigrant Jew. [64] Koven recalled that when his daughter and the director Martin Scorsese wanted to include the expletive *fuck* in a film they were producing, they consulted Fortas, who patiently took them through an exposition of their First Amendment rights. "But . . . I don't think it would help sell the film," he concluded. "That was the only thing that impressed them," Koven chuckled. [65] Fortas remained involved in Puerto Rican issues and willing to use his influence on the island's behalf, though Muñoz was no longer in power. The new governor of Puerto Rico used him as an intermediary to request a meeting with Richard Nixon in 1973, and Hubert Humphrey was Fortas's messenger to Jimmy Carter on a Puerto Rican issue four years later. [66]

Fortas also donated a great deal of free legal work to cultural institutions. He had continued to served on the board of directors of Carnegie Hall while he was on the Court, and he now joined its executive board. He had been a member of the Kennedy Center's board of trustees since the center's inauguration in 1964, but he had more time for that job after his resignation from the Court. He became chairman of the board of a sister organization, Kennedy Center Productions,

Inc. Typically on Sundays the Kennedy Center chair, Roger Stevens, whose appointment Fortas had made possible and who was said to consider the attorney "the greatest gift to mankind since fire," came by his house for hours of legal advice.[67] Fortas appreciated the visits. "The Kennedy Center saved his life," Mercedes Eichholz emphasized. After he left the Court, his work for the center "helped him save face because everybody knew how important he was to its success."[68] In essence, Fortas acted as unpaid general counsel to the center. He was not shy about expressing his disagreement with its attorneys of record.[69] Nor did he hesitate to express his opinions in meetings. A resident opera company was one of the most cherished desires of the center's executive director, who pressed the board at a meeting to sign a contract that would have obligated the center to assume artistic management of the Washington Opera. After extensive discussion a consensus in favor of accepting the contract developed. Senator Charles Percy of Illinois, a member of the board, indicated he would like "a lawyer's opinion" of the contract. Fortas, who had remained silent until this point, first effusively praised the executive director, then proceeded to give a forceful exposition of the reasons the center should not sign the contract. When he finished, the board voted the contract down.[70]

Once again Fortas was a Washington lawyer who combined causes in which he believed with a roster of affluent clients who expected him to use his knowledge of government to achieve the impossible. He still had influence with high-ranking government officials. By 1970 he was even proving his usefulness to the Nixon administration. Fortas wanted to find a way around Civil Aeronautics Board regulations in order to enable musicians to store their large instruments on airplanes with extra space, so he telephoned Nixon's counsel, Leonard Garment, who invited him to the White House. In a virtuoso performance, Fortas asked for help with the CAB and along the way endeared himself to Garment, who had been Nixon's co-counsel in *Time v. Hill,* by apologizing for not having been "more effective" in that case. Following this meeting, Garment began to consult Fortas "from time to time . . . for private advice." Fortas impressed Garment. "I could see why President Johnson couldn't break his habit of turning to Fortas as his counsellor of first or last resort, even when Fortas ascended to the supposedly cloistered life of a Supreme Court justice," he admitted.[71] In 1971 Victor Navasky asked former internal revenue commissioner Mortimer Caplin if Fortas's telephone calls to government officials would command the same attention as before. Caplin replied: "You don't not return the call of Abe Fortas—I don't care *what* your politics are."[72]

Since the press and such younger lawyers as Ralph Nader had become so sensitive to the activities of Washington lawyers, however, Fortas was more careful than ever to insist that he did not use his influence on behalf of his clients.[73] In the summer of 1970 the *New York Times* reported that he had registered as a lobbyist on behalf of John Loeb's investment banking firm.[74] Fortas respected lobbyists and once told a colleague that he did not understand why they had a bad reputation. As he pointed out, it was less expensive to persuade Congress not to pass a law then to challenge it in the courts after its enactment.[75] Since he knew many did not share his views, he downplayed the significance of his own registration as a lobbyist. "Why in the world the press considers this news is beyond me," he told a reporter. "I assume you know that the Lobbying Act is so broad and ambiguous that a good many lawyers—including my old firm and myself—register even when their communications to Congress or Congressmen are limited, and even where they may be confined to efforts to be helpful on technical matters."[76]

Fortas did more than lobby. His practice combined work for steady clients such as Loeb and Bernhard with troubleshooting for lawyers who needed help in devising litigation strategies. After losing a lawsuit for Hughes Aircraft, for example, the Los Angeles firm of Latham & Watkins consulted him. Fortas became involved in the litigation, which constituted one of the largest patent cases to work its way through the federal courts. Once again other lawyers were looking to him to pull their irons out of the fire. In this case, as in others, he successfully did so.[77] Fortas's recovery was not complete. Perhaps it never could be. Nevertheless, to a remarkable degree, his life was assuming the contours it had had before Kennedy was assassinated and Lyndon Johnson had begun to dominate his life. As Fortas would have put it, "Washington is just too much fun" to remain forever embittered about the past.[78]

He seemed a kinder colleague now. Friedman & Koven regularly dispatched Sheldon Karon to aid Fortas. Once, when Karon was working on a case in New York, Fortas appeared to take him out on the town. They saw the opening of a Tennessee Williams play, went backstage to see Isaac Stern at Lincoln Center, and went to a party. "I realized in the middle of it all that it was my birthday, and he had come to town especially to see that I wasn't lonely by myself so far away from home," Karon remembered. Years later, he could not speak about Fortas without smiling.[79]

Fortas's standards did not diminish. He never suffered fools gladly. When he did not like an attorney Friedman & Koven sent him, he quickly let the firm know that "I don't think he's good enough, and he didn't want to work until Saturday at midnight."[80] Whenever Karon thought he had submitted a final product, he was disappointed. Fortas usually began with a compliment: "This is superb!" Then came the inevitable letdown: "This is a good start. We have to make this sing." The two men would take the document apart. "I think it's beginning to hum now," Fortas would say eventually. "You always used to wonder when the damn thing was going to sing," Karon recalled.[81] Harold Burson thought that by demanding the best, his cousin brought it out in other people. Fortas was determined, for instance, to provide a home for chamber music in Washington, and at his request Burson raised $3 million from the Japanese government as its bicentennial gift to the United States for construction of the Terrace Theater at the Kennedy Center. He did not do it out of love for his cousin. "In my view, he was not a very loveable person (and I think I *liked* him more than most who knew him well)," Burson explained.[82] He elaborated, "I wanted to prove to him that I could do it."[83] That seems an odd comment from the founder of one of the world's most important public relations firms and suggests that Fortas constantly made people prove themselves to him, regardless of their stature.

Though he continued to work "seven days a week,"[84] Fortas increasingly took time to relax. He valued music more than ever. The quartet played at his house every Sunday without fail, and Fortas considered the sessions vital to living. He joked with Alexander Schneider about starting a conservatory exclusively for second violinists, where musicians would learn to play "The Sascha Schneider Shymphonic Shtomp for Second Violinists Exclusively: No First Violinists Needed."[85] Though Fortas's interest in Judaism as a religion remained slight, he seemed more intrigued by Jewish culture. He peppered his communications with other Jews with Yiddish expressions ever more frequently.[86] He served as a director of Israel's Red Cross and in 1974 finally visited Israel. He took more skiing holidays and pleasure trips as well. In 1979 Fortas went to Peru to lecture to its supreme court and then joined his godson and members of an Andean expedition from Harvard on a mountain climbing trip to Cuzco and Machu Picchu. Perhaps life sometimes seemed a bit slow after the excitement of the White House and the Supreme Court in the 1960s, but Fortas appeared to like it that way.

No one could be sure that he did, however, for his core remained hidden. As always, he displayed different personas to different people. To Leonard Garment, Fortas at times seemed "elfin," at others "cold and difficult."[87] He was increasingly willing to speak with historians about the New Deal and Lyndon Johnson,[88] but when a journalist wrote a book about him, he threatened a libel suit.[89] The lawyer who was so comfortable in front of the most rigorous judges was "thrilled" to be allowed to test the acoustics of the Terrace Theater in a performance for invited guests.[90] Clients worshipped him, and students turned to him for advice.[91] Even when he was in his late sixties, women still adored him. He carried on a long, silly correspondence with Abigail Van Buren of "Dear Abby" and made new personal conquests as well.[92] But he remained intensely private. Karon believed he saw a glimpse of the real Abe Fortas on only a few occasions. One occurred soon after they began working on the Hughes litigation.

The atmosphere was tense, since the lawyers who were consulting Fortas seemed desperate. When Fortas and Karon excused themselves during one meeting, Fortas had a twinkle in his eye. "This is fun," he said when he and Karon were alone in the washroom. "Find me another one like this." But that was a rare moment.[93] "There was an inner reserve, and I think the important thing was not to get to the borderline," Koven said. Questions about his resignation crossed the boundary. They were "taboo," another friend remembered.[94]

Inevitably his business brought him into contact with his former colleagues. Fortas first returned to the Court to move the admission of Karon into the Supreme Court bar. His secretary drove Fortas and Karon from their office to the Court. No one spoke. "The atmosphere was charged," Karon said.[95] On another occasion Fortas was standing with the other lawyers in the Court when his eyes met his successor's. "He kind of nodded," Justice Harry Blackmun remembered. "I wondered what was going through his mind." When he saw Fortas at a dinner party soon afterward, Blackmun asked him if he recalled the incident. "I'll never forget it," Fortas answered. Blackmun considered it remarkable that Fortas did not show "an ounce of antagonism or resentment."[96]

Fortas remained closest to Douglas, of all the justices. Originally his mentor contemplated retiring in the wake of Fortas's resignation. "My ideas are way out of line with current trends," he wrote to Fortas, "and I see no particular point in staying on and being obnoxious."[97] But Douglas did remain on the Court until illness forced his retirement in 1975. By that time, most of his colleagues were relieved to see him go.[98] Until Douglas's death, however, Fortas remained one of his most loyal supporters. During the congressional investigation of Douglas in 1969 and 1970, Fortas publicly spoke out on his friend's behalf in lectures throughout the country. He wrote a glowing appraisal of the first volume of Douglas's memoirs and tried to dissuade a friend from publishing a negative appraisal that Fortas considered "fundamentally unjust to Douglas."[99] Fortas was less enthusiastic about the second volume of the autobiography. He tried unsuccessfully to persuade Douglas to moderate his description of Lyndon Johnson, and when the book was published in 1980, Fortas to wrote Warren Burger to apologize for some of his friend's overly candid, and incorrect, revelations about the Court.[100] To his death, Douglas remained one friend and client whose behavior Fortas could not control, but disagreement did not damage their relationship. "We have enjoyed the kind of friendship which people these days have mostly forgotten," Douglas told Fortas in 1979.[101]

Though Fortas was regularly invited to functions involving the Court as a body, he kept a lower profile where that institution was concerned than most former justices.[102] In 1971 Chief Justice Burger appointed a prominent committee of lawyers and law professors headed by Paul Freund of Harvard to examine ways of relieving the Court's workload. The Freund Report, delivered in the following year, proposed the establishment of a national court of appeals that would screen petitions for review submitted to the Supreme Court. Retired chief justice Earl Warren bitterly denounced the proposal, and Douglas, who condemned the Freund Report as "a beginning of the scuttling of the Court," wanted Fortas to do so too. [103] But Fortas was reluctant. Privately, he made it clear that he considered the proposal "ill-advised and extremely unwise," and contemptuously remarked that it originated out of "the distress of new Justices who had not yet gone around the bases." [104] But he expressed that alarm in a very polite letter to Chief Justice Burger. [105] While a friendly private letter detailing his own views represented a fundamental element of the Fortas style, part of his approach in this instance derived from the particular circumstances. "I have been a bit reluctant to engage in the controversy because of some sensitivity—perhaps unwarranted—about seeming to argue publicly with the Chief Justice," he admitted. [106]

While Fortas remained in the Court's shadows, his reputation as a justice was improving. In 1972 sixty-five leading legal scholars were asked to identify past Supreme Court justices as *great, near great, average, below average,* or *failure.* They ranked Fortas *near great,* a category that included William Howard Taft, Robert Jackson, the younger John Harlan, William O. Douglas, and William Brennan. Only a dozen justices in the Court's entire history were ranked as *great,* and of all the justices in the top two categories, Fortas had been at the Court the shortest period. [107] "Did you ever wonder what they would have done to you if you'd only been average?" a friend asked Fortas. In replying, Fortas joked that he would have had a chance at being "acceptable" only if he had been "subnormal." [108]

Despite that acclaim for his work, his resignation continued to haunt him. Though he said he had been "going to seed" on the Court, [109] he would have preferred to leave the job some other way. Nevertheless, his relationship with Louis Wolfson remained cordial, and in 1973 the financier once again offered him $20,000 annually to become a consultant on issues of crime and juvenile delinquency to the Wolfson Family Foundation. The arrangement would be on a year-to-year basis instead of for life. Fortas declined in a cordial letter explaining that he was deeply moved but too busy. [110] Four years later, Fortas awoke on a Sunday morning to find that reporter Bob Woodward had provided further details of his earlier relationship with Wolfson in the *Washington Post.* Relying on a transcript of a conversation between Fortas and Wolfson in 1971 that the financier had taped, Woodward claimed that the justice had been "very heavily involved in advising Wolfson on legal difficulties he had with the Securities and Exchange Commission," and that he had agreed to intervene on the millionaire's behalf with the chairman of the SEC but had been too fearful of the consequences to follow through on his promise.[111]

The story's appearance was the fault of one of Wolfson's attorneys. He had hoped that Woodward would write a story about the Justice Department's leaks to *Life* magazine in 1969 about Fortas's relationship with Wolfson that might help the financier to obtain a reversal of his convictions. In the process of courting the reporter, he had given him "a background file on Wolfson" in which he had "inadvertently" included the transcript in question.[112] His blunder further damaged Fortas's reputation. Instead of declaring that the mystery of whether the justice had spoken with the SEC chair had finally been solved with a negative answer, newspapers seemed more interested in the fact that the justice had contemplated intervention on the financier's behalf.[113]

In view of the circumstances of his departure from the Court, Fortas might have been expected to feel great hostility toward Richard Nixon. His wife did. In 1972 when the Democrats veered to the left and selected as their presidential candidate Senator George McGovern, who had bitterly criticized Johnson's policies in Vietnam, Carol Agger donated five hundred dollars to the senator's campaign. "Some years ago I evolved Agger's Law #1 of Politico-Dynamics," she explained to a friend when she mailed in her check for Richard Nixon's opponent. "In laymen's terms," the law stated: "Always support whatever candidate is running against Congressman Broyhill (from Northern Virginia, whom I bitterly hate), no matter how unlikely the candidate is to succeed, and no matter that I disagree with the candidate on many issues. More recently I have discovered that this Law has a broader application than I had originally supposed."[114] For his part, Fortas publicly branded Nixon's first term as "a dangerous phase . . . of retrenchment, perhaps of reaction, against the amazingly revolutionary change of the last decade," but insisted he did not hate Nixon.[115] In the summer of 1972 Fortas even wrote Lyndon Johnson a long letter applauding the former President for refusing "to join in condemnation of the young people and the nonprofessional, miscellaneous group that dominated the Convention and formed the core of McGovern's support." Fortas was "extremely proud" to be regarded as "a Johnson man," but he thought that "the young people and the nonprofessionals have some points of profound importance; and I believe that, now that they have scored this fantastic victory, they represent the future of the Democratic Party— and hopefully, of the country. I don't think that my attitude is based upon animosity to President Nixon. On the contrary, I think he has done an extremely skillful job. But the future certainly does not belong to him and to the Vice President."[116]

Even before it turned out that Fortas's prediction was wrong, Nixon reappointed him as a Kennedy Center trustee. Fortas confided to Wolfson that the

President's action had surprised him.[117] He wrote effusive letters of thanks to the President and to White House staff member H. R. Haldeman, assuring them both that "I will do everything that I can to prevent the problems of the Kennedy Center from adding to the President's burdens."[118] That did not mean that Fortas placed criticism of Nixon himself off limits, but the former justice took the high road. He professed admiration for Nixon's "spectacular achievements in the foreign policy field" to a reporter in 1973 while simultaneously remarking that the President "was trying to halt—or at least slow down—a vast historical process toward democratization of the benefits of a highly developed society. The question is, can he succeed in doing it without highly repressive measures?"[119]

When it turned out that Nixon could not, Fortas became a constitutional adviser to those trying to limit the President's power. The Speaker of the House, Carl Albert, asked Fortas in 1973 to become a member of "an informal advisory group to work on constitutional questions involving problems the Congress is having with the President."[120] In that capacity, Fortas strenuously objected when his onetime nemesis, Sam Ervin, introduced a bill requiring the President to report all impoundments of funds to Congress and establishing machinery by which Congress could override Nixon's action. Fortas's objection related to the bill's implicit acknowledgement that the President could nullify a congressional authorization to obligate funds or could refuse to spend monies appropriated by Congress. "I believe that there is no justification in principle on the basis of our Constitution for such impoundment."[121] When Senator Edmund Muskie of Maine was deciding whether to introduce a bill that would have enabled Congress to make public certain matters which the Executive Branch had designated as secret, his staff also consulted Fortas about the limits of executive privilege.[122]

As Watergate unfolded, Fortas hoped that Nixon would follow his own example. "In the name of God and country, President Nixon should resign," Fortas wrote his godson in the fall of 1973. "This marvelous nation is entitled to no less than that."[123] Indeed the former justice was so anxious to secure the President's departure that he publicly suggested Congress enact a law promising Nixon immunity from criminal prosecution if he quit. Fortas likened his proposal to "plea bargaining in advance" and speculated that it might make relinquishing the Presidency more attractive to Nixon.[124] The specter of impeachment proceedings if Nixon stayed on horrified Fortas. It was, he said in a public lecture, "staggering to contemplate the amount of time that a Senate trial of impeachment charges will require; the inevitable fury that it will provoke; and the divisions, diversions, and hostilities that it will engender."[125] Fortas also worried that "if the Senate fails to convict, there will be a wave of disillusionment in the country, particularly among younger people."[126]

The House Judiciary Committee's hearings to determine whether Nixon had

committed impeachable offenses stalled another project Fortas's: finding a constitutional alternative to impeachment. In the summer of 1973 he had written an
article urging Congress to enact a constitutional amendment that would provide
a new remedy in the event of presidential misconduct: if two-thirds of the Senate
and the House enacted a concurrent resolution that the President had failed to
execute the laws Congress enacted, that he had willfully exceeded his constitutional or legal powers, or that he was responsible for illegal invasions of the rights
of American citizens, "Congress shall, by legislation which becomes law without
the President's consent, provide for an election for President and Vice-President
to be held within three months of the effective date of the legislation." The
persons elected would serve out the remainder of the President's and Vice-
President's terms. Perhaps remembering how close he himself had come to being
impeached, Fortas maintained that the consequences of impeachment "are too
extreme except, possibly in the most flagrant circumstances—perhaps like
Watergate." After all, impeachment not only removed an official from office but
disqualified him from holding any other office of "honor, trust or profit under the
United States" and left him vulnerable to criminal prosecution as well. In contrast, Fortas's proposal would have allowed both the President and Vice-President
who had been the target of such a concurrent resolution to stand as candidates for
reelection.[127]

As he was about to send this piece off to the *New York Times,* Fortas mentioned his idea at a luncheon with some members of Congress. Congresswoman
Edith Green of Oregon called later to ask him for further information, indicating
that she would consider sponsoring such a constitutional amendment. In August
1973 Green introduced H.J. Res. 697, which incorporated Fortas's proposal.
Without ever taking credit publicly for the bill, Fortas gave Green's resolution as
much publicity as he could, making it the cornerstone of a major public lecture.[128] The resolution stalled. Though some members of the House Judiciary
Committee favored the alternative to impeachment the amendment offered, by
the spring of 1974 they had "travelled down the impeachment road so far" that
many concluded hearings on the constitutional amendment should be deferred
until after they had made a recommendation to Congress regarding impeachment.[129] Though Fortas thought they were right, he still liked his idea, and he
told Green that if the Senate failed to convict Nixon, he hoped "a vigorous
campaign would be mounted quickly to secure adoption of your amendment."[130]
As it turned out, the threat of impeachment by the House and conviction by the
Senate were sufficient to convince Nixon to resign.

Fortas might have been expected to chortle, and Nixon's fate did amuse him.
On the night of his own resignation from the Court, Nixon had telephoned him
and reassured him at great length that he had done the right thing. Fortas, who

was contemptuous of Nixon's gesture, joked to a former clerk that it was his turn to telephone Nixon.[131] Yet when Leonard Garment, who described himself as "one of the handful of Nixon staffers who were allowed to remain in the Ford White House and thus escape much of the Watergate taint," asked Fortas whether Nixon should receive a presidential pardon, Fortas was enthusiastic. It was "Ecclesiastes time—a time for repair and reconciliation, and not 'the horror' of a long state trial of the former President."[132] Fortas worried most about the damage Watergate had inflicted upon the Presidency.[133] He continued to speak about on behalf of the Green Resolution. At first glance, it seemed odd that he had written a resolution which veered toward parliamentary government by allowing Congress to call special elections when it had lost confidence in a President. For so long Fortas had espoused a powerful executive branch and reviled Congress. But he was trying to legitimate rather than weaken the presidency. Indeed in the first sentence of a piece he wrote championing a constitutional amendment which would provide an alternative to impeachment, he claimed that "the enormous growth of presidential power from FDR to Lyndon Johnson was a necessary and an inevitable adaptation of our constitutional system to national needs." His proposal represented an attempt to avert the backlash against a strong presidency which Watergate—and, though Fortas would not admit it, Lyndon Johnson—had caused. Fortas claimed that the creation of an easier method of removing presidents who had exceeded the bounds of office might make increase public willingness to accept the inevitable. "It is Presidential leadership that has animated our Nation in the 30 years of our current revolution; and, whether we like it or not, the probability is that we shall continue to need a strong presidency," he said in a message to "liberals" on the sixtieth anniversary of the *New Republic* magazine. "It is improbable that Congress will provide an effective alternative."[134] Even Richard Nixon did not make Fortas admire Congress.

Generally, his beliefs remained remarkably consistent. At the end of his life, Fortas was still railing against the 535 members of Congress for acting as if they alone had the authority to set foreign policy.[135] Nor had his sympathy for the press increased. He retained a particular antipathy for the periodical which he blamed for causing his departure from the Court. When a friend referred to *Life* magazine, Fortas immediately corrected him. "We call it *Knife*."[136] Occasionally he took on new issues. In the late 1970s, for example, he spoke out vigorously against capital punishment, arguing that neither deterrence nor revenge justified the penalty, and that America's discriminatory system of justice ensured that it was meted out to a disproportionate number of Blacks.[137] But he reserved his most fervent political faith for a strong presidency, which he believed represented the last, best hope for further social reform. Though all of the New

Dealers with whom he had reached political maturity seemed to be dying by the mid-1970s, he clung to their principles.

He had little sympathy for onetime liberals who became neoconservative supporters of Ronald Reagan. A Memphis reporter who suggested that Fortas himself had joined that group—the "liberal stalwart during his brief, but dramatic, career on the U.S. Supreme Court in the 60's . . . now expresses support for President Reagan's conservative policies aimed at eliminating numerous social programs"—was quickly rebuked. The incident represented one of the few times in his life in which Fortas demanded and received a public apology from the press.[138] Fortas seemed to hold Reagan in even lower regard than he had held Nixon. He characterized "the Reagan Revolution" as truly radical. "The Reagan Administration's program is not really the fiscal adjustment; it is not a budget-balancing program; it is a program for increasing the after-tax income of the rich and upper-middle class, and depressing the standards of the lower-middle class and the disabled," he said several months before his death. "It does not merely repeal the Twentieth Century; as a minimum, it turns its back on the principle of 'entitlement,' which was recognized and established in the reign of Queen Elizabeth I; in fact, it turns its back on the biblical principle of tithing—which the Bible states as a moral and religious *obligation* and not merely as a voluntary act."[139]

## LAST THINGS

The last case Abe Fortas argued involved Puerto Rico. With the close of the Muñoz era, its politics had become more volatile. In the close electoral race between the pro-statehood New Progressive Party (NPP) and Muñoz's pro-commonwealth Popular Democratic Party (PDP) in 1980 the NPP retained power, but the election gave rise to two cases. One centered on the fact that PDP voters had mismarked their ballots in elections throughout the island. The PDP won a circuit court ruling that contested ballots should be counted in accordance with the voters' intent. When the NPP filed for certiorari in the Supreme Court, Fortas was asked to help draft the PDP's brief in opposition to the petition. He was so happy to "be of some service to Puerto Rico and my dear friends" that he did not charge. The Supreme Court denied certiorari.[140] The second case arose because of the death of a member of the Puerto Rican legislature. In nominating another party member to serve out his term, the PDP followed Puerto Rican law. The NPP charged that this provision of Puerto Rican law was unconstitutional, however, and argued that a general election open to candidates of all parties should be held. The PDP won the case in the Supreme Court of Puerto Rico. This time the United States Supreme Court agreed to hear the case, which was set for argument in March 1982.

"It came as a surprise when the Supreme Court noted jurisdiction," the PDP attorney Rafael Hernández Colón recalled. "I knew I had to call Abe." Fortas told Hernández Colón he wished he had been consulted earlier. He was not certain he could win the case but promised "to do what I can to salvage it."[141] Since it involved major litigation, he would charge the island, but not at his usual rate. "He devoted himself to that case with a dedication, zest and vigor I hadn't seen in any lawyer," Hernández Colón said. "He was continuously calling me to get more documents."[142] Fortas told Jaime Benítez that he did not "recall ever having worked so hard on a brief.—Perhaps because of its emotional background, so far as I am concerned, and partly because of the difficulty in dealing with the Puerto Rican source materials."[143] The brief reflected Fortas's longstanding belief in commonwealth status. In his eyes, the designation of commonwealth remained a "unique" and "autonomous" status which required the Court to treat the island with "the greatest consideration and deference." Puerto Rico had special governmental and economic reasons for holding elections only once every four years. "Its poverty is well known; the need for relative freedom from the pressures of political campaigns in the intervening years is unusually compelling; the passions aroused by the statehood/assimilation, commonwealth/autonomy, and independence/separatist conflicts, are particularly divisive."[144]

The case might have posed an intellectual dilemma for Fortas. His brief relied on an opinion Hugo Black had written in 1966 in *Fortson v. Morris.*[145] There, Fortas reminded his former colleagues, "this Court sustained a Georgia constitutional provision providing that if no candidate for Governor received a majority of the votes, the legislature shall elect a Governor from the two persons receiving the highest number—a provision which would permit the legislature to appoint the candidate receiving *fewer* votes than his opponent." In Fortas's brief, *Fortson* stood for the proposition that "the method of interim appointment is a matter for state decision and is not, within any practically foreseeable limits, offensive to the Federal Constitution."[146] At the time *Fortson* was decided, however, Fortas had objected vigorously to allowing anyone other than the people to choose the occupant of an elective office, and taken to its logical extreme, his dissent had implied that all state officials must be elected.[147] But Fortas was never concerned about challenging the positions he had espoused in previous roles. He did, however, worry about his former colleagues on the Court. Warren, Brennan, and Douglas had also dissented in *Fortson,* and though Warren and Douglas were gone, Brennan had been joined by Thurgood Marshall, Warren's "judicial adjunct."[148] Fortas wanted to carry Marshall and Brennan, and he worried that he would not be able to do so.[149] José Trías Monge, who had now become chief justice of the Puerto Rican Supreme Court and who had heard the case when it was working its way through the island courts, thought his old friend would win the case by a seven-to-two margin.[150] Even the attorneys who opposed Fortas were convinced they would receive at least two votes: Brennan's and Marshall's.[151]

The case was set for argument on Monday, March 22, 1982. As Fortas and Hernández Colón prepared their oral argument in the last hectic few days, Fortas tried to anticipate questions and prepare answers. He was smoking a great deal. On Sunday, however, he refused to work. Instead he invited Hernández Colón to lunch and to hear his quartet. There the attorney saw another side of Abe Fortas. "Abe was playing very enthusiastically. He was very relaxed. That day, the case was not mentioned at all."[152] Fortas's calmness that Sunday was surprising, for it would be his first oral argument before the Court since his resignation. Because he was the attorney, reporters were paying special attention to the case.[153] Though he said nothing about his resignation while they labored, Hernández Colón thought Fortas was "very emotional" about returning to the Court. Carol Agger even accompanied him, "and she was not one to follow Abe around. He prepared as if it was his first case." Did he also know that it would be his last? Fortas twice asked whether Hernández Colón would prefer to present the case. Both times the Puerto Rican declined. There was "no way I'd argue the case with him on board."[154] In retrospect, Hernández Colón wondered if Fortas had a premonition of the end. Warren Burger later told Howard Koven that the justices thought their old colleague seemed "a little down physically and that he wasn't as charismatic and electrifying as he would have been even in chambers."[155]

Nevertheless, Fortas's presentation went well. The justices tormented Fortas's opponent with questions. Perhaps remembering their former colleague's bias against interruption of attorneys during oral argument, they asked Fortas almost nothing. When Fortas concluded, he told the justices how pleased he was to have been with them.[156] "Lawyers on occasion do that, but not very often," Justice Harry Blackmun remarked. "It came from the heart of Abe Fortas that day."[157] Fortas and Hernández Colón left the Court feeling "very euphoric."[158] Later, Fortas offered to bet a friend ten dollars he had won.[159]

Fortas was right. The decision in his favor was unanimous, but he never knew it.[160] He was not feeling well, but thinking that only his gall bladder was bothering him, he kept working.[161] During the two weeks following his oral argument, he wrote another Supreme Court brief. His godson was now in law school, and on April 5, 1982, Fortas sent him a copy of the document. "The final draft of this brief was turned out in Chicago by my Chicago associates to reflect the results of a conference between them and me here in Washington, at which I was largely responsible for insisting upon drastic changes in the prior draft," he explained. Though he admired his colleagues' speed, Fortas was still apologetic: "I should tell you that this is the only time I have permitted a brief bearing my name to be filed without my having worked over the final, final, final, final draft, and I also want you to know that if I had seen the final draft, I would not have, tolerated the split infinitives."[162] Appropriately, one of his last acts was to affirm his faith in a meticulous law practice. That night he died of a ruptured aorta.

The audience at the Kennedy Center for Fortas's memorial service included members of the Supreme Court, Congress, and the diplomatic corps, and a former First Lady. Isaac Stern and the other musicians there, as well as the public servants, had come to pay tribute to one of their own. The *Washington Post* billed it as a "requiem for a friend."[163] Roger Stevens, chairman of the Kennedy Center, spoke first and lauded Fortas's advocacy of the arts. He had depended on the attorney so much, Stevens explained, "because of his vast knowledge of governmental affairs as well as his understanding of the arts—and the artists." Eric Sevareid then talked of Fortas as a lawyer and Supreme Court justice and described Fortas's resignation from the Court as "an act of conscience, proving of course that he was exactly the kind of man the Court should never be without." He praised his friend for his defense of the poor and reminded the audience that no one had battled more vigorously against Senator Joe McCarthy than Abe Fortas. "We cannot explain a man like this," Sevareid said, "but we can be glad he was around." Isaac Stern followed, recounting his memories of Fortas as an amateur violinist who loved music and played quartets with a group of friends every Sunday evening. "What can we musicians say?" he concluded. "How many ways can we say 'I love you' to Abe Fortas?"

They chose to do it through music. Stern joined Walter Trampler and the members of Fortas's chamber music group in playing their friend's favorite piece, the andante movement from Mozart's string quartet in C. Eugene Istomin, Leonard Rose, Mstislav Rostropovich, and others played from Brahms, Rachmaninoff, and Schubert. Mercedes Eichholz remembered the music. As Fortas had not been an observant Jew, it seemed appropriate that the service for him "took religion out . . . and made music fill its place."[164] But what stood out in Lady Bird Johnson's memory was the variety in the eulogies.[165] Each speaker had emphasized a different facet of her friend. It was a fitting tribute to someone of his complexity.

# Notes

The following abbreviations are used in these notes:

A&P OF          Arnold & Porter Office Files
AFP OF, FLMM    Arnold, Fortas & Porter Office Files, Fundación Luis Muñoz Marín
AFSC            Abe Fortas Supreme Court Papers, Yale University Archives
COHP            Columbia Oral History Project, Columbia University
FDRL            Franklin D. Roosevelt Library
FFS             Fortas Family Scrapbook
FP              Abe Fortas Papers (privately held)
LBJL            Lyndon B. Johnson Library
LBJOH           Lyndon B. Johnson Library Oral History Collection
MS Diary        Harold LeClaire Ickes Manuscript Diary, Library of Congress
RG              Record Group, National Archives
WODP            William O. Douglas Papers, Library of Congress

## PROLOGUE

1. Fortas to Peter Lehner, May 18, 1977, FP.

2. Quoted in Bruce Murphy, *Fortas: The Rise and Ruin of a Supreme Court Justice* (New York: William Morrow, 1988), p. 210. In a letter to Alexander Calder (Dec. 28, 1956, A&P OF) Fortas noted that if biographies were "any good at all," their subjects never felt "entirely happy" with them. He explained, "This is not merely because of egocentricity but mainly because each person sees himself in a perspective that is due to long and intimate association and which is never the perspective in which he is seen by others."

3. Stanley Murphy to Fortas, May 30, 1968; Fortas to Murphy, July 7, 1968; both in FP.

4. See Kermit Hall, *The Magic Mirror: Law in American History* (New York: Oxford University Press, 1989), p. 284; G. Edward White, "Recapturing New Deal Lawyers," *Harvard Law Review* 102 (1988): 512–19.

5. Johnson's close adviser and secretary of defense Clark Clifford began his political life as one of Harry Truman's Fair Dealers. In the 1960s Lyndon Johnson viewed Dean Acheson, Truman's secretary of state, as window dressing. Roosevelt adviser Benjamin Cohen and Justice William O. Douglas alienated Johnson by their opposition to the war in Vietnam. Johnson relied on James Rowe, who had been administrative assistant to FDR, primarily for matters of patronage. He had tired of another Roosevelt adviser, Thomas Corcoran, by the time he became President. Roosevelt's SEC chair and Office of Civil Defense head, James Landis, had died in 1964, and Justice Felix Frankfurter was dying.

## 1. OUTSIDER

1. Biographical information in this chapter is based largely on interviews with Esta Fortas Bloom (Sept. 1984); on information in Charles Edmundson, "The Great Persuader," *Memphis Commercial Appeal,* Dec. 11, 1966; and on the Fortas Family Scrapbook. Some of the newspaper clippings in this scrapbook are undated or lack newspaper name.

2. Quoted in Charles Seib and Alan Otten, "Abe,—Help!—LBJ," *Esquire,* June 1965, p. 142.

3. Abe Fortas to Frederick Michael Fortas, Oct. 2, 1978, FP.

4. Steve Stern, "Echoes of the Pinch," *Memphis* 8 (1984).

5. Fortas, LBJOH, p. 36.

6. George Lee, *Beale Street: Where the Blues Began* (College Park, Md.: McGrath, 1969), p. 13.

7. "Fiddlin' Abe Fortas Visiting Homefolk Here," (ca. 1937), FFS, FP; and "DeMolays Danced to Their Tunes" (ca. 1927), ibid.

8. Interview with Colie Stolz, Sept. 1984.

9. "Abe Fortas No Protege of McKellar or Stewart," *Memphis Press-Scimitar,* June 20, 1942.

10. Quoted in James Simon, *Independent Journey: The Life of William O. Douglas* (New York: Harper and Row, 1980), p. 218.

11. Quoted in Edmundson, "Great Persuader."

12. See Gary Goodman, "Fortas' Genius Showed at Early Age" (ca. 1965), FFS, FP.

13. Quoted in "Teacher Leads Cheers for Fortas," (ca. June 1965), FFS, FP.

14. Quoted in Edmundson, "Great Persuader."

15. Edmundson, "Great Persuader."

16. Interview with Carol Agger, May 1987. (This is the name by which Carolyn Agger Fortas was known in her professional life.)

17. "Southside Lad Wins Peres Scholarship" (ca. Sept. 8, 1928), FFS, FP.

18. Interview with Goodbar Morgan, Sept. 1984.

19. Gerald Capers to Fortas, Sept. 11, 1980, FP.

20. Interview with Agger.

21. *Lynx,* Southwestern College yearbook, 1929–30, FP.

22. Fortas, "The Role of Law in the Future of Our Nation" (Speech delivered at Southwestern College, May 1, 1981), Southwestern Alumni Records; *Lynx,* 1929–30; Fortas, "An Approach to Progressive Policy" (Speech delivered at Southwestern College, June 3, 1946), Box 57, Harold LeClaire Ickes Papers, Library of Congress.

23. Quoted in Robert Shogan, *A Question of Judgment: The Fortas Case and the Struggle for the Supreme Court* (Indianapolis, Ind.: Bobbs-Merrill, 1972), p. 30.

24. Quoted in "Fortas Made Hit at Southwestern," *Memphis Press-Scimitar,* July 30, 1965.

25. Robert D. Franklin, "Remembered," *Memphis Commercial Appeal,* April 18, 1982.

26. Interview with Morgan.

27. David Alexander to Laura Kalman, July 12, 1985.

28. Quoted in Goodman, "Fortas' Genius Showed At Early Age."

29. Fortas to William O. Douglas, April 6, 1973, FP.

30. Interview with Bloom.

31. Franklin, "Remembered."

32. Charles Edmundson to Fortas, Dec. 18, 1966, FP. Fortas replied to Edmundson, a reporter (Dec. 23, 1966, ibid.): "I have no recollection whatever of the 1928 speech, but I am grateful to you for ignoring it."

33. "Southwestern Will Meet Northwestern In Debate on Foreign Policy of U.S.," *Memphis Commercial Appeal* (ca. April), FFS, FP; William F. Orr to Fortas, July 29, 1965, FP.

34. "Fiddling Abe Fortas, 22, Leaves Memphis Dances for High Legal Post with Uncle Sam's Farm Bureau," *Memphis Press-Scimitar,* Nov. 27, 1933.

35. *Lynx,* 1929–30.

36. Franklin, "Remembered."

37. Fortas to Allen Cabaniss, Aug. 21, 1965, FP.

38. Fortas, "The Problems of Age" (Unpublished manuscript), ibid.

39. Quoted in Shogan, *A Question of Judgment,* p. 31.

40. Fortas, Speech delivered to the Anti-Defamation League of B'nai Brith, New York City, June 26, 1972, FP.

41. Fortas, Speech delivered at a convocation of the Jewish Theological Seminary, Philadelphia, Penna., Dec. 12, 1965, FP.

42. Fortas, LBJOH, p. 31.

43. Interview with Bloom; *Lynx.* In the summer of 1929 when he attended the University of Wisconsin's summer session, Fortas may have been amused to learn that he had followed the example of the prominent Progressive Robert LaFollette, whose political clout on the Madison campus derived from his organization of the "scrubs" who had been excluded from fraternities (Belle and Fola LaFollette, *Robert M. LaFollette* [New York: Macmillan, 1953] 1:28–29).

44. Alexander to Kalman, July 12, 1985.

45. Fortas to James Linn (quoting Paul Porter), July 21, 1975, FP.

46. Alexander to Kalman, July 12, 1985.

47. Fortas to William Connell, April 2, 1965, FP.

48. Interviews with Raenell Gold and Esta Bloom, Sept. 1984.

49. Quoted in Goodman, "Fortas' Genius Showed at Early Age."

50. Edmundson, "Great Persuader."

51. Thurman Arnold to John Loomis, Dec. 12, 1935, Thurman Arnold Papers, American Heritage Center, University of Wyoming (hereafter, Arnold Papers).

52. Ibid.

53. "Memphis Man Awarded Honor" (ca. 1930), FFS, FP.

54. Edmundson, "The Great Persuader."

55. Thurman Arnold to Leon Green, Feb. 25, 1936, reprinted in *Voltaire and the Cowboy: The Letters of Thurman Arnold.* ed. Gene Gressley (Boulder Colo.: Colorado Associated University Press, 1977), p. 222. Emphasis in the original.

56. He had been surprised, Fortas added, when in the 1970s he had come across a letter Arnold wrote to a friend at Northwestern when Fortas was teaching at Yale in the late 1930s "saying he ought to get me out to Northwestern and there was a problem at Yale because I was Jewish" (interview with Abe Fortas, May 1981).

57. Interview with J. Howard Marshall, Sept. 1984.

58. Interviews with Frances Arnold and Thurman Arnold, Jr., July 1984.

59. See, e.g., Thurman Arnold to Tracy Voorhies, Jan. 4, 1936, Arnold Papers.

60. Leon Green to Thurman Arnold, Feb. 28, 1936, ibid.

61. E. J. Dimock to Arnold, Nov. 25, 1935, ibid.

62. Horace C. Hitchcock to Arnold, Dec. 31, 1935, ibid.

63. Charles E. Clark to James Rowland Angell, Sept. 27, 1935, Box 39, Folder 389, Provost's Papers, Yale University Archives.

64. Fortas to Peter Lehner, Oct. 6, 1981, FP.

65. Interview with Thomas Emerson, April 1985.

66. Confidential interviews 1 and 2. To protect the anonymity of some interviewees in discussions of certain points, I have assigned those interviews, or parts of interviews, numbers. Readers can use the numbers to link an individual's various comments.

67. Information on Fortas's second-year status is from Yale Law School Faculty Minutes, Sept. 27, 1932, Yale University Archives (hereafter, YLS Faculty Minutes). Data on Finlay appears in YLS Faculty Minutes, Sept. 28, 1933, and Charles E. Clark to the Committee on

Faculty Appointments, Jan. 28, 1935, Arnold Papers. The law journal appointment is discussed in YLS Faculty Minutes, Jan. 28, 1932.

68. Quoted in Arthur Sutherland, *The Law at Harvard* (Cambridge, Mass.: Belknap Press of Harvard University Press, 1967), p. 175.

69. See, e.g., Morton White, *Social Thought in America: The Revolt Against Formalism* (Boston: Beacon Press, 1970).

70. For an extended discussion of legal realism and its impact on legal education see Laura Kalman, *Legal Realism at Yale, 1927–1960* (Chapel Hill, N.C.: University of North Carolina Press, 1986).

71. Interview with Fortas.

72. Thurman Arnold, *Fair Fights and Foul: A Dissenting Lawyer's Life* (New York: Harcourt, Brace and World, 1965), p. 263.

73. In Jerome Frank, "A Plea for Lawyer-Schools," *Yale Law Journal* 56 (1947): 1303.

74. Fortas to Jerome Frank, June 13, 1932, Box 7, Folder 184, Jerome Frank Papers, Yale University Archives.

75. Jerome Frank, "Why Not A Clinical Lawyer-School?" *University of Pennsylvania Law Review* 81 (1933): 907–23.

76. Interview with Fortas.

77. Ibid.; see also Kalman, *Legal Realism at Yale,* pp. 115–20.

78. Thurman Arnold to Joe Alsop, Aug. 26, 1939, Arnold Papers.

79. Quoted in William N. Stokes, "Regnier and Stokes—The Chorus Girls—and Mr. Arnold" (Unpublished manuscript), FP.

80. Kalman, *Legal Realism at Yale,* pp. 119, 131.

81. See, e.g., William O. Douglas, "A Functional Approach to the Law of Business Associations," *Illinois Law Review* 33 (1929): 673–82.

82. William Clark, William O. Douglas, and Dorothy Thomas, "The Business Failures Project—A Problem in Methodology," *Yale Law Journal* 39 (1930): 1013.

83. Quoted in *Progressivism,* ed. David M. Kennedy (Boston: Little, Brown, 1971), p. 56.

84. Confidential interview 3.

85. Interview with Myres McDougal, May 1981.

86. Interview with Gerhard Gesell, July 1985.

87. Interview with Fortas.

88. Interview with Agger.

89. Interview with Mercedes Eichholz, May 1986.

90. For a description of Douglas's early life, see Simon, *Independent Journey,* pp. 17–65.

91. Interview with Fortas.

92. William O. Douglas to Felix Frankfurter, Oct. 3, 1932, Box 6, WODP.

93. Douglas to Leon Henderson, March 21, 1932, Box 8, ibid.

94. *State Street Furniture* v. *Armour Company,* 345 Ill. 160 (1931).

95. See exchange of letters (Coit to Douglas, Nov. 27, 1931; Douglas to Coit, March 12, 1932; Coit to Douglas, March 15, 1932; May 13, 1932; May 15, 1932; May 19, 1932), Box 6, WODP.

96. William O. Douglas, "Wage Earner Bankruptcies—State v. Federal Control," *Yale Law Journal* 42 (1933): 638.

97. Douglas to Fortas, June 28, 1932, Box 6, WODP.

98. Interview with Fortas.

99. Fortas to Douglas, June 27, 1932, Box 6, WODP.

100. Fortas, "Wage Assignments in Chicago—State Street Furniture Co. v. Armour & Co.," *Yale Law Journal* 42 (1933): 528, n. 5.

101. Henry Coit to Douglas, July 13, 1932, Box 26, WODP. See also Coit to Douglas, July 26, 1932, ibid.

102. Peter Nehemkis to Douglas, June 30, 1932, Box 11, ibid.

103. Henry Coit to Donald Slesinger, Aug. 19, 1932, Box 26, ibid.

104. Fortas to Harold Burson, March 30, 1978, FP.

105. Fortas, "Wage Assignments in Chicago," p. 531.

106. John Schlegel, "American Legal Realism and Empirical Social Science: From the Yale Experience," *Buffalo Law Review* 28 (1979): 459–586.

107. Fortas, "Wage Assignments in Chicago," pp. 557–58.

108. Richard Hofstadter, *The Age of Reform: From Bryan to F.D.R.* (New York: Vintage, 1955), pp. 316–17.

109. YLS Faculty Minutes, Oct 27, 1932; and Sept. 27, 1932.

110. I have read the Yale Law School faculty minutes between 1927 and 1960 and do not recall seeing the name of any other editor in chief appear so frequently.

111. See Thurman Arnold, "Law Enforcement—An Attempt at Social Dissection," *Yale Law Journal* 42 (1932):1–24; Underhill Moore, Gilbert Sussman, and C. E. Brand, "Legal and Institutional Methods Applied to Orders to Stop Payments of Checks," (1933):817–62; Walton Hamilton, "In Re the Small Debtor" (1933): 473–86; Max Lerner, "The Supreme Court and American Capitalism" (1933): 668–701.

112. Interview with Ernest Meyers, Aug. 1985.

113. Confidential interview 4.

114. Confidential interview 2.

115. Confidential interviews 1 and 2.

116. Confidential interview 2.

117. Gordon Gray to Fortas, Aug. 21, 1964, FP.

118. Confidential interviews 1, 4, and 2. Peter Nehemkis's piece on the Boston debtor court was also signed. See Peter Nehemkis, "The Boston Poor Debtor Court—A Study in Collection Procedure," *Yale Law Journal* 42 (1933): 561–90.

119. YLS Faculty Minutes, Oct. 27, 1932.

120. Confidential interview 1.

121. Confidential interview 2.

122. Douglas to Emory Buckner, Dec. 12, 1932, Box 6, WODP.

123. Douglas to William Donovan, Dec. 12, 1932, ibid.

124. Douglas to Walter Pollak, Dec. 12, 1932, ibid.

125. Interview with Fortas. The individual was Thomas Emerson, who later became Fortas's housemate.

126. Douglas to Donald Slesinger, June 27, 1932, Box 15, WODP.

127. YLS Faculty Minutes, Jan. 19, 1933.

128. Interview with Fortas.

## 2. "THE GREATEST LAW FIRM IN THE COUNTRY"

1. Gardner Jackson, COHP, p. 507.

2. Beverly Smith, "Uncle Sam Grows Younger," *American Magazine* 117 (1934).

3. Interview with Ernest Meyers, Aug. 1985.

4. Quoted in William E. Leuchtenburg, *Franklin D. Roosevelt and the New Deal* (New York: Harper and Row, 1963), p. 64.

5. Interviews with Thomas Emerson, April 1985; Leon Keyserling, July 1985; Ambrose Doskow, Aug. 1985.

6. Jerome Frank, COHP, p. 128. See also Robert Jerome Glennon, *The Iconoclast as Reformer: Jerome Frank's Impact on American Law* (Ithaca, N.Y.: Cornell University Press, 1985), pp. 78–80; Peter Irons, *The New Deal Lawyers* (Princeton, N.J.: Princeton University Press, 1982), pp. 126–28.

7. Interview with Elizabeth Wickenden, Dec. 1983.

8. Thomas Emerson, who could have gotten a job anywhere he wanted, enlisted with the New Deal because of idealism and "the opportunity you had as a young lawyer just out of law school. . . . You'd be crossing swords with the best of the Wall Street lawyers" (interview with Emerson).

9. Fortas is quoted in Katie Lonchheim, *The Making of the New Deal: The Insiders Speak* (Cambridge, Mass.: Harvard University Press, 1983) pp. 223–25. Cf. Bruce Murphy, *Fortas: The Rise and Ruin of a Supreme Court Justice* (New York: William Morrow, 1988), pp. 16, 25, 48, which contends that Fortas lacked ideology.

10. "We were fortunate that the Democrats under President Roosevelt were essentially conservatives who saw and met the need for adaptation of our institutions and rejected the siren call to uproot them," Fortas said later (Fortas, "The Social and Political Attitudes Affecting Washington Regulation of Wall Street," [Speech before the Investment Association of New York, Oct. 26, 1972], FP). See also Fortas interview printed in Louchheim, *Making of the New Deal*, pp. 225–26.

11. Fortas, interview by Katie Louchheim, Sept. 1981. I am indebted to Katie Louchheim for giving me a transcript of this interview. Information on Fortas's first days in Washington is taken from Fortas to Richard Rovere, Oct. 25, 1946, Richard Rovere Papers, FDRL; and Lee Pressman to Jerome Frank, July 19, 1933, General Correspondence, Jerome Frank, RG 145.

12. Interview with Fortas, May 1981. See G. Edward White, "From Sociological Jurisprudence to Realism: Jurisprudence and Social Change in Early Twentieth Century America," *Virginia Law Review* 58 (1972): 999–1028.

13. Jerome Frank, "Realism in Jurisprudence," *American Law School Review* 7 (1934): 1063, reprinted sub. nom. "Experimental Jurisprudence and the New Deal," *Cong. Rec.* 73d Cong., 2d sess., 1934, pt. 11: 12412–14.

14. In one novel by Louis Auchincloss the key assistant to a conservative Wall Street lawyer who spent his time challenging the constitutionality of the New Deal explained that he wrote his briefs before reading the relevant cases: "A good lawyer should be able to find a precedent for anything." His irritated colleague replied, "I hope you don't air these views outside the firm." See Auchincloss, *The House of the Prophet* (Boston: Houghton Mifflin, 1980), pp. 124–25. Frank and other New Dealers operated under no such constraints.

15. Quoted in Nathan Miller, *FDR: An Intimate History* (New York: Doubleday, 1983), p. 327. See also Lee Pressman, COHP, p. 20.

16. See generally Arthur Schlesinger, Jr., *The Coming of the New Deal* (Boston: Houghton Mifflin, 1955), pp. 27–176; id., *The Politics of Upheaval* (Boston: Houghton Mifflin, 1960), pp. 385–408; id., "Getting FDR's Ear," *New York Review of Books*, Feb. 16, 1989, pp. 20–23; Ellis Hawley, *The New Deal and the Problem of Monopoly: A Study in Economic Ambivalence* (Princeton N.J.: Princeton University Press, 1966), pp. 3–148, 283–303.

17. Jerome Frank, COHP, pp. 14, 65–66; Glennon, *Iconoclast as Reformer*, p. 73.

18. Interview with Eugene Bogan, May 1985.

19. Fortas to Rovere, Oct. 25, 1946.

20. Ibid.

21. Frank, COHP, p. 150.

22. Quoted in Louchheim, *Making of the New Deal*, p. 224.

23. Quoted in Schlesinger, *Coming of the New Deal*, p. 77. Wallace made this comment about relations between Tugwell and Peek's successor, Chester Davis, but it applies even more aptly to the situation between Frank and Peek. For a more detailed account of this tension, which ultimately forced out Peek, see Schlesinger, ibid., pp. 46–52, 74–77; Edwin Nourse, *Marketing Agreements under the AAA* (Washington, D.C.: Brookings Institution, 1935), pp. 37–45; Theodore Saloutos, *The American Farmer and the New Deal* (Ames, Ia.: Iowa State University Press, 1982), pp. 62–65, 88–90; David Conrad, *The Forgotten Farmers* (Urbana, Ill.: University of Illinois Press, 1965), pp. 38–39, 105–19; Gilbert Fite, *George N. Peek and the Fight for Farm Parity* (Norman, Okla.: University of Oklahoma Press, 1954), pp. 253–66;

Bernard Sternsher, *Rexford Tugwell and the New Deal* (New Brunswick N.J.: Rutgers University Press, 1964), pp. 194–200; Rexford Tugwell, *Roosevelt's Revolution* (New York: Macmillan, 1977), pp. 122–25.

24. Chester Davis, COHP, p. 291; Glennon, *Iconoclast as Reformer*, pp. 94–99.

25. Russell Lord, *The Wallaces of Iowa* (Boston: Houghton Mifflin, 1947), p. 400.

26. Gardner Jackson to Richard Rovere, Dec. 18, 1946, Rovere Papers.

27. Fortas to Rovere, Oct. 25, 1946.

28. Interview with Carol Agger, May 1987.

29. See, e.g., Jerome Frank to Walton Hamilton, Aug. 28, 1934, Box 12, Folder 97, Jerome Frank Papers, Yale University Archives (hereafter, JFP); Thurman Arnold to Jerome Frank, May 27, 1938, Box 21, Folder 17, JFP.

30. Fortas, interview by Louchheim.

31. Fortas to Rovere, Oct. 25, 1946.

32. Ernest Brown, Howard Corcoran, and Alger Hiss to Jerome Frank, July 21, 1933, OF 1K, Box 12, FDRL.

33. Rexford Tugwell to Franklin D. Roosevelt, Aug. 3, 1933, ibid.

34. Irons, *New Deal Lawyers*, p. 313, n. 45.

35. See Thomas McCraw, *Prophets of Regulation* (Cambridge, Mass.: Harvard University Press, Belknap Press, 1984), pp. 210–21; Cass Sunstein, "Constitutionalism After the New Deal," *Harvard Law Review* 101 (1987): 437–41.

36. Quoted in Donald Ritchie, *James M. Landis* (Cambridge, Mass.: Harvard University Press, 1980), p. 177.

37. Tugwell to Roosevelt, Aug. 3, 1933.

38. Alger Hiss, *Recollections of a Life* (New York: Seaver Books, 1988), p. 70.

39. Tugwell to Roosevelt, Aug. 3, 1933.

40. Frank Freidel, Foreword, Louchheim, *Making of the New Deal*, p. xiii.

41. Roosevelt to Rexford Tugwell, Aug. 7, 1933, OF 1K Box 12, FDRL; Schlesinger, *Coming of the New Deal*, p. 530.

42. Quoted in Chester Davis, COHP, p. 295.

43. Ibid.

44. Julien Friant to Jerome Frank, Oct. 30, 1934, Box 12, Folder 86, JFP.

45. See Lord, *Wallaces of Iowa*, p. 353.

46. Interview with Thomas Emerson, April 1985.

47. Michael E. Parrish, *Felix Frankfurter and His Times: The Reform Years* (New York: Free Press, 1982), pp. 27–28. See generally, G. Edward White, "Felix Frankfurter, The Old Boy Network and the New Deal: The Placement of Elite Lawyers in Public Service in the 1930s," *Arkansas Law Review* 39 (1986): 631–67.

48. Frank to Chester Davis, Oct. 17, 1933, Abe Fortas, General Correspondence, RG 145.

49. Interview with H. Thomas Austern, Dec. 1983. For the crisis in the peach industry, see Nourse, *Marketing Agreements*, p. 166.

50. Interview with Austern.

51. Nourse, *Marketing Agreements*, p. 165.

52. See generally Nourse, *Marketing Agreements*, pp. 275–90.

53. Agricultural Adjustment Act, sec. 8(3), 48 *Stat.* 31 (1933); Nourse, *Marketing Agreements*, pp. 276–83. Austern maintained that his and Fortas's concern about the federal government's authority under the commerce clause to regulate items such as peaches in intrastate commerce led them to develop a prefatory clause that he said found its way into subsequent NRA codes and AAA marketing agreements: the intrastate commerce in the item was "inextricably intermingled" with interstate commerce (interview with Austern).

54. Agricultural Adjustment Act, sec. 8(2).

55. Jerome Frank, COHP, pp. 83, 86. See also Irons, *New Deal Lawyers*, p. 135; Nourse,

*Marketing Agreements,* pp. 275–76; Forrest Revere Black, "Does Due Process of Law Require An Adequate Notice and Hearing Before a License is Issued Under the Agricultural Adjustment Act?" *University of Chicago Law Review* 2 (1935): 270–90.

56. See, e.g., "Concerning the Books and Records Clause in Marketing Agreements," Jan. 27, 1934; Box 13, Folder 42, JFP.

57. Jerome Frank, COHP, pp. 83–84.

58. Ibid., p. 86; Irons, *New Deal Lawyers,* pp. 140–41.

59. Jerome Frank, COHP, pp. 86–87.

60. Thurman Arnold to F. E. Singleton, Nov. 12, 1935, Thurman Arnold Papers, American Heritage Center, University of Wyoming (hereafter, Arnold Papers); Fortas is quoted in Louchheim, *Making of the New Deal,* p. 221.

61. Arnold to Singleton, Nov. 12, 1935; Nourse, *Marketing Agreements,* p. 273, n. 14.

62. Jerome Frank to Charles E. Clark, Sept. 15, 1933, Box 9, Folder 19, JFP; Irons, *New Deal Lawyers,* p. 139.

63. Memorandum Brief in Support of Application for a Temporary Injunction, *United States v. Calistan Packers,* File 106-8-11, RG 60.

64. Quoted in Louchheim, *Making of the New Deal,* p. 221.

65. *People v. Stafford Packing Company* 193 Cal. 719 (1924). See Memorandum in Support of Application for a Temporary Injunction, *United States v. Calistan Packers,* pp. 33–34.

66. Thurman Arnold, James Lawrence Fly Project, COHP, p. 2.

67. "U.S. Upheld in Test Suit to Close Cannery," *San Francisco Examiner,* Oct. 3, 1933: "Donald MacLean, president of the [Calistan] Company, and himself an attorney, explained his stand as follows: 'We are not attacking the Government or the Act. We do complain, however, about the manner in which the agreement has been administered. We feel that the large canners are obtaining an advantage over the small, independent canners. We want to co-operate with the Government.'"

68. Thurman Arnold, COHP, p. 30.

69. The author of a contemporary memorandum contemplating a license revocation case against another group in the peach industry warned: "We cannot be certain that this case will be tried before St. Sure. We shall, in all probability have to contend with much stouter resistance from this Defendant than was offered by Calistan Packers, Inc." (Albert D. Hadley to Jerome Frank, Nov. 13, 1933, File 106-11-8, RG 60). Not until five days before decision was rendered in favor of the government, by which point the lawyers had convinced Calistan to default and surely knew who their judge would be, did Fortas and Arnold wire Frank not to announce a settlement of the case: "Our present plans contemplate ex parte argument before Judge in order to obtain constitutional decision" (Fortas and Arnold to Jerome Frank, Sept. 28, Abe Fortas, General Correspondence, RG 145).

70. *United States v. Calistan Packers,* 4 F. Supp. 660, 661 (N.D. Cal., 1933); see also Memorandum Brief in Support of Application for a Temporary Injunction, *United States v. Calistan Packers;* Irons, *New Deal Lawyers,* pp. 39–40. For comment on the significance of the case, see Note, *Virginia Law Review* 20 (1934): 671–77; "Recent Decisions," *Georgetown Law Journal* 22 (1933): 100–101; Karl Houston, Note and Comment, *Oregon Law Review* 13 (1934): 245–49.

71. Thurman Arnold to Royal H. Balcon, March 26, 1934, Arnold Papers. See also Arnold to F. E. Singleton, Nov. 12, 1935.

72. *Nebbia v. New York,* 291 U.S. 502 (1934).

73. Interview with Bogan. On Whitehair's sensitivity, see also "Text of Akerman's Ruling Declaring Control Act Invalid," *Tampa Morning Tribune,* Jan. 31, 1934. Whitehair quickly came to respect Fortas and later said, "Fortas's thinking machine was so good that it would require two bodies to serve it." The two men became lifelong friends. Whitehair later worked ceaselessly in what he characteristically exaggerated as a "one-man crusade" to broaden support for Fortas's nomination as chief justice (interview with Bogan; Francis P. Whitehair to Eugene Bogan, Sept. 5, 1968, Box 5, Paul Porter Papers).

74. Irons, *New Deal Lawyers*, p. 142.

75. Fortas to Peter Irons, July 29, 1981, FP.

76. Ashley Sellers to Harold Stephens, Feb. 3, 1934, File 106-18-1, RG 60. See generally Forrest Revere Black, "At What Stage May a Licensee Seek Equitable Relief under the Agricultural Adjustment Act?" *New York University Law Quarterly* 12 (1935): 354–87.

77. James L. Fly to Harold Stephens, Jan. 24, 1934; Sellers to Stephens, Feb. 3, 1934; both in File 106-18-1, RG 60.

78. Sellers to Stephens, Feb. 3, 1934.

79. Fortas, James L. Fly Project, COHP, pp. 5–6.

80. Sellers to Stephens, Feb. 3, 1934.

81. A Florida newspaper reported this example. "'Just a minute,' interrupted Judge Akerman, jumping into doggerel." He recited:
"Don't waste any sympathy on the court.
"Shall and shan't.
"Will and won't.
"Be damned if you do,
"And be damned if you don't.
"No, don't waste any sympathy on the Court."
("Government Fights Citrus Injunction Suit—Denies Court Here Holds Jurisdiction Over Wallace," *Tampa Morning Tribune,* January 30, 1934).

82. E. Hood Wilkerson to Fortas, July 4, 1968, FP.

83. *Hillsborough Packing v. Wallace,* File 106-18-1, RG 60. See "Farm Recovery Act Held Unconstitutional by Federal Judge in Florida Citrus Case," *New York Times,* Jan. 31, 1934; "AAA Illegal, Judge Rules; U.S. to Appeal," *Washington Post,* Jan. 31, 1934; "Akerman Knocks It Out," *Tampa Morning Tribune,* Jan. 31, 1934. The *Tribune* editorialized that Akerman's decision returned the Florida citrus industry to "a condition of disorganization, selfish and destructive competition—every man for himself and the Devil take the industry" ("Unfortunate for Florida," ibid.).

84. Jerome Frank to Harold Stephens, March 15, 1934, Box 17, Folder 24, JFP.

85. James L. Fly to Harold Stephens, Jan. 31, 1934; Rexford Tugwell to Homer Cummings, Feb. 2, 1934; both in File 106-18-1, RG 60.

86. *Yarnell v. Hillsborough Packing Company,* 70 F. 2d 435 (1934). See also Irons, *New Deal Lawyers*, p. 144, and "Injunction against AAA Ended," *New York Times,* April 15, 1934. The vindication of the AAA's tactics came too late to prevent Justice from using such interagency disputes to seize complete authority over all federal litigation. See Irons, *New Deal Lawyers,* p. 146.

87. Interview with Emerson, April 1985.

88. Complaint quoted by Congressman D. C. Dobbins, Sept. 14, 1933, OF 1K, Box 12, FDRL.

89. Gardner Jackson, COHP, pp. 506–07. For equally laudatory appraisals, see Frederick Henshaw, COHP, p. 33; Jerome Frank, COHP, p. 150.

90. Smith, "Uncle Sam Grows Younger," pp. 63, 122.

91. Confidential interviews 5 and 6.

92. Quoted in Louchheim, *Making of the New Deal* p. 224.

93. Interview with Keyserling.

94. Interviews with Emerson, Doskow, and Keyserling.

95. Smith, "Uncle Sam Grows Younger," p. 122.

96. She had known Rex Tugwell, for example, since she was fourteen years old. (Carol Agger, "Application for Position," Box 16, Folder 233, JFP). Underhill Moore, of Columbia and Yale law schools, had been her babysitter when she was a child and had taught her how to play poker (Carol Agger to Underhill Moore, n.d., Box 9, Underhill Moore Papers, Yale University Archives).

97. Interview with Helen Muller, Jan. 1987.

98. Carol Agger to Underhill Moore, n.d.; Agger to Moore, April 25, 1934; both in Box 9, Underhill Moore Papers.

99. Interview with Carl Siegesmund, May 1987.

100. Interview with Agger.

101. Interview with Muller.

102. Jerome Frank, Recommendation for Carol Agger, n.d., Box 16, Folder 223, JFP.

103. Interview with Agger.

104. Interviews with Emerson, Keyserling, Doskow, and C. Girard Davidson (July 1984).

105. Interview with Agger.

106. G. Edward White, "Recapturing the New Deal Lawyers," *Harvard Law Review* 102 (1988): 513.

107. Interview with Esta Bloom, Sept. 1984.

108. Interview with Liz Carpenter, May 1986.

109. William O. Douglas, *Go East, Young Man, The Early Years: The Autobiography of William O. Douglas* (New York: Delta, 1974), p. 423.

110. Fortas to William O. Douglas, Oct. 16, 1933, Box 6, WODP.

111. Fortas to Douglas, Aug. 29, 1934; and July 10, 1934, ibid.

112. See Douglas to Fortas, Aug. 2, 1934, Fortas to Douglas, Aug. 4, 1934, and Fortas to Douglas, Friday (ca. July 1934), ibid.

113. Fortas to Douglas, Aug. 26, 1934, ibid.

114. Charles E. Clark to Charles Seymour, June 15, 1934, Box 39, Folder 389, Provost's Papers, Yale University Archives.

115. Charles E. Clark to Douglas, Sept. 13, 1934, Box 3, WODP.

116. Fortas to Douglas, Aug. 26, 1934, Box 6, ibid; Fortas to Douglas, Aug. 29, 1934, ibid.

117. Fortas to Douglas, Sept. 14, 1934, ibid.

118. Douglas to Fortas, Oct. 8, 1934, and Oct. 11, 1934; both in ibid.

119. Fortas to Douglas, n.d. (ca. Oct. 12, 1934), ibid.

120. Fortas to Douglas, Oct. 8, 1934.

121. Fortas to Douglas, n.d. (ca. Oct. 12, 1934).

122. Wesley Sturges to Jerome Frank, Oct. 31, 1934, ibid.

123. Jerome Frank to Douglas, Nov. 3, 1934, ibid.

124. See Murphy, *Fortas*, p. 25.

125. Interview with Agger.

## 3 · PROFESSOR AND INQUISITOR

1. Laura Kalman, *Legal Realism at Yale, 1927–1960* (Chapel Hill N.C.: University of North Carolina Press, 1986), pp. 126–40.

2. Charles E. Clark to James Rowland Angell, May 18, 1934, Box 121, Folder 1251, James Rowland Angell Papers, Yale University Archives.

3. See Charles E. Clark to William O. Douglas, July 22, 1934, Box 3, WODP; Charles E. Clark to Charles Seymour, June 15, 1934, Box 39, Folder 389, Provost's Papers, Yale University Archives; and Kalman, *Legal Realism at Yale*, p. 274, n. 172.

4. Interview with Fortas, May 1981.

5. Interview with Myres McDougal, April 1985.

6. Fortas to Douglas, Aug. 29, 1934, Box 6, WODP.

7. Charles E. Clark to James Rowland Angell, Jan. 30, 1936, Box 39, Folder 388, Provost's Papers, Yale University Archives.

8. Fortas, "The Training of the Practitioner" (Paper delivered at seminar at Rutgers Law School, Sept. 10, 1966), FP.

9. Interview with Fortas.

10. Underhill Moore, Memorandum, n.d., Box 22, WODP.

11. Fortas to Douglas, April 30, 1936, ibid.

12. Kalman, *Legal Realism at Yale*, p. 136.

13. By 1937 Fortas surmised that Yale's attitude made it pointless for him to continue "to struggle for the law-business idea" (Fortas to Douglas, Jan. 16, 1937, Box 6, WODP), and he was right. The business-law program was discontinued in 1938. It had not failed, Fortas emphasized years later. Rather, "it was extraordinary that it ever started because there was first, geographical distance; second, the rivalry between the two institutions played a very important part in it; and third, it really depended on personalities, and for all those reasons it was not at all remarkable that it faded out" (interview with Fortas).

14. Fortas to Douglas, June 5, 1936, Box 22, ibid.

15. Douglas to Charles E. Clark, June 8, 1936, ibid.

16. Interview with McDougal, April 1985. For a different view, see Bruce Murphy, *Fortas: The Rise and Ruin of a Supreme Court Justice* (New York: William Morrow, 1988), p. 28.

17. Interviews with Eugene Rostow (July 1985), Norman Diamond (May 1985), and Lloyd Cutler (June 1985). See also Eugene Rostow, "Professor Fortas—A Student's Reminiscence," *Yale Law Report* 12 (Fall 1965): 2.

18. "Fiddlin' Abe Fortas Visiting Homefolk Here," (ca. Sept. 1937), FFS, FP.

19. Interviews with Myres McDougal, May 1981 and April 1985.

20. Interview with Allen Throop, July 1985.

21. Interview with McDougal, April 1985.

22. Fortas to Douglas, Feb. 8, 1936, Box 6, WODP.

23. Interviews with McDougal (April 1985) and Diamond.

24. See, e.g., Fortas to Douglas, Nov. 22, 1936, Box 6, WODP: "I am pretty well fed up. When I was younger . . . [he was now 26] I could take it, but hyperacidity and reaction is too much. I'll try to stick it out and be sufficiently good not to be kicked out until February, 1938 [Agger's graduation date], but who knows?" See also Fortas to Douglas, April 30, 1936, ibid.

25. Interview with Fortas.

26. Interview with Carol Agger, May 1987.

27. Quoted in Katie Louchheim, *The Making of the New Deal: The Insiders Speak* (Cambridge, Mass.: Harvard University Press, 1983), p. 223. Louchheim comment from interview with Katie Louchheim, July 1985.

28. Interview with Fortas.

29. Fortas to Joel Seligman, July 29, 1980, FP.

30. William O. Douglas, *Go East, Young Man, The Early Years: The Autobiography of William O. Douglas* (New York: Delta, 1974), p. 465.

31. Thomas McCraw, *Prophets of Regulation* (Cambridge, Mass.: Harvard University Press, Belknap Press, 1984), p. 153.

32. Fortas, "The Social and Political Attitudes Affecting Washington Regulation of Wall Street" (Speech delivered at Investment Association of New York, Oct. 26, 1972), FP.

33. SEC, *Report of the Study and Investigation of the Work, Activities, Personnel and Functions of Protective and Reorganization Committees* [hereafter, *Report*], pt. 1, *Strategy and Techniques of Protective and Reorganization Committees* (Washington: GPO, 1937), p. 863–68.

34. Fortas to Seligman, July 29, 1980.

35. *Report*, pt. 1, *Strategy and Techniques*, pp. 184–191; *Report*, pt. 3, *Committees for the Holders of Real Estate Bonds* (Washington: GPO, 1936), pp. 167–77.

36. Typed excerpt from "The Profits of Congressional Investigation," *Chicago Daily Tribune*, Dec. 9, 1935, Box 27, WODP.

37. Fortas to Seligman, July 29, 1980.

38. Fortas to Mr. Farnham, Dec. 24, 1935, Box 27, WODP. Some of the Sabath committee's investigations proved useful to the Protective Committee Study ( pt. 3, *Committees for the Holders of Real Estate Bonds*, pp. 51–52).

39. William O. Douglas to Fortas, Jan. 3, 1936, Box 27, ibid.

40. "False Ideas Seen in Lea Bill for SEC," *New York Times,* June 13, 1937. The *Herald-Tribune* believed that, as originally drawn, the Lea Bill "supplied the S.E.C. with axes that might well be used to chop heads indiscriminately whatever the intent of those concerned with reorganizations" ("Lea Bill," *New York Herald-Tribune,* Aug. 1, 1937).

41. Joel Seligman, *The Transformation of Wall Street: A History of the Securities and Exchange Commission and Modern Corporate Finance* (Boston: Houghton Mifflin, 1982), pp. 190–91. ("Quietly disappeared" is on p. 191.) The Trust Indenture Act is discussed in ibid., pp. 192–97, and in Douglas, *Go East, Young Man,* p. 260.

42. Fortas to Seligman, July 29, 1980.

43. Douglas to Fortas, Jan. 10, 1936; Fortas to Samuel O. Clark, Sept. 26, 1935; both in Box 6, WODP.

44. Douglas, *Go East, Young Man,* p. 282.

45. See, e.g., Fortas to Douglas, April 30, 1935; Douglas to John Flynn, May 6, 1935, both in Box 6, WODP.

46. Douglas, *Go East, Young Man,* p. 259.

47. Fortas to Seligman, July 29, 1980.

48. *Report,* pt. 6, *Trustees under Indentures* (1936), pp. 86–87, n. 179.

49. Fortas to Douglas, March 1, 1937, Box 6, WODP.

50. Fortas to Douglas, Saturday, Box 6, ibid.

51. *Report,* pt. 1, *Strategies and Techniques,* pp. 777–91.

52. Fortas to Douglas, March 1, 1937, Box 26, WODP.

53. Fortas to Douglas, Feb. 17, 1937, ibid.

54. Ibid.

55. Fortas to Douglas, March 1, 1937.

56. Fortas to Douglas, Feb. 17, 1937.

57. Douglas, *Go East, Young Man,* p. 150.

58. Fortas to Douglas, April 29, 1935; Fortas to Douglas, May 1, 1935; and Fortas to Samuel O. Clark, May 3, 1935; all in Box 6, WODP.

59. Interview with Ernest Meyers, Aug. 1985.

60. Interview with Martin Riger, May 1987.

61. Fortas to Douglas, n.d., Box 6, WODP.

62. Douglas to Fortas, Dec. 5, 1936, Box 24, ibid.

63. Fortas to Douglas, Dec. 7, 1936, ibid.

64. Douglas to Fortas, Dec. 9, 1936, Box 6. WODP. See Abe Fortas, "The Securities Act and Corporate Reorganizations," *Law and Contemporary Problems* 4 (1937): 218–40.

65. For the AAA period see, e.g., Fortas to Douglas, Thursday; Fortas to Douglas, July 16, 1934, both in Box 6, WODP. For the SEC study period see the numerous letters between Fortas and Douglas in ibid. and in the Protective Committee Study Confidential File, Box 27, ibid.

66. Douglas, *Go East, Young Man,* p. 264; James Simon, *Independent Journey: The Life of William O. Douglas* (New York: Harper and Row, 1980), pp. 139–41.

67. See, e.g., Fortas to Thomas Farnham, Dec. 24, 1935, Box 27, WODP. Douglas described Fortas, Martin Riger and Samuel O. Clark as "the dynamo of the study" (Douglas to James M. Landis, Oct. 15, 1935, Box 9, ibid).

68. Fortas to Douglas, March 28, 1935, Box 6, ibid.

69. Fortas to Douglas, May 10, 1935, and May 8, 1935, ibid.

70. Fortas to Douglas, Dec. 10, 1934, ibid.

71. Interview with Milton Freeman, Dec. 1983.

72. Interview with Throop.

73. Interview with Charles Reich, Dec. 1985.

74. Interviews with Margaret Rioch, July 1985, and Carl Siegesmund, June 1987.

75. Interview with Mercedes Eichholz, May 1986.

76. Quoted in Louchheim, *Making of the New Deal*, p. 222.

77. Fortas to Edith Waters, May 20, 1936, Box 6, WODP.

78. Douglas, *Go East, Young Man*, p. 270.

79. Fortas, interview by Katie Louchheim. I am indebted to Miss Louchheim for giving me a transcript of this interview.

80. Fortas to Douglas, Jan. 23, 1936; Douglas to Fortas, Jan. 25, 1936; both in Box 6, WODP. For Fortas's efforts to place committee members, see Fortas to Douglas, Jan. 17, 1936 and Jan. 23, 1936; Fortas to James M. Landis, Jan. 13, 1936; all in Box 27, ibid.

81. Robert Kintner, in "Financial Washington—Treasury Aid," *New York Herald-Tribune*, June 27, 1937, reported that the Department of the Treasury had drafted Fortas, who "bids fair to be the leading Treasury sleuth in uncovering examples of the need for 'plugging the loopholes' in tax reform."

82. In a radio speech, for instance, he rebuked conservative members of the Court for the judicial activism realists abhorred when it did not suit their purposes ("The Court Issue," Speech delivered on Station WDRC, Hartford, April 13, 1937, Box 21, WODP). Fortas also undertook a project for Douglas analyzing recent Supreme Court opinions for statements on the Court's function and motivation that might embarrass the conservative majority (Fortas to Douglas, Feb. 12, 1936, Box 20, ibid).

83. Seligman, *Transformation of Wall Street*, p. 131.

84. See, e.g., Arthur Schlesinger, Jr., *The Politics of Upheaval* (Boston: Houghton Mifflin, 1960), pp. 394–95; William E. Leuchtenburg, *Franklin D. Roosevelt and the New Deal* (New York: Harper and Row, 1963), pp. 154–57, 163.

85. Jerome Frank to Thomas Corcoran, April 1, 1939, Box 24, Folder 127, Jerome Frank Papers, Yale University Archives (hereafter, JFP).

86. Interview with Walter Freedman, May 1985.

87. Fortas to Seligman, July 29, 1980.

88. Fortas quoted in Louchheim, *Making of the New Deal*, p. 223.

89. Frank to Corcoran, April 1, 1939.

90. Seligman, *Transformation of Wall Street*, p. 182.

91. Joseph Alsop and Robert Kintner, "The Capital Parade," *Washington Evening Star*, Oct. 8, 1938. See also "Standard Gas' New Chairman Is SEC's Choice," *Chicago Sunday Tribune*, Oct. 9, 1938, Box 38, Folder 644, JFP.

92. Jerome Frank to Robert Healy and Roy Smith, Dec. 29, 1938, Box 38, Folder 643, ibid.

93. Frank to Corcoran, April 1, 1939. "I do not remember any personal unpleasantness with Smith . . . but I doubt if we were ever in agreement on any issue affecting the . . . 'death sentence' provisions," Fortas told Seligman many years later (Fortas to Seligman, July 29, 1980).

94. Jerome Frank to the Commission, Dec. 28, 1938, Box 25, Folder 166, JFP; Draft Memorandum, Nov. 15, 1938, Box 38, Folder 644, ibid.

95. Roy Smith to Jerome Frank, Dec. 2, 1938, Box 38, Folder 643, ibid.

96. Frank to Corcoran, April 1, 1939.

97. See, e.g., Memorandum, "Adequacy of Administration by Roy Smith of the Utilities Division," Nov. 22, 1938; Robert Healy to Jerome Frank, Dec. 5, 1938; Frank to Healy, Dec. 27, 1938; Frank to the Commission, Dec. 28, 1938; Frank to Commissioner Healy and Roy Smith, Dec. 29, 1938, all in Box 38, Folder 644, JFP.

98. Confidential interview 7.

99. Interview with Freedman.

100. Seligman, *Transformation of Wall Street*, pp. 182–83.

101. When members of Congress objected that, although he had been born in the state of Washington, Douglas was really an Easterner, and so did not satisfy FDR's promise to appoint a Westerner to the next vacancy on the Court, Fortas asked an attorney in his division, Walter

Freedman, to review Supreme Court decisions of the last ten years to determine how many favorable opinions on "western" issues such as irrigation and reclamation had been written by justices from the West. Freedman spent a long Saturday compiling a document that showed most pro-Western opinions had not been written by Westerners. He believed that Fortas gave his tabulations to a newspaper (interview with Freedman).

102. Frank to Corcoran, April 1, 1939. Emphasis in the original.

103. Douglas, *Go East, Young Man*, p. 465.

### 4. THE LAWYER AS BUREAUCRAT

1. Barry Karl, *The Uneasy State: The United States from 1915 to 1945* (Chicago: University of Chicago Press, 1983), p. 181. On the Third New Deal, see ibid., pp. 155–81, and Otis Graham, "New Deal," in *Franklin D. Roosevelt: His Life and Times*, ed. Otis Graham and Meghan Wander (Boston: G. K. Hall, 1985), p. 286.

2. MS Diary, Nov. 28, 1942.

3. Presidential Memorandum for Harold Ickes, Feb. 22, 1943 (quoting note from Ickes dated Feb. 15, 1943), OF 6, Box 6, FDRL.

4. Interview with Arthur ("Tex") Goldschmidt, Dec. 1983.

5. Harold Ickes to Robert M. Sperry, Feb. 2, 1942, Box 215, Harold LeClaire Ickes Papers, Library of Congress (hereafter, Ickes Papers). Even Jane Ickes, who adored her husband, was frank in emphasizing his "truculent candor." She said, "It is no secret that he did not like to pull his punches and that he did like a fight" (Jane Ickes, Preface, in Harold L. Ickes, *The First Thousand Days: The Secret Diary of Harold Ickes* [New York: Simon and Schuster, 1954], p. vi).

6. Ickes, *First Thousand Days*, p. 122. See also Michael Stoff, "Managing the 'Official Family': Franklin D. Roosevelt, His Cabinet, and the Case of Harold Ickes," *Power and Responsibility: Case Studies in American Leadership*, ed. David Kennedy and Michael Parrish (San Diego: Harcourt Brace Jovanovich, 1986), pp. 1–28.

7. MS Diary, March 1, 1942. Ickes also described it as being "put into a doghouse from which I was not permitted to emerge even on a leash" (ibid., Nov. 16, 1944).

8. For quote on Hopkins, see Feb. 27, 1943; on Wallace: April 19, 1942; on Henderson: July 12, 1942; on Stimson: March 1, 1942; on Rosenman: Aug. 1, 1942; on Jones: Jan. 4, 1942; all in Ickes MS Diary. On Morganthau, see Ickes, *First Thousand Days*, p. 239.

9. Walter Gellhorn, COHP, p. 484.

10. Arthur Goldschmidt, "Harold Ickes," in Katie Louchheim, *The Making of the New Deal: The Insiders Speak* (Cambridge, Mass.: Harvard University Press, 1983), p. 248.

11. Graham White and John Maze, *Harold Ickes of the New Deal: His Private Life and Public Career* (Cambridge, Mass.: Harvard University Press, 1985), p. 137.

12. Quoted in Michael B. Stoff, "Rewriting History to Reshape a Life: Harold Ickes, the Department of Conservation and the Ballinger-Pinchot Affair" (Unpublished manuscript). Ickes's huffiness was well known. He was invited to become a charter member of the Grouch Club of America in 1939 ("Ickes Invited to Grouch Club," *New York Times*, Nov. 9, 1939). For good contemporary portraits of Ickes, see "Nobody's Sweetheart," *Time*, Sept. 15, 1941, pp. 14–16; "Somebody's Sweetheart Now," Dec. 14, 1942, p. 29, ibid; Walter Davenport, "Holy Harold," *Collier's*, Oct. 11, 1941.

13. Goldschmidt, "Harold Ickes," p. 249.

14. See generally Arthur Schlesinger, Jr., *The Coming of the New Deal* (Boston: Houghton Mifflin, 1958), pp. 282–96. In its "liquidation phase" in 1939, the agency still employed two thousand individuals.

15. MS Diary, April 8, 1939.

16. Record Employment of Mr. Abe Fortas, FP.

17. Ickes to Raymond Robins, July 17, 1939, Box 162, Ickes Papers. Ickes suspected that "this is another case of the President's being flattered into believing that here is a great man. He has these sudden crushes" (MS Diary, June 25, 1939).

18. Ickes to Frank Knox, July 5, 1939, Box 162, Ickes Papers.

19. MS Diary, June 25, 1939.

20. See, e.g., John Flynn, "Coal Black and the Seven Dwarfs," *Collier's,* July 9, 1938; Ickes to William E. Leuchtenburg, Jan. 5, 1951, Box 71, Ickes Papers.

21. Ickes to Franklin Roosevelt, Oct. 2, 1939, OF 6A, Box 19, FDRL.

22. 4 *Federal Register* 2731 (1939).

23. Interview with Norman Diamond, May 1985.

24. Eugene V. Rostow, "Bituminous Coal and the Public Interest," *Yale Law Journal* 50 (1941): 567.

25. Ickes to Roosevelt, Oct. 2, 1939.

26. Ickes to Ezra Brudno, March 17, 1942; Ezra Brudno to Ickes, March 10, 1942; both in Box 97, Ickes Papers.

27. Interview with David Lloyd Kreeger, May 1985. Norman Diamond has confirmed this incident in a letter to the author, July 10, 1989.

28. Interview with Norman Diamond, May 1985. Although Congress ultimately did renew the act, for most of Fortas's tenure it was by no means clear that it would do so, and scholars debated over whether it should. See, e.g., Rostow, "Bituminous Coal and the Public Interest," *Yale Law Journal* 50 (1941): 543–94; Walton Hamilton, "Coal and the Economy—A Demurrer," ibid., pp. 595–612; Eugene Rostow, "Joinder in Demurrer," ibid., pp. 613–20.

29. 15 U.S.C. 833.

30. Interview with Kreeger.

31. Rostow, "Bituminous Coal and the Public Interest," pp. 569–71.

32. Rostow, "Bituminous Coal and the Public Interest," p. 569, n. 69.

33. Interviews with Kreeger and Arnold Levy, May 1985.

34. Interviews with Diamond and Kreeger; Harold Leventhal, "An Appreciation" (Remarks at Memorial Service for Jesse B. Messitte, Nov. 15, 1970), FP.

35. Interview with Diamond.

36. Interview with Levy.

37. Fortas to Howard Gray, June 21, 1941, RG 222, File: Abe Fortas.

38. Philip Fungiello, *Toward a National Power Policy* (Pittsburgh, Pa: University of Pittsburgh Press, 1973) pp. 246–52.

39. Quotes from MS Diary, April 20, 1941. See also Ickes, *Secret Diary,* vol. 3, *The Lowering Clouds,* p. 427; and also see generally Linda Lear's excellent article, "The Struggle for Control of National Power Policy, 1941–3" (Paper presented at the Western History Association meeting, Salt Lake City, Utah, Oct. 14, 1983).

40. Quoted in Clayton R. Koppes, "Environmental Policy and American Liberalism in The Department of Interior, 1933–53," *Environmental Review* 7 (1983): 244. Bruce Murphy disagrees, in *Fortas: The Rise and Ruin of a Supreme Court Justice* (New York: William Morrow, 1988), p. 37: "Though Fortas was not ideologically committed to public power, he was once more the 'technician,' designing the solutions regardless of the ends being sought."

41. Lear, "Struggle for Control," p. 11.

42. Ickes, *Secret Diary,* vol. 3, *Lowering Clouds,* p. 587.

43. Leland Olds, "Preliminary Notes on Fortas Draft for Power Policy Report on FPC Plan," Aug. 12, 1941, Box 108, Leland Olds Papers, FDRL.

44. "Power," *Time,* Nov. 17, 1941, p. 15. "The New Dealers warred, brother against brother" (p. 16). See also Richard L. Neuberger, "Columbia Dam Row Near End," *New York Times,* Aug. 24, 1941.

45. Quoted in Louchheim, *Making of the New Deal.*

46. Walter Pierce to F. E. Coulter, Nov. 26, 1937, Walter M. Pierce Papers, University of Oregon Library (hereafter, Pierce Papers).

47. S. 1852, 77th Cong., 1st sess. (1941).

48. Neuberger, "Columbia Dam Row Near End."

49. Ickes to Roosevelt, Jan. 13, 1945, Box 364, Ickes Papers.

50. Ickes to Roosevelt, April 5, 1945, Box 212, ibid.

51. Ickes to Leuchtenburg, Jan. 5, 1951.

52. Homer Bone to Daniel Ogden, Sept. 9, 1948, Homer Bone Papers, University of Puget Sound Library (hereafter, Bone Papers).

53. Form letter from George Norris to My Dear Mr. _____, April 23, 1941, copy in Joe Smith Papers, University of Washington Archives (hereafter, Joe Smith Papers).

54. Homer Bone to Saul Haas, Dec. 29, 1953, Bone Papers. See also Statement of Senator Homer T. Bone and Representative Martin F. Smith, *Cong. Rec.*, 77th Cong., 1st sess., Oct. 6, 1941, 87, pt. 13: A 4475–76; and Bone to Walter Pierce, Aug. 9, 1941, Pierce Papers: "Mr. Ickes may not be here to 'see it through' at the most critical time of its development—three years hence. What a mess if we saw our power baby slip into hostile hands—and be forced to rail against the change—all in vain." Pierce agreed (Walter Pierce to J. V. Mitchell, Jan. 6, 1941, ibid).

55. Bone to Haas, Dec. 29, 1953.

56. Ickes to Roosevelt, Oct. 25, 1941, OF 2882, Box 2, FDRL. Ickes, "A One-Man Job."

57. Interview with C. Girard Davidson, July 1984.

58. Fortas to Walter M. Pierce, June 2, 1941, Pierce Papers.

59. MS Diary, July 20, 1941.

60. Ibid., Oct. 25, 1941.

61. Interview with Goldschmidt.

62. Fortas to Lilian Syten, Jan. 17, 1942, Houghton, Cluck, Coughlin and Schubat Papers, University of Washington Archives (hereafter, Houghton, Cluck Papers).

63. Homer Bone to Clark Squire, April 3, 1942, Houghton, Cluck Papers; *Cong. Rec.*, 77th Cong., 2d sess., April 1, 1942, 88, pt. 3: pp. 3279–81 (Remarks of Senator Bone). See S. 2430, 1942. Bone had introduced a bill similar to the 1942 compromise two years earlier, but it failed because of his own lack of commitment to it and because of the opposition of Senator Norris and the Northwest public power lobby (Fungiello, *Toward a National Power Policy,* pp. 221–23).

64. Lowell Mellett to Fortas, April 8, 1942, Box 4, Lowell Mellett Papers, FDRL.

65. Ickes to Roosevelt, April 3, 1942, OF 2882, Box 2, FDRL.

66. Fortas to Saul Haas, April 25, 1942, Saul Haas Papers, University of Washington.

67. Bone to Ogden, Sept. 9, 1948.

68. Richard Lowitt, *The New Deal and the West* (Bloomington, Ind.: Indiana University Press, 1984), p. 170.

69. Fortas to William O. Douglas, Oct. 13, 1937, Box 6, WODP.

70. MS Diary, May 25, 1941.

71. Jerome Frank to Roosevelt, Dec. 23, 1941, OF 1060 A, Box 15, FDRL.

72. Douglas to Roosevelt, Dec. 24, 1941, ibid.

73. Edward Eicher to Roosevelt, Dec. 24, 1941, ibid.

74. James M. Landis to Roosevelt, Dec. 26, 1941, ibid.

75. MS Diary, Jan. 4, 1942.

76. Ibid., Sept. 20, 1941.

77. Ickes denied the charge. (Minutes of Staff Meeting, May 11, 1938, Box 164, Ickes Papers.

78. MS Diary, Sept. 20, 1941.

79. Ibid.

80. Ibid., Jan. 4, 1942.

81. Ibid., May 31, 1942.
82. Ibid., June 14, 1942.

## 5. UNDER SECRETARY

1. Interview with Jaime Benítez, Aug. 1985.
2. Rexford Tugwell, *The Stricken Land: The Story of Puerto Rico* (Garden City N.Y.: Doubleday, 1947), p. 347.
3. Fortas, "Check and Double-Check: Congress and the Executive" (Unpublished paper), Box 53, Folder 314, Jerome Frank Papers, Yale University Archives.
4. Ickes, MS Diary, July 25, 1943.
5. John Morton Blum, *V Was for Victory: Politics and American Culture during World War II* (New York: Harcourt Brace Jovanovich, 1976), p. 120.
6. Interview with John McCloy, Dec. 1983.
7. "The Home Fires, Too," *New Republic*, Nov. 17, 1941, p. 638.
8. A farm owned by a husband and wife could qualify for water at up to 320 acres.
9. H.R. 3961, 78th Cong., 2d sess., 1944 (1).
10. "Friant Dam Valve Fills Canal Today," *New York Times*, June 4, 1944. See also "Ickes Accused of Plot in Central Valley Inquiry," *San Francisco Examiner*, June 2, 1944.
11. Paul Taylor Oral History, "California Social Scientist: California Water and Agricultural Labor" (3 vols.), Berkeley, California, Regional Oral History Office, Bancroft Library, 2:180 (hereafter, Taylor, Oral History).
12. Fortas to Ickes, Nov. 10, 1944, Box 258, Harold LeClaire Ickes Papers, Library of Congress (hereafter, Ickes Papers).
13. Fortas to Ickes, Aug. 22, 1944, and Aug. 24, 1944, Box 93, ibid.
14. Taylor, Oral History, 2:180.
15. Richard Lowitt, *The New Deal and the West* (Bloomington, Ind.: Indiana University Press, 1984), p. 224.
16. Harry Bashore, quoted in Linda Lear, "The Struggle for Control of National Power Policy, 1941–3" (Paper presented at the Western History Association, Salt Lake City, Utah, Oct. 14, 1983).
17. "Hawaiian Feud," *Newsweek*, Sept. 6, 1943, p. 22.
18. Quote in Fortas to Walter Armstrong, Oct. 15, 1943, Box 1, RG 48. See Walter P. Armstrong, "Martial Law in Hawaii," *American Bar Association Journal* 29 (1943).
19. Ickes to Henry Stimson, April 20, 1944, Box 1, RG 48; John Frank to Fortas, April 15, 1944, ibid.; John Frank to John McCloy, June 26, 1944, ibid.
20. Fortas to John McCloy, July 12, 1944, Box 1, RG 48.
21. Fortas to James Forrestal, July 12, 1944, ibid. Fortas professed not to blame top War Department officials such as McCloy for the stalemate. Rather, he told Forrestal, "there seems to be difficulty down the line among both the Army and Navy officers."
22. See Fortas to Harold Ickes, July 19, 1944, ibid.
23. See First Draft, Executive Order, ibid.
24. Fortas to John McCloy, Sept. 1, 1944, ibid.
25. Interview with Warner Gardner, Dec. 1983.
26. MS Diary, March 1, 1942.
27. Ibid., April 10, 1943; and March 1, 1942.
28. Fortas to Ickes, Jan. 15, 1944 [A File of Documents Declassified in 1970], Box 1, RG 48.
29. See Fortas, "Effects of Prejudice," Letter to the editor of the *Washington Post*, Dec. 9, 1945. "What happened here, was, I think, to a large extent, the judgment of a single Army general," Fortas later told the Commission on Wartime Relocation established by Congress in

1980. "When I say this, I always try to remind myself, remember Pearl Harbor; remember that it was war, and even as to those whose actions I must criticize, one must be compassionate. I always think, when I think of General De Witt [Lieutenant General John De Witt, Commanding General of the Western Defense Command, with responsibility for security on the West Coast] . . . of something that General Wheeler said to me long ago in connection with Vietnam. He said 'The trouble is that in my business there are no prizes for coming in second.' And it may be that the lesson to be learned after that story and from what happened here is that we should re-examine the authority that is given to the military commander within the United States and the degree to which that authority can be confirmed and circumscribed" (Statement by Abe Fortas, Commission on Wartime Relocation and Internment of Civilians, Oct. 19, 1981, FP; hereafter, Statement by Fortas, Commission on Wartime Relocation.)

30. MS Diary, Jan. 16, 1944.

31. Fortas to Eugene Rostow, June 28, 1945, Box 11, RG 48. See also Fortas to Rostow, Sept. 26, 1944, ibid.; and Rostow, "The Japanese American Cases—A Disaster," *Yale Law Journal* 54 (1945): 489–533.

32. Francis Biddle, "Memorandum for the President," Dec. 30, 1943; James F. Byrnes to Roosevelt, Feb. 10, 1944; Ickes to Roosevelt, Feb. 17, 1944; all in OF 4849, Box 1, FDRL.

33. Statement by Fortas, Commission on Wartime Relocation.

34. Fortas to Mr. Ryckman, May 12, 1944, Box 12, RG 48.

35. Fortas to Dillon Myer, July 21, 1944, ibid.

36. Peter Irons, *Justice at War: The Story of the Japanese American Internment Cases* (New York: Oxford University Press, 1983), pp. 102–03.

37. Fortas to Rostow, June 28, 1945. For Fortas's Oct. 13, 1944 letter to Fahy for transmittal to the Court, see Box 36, Charles Fahy Papers, FDRL.

38. Irons, *Justice at War,* p. 324. But Fahy submitted Fortas's letter reluctantly, telling Chief Justice Stone: "I should have thought such assurance unnecessary and that no one could doubt that any writ required to be issued by the decision of this Court or issued by this Court would be obeyed. In oral argument I stated that the Government would assist the Marshal in making service should a writ issue" (Charles Fahy to Harlan Fiske Stone, Oct. 14, 1944, Box 36, Charles Fahy Papers).

39. Irons, *Justice at War,* p. 318.

40. *Ex Parte Endo,* 323 U.S. 283 (1944).

41. Adrian Fisher, quoted in Robert Shogan, *A Question of Judgment: The Fortas Case and the Struggle for the Supreme Court* (Indianapolis, Ind.: Bobbs-Merrill, 1972), p. 53.

42. Draft A, n.d., transmitted from Fortas to Ickes (Statement to be issued by Ickes in San Francisco regarding the program of the War Relocation Authority), April 6, 1944, Box 12, RG 48.

43. Dillon Myer to Fortas, Dec. 9, 1944; and attached statement, n.d. (for Ickes to release the day after the War Department announced revocation of the exclusion order); both in ibid.

44. Fortas, Draft A, ibid.

45. Baruch Bernstein to Fortas, Nov. 5, 1942, Box 2, RG 48.

46. Fortas to Herbert S. Goldstein, March 11, 1943, ibid.

47. Blum, *V Was for Victory,* pp. 175–81.

48. Fortas to Dillon Myer, June 13, 1944, Box 12, RG 48.

49. Fortas to Ickes, March 17, 1945, Box 11, ibid.

50. See generally Blum, *V Was for Victory,* pp. 281–88.

51. Fortas, Memorandum for the Files, Dec. 5, 1942, Box 9, RG 48.

52. Memorandum Concerning Alternative Drafts of Message Relating to Philippines Independence, Sept. 27, 1943, ibid.

53. 58 *Stat.* 625, 626 (1944). Alejandro Fernandez, *The Philippines and the United States* (Quezon City: NSDB-UP Integrated Research Program, 1977), pp. 197–99; Raymond Bonner, *Waltzing with a Dictator* (New York: Times Books, 1987), pp. 31–32.

54. Samuel Rosenman, Memorandum for the President, Aug. 29, 1944, OF 400, Box 26, FDRL.

55. Fortas to Joseph Jones, Feb. 22, 1944, Box 10, RG 48.

56. See generally Tugwell, *Stricken Land*, pp. 3–7.

57. Ibid., p. 75, n. 2; and generally pp. 3–7.

58. Diary, Aug. 1, 1943, Box 18, Rexford Tugwell Papers, FDRL (hereafter, Tugwell Diary); Ickes to Roosevelt, March 9, 1942, Box 256, Ickes Papers.

59. For example, Tugwell would refer to Muñoz as "Luis" rather than "Don Luis" or "Muñoz" (interview with Teodoro Moscoso, Aug. 1985).

60. Tugwell Diary, Nov. 24, 1942, Box 18.

61. Ibid., Nov. 18, 1942.

62. Ibid., April 26, 1943.

63. Roosevelt to Ickes, March 9, 1943, OF 400, Box 26, FDRL.

64. Tugwell Diary, July 23, 1943, and July 23, 1943.

65. *Meeting of the President's Committee To Revise the Organic Act of Puerto Rico*, reprinted as Appendix to *Hearings before a Subcommittee of the Committee on Territories and Insular Affairs, on S. 1407*, United States Senate, 78th Congress, 1st Session (Washington: GPO, 1943), p. 364. (Hereafter Appendix, *Hearings on S. 1407*). See Ickes to Roosevelt, Aug. 31, 1943, OF 400, Box 26, FDRL.

66. See, e.g., Appendix to *Hearings on S. 1407*, pp. 525–26. "I—and I believe Secretary Ickes—at all relevant times was deeply influenced by the practical limitations imposed by the Congressional situation," Fortas later recalled. "It was clear that Congress could not be induced to make a bold forward move as the first step toward achieving improved status for Puerto Rico. It was clear that the task had to be accomplished by successive moves" (Fortas to Surendra Bhana, June 9, 1971, FP).

67. Fortas, "Puerto Rico Challenge to Americans' Belief in Others' Freedom," *Washington Post*, May 6, 1945.

68. Tugwell Diary, July 21, 1943.

69. Appendix to *Hearings on S. 1407*, pp. 491–92.

70. Tugwell Diary, Aug. 4, 1943.

71. Appendix to *Hearings on S. 1407*, p. 496.

72. Tugwell Diary, Aug. 1, 1943.

73. Ibid., Aug. 4, 1943.

74. Ickes to Roosevelt, Aug. 31, 1943.

75. 61 *Stat.* 770 (1947).

76. Jose Trías Monge, *Historia Constitucional de Puerto Rico* (Rio Piedras: Universidad de Puerto Rico, 1981), 2:296.

77. Fortas, "The Art of Living Together" (Speech given at the hundredth anniversary of the City College of New York), reprinted in *Young Democrat*, January 1946.

78. Fortas, Memorandum for the File, No. 7, Jan. 9, 1946, FP.

79. See Fortas to Ickes, Nov. 12, 1946, FP; and Fortas to Ickes, March 10, 1945, Box 8, RG 48.

80. Fortas, "What Should the United States Do about Pacific Bases?" Feb. 18, 1946, FP. To Robert Dallek, Roosevelt's commitment to trusteeships provided a "good example of how he used an idealistic idea to mask a concern with power" (Robert Dallek, *Franklin D. Roosevelt and American Foreign Policy, 1932–45* [New York: Oxford University Press, 1979], p. 536).

81. Jack Fahy to Fortas, Jan. 3, 1945, RG 48, Box 8.

82. Fortas to John McCloy, Feb. 8, 1945, ibid.

83. Fortas to James Forrestal, Sept. 5, 1945.

84. Fortas to Ickes, Nov. 12, 1946, See generally Ralph J. Bunche, "Trusteeship and Colonies," *New Republic*, October 28, 1946, pp. 542–44.

85. Memorandum for the File, No. 1, Dec. 31, 1945, FP.

86. See, e.g., Memorandum for the File, No. 3, Jan. 4, 1946; and No. 6, Jan. 8, 1946; both in FP; Fortas to Ickes, Nov. 12, 1946.

87. Fortas to Ickes, Nov. 12, 1946.

88. See, e.g., John Gaddis, *The United States and the Origins of the Cold War* (New York: Columbia University Press, 1972), pp. 224–30, 292–94.

89. MS. Diary, Oct. 13, 1945: "This policy [of Attempting to keep the atomic bomb formula an American secret] was announced while I was away by President Truman. There has been some discussion in the Cabinet with a rather sharp division of sentiment. In representing me, Abe properly took the position that the secret ought to be shared with other friendly nations that could be trusted. . . . I can't see much chance for peace in the world if we are to regard our Allies with such suspicion as is evidenced by our announcement that we will not share with Russia and other countries the information as to atomic energy."

90. "An Approach to Progressive Policy" (Speech delivered at Southwestern College), June 3, 1946, Box 57, Ickes Papers.

91. Fortas, "The Atomic Age and Survival," n.d., FP.

92. See report on a speech by Fortas in Editorial, *Progressive,* July 24, 1944, p. 12.

93. The term comes from Arthur Schlesinger, Jr., *The Coming of the New Deal* (Boston: Houghton Mifflin, 1958), pp. 534–36.

94. Interview with John McCloy, Dec. 1983.

95. See Fortas to Harold Ickes, Aug. 18, 1944, Box 212, Ickes Papers.

96. Interview with Stanley Schroetel, Sept. 1984.

97. Fortas to Ickes, Aug. 24, 1942, Box 7, RG 48.

98. Ibid.

99. See Fortas to Ickes, Feb. 8, 1945, Box 11, RG 48; Dillon Myer to Ickes, March 31, 1945, ibid; Roger Baldwin to Ickes, April 19, 1945, ibid; *Personal Justice Denied: Report of the Commission on Wartime Relocation and Internment of Civilians* (Washington, D.C.: GPO, 1982), pp. 240–41.

100. See Fortas to Roger Baldwin, April 24, 1945, Box 11, RG 48; Fortas to Ickes, May 18, 1945, ibid; Herbert Wechsler to Fortas, May 16, 1945, ibid.

101. Fortas to Herbert Wechsler, May 17, 1945, ibid.

102. For another example, see Fortas to Ferdinand Eberstadt, Nov. 10, 1942, Box 14, RG 48.

103. See Harold Ickes to Raymond Robins, May 8, 1943, Box 163, Ickes Papers. According to Melvyn Dubofsky and Warren Van Tine, Lewis "viewed Ickes as one of the few reasonable men in Washington" and as "a man with whom he could do business" (Melvyn Dubofsky and Warren Van Tine, *John L. Lewis* [New York: Quadrangle Books, 1977], pp. 428–29).

104. Nelson Lichtenstein, *Labor's War at Home: The CIO in World War II* (New York: Cambridge University Press, 1982), pp. 165–66.

105. Ickes to Raymond Robins, May 8, 1943.

106. Dubofsky and Van Tine, *John L. Lewis,* pp. 425, 431; MS Diary, June 21, 1943; Lichtenstein, *Labor's War at Home,* p. 166.

107. Dubofsky and Van Tine, *John L. Lewis,* p. 431.

108. Lichtenstein, *Labor's War at Home,* pp. 166–67.

109. Drew Pearson, "The Washington Merry-Go-Round," *Washington Post,* June 8 and June 16, 1943. For an example of the board's sensitivity about its jurisdiction, see Wayne Morse, "The National War Labor Board Puts Labor Law Theory into Action," *Iowa Law Review* 29 (1944): 175–201.

110. Ickes to Margaret Robins, June 22, 1943, Box 163, Ickes Papers.

111. MS Diary, June 6, 1943.

112. Ibid.

113. The Toledo, Peoria and Western Railroad executive order gave Eastman less power than the Puerto Rican Railroad order. But even the Toledo order left open the possibility that

Eastman could alter the wage structure "pending such termination of the existing dispute as may be approved by the National War Labor Board." See Executive Order 9108, 7 *Fed. Reg.* 2201 (March 21, 1942). Cf. Executive Order 9341, 8 *Fed. Reg.* 6323 (May 15, 1943).

114. MS Diary, June 6, 1943.

115. Morse's letter of June 4, 1943, referring to Fortas's letter to the President is summarized in OF 6, Box 6, FDRL.

116. Fortas to Wayne Morse, June 4, 1943, quoted in A. Robert Smith, *The Tiger in the Senate* (Garden City, N.Y.: Doubleday, 1962), pp. 58–59.

117. Ibid; Morse to Fortas, June 7, 1943, quoted in Smith, *Tiger in the Senate*, pp. 59–60.

118. See Fortas to Morse, June 7, 1943; Morse to Fortas, June 8, 1943; Fortas to Morse, June 8, 1943; Ickes to Morse, June 11, 1943; Morse to Ickes, June 14, 1943; all quoted in Smith, *Tiger in the Senate*, pp. 60–64.

119. MS Diary, June 12, 1943.

120. The miners, who had traditionally been paid only when they reached the face of the mine, hoped to contravene the Little Steel formula and the "hold the line" order limiting the War Labor Board's authority to grant wage increases by arguing that they should be paid from the time they passed through the mine's portal until they returned to the portal at the end of the day (Dubofsky and Van Tine, *John L. Lewis*, pp. 421–23). Since two court decisions had affirmed portal-to-portal pay for metal workers, they seemed to have a case. (See Oscar Cox, "Memorandum for the Attorney General, July 22, 1943, Box 59, Oscar Cox Papers, FDRL for an assessment of how good the miners' case was.)

121. Fortas to Ickes, June 19, 1943, Box 148, Ickes Papers. For the draft in Fortas's hand, see Box 1, RG 48.

122. Roosevelt to James Byrnes, June 24, 1943, OF 407-B, FDRL.

123. Lichtenstein, *Labor's War at Home*, pp. 169–70.

124. Nathan Robertson, "Inside Story of the Elk Hills Oil Scandal: How New Dealers Exposed Standard Grab," *P.M.*, June 13, 1943.

125. Norman Littell, *My Roosevelt Years*, ed. Jonathan Denbo (Seattle, Wash.: University of Washington Press, 1987), pp. 165–67.

126. Fortas to Ronald Kent, March 19, 1945, FP.

127. Interview with Arthur ("Tex") Goldschmidt, Dec. 1943.

128. See Fortas to Ickes, Dec. 9, 1937, Box 294, Ickes Papers.

129. See Fortas to Robert Morss Lovett, May 20, 1943, Box 1, RG 48.

130. Interview with Goldschmidt.

131. Ibid.

132. See Tugwell, *Stricken Land*, pp. 375–81.

133. Fortas to Rexford Tugwell, Sept. 5, 1942, Box 3, RG 48.

134. Tugwell Diary, Sept. 7, 1942, Box 18, Tugwell Papers.

135. Tugwell Diary, Sept. 14, 1942, ibid.

136. Tugwell, *Stricken Land*, p. 381. Food shortages continued to be a problem, in part because of American cultural stereotypes. Fortas sent Tugwell's assistant, Teodoro Moscoso, over to the Department of Agriculture when Moscoso complained that every shipload contained tons of raisins and that funds should be allocated more wisely. Moscoso remembered descending into the bowels of the building, where he found an elderly woman in charge of setting food shipments. When he asked her why she was sending so many raisins she told him that Puerto Rico requested so much rice each year that she had assumed the island would want the correct proportion of raisins to make a good rice pudding (interview with Moscoso).

137. Tugwell Diary, Jan. 16, 1943, Box 18, Tugwell Papers.

138. Ickes to Fortas, April 8, 1944, Box 10, RG 48.

139. Tugwell to Fortas, Nov. 22, 1943, Box 27, Tugwell Papers.

140. Ickes to Tugwell, Jan. 10, 1945, Box 256, Ickes Papers.

141. Clifford Durr, COHP, p. 84.

142. Interview with Goldschmidt.
143. Interview with Warner Gardner, Dec. 1983.
144. Interview with Elliot Janeway, May 1987.
145. Robert Caro, *The Years of Lyndon Johnson,* vol. 1, *The Path to Power* (New York: Alfred A. Knopf, 1982), pp. 462–66.
146. See, e.g., Fortas to Lyndon Johnson, Jan. 29, 1943, Feb. 27, 1943; June 2, 1943; Johnson to Fortas, June 28, 1943; Fortas to Ralph Davies, July 2, 1943; Johnson to Fortas, Oct. 5, 1943; Fortas to Johnson, Oct. 13, 1943, all in Box 1, RG 48.
147. Fortas to Johnson, Nov. 15, 1943, FP.
148. Fortas to Howard McMurray, Oct. 11, 1943. See also, e.g., Fortas to Charles Leavy, July 13, 1942, Box 1, RG 48: "I don't want you to think that I am flattering you, but I am persuaded that if you had been in the Congress this past season things would have been somewhat different. . . . One man such as you would have made an enormous difference." For other examples, see Fortas to Howard McMurray, Oct. 11, 1943, Box 1; Fortas to Clinton P. Anderson, Aug. 26, 1942, Box 3, both in RG 48.
149. Fortas to Mary B. Palmer, July 12, 1943, Box 1, RG 48; see "Ickes' Field Marshal," *Newsweek,* July 5, 1943, p. 52. See also Fortas to Jones, Feb. 22, 1944, FP.
150. Natalie Davis Springarn, "What It Takes To Work for Uncle Sam," *P.M.,* April 28, 1946.
151. Interview with J. Howard Marshall, Sept. 1984.

### 6. FROM PUBLIC SERVICE TO THE PRIVATE SECTOR, I

1. "The Wings of Ickes," *Time,* June 29, 1942.
2. Quoted in interview with Elliot Janeway, May 1987.
3. Interview with Carol Agger, May 1987.
4. See, e.g., Harold Ickes, MS Diary, June 28, 1942; Sept. 19, 1942; Nov. 28, 1942; Dec. 6, 1942.
5. Quote in ibid., Aug. 31, 1942.
6. Memorandum of letter from Ickes to Roosevelt, Dec. 15, 1941, PPF 3650, FDRL.
7. MS Diary, June 27, 1943.
8. Ibid., Oct. 4, 1942.
9. Francis Biddle Diary, Oct. 2, 1942, Box 1, Francis Biddle Papers, FDRL.
10. MS Diary, Oct. 2, 1942.
11. Ibid.
12. Walter Gellhorn, COHP, p. 467.
13. See M. H. McIntyre to William H. McReynolds, Jan. 13, 1943; Jan. 26, 1943; Jan. 27, 1943 (transmitting Fortas's requests); all in OF 6, Box 6, FDRL.
14. When Fortas nominated Michael Straus as assistant secretary at the beginning of 1943, Ickes, who had been worrying "whether I ought to appoint another Jew as Assistant Secretary," told Fortas that there was "a good reason" why Straus should not be appointed. "Fortas replied that he understood the reason," Ickes recorded. "He considered it a good one, but remarked that he, himself, could get into the army. Of course, I couldn't consent to that. Fortas is too valuable a man" (MS Diary, Feb. 7, 1943).
15. M. H. McIntyre to William H. McReynolds, Jan. 11, 1943, OF 6, Box 6, FDRL.
16. Interview with Warner Gardner, Dec. 1983.
17. Walter Gellhorn, COHP, p. 468.
18. Fortas to Roosevelt, April 30, 1943, OF 6, Box 6, FDRL.
19. Ickes's letter to the President is quoted in "Roosevelt Rejects Fortas' Resignation from Interior Post," *Washington Evening Star,* May 11, 1943.
20. Roosevelt to Fortas, May 11, 1943, OF 6, Box 6, FDRL.

21. MS Diary, May 16, 1943.

22. George Morris, "Unhappy Draftees," FFS. (Neither the name of the newspaper in which the article appeared nor the dateline is included.) See also "Roosevelt Rejects Fortas' Resignation From Interior Post" and "President Forbids Abe Fortas To Quit Cabinet Job for Draft," *Washington Post,* May 12, 1943; "President Refused To Let Fortas Quit," *New York Times,* May 12, 1943.

23. Hamilton Fish (R., N.Y.) and Dennis Chavez (D., N.M.) are quoted in "Ickes Releases Aide to Draft—Well, Almost!" *Chicago Tribune,* Sept. 5, 1943.

24. May 14, 1943, *Cong. Rec.,* 78th Cong., 1st sess., 89, pt. 4: 4475 [Remarks of Congressman Forest Harness, R., Ind.].

25. Fortas to Ickes, Aug. 31, 1943, Box 161, Harold LeClaire Ickes Papers, Library of Congress (hereafter, Ickes Papers).

26. MS Diary, Sept. 5, 1943; Ickes to Fortas, Sept. 2, 1943, Box 161, Ickes Papers.

27. Abe Fortas, "Check and Double-Check: Congress and the Executive" (Unpublished MS), Box 53, Folder 314, Jerome Frank Papers, Yale University Archives.

28. Fortas, "Check and Double-Check."

29. Interview with Janeway.

30. Interview with Agger.

31. Fortas to Ickes, Tuesday (ca. Nov. 1943), Box 161, Ickes Papers.

32. Fortas to Saul Haas, Oct. 26, 1943, Saul Haas Papers, University of Washington.

33. Fortas to Ickes, Nov. 4, 1943, Box 161, Ickes Papers.

34. MS Diary, Nov. 7 and Nov. 21, 1943. When he learned that Stettinius suspected him of leaking information about the United Nations conference to the press two years later, Fortas denied doing so (Fortas to Edward Stettinius, June 12, 1945, FP), but he did sometimes leak information, and he may have had the motivation for doing so in this particular instance.

35. "Exit Despite Flowers," *Time,* Nov. 17, 1943, p. 21.

36. Nov. 7, 1943, *Cong. Rec.,* 78th Cong., 2d Sess., 89, pt. 7: 9628.

37. Fortas to Ickes, Nov. 15, 1943, Box 161, Ickes Papers.

38. Ickes to Fortas, Nov. 17, 1943, ibid.

39. Roosevelt to Fortas, Nov. 17, 1943, OF 6, Box 6, FDRL.

40. Interview with Gardner.

41. MS Diary, Sept. 5, 1943.

42. Gellhorn, COHP, p. 471.

43. Interview with Agger.

44. Confidential interview 9.

45. Dr. Benjamin Rones, Resume of Mr. Abe Fortas, Nov. 15, 1943, Box 161, Ickes Papers.

46. MS Diary, Sept. 5, 1943.

47. Ibid., Oct. 3, 1943.

48. Ibid., Nov. 7, 1943. Secretary of the Navy Frank Knox promised Ickes that a position "commensurate with his ability" would be found for Fortas in the Navy after he completed boot camp, but Ickes was not satisfied. "I shot back at him that there was no such job in the Navy" (MS Diary, Nov. 21, 1943).

49. Fortas to Lyndon B. Johnson, Nov. 15, 1943, FP.

50. Fortas to Ickes, Saturday (ca. Nov. 1943), Box 161, Ickes Papers. The reason he failed the Navy examination is unclear, but it probably had something to do with his eyes. Fortas told one of the President's administrative assistants that his experience was "by no means unusual. Exactly the same thing that happened to me occurred to a number of others who arrived at the receiving center at the same time that I did; and as I observed, there was hardly a group of recruits which did not include some men who had been passed at the induction center but who were discharged after naval examination" (Fortas to Jonathan Daniels, Jan. 11, 1944, FP).

51. Fortas to Ickes, Tuesday (ca. Nov. 1943), Box 161, Ickes Papers.

52. Fortas to Jane Ickes, Nov. 25, 1943, Box 27, Ickes Papers.

53. Fortas to William O. Douglas, Nov. 26, 1943, Box 327, WODP. "I've spent some time writing letters for two men who are completely illiterate," he said in another letter. "Both are men of Anglo-Saxon stock, and are 2d or 3d generation Americans" (Fortas to Douglas, Dec. 6, 1943, ibid).

54. Fortas to Jane Ickes, Nov. 25, 1943.

55. MS Diary, Dec. 11, 1943.

56. Conversation with Carol Agger, July 1986.

57. Fortas to Clifford Davis, Jan. 7, 1944, FP.

58. Fortas to Ickes, Saturday (ca. Nov. 1943).

59. Ickes to Fortas, Nov. 25, 1943, Box 161, Ickes Papers.

60. MS Diary, Dec. 19, 1943.

61. Interview with Agger.

62. MS Diary, Dec. 19, 1943.

63. Years later, Carol Agger emphasized how "absolutely incredible" the "old gentlemen" at Lord, Day and Lord found it to have a woman colleague. They repeatedly entered her office to ask if she was working too hard. Agger, who had put in long hours at the Department of Justice, was nonplussed (interview with Agger).

64. Confidential interviews 9 and 10.

65. MS Diary, Dec. 19, 1943.

66. Interview with Agger.

67. Discussed in MS Diary, Dec. 19, 1943.

68. (Kenny so paraphrased Douglas's comment.) Robert Kenny to Fortas, June 23, 1944, Box 6, Robert Kenny Papers, Bancroft Library, University of California at Berkeley.

69. Interview with Janeway.

70. Douglas quoted in Ickes, MS Diary, Dec. 19, 1943. Fortas had intimated that it had been his own decision not to go to the Middle East (Fortas to Douglas, Nov. 15, 1943, Box 327, WODP).

71. MS Diary, Dec. 19, 1943.

72. Fortas to Ickes, Dec. 21, 1943, Box 161, Ickes Papers.

73. MS Diary, Jan. 1, 1944; Roosevelt to Fortas, n.d., Box 161, Ickes Papers.

74. MS Diary, Jan. 9, 1944.

75. MS Diary, Feb. 12, 1944.

76. Ibid. He received some support. A member of the House Committee on Military Affairs, Clifford Davis, wrote Fortas: "Bother not about the sniping of some who have neither the ability nor the desire to serve their Government as you have so well served" (Clifford Davis to Fortas, Dec. 30, 1943, FP).

77. MS Diary, Jan. 8, 1944.

78. Memorandum for the Solicitor, n.d., (ca. March 1945), Box 10, RG 48.

79. See, e.g., MS Diary, April 10 and April 17, 1944.

80. Ibid., March 10, 1945.

81. MS Diary, April 23, 1944. See Fortas to Ickes, April 8, 1944; Ralph Davies to Ickes, April 10, 1944; Fortas to Ickes, April 12, 1944; Davies to Ickes, April 24, 1944; all in Box 161, Ickes Papers.

82. MS Diary, April 23, 1944. The memorandum from Fortas to Ickes dated April 12, 1944, is included in Box 161 of the Ickes Papers. It is arrogant.

83. MS Diary, April 23, 1944. Ickes did not record the exact language Fortas used.

84. Interview with Arnold Levy, May 1985.

85. MS Diary, April 23, 1944.

86. Ibid.

87. Ibid. Fortas kept in a scrapbook a birthday card illustrated with a cartoon of himself perspiring in a suit while Lewis stared wrathfully at him. The message read: "If it gets too

hot / Just shed your coat / And don't let Lewis / Get your goat" ("Happy Birthday Greetings," n.d., FP).

88. MS Diary, April 23, 1944.

89. Melvyn Dubofsky and Warren Van Tine, *John L. Lewis* (New York: Quadrangle Books, 1977), p. 440.

90. Fortas to Howard McMurray, June 17, 1943, Box 2, RG 48.

91. Conversation with Carol Agger, July 1986.

92. Interview with Levy.

93. Interview with Janeway.

94. Telegram, United Mine Workers to Ickes, Sept. 19, 1944, Box 237, Ickes Papers.

95. In the same vein, Fortas allied himself with Tom Corcoran and other liberals who joined forces with the right-wing Democratic bosses to persuade the White House to dump Henry Wallace as Vice-President in 1944. "Fortas did everything he could against me prior to the 1944 convention and was responsible for stirring up Ickes against me," Wallace later said (COHP, pp. 4106–07). Fortas did, however, urge Ickes to lobby Roosevelt to appoint Wallace to the cabinet position Wallace wanted after the election (MS Diary, Dec. 2, 1944).

96. MS Diary, March 17, 1945.

97. Ibid., April 29, 1945.

98. See complaints about press leaks on ibid., March 4, 1945; May 20, 1945; Oct. 13, 1945.

99. See complaints in Ickes to Fortas, May 19, 1944, Box 161, Ickes Papers. "Ambitious" quote and "Fortas is always seeing . . ." are in MS Diary, Jan. 7, 1945.

100. Interview with John McCloy, Dec. 1983.

101. MS Diary, Feb. 7, 1943. (See n. 14, this chapter.)

102. Reported in ibid., Nov. 26, 1944; Oct. 13, 1945.

103. "Dictatorial" quote in ibid., Nov. 26, 1944; "sadist" remark in ibid., Oct. 13, 1945. Also see ibid., July 8, 1945; Oct. 13, 1945; Feb. 10, 1946.

104. See MS Diary, Oct. 13, 1945. See also Virginia Durr to Thomas Corcoran, June 21, 1945, Corcoran Wiretap, President's Secretaries File, Harry S Truman Library (hereafter, Corcoran Wiretap). In the transcripts of conversations, the name of the person initiating the call is cited first. (Either J. Edgar Hoover of the FBI or Attorney General Tom Clark ordered the wiretap installed in May 1945, apparently because Truman was concerned about Corcoran's lobbying activities. See generally Robert Donovan, *Conflict and Crisis: The Presidency of Harry S Truman, 1945–1948* [New York: W. W. Norton, 1977], pp. 29–30; Kai Bird and Max Holland, "Tapping of Tommy the Cork," *Nation*, Feb. 8, 1986.)

105. MS Diary, June 17, 1945.

106. Durr to Corcoran, June 21, 1945, Corcoran Wiretap.

107. See Harold Ickes to Charles Harwood, May 17, 1944, Fortas to Ickes, May 18, 1944; Ickes to Fortas, May 20, 1944; Fortas to Ickes, May 29, 1944; all in Box 39, Ickes Papers.

108. Thomas Corcoran to Fortas, Sept. 15, 1945, Corcoran Wiretap.

109. See, e.g., "Mr. Smith's Budget," *Time*, July 1, 1946; "Why Career Men Resign: Attraction of Higher Pay," *United States News*, June 28, 1946.

110. Thurman Arnold to Corcoran, July 2, 1945, Corcoran wiretap.

111. Thomas Corcoran to Elliot Janeway, Sept. 13, 1945, ibid.

112. Jerome Frank to Cabell Phillips, Box 69, Folder 774, Jerome Frank Papers, Yale University Archives.

113. Phillips to Frank, Oct. 4, 1946; Frank to Phillips, Oct. 7, 1946; both in Jerome Frank Papers.

114. Fortas, "Thurman Arnold and the Theatre of Law," *Yale Law Journal* 79 (1970): 991.

115. See Laura Kalman, *Legal Realism at Yale, 1927–1960* (Chapel Hill, N.C.: University of North Carolina Press, 1986), p. 148; Fortas to Douglas, July 30, 1945, Box 327, WODP.

116. Interview with Norman Diamond, May 1985. "My only specific project thus far is the

American Molasses connection," Fortas confided to William O. Douglas. "The proposal there is that I become a Director and Treasurer of the Company as well as special counsel. But the retainer offered is only $500 a month" (Fortas to Douglas, July 30, 1945).

117. Interview with Agger.

118. John Burns to Corcoran, June 22, 1945, Corcoran Wiretap.

119. Bennett Clark to Corcoran, Jan. 17, 1946, ibid.

120. Corcoran to Edward Prichard, Aug. 20, 1945, ibid.

121. Ibid; Thurman Arnold to Corcoran; Ickes to Corcoran; all on Aug. 20, 1945, Corcoran Wiretap.

122. Corcoran to Fortas, Aug. 20, 1945, ibid; Fortas to Douglas, August 21, 1945, Box 327, WODP.

123. Corcoran to Ickes; Corcoran to Fortas, both on Aug. 30, 1945, Corcoran Wiretap. Ickes agreed that Truman's appointments made the D.C. Circuit Court "more conservative than it was" (MS Diary, Oct. 13, 1946). For Corcoran, the appointments of Bennett Clark, Barrett Prettyman, and Wilbur Miller to that court ended "the S.E.C., the Labor Board, the Wage and Hour Board" because "these people will kill the administrative agencies" (Corcoran to Elliot Janeway, Sept. 13, 1945, Corcoran Wiretap).

124. Corcoran to Fortas, Aug. 3, 1945, Corcoran Wiretap.

125. See, e.g., Alexander Holtzoff, *New Federal Procedure and the Courts* (Chicago: American Bar Association, 1940).

126. Corcoran to Tom Clark; Corcoran to Ickes (describing his conversation with Clark), both Aug. 31, 1945, Corcoran Wiretap.

127. Corcoran to Fortas, ibid.

128. MS Diary, Sept. 2, 1945.

129. Conversation with Mercedes Eichholz, Aug. 1988; Corcoran to Eddie, Dec. 27, 1945, Corcoran Wiretap; Corcoran to Sam Clark, Jan. 13, 1946, ibid.

130. MS Diary, Dec. 23, 1945.

131. Ibid., Dec. 29, 1945.

132. Harry Truman to Bill, n.d., OF 6, Harry S Truman Library.

133. He added, "However, probably no such questions will be asked unless I plant them and that I will not do. Of course when Pauley's name goes up for Secretary of the Navy the situation may be different" (MS Diary, Jan. 20, 1946). It is possible that Ickes or someone close to him planted the questions. The *Washington Post* columnist Joe Alsop told Corcoran, "You could get hold of—I could get hold of the right Republicans, and if they were told what questions might desirably be asked, why you'd have quite a little thing fixed up, you see?" As Corcoran suspected his telephone was being tapped, he promised to reply from another telephone, and there is no record of his final response (Alsop to Corcoran, Jan. 22, 1946, Corcoran Wiretap).

134. Donovan, *Conflict and Crisis*, p. 181.

135. MS Diary, Feb. 3, 1946.

136. Quoted in Thomas Corcoran to Lyndon Johnson, Feb. 1, 1946, Corcoran Wiretap. The two men were reading newspaper stories aloud to each other.

137. MS Diary, Feb. 3, 1946.

138. Donovan, *Conflict and Crisis*, p. 181.

139. Corcoran to Johnson, Feb. 1, 1946, Corcoran Wiretap.

140. "Invite Yourself Out, A Senator Advises Pauley," *Chicago Daily Tribune*, Feb. 21, 1946.

141. Eben Ayers's diary offers some insight into Truman's state of mind. After Ickes resigned, Truman told his staff, according to Ayers, that "he did not know whether Pauley said the things to Ickes that Ickes testified he did or not. But, he said, Pauley never asked him to do anything for anyone and that Pauley did not ask him for this job. . . . The President, referring to all the attacks and the many problems now, said this is war. He added that it is worse than a

shooting war—he said he had been in both—and in a shooting war you could shoot back. All of these attacks, the criticism of Pauley and of John Snyder, the President felt were to get at him the President" (Eben Ayers Diary, Feb. 13, 1946, Harry S Truman Library).

142. D. Worth Clark to Corcoran, Feb. 12, 1946. "Nobody'd ever dreamed how deeply he planned this thing," Corcoran said of Ickes's resignation (D. Worth Clark to Corcoran, Feb. 13, 1946). Ickes, of course, denied this (MS Diary, Feb. 17, 1946).

143. William O. Douglas to Corcoran, Feb. 13, 1946, Corcoran Wiretap. Truman offered Ickes's position to William O. Douglas, who decided to stay at the Court (Douglas to Truman, Feb. 23, 1946, President's Secretaries File, File: William O. Douglas, Harry S Truman Library).

144. MS Diary, Feb. 10, 1946.

145. Corcoran to Fortas, Feb. 8, 1946, Corcoran Wiretap.

146. Fortas to Corcoran, Feb. 11, 1946, ibid.

147. MS Diary, Feb. 10, 1946.

148. Ibid.

149. Arthur Krock, "Implications of the Ickes-Pauley Episode," in "In the Nation" column, *New York Times,* Feb. 15, 1946.

150. Quoted in Drew Pearson, "The Washington Merry-Go-Round" column, *Washington Post,* June 26, 1945.

151. Fortas to Rexford Tugwell, Feb. 19, 1946, Box 27, Rexford Tugwell Papers, FDRL. Fortas actually believed that the issue was more complex. He thought that the White House was engaged "in a desperate hunt for liberals and good government men," but that none of the liberals were biting (ibid).

152. Corcoran to Fortas, Feb. 8, 1946, Corcoran Wiretap.

153. Ibid.; Fortas to Tugwell, Feb. 19, 1946.

154. Corcoran to Martin Pendergast, Feb. 10, 1946, Corcoran Wiretap.

155. Testimony of Abe Fortas before Committee on Naval Affairs, Feb. 20, 1946, Box 28, Edwin Pauley Papers, Harry S Truman Library.

156. *New York Times,* Feb. 21, 1946; *Chicago Tribune,* Feb. 21, 1946.

157. Testimony of Abe Fortas before Committee on Naval Affairs.

158. Corcoran to Fortas, Feb. 20, 1946, Corcoran Wiretap.

159. Fred Vinson to Thomas Corcoran (and Benjamin Cohen on extension), Feb. 21, 1946, ibid.

160. Corcoran to George Killion, Feb. 22, 1946, ibid.

161. MS Diary, Feb. 24, 1946.

162. Confidential interview 11.

163. Oscar Chapman, Harry S Truman Oral History Collection, p. 551.

164. Fortas to Ickes, Nov. 14, 1943.

165. Walter Gellhorn, COHP, p. 484.

### 7. COLD WAR DISTRACTIONS

1. John Morton Blum, *V Was for Victory: Politics and American Culture during World War II* (New York: Harcourt Brace Jovanovich, 1976), pp. 131–35.

2. This account relies largely on information in Thurman Arnold to Mrs. C. P. Arnold, June 26, 1945; Dec. 14, 1945; March 21, 1946; in Thurman Arnold Papers, American Heritage Collection, University of Wyoming (hereafter, Arnold Papers); and interview with Reed Miller, May 1985.

3. Quoted in Milton Freeman, "Speech at the Twenty-Fifth Anniversary Dinner of Arnold and Porter," Dec. 17, 1971, A&P OF.

4. Charles E. Clark to Arnold, July 16, 1945, Arnold Papers.

5. Arnold to J. R. Sullivan, March 30, 1946, ibid. Monthly income noted in Arnold to Mrs. C. P. Arnold, April 23, 1946, ibid.

6. Fortas to Freda Kirchwey, May 26, 1947, FP; Fortas to William O. Douglas, Aug. 18, 1947, ibid; interview with Milton Freeman, July 1989. See also Memorandum by Simon Rifkind, Jerome Frank, Stanley Fuld, Abraham Tullin, Milton Handler, Murray Gurfein, Abe Fortas, Lawrence Eno, "The Basic Equities of the Palestine Problem," New York, Sept. 10, 1947. I am grateful to Milton Freeman and Avraham Harman for providing me with copies of this statement, which was apparently privately circulated and never published.

7. Fortas, "Thurman Arnold and the Theatre of Law," *Yale Law Journal* 79 (1970): 991.

8. For an interesting comparison of the two red scares see Allan Nevins's "What Is a Communist? How Can You Spot Him?" *New York Times Magazine,* May 2, 1948.

9. "How To Spot a Communist," Paul Tillett Papers, Princeton University Library (hereafter, Tillett Papers). The Army rescinded the pamphlet after protest by the American Civil Liberties Union ("Army Rescinds Pamphlet 'How To Spot a Communist' After ACLU Protest," Weekly Bulletin 1704, American Civil Liberties Union, June 27, 1955, ibid.).

10. Gerald Pomper to B. J. Hauser, Oct. 7, 1958, ibid.

11. See generally Stanley Kutler, *The American Inquisition: Justice and Injustice in the Cold War* (New York: Hill and Wang, 1982), pp. 34–39.

12. Milton Freeman to Laura Kalman, July 20, 1989.

13. "Communism in Government—Questions and Answers," Series 5, Box 16, Folder 5-16-2, Americans for Democratic Action Papers, State Historical Society of Wisconsin (hereafter, ADA Papers).

14. Memorandum Concerning Loyalty Cases, (Describing the case of "Mr X.") n.d., A&P OF.

15. Hearing transcript, *In the Matter of* "A," U.S. Department of Commerce Loyalty Board, Feb. 18, 1949, ibid. The individual's name has been withheld to protect confidentiality.

16. See Max Lerner, "The Long March," *P.M.,* Jan. 9, 1947, Series 7, Box 80, Folder 7-80-4, ADA Papers; and, generally, Steven Gillon, *Politics and Vision: The ADA and American Liberalism, 1947–1985* (New York: Oxford University Press, 1987), pp. 72–74.

17. See generally Terence Halliday, "The Idiom of Legalism in Bar Politics: Lawyers, McCarthyism, and the Civil Rights Era," *American Bar Foundation Research Journal* 1982: 911–88.

18. Kutler, *American Inquisition,* pp. 152–55.

19. John Frank, "The United States Supreme Court, 1950–51," *University of Chicago Law Review* 19 (1951): 200. See also Irving R. Kaufman, "Representation by Counsel: A Threatened Right," *American Bar Association Journal* 40 (1954): 299–302.

20. Milton Freeman did not believe "that Fortas would want to 'catch' a mailman in Topeka, Kansas, who belonged to the Communist Party, or any other functionary where the political affiliation of the employee was not damaging to any legitimate interest of the U.S. government" (Freeman to Kalman, July 20, 1989).

21. Interview with Eric Sevareid, June 1985.

22. Abe Fortas, "Outside the Law," *Atlantic Monthly,* August 1953, p. 42.

23. Fortas to Herbert Gaston, Oct. 12, 1953, A&P OF.

24. Fortas, "Outside the Law," p. 43.

25. Fortas to Harry Barnard, April 11, 1958, Box 70, Harry Barnard Papers, American Heritage Collection, University of Wyoming Archives; Fortas to Meyer Fortes, May 12, 1958, FP. For a fascinating discussion of Pound's "custody" and the case see Kutler, *American Inquisition,* pp. 59–88.

26. Fortas to Gardner Jackson, Aug. 30, 1962, Box 27, Gardner Jackson Papers, FDRL.

27. Quoted in Milton Freeman, "Abe Fortas: A Man of Courage," *Yale Law Journal* 91 (1982): 1055. That was an overstatement, as both Freeman and Fortas recognized (ibid., p. 1054, n.6; Fortas, "Thurman Arnold and the Theatre of Law," p. 994), but few lawyers actively

opposed the program. Fortas liked to recount the story Paul Porter told "of this barbed exchange with a fellow lawyer whom he encountered at a golf club and who reflected the hostility of much of the bar to this work (Fortas, "Thurman Arnold and the Theatre of Law," p. 994):

> Lawyer: "Paul, I understand your firm is engaged in defending homosexuals and Communists."
>
> Porter: "That's right. What can we do for you?"

28. See, e.g., Thurman Arnold to Harry P. Cain, Jan. 18, 1955, A&P OF, congratulating Cain on his "hard-hitting speech on the security program. This comes with a special force from you because of your conservative history and the responsible position you now occupy"; and Milton Freeman to John Lord O'Brian, March 2, 1948, ibid., comparing O'Brian's criticism of the loyalty program to "former Chief Justice Hughes' participation on the side of reason in the case of a previous attack of national hysteria."

29. Fortas, "Outside the Law," pp. 44–45.

30. Ibid., p. 45.

31. Fortas, "Thurman Arnold and the Theatre of Law," p. 992.

32. "In my view the fact that liberals like yourself have not made an all-out attack on this kind of procedure is one of the principal reasons for its continuance," Arnold told one reformer who had proposed methods for improving the loyalty program (Arnold to Herbert Cornell, Nov. 7, 1951, A&P OF).

33. Abe Fortas Freedom of Information Act File.

34. Fortas to Stuart Chase, May 11, 1949, A&P OF.

35. Senate Committee on the Judiciary, *Hearing on the Nomination of Abe Fortas,* 89th Cong., 1st sess., (Washington: GPO, 1965), p. 39. According to Virginia Durr, Fortas *had* been a member of the Southern Conference for Human Welfare (Virginia Durr, *Outside the Magic Circle: The Autobiography of Virginia Foster Durr,* ed. Hollinger Barnard [University (Tuscaloosa), Ala: University of Alabama Press, 1985], p. 116).

36. Confidential interview 12.

37. Fortas to Catherine Bauer Wurster, July 21, 1949, Catherine Bauer Wurster Papers, Bancroft Library, University of California at Berkeley.

38. Joseph Borkin, interviewed by Paul Tillett, n.d., Tillett Papers.

39. Joseph Fanelli, interviewed by Paul Tillett, March 1, 1962, ibid.

40. L. A. Nikoloric to Sheila N. Schwartz, April 28, 1950, A&P OF.

41. Fortas to Norman P. Moore, July 25, 1953, ibid.

42. Borkin, interviewed by Tillett. See also Arnold's Tenth Commandment in Thurman Arnold, "How *Not* to get Investigated," *Harper's,* Nov. 1948, p. 62.

43. Interviews with G. Duane Vieth, Dec. 1985, and Milton Freeman, Dec. 1983. Porter estimated that the firm had handled more than fifty loyalty cases by the beginning of 1949 (Paul Porter to Herbert M. Levy, Feb. 18, 1949, A&P OF).

44. G. Duane Vieth to Laura Kalman, Aug. 23, 1989.

45. Adam Yarmolinsky, "How a Lawyer Conducts a Security Case," *Reporter* 10 (March 2, 1954): 18–19.

46. Fortas to Joseph Nessenfeld, Dec. 7, 1950 A&P OF; interview with Vieth, July 1989.

47. Interview with Vieth, July 1989; Interview with Freeman, July 1989. See also *Friedman* v. *Schwellenbach,* 65 F. Supp. 254, 257–58 (1946) for a discussion of the significance of a government employee's membership in the American Peace Mobilization.

48. Interviews with Vieth (July 1989) and Freeman (July 1989).

49. Fortas to Nessenfeld, Dec. 7, 1950.

50. Interviews with Vieth (July 1989) and Freeman (July 1989).

51. Interview with Vieth, July 1989.

52. Freeman to Kalman, July 20, 1989; interviews with Vieth (July 1989) and Freeman (July 1989).

53. Interview with Freeman, July 1989. See "Lovett Bars Any Appeal in Loyalty Cases,"

*New York Herald Tribune*, Nov. 3, 1947. Andrews quoted a letter from Arnold, Fortas, and Porter branding the procedure employed by the State Department as "tragically analogous to the tactics employed in the police states dominated by Communists and Fascists."

54. Fortas to George M. Norris, Feb. 1, 1951, A&P OF.

55. Interview with Vieth, July 1989.

56. Ibid., and interview with Freeman, July 1989.

57. Department of Commerce, *Hearing before the Loyalty Board, In the Matter of "B,"* March 16, 1949, A&P OF. (Name withheld to protect confidentiality.)

58. See generally Jerold Auerbach, *Unequal Justice* (New York: Oxford University Press, 1976), pp. 241–42; Kutler, *The American Inquisition*, pp. 152–59.

59. Interview with Joseph Rauh, Dec. 1983.

60. Clifford Durr, COHP, p. 220.

61. Interview with Thomas Emerson, April 1985.

62. See Bruce Murphy, *Fortas: The Rise and Ruin of a Supreme Court Justice* (New York: William Morrow, 1988), p. 85.

63. Interview with Vieth, Dec. 1985; Freeman to Kalman, July 20, 1989.

64. Interview with Milton Freeman, July 1989.

65. Interview with Vieth, Dec. 1985.

66. William Wright, *Lillian Hellman: The Image, The Woman* (New York: Simon and Schuster, 1986), pp. 245, 250; and confidential interview 9.

67. Arnold, Fortas, and Porter's letter to the *Washington Post* responded to the column "Counsel for Pariahs," (Nov. 20, 1950), which condemned the bar for refusing to defend Communists who were appealing their Smith Act convictions to the Supreme Court. Chastened, the *Post* reprinted their letter on Nov. 28, 1950 (see "Communists in Court"), along with the admission that "we failed to point out . . . the possibility that the Communists were seeking to impose terms that no lawyer regarding himself as a 'minister of justice' could accept."

68. Fortas to Jaime Benítez, March 29, 1951, A&P OF.

69. Interview with Mary Keyserling, July 1985.

70. Paul Porter to Martin R. Haskell, Sept. 3, 1948, A&P OF.

71. Statement of United Public Workers of America (CIO) as Amicus Curiae in Support of Petition for Rehearing, *Friedman v. Schwellenbach*, Supreme Court of the United States, April 1947 (No. 990), A&P OF. See also Thurman Arnold, *Fair Fights and Foul: A Dissenting Lawyer's Life* (New York: Harcourt, Brace and World, 1965), pp. 205–06.

72. Fortas to Chester Lane, March 16, 1954, A&P OF.

73. See Newbold Noyes, "The Story of Dorothy Bailey," *Washington Evening Star*, March 27, 1949.

74. Transcript of Proceedings, Dorothy Bailey Loyalty Review Board Hearing, Dec. 8, 1948, p. 11, A&P OF.

75. Petition for a Writ of Certiorari to the United States Supreme Court, *Dorothy Bailey v. Seth Richardson*, October Term 1950 (No. 49), pp. 8–9, ibid.

76. Ibid., p. 2.

77. *Bailey v. Richardson*, 182 F. 2d 46, 66 (1950); "Edgerton on Liberty," *New Republic*, April 3, 1950, pp. 13–14; "Bailey Case," *Washington Post*, August 3, 1949.

78. Richard Rovere, "Letter from Washington," *New Yorker*, Oct. 8, 1949, pp. 86–89. See Rovere to Arnold, Oct. 1, 1949, A&P OF.

79. Arnold to J. Howard McGrath, Oct. 17, 1949, A&P OF.

80. Porter to Max Lerner, April 18, 1950, ibid.

81. Porter to Edward F. Prichard, Jr., Oct. 13, 1950, ibid.

82. Ibid.

83. Arnold to Arthur Krock, Dec. 20, 1950, ibid.

84. Porter to Prichard, Oct. 13, 1950.

85. Ibid.

86. *Bailey* v. *Richardson*, 341 U.S. 918 (1951).

87. *Joint Anti-Fascist Refugee Committee* v. *Mc Grath*, 341 U.S. 123 (1951).

88. See opinions of justices Jackson, 341 U.S. 186; Douglas, 341 U.S. 177–83; and Black, 341 U.S. 145, n. 3. On the wake of confusion left by the two decisions, see B. E. Reardon and R. S. Hope, "The Government Loyalty Program Cases," *Georgetown Law Review* 20 (1952): 294–313; "The Court Turns Its Back," *New Republic,* May 1951, p. 6; Arthur Krock ("In the Nation" column), "Effects of Burton Decision Are Doubtful," *New York Times,* May 3, 1951. For adverse comment on the *Bailey* decision see "Bailey Decision," *Washington Post,* May 1, 1951; George Gardner, "Bailey v. Richardson and the Constitution of the United States," *Boston University Law Review* 33 (1953): 173–203.

89. She replaced Evelyn Chavoor, a former employee of Helen Gahagan Douglas. After Richard Nixon had smeared Douglas as "the pink lady" in the 1950 senate race in California, Douglas left Congress. In part because she had "a liberal tinge," Chavoor was unable to find a job, and Arnold, Fortas & Porter hired her. When Chavoor obtained the position she wanted in Congress, she submitted her resignation to Fortas. "God moves in mysterious ways," he told her. "Your leaving makes it possible for Dorothy Bailey to take over your job" (interview with Evelyn Chavoor, May 1985; Chavoor to Helen Gahagan Douglas, n.d., Box 194, Folder 9, Helen Gahagan Douglas Papers, Carl Albert Center, University of Oklahoma).

90. Transcript of Argument on Behalf of the Petitioner, *Peters* v. *Hobby,* United States Supreme Court, April 19, 1955, pp. 4–5 (hereafter Transcript, *Peters*), A&P OF.

91. Arnold to John Peters, Feb. 26, 1954, ibid.

92. Arnold to Peters, Dec. 6, 1954, ibid.

93. Ibid.

94. Brian Gilbert, "The Irony of the Peters Case," *New Republic,* June 13, 1955 p. 13.

95. Peters to Arnold, Jan. 10, 1955, A&P OF. See also Arnold to Fowler Harper, Jan. 4, 1955, ibid. Although the brief in *Peters,* as in *Bailey,* rested on the right to confrontation as an aspect of due process, Arnold was coming to think that the right to confront secret witnesses or evidence would not make loyalty proceedings significantly fairer and might even prove more harmful to the accused. He told one attorney: "My own belief is . . . that there is no possibility of conducting such hearings in a fair way. Take the Oppenheimer case, for example. Unlike Dr. Peters, Oppenheimer was confronted with the evidence against him. It did no possible good. The reason is that there is no such thing as a fair trial of a man's character. These trials of course are trials not of what a man has done but what he might do because of tendencies. A stigma is put on him with the appearance of trial" (Arnold to Hiram Todd, May 10, 1955, ibid).

96. Arnold to Peters, Jan. 4, 1955, ibid.

97. Michael Mayer, "An Office and a Conscience: The Role of the Solicitor General in the Peters Case" (M.A. thesis, Duke University, 1974), A&P OF.

98. Anthony Lewis, "Did Burger Say 'Yes' But Mean 'No' in Peters Case?" *Washington Daily News,* April 21, 1955.

99. Transcript, *Peters,* p. 14.

100. See exchange in Transcript, *Peters,* pp. 15–16. See also Anthony Lewis, "Both Sides Beg High Court To Settle 'Accusers' Issue," *Washington Daily News,* April 22, 1955.

101. *Peters* v. *Hobby,* 349 U.S. 331 (1955). For Warren, see esp. p. 338. For concurrences, see pp. 349–52.

102. Arnold to Peters, June 29, 1955, A&P OF.

103. Fortas to Fowler Harper, June 13, 1955, ibid.

104. Arnold, *Fair Fights and Foul,* pp. 210–13.

105. See generally Bert Andrews, *Washington Witch Hunt* (New York: Random House, 1948), pp. 133–45. For two interesting and different perspectives on the case see Henry Wallace, "The Case of Dr. Condon," *New Republic,* March 15, 1948, p. 10; and J. Parnell Thomas, "Russia Grabs Our Inventions," *American Magazine,* June 1947, p. 19.

106. Fortas to Clifford Forster, April 6, 1948, A&P OF.

107. Arnold, Fortas, Porter to Chairman, Committee on Un-American Activities, March 29, 1948, ibid. See, e.g., Jack Steele, "Three Condon Attorneys Warn Thomas Group," *New York Herald Tribune,* March 30, 1948.

108. April 1, 1948, *Cong. Rec.,* 80th Cong., 2d sess., 94, pt. 3: 3999 (Remarks of Representative McDowell).

109. Fortas to Walter Gellhorn, April 7, 1948, A&P OF.

110. Kutler, *American Inquisition,* pp. 185–87; Robert Griffith, *The Politics of Fear* (Rochelle Park, N.J.: Hayden, 1970), pp. 76–77, n. 66.

111. Owen Lattimore, *Ordeal by Slander* (Boston: Little, Brown, 1950), p. 4.

112. Ibid., p. 15.

113. Ibid., pp. 21–22.

114. Lattimore to Kalman, May 21, 1987: "In the periods of greatest tension, they kept me out of many of their discussions. They knew that when I was there it increased the pressure on me and when I was working on other aspects of the problem the tension was relieved."

115. Paul Tillett, "Lattimore—ordeal by slander," n.d., Tillett Papers.

116. "Dave Boothe Says," n.d., A&P OF.

117. Lattimore to Kalman, May 21, 1987.

118. Draft statement, n.d., A&P OF. Lattimore actually released a different but equally vituperative statement, in which he labeled McCarthy "a madman" (see "Text of Professor Lattimore's Statement Denying He Is a Communist and Denouncing Senator McCarthy," *New York Times,* April 2, 1950).

119. Lattimore, *Ordeal by Slander,* p. 201. Emphasis in the original.

120. *Hearings Before a Subcommittee of the Committee on Foreign Relations, Pursuant to S. Res. 231, State Department Employee Loyalty Investigation,* U.S. Senate, 81st Cong., 2d sess., pt. 1 (1950), vol. 1, p. 471 (hereafter, *Hearings,* Tydings committee).

121. Ibid., pp. 473–74.

122. Lattimore, *Ordeal By Slander,* pp. 107–08.

123. Ibid; interview with Vieth, Dec. 1985.

124. Fortas to Wilbur Baldinger, April 27, 1950, A&P OF.

125. Drew Pearson, *Diaries, 1949–1959,* ed. Tyler Abell (New York: Holt, Rinehart and Winston, 1974), April 12, 1950, p. 119. For a sense of Budenz's style see, e.g., Louis Budenz, "Capture of the Innocents," *Colliers,* Nov. 27, 1948; "Louis Budenz Meets the Press," *American Mercury,* July 1950, pp. 90–99.

126. Quoted in Lattimore, *Ordeal by Slander,* pp. 111–112.

127. Interview with Mercedes Eichholz, Sept. 1988.

128. See Questions, A&P OF.

129. Lattimore, *Ordeal By Slander,* p. 125.

130. *Hearings,* Tydings committee, pp. 506, 511.

131. U.S. Senate, *Hearings Before the Subcommittee to Investigate the Administration of the Internal Security Act and Other Internal Security Laws of the Committee on the Judiciary, The Institute of Pacific Relations,* 82d Cong., 2d sess., pt 7 (1952), p. 2966 (hereafter, *Hearings,* McCarran committee). Fortas here admitted giving information to the Tydings Committee.

132. *Hearings,* Tydings committee, pp. 529–31.

133. As they did when she ultimately appeared (ibid., pp. 639–60).

134. Quoted in Lattimore, *Ordeal by Slander,* pp. 114–15.

135. *Hearings,* McCarran committee, p. 2934.

136. *Hearings,* McCarran committee, p. 2935. See Brian Gilbert, "New Light on the Lattimore Case," *New Republic,* Dec. 27, 1954, p. 9: "Lattimore was uncooperative, sarcastic, convinced that he was being lynched. McCarran was a prosecutor."

137. Fortas, "Methods of Committees Investigating Subversion—A Critique," Notre Dame University Symposium, Dec. 9, 1953, Box 27, Gardner Jackson Papers, FDRL.

138. *Hearings,* McCarran committee, p. 2935.

139. See ibid., pp. 3022–23; 3115–16; 3081.

140. Arnold to Robert Maynard Hutchins, March 25, 1952, Arnold Papers.

141. *Hearings*, McCarran committee, p. 3676. McCarran had forced Truman's new attorney general, James McGranery, to promise at his confirmation hearing in 1952 to prosecute Lattimore for perjury (see Arnold, *Fair Fights and Foul*, p. 217).

142. Those proceedings are ably described by Stanley Kutler in *American Inquisition*, pp. 203–11; and Thurman Arnold, *Fair Fights and Foul*, pp. 217–27.

143. Kutler, *American Inquisition*, p. 212.

144. Arnold to Hutchins, March 25, 1952, Arnold Papers. As an example, Arnold gave the case of Lauchlin Currie. The McCarran committee had called Currie, with whom Lattimore sometimes consulted. Currie asked Arnold, Fortas & Porter to represent him, but the firm declined because of a possible conflict of interest. Lattimore and Currie might have remembered the same events in the past fourteen years differently, "particularly in light of the traps which are set by the committee." Arnold was unable to find a lawyer "of standing" to represent Currie (ibid).

145. Interview with Rauh.

146. Interview with Freeman, Dec. 1983.

147. Quoted in Louis Cassels, "Arnold Fortas, Porter and Prosperity," *Harper's*, Nov. 1951, p. 67.

148. Quoted in ibid., p. 67.

149. Ibid., p. 62.

150. Interview with Freeman, Dec. 1983. Fortas 1952 earnings from Federal income tax return, 1953, FP.

## 8. THE WASHINGTON LAWYER

1. Charles Horsky, *The Washington Lawyer*, (Boston: Little, Brown, 1952), p. 17. Emphasis in the original.

2. Louis Cassels, "Arnold, Fortas, Porter and Prosperity," *Harper's*, Nov. 1951, p. 65.

3. Draft internal synopsis, n.d., A&P OF.

4. Abe Fortas, Book Review, *Northwestern University Law Review* 48 (1953): 121.

5. Interview with Joseph Rauh, Dec. 1983.

6. Fortas, "Thurman Arnold and the Theatre of Law," *Yale Law Journal* 79 (1970): 996.

7. William Simon, "The Ideology of Advocacy: Procedural Justice and Professional Ethics" (1978), reprinted in *Ethics and the Legal Profession*, ed. Michael Davis and Frederick A. Elliston (Buffalo: Prometheus Books, 1986), p. 228.

8. Fortas to Rexford Tugwell, March 13, 1945, Box 10, RG 48. Part of Fortas's disapproval of the arrangement probably was attributable to the particular attorney Tugwell wanted to hire, "an elderly man of demonstrable incompetence" (interview with Warner Gardner, Dec. 1983).

9. When Tugwell retained Fortas, Warner Gardner, who had remained at Interior, wrote the governor saying that the arrangement was one Fortas himself had condemned (Warner Gardner to Tugwell, March 8, 1946, Box 27, Rexford Tugwell Papers, FDRL). "I had a splendid time . . . quoting his letter to Tugwell and thought no more of it," Gardner remembered. "Months later there was the damn thing in the press." Gardner subsequently learned that Oscar Chapman, of Interior, had leaked the story. "For the next decade or two, whenever Abe got into trouble . . . somebody . . . would dash out that damned letter. And I always wanted to write or telephone Abe, and say: 'Look, honest . . . I never turned that letter loose. It was Oscar.' But it seemed too self-defensive to be doing it, so I never did" (interview with Gardner).

10. See, e.g., Marquis Childs ("Washington Calling" column), "Law Industry," *Wash-*

*ington Post,* May 22, 1946; reprinted in U.S. Senate, *Hearings Before the Committee on the Judiciary on the Nominations of Abe Fortas and Homer Thornberry,* 90th Cong., 2d sess. (Washington: GPO, 1968), p. 1114.

11. Simon, "Ideology of Advocacy," p. 236.

12. See Ellis Hawley, *The New Deal and the Problem of Monopoly: A Study in Economic Ambivalence* (Princeton, N.J.: Princeton University Press, 1966), pp. 429–30, 450.

13. See John Morton Blum, *V Was for Victory: Politics and American Culture during World War II* (New York: Harcourt Brace Jovanovich, 1976), pp. 132–35.

14. Thurman Arnold, "The Economic Purpose of Antitrust Laws," *Mississippi Law Journal* 26 (1955): 212.

15. Carl Kaysen, "Big Business and the Liberals, Then and Now," *New Republic,* Nov. 22, 1954, p. 120.

16. Interviews with Julius Greisman, June 1985; Dennis Lyons, Dec. 1985.

17. Interview with Norman Diamond, May 1985.

18. Defendant's Reply Memorandum on the Motion and Cross-Motion for Summary Judgment, *Tampa Electric Co.* v. *Nashville Coal Co.,* District Court of the United States for the Middle District of Tennessee, July 29, 1958, Civil Action 2418, p. 17, FP. Emphasis in the original.

19. Interview with Reed Miller, July 1985.

20. Interviews with Diamond, May 1985; and Milton Freeman, Dec. 1983.

21. Interview with Maurice Lazarus, Sept. 1985.

22. Interview with Abe Krash, May 1987.

23. Post-Trial Brief of Defendant Lever Brothers Company, *United States of America* v. *Lever Brothers Company and Monsanto Chemical Company,* District Court of the United States for the Southern District of New York, April 1, 1963, Civil Action No. 135-219, pp. 50–51, FP.

24. Interview with G. Duane Vieth, Dec. 1985.

25. Interview with Lloyd Cutler, May 1985.

26. Brief for Appellant, *Kaiser-Frazer Corporation* v. *Otis and Co.,* United States Court of Appeals for the Second Circuit, p. 37, FP.

27. Interview with Vieth, Dec. 1985.

28. Interviews with Diamond and Freeman.

29. *Kaiser-Frazer Corp.* v. *Otis and Co.,* 195 F. 2d 838 (1952).

30. Interview with Vieth, Dec. 1985.

31. Interview with Cutler.

32. Supplemental Statement of Petitioners, *Bank of America National Savings and Trust Association, and A.P. Giannini* v. *Board of Governors of the Federal Reserve System,* Supreme Court of the United States, October Term 1950, No. 323, p. 1, FP.

33. Reply Brief for Appellants, *Kukatash Mining Corporation* v. *Securities and Exchange Commission,* United States Court of Appeals for the District of Columbia Circuit, Feb. 27, 1962, No. 16, 734, p. 4.

34. Interview with William Rogers, May 1987.

35. Edward Howrey, *Washington Lawyer* (Iowa City, Ia.: University of Iowa College of Law, 1983), p. 83.

36. Interview with Greisman, June 1985.

37. Interview with Victor Kramer, Dec. 1984.

38. Reed Miller to Abe Fortas, Aug. 2, 1965, A&P OF.

39. Interview with Paul Berger, May 1985.

40. Term used in Robert Nelson, "Practice and Privilege: Social Change and the Structure of Large Law Firms," *American Bar Foundation Research Journal* 1981 (1981): 121.

41. Interview with Martin Riger, May 1987.

42. Interview with Paul Warnke, May 1985.

43. Interview with Maurice Lazarus.

44. Interview with Ralph Lazarus, Sept. 1984.

45. Maurice Lazarus to Laura Kalman, Aug. 4, 1989.

46. Fortas to James F. Henry, May 21, 1981, FP.

47. Nelson, "Practice and Privilege," pp. 111–15.

48. Draft internal synopsis.

49. Interview with Patrick Macrory, June 1987.

50. Perhaps the few Washington "superlawyers" whose names would add luster to any board often acted as both fiduciaries and special agents, and that dual status was one of their distinctive characteristics.

51. Fortas, "Thurman Arnold and the Theatre of Law," p. 996.

52. Confidential interview 12.

53. Interview with Vieth, Dec. 1985.

54. Interview with Charles Reich, Dec. 1985.

55. Louis Brandeis, "Opportunity in Law," *Business—A Profession* (Boston: Hale, Cushman and Flint, 1933), pp. 330, 337–39.

56. Indeed corporate lawyers had even less professional autonomy than lawyers in the personal sector of law practice. See generally John Heinz and Edward Laumann, *Chicago Lawyers: The Social Structure of the Bar* (New York: Russell Sage Foundation and American Bar Foundation, 1982) pp 108–09, 370–73; John Heinz, "The Power of Lawyers," *Georgia Law Review* 17 (1983): 891–911; Robert Nelson, "Ideology, Practice and Professional Autonomy: Social Values and Client Relationships in the Large Law Firm," *Stanford Law Review* 37 (1985): 545, 506–07; Robert A. Kagan and Robert E. Rosen, "On the Social Significance of Large Law Firm Practice," *Stanford Law Review* 37 (1985): 429–30 and 433–35. Cf. Erwin Smigel, *The Wall Street Lawyer* (New York: The Free Press of Glencoe, 1964), p. 331.

57. Stewart Macaulay, "Lawyers and Consumer Protection Laws," *Law and Society Review* 14 (1979): 163.

58. Heinz, "Power of Lawyers," p. 901.

59. Robert Gordon, "The Ideal and the Actual in the Law: Fantasies and Practices of New York City Lawyers, 1870–1910," *The New High Priests*, ed. Gerard Gawalt (Westport, Conn.: Greenwood Press, 1984), p. 65. See also idem., "Legal Thought and Legal Practice in the Age of American Enterprise, 1870–1920," *Professions and Professional Ideologies in America*, ed. Gerald Geison (Chapel Hill, N.C.: University of North Carolina Press, 1983), p. 99.

60. Fortas to M. G. deBaat, Feb. 13, 1956, FP.

61. Fortas, In Memoriam, Louis Eisenstein, (transcript of eulogy), Jan. 9, 1966, ibid.

62. Fortas, "Thurman Arnold and the Theatre of the Law," pp. 990–92.

63. Interview with Ralph Lazarus.

64. See this chapter below and chap. 10.

65. Judy Hennessee, "The Washington Legal Establishment," *Washingtonian*, August 1967, p. 37.

66. Interview with Diamond.

67. Quoted in Cassels, "Arnold, Fortas, Porter and Prosperity," p. 68. Emphasis in the original.

68. Interview with Vieth, Dec. 1985.

69. Fortas to William O. Douglas, Jan. 13, 1958, A&P OF.

70. Fortas to Stanley Marcus, March 5, 1958, ibid.

71. Interview with John Loeb, Dec. 1983.

72. Interview with Lyons.

73. Interview with Freeman. Paul Warnke considered Fortas's relationship with Johnson "a distinct asset. . . . What it does is to lead people to feel that this is a very important guy. . . . It's like my partner, Clark Clifford. It's not that he can go to some particular Senator and say 'I'd like you to influence the decision at the Eighth Circuit.' Of course he can't do a damn thing

about it. It's just that he becomes a prominent Washington figure, and then people like to be represented by prominent Washington figures. And they're impressed that they come in and talk to their lawyer Abe Fortas . . . and Abe Fortas says, 'When I was talking to Lyndon the other day,' and it's sort of ego-thrilling as much as anything else. I think that people sometimes think that businessmen, corporate leaders, are looking for some sort of advantage, when in many instances, they're just impressionable. And they're kind of star-happy" (interview with Warnke).

74. Hennessee, "Washington Legal Establishment," p. 37.

75. Interview with Vieth, Dec. 1985.

76. Ibid.

77. Horsky, *Washington Lawyer*, p. 154.

78. Hennessee, "Washington Legal Establishment," p. 34.

79. Fortas to Corcoran, Jan. 27, 1946, Corcoran Wiretap, President's Secretaries File, Harry S Truman Library; Corcoran to William Leahy, ibid.

80. Corcoran to Fortas, Feb. 8, 1946, ibid.

81. Fortas to Hiram Cancio, March 9, 1963, AFP OF, FLMM.

82. Quoted in "They Build A Bridge to Washington," *Business Week*, April 23, 1966, p. 87.

83. Interview with G. Duane Vieth, July 1989.

84. See Horsky, *Washington Lawyer*, pp. 33, 51–54.

85. Interview with Vieth, July 1989.

85. Interview with Rogers.

86. Kagan and Rosen, "On the Social Significance of Large Law Firms," p. 408.

87. Elizabeth Drew, "The Quiet Victory of the Cigarette Lobby," *Atlantic Monthly*, September 1965, p. 77.

88. So Drew suggested in "Quiet Victory of the Cigarette Lobby," p. 77. See also Joseph Goulden, *The Superlawyers* (New York: Weybright and Talley, 1972), p. 131.

89. See, e.g., Goulden, *Superlawyers*, pp. 139–140; Mark Green, Beverly C. Moore, Jr., Bruce Wasserstein, *The Closed Enterprise System; Ralph Nader's Study Group on Antitrust Enforcement* (New York: Grossman Publishers, 1972), pp. 340–41.

90. *In the Matter of Broadway-Hale Stores, Inc.*, 75 F.T.C. 374 (March 5, 1959), Separate Statement of Commissioner Mac Intire at 381.

91. Green, Moore, and Wasserstein, *Closed Enterprise System*, p. 340.

92. Interview with Ralph Lazarus.

93. *Barenblatt v. United States*, 360 U.S. 109 (1959).

94. Thurman Arnold to Hugo Black, June 10, 1959, Thurman Arnold Papers, American Heritage Center, University of Wyoming.

95. Fortas to William O. Douglas, Aug. 18, 1947, A&P OF. For Fortas's remarks on the Transparent Wrap case see Fortas to Douglas, July 14, 1947, and Aug. 18, 1947, both in Box 327, WODP. Fortas had begun writing Douglas letters commenting on the justice's opinions while he was in government (see Fortas to William O. Douglas, June 16, 1942, and June 27, 1945, A&P OF).

96. Fortas to Douglas, April 8, 1959, A&P OF.

97. Fortas to Tom and Mary Clark, Nov. 16, 1963, ibid.

98. See, e.g., Fortas to Douglas, Aug. 18, 1947, and June 11, 1948, ibid.

99. Douglas to Roger Straus, June 4, 1949; Douglas to Fortas, June 4, 1949; both in ibid.

100. Interview with Milton Freeman, July 1989.

101. Fortas to Saul Haas, Elon Gilbert, David Ginsburg, Ganson Purcell, Clark Clifford, July 23, 1959, A&P OF; Fortas to Elon Gilbert, March 10, 1959, ibid.

102. John Frank, "Disqualification of Justices," *Yale Law Journal* 56 (1949): 617.

103. J. Woodford Howard, Jr., "Advocacy in Constitutional Choice: The *Cramer* Treason Case, 1942–1945," *American Bar Foundation Research Journal* 1986 (1986): 402.

104. By 1945, when Justice Jackson criticized Justice Black "for participating in a case

argued by a man who twenty years before had been Black's law partner," the subject of judicial disqualification was coming "sharply into the focus of public and professional attention," John Frank noted in his classic article on judicial disqualification (Frank, "Disqualification of Justices," p. 606). But at the time, "the overwhelming American practice" was against disqualification for close personal friendship (ibid., p. 622). Frank argued: "A judge, of course, is often closely associated with attorneys not in the ex-partner class. Close friendships formed at the bar with other practitioners naturally outlive elevation to the bench. And, presumably, if the ex-practitioner judge is equally intimate with former partners, the ex-teacher judge is equally intimate with former faculty colleagues. . . . None of these grounds, however, is usually considered sufficient to warrant disqualification. For example, Justice Frankfurter does not disqualify himself when his former Harvard colleague and good friend Paul Freund is of counsel, nor does Justice Douglas decline to sit when he finds the names of his old Yale associates Thurman Arnold, Abe Fortas and Walton Hamilton on the briefs. . . . Indeed, no one has ever suggested the desirability of disqualification in such instances" (ibid., p. 621). Nor at the time was former partnership generally considered grounds for disqualification. "It is common practice to sit in cases argued by ex-partners," as long as the case came to the office after the dissolution of the partnership (ibid., p. 630). Twenty years later, however, Fortas would routinely disqualify himself whenever Arnold & Porter had a case in the Supreme Court, regardless of whether the case had come to the firm while he was there or after he had left.

105. Robert Nelson and John Heinz, with Edward Laumann and Robert Salisbury, "Lawyers and the Structure of Influence in Washington" (Unpublished paper).

106. Interview with Rogers.

107. Fortas to Teodoro Moscoso, July 8, 1950, AFP OF, FLMM.

108. Interview with Rogers.

109. Interview with Jose Trías Monge, Aug. 1985.

110. See generally Donald Robinson, "Muñoz Marín—Puerto Rico's 'Poet Leader,' " *Reader's Digest* 69 (1956); "Muñoz: Energetic Idealist," *Life*, March 11, 1957.

111. Fortas to Jaime Benítez, Oct. 3, 1946, AFP OF, FLMM.

112. Fortas to Thomas Corcoran, May 10, 1957, ibid.

113. José Ferrer to Muñoz Marín, Nov. 30, 1954, ibid.

114. Fortas to Luis Muñoz Marín, Dec. 8, 1954, ibid.

115. Interview with Inés Muñoz Marín, Aug. 1985.

116. Interview with Roberto Sánchez Vilella, Aug. 1985.

117. Interview with Inés Muñoz Marín, Aug. 1985.

118. Interview with Sánchez Vilella.

119. Interview with Trías Monge.

120. Sánchez recalled this figure as the amount Arnold, Fortas & Porter charged in 1959–60 (interview with Sánchez Vilella). In 1963 one member of the firm estimated that its legal fees just for representing the Commonwealth in proceedings before the Civil Aeronautics Board, the Federal Maritime Commission, and the Maritime Administration would amount to $100,000 (John Rigby to Ruben Sanchez, August 16, 1963, AFP OF, FLMM).

121. Interview with Sánchez Vilella.

122. Message for Fortas left by James Rowe, July 12, 1956, AFP OF, FLMM.

123. Muñoz Marín to Dwight Eisenhower (letter drafted by Fortas), Oct. 13, 1957, ibid. See S. 4129, H.R. 10906, 85th Cong., 2d sess.

124. Muñoz Marín to Lyndon B. Johnson, July 10, 1958; Fortas to Muñoz Marín, July 25, 1958; both in AFP OF, FLMM.

125. Thurman Arnold to Fortas, Aug. 22, 1958; Arnold to Muñoz Marín, Aug. 23, 1958; ibid.

126. Symington sent Fortas a copy of a letter he had written to Muñoz Marín (Aug. 25, 1959) and added this comment at the bottom (in AFP OF, FLMM).

127. Symington to Fortas, Jan. 12, 1959, ibid.

128. Fortas to Symington, Aug. 24, 1958, ibid.

129. Interview with Inés Muñoz Marín.

130. Interview with Sánchez Vilella.

131. José Cabranes, Book Review, *Harvard Law Review* 100 (1986): 454. Emphasis in the Cabranes essay.

132. Surendra Bhana, *The United States and the Development of the Puerto Rican Status Question, 1936–1968* (Lawrence, Kans.: The University Press of Kansas, 1975), p. 45. The discussion that follows relies on information in this work.

133. "Muñoz: Energetic Idealist," p. 81. See also "Operation Bootstrap Score: 400th New Factory," *Life*, May 21, 1956, pp. 38–43.

134. Walton Hamilton to Luis Muñoz Marín, April 16, 1953, AFP OF, FLMM.

135. P.L. 600, 64 *Stat.* 319, Sec. 1 (1950).

136. Fortas to Muñoz Marín, June 9, 1950, AFP OF, FLMM.

137. Interview with Trías Monge.

138. 39 *Stat.* 95, Sec. 1 (1917).

139. Interview with Benítez.

140. See Jose Trías Monge, *Historia Constitucional de Puerto Rico* (Rio Piedras: Editorial de la Universidad de Puerto Rico, 1982), 3:40–56.

141. Both Muñoz and Férnos are quoted in Juan Torruella, *The Supreme Court and Puerto Rico: The Doctrine of Separate and Unequal* (Rio Piedras: Editorial de la Universidad de Puerto Rico, 1985), p. 149.

142. Constitution of the Commonwealth of Puerto Rico, 1952, Section 1. In 1950 Trías and Fortas wrote one of the two preparatory studies which served as the basis for the constitution the constitutional convention drafted. See Trías Monge, *Historia Constitucional*, 3:64–70. Muñoz is quoted in Torruella, *Supreme Court and Puerto Rico*, p. 131.

143. Torruella, *Supreme Court and Puerto Rico*, pp. 153–59; Trías Monge, *Historia Constitucional*, 3:272–311.

144. Fortas to Jaime and Luz Benítez, Jan. 25, 1952, AFP OF, FLMM.

145. "The laws enacted by the Government of the Commonwealth pursuant to the compact cannot be repealed or modified by external authority," stated Muñoz's draft letter to Truman formally requesting that the U.S. government notify the United Nations that Puerto Rico was no longer a non-self-governing area. "Our status and the terms of our association with the United States cannot be changed without our full consent" (Draft letter, Luis Muñoz Marín to the President of the United States, Jan. 17, 1953, ibid).

146. Fortas to Trías Monge, Feb. 21, 1953, AFP OF, FLMM.

147. *Mora v. Torres*, 113 F. Supp. 309, 315 (1953).

148. Report by Hon. Frances P. Bolton and James P. Richards on the Eighth Session of the General Assembly of the United Nations, April 26, 1954, quoted in Trías Monge, vol. 4 (1983) *Historia Constitucional*, p. 43.

149. Quoted in Brief of the Commonwealth of Puerto Rico as Amicus Curiae, *James W. S. Davis v. Trigo Brothers Packing Company*, United States Court of Appeals for the First Circuit, Jan. 22, 1959, No. 5385, p. 32, FP (hereafter, Brief, *Davis v. Trigo Brothers*).

150. *Mora v. Mejías*, 206 F. 2d 377, 387 (1953).

151. Fortas to Jose Trías Monge, July 29, 1953, AFP OF, FLMM.

152. Brief, *Davis v. Trigo Brothers*, p. 2.

153. Ibid., p. 18.

154. For an example of a victory, see *Figueroa v. People of Puerto Rico*, 232 F. 2d 615, 620 (1958). For an analysis of less helpful cases, see Torruella, *Supreme Court and Puerto Rico*, pp. 167–194.

155. Interview with Sánchez Vilella; Fortas to Jose Trías Monge, April 10, 1954, AFP OF, FLMM; Fortas to Luis Muñoz Marín, Feb. 10, 1958, ibid.

156. Antonio Férnos Isern and Fortas to Luis Muñoz Marín, Jan. 13, 1959, ibid.

157. Memorandum for the President of the United States from the Governor of the Commonwealth of Puerto Rico, June 17, 1959, ibid.

158. Fortas to Muñoz Marín, June 26, 1959, ibid.

159. Fortas had noted it was imperative "that we try to make sure [Jackson] has complete understanding of the bill and will support it wholeheartedly" (Fortas to Muñoz Marín, March 17, 1959, ibid.). He met with the senator for this purpose, conveying "our full realization of Jackson's key position and our great regard for his assistance and guidance" (Fortas to Muñoz Marín, May 25, 1959, ibid.).

160. U.S. Senate, *Hearings before the Committee on Interior and Insular Affairs on*`S. 2023, 86th Cong., 1st sess. (Washington: GPO, 1959), pp. 20–21.

161. Fortas to Roberto Sánchez Vilella, June 20, 1959, AFP OF, FLMM.

162. Fortas to Muñoz Marín, Dec. 19, 1960, ibid.

163. Fortas to Muñoz Marín, June 25, 1959, ibid.

164. See generally Bhana, *United States and Puerto Rican Status Question*, pp. 176–80.

165. Brief for Appellees, *Jesus Rivera Rodríguez v. Popular Democratic Party*, Supreme Court of the United States, October term 1981, No. 81-328, pp. 10–13, FP.

166. On Muñoz, see "Free Spirit of Puerto Rico Politics," *Los Angeles Times*, April 21, 1989. For the judge's comments, see Cabranes, Book Review, p. 463.

167. Fortas, Memorandum to Partners and Associates, May 27, 1955, AFP OF, FLMM.

168. Fortas to Hiram Cancio, Feb. 14, 1959, ibid.

169. Fortas to Jacob Davis, April 1, 1954, ibid.

170. Fortas to Teodoro Moscoso, March 10, 1959, ibid.

171. Fortas to Rafael Durand, June 4, 1957, ibid.

172. Fortas to Teodoro Moscoso, Dec. 12, 1956, ibid.

173. Fortas to Lazarus, Dec. 3, 1957, ibid.

174. Fortas to Harold Hartog, June 22, 1958, ibid.

175. Interview with Marta Casals Istomin, May 1985.

176. Fortas to Luis Muñoz Marín and Inés Muñoz Marín, April 30, 1957.

177. Interview with Casals Istomin.

178. Robert Shogan, *A Question of Judgment: The Fortas Case and the Struggle for the Supreme Court* (Indianapolis, Ind.: Bobbs-Merrill, 1972), p. 73.

179. Fortas to Isaac Stern, Nov. 18, 1961, A&P OF.

180. Fortas to Pablo Casals, Dec. 20, 1961, AFP OF, FLMM.

181. Fortas to Marta Casals, May 30, 1962, ibid.

182. Fortas to Mortimer W. Caplin, July 19, 1962, ibid.

183. "Institute Honors Justice," *Washington Post*, Nov. 22, 1965. For examples of Fortas's work on behalf of the Humane Slaughter Bill (1958), see Fortas to Leo Pfeffer, Oct. 19, 1957; Fortas to Christine Stevens, Dec. 31, 1957, and Nov. 22, 1957; Fortas to Fred Myers, Dec. 31, 1957; all in FP.

184. Fortas, "The Legal Interview," *Psychiatry* 15 (1952): 91–92; Fortas, "A Time for Putting Together Again" (Speech delivered at the William Alanson White Institute of Psychiatry), Feb. 6, 1954, FP.

185. Fortas, "The Rule in Durham's Case" (Speech to the Federal Bar Association, March 20, 1958), FP.

186. *Tatum v. United States*, 190 F. 2d 612, 615 (1951).

187. *Durham v. United States*, 214 F. 2d 862, 866, 869 (1954).

188. Abe Fortas, "Durham's Case: Mad or Bad?" (Paper delivered at a conference on Insanity and the Law, University of Chicago Law School, Feb. 28, 1955), FP.

189. Interview with Abe Krash, May 1987.

190. Ibid.

191. Supplemental Brief for Appellant on Reargument, *Monte W. Durham* v. *United States of America,* United States Court of Appeals for the District of Columbia Circuit, Jan. 5, 1954, No. 11,859, FP (hereafter, Brief, *Durham*).

192. Brief, *Durham,* p. 21.

193. Ibid., pp. 22–25, 28–29; interview with Margaret Rioch, May 1985.

194. Brief, *Durham* pp. 26–32.

195. Fortas, "Durham's Case: Mad or Bad?"

196. *Durham* v. *United States,* 214 F. 2d 869.

197. Ibid., at 874–75. See also John Hughes, *In the Law's Darkness: Isaac Ray and the Medical Jurisprudence of Insanity in Nineteenth-Century America* (New York: Oceana, 1986), especially, pp. 112–13; John Reid, "Understanding the New Hampshire Doctrine of Criminal Insanity," *Yale Law Journal* 69 (1960): 360–420; idem, *Chief Justice: The Judicial World of Charles Doe* (Cambridge, Mass.: Harvard University Press, 1967), pp. 109–21.

198. Fortas to William O. Douglas, Oct. 19, 1954; and Fortas to David Bazelon, Aug. 17, 1954; both in FP. The newspaper was the *Evening Sun.*

199. See, e.g., Judge Warren Burger's dissent in *Blocker* v. *U.S.,* 288 F. 2d 857–72 (1961); and Judge Miller's dissent (joined by Judge Bastian) in ibid., at 877–78. See also *U.S.* v. *Fielding,* 148 F. Supp. 51–52 (1957).

200. Abe Fortas, "Implications of Durham's Case" (Speech delivered at meeting of the American Psychiatric Association, Chicago, May 3, 1956), FP.

201. William O. Douglas, "The Durham Rule: A Meeting Ground for Lawyers and Psychiatrists," *Iowa Law Review* 41 (1956): 485–95. See, e.g., Francis Rabb, "A Moralist Looks at the Durham and M'Naghten Rules," *Minnesota Law Review* 46 (1961): 327–36; Wilber Katz, "Law, Psychiatry and Free Will," *University of Chicago Law Review* 22 (1955): 397–404; Harry Kalven, Jr., Introduction to symposium "Insanity and Criminal Law," ibid., pp. 317–19; Henry Weihofen, "The Flowering of New Hampshire," ibid., pp. 356–66; Edward De Grazia, "The Distinction of Being Mad," ibid., p. 340, n. 8. But contrast, e.g., Herbert Wechsler, "The Criteria of Criminal Responsibility," ibid., pp. 367–76; P. P. Lynch, "Insanity as a Defence to Crime," *New Zealand Law Journal* 31 (1955): 216–27.

202. Winfred Overholser to Fortas, April 2, 1955, FP. See also editorial "A Century of Progress: The Durham Case," *Journal of Forensic Sciences* 1, no. 4 (1956): 41–42; H. B. Dearman, "Criminal Responsibility and Insanity Tests: A Psychiatrist Looks at Three Cases," *Virginia Law Review* 47 (1961): 1388–98; Philip Roche, "Criminality and Mental Illness: Two Faces of the Same Coin," *University of Chicago Law Review* 22 (1955): 320–24; Manfred Guttmacher, "The Psychiatrist as an Expert Witness," ibid., p. 325; Gregory Zilborg, "A Step Toward Enlightened Justice," ibid., pp. 331–35.

203. See *United States* v. *Brawner,* 417 F. 2d 969 (1972), overruling *Durham.*

204. *Betts* v. *Brady,* 316 U.S. 445 (1942).

205. See generally Anthony Lewis, *Gideon's Trumpet* (New York: Vintage Books, 1964); Bernard Schwartz, *Super Chief: Earl Warren and His Supreme Court—A Judicial Biography* (New York: New York University Press, 1983), pp. 458–59.

206. See generally Draft, Fortas to Criminal Rules Advisory Committee, June 14, 1961, FP. In 1961 Fortas had drafted a rule for the committee requiring police officers to advise defendants at the time of arrest that they were not required to make a statement and that anything they said might be used against them and to permit defendants to see or speak with whomever they wished (Draft, Fortas to Criminal Rules Advisory Committee, June 14, 1961). He had written William O. Douglas in 1959, "My own feeling is that immediately [after] a person is arrested or accused . . . he should be supplied with a 'friend,' presumably a lawyer, and that no further interrogation, and certainly no confession or admission should be tolerated until he has had an opportunity to talk with the friend or lawyer" (Fortas to William O. Douglas, March 10, 1959, A&P OF).

207. Fortas to Philip Abbott, Nov. 1, 1974, FP.

208. Brief for the Petitioner, *Clarence Earl Gideon* v. *H. G. Cochran, Jr.,* United States Supreme Court, October Term 1962, No. 155, p. 5, FP (hereafter, Brief, *Gideon*).

209. Quoted in Jonathan D. Casper, *Lawyers before the Warren Court: Civil Liberties and Civil Rights, 1957–66* (Urbana, Ill.: University of Illinois Press, 1972), pp. 95–96.

210. Ibid., p. 119.

211. Interview with Harold Burson, May 1987.

212. Fortas to Abbott, Nov. 1, 1974.

213. Fortas to Abbott, Nov. 1, 1974. For Fortas's letter to Gideon, see Lewis, *Gideon's Trumpet,* pp. 64–65.

214. Brief, *Gideon,* pp. 13–14, 41.

215. Abe Krash, "The Right to a Lawyer," *Notre Dame Lawyer* 39 (1964), p. 153.

216. Lewis, *Gideon's Trumpet,* pp. 126–27.

217. Brief, *Gideon,* pp. 8, 33. See also pp. 11–12.

218. Quoted in Lewis, *Gideon's Trumpet,* p. 127.

219. Ibid., pp. 171–72.

220. Interview with Potter Stewart, Sept. 1985.

221. Interview with Gerhard Gesell, May 1985.

222. William O. Douglas, *The Court Years, 1939–1975: The Autobiography of William O. Douglas* (New York: Random House, 1980), p. 187.

223. Lewis, *Gideon's Trumpet,* p. 174.

224. *Gideon* v. *Wainright,* 372 U.S. 335 (1963).

225. Interview with Krash.

226. Lewis, *Gideon's Trumpet,* p. 48.

## 9. THE ACTOR

1. Interview with Nicholas Katzenbach, Dec. 1983.

2. Interview with Norman Diamond, May 1985.

3. Interview with Charles Reich, Dec. 1985.

4. Eric Sevareid, Remarks delivered at a memorial service for Paul Porter, Dec. 11, 1975, FP.

5. Interview with Abe Krash, May 1987.

6. Richard Rovere, *Howe and Hummel: Their True and Scandalous History* (New York: Farrar, Straus, 1974), pp. 18, 16; interview with Milton Freeman, Dec. 1983.

7. Interview with Theodor Muller, Jan. 1987.

8. Interview with Louis Pollak, July 1985; interview with Katzenbach.

9. Interview with William Rogers, May 1987.

10. Interview with Edgar H. Brenner, Dec. 1984.

11. Interview with Diamond.

12. Interview with Thurman Arnold, Jr., July 1984.

13. Interview with Carl Siegesmund, May 1987.

14. Confidential interview 8.

15. Confidential interview 13.

16. Interview with Carol Agger, May 1987.

17. Interview with Rogers.

18. Robert Nelson, "Practice and Privilege: Social Change and the Structure of Large Law Firms," *American Bar Foundation Research Journal* 1981, table I, pp. 105–07. In 1950 a nine-person firm was not considered minuscule. When Robert B. Siddal surveyed large American law firms in 1956, he defined a large firm as one including nine or more members (Siddal, *A Survey of Large Law Firms in the United States* [New York: Vantage Press, Inc., 1956]). Yet Arnold, Fortas & Porter was one of the smallest of the "large" firms. Only one of the fifty largest

firms in 1979 had been smaller during the 1950s and 1960s than Arnold, Fortas & Porter (Nelson, "Practice and Privilege," 105–07). The presence of only three Washington firms in that 1979 group suggests that Washington firms historically may have been smaller than their New York and Chicago counterparts, but Arnold, Fortas & Porter was significantly smaller than even the other two Washington firms included, Covington & Burling (53 lawyers) and Hogan & Hartson (36 lawyers). Even after the firm doubled in size in 1961, it remained relatively small.

19. See, e.g., the description in Judy Hennessee, "The Washington Legal Establishment," *Washingtonian,* Aug. 1967, p. 34: "Arnold & Porter (Abe Fortas's old firm), has an off-beat, youthful, racy personality that makes stuffy people nervous, but all things considered, it probably has more quality per square inch than any other firm. It is also the most likable. Lawyers speak happily of it, almost as if they slept better at night knowing it was there."

20. Thurman Arnold to Wallace J. Burgess, May 5, 1966, A&P OF.

21. Nelson, "Practice and Privilege," pp. 118–26. Nelson suggested that these roles corresponded to the three significant roles the historian of business Alfred Chandler found in the multidivisional corporation—entrepreneurs, managers, and workers (see Alfred D. Chandler, Jr., *Strategy and Structure: Chapters in the History of American Industrial Enterprise* [Cambridge, Mass.: Harvard University Press, 1967]).

22. Interviews with Dennis Lyons, Dec. 1985; and G. Duane Vieth, Dec. 1985.

23. Confidential interview 14.

24. Interview with Diamond.

25. Confidential interview.

26. Robert Swaine, *The Cravath Firm and Its Predecessors* (New York: Ad Press, 1948), II: 12. See also Erwin Smigel, *The Wall Street Lawyer* (New York: The Free Press of Glencoe, 1964) p. 237. By 1964 Smigel thought that "the dictator senior partner is disappearing" and that firms were becoming more democratic. But see Nelson, "Practice and Privilege", pp. 23–24, 413–14.

27. Information in this paragraph is taken from confidential interviews 11, 14, 15, and 16.

28. Confidential interviews 14, 15, 16, and 17.

29. Confidential interviews 15, 18, and 19.

30. Interview with Rogers.

31. Interview with Krash.

32. Interview with Reich.

33. Interview with Krash.

34. Confidential interview 14.

35. Confidential interviews 17 and 18.

36. Confidential interviews 18, 17, 20, and 21.

37. Interviews with Lyons, Vieth, and Reich.

38. Interview with Vieth.

39. Confidential interview 17.

40. Interview with Krash.

41. Reed Miller, Remarks delivered at a memorial service for Paul Porter, Dec. 11, 1975, FP.

42. Confidential interview 14.

43. Charles Reich, *The Sorcerer of Bolinas Reef* (New York: Random House, 1976), p. 32.

44. Reich to Kalman, Oct. 10, 1986.

45. Interview with Reich.

46. Interview with Patrick Macrory, June 1987.

47. Rex Lee, "In Memoriam: Abe Fortas," Supreme Court Historical Society, *Yearbook 1983,* pp. 8–9.

48. Confidential interview 22.

49. Interview with Helen Muller, Jan. 1987.

50. Interview with Mercedes Eichholz, July 1988.

51. Interview with Macrory.
52. Interview with Vieth.
53. Interviews with Helen Muller and Mercedes Eichholz, May 1986.
54. See Fortas to Leonard C. Jones, June 12, 1964; Fortas to Clark Clifford, June 12, 1964; both in A&P OF.
55. Fortas to Isaac Stern, March 31, 1961, ibid.
56. Interviews with Isaac Stern, Jan. 1987, and Alexander Schneider, May 1987.
57. Interview with Barbara Winslow, May 1985.
58. Interviews with Helen Muller and Theodor Muller.
59. Interview with Stern.
60. Interview with Margot Collins, June 1985.
61. Interview with Stern.
62. Interviews with Collins and Winslow.
63. Interview with Marta Casals Istomin, May 1985.
64. Confidential interviews 17 and 18.
65. Fortas to Arthur Goldschmidt, March 21, 1962, FP.
66. Fortas to Alexander Schneider, Sept. 15, 1961, ibid; interview with Agger.
67. Interview with Krash; interview with Martin Riger, May 1987.
68. Interview with Theodor Muller.
69. Confidential interview 10.
70. Interview with Steven Gold, Sept. 1984.
71. Confidential interview 11.
72. Patrick Macrory to Laura Kalman, July 24, 1989.
73. Interview with Agger.
74. Confidential interviews 23, 24, and 27.
75. Confidential interview 14.
76. Interview with Kramer.
77. Confidential interview 25.
78. Interview with David Ginsburg, Dec. 1983.
79. Confidential interview 26.
80. Interview with Liz Carpenter, May 1986.
81. Interview with Lady Bird Johnson, May 1986.
82. Ibid.
83. Confidential interviews 9, 10, 23, and 24.
84. Confidential interview 27.
85. Confidential interview 9.
86. Confidential interviews 9, 23, 24, and 27.
87. Confidential interview 10.
88. Interview with Harold Burson, May 1987.

## 10. THE ADVISER, I

1. Abe Fortas, "Portrait of a Friend," in *Portraits of American Presidents*, ed. Kenneth W. Thompson (Lanham, Md: University Press of America, 1986) vol. 5, *The Johnson Presidency: Twenty Intimate Perspectives of Lyndon B. Johnson*, p. 17.
2. Goldschmidt is generally credited with having introduced Fortas and Johnson to each other, though he is not certain he did so (interview with Arthur ("Tex") Goldschmidt, Dec. 1983).
3. Interview with Lady Bird Johnson, May 1986.
4. Ibid.
5. Paul Porter to Lyndon B. Johnson, May 24, 1948, LBJA, Selected Names, Box 30, Paul Porter File, LBJL.

6. Paul Porter, LBJOH, p. 16; Robert Caro, *The Years of Lyndon Johnson,* vol. 2, *Means of Ascent* (New York: Alfred A. Knopf, 1990) pp. 309–13.

7. Abe Fortas, LBJOH, p. 8.

8. Texas law would permit Johnson's name to appear on the ballot only if county election officials received notice of his certification by the secretary of state of Texas thirty days before the general election on November 2. Certification mailing would take several days.

9. Fortas, LBJOH, p. 6.

10. Interview with Lady Bird Johnson.

11. Fortas, LBJOH, p. 8.

12. See Francis Biddle, Thurman Arnold, and James Rowe to Alvin Wirtz, Sept. 18, 1948, Stegall Files, Box 61, LBJL.

13. Fortas, LBJOH, p. 6.

14. Porter, LBJOH, p. 12.

15. Interview with Joseph Rauh, Dec. 1983.

16. Joseph Rauh, LBJOH, p. 4; and interview with Rauh.

17. William O. Douglas, *The Court Years, 1939–1975: The Autobiography of William O. Douglas* (New York: Random House, 1980), p. 335.

18. "AF Draft," Aug. 29, 1977, FP. There is no way to be certain Fortas sent this document to Douglas, as there is no reply in these papers. By the time he wrote *The Court Years* Douglas had developed very different ideas about Johnson than those held by Fortas.

19. Quoted in Merle Miller, *Lyndon: An Oral Biography* (New York: G. P. Putnam's Sons, 1980), p. 133.

20. Johnson to Fortas, Oct. 1, 1948, LBJA, Selected Names, Abe Fortas File, Box 18, LBJL.

21. Interview with Clark Clifford, July 1985.

22. James Rowe to Johnson, Aug. 24, 1960, LBJA, Selected Names, James Rowe File, Box 32, LBJL; and Rowe to Johnson, "The Liberal Revolt," Dec. 4, 1958, ibid.

23. See, e.g., Rowe to Johnson, April 4, 1956; Dec. 21, 1954; July 3, 1957; July 7, 1959; Aug. 24, 1960; all in ibid.

24. Fortas to Johnson, Aug. 9, 1956, LBJA, Selected Names, Abe Fortas File, Box 18, LBJL.

25. Fortas to Johnson, Aug. 20, 1957, ibid.

26. Fortas to Johnson, Dec. 31, 1957, FP.

27. "AF Draft." Emphasis in original.

28. Ibid. Emphasis in original.

29. Reported in confidential interview 9.

30. Fortas, "Portrait of a Friend," p. 14.

31. "AF Draft." Douglas did not. The exchange between Douglas and Johnson is quoted in Douglas, *Court Years,* p. 329.

32. See, e.g., Fortas, "Portrait of a Friend," pp. 7–8, 13, 16.

33. Interview with Frances Arnold, July 1984. When an acquaintance sent Fortas a draft of an article suggesting that William Howard Taft and Andrew Carnegie belonged to the "ultimate level" of the American Establishment, while Fortas did not, Fortas waspishly replied, "Comparison in these terms is offensive—regardless of who is preferred and who is denied" (Fortas to John Frank, Aug. 7, 1970, FP).

34. Interview with Lady Bird Johnson. For an example of Fortas's comments on Johnson as a Southerner, and Fortas's sometimes disingenuous approach to Southern history, see an undated draft of a speech to the Memphis Bar Association, FP: "I know of no place which is so rich in human warmth, hospitality and personal kindness. . . . This is the special quality of the South and it is this quality that makes me proud to be a Southerner and a Memphian. . . . I am glad that we have a President who *knows* that these are the true qualities of the South—a President who shares this heritage—who does not have to try to learn or to be *told* that the people of the South are good and kind and generous and warm-hearted—and that they feel and act this way towards all of God's children, whatever their race or religion might be." Compare

the comment on Southern history quoted in chapter 1, p. 12. (from a speech to the Anti-Defamation League of B'nai Brith).

35. Harry McPherson, LBJOH, 1, Tape 2, p. 28.

36. Interview with Lady Bird Johnson.

37. Interview with Agger.

38. Interview with Clifford.

39. Harry McPherson, LBJOH, 3, tape 1, p. 29; and interview with McPherson, May 1985.

40. Interview with George Reedy, Sept. 1984.

41. Bill Lloyd to Johnson, March 24, 1960, Prepresidential Memos File, Box 6, LBJL.

42. George Reedy to Johnson, March 24, 1960, Office Files of George Reedy, box 430, LBJL.

43. Interview with Reedy.

44. "The Enemies of Leland Olds," *New Republic*, Oct. 17, 1949, Senate Appointment Files, File: Leland Olds," Box 320, LBJL.

45. Miller, *Lyndon*, p. 146.

46. Ibid., p. 147. Fortas wrote Rauh a letter denying the charge (interview with Rauh).

47. Interview with Walter Jenkins, Sept. 1984.

48. Dan and Jack Danciger to Johnson, Oct. 4, 1949, Box 320, Olds Appointment File, LBJL.

49. Interview with Jenkins.

50. James Rowe to Johnson, June 9, 1958, LBJA, Selected Names, James Rowe File, Box 32, LBJL.

51. Fortas to Walter Jenkins, June 8, 1955, LBJA, Selected Names, Abe Fortas File, Box 18, ibid.

52. Interview with Jenkins.

53. Fortas to Arthur Goldschmidt and Elizabeth Wickenden, Dec. 31, 1957, FP.

54. Fortas to Meyer Fortes, Nov. 13, 1958, ibid.

55. Fortas to Mrs. Edward Macauley, Jan. 14, 1958, ibid.

56. Fortas to Stuart Symington, May 27, 1960, ibid.

57. Fortas to William O. Douglas, July 25, 1960, A&P OF.

58. See Steven Gillon, *Politics and Vision: The ADA and American Liberalism, 1947–1985* (New York: Oxford University Press, 1987), pp. 131–35.

59. Bill Taylor to Vi Gunther, March 1, 1960, Box 18, Americans for Democratic Action Papers, The State Historical Society of Wisconsin.

60. Quoted in Charles Seib and Alan Otten, "Abe, Help!—LBJ," *Esquire* (June 1965), pp. 88, 147.

61. Fortas to Macauley, Jan. 14, 1958.

62. James Rowe to Ancil Payne, March 26, 1959, C. Girard Davidson Papers, University of Oregon Archives.

63. Rowe to Johnson, Jan. 17, 1959, LBJA, Selected Names, James Rowe File, Box 32, LBJL. Emphasis in the original.

64. Reedy to Johnson, March 24, 1960.

65. Diary File, June 15, 1960, Box 219, Adolf Berle Papers, FDRL.

66. Fortas to Symington, May 27, 1960.

67. Fortas to Douglas, July 25, 1960.

68. Quoted in Bruce Murphy, *Fortas: The Rise and Ruin of a Supreme Court Justice* (New York: William Morrow, 1988), p. 108.

69. Fortas to Johnson, April 10, 1959, Box 1, Special File Pertaining to Abe Fortas and Homer Thornberry, LBJL (hereafter, Fortas-Thornberry File). See *Parr* v. *United States*, 268 F. 2d 894 (1959); *rehearing denied* 268 F. 2d 959 (1959).

70. See, e.g., Fortas to Johnson, Dec. 8, 1959; Telephone conversation between Abe Fortas and Walter Jenkins, Dec. 14, 1959, LBJL; *Parr* v. *United States*, 363 U.S. 1171 (1960).

71. Interview with Reedy.

72. Fred Korth, LBJOH, p. 28.

73. Fortas to William O. Douglas, Feb. 27, 1962, FP.

74. William S. White, *The Professional: Lyndon B. Johnson* (Greenwich, Conn.: Fawcett Publications, 1964), p. 145.

75. Leonard Baker, *The Johnson Eclipse: A President's Vice-Presidency* (New York: Macmillan, 1966), p. 149.

76. Fortas to Eleanor Roosevelt, March 17, 1961, FP.

77. Harris Wofford, Oral History, John F. Kennedy Library, p. 125; and Hobart Taylor, Oral History, ibid., p. 13.

78. Fortas to Eleanor Roosevelt, March 17, 1961, FP.

79. Baker, *Johnson Eclipse*, p. 148.

80. Fortas to George Reedy, May 24, 1961, FP.

81. Fortas, Memorandum for the Vice-President, March 9, 1961, ibid.

82. Fortas to George Reedy, Aug. 31, 1961 (enclosing draft of talking points to be used by Johnson in discussion of the EEOC with Kennedy).

83. Baker, *Johnson Eclipse*, p. 156.

84. See, e.g., Fred Lazarus to Robert Troutman, Jr., Jan. 3, 1962; Fortas to George Reedy, Jan. 4, 1962; Fortas, "Memorandum Concerning the President's Committee on Equal Employment Opportunity," Jan. 18, 1962; Fortas to Troutman, Jan. 27, 1962; all in FP.

85. See Baker, *Johnson Eclipse*, pp. 159–62; Arthur Schlesinger, Jr., *Robert F. Kennedy and His Times* (Boston: Houghton Mifflin, 1978) pp. 312–13.

86. "A Partial Transcript of an Interview with Justice Fortas," March 27, 1967, FP.

87. Interview with Abe Krash, May 1987.

88. Quote in Fortas, "Portrait of a Friend," p. 6. See also Murphy, *Fortas*, pp. 121–23.

89. Fortas, "Portrait of a Friend," p. 7; "some corn pone" in Murphy, *Fortas*, p. 119.

90. See Richard Goodwin, *Remembering America: A Voice From the Sixties* (Boston: Little, Brown and Company, 1988), p. 71.

91. Fortas, Memorandum for the President, Dec. 1, 1963, Diary Backup, Box 2, LBJL. See also Murphy, *Fortas*, pp. 119–20.

92. Draft, n.d., State Messages, Statements File, Box 89, LBJL.

93. Ibid.

94. Horace Busby, Memorandum to the President and Mrs. Johnson, Nov. 24, 1963, Ex FG 400, WHCF, Box 321, LBJL.

95. Seib and Otten, "Abe, Help!—LBJ," p. 88.

96. Ibid.

97. See generally John M. Blum, *Roosevelt and Morgenthau* (Boston: Houghton Mifflin, 1972), pp. 173–209.

98. See generally James M. Burns, *Roosevelt: The Lion and the Fox* (New York: Harcourt, Brace and World, 1956), pp. 328–36.

99. Quoted in Allen Matusow, *The Unraveling of America: A History of Liberalism in the 1960s* (New York: Harper and Row, 1984), p. 53.

100. Fortas to Johnson, Dec. 25, 1963, FP.

101. Fortas, Memorandum for Theodore C. Sorensen, Dec. 25, 1963, FP.

102. Draft, n.d., State Messages. Emphasis added.

103. "Program for Thrift and Frugality," Nov. 30, 1963, FP.

104. Memorandum for the Files, Meeting with Equity Managers, June 26, 1968, Meeting Notes, Box 3, LBJL: "The President reminisced on the conflict between business and Government during the New Deal. He said he thought that perhaps the most significant development of the past generation was the new social consciousness of business."

105. Fortas, Draft of speech, "For the Business Advisory Committee," n.d., FP. (Fortas probably was referring to the Business Advisory Council, which had reconstituted itself as the Business Council during the Kennedy administration.)

106. Maurice Lazarus to Fortas, Sept. 11, 1964; Fortas to Lazarus, Sept. 15, 1964, ibid.

107. Fortas to Nicholas Katzenbach, Feb. 12, 1965, FP; "List of Names Suggested by Fred Lazarus, Jr., 1/29," ibid.

108. Fortas to Bill Moyers, Jan. 21, 1964, ibid.

109. Fortas to Ralph Lazarus, Oct. 12, 1964, ibid.

110. Fortas to Jack Valenti, Jan. 31, 1964, ibid.

111. Fortas to Norman Diamond, July 23, 1964, ibid.

112. Johnson to Paul Porter, March 4, 1964, Paul Porter Name File, WHCF, Box 266, LBJL.

113. Fortas, Memorandum for the President, n.d. (ca. November, 1963), FP.

114. Sargent Shriver to Fortas, Sept. 26, 1966, and Fortas, Remarks at the Opening Ceremony of Bridgeport Legal Services Committee, n.d. [ca. Summer 1966], both in ibid.

115. Fortas to Lt. Richard Nelson, Oct. 12, Box 1, Fortas-Thornberry File, LBJL.

116. Fortas to Bill Moyers, April 30, 1964, FP.

117. McPherson, LBJOH, 3, Tape 1, p. 39; interview with Lady Bird Johnson; interview with Clifford; Eric Goldman quoted in Richard Rovere Diary, Feb. 13, 1964, Box 17, Richard Rovere Papers, State Historical Society of Wisconsin.

118. Fortas to Troy Post, Dec. 30, 1963, FP.

119. Walter Jenkins, "Various Conversations Today," Nov. 25, 1963, Ex FG 1, LBJL; Fortas, Memorandum (concerning conversation with Dean Acheson), Nov. 25, 1963, FP.

120. AF Draft, Aug. 29, 1977. Cf. Murphy, *Fortas*, pp. 116–17.

121. AF Draft, Aug. 29, 1977.

122. Fortas, Conference Re Investigation Procedures, Dec. 2, 1963, FP.

123. Paul Taylor to Fortas, Feb. 17, 1964; "New Udall Water Plan for West," *Oakland Tribune*, Feb. 16, 1964; Fortas to Taylor, Feb. 20, 1964; all in FP. See chap. 5.

124. E. U. Condon to Fortas, Jan. 12, 1964; Fortas to Condon, Feb. 8, 1964; FP.

125. Jack Valenti, Memorandum for the President, Dec. 28, 1963, Ex FE 2–11, WHCF, Box 2, LBJL.

126. Fortas to Bill Moyers, Nov. 9, 1964; Fortas to John W. Macy, Dec. 19, 1964; Fortas to Nicholas Katzenbach, Feb. 12, 1965; Fortas to Marvin Watson, March 20, 1965; Fortas to R. Sargent Shriver, Feb. 1, 1965; Fortas to John Macy, March 31, 1965; all in FP. Cf. Bruce Murphy's presentation of Fortas as a "public relations counsellor," who was "more concerned with the *symbolic appearance* of an action [by Johnson] than its substance" in *Fortas*, pp. 108, 126, 132.

127. Fortas to Macy, Nov. 21, 1964, ibid.

128. See, e.g., Fortas to Luis Muñoz Marín, July 30, 1964, FP; George Reedy to President, Aug. 17, 1964, WHCF, Ex PL 10/ST 51–2, Box 135; LBJL.

129. Fortas to Muñoz Marín, Nov. 14, 1964; Fortas to John Macy, Nov. 27, 1964; Fortas to Macy, Dec. 7, 1964; FP.

130. Fortas to Teodoro Moscoso, Dec. 8, 1964, ibid. See, e.g., Fortas to Ralph Dungan, Nov. 14, 1964; Fortas to Henry Fowler, July 23, 1965; both in ibid.

131. Fortas to Luis Laboy, June 5, 1965, ibid.

132. He liked to compare the presidential adviser to "the little boy who looks at a baseball game through a knothole in the fence." Just as the boy might think that since he could only see right field, the entire game was occurring there, so the presidential adviser might believe, wrongly, that he could understand White House activity. In fact, the two qualifications Fortas believed an adviser most needed were "the courage to assert one's views and the capacity for humility" (Fortas, Interview with Emmet Hughes, "The Presidency As I Have Seen It," ibid).

133. Fortas to C (name withheld to protect confidentiality), April 10, 1964, ibid. Other appointments made Fortas more hopeful. Mary Keyserling, whose clearance he had secured from a loyalty board, was among those he endorsed for a high government position. "In the early 1950's, while the hysteria was at its height, loyalty charges were proffered against her—as against most good people of her generation," Fortas explained to the President's staff. "I am

familiar with the facts and it was one of the more outrageous instances of accusation on account of consanguinity" (Fortas to Jack Valenti, Feb. 20, 1964, ibid). Keyserling received the appointment.

134. Fortas to Christine Stevens, April 8, 1966; Fortas to Johnson, Feb. 10, 1966; both in ibid; Murphy, *Fortas*, pp. 204–05.

135. Fortas, Remarks at Memorial Service for Joseph H. Hirshhorn, Sept. 16, 1981; Dillon Ripley to Lyndon Johnson, Feb. 19, 1971; both in FP.

136. Fortas to Julius Bloom, June 4, 1964; Fortas to Bess Abell, June 11, 1964; ibid. See also "Justice Fortas Is Talent Scout for White House," *Washington Post*, Sept. 27, 1967.

137. Fortas to Hubert Humphrey, Jan. 24, 1964, FP.

138. Fortas to Jack Valenti, Dec. 6, 1964, ibid.

139. Fortas to Arthur Schlesinger, Jr., Dec. 1, 1963, ibid. Kennedy had not understood why Goodwin wanted the position either (Goodwin, *Remembering America*, p. 222).

140. Fortas, Memorandum for the President, Jan. 29, 1964; Fortas to Jack Valenti, Dec. 6, 1964; both in FP.

141. Fortas to Lucius Battle, Pierre Salinger, and Isaac Stern, Jan. 31, 1964, ibid. Stern replied, "So what else is new?" (Stern to Fortas, Feb. 8, 1964, ibid).

142. Fortas, Memorandum for the President, March 10, 1964, ibid.

143. Fortas to Valenti, Dec. 6, 1964.

144. See, e.g., Kathleen Turner, *Lyndon Johnson's Dual War: Vietnam and the Press* (Chicago: University of Chicago Press, 1985), pp. 46–47, 93, 104–106, 167; Carl Solberg, *Hubert Humphrey: A Biography* (New York: W. W. Norton, 1984), pp. 278–79, 302–03, 347–48.

145. Harry McPherson, LBJOH, 1, Tape 2, pp. 19–20.

146. Interview with Krash.

147. "Paul Berry's Washington" (Transcript of radio show taped Nov. 8, 1977), FP. Jenkins assured Fortas that he had never consulted either Fortas or Clifford. Fortas summarized his conversation with Jenkins in a memorandum to the files: "It was felt that he should not talk with either Clark Clifford or me because of the desire that the entire matter be disassociated from the White House." Fortas warned the radio station that if it broadcast the portion of the interview implying he had committed a crime, he might sue (Fortas, Memorandum to the Files, Nov. 9, 1977).

148. Quoted in Eric Goldman, *The Tragedy of Lyndon Johnson* (New York: Alfred A. Knopf, 1969), p. 83. See also George Reedy, LBJOH, III, Tape 1, pp. 37–38.

149. Interview with Reedy.

150. Interview with Clifford; McPherson, LBJOH, 3, Tape 1, p. 39.

151. Interview with Clifford.

152. "Replies to Bill Manchester letter," (ca. June 1965); Memorandum for Jack Valenti, May 10, 1965; FP.

153. Fortas to Johnson, Nov. 29, 1965, ibid.

154. Ibid.

155. Fortas, "The Organization of the Office of the President", Nov. 2, 1964, ibid.

156. Goldman, *Tragedy of Lyndon Johnson*, pp. 154–56. See also Richard Rovere Diary, May 13, 1964, Box 17, Richard Rovere Papers: "EG took the whole thing . . . to Abe Fortas, who said it sounded great but pointed out that LBJ's attitude toward his staff made it all impossible."

157. Eric Goldman to Fortas, May 13, 1964, FP.

158. Goldman, *Tragedy of Lyndon Johnson*, p. 38.

159. Jack Valenti to Fortas, n.d., FP.

160. Bill Moyers to Fortas, Dec. 29, 1967; Fortas to Moyers, Jan. 5, 1968; FP.

161. Interview with Lady Bird Johnson.

162. See generally David Wise, "How the Jenkins Case Unfolded," *Chicago Sun-Times*, Oct. 18, 1964; and "Johnson Friends Called on Press," *New York Times*, Oct. 16, 1964.

163. Liz Carpenter, LBJOH, 4, LBJL, pp. 33–35.

164. Interview with Liz Carpenter, May 1986.

165. U.S. Senate, *Hearing before the Committee on the Judiciary,* 89th Cong., 1st sess., Nomination of Abe Fortas (Washington: GPO, 1965) (hereafter, *Nomination Hearing*), pp. 48–49. Fortas reconstructed his conversation with Jenkins for the committee.

166. Seib and Otten, "Abe, Help!—LBJ," pp. 86–87. Fortas subsequently wrote Adolf Berle that Jenkins's act "was the symbolic suicide of a man whose nervous apparatus and personality structure finally broke under inhuman strain. I do not hesitate to say that he is as fine a man as I have ever known; intensely and deeply moral, profoundly religious and dedicated beyond comparison to his work and the public interest" (Fortas to Adolf Berle, Oct. 27, 1964, Box 86, Adolf Berle Papers, FDRL).

167. The President's Daily Diary, Box 2, October 14, 1964, LBJL.

168. Wise, "How the Jenkins Case Unfolded."

169. Interview with Carpenter.

170. Interview with Jenkins.

171. Fortas to Harold Burson, Oct. 29, 1964, FP.

172. Fortas to M. B. Schnapper, May 9, 1964, FP.

173. *Nomination Hearing,* p. 49.

174. Portions of that interview subsequently appeared in a piece entitled "Abe, Help!—LBJ," which was illustrated with some unflattering caricatures of Fortas. When Seib wrote to say that he and his coauthor had "tried to do an honest bit of journalism, neither puff piece nor hatchet job" and added that they had nothing to do with the selection of the title or the cartoons, (Charlie Seib to Fortas, May 18, 1965, FP), Fortas quickly reassured him. "Don't be concerned about the title or cartoons," he replied. "I know you called it as you see it—and you know that I wanted to help as an indication of my profound appreciation of your humanity in the Walter Jenkins affair" (Fortas to Seib, May 20, 1965, FP). See also *Nomination Hearing,* p. 49.

175. Fortas to John O'Rourke, Dec. 19, 1964, FP.

## 11. NEW ROLES

1. Bill Moyers to Fortas, March 17, 1965, Abe Fortas Name File, LBJL.

2. Fortas to Hal Gerber, Dec. 10, 1963, FP.

3. Fortas to Simon Lazarus, Jr., Dec. 23, 1963, ibid.

4. Fortas to Walter A. Rudlin, Dec. 23, 1963, ibid.

5. Quoted in Leonard Lyons, "The Lyons Den" column (date not included), ibid.

6. Confidential interviews 14 and 17.

7. Fortas to Dorothy Page, Feb. 7, 1964, FP.

8. Troy Post to Fortas, March 3, 1964, ibid.

9. Piute Pete to Fortas, March 5, 1964, ibid.

10. Sister Mary James to Fortas, April 26, 1964, ibid.

11. Fortas to Roger Stevens, Sept. 26, 1964 (transmitting Irma Lazarus's letter), ibid.

12. Arthur Goldschmidt to Fortas, Feb. 11, 1964, ibid.

13. Fortas to Roger Stevens, Sept. 25, 1964, ibid.

14. Fortas to Dorothy Page, Feb. 7, 1964.

15. Fortas to Troy Post, March 12, 1964, ibid.

16. Fortas to Irma Lazarus, Sept. 26, 1964, ibid.

17. Fortas to Arthur Goldschmidt, Feb. 13, 1964, ibid.

18. Fortas to Bess Abel, March 13, 1964, ibid.

19. Fortas to Richard Nelson, May 2, 1964, Box 1, Special File Pertaining to Abe Fortas and Homer Thornberry, LBJL.

20. Fortas to Jack Valenti, Nov. 26, 1964, ibid.

21. Fortas to John Frank, August 7, 1970, FP.

22. Confidential interviews 14 and 17.

23. Confidential interview 17.

24. Charles Seib and Alan Otten, "Abe, Help!—LBJ!," *Esquire,* June 1965, p. 87.

25. Interview with Carol Agger, May 1987.

26. Interview with Lady Bird Johnson, May 1986.

27. Interview with Barbara Winslow, May 1985.

28. Fortas to Harold Hartog, December 23, 1963, FP.

29. I am indebted to Carol Agger for supplying me with a summary of Fortas's 1964 tax returns.

30. Interview with Agger.

31. See Jerome Slater, *Intervention and Negotiation,* (New York: Harper and Row, 1970), pp. 23–24.

32. Quoted in John Bartlow Martin, *Overtaken by Events: The Dominican Crisis from the Fall of Trujillo to the Civil War* (New York: Doubleday, 1966), p. 661.

33. Lyndon Johnson, *The Vantage Point: Perspectives of the Presidency, 1963–1969* (New York: Holt, Rinehart and Winston, 1971), p. 202.

34. Interview with Agger. Fortas was in Boston visiting Maurice Lazarus on May 1 when Johnson telephoned to tell him that the United States was sending in additional troops. Fortas told Lazarus he had commented that the number of Marines the President planned to send would "tip over the island" (interview with Maurice Lazarus, Sept. 1985).

35. Fortas, LBJOH, pp. 29–30.

36. Confidential source. For Fortas's explanation of the "moral" argument that could be advanced to justify intervention, see Fortas to McGeorge Bundy, May 6, 1965, National Security File, History, Dominican Republic invasion, LBJL. See also Len Meeker, Memorandum, "Legal Basis for United States Actions in the Dominican Republic," May 7, 1965, ibid.

37. Interview with McGeorge Bundy, March 1989.

38. White House records indicate that Johnson spoke with Bundy by telephone eighty-six times during that period, and with Fortas 40 times. The next most frequently telephoned participant was Secretary of Defense Robert McNamara, who had thirty-one conversations with the President during this period. Yet Johnson met with Fortas about the crisis relatively infrequently (Memorandum to the President, May 12, 1965, National Security File, McGeorge Bundy Memos to the President, Box 3, LBJL).

39. Bruce Murphy, *Fortas: The Rise and Ruin of a Supreme Court Justice* (New York: William Morrow, 1988), pp. 145–46, 149. See also Bundy Notes, May 10, 1965, National Security File, Country File, Dominican Republic, Davidson File, Box 51, LBJL: "Abe Fortas says Munoz: Venezuela OAS.—President plead with them to send a team."

40. Benítez, one of Bosch's most important advisers throughout the crisis, telephoned Fortas's office the day after Caamaño's coup and dictated a statement for possible use by the State Department emphasizing Washington's "traditional non-intervention policy" and its hope "for the resumption at the earliest possible time of constitutionality and order" (Helen to Fortas, April 26, 1965, FP.)

41. Information about Fortas's conversation with LBJ and his subsequent conversation with Bosch appears in Fortas, Memorandum, May 1, 1965, FP.

42. Ibid. See Abraham Lowenthal, *The Dominican Intervention* (Cambridge, Mass.: Harvard University Press, 1972), p. 127, for a different account of Fortas and Bosch's conversation: "Caamaño then telephoned Bosch in San Juan, who interrupted a 'Face the Nation' interview being taped by CBS TV to instruct Caamaño to tell his forces not to resist the American advance. . . . Soon Fortas was talking by telephone with Bosch, who informed Fortas of the advice he had just given Caamaño; Fortas expressed his gratitude."

43. Fortas, Memorandum, May 1, 1965. Bosch's account of the conversation suggests Fortas was less forthcoming about helping Bosch return to Santo Domingo than the attorney indicated in his notes and that Bosch did not tell Fortas he had decided against going back to Santo Domingo: "When Fortas told me by phone that in 10 minutes the Marines would receive

the order to attack the constitutionalist forces, I responded that in my judgment, at that moment there was only one solution: my going to Santo Domingo. I requested a plane for the trip, but Fortas gave no indication that his government would accede to my request. . . . Fortas had responded with silence" (Bosch, "A Tale of Two Nations," *New Leader,* June 21, 1965, pp. 4, 7).

44. Homer Bigart, "U.S. and Bosch: A Story of Blunders," *New York Times,* May 6, 1965.

45. John Bartlow Martin to Secretary of State, Cable, May 3, 1965, National Security File, National Security Council History, File: Dominican Crisis, 1965, Chronology, May 4–10, 1965, Box 10, LBJL.

46. Martin, *Overtaken by Events,* p. 676.

47. McGeorge Bundy to Lyndon Johnson, May 3, 1965, National Security File, McGeorge Bundy Memos to the President, Box 3, LBJL.

48. Fortas notes, May 3, 1965, FP; see also Bundy to Johnson, May 3, 1965.

49. Bosch, "A Tale of Two Nations," p. 7. See also Theodore Draper, *The Dominican Revolt* (New York: Commentary Reports, 1968), p. 158: "Since Martin had already committed himself publicly to the "Communist takeover," not merely the danger, and Bosch had already denounced the U.S. intervention, precisely because he considered the entire Communist issue an indefensible red herring, it is hard to see how Martin or Fortas could have chosen to ask him to sign a more obnoxious and self-destroying statement."

50. See Martin, *Overtaken by Events,* pp. 679–95, for following account.

51. Quoted in U.S. Senate, Committee on Foreign Relations, *Background Relating to the Dominican Republic,* 89th Cong., 1st sess., p. 23.

52. "Bosch Charge," May 9, 1965, FP.

53. John Bartlow Martin, *It Seems Like Only Yesterday: Memoirs of Writing, Presidential Politics and the Diplomatic Life* (New York: William Morrow, 1986), pp. 253–54.

54. Quoted in Slater, *Intervention and Negotiation,* p. 67. As Draper has observed in *The Dominican Revolt,* pp. 176–77: "After April 29 . . . a struggle went on in Washington for the conscience and comprehension of President Johnson and those closest to him. If some of them had not been deeply disturbed by the events and their own part in them, they would not have gone to the trouble of bringing three of the most respected and most progressive Latin American elder statesmen to advise them. In effect, one arm of U.S. policy was working against Bosch and one arm was tentatively working with him."

55. Bigart, "U.S. and Bosch: A Story of Blunders."

56. Confidential source.

57. Bosch's own account of his negotiations with John Bartlow Martin suggested that he never came around to the American interpretation of the Dominican intervention, which would have required him to concede that "the Dominican constitutionalist movement was under Communist domination" (Bosch, "A Tale of Two Nations," p. 3).

58. Fortas, Events of 12 May 1965, ibid.

59. Carol Agger to Laura Kalman, Feb. 11, 1986.

60. Interview with Patrick Macrory, May 1987.

61. Interview with Agger.

62. Interview with Agger.

63. See Fortas, "Several Appointment Possibilities," n.d., FP, in which he gave Davidson an "AAA" rating"; Fortas to Bill Moyers, Nov. 9, 1964, ibid.: "I am still unable to understand why C. Girard Davidson (Jebby Davidson) has not been utilized. The fact that he opposed Kennedy for the nomination should by now be irrelevant"; Fortas to C. Girard Davidson, March 13, 1964, ibid.: "I wish that you were here in an important official post. I urge this, but there is some static in the internal channels. I suspect you know what I mean."

64. Interview with Jaime Benítez, August 1985.

65. Jaime Benítez to John Kenneth Galbraith, Jan. 30, 1986 (copy given me by Carol Agger); interview with Benítez.

66. Statement agreed to by Juan Bosch, 12 May 1965, with Davidson, FP.

67. E.g., Slater, *Intervention and Negotiation,* p. 88.

68. The account in this paragraph draws on Fortas, Events of 12 May 1965.

69. Interview with Benítez.

70. Interview with Benítez.

71. Fortas, Events of 12 May 1965.

72. Fortas, Statement to be made by the President of the U.S., (Written in Benítez's hand) May 13, 1965, FP.

73. Agreed to between Juan Bosch and Davidson, May 13, 1965 (memorandum), FP. According to Fortas's notes, Bosch had suggested Elmilio Alimonte Jimenez, a hydraulic engineer, as president the previous night, but they had not settled upon him (Fortas, Events of 12 May 1965).

74. Johnson quoted in McGeorge Bundy Notes, May 14, 1965, National Security File, National Security Council History, Dominican Crisis 1965, Box 11, LBJL.

75. Slater, *Intervention and Negotiation,* pp. 92–97, 106–35. Guzman was elected president of the Dominican Republic twelve years later.

76. McGeorge Bundy to the President, June 11, 1965, National Security File, McGeorge Bundy Memos to the President, Box 3, LBJL.

77. Henry Wallace to Fortas, May 31, 1965, FP.

78. Fortas to Henry Wallace, June 5, 1965, ibid.

79. Johnson, *The Vantage Point,* pp. 543–44.

80. Interview with Arthur Goldberg, Dec. 1983.

81. Quoted in Murphy, *Fortas,* p. 171.

82. Paul Porter, LBJOH, p. 29.

83. Interview with Nicholas Katzenbach, Dec. 1983.

84. Interview with Lady Bird Johnson.

85. Interviews with Milton Freeman, Dec. 1983; William Rogers, May 1987; Paul Berger, May 1985; G. Duane Vieth, Dec. 1985. See also Porter, LBJOH, pp. 28–29.

86. Interview with Mercedes Eichholz, May 1986.

87. Confidential interview 27.

88. Quoted in Johnson, *Vantage Point,* pp. 544–45.

89. Fortas, LBJOH, p. 24.

90. Interview with Carl Siegesmund, May 1987.

91. See pp. 46–48.

92. Interview with Agger.

93. Confidential interview 9.

94. Interviews with Eichholz and Agger.

95. Robert Shogan, *A Question of Judgment: The Fortas Case and the Struggle for the Supreme Court* (Indianapolis, Ind.: Bobbs-Merrill, 1972), p. 110.

96. Confidential interviews 28, 29, and 30.

97. Interview with Agger.

98. Interview with William Rogers, May 1987.

99. Interview with Abe Krash, May 1987; interview with Rogers; confidential interviews 25 and 31.

100. William O. Douglas to Fortas, July 20, 1965, FP.

101. Mercedes Eichholz to William O. Douglas, July 21, 1965. I am grateful to Melvin Urofsky for giving me a copy of this letter.

102. Interview with Lady Bird Johnson.

103. Johnson, *Vantage Point,* p. 545.

104. Fortas, LBJOH, pp. 24–25.

105. *Washington Post,* July 30, 1965.

106. Michael Parrish, *Felix Frankfurter and His Times: The Reform Years* (New York: Free Press, 1982), p. 275.

107. Interviews with Isaac Stern (Jan. 1987) and Eichholz.

108. Interview with Berger.

109. Interview with Eichholz.

110. Interview with Agger.

111. Porter, LBJOH, p. 31.

112. Ibid., and confidential interviews 9, 23, and 32.

113. Interview with Goldberg; Dorothy and Arthur Goldberg to Fortas, July 28, 1965.

114. "The Colonel [Parker]" to Fortas, July 29, 1965; Cartha DeLoach to Fortas, July 28, 1965; both in FP.

115. Florence Frank to Fortas, Aug. 1, 1965, ibid.

116. Benjamin V. Cohen to Fortas, Aug. 13, 1965, ibid; Fortas to Cohen, Aug. 23, 1965, ibid.

117. Fortas to Alexander Schneider, Aug. 12, 1965, ibid.

118. Fortas to Adolf Berle, Aug. 10, 1965, Box 86, Adolf Berle Papers, FDRL.

119. Fortas to William O. Douglas, Aug. 11, 1965; William Brennan to Fortas, n.d.; Fortas to William Brennan, Aug. 11, 1965; Fortas to Tom Clark, Aug. 11, 1965; all in FP.

120. Norman Diamond to Fortas, July 29, 1965, ibid.

121. Philip Hart to Thurman Arnold, Aug. 5, 1965, Thurman Arnold Papers, American Heritage Collection, University of Wyoming.

122. Fortas to Patrick Macrory, Aug. 10, 1965, FP.

123. Fortas to Fred Lazarus, Aug. 23, 1965, ibid.

124. Interview with Ernest Meyers, July 1985.

125. Interview with Norman Diamond, May 1985.

126. Interview with Mercedes Eichholz, Sept. 1988.

127. Elizabeth Wickenden to Fortas, Aug. 3, 1965, FP.

128. U.S. Senate, *Hearing before the Committee on the Judiciary, Nomination of Abe Fortas,* 89th Cong., 1st sess., (Washington: GPO, 1965), p. 50 (hereafter, *Nomination Hearing*).

129. See *Reynolds v. Sims,* 377 U.S. 533 (1964).

130. *Nomination Hearing,* pp. 51–56.

131. Fortas to David Bazelon, July 12, 1965, FP. It is unclear whether Fortas sent the letter.

132. *Nomination Hearing,* p. 45.

133. Ibid., pp. 45–47.

134. Ibid., p. 11.

135. Fortas to I. F. Stone, Sept. 16, 1965; Fortas to James O. Eastland, Sept. 16, 1965; both in FP.

136. William O. Douglas to Fortas, Oct. 4, 1965, ibid.

## 12. THE LAWYER AS JUSTICE

1. Llewellyn devoted three pages in *The Bramble Bush: On Our Law and Its Study,* published in 1950, to explaining how critics had wrenched his statement out of context. (Karl Llewellyn, *The Bramble Bush* [reprint; Dobbs Ferry, New York, Oceana, 1978], pp. 8–10).

2. Abe Fortas, *Concerning Dissent and Civil Disobedience* (New York: New American Library, 1968), p. 59. Emphasis in original.

3. Cf. Robert Burt's description of Brandeis and Frankfurter in *Two Jewish Justices: Outsiders in the Promised Land* (Berkeley, Calif.: University of California Press, 1988), pp. 34–35, 44–48.

4. Daniel Levitt, Remarks at Supreme Court memorial service for Fortas (hereafter, Remarks), 102 S. Ct. 36 (1982).

5. See Abe Fortas, "Beyond *Gault:* The Juvenile Offender" (Paper delivered to the Juvenile Court Practice Institute, Washington, D.C., Nov. 20, 1969), FP.

6. Ibid.

7. Fortas, Draft, *Kent* v. *United States*, AFSC.

8. *Kent* v. *United States*, 383 U.S. 541, 555, 562 (1966).

9. In the process of making its way to the United States Supreme Court, further reasons for questioning Juvenile Court Judge McGhee's decision emerged. Since Arizona law did not provide the right of appeal in juvenile cases, Gault filed a habeas corpus petition with the Arizona Supreme Court, which referred his case to the local superior court for a hearing. There Judge McGhee explained that he had based his decision to commit Gault on two state statutes. One prohibited the use of lewd language and provided that an adult violator would be fined between five and fifty dollars or imprisoned for up to two months. Yet McGhee had deprived Gault of his freedom for six years. The other statute defined a delinquent as a child who was habitually involved in immoral matters. The judge had reached the determination that Gault fit within the purview of this latter statute because he thought Gault had admitted making similar telephone calls in the past and because two years earlier the boy was said to have stolen a baseball glove. McGhee admitted that there had been insufficient evidence to hold a hearing on the baseball glove charge and that he had never informed either Gault or his parents that he had used the alleged incident as evidence against the boy. After the superior court dismissed the writ and the Arizona Supreme Court affirmed its decision, Gault's lawyers appealed to the United States Supreme Court (*In re Gault*, 387 U.S. 1, 8–9 [1967]).

10. Griffiths, Memorandum, *In re Gault*, AFSC.

11. Interview with John Griffiths, June 1987.

12. *In re Gault*, 387 U.S. 1, 4 (1967).

13. Interview with Griffiths.

14. 387 U.S. 12–13. The two other cases were *Haley* v. *Ohio*, 332 U.S. 596 (1948) and *Gallegos* v. *Colorado*, 370 U.S. 49 (1962).

15. 387 U.S., pp. 26, 21, and 20.

16. Ibid., p. 28.

17. Ibid., p. 26.

18. See Alan Neigher, "The Gault Decision: Due Process and the Federal Courts," *Federal Probation* 31 (Dec. 1967): 17.

19. Fortas, Conference Notes, No. 116, *In re Gault*, AFSC.

20. Thus, for example, Fortas told his brethren soon after *Gault* that he was inclined to grant a right to trial by jury for juveniles with respect to all offenses that would be considered felonies if committed by adults (Fortas, Memorandum for the Conference, No. 701, *In the Matter of Buddy Lynn Whittington*, ibid).

21. 387 U.S. 61.

22. Ibid., p. 22. See Richard A. Michael and William C. Cunningham, "From Gault to Urbasek: For the Young the Best of Both Worlds," *Chicago Bar Record* (January 1968): 163.

23. Earl Warren to Fortas, March 17, 1967; Norman Dorsen to Fortas, May 22, 1967; William H. Robinson to Fortas, June 23, 1967; Inés Muñoz Marín to Fortas, May 16, 1967; "Juvenile Courts," *New York Times* (the date of the article is not included); "Justice for Children," *Washington Post*, May 16, 1967; all in AFSC.

24. John Griffiths, Speech to a Connecticut Bar Association panel on *In re Gault*, Oct. 16, 1967.

25. 387 U.S. 79.

26. All of these complaints are in the *Gault* file, AFSC. None is signed. Emphasis in the original.

27. *Giles* v. *Maryland*, 386 U.S. 66, 100 (1967).

28. *Johnson* v. *Avery*, 393 U.S. 483 (1969). See "The Supreme Court, 1968 Term," *Harvard Law Review* 83 (1969): 198–200.

29. Levitt, Remarks.

30. Bernard Schwartz, *Super Chief: Earl Warren and His Supreme Court, A Judicial Biogra-*

*phy* (New York: New York University Press, 1983), p. 593. See *Miranda* v. *Arizona,* 384 U.S. 436 (1966).

31. Levitt, Remarks.

32. Fortas, Notes, April 25, 1966, *Schmerber* v. *California,* AFSC.

33. *Schmerber* v. *California,* 384 U.S. 757, 779 (1966).

34. *U.S.* v. *Wade,* 388 U.S. 218, 261–62 (1967). For the same reason, Fortas dissented in part in *Gilbert* v. *California,* the companion case to *Wade,* in which a majority held that an accused could be forced to provide an example of his handwriting (388 U.S. 263, 292 [1967]).

35. *Alderman* v. *U.S.,* 394 U.S. 165, 208 (1969).

36. Ibid. at 209–11.

37. Bruce Murphy, *Fortas: The Rise and Ruin of a Supreme Court Justice* (New York: Morrow, 1988), p. 533.

38. *Bloom* v. *Illinois,* 391 U.S. 194, 214–15 (1968). Discussed in Murphy, *Fortas,* p. 533.

39. Fortas to William Brennan, March 4, 1966, *Cheff* v. *Schnackenberg* (384 U.S. 373 [1966]), AFSC.

40. *Robinson* v. *California,* 370 U.S. 660 (1962).

41. Interview with H. David Rosenbloom, May 1985. See also Fortas's dissent from denial of certiorari in *Budd* v. *California,* 385 U.S. 909 (1966).

42. Fortas, Draft, *Powell* v. *Texas,* AFSC.

43. Draft, circulated April 23, 1968, ibid. Emphasis added.

44. Hugo Black, Draft circulated May 16, 1968, ibid. According to Black, "Constitutional questions will now be raised by every state effort to regulate the admissibility of evidence relating to 'disease' and 'compulsion,' and by every state attempt to explain these concepts in instructions to the jury."

45. Levitt, Remarks, 102 S. Ct. 32–33.

46. Interview with Potter Stewart, Sept. 1985.

47. Byron White to Fortas, May 8, 1968, AFSC.

48. Interview with Rosenbloom.

49. The test for criminal liability Fortas endorsed in his dissent was only slightly more restrictive than the one he had asserted in earlier circulated drafts. Fortas now suggested that "a person may not be punished if the condition essential to constitute the defined crime is part of the pattern of his disease *and is occasioned by a compulsion symptomatic of the disease*" (*Powell* v. *Texas,* 392 U.S. 514, 569 [1968]). Emphasis added.

50. Ibid. at 536.

51. Handwritten on the dissent Black circulated on June 12, 1968, Box 16, AFSC.

52. William O. Douglas to Fortas, April 23, 1968, Box 16, AFSC.

53. *Harper* v. *Virginia Board of Elections,* AFSC. Ultimately Fortas did not issue this concurrence. See *Harper* v. *Virginia Board of Elections,* 383 U.S. 663 (1966).

54. *Katzenbach* v. *Morgan,* 384 U.S. 641 (1966).

55. William O. Douglas, Draft, Jan. 25, 1966, *Cardona* v. *Power,* AFSC.

56. Fortas to William O. Douglas and William Brennan, June 2, 1966, ibid.

57. William O. Douglas, Draft, circulated June 13, 1966, ibid. See also final opinion, *Cardona* v. *Power,* 384 U.S. 672, 675, n.1 (1966).

58. *Reynolds* v. *Sims,* 377 U.S. 533 (1964).

59. *Kirkpatrick* v. *Preisler,* 394 U.S. 526 (1969).

60. Ibid. at 538–39.

61. *Avery* v. *Midland County,* 390 U.S. 474 (1968).

62. Ibid. at 497. See also Fortas's dissent in *Wells* v. *Rockefeller,* 394 U.S. 542, 549 (1969).

63. 390 U.S. 500, n. 5.

64. Ibid. at 510.

65. *Griswold* v. *Connecticut,* 381 U.S. 479, 484 (1965).

66. Levitt, Remarks, 102 S. Ct. 33–34.

67. Quote from Burt, *Two Jewish Justices*, p. 11.

68. Interview with Griffiths.

69. Levitt, Remarks.

70. *New York Times Company v. Sullivan*, 376 U.S. 254 (1964).

71. Leonard Garment, "Annals of Law," *New Yorker*, April 17, 1989, p. 94.

72. Although Hayes knew of the Hills' experience, he denied that it had provided the basis for his novel.

73. Quotation in magazine article cited in statement of facts taken from Fortas draft majority opinion (hereafter, Fortas draft), reprinted in Bernard Schwartz, ed., *The Unpublished Opinions of the Warren Court* (New York: Oxford University Press, 1985), pp. 245–49.

74. Garment, "Annals of Law," p. 97.

75. Schwartz, *Super Chief*, p. 643.

76. Fortas draft, in Schwartz, *Unpublished Opinions*, p. 250.

77. Ibid., p. 251.

78. Ibid., pp. 251–52.

79. Ibid., p. 253.

80. Ibid., pp. 263–64.

81. Fortas draft, p. 255.

82. William O. Douglas draft, in Schwartz, *Unpublished Opinions*, p. 265.

83. Byron White draft, in Schwartz, *Unpublished Opinions*, pp. 288–89.

84. See ibid. and Schwartz's discussion of the changes Fortas made in his draft (ibid., p. 298). For the Court's eventual agreement with Fortas's understanding of New York law, see *Time v. Hill*, 385 U.S. 374, 383 (1967).

85. Hugo Black, Memorandum, in Schwartz, *Unpublished Opinions*, pp. 274–75. Emphasis in the original.

86. Ibid.; 381 U.S. 508–510.

87. Black, Memorandum, in Schwartz, *Unpublished Opinions*, pp. 278–79, 283, 287.

88. 375 U.S. 398 (1967).

89. Ibid., pp. 411, 415.

90. Interview with Rosenbloom.

91. *St. Amant v. Thompson*, 390 U.S. 727, 734 (1968).

92. Murphy, *Fortas*, pp. 224, 227; and see p. 534. See also Fred Graham, "Abe Fortas," *Justices of the Supreme Court, 1789–1969*, eds. Leon Friedman and Fred Israel (New York: Chelsea House in association with R. R. Bowker, 1969), 5 vols., 4:3023: "Fortas broke sharply with the 'liberal' Justices over the majority's attitude toward corporate mergers and regulatory agencies." Even businessmen thought Fortas was on their side, or so some who supported him for the chief justiceship claimed. (see p. 329.)

93. 15 U.S.C. § 25 (1964).

94. *FTC v. Dean Foods*, 384 U.S. 597, 609 (1966).

95. Levitt, Remarks.

96. Fortas, Memorandum to the Conference, *FTC v. Dean Foods*, circulated April 20, 1966, AFSC.

97. "The Supreme Court, 1965 Term," *Harvard Law Review* 80 (1965): 253, 256.

98. 384 U.S. 621.

99. See Fortas, Notes, Dean Foods dissent, AFSC.

100. Comment, "Preliminary Injunctions for the FTC in Merger Cases," *Cornell Law Quarterly* 52 (1967): 461.

101. 384 U.S. 636–40 (1966).

102. "The Supreme Court: 1965 Term," p. 253.

103. See "Preliminary Injunctions for the FTC in Merger Cases," p. 469; "FTC v. Dean Foods," *Villanova Law Review* 12 (1967): 347; "FTC v. Dean Foods," *Georgetown Law Journal* 55 (1966): 367; Thomas E. Kauper, "The 'Warren Court' and the Antitrust Laws: Of Economics,

Populism, and Cynicism," *Michigan Law Review* 67 (1968): 341. But see "FTC Preliminary Relief Powers under Section 7 of the Clayton Act," *Washington Law Review* 42 (1967): 636. ("The dissent pursues a phantom in attempting to infer Congressional intention from insterstices.")

104. "The Supreme Court, 1966 Term," *Harvard Law Review* 81 (1967): 226.

105. *Gardner v. Toilet Goods Association*, 387 U.S. 167, 176 (1967).

106. See generally Cass Sunstein, "Constitutionalism after the New Deal," *Harvard Law Review* 101 (1987): 438–44.

107. *Vaca v. Sipes*, 386 U.S. 171 (1967).

108. Ibid. at 182. See especially note 8.

109. See, e.g., Comment, "Individual Control over Personal Grievances under *Vaca v. Sipes*, *Yale Law Journal* 77 (1968): 564–70; David Feller, "A General Theory of the Collective Bargaining Agreement," *California Law Review* 61 (1973): 814–17; Katherine Van Wezel Stone, "The Post-War Paradigm in American Labor Law," *Yale Law Journal* 90 (1981): 1536–37, 1541–42; idem, "Re-Envisioning Labor Law: A Response to Professor Finkin," *Maryland Law Review* 45 (1986): 1000–1001.

110. 386 U.S. 199.

111. *Baltimore and Ohio Railroad v. United States*, 386 U.S. 372, 478 (1967).

112. Interview with Griffiths.

113. Interview with Rosenbloom.

114. See, e.g., *FTC v. Borden Company*, 383 U.S. 637 (1966); *FTC v. Mary Carter Paint Company*, 382 U.S. 46 (1966); *Utah Pie Company v. Continental Baking Company*, 386 U.S. 685 (1967). See also Fortas's opinion for the Court in *United States v. Sealy*, 388 U.S. 350 and his concurrences cited in note 115.

The four significant exceptions to this generalization are *FTC v. Dean Foods; Baltimore and Ohio Railroad v. United States*, 386 U.S. 459 (1967); *U. S. v. Grinnell Corporation*, 384 U.S. 563, 585 (1966); and *Fortner v. U. S. Steel Corporation*, 394 U.S. 495, 520 (1969).

115. See, e.g., *United States v. Pabst Brewing Company*, 384 U.S. 546, 561 (1966); *Perma Life Mufflers v. International Parts Company*, 392 U.S. 134, 147 (1968); *FTC v. Fred Meyer, Inc.*, 390 U.S. 341, 358 (1968); *United States v. Container Corporation of America*, 393 U.S. 333, 338 (1968).

116. 384 U.S. 628.

117. See, e.g., his dissent in *Baltimore and Ohio Railroad v. United States;* his dissent in *U. S. v. Grinnell Corporation* and Fortas to Earl Warren, April 11, 1966, *U. S. v. Grinnell Corporation*, AFSC.

118. For Warren on antitrust, see *U. S. v. Pabst Brewing Company*, 384 U.S. 546; and G. Edward White, *Earl Warren: A Public Life* (New York: Oxford University Press, 1982), p. 294.

119. *U.S. v. Arnold, Schwinn and Company*, 388 U.S. 365, 378–80 (1967).

120. Karl Llewellyn, *Cases and Materials on the Law of Sales* (Chicago: Calaghan, 1930), Preface.

121. 388 U.S. 392.

122. Quote and numerous citations of articles in *Continental T.V. v. GTE Sylvania*, 433 U.S. 36, 48, n. 13 (1977).

123. 433 U.S. 59.

124. Interview with Griffiths.

125. Ibid.

126. Murphy, *Fortas*, p. 218.

127. Interviews with Griffiths, Martha Field (Sept. 1985), and H. David Rosenbloom (May 1985).

128. See *Snyder v. Harris*, 394 U.S. 332, 351–52 (1969).

129. Ibid. at 341.

130. Ibid. at 343–44, 346.

131. See, e.g., "The Supreme Court, 1968 Term," *Harvard Law Review* 83 (1969): 202–12; "Federal Courts and Procedure—Aggregation of Claims in Class Actions," *Tennessee Law Review* 37 (1969): 103–08. Even one observer who remained "undecided on the issue" because he believed that both Black and Fortas's positions "have merit," believed that "avoidance . . . seems to be the primary motive" behind Black's stance (Steve Hixon, Comment, *Kentucky Law Journal* 58 [1970]: 403–07).

132. Charles Alan Wright to Fortas, March 28, 1969, AFSC.

133. *Scopes v. State,* 154 Tenn. 105 (1927).

134. *Epperson v. Arkansas,* 393 U.S. 97, 101, n. 7 (1968).

135. Peter Zimroth, Memorandum, *Epperson and Blanchard v. Ark,* Dec. 20, 1967, AFSC.

136. Transcript, *Epperson v. Arkansas,* pp. 7–9, ibid.

137. Notes, Oct. 16, 1968, ibid.

138. *Meyer v. Nebraska,* 262 U.S. 390 (1923).

139. See Fortas, Conference notes, *Epperson v. Arkansas,* AFSC. Warren also suggested that the statute might be held overbroad on the basis of *Butler v. Michigan,* 352 U.S. 380 (1957).

140. Schwartz, *Super Chief,* p. 754.

141. Fortas, Conference notes, *Epperson v. Arkansas,* AFSC.

142. Quoted in Schwartz, *Super Chief,* pp. 754–55.

143. Peter Irons, *The Courage of Their Convictions* (New York: Free Press, 1988), p. 214.

144. Fortas to Arthur Goldschmidt, Nov. 19, 1968; Melvyn Douglas to Fortas, Dec. 18, 1968; AFSC.

145. Interview with Louis Pollak, July 1985.

146. 393 U.S. 103.

147. Ibid. at 115.

148. Ibid. at 112, 114.

149. Ibid. at 109, 103.

150. *McLean v. Arkansas Board of Education,* 529 F. Supp. 1255 (1982); *Aguilard v. Edwards,* 765 F.2d 1251 (1985); *Edwards v. Aguilard,* 482 U.S. 578 (1987).

151. 393 U.S. 105–06.


## 13. REVOLUTION

1. Abe Fortas, "Lawyers and Social Revolutions," Jan. 13, 1962, FP. I could not discover if or when this speech was delivered.

2. *Edwards v. South Carolina,* 372 U.S. 229, 235 (1963).

3. See, e.g., *Cox v. Louisiana* (II), 379 U.S. 559 (1965).

4. Harry Kalven, "The Concept of the Public Forum: Cox v. Louisiana," *Supreme Court Review* 1965: 12.

5. *Cox v. Louisiana* (I), 379 U.S. 536 (1965). The other two cases were *Garner v. Louisiana* 368 U.S. 157 (1961) and *Taylor v. Louisiana* 370 U.S. 154 (1962).

6. Fortas, Handwritten Draft, n.d., *Brown v. Louisiana,* AFSC. (Unless otherwise noted, internal Court documents cited in this chapter are undated.) Fortas deleted the remark beginning "after these decisions . . ." from the final version of *Brown v. Louisiana,* 383 U.S. 131 (1966). The phrase "unquestionably lawful" appears in a draft circulated Dec. 30, 1965. For a critique of Fortas's use of the "no evidence doctrine," see "The Supreme Court, 1965 Term," *Harvard Law Review* 80 (1966): pp. 152–53.

7. Fortas, Draft, *Brown v. Louisiana,* Dec. 30, 1965, AFSC.

8. Jim Hale, Memorandum, Jan. 1, 1966, Earl Warren Papers. I am indebted to Mark McGuire for providing me with a copy of this document.

9. 379 U.S. 551–52; 544–550.

10. Fortas, Draft, *Brown v. Louisiana,* Dec. 30, 1965, n. 4.

11. Justice Brennan, the Court's expert on overbreadth, observed in his concurrence in *Brown* v. *Louisiana* that as the overbroad nature of the breach of peace statute "clearly requires the reversal of these convictions, it is wholly unnecessary to reach let alone rest reversal, as the prevailing opinion seems to do, on the proposition that even a narrowly drawn 'statute cannot constitutionally be applied to punish petitioners' actions in the circumstances of this case'" (383 U.S. 149–50).

12. Fortas, Draft, *Brown* v. *Louisiana.*

13. This argument is made convincingly in an unpublished senior thesis by Mark McGuire in my possession (hereafter cited as McGuire MS.).

14. 383 U.S. 142.

15. "Supreme Court, 1965 Term," p. 154.

16. 383 U.S. 143–150.

17. Ibid. at 150–151.

18. Earl Warren to Fortas, Jan. 12, 1966, *Brown* v. *Louisiana*, AFSC.

19. 383 U.S. 160, 166.

20. For a critique of Black's approach, see Sheila Cahill, "The Public Forum: Minimum Access, Equal Access, and the First Amendment," *Stanford Law Review* 28 (1975): 126–30; Harry Kalven, "Upon Rereading Mr. Justice Black on the First Amendment," *UCLA Law Review* 14 (1967): 447–53.

21. 383 U.S., especially pp. 167–168.

22. Douglas to Fortas, both notes n.d., *Brown* v. *Louisiana*, AFSC.

23. *Adderly* v. *Florida*, 385 U.S. 39, 48 (1966).

24. *Walker* v. *Birmingham*, 388 U.S. 307 (1967).

25. John Griffiths, Memorandum, *Walker* v. *Birmingham*, AFSC.

26. The comment of Fortas's clerk is included on the draft Brennan circulated on June 6, 1967 (ibid). Brennan deleted this remark in the final version, but even there he maintained that the majority's personal views about the increasingly violent nature of the civil rights movement explained its restriction of the "breathing room" that the First Amendment required. According to him, "we cannot permit fears of 'riots' and 'civil disobedience' generated by slogans like 'Black Power' to divert our attention from what is here at stake" (388 U.S. 349).

27. Fortas (Speech written for meeting of the American Booksellers Association, Washington, D.C., June 5, 1968), FP. Because of the assassination of Robert Kennedy, Fortas did not deliver the speech.

28. Confidential interview 33.

29. Fortas (Meiklejohn Lecture, delivered at the University of Wisconsin, Nov. 20, 1967), FP.

30. See generally Dean Alfange, Jr., "Free Speech and Symbolic Conduct: The Draft Card Burning Case," *Supreme Court Review* (1968): 3–10, Rivers quoted at p. 5, n. 20.

31. Bernard Schwartz, *Super Chief: Earl Warren and His Supreme Court, A Judicial Biography* (New York: New York University Press, 1983), pp. 683–84.

32. The chief justice's draft opinion in *O'Brien* formulated a test for determining whether nonverbal activity was speech. It suggested that "an act unrelated to the employment of language or other inherently expressive symbols is not speech within the First Amendment if as a matter of fact the act has an immediate harmful impact not completely apart from any impact arising by virtue of the claimed communication itself." Since the burning of a draft card had "an immediate harmful impact" unrelated to the impact of First Amendment expression, draft card burning was not speech (ibid., p. 684).

33. Warren, Draft, *United States* v. *O'Brien*, circ. April 12, 1968, AFSC. Emphasis in the original. Fortas's comments were made on his copy of Warren's draft majority opinion.

34. 383 U.S. 142.

35. Ibid at 376; Schwartz, *Super Chief*, p. 684. Even assuming O'Brien had brought the First Amendment into play when he burned his draft card, Warren contended in his final

opinion, a countervailing "substantial" state interest mitigated against the protection of such activity. The statute prohibiting draft card destruction represented a legitimate attempt to insure "the continued availability of Selective Service certificates issued" (*U. S.* v. *O'Brien, 391* U.S. 367, 381 [1968]). This reasoning made little sense. It implied that the statute was overnarrow because it only prohibited draft card burning and did not penalize the individual who left his draft card at home. See Melville Nimmer, "The Meaning of Symbolic Speech under the First Amendment," *UCLA Law Review* 21 (1973): 40–41; Kenneth Karst, "Equality and the First Amendment," *University of Chicago Law Review* 43 (1975): 29, n. 45.

36. According to Warren: "We think it clear that a government regulation is sufficiently justified if it is within the constitutional power of the Government; if it furthers an important or substantial government interest; if the governmental interest is unrelated to the suppression of free expression; and if the incidental restriction on First Amendment freedoms is no greater than is essential to the furtherance of that interest" (391 U.S. 377). Whereas Fortas proposed giving the Court discretion to punish the protest of a reasonable constitutional law whenever the means of protest selected was "not essential to the communication," the Chief Justice's opinion required a showing that the restriction of First Amendment rights was "essential" to the furtherance of a "substantial state interest."

37. Fred Graham, "Fortas Hits Student Law Violations," *Atlanta Constitution*, May 24, 1968, FP. In fact, Fortas meant to coax rather than to condemn. See n. 62.

38. Abe Fortas, *Concerning Dissent and Civil Disobedience* (New York: A Signet Special Broadside published by the New American Library, 1968), p. 124.

39. Ibid., pp. 34–35.

40. See Michael Tigar, Book Review, *Michigan Law Review* 67 (1969): pp. 613–14. The review discusses the inconsistency between Fortas's interpretation of *Brown* in *Concerning Dissent and Civil Disobedience* and his opinion in the case itself.

41. *Gregory* v. *Chicago* involved the Black comedian Dick Gregory's appeal of his conviction under a disorderly conduct statute during a march he led to protest the city of Chicago's slowness in desegregating its schools. Though the march was orderly, Gregory and the other demonstrators had defied a police directive to disperse, and a majority of the Court reversed the conviction. Fortas's proposed concurrence, which he did not issue, reaffirmed the commitment to peaceful demonstrations he had expressed in *Brown* (Fortas, Draft, *Gregory* v. *Chicago,* AFSC). See also Fortas's comments on a draft circulated by Justice Black, Jan. 15, 1969, ibid.; and *Gregory* v. *Chicago,* 394 U.S. 111 (1969).

42. *Street* v. *New York,* 394 U.S. 576, 577–81 (1969).

43. Transcript, Oral Argument, *Street* v. *New York,* pp. 12, 32–33, 41, AFSC.

44. *Street* v. *New York,* 394 U.S. 589, 585, 581.

45. The first draft dissent Warren wrote was markedly different from his second draft and from his final dissent, both of which paid less attention to the distinction between speech and conduct and focused on a critique of Harlan's opinion.

46. Fortas, Draft, *Street* v. *New York,* circulated Dec. 11, 1968, AFSC.

47. Fortas, Memorandum to the Conference, March 19, 1969, ibid.

48. 394 U.S. 616.

49. Ibid. at 616–17. See *Texas* v. *Johnson,* slip opinion, No. 88–155 (June 21, 1989), Dissent of Chief Justice Rehnquist, Justice White, and Justice O'Connor, p. 12.

50. Fortas wrote this comment on a memorandum written by his clerk Peter Zimroth on *Tinker* v. *Des Moines School District,* Feb. 14, 1968, AFSC.

51. Transcript, pp. 19–20, *Tinker* v. *Des Moines School District,* AFSC.

52. *Tinker* v. *Des Moines School District,* 393 U.S. 503, 506–08.

53. See Theodore Denno, "Mary Beth Tinker Takes the Constitution to School," *Fordham Law Review* 38 (1969): 43–44.

54. 393 U.S. 513.

55. See, e.g., Charles Alan Wright, "The Constitution on the Campus," *Vanderbilt Law*

*Review* 22 (1969): 1053; and "The Supreme Court, 1968 Term," *Harvard Law Review* 83 (1969): 159, which noted: "In short, the Court adopted the view that the process of education in a democracy must be democratic."

56. 393 U.S. 511.

57. Compare 391 U.S. 377 and 393 U.S. 513. See also McGuire MS.

58. 393 U.S. 508–09.

59. Interview with Martha Field, Sept. 1985; *Terminiello v. Chicago,* 337 U.S. 1. (1949).

60. Jaime Benítez to Fortas, April 21, 1969 (enclosed his April 21, 1969, letter to Russell Thackrey), FP.

61. Fortas to Benítez, April 25, 1969, ibid.

62. Fortas to Fred Lazarus, May 21, 1968, ibid. Fortas' great desire to promote "reasoned" communication on college campuses was also indicated by his concession in *Concerning Dissent and Civil Disobedience* that although civil disobedience represented a violation of law, "a moral (although not a legal) defense of law violation can be urged" when the law protested was "profoundly immoral or unconstitutional" (pp. 124–25). When a bewildered Eugene Rostow wrote to ask why he had not given greater weight to the moral duty of obeying all law (Eugene Rostow to Fortas, May 13, 1968, FP), Fortas replied that he had "soft-pedaled the 'moral' duty" because he had written the pamphlet "for a purpose. That is: to appeal to young faculty members on college staffs—and perhaps even to some students. . . . Based on my visits to a great many colleges during the past two years, I think that nothing could defeat my purpose so much as emphasizing the 'moral' duty of obedience to law—although I profoundly believe in it" (Fortas to Eugene Rostow, May 28, 1968, FP).

63. *Barker v. Hardway,* 394 U.S. 905 (1969).

64. 393 U.S. 515, 518, 525.

65. Ibid., p. 518.

66. Quoted in Gerald Dunne, *Hugo Black and the Judicial Revolution* (New York: Simon and Schuster, 1977), 361.

67. 393 U.S. 521–22.

68. Ibid. at 520.

69. *West Virginia v. Barnette,* 319 U.S. 624, 643 (1943).

70. Fortas's comments are written on his copy of Black's draft, AFSC.

71. Fortas, Draft, circulated April 18, 1969, *Brandenburg v. Ohio,* AFSC. Because of Fortas's resignation, he did not receive credit for writing the opinion. Instead the Court issued *Brandenburg* as a *per curiam* opinion (395 U.S. 444 [1969]).

72. See discussion of *Gunn v. University Committee to End the War in Vietnam,* 399 U.S. 383 (1970), in Schwartz, *Super Chief,* pp. 737–38.

73. Louis Henkin, "The Supreme Court, 1967 Term Foreword: On Drawing Lines," *Harvard Law Review* 82 (1968): pp. 80, 64.

74. Charles Coleman to Fortas, Feb. 24, 1969; Nick Pettenger to Fortas, Feb. 26, 1969; Edward Beatty to Fortas, Feb. 28, 1969; William R. Johnson to Fortas, Feb. 28 1969; Coleman to Fortas, Feb. 24, 1969; all in AFSC.

75. Fortas to Benítez, April 25, 1969.

76. Howard Zinn, *Disobedience and Democracy: Nine Fallacies on Law and Order* (New York: Random House, 1968), p. 7.

77. I am indebted to Richard Abrams for reminding me of this possibility.

### 14. THE ADVISER, II

1. Fortas to Abe Krash, July 10, 1967, FP.

2. Confidential interview 35.

3. McGeorge Bundy to Lyndon Johnson, Nov. 2, 1964, National Security File, McGeorge Bundy Memos to the President, Box 15, LBJL.

4. J. D. Pomfret, Memorandum on visit with Lyndon Johnson, June 24, 1965, Arthur Krock Papers, Princeton University Library (hereafter, Krock Papers).

5. Confidential interviews 9 and 36.

6. Abe Fortas, interview by William Gibbons and Patricia McAdams, Sept. 9, 1980.

7. Ibid.

8. Chester Cooper, Memorandum for the record, July 22, 1965, filed under Meetings on Vietnam, July 21, 1965, Meeting Notes File, Box 1, LBJL (hereafter, Meeting Notes).

9. Interview with Katie Louchheim, July 1985. (The conversation between Fortas and Cohen occurred at a dinner party at Louchheim's home.)

10. Quoted in Jules Witcover, *85 Days: The Last Campaign of Robert Kennedy* (New York: G. P. Putnam's Sons, 1969), p. 38.

11. U.S. Senate, *Hearings Before the Committee on the Judiciary on the Nominations of Abe Fortas and Homer Thornberry,* 90th Cong., 2d sess. (Washington: GPO, 1968), p. 104 (hereafter, *Nomination Hearings*).

12. Bundy to Johnson, Nov. 27, 1965, National Security File, McGeorge Bundy Memos to the President, Box 5, LBJL. For other articulations of the need for a bombing pause to satisfy public opinion, see Bundy to Johnson, Dec. 9, 1965, ibid.; Jack Valenti, Notes on meeting, May 16, 1965, 6:45 P.M.; and Notes on meeting, December 18, 1965, 12:35 P.M.; Meeting Notes, Box 1, LBJL.

13. Valenti, Notes on meeting, Dec. 18, 1965. Johnson subsequently described Fortas's advice somewhat differently to Hugh Sidey: "I had a meeting here, which included Fortas and Clifford. Fortas was against it. He said it would telegraph a signal that we were too anxious, and that the oriental mind would decide this was the time to hold out. Clifford was also eloquent against a pause. McNamara told me I had brought in a couple of ringers" (Meeting of the President with Hugh Sidey, Feb. 8, 1967, Box 3, Meeting Notes).

14. Asked in 1980 whether he thought that the United States should have used greater force once it had committed itself to the conflict, Fortas replied affirmatively, adding: "And I'm not afraid to say that. I thought the cessation of bombing at various times was ill-advised" (Gibbons and McAdams interview with Fortas).

15. Fortas, interview by Gibbons and McAdams. So, too, when William O. Douglas said that the President had allowed Harry Ashmore to send positive signals to Ho Chi Minh with his "right hand," while torpedoing the Ashmore mission with his left (William O. Douglas, *The Court Years, 1939–1975: The Autobiography of William O. Douglas* [New York: Random House, 1980], pp. 320–22), Fortas vigorously objected. "Ashmore was one of the many who appeared with proposals, allegedly cleared with Ho Chi Minh which L. B. J. eagerly greeted only to find that they were unacceptable to Ho Chi Minh," he told Douglas. "I believe I am justified in saying that L. B. J. was desperately seeking initiation of talks" (AF Draft, Aug. 29, 1977, FP).

16. Fortas, interview by Gibbons and McAdams. For opposing view, see Ned Kenworthy to Tom Wicker, Impressions from trip with Humphrey, June 9–10, 1965, Krock Papers.

17. Interview with Mercedes Eichholz, May 1986. (William O. Douglas's second wife married Robert Eichholz in 1963.)

18. Fortas to Johnson, Jan. 7, 1966, FP.

19. Ibid.

20. Meeting in President's Office (from Jack Valenti's notes of meeting), Jan. 29, 1966, 11:34 A.M.–12:40 P.M., Meeting Notes, Box 1, LBJL.

21. Memorandum for the President, Jan. 30, 1966, FP. Although Fortas did not sign the memorandum, he surely wrote it, perhaps with Clark Clifford. It was housed in his files, the style was his, and the date was noted in the handwriting of his secretary, Gloria Dalton.

22. Fortas to John Frank, Aug. 7, 1970, FP.

23. Annual Message to Congress on the State of the Union, Jan. 12, 1966, LBJ Statements, Box 173, LBJL (hereafter, State of the Union Message, 1966).

24. State of the Union Message, 1966. Johnson was stating more forcefully an idea that

also appeared in Fortas's draft: "So far as our domestic programs are concerned, we shall have no difficulty in continuing them on a totally adequate basis, with undiminished vigor—and we shall do so" (Fortas, Handwritten revisions of State of the Union Message, 1966, LBJ Statements, Box 173, LBJL).

25. Fortas to Fred Lazarus, Dec. 12, 1966; Fortas to Maurice Lazarus, Dec. 12, 1966; FP.

26. *Nomination Hearings,* p. 168.

27. Interview with Ralph Lazarus, Sept. 1984.

28. See, e.g., Joe Califano to Johnson, Feb. 12, 1967, Box 1, Special File Pertaining to Abe Fortas and Homer Thornberry, LBJL.

29. George Christian to the President, Notes on Aug. 10, 1967 Luncheon Meeting with Business Leaders, Aug. 15, 1967, Box 2, Meeting Notes, LBJL. Johnson decided to delay asking Congress for a tax increase until 1968.

30. Fortas to Esta Bloom, Aug. 25, 1966, FP.

31. See, e.g., Fortas to Lyndon Johnson, March 10, 1966, ibid. (advising the President to accept an invitation he had received from the American Jewish Committee). Fortas had sometimes communicated messages from Jewish groups to the White House before he joined the Court. See, e.g., Fortas to William Moyers, Jan. 15, 1964, Ex PP 13–4, WHCF, Box 103, LBJL.

32. Jim Jones to Marvin Watson, July 14, 1966, Abe Fortas Name File, LBJL (reporting Fortas's message).

33. See the correspondence between Fortas and Kollek in FP; interview with Agger.

34. Confidential interview 35. See also "LBJ Withdraws Fortas Nomination," *Washington Post,* Oct. 3, 1968.

35. Donald Neff, *Warriors for Jerusalem: The Six Days that Changed the Middle East* (New York: Linden Press, 1984), p. 175.

36. The planned breakfast meeting was cancelled. When Harman and Ben-Gurion arrived at Fortas's house, they learned that Johnson had been called away from Washington to attend the funeral of the late Senator Robert Kerr. Johnson did telephone Ben-Gurion from his car on his way to the airport (Avraham Harman to Laura Kalman, Sept. 27, 1989).

37. Ibid.

38. Daniel Levitt to Laura Kalman, September 7, 1989.

39. Avraham Harman to Laura Kalman, October 25, 1989.

40. Ibid.; Levitt to Kalman, September 7, 1989; interview with John Griffiths, June 1987. Fortas also attended an important White House meeting on the Middle East on May 26 (The President's Daily Diary, May 26, 1967, LBJL).

41. Neff, *Warriors for Jerusalem,* p. 164.

42. Levitt to Kalman, Sept. 7, 1989.

43. Harman does not recall the scene Levitt described. "I must emphasize that I have kept no papers and am relying only on memory," he added (Harman to Kalman, Oct. 25, 1989.)

44. Fortas's comment to Harman bore a striking similarity to advice Foreign Minister Abba Eban received about the same time. On the afternoon of June 1, two days before Harman returned to Tel Aviv, Eban "received a document in the late afternoon which had a decisive effect on my attitude. An American, known for his close contact with government thinking, had described the situation to one of our friends in Washington as follows: 'If Israel had acted alone without exhausting political efforts it would have made a catastrophic error. It would then have been almost impossible for the United States to help Israel and the ensuing relationship would have been tense. The war might be long and costly for Israel if it broke out. If Israel had fired the first shot before the United Nations discussion she would have negated any possibility of the United States helping her. Israelis should not criticize [Prime Minister Levi] Eshkol and Eban; they should realize that their restraint and well-considered procedures would have a decisive impact when the United States came to consider the measure of its involvement.' The American friend whose thinking seemed typical of the current Washington view understood that 'time was running out and that it was a matter of days or even hours.' But he believed that

'if the measures being taken by the United States [in the United Nations] prove ineffective, the United States would now back Israel.'" What Eban "found new in this information was the absence of any exhortation to us to stay our hand much longer. Our restraint in the past was strongly praised; its continuation in the future was not suggested.'" Abba Eban, *Abba Eban: An Autobiography* (London: Weidenfeld and Nicolson, 1977), pp. 384–85. Eban has never identified the American who sent the message. The individual could have been Fortas or anyone of several other Presidential advisers who were highly sympathetic to Israel.

45. Harman to Kalman, Oct. 25, 1989.

46. The President's Daily Diary, June 4, 1967, Box 11, LBJL.

47. Interview with John Loeb, Dec. 1983. Loeb subsequently wrote to Fortas: "You were prophetic about the Middle East. Thank the Lord the President has you as a friend and counsellor" (John Loeb to Fortas, June 6, 1967, FP).

48. The President's Daily Diary, June 4, 1967.

49. Johnson, *The Vantage Point: Perspectives of the Presidency, 1963–1969* (New York: Holt, Rinehart and Winston, 1971), pp. 287, 297.

50. Joe Califano to Lyndon Johnson, June 5, 1967, National Security File, National Security Council History, Middle East Crisis, Box 18, LBJL.

51. Joe Califano to Lyndon Johnson, June 7, 1967, 10:15 A.M., Abe Fortas Name File, LBJL. Fortas thought "we have taken care of that with the American-Jewish community and he has deep reservations about the applicability of the Neutrality Act to this situation" (ibid).

52. John Loeb to Fortas, June 12, 1967, FP.

53. Fortas to Loeb, June 15, 1967, ibid.

54. Interview with Griffiths.

55. Isaac Stern to Fortas, Aug. 11, 1967; Fortas to Stern, Aug. 24, 1967; FP.

56. Fortas to John Loeb, July 6, 1967, ibid.

57. "The President could never understand why there were so many Jews who were anti-Viet Nam. . . . To him this was a small country fighting aggression. And these people had suffered from aggression. They had suffered from the reluctance of major powers to step in and stop aggression early. Couldn't they see that the same thing was going on in Viet Nam? He said, 'Dammit, they want me to protect Israel, but they don't want me to do anything in Viet Nam'" (Harry McPherson, LBJOH, pt. 3, tape 1, pp. 36–37).

58. Joe Califano to the President, June 5, 1967, National Security File, National Security Council History, Middle East Crisis, Box 18, LBJL.

59. Fortas to Stern, Aug. 24, 1967 (responding to Stern's letters of Aug. 11 and Aug. 20).

60. Interview with Eichholz.

61. Fortas to Herbert Cohen, Oct. 27, 1967, FP.

62. Fortas to Johnson, n.d. (ca. Oct. 1967), National Security File, Country File, Vietnam 7 E (1) b September–October 1967, 21-f, Box 99, LBJL. Emphasis in the original.

63. Jim Jones to Lyndon Johnson, Nov. 8, 1967, Diary Backup, Box 81, LBJL.

64. Fortas to Johnson, Nov. 5, 1967, National Security File, Country File, Vietnam, Box 127, Folder labeled March 19, 1970, Memo to the President, "Decision to Halt the Bombing with Copies of Documents", LBJL. Emphasis in the original. Fortas may have drafted Johnson's statement "promoting" McNamara to the World Bank (see "The President's Statement," n.d., FP).

65. Kathleen Turner, *Lyndon Johnson's Dual War: Vietnam and the Press* (Chicago: University of Chicago Press, 1965), p. 219.

66. John Loeb to Fortas, Feb. 20, 1968; Fortas to Loeb, Feb. 29, 1968; FP.

67. Fortas to Johnson, Feb. 19, 1968, sent to White House on March 12, 1968, Special File Pertaining to Abe Fortas and Homer Thornberry, Box 1, LBJL (hereafter, Fortas-Thornberry File). Emphasis in the original. When Lyndon Johnson remarked that he would only strengthen the Republican right wing if he behaved in "too-dove-like fashion," Nicholas Katzenbach was sure he had been speaking with Fortas: "I feel [it was] such a sophisticated view that I always assumed he got it from Abe" (interview with Nicholas Katzenbach, Dec. 1983).

68. Fortas to Johnson, Feb. 19, 1968. Emphasis in the original.

69. Johnson was sufficiently taken with it to order a revised version sent to Clark Clifford and Dean Rusk (note from Lyndon Johnson, March 12, 1968, Box 1, Fortas-Thornberry File).

70. Meeting Notes, March 19, 1968, Meeting Notes, Box 2.

71. Herbert Schandler, *Lyndon Johnson and Vietnam: The Unmaking of a President* (Princeton, N.J.: Princeton University Press, 1977), pp. 259–65.

72. Fortas made endorsements ranging from Arthur Schlesinger as a member of the Kennedy Center Board (Fortas to Lyndon Johnson, Nov. 25, 1966, FP) to his old friend Theodor Muller for the Fine Arts Commission (Fortas to Lady Bird Johnson, July 11, 1967, ibid.).

73. *Nomination Hearings*, p. 103. See Jack Valenti to Johnson, March 29, 1966 (forwarding letter from Fortas recommending Simon Lazarus, Jr., for a judgeship), Office Files of John Macy, Box 190, LBJL; Fortas to Johnson, July 19, 1967, Re: Appointment to the United States Court of Appeals for the Ninth Circuit—Joseph A. Ball, FP; Fortas to John Macy, Jr., Nov. 30, 1965, FP; and Fortas to Nicholas Katzenbach, Nov. 30, 1965, Re: U.S. District Judge in Portland, Oregon (recommending Allan Hart); FP.

74. Conversation with Carol Agger, April 1988.

75. Confidential interview 37.

76. Fortas to Ramsey Clark, Oct. 9, 1967, FP.

77. Joe Califano to Johnson, May 23, 1967, WHCF, Ex LE/PL 2, Box 149, LBJL; Califano to Fortas, Feb. 11, 1967, FP.

78. See, e.g., Califano to Johnson, May 1, 1967, Legislative Background, Rail Strike Settlement, Box 1, LBJL.

79. Carl Solberg, *Hubert Humphrey: A Biography* (New York: W. W. Norton, 1984), p. 297.

80. McPherson, 4, LBJOH, tape 2, p. 22.

81. Johnson, *Vantage Point*, pp. 167–68.

82. Quoted in Bruce Murphy, *Fortas: The Rise and Ruin of a Supreme Court Justice* (New York: Morrow, 1988), p. 393. See also, Johnson, *Vantage Point*, p. 170.

83. Notes of the President's Meeting with Attorney General Clark, Secretary McNamara and Others on the Detroit Riot, July 24, 1967, Diary Backup, Box 71, LBJL.

84. Interview with Harry McPherson, May 1985; and McPherson, LBJOH, 5, Tape 1, p. 21.

85. ·Notes of the President's Meeting with Secretary McNamara, Abe Fortas and George Christian, July 24, 1967, Diary Backup, Box 71, LBJL: "The President reviewed a statement drafted by Mr. Abe Fortas. He suggested changes and asked that George Christian read over the proposed statement."

86. Interview with McPherson; and McPherson, LBJOH, 5, Tape 1, p. 21.

87. Harry McPherson, *A Political Education* (Boston: Little, Brown, 1972), p. 359.

88. McPherson, LBJOH, 5, Tape 1, p. 22.

89. Interview with McPherson.

90. "He was terribly valuable not just to Johnson but to the whole country with that book [*Concerning Dissent and Civil Disobedience*, which had not been published by the time of the Detroit riots] and the talks he made around it in the country [which began well before Fortas wrote the broadside] because the public was looking for some kind of guidance [on the question]: how do we deal . . . with violent dissent?" (interview with McPherson).

·91. McPherson, LBJOH, 5, Tape 1, pp. 21–22; McPherson, *A Political Education*, p. 360.

92. *Nomination Hearings*, p. 105.

93. McPherson to Johnson, July 26, 1967, Office Files of Harry McPherson, Box 32 (Riots, Folder 3), LBJL. The President replied, "I rather agree—see what you can develop" (Lyndon Johnson to Harry McPherson, July 26, 1967, ibid). Johnson's announcement of the establishment of the Kerner Commission was accompanied by a request that all Americans work and pray for an end to violence and by his designation of Sunday as a "national day of prayer for peace and reconciliation" (UPI Wire, ibid., Folder 4).

94. McPherson to Johnson, July 26, 1967.

95. Charles Horsky to Lyndon Johnson, Nov. 3, 1966, Ex LE/FG 216, WHCF, Box 45, LBJL: "H.R. 5688 is (1) a Southern Democrat-Republican creation, opposed by Administration supporters on the District Committee and by Democratic liberals generally, and (2) accepted by a very reluctant Senate as the price it had to pay to achieve other District measures which you were urging and which it knew to be of prime urgency."

96. McPherson, LBJOH, 3, p. 39.

97. Harry McPherson and Joe Califano to Lyndon Johnson, Nov. 9, 1966, Ex LE/FG 216, WHCF, Box 45, LBJL.

98. Ibid.; Cable, Califano to Johnson, Nov. 12, 1966; The President's Statement of Disapproval on H.R. 5688, both in ibid.

99. McPherson and Califano to Johnson, Nov. 9, 1966.

100. Johnson, *Vantage Point*, p. 335.

101. *Mallory* v. *U.S.*, 354 U.S. 449 (1957).

102. Califano to Johnson, Feb. 24, 1967, Ex LE/FG 216, WHCF, Box 45, LBJL (reporting Fortas's message).

103. Cable, Larry Levinson to Jim Jones, Dec. 27, 1967 (confirming Fortas's help), ibid.

104. Fortas, "Crime Message," n.d., Legislative Background—Safe Streets, Box 6, LBJL.

105. William O. Douglas to Fred Rodell, July 25, 1968, Fred Rodell Papers, Treasure Room Collection, Haverford College.

106. Interview with Potter Stewart, Sept. 1986. See, e.g., *Mitchell* v. *United States*, 386 U.S. 972 (1967); *Morav. McNamara*, 389 U.S. 934 (1967).

107. Fortas to Marvin Watson, Aug. 1, 1967, FP. Fortas also insisted that those who protested the war should not be permitted to disrupt Congress. If they became "unruly" following the announcement of the new law increasing security in the Capitol, the justice advised the President to "come out swinging with the toughest statement you can make" (Reactions to [the Proposed Presidential] Statement, Matthew Nimetz Files, n.d. [weekend of Oct. 21, 1967, Pentagon demonstration], Box 14, Folder 2, LBJL).

108. Interview with Harold Burson, May 1987.

109. Confidential interview 35.

110. Confidential interviews 38 and 33.

111. Thomas Schoenbaum, *Waging Peace and War: Dean Rusk in the Truman, Kennedy, and Johnson Years* (New York: Simon and Schuster, 1988), p. 415.

112. Interview with Eugene Rostow, July 1985.

113. Muriel to Joe Califano, Feb. 6, 1968, Legislative Background, Safe Streets and Crime Control Act of 1967, Box 6, LBJL.

114. Interview with McGeorge Bundy, March 1989.

115. Louis Jaffe, "Professors and Judges as Advisors to Government: Reflections on the Roosevelt-Frankfurter Relationship," *Harvard Law Review* 83 (1969): 373–74.

116. Interview with William Brennan, Dec. 1985.

117. Interview with Arthur Goldberg, Dec. 1983.

118. Interview with Lady Bird Johnson, May 1986.

119. J. Edgar Hoover to Ramsey Clark, July 12, 1966, FP.

120. For a full account of the Black case, see Athan Theoharis and John Cox, *The Boss: J. Edgar Hoover and the Great American Inquisition* (Philadelphia: Temple Univerity Press, 1988), pp. 368–93.

121. Andrew Kopkind, "Brennan v Tigar," *New Republic*, Aug. 27, 1966, p. 21.

122. Quoted in Nat Hentoff, "The Constitutionalist," *New Yorker*, March 12, 1990, pp. 61–62.

123. The memorandum from Cartha DeLoach to Clyde Tolson, June 14, 1966, will be reprinted in full in the section on J. Edgar Hoover, Robert Kennedy, FBI wiretapping and bugging activities, and the Fred Black case in Athan Theoharis, ed., *The Secret Files of J. Edgar*

*Hoover* (Frederick, Md: Twenty-First Century Books, 1990). As Fortas predicted, the Supreme Court did confirm Hoffa's conviction, but Fortas ultimately decided against participating in the Hoffa case (*Hoffa v. United States*, 355 U.S. 293 [1966]).

124. J. Edgar Hoover, Memorandum for Personal Files, June 14, 1966, reprinted in ibid.

125. See the memoranda from Cartha DeLoach to Clyde Tolson, June 21, 1966, and June 23, 1966, reprinted in ibid.

126. Theoharis and Cox, *The Boss,* p. 392.

127. *Black v. United States*, 385 U.S. 26 (1966).

128. DeLoach to Tolson, June 23, 1966.

129. Quoted in Theoharis and Cox, *The Boss,* p. 393.

130. Ibid., pp. 9, 11–12.

131. Interview with Isaac Stern, Jan. 1987.

132. Interview with Nicholas Katzenbach, Dec. 1983.

133. Confidential interview 33.

134. Interview with Liz Carpenter, May 1986.

135. Fortas to Johnson, Sept. 29, 1966, FP.

136. Fortas, "From the Bill White Universe-News Syndicate," n.d., ibid.

137. Interview with David Lloyd Kreeger, May 1985.

138. Interview with Clark Clifford, July 1985.

139. Fortas to Johnson, Aug. 28, 1967, Ex PP 2-1/F, WHCF, Box 22, LBJL.

140. AF Draft, Fortas to William O. Douglas, Aug. 29, 1977, FP.

141. Abe Fortas, "Portrait of a Friend," in *Portraits of American Presidents*, ed. Kenneth W. Thompson (Lanham, Md,; University Press of America, 1986), vol. 5, *The Johnson Presidency: Twenty Intimate Perspectives of Lyndon B. Johnson*, p. 19.

## 15. ON THE DEFENSIVE

1. Fortas to Luis Muñoz Marín, Oct. 15, 1968, FP.

2. Interviews with Walter Slocombe, May 1985; David Rosenbloom, May 1985; Martha Field, Sept. 1985; and John Griffiths, June 1987.

3. See, e.g., Fred Graham, "Abe Fortas," in *Justices of the Supreme Court,* ed. Leon Friedman and Fred Israel (New York: Chelsea House in association with R. R. Bowker, 1969), pp. 3018–19.

4. Interview with Potter Stewart, Sept. 1985.

5. Interview with William Brennan, Dec. 1985. As solicitor general, Erwin Griswold argued four cases before Fortas and found the justice "a keen and alert participant. He asked a moderate amount of questions but not too many, as . . . Frankfurter had." (interview, May 1985). Cf. Bruce Murphy, *Fortas: The Rise and Ruin of a Supreme Court Justice* (New York: William Morrow, 1988), p. 218.

6. *Loving v. Virginia*, 388 U.S. 1 (1967); "Loving v. State of Virginia," April 10, 1967 (poem), FP.

7. Interviews with Brennan and Stewart, and interview with Carol Agger (May 1987).

8. Fortas to Monique Lehner, May 2, 1968, FP.

9. See, e.g., Fortas to Frank Dillingham, Nov. 21, 1966, ibid.

10. Interview with Stewart.

11. Hugo L. Black and Elizabeth Black, *Mr. Justice and Mrs. Black: The Memoirs of Hugo L. Black and Elizabeth Black* (New York: Random House, 1986), pp. 120–21.

12. Hugo Black to Fortas, Nov. 14, 1965, *United Steel Workers of America v. R. H. Bouligny,* AFSC.

13. Both Potter Stewart and one of Fortas's clerks, John Griffiths, believed that this case marked the beginning of the friction between Black and Fortas (interviews with Stewart and with Griffiths, June 1987).

14. *U.S.* v. *Yazell,* 382 U.S. 341, 359 (1966). See John Harlan to Fortas, n.d., *U.S.* v. *Yazell,* AFSC.

15. Hugo Black to Fortas, n.d., *Brown* v. *Louisiana,* ibid.

16. Benno Schmidt, COHP, p. 217.

17. Confidential interview 35.

18. Black and Black, *Mr. Justice and Mrs. Black,* p. 144.

19. Interview with Slocombe.

20. Fortas wrote the first comment in the margin of Black's draft dissent in *Hunter* v. *Erickson* (AFSC), which said: "For some time I have been filing my protests against the Court's use of the Due Process Clause to strike down state laws that shock the Court's conscience, offend the Court's sense of what it considers to be 'fair' or 'fundamental' or 'arbitrary' or 'contrary to the beliefs of the English-speaking people.'" He wrote the second comment in the margin of his clerk's memorandum on *Hanson* v. *Chesapeake & Ohio Railway Company* (ibid.).

21. Interview with Agger.

22. Interviews with Helen and Theodor Muller, Jan. 1987, and Isaac Stern, Jan. 1987.

23. Interview with Harold Burson, May 1987.

24. Fortas to Stanley Marcus, Nov. 30, 1966, FP.

25. Fortas to Carolyn Kizer, May 10, 1966 (reporting that Black worried about the propriety of accepting a ride on one of President Johnson's airplanes); Fortas to Alice Kaplan, June 9, 1967, both in ibid.

26. Fortas to Paul Smith, Aug. 25, 1966; Fortas to Gustave Levy, Dec. 19, 1966, both in ibid.

27. Fortas to Levy, Dec. 19, 1966.

28. Interview with Arthur Goldberg, Dec. 1983.

29. Confidential interviews 39, 40, and 15.

30. Robert Shogan, *A Question of Judgment: The Fortas Case and the Struggle for the Supreme Court* (Indianapolis, Ind.: Bobbs-Merrill, 1971), pp. 189–90.

31. Louis Wolfson to Fortas, July 22, 1965 (letter given me by Louis Wolfson).

32. Draft—Possible Letter to Mr. Fortas, n.d. (letter given me by Louis Wolfson).

33. William O. Douglas, *The Court Years, 1939–1975: The Autobiography of William O. Douglas.* (New York: Random House, 1980), pp. 361–62.

34. Interview with Mercedes Eichholz, Oct. 1988.

35. Fortas to John Frank, Aug. 7, 1970, FP.

36. Interview with Agger.

37. Fortas to Louis Wolfson, May 17, 1966 (letter given me by Louis Wolfson).

38. Ibid.

39. Stewart, who knew that Fortas was in Florida but who was not told why the justice had gone there, presented the budget instead (interview with Stewart).

40. Interview with Griffiths. See Shogan, *A Question of Judgment,* p. 211.

41. Shogan, *A Question of Judgment,* pp. 211–12.

42. Fortas noted on his January 1966 statement (FP): "This includes the Wolfson Family Foundation check ($20,000) repaid December 15, 1966 which was offset by my check in the same amount to the Wolfson Family Foundation (No. 793)."

43. Sol Linowitz to August Heckscher, May 18, 1966, FP.

44. Adolf Berle to August Heckscher, May 27, 1966, ibid.

45. Fortas to Adolf Berle, July 12, 1966, ibid.

46. Fortas to Oscar Ruebhausen, Sept. 16, 1966, ibid.

47. Many confirmations of Fortas's speaking dates, which include the amount of fees involved, are in FP.

48. Fortas to Walter Gellhorn, January 30, 1968, FP.

49. B. J. Tennery to Paul Porter, Nov. 2, 1967, Box 5, Paul Porter Papers, LBJL (hereafter, Porter Papers). Projected Budget for Inter-Disciplinary Program for Contemporary Legal Problems, Summer Session, 1968, ibid.

50. See, e.g., Paul Porter to Gustave Levy, Feb. 2, 1968, Porter Papers.

51. Interview with Clark Clifford, July 1985.

52. Lyndon Johnson, *The Vantage Point: Perspectives of the Presidency* (New York: Holt, Rinehart and Winston, 1971), p. 545.

53. Interview with Clifford.

54. Johnson may have had a historical precedent in mind when he chose Thornberry. In 1937 many conservative Southern senators who opposed Franklin Roosevelt's court packing plan in principle had acquiesced to it because they knew that the President had promised a seat on the Court to their colleague, Senate Majority Leader Joe Robinson. When Robinson died in the middle of the floor debate on court packing, Southern support for the plan collapsed. See William Leuchtenburg, "Court-Packing Plan," *Franklin D. Roosevelt; His Life and Times: An Encyclopedic View,* ed. Otis L. Graham and Meghan Wander (Boston: G. K. Hall, 1985) p. 86.

55. Interview with Clifford. See also Johnson, *Vantage Point,* p. 545.

56. John Masarro, "LBJ and the Fortas Nomination for Chief Justice," *Political Science Quarterly* 97 (Winter, 1982–1983): 606–07.

57. Earl Warren to Lyndon Johnson, June 13, 1968, Box 1, Special File Pertaining to Abe Fortas and Homer Thornberry, LBJL (hereafter, Fortas-Thornberry File).

58. Warren Christopher to Larry Temple, Dec. 20, 1968, Memorandum on the Fortas and Thornberry Nominations (hereafter, Chronology), Box 3, Fortas-Thornberry File.

59. "Another Letter, Please," *Washington Post,* June 28, 1968.

60. Mike Manatos to Johnson, June 26, 1968, 3:00 P.M., Box 1, Fortas-Thornberry File.

61. Ibid. The twelve senators were Daniel Brewster (Md.), Fred Harris (Okla.), Philip Hart (Mich.), Ernest Hollings (S.C.), Daniel Inouye (Hawaii), Henry Jackson (Wash.), George McGovern (S.D.), Walter Mondale (Minn.), Mike Monroney (Okla.), Frank Moss (Utah), Gaylord Nelson (Wisc.), and William Spong (Va.). See also Manatos to Johnson, June 26, 1968, 5:30 P.M., ibid., reporting that "Senator [Edward] Long of Missouri is enthusiastic about these appointments—particularly Fortas."

62. Manatos to Johnson, June 25, 1968, 4:15 P.M., ibid.

63. The President's Daily Diary, Oct. 7, 1966, Box 8, LBJL.

64. James Eastland, LBJOH, p. 18.

65. Chronology; Manatos to Johnson, June 25, 1968, 3:00 P.M., Box 1, Fortas-Thornberry File.

66. Manatos to Johnson, June 26, 1968, 5:30 P.M.

67. Manatos to Johnson, June 25, 1968, 3:00 P.M.

68. Manatos to Johnson, June 25, 1968, 4:15 P.M. Compare with Manatos to Johnson, June 26, 1968, 9:30 A.M.: "Robert Byrd called me last night about 8:30 to say that upon reflection he thought his comments were too harsh with respect to Abe Fortas—that while he disagreed with most of the positions Fortas has taken as a member of the Supreme Court, he (Fortas) is a friend of the President—that the President 'has been a good friend of mine' and ought to be free to name a Chief Justice without meeting any organized resistance on the part of Bob Byrd. Consequently, while he would probably cast a vote against Fortas, he would neither organize nor participate in any way in any campaign aimed at bringing about the rejection of Fortas' nomination."

69. Manatos to Johnson, June 25, 1968, 4:15 P.M.

70. The President's Daily Diary, June 25, 1968, Box 16, LBJL.

71. Shogan suggested that Russell controlled at least a dozen votes; Murphy maintained the number was fourteen. Cf. Shogan, *A Question of Judgment,* p. 159, with Murphy, *Fortas,* p. 335.

72. Murphy, *Fortas,* p. 301.

73. Larry Temple to Johnson, May 20, 1968, Abe Fortas Name File, WHCF, LBJL: "The Justice said that he 'would not be outraged if the President went ahead with this appointment.' He said he admired Ramsey for the courage of his position. But this is a reasonable price to pay for the essential good will of Senator Russell and he sees nothing wrong with the making of the

appointment." See also Jim Jones to Johnson, June 24, 1968, ibid., reporting that Fortas had read a letter from Lawrence portraying himself as an individual who would enforce the law no matter how strongly he disagreed with it and now advised the White House "to go ahead on this [appointment] now for sure."

74. Richard Russell to Johnson, July 1, 1968, Office Files of Larry Temple, Box 1, LBJL. For a detailed account of this incident see Murphy, *Fortas,* pp. 329–59.

75. Everett Dirksen, LBJOH, pp. 13–14.

76. Murphy, *Fortas,* pp. 292–99.

77. Richard Denny to Everett Dirksen, Sept. 25, 1968; and Dirksen to George Abell, July 19, 1968; both in Box B 129–32, Gerald R. Ford Papers, Gerald R. Ford Library.

78. July 1, 1968, *Cong. Rec.,* 90th Cong., 2d sess., 114, pt. 15: 19543–44.

79. Ibid., June 21, 1968, p. 18171.

80. Murphy, *Fortas,* p. 302.

81. "Wash[ingto]n—Add[itional] Court Opposition," June 27, 1968, Box 1, Fortas-Thornberry File.

82. Barefoot Sanders to the President, June 28, 1968, 4:30 P.M.

83. Michael Manatos to Johnson, July 2, 1968, 6:40 P.M., Box 2, ibid.

84. Although Robert Shogan suggests that Russell telephoned Griffin to promise his support over the holiday weekend, Bruce Murphy argues that the pledge was made in Russell's office before the weekend began. Cf. Shogan, *A Question of Judgment,* pp. 158–59 with Murphy, *Fortas,* p. 359, and p. 645, n. 92.

85. Chronology.

86. Michael Manatos to Johnson, July 15, 1968, 6:15 P.M., Box 2, Fortas-Thornberry File.

87. Ramsey Clark to Johnson, Box 1, ibid. (transmitting copy of the memorandum, entitled "Judicial Restraint in the Opinions of Mr. Justice Fortas"); Chronology.

88. Charles Fairman to Warren Christopher, June 30, 1968, Box 2, ibid. (transmitted from Christopher to Larry Temple on July 2, 1968).

89. Warren Christopher, Memorandum and attachment, July 12, 1968, ibid. See also Memorandum for Justice Abe Fortas (apparently written by John Frank), "Justices and Presidents," July 17, 1968, 8:45 A.M., ibid.

90. See, e.g., Irv Sprague to Barefoot Sanders, July 2, 1968, 11:00 A.M., (reporting on *Los Angeles Times*), ibid.; Harry McPherson to Lyndon Johnson, July 11, 1968, 7:00 P.M., Box 5, ibid. (regarding Alan Barth of the *Washington Post* and columnists Rowland Evans and Robert Novak. Also see Paul Porter to John Sigenthaler of the *Nashville Tennessean,* July 1, 1968; Porter to Harold Clancy of the *Boston Herald Traveler,* July 1, 1968; Porter to E. Palmer Hoyt of the *Denver Post,* July 1, 1968, all in Box 5, Porter Papers.

91. Quote in Jim Gaither to Joe Califano, Box 2, Fortas-Thornberry File. For Coca-Cola, see Larry Levinson to Larry Temple, July 10, 1968, Box 2, ibid; For Lazarus, see Jim Jones, Memorandum, "Justice Fortas called with the following," June 27, 1958, 10:50 A.M., Box 4, ibid.: "Fred Lazarus is working on [Senator from Utah] Wallace Bennett; Fortas to Paul Porter, n.d., Box 3, Porter Papers; Ralph Lazarus to Fortas, August 9, 1968, FP: "I have also done everything that I knew how to do through those contacts I have and will continue." For American Airlines, see Paul Porter to George Spater, July 1, 1968, Box 5, Porter Papers. For Eastern, see Jim Gaither to Joe Califano, July 2, 1968, Box 4, Fortas-Thornberry File.

92. "Chronology—Events Relating to Supreme Court Nominations," Box 2, ibid; transcript of article by Steven Gerstel, July 2, 1968, ibid.

93. Jim Gaither to Joe Califano, July 2, 1968.

94. Eric Goldman, *The Tragedy of Lyndon Johnson* (New York: Alfred A. Knopf, 1969), p. 57.

95. See, e.g., *Cong. Rec.,* 90th Cong., 2d sess., 114, pt. 14: p. 18790 (Remarks of Senator Gore); ibid, pt. 15: 19533–41 (Remarks of Senator Smathers); ibid., pt. 15: 20284–85 (Remarks of Senator Morse).

96. Larry Temple to Jim Jones, July 13, 1968, Box 7, Fortas-Thornberry File.

97. Eugene Bogan to Paul Porter, n.d., Box 5, Porter Papers: "Stu Symington owes Abe one hell of a lot—enuff to work a 25 hour day on the floor for him. How do we activate SS?" See *Cong. Rec.*, 90th Cong., 2d sess., 114, pt. 14: 19242–43, for speech by Symington on Fortas's behalf.

98. Fortas to Muñoz, Oct. 15, 1968.

99. Interview with Louis Pollak, July 1984.

100. Interview with William Brennan, Dec. 1985.

101. Interview with Martha Field, Sept. 1985.

102. Michael Parrish, "Little Daily Questions and Shooting Tiger," in *Power and Responsibility: Case Studies in American Leadership*, ed. David Kennedy and Michael Parrish (New York: Harcourt Brace Jovanovich, 1986), p. 142.

103. Jones, Memorandum, "Justice Fortas called with the following."

104. "When Abe . . ." in Lady Bird Johnson, *A White House Diary* (New York: Holt, Rinehart and Winston, 1970), p. 713; quote about Paul Porter is from interview with Lady Bird Johnson, May 1986.

105. Fortas, "Abe Fortas Should Be Confirmed Now," n.d., FP. Ribicoff's office released this statement on June 27, 1968.

106. Quoted in Murphy, *Fortas*, p. 366.

107. Fortas to Porter, n.d., Box 3, Porter Papers.

108. Confidential interview 35.

109. Warren Christopher, LBJOH, Tape 1, pp. 12, 14.

110. Statement, n.d., FP.

111. U.S. Senate, *Hearings Before the Committee of the Judiciary on the Nominations of Abe Fortas and Homer Thornberry* (Washington: GPO, 1968) (hereafter, *Nomination Hearings*), p. 103.

112. The day before Fortas's first appearance, Philip Hart, a member of the Judiciary Committee, told Christopher what the White House had already guessed: Justice Fortas's role in advising the President would be made an important issue by the opposition (Chronology).

113. *Nomination Hearings*, p. 49.

114. Cf. Murphy, *Fortas*, pp. 370–71: Fortas "had developed a certain style of advocacy before congressional committees, but not everyone appreciated it. For him, truth was secondary when there was a battle to be won." I would suggest instead that until the hearings on his appointment as chief justice, Fortas's statements to congressional committees were characterized by their legalistic nature. They were generally technically correct, if not always fully informative.

115. *Nomination Hearings*, pp. 103–05.

116. Ibid., pp. 105–06. See also Fortas's testimony at p. 213: "Senator, yesterday and the day before, and the day before that, in response to a question, I stated that I do not believe that the Supreme Court of the United States should or can appropriately make policy or seek to bring about social, political or economic change in this country."

117. Ibid., p. 110.

118. Ibid., p. 200.

119. Ibid., p. 226.

120. Ibid., p. 106.

121. Ibid., pp. 52–54.

122. Ibid., pp. 164–66.

123. Fred Graham had already reported that Fortas had telephoned a friend on this occasion, but he had misidentified the friend (Graham, "The Many-Sided Justice Fortas," *New York Times Magazine*, Jan. 4, 1967).

124. *Nomination Hearings*, pp. 167–68.

125. Michael Manatos to Johnson, July 16, 1968, 1:30 P.M., Box 2, Fortas-Thornberry File.

126. *Nomination Hearings*, pp. 169–70.

127. "Fortas Concedes Move To Correct War-Cost Critic," *Washington Post,* July 18, 1968.
128. "Mr. Fortas and the President," ibid.
129. *Nomination Hearings,* p. 191. The incident is described in "Fortas Berated for Two Hours," *Washington Post,* July 19, 1968.
130. *Nomination Hearings,* p. 182.
131. Ibid., p. 173
132. See ibid., p. 189, where Fortas hinted that his dissent in the case of *Fortson* v. *Morris,* 385 U.S. 231, 242 (1966) was based on existing law, not law as he would write it.
133. *Nomination Hearings,* p. 191.
134. Ibid., p. 219.
135. Ibid., pp. 214–15.
136. See, e.g., "Fortas Concedes Move To Correct War-Cost Critic."
137. *Nomination Hearings,* pp. 227–28.
138. Larry Temple, LBJOH, 4, Tape 2, p. 3.
139. Murphy, *Fortas,* pp. 442–43.
140. *Nomination Hearings,* p. 300. See also pp. 292–97.
141. Ibid., pp. 297–98, 302. See 388 U.S. 454 (1967).
142. Ibid., p. 309.
143. Murphy, *Fortas,* pp. 459–60.
144. Quoted in Samuel Shaffer, *On and Off the Floor: Thirty Years as a Correspondent on Capitol Hill* (New York: Newsweek Books, 1980), p. 91.
145. See *Ginsberg* v. *United States,* 390 U.S. 629, 673 (1968). See also Murphy, *Fortas,* pp. 457–58.
146. *Ginzburg* v. *U.S.,* 383 U.S. 463 (1966).
147. Quoted in Bernard Schwartz, *Super Chief: Earl Warren and His Supreme Court, A Judicial Biography* (New York: New York University Press, 1983), p. 619.
148. Fortas to William O. Douglas, April 15, 1966, *Ginzburg* v. *United States,* AFSC.
149. Interview with Mercedes Eichholz, Oct. 1988.
150. Thurman Arnold to Fortas, March 29, 1966, *Ginzburg* v. *U.S.* AFSC. The journalist Anthony Lewis considered the Court's decision intellectually dishonest (Anthony Lewis to Fred Rodell, May 2, 1966, Fred Rodell Papers, Treasure Room Collection, Haverford College; hereafter, Rodell Papers). Rodell, generally among Fortas's and Brennan's most ardent boosters, agreed that "the Ginzburg decision was unfortunate and unwarranted" (Rodell to Anthony Lewis, June 10, 1966, ibid.) and told Fortas that he disagreed with it (Rodell to Fortas, June 24, 1966, ibid).
151. Interview with Griffiths.
152. Fortas to Douglas, April 15, 1966.
153. See the draft of Fortas's opinion in *Redrup* v. *New York,* circulated Dec. 7, 1966, AFSC.
154. Quoted in Murphy, *Fortas,* p. 460.
155. Ibid., pp. 460–61.
156. Joe Califano to Johnson, July 24, 1968, 8:30 P.M., Box 2, Fortas-Thornberry File; Murphy, *Fortas,* p. 447.
157. Mike Manatos to Johnson, July 25, 1968, 7:00 P.M., Box 7, Fortas-Thornberry File.
158. See generally Murphy, *Fortas,* pp. 447–62.
159. Carolyn Agger to Mercedes and Robert Eichholz, Aug. 9, 1968 (letter given me by Mercedes Eichholz). Initially, Agger had confused Richard Nixon with the Republican candidate of 1948, Thomas Dewey. "What a Freudian slip," she wrote.
160. Paul Porter to Gustave Levy, Sept. 24, 1968, Box 5, Porter Papers.
161. Eugene Bogan to Jack Miller, July 16, 1968, ibid.
162. Eugene Bogan to Paul Porter, July 16, 1968, ibid; interview with Eugene Bogan, May 1985; Larry Temple, "Paul Porter sent this over for the President to See," July 17, 1968, Box 2, Fortas-Thornberry File.
163. Interview with Bogan.

164. John Ehrlichman, *Witness to Power: The Nixon Years* (New York: Simon and Schuster, 1982), p. 113. According to Murphy, however, there is "no hard evidence" to show conclusively that there was "a formal deal . . . between Nixon and the conservatives" (Murphy, *Fortas*, p. 658, n. 38).

165. Interview with Bogan.

166. Paul Porter to William P. Rogers, Aug. 22, 1968, Box 5, Porter Papers.

167. Transcript of Taped Conversation, July 3, 1968, Box 3, Fortas-Thornberry File.

168. According to Murphy, *Fortas*, p. 299, Eastland was overheard making this remark at a cocktail party.

169. Jones, "Justice Fortas called with the following."

170. Quoted in interview with Robert Griffin conducted by CBS newsmen Nelson Benton, Bruce Morton, and Hal Walker, July 2, 1968, Box B 129–32, Gerald R. Ford Library.

171. Irv Sprague to Barefoot Sanders, June 28, 1968, 2:30 P.M., Box 4, Fortas-Thornberry File; Memorandum of message left by Eugene Wyman, June 28, 1968, 9:00 P.M., Box 1, ibid.

172. Murphy, *Fortas*, p. 362.

173. Harry McPherson to Johnson, July 11, 1968, Box 4, Fortas-Thornberry File.

174. See generally Murphy, *Fortas*, pp. 469–71.

175. Fortas to Porter, n.d., Box 6, Porter Papers. Cf. Murphy, *Fortas*, p. 471, for a literal reading of Fortas's remark.

176. See *Cong. Rec.*, 90th Cong., 2d sess., 114, pt. 21: 28299 (Remarks of Senator Javits).

177. Nixon's comments that he neither supported Fortas nor opposed him and that he opposed a filibuster of the Fortas nomination just as he opposed "any filibuster" came too late to have any impact, and Republicans wondered how sincere they were. See Shogan, *A Question of Judgment*, p. 180; Murphy, *Fortas*, p. 475.

178. Fortas to Douglas, July 26, 1968, FP. Bruce Murphy has suggested that the confirmation fight strained Fortas's relationship with Douglas (Murphy, *Fortas*, p. 529). It is true that Douglas told Fred Rodell that Fortas "had to establish that I who was his mentor was too leftist. He (Fortas) relied on 'reason and history,' while WOD relies on what he thinks should be the result of the case." But Douglas thought "it was a neat way of getting rid of too close an identification with me," though he added that in days ahead, Fortas might find the price of having distanced himself "excessive" (William O. Douglas to Fred Rodell, July 27, 1968, Rodell Papers). Murphy writes, "Whether this was a prediction, a hope, or a promise was not clear" (Murphy, *Fortas*, p. 529). It could not have been a hope or a promise, for Douglas's correspondence with Fortas indicated their continued closeness. See, e.g., Douglas to Fortas, July 31, 1968, FP: "The news of the hearings out here was skimpy and quite superficial. If Washington State is a barometer they don't give a damn one way or the other, except the hard core of John Birchers who would like (a) to destroy the Court (b) occupy Vietnam and (c) march on to China." After the Senate Judiciary Committee decided to delay reporting out Fortas's nomination, Douglas wrote again: "The wire story here (quite brief) was that the odds are against you. I hope & pray that is not correct. If there is anything I can do, you have but to tell me" (Douglas to Fortas, Aug. 3, 1968, ibid). Perhaps Douglas meant Fortas would pay an excessive price in terms of alienating liberals, rather than in terms of their personal relationship.

179. Fortas, Speech, American College of Trial Lawyers, Aug. 3, 1968, ibid.

180. Paul Porter to James R. Jones, Aug. 7, 1968, Box 5, Porter Papers.

181. Fortas to Douglas, July 26, 1978.

182. Fortas to Earl Warren, July 25, 1968, FP.

183. Murphy, *Fortas*, pp. 524–25, 539.

184. John Harlan to Fortas, July 21, 1968, FP.

185. Fortas to Harlan, July 24, 1968, ibid.

186. Larry Temple, LBJOH, p. 42.

187. Barefoot Sanders to Johnson, July 30, 1968, 8:45 P.M., Box 7, Fortas-Thornberry File.

188. George Reedy to Johnson, July 30, 1968, ibid.

189. Joe Califano to Johnson, Aug. 13, 1968, ibid.

190. Johnson, *Vantage Point*, p. 547.

191. "On a note of defeat" from George Reedy to Johnson, Sept. 20, 1968, Box 7, Fortas-Thornberry File. For Johnson on Fortas, see Joe Califano, *A Presidential Nation* (New York: W. W. Norton, 1975), p. 202. Cf. Murphy (*Fortas*, p. 462), who suggests that Johnson continued the fight "because no one said no to Lyndon Johnson, certainly not the United States Senate."

192. Barefoot Sanders to Johnson, July 30, 1968, Box 7, Pertaining to Fortas-Thornberry File. Emphasis in original.

193. Eugene Bogan to Porter, n.d., Box 3, Porter Papers. For the extensive activities Porter and Bogan undertook on behalf of the Fortas nomination see Porter Papers. For the White House's role see, e.g., Sanders to Johnson, July 30, 1968.

194. Agger to M. and R. Eichholz, Aug. 9, 1968.

195. Porter to John Kenneth Galbraith, Sept. 16, 1968, Box 3, Porter Papers.

196. Joseph Rauh to Porter, September 20, 1968, ibid.

197. Daniel Yergin, "How Does Dick Goodwin Get Away with Making All Those Jumps?" *New York Magazine*, July 22, 1968; quoted in *Nomination Hearings*, pp. 1369–70.

198. "Too-Lenient Judges Criticized by Allott," *Denver Post*, Aug. 25, 1968.

199. Robert P. Griffin, Memorandum to the Chairman and Members of the Committee on the Judiciary, Sept. 9, 1968; quoted in *Nomination Hearings*, pp. 1369–70; ibid. p. 1285.

200. Murphy, *Fortas*, pp. 440, 497.

201. *Nomination Hearings*, pp. 1286–1304.

202. Califano, *A Presidential Nation*, p. 201.

203. Porter to Clark Clifford, Sept. 24, 1968, Box 5, Porter Papers. Emphasis in the original.

204. Fortas to Porter, Feb. 27, 1968, FP. Porter to Fortas, Feb. 28, 1968, ibid.

205. Porter to Troy Post, Feb. 7, 1968; Porter to Gustave Levy, Feb. 9, 1968, both in Box 5, Porter Papers. See also Porter to Maurice Lazarus, Feb. 9, 1968, and Porter to John Loeb, Feb. 14, 1968 (indicating he would tell Fortas of Lazarus's and Loeb's contributions), both in ibid.. Porter's letters led Murphy to argue that Fortas knew the contributors' identities (Murphy, *Fortas*, p. 507, and p. 664, n. 45). But Fortas's letter to Porter indicates that he did not. See also Fortas to John Frank, August 7, 1970, FP: "I knew nothing about that."

206. *Nomination Hearings*, p. 1289; student evaluations in Box 3, Porter Papers, LBJL.

207. Murphy, *Fortas*, pp. 500–501.

208. Fortas to Paul Porter, n.d., Box 3, Porter Papers, LBJL.

209. *Nomination Hearings*, p. 1306.

210. Ibid., p. 1298, 1300. Fortas argued that "the $15,000 fee included preparing a set of materials which were turned over to American University for use. I expect that if I had published them myself, my compensation and royalties would have been much greater" (Fortas to John Frank, Aug. 7, 1970, FP).

211. Interview with Martha Field, Sept. 1986.

212. *Nomination Hearings*, p. 1291. See also, e.g., *Cong. Rec.*, 90th Cong., 2d sess., 114, pt. 21: 28119 (Remarks of Senator Griffin).

213. Confidential interview 35.

214. Interview with Bogan.

215. *Nomination Hearings*, pp. 1332–34, 1314, 1346.

216. Ibid., p. 1331.

217. Ibid., p. 1349.

218. See DeVier Pierson to Lyndon Johnson, Sept. 11, 1968, Box 7, Fortas-Thornberry File; *Nomination Hearings*, p. 1347.

219. Ibid., p. 1350.

220. Ibid., p. 1351–52, 1375–76. A majority of the committee recognized that "there has long been a distinction between a Justice's voluntarily expressing his views on legal subjects and his being interrogated about judicial opinions by a Senate committee" (Report, *Nomination of*

*Abe Fortas*, 90th Cong., 2d sess., U.S. Senate, Executive Report No. 8 [Washington: GPO, 1968], p. 5).

221. Michael Manatos to Johnson (including "movies" quote from Dirksen), Sept. 16, 1968, 4:15 P.M., Box 3, Fortas-Thornberry File.

222. The original vote was 10–6. Senator Long, who was absent for that vote, later voted with the majority, making Fortas's margin 11–6 (Chronology).

223. Harry McPherson to Michael Manatos, Sept. 20, 1968, 12:45 P.M., Box 3, Fortas-Thornberry File.

224. Memorandum written by Ernest Goldstein, n.d., ibid.

225. Barefoot Sanders to Johnson, Sept. 12, 1968, ibid.

226. Quoted in Chronology.

227. *Cong. Rec.* 90th Cong., 2d sess., 114, pt. 21: 28114.

228. See Murphy, *Fortas,* p. 521; Masarro, "LBJ and the Fortas Nomination," pp. 611–12.

229. Quoted in Manatos to Johnson, Sept. 16, 1968.

230. Thurgood Marshall to Fortas, n.d., FP.

231. Quoted in Shogan, *A Question of Judgment,* p. 183.

232. Fortas to Luis Muñoz Marín, Oct. 15, 1968, FP.

233. Interview with Nicholas Katzenbach, Dec. 1983.

234. Quoted in Murphy, *Fortas,* p. 286.

235. Fortas, LBJOH, p. 33.

236. See generally Masarro, "LBJ and the Fortas Nomination," pp. 620–21.

237. Interview of Robert Griffin by Nelson Benton, Bruce Morton, and Hal Walker.

238. Interview with Lady Bird Johnson.

239. Fortas to Muñoz, Oct. 15, 1968.

## 16. FROM PUBLIC SERVICE TO THE PRIVATE SECTOR, II

1. Hugo L. Black and Elizabeth Black, *Mr. Justice and Mrs. Black: The Memoirs of Hugo L. Black and Elizabeth Black* (New York: Random House, 1986), p. 206.

2. Robert Shogan, *A Question of Judgment: The Fortas Case and the Struggle for the Supreme Court* (Indianapolis, Ind.: Bobbs-Merrill, 1971), pp. 205–14. The discussion of the Wolfson episode on the following pages is based in part on the account in Shogan's book.

3. Bruce Murphy, *Fortas: The Rise and Ruin of A Supreme Court Justice* (New York: William Morrow, 1988), p. 518.

4. Cartha DeLoach to Mr. Tolson, Sept. 23, 1968, Abe Fortas Freedom of Information Act file.

5. Ramsey Clark, LBJOH, pp. 19–21.

6. Louis Wolfson to Fortas, June 14, 1967, FP.

7. Fortas to Florence Wolfson, Jan. 4, 1968, ibid.

8. Fortas to Caroline Dahl, March 7, 1969, ibid.

9. For example, Wolfson sent Fortas an article from the December 1968 issue of *Fortune* entitled "Judgeship for SEC's Cohen?" with the note: "Hope this does not come to pass until the facts are known" (n.d., ibid). He also sent a *Wall Street Journal* article describing a light prison sentence an alleged Mafia figure had received with a note explaining that the judge in that case had been his judge. See "Alleged Mafia Figure Arrested in New York In Bond-Theft Case," *Wall Street Journal,* Dec. 13, 1967 and Wolfson, memorandum, n.d., ibid.

10. "Winners and Losers," *Life,* Jan. 10, 1969, p. 98.

11. Fortas to Hedley Donovan, Jan. 10, 1969, *Time, Inc.* v. *Hill,* Box 31, AFSC. Fortas sometimes released his frustration at the press by writing angry letters that he did not mail. On one occasion when he was still practicing law, he did send a reply to a journalist who had criticized one of his clients, but the letter included only the salutation and his signature at the bottom of the page. The area between was blank. When the bewildered reporter telephoned

Fortas, the attorney explained that he had originally begun to dictate his comments on the article. "'But then I thought about the laws of libel . . . and just signed it and sent it on.' The reporter recalls that Fortas did not laugh when he said this" (Fred Graham, undated draft of article on Fortas, Box 8, Fred Graham Papers, Library of Congress; hereafter, Graham Papers).

12. Shogan, *A Question of Judgment,* pp. 223–24.

13. "Bill Lambert," n.d., Box 8, Graham Papers.

14. Quoted in Murphy, *Fortas,* p. 551. See generally Shogan, *A Question of Judgment,* pp. 226–27; Murphy, *Fortas,* pp. 549–51.

15. Memorandum for Messrs. Tolson, DeLoach, Gale, Rosen, Sullivan, Bishop, April 23, 1969 (recounting Hoover's conversation with Nixon) Fortas Freedom of Information Act File. While Hoover did not sign the portion of the memorandum that has been declassified, the context indicates that only he could have written it.

16. Fortas and Lambert quoted in Shogan, *A Question of Judgment,* p. 224.

17. Memorandum for Tolson, De Loach, Gale, Rosen, Sullivan, Bishop.

18. See Bob Woodward, "Fortas Tie to Wolfson Is Detailed," *Washington Post,* Jan. 23, 1977.

19. Murphy, *Fortas,* p. 554.

20. "Wolfson Is Convicted on No-Contest Plea, Fined $10,000, Let Go," *Wall Street Journal,* Dec. 1, 1972.

21. Confidential interview 41. I have placed my notes from this interview under seal at the Yale University Archives. They will be available to researchers upon the deaths of all parties involved.

22. Hoover quoted in Bob Woodward and Scott Armstrong, *The Brethren* (New York: Simon and Schuster, 1979), p. 18.

23. Murphy, *Fortas,* p. 555–56.

24. *Life,* May 9, 1966, pp. 32–37. *Life* released advance copies of the article to the press on May 4 (Shogan, *A Question of Judgment,* p. 235).

25. Interview with Joseph Rauh, Dec. 1983.

26. Fortas to Earl Warren, May 14, 1969, FP (reprinted in Shogan, *A Question of Judgment,* pp. 279–82); "Fortas on His Resignation: 'There Wasn't Any Choice for a Man of Conscience,'" *U. S. News and World Report,* May 26, 1969.

27. Fortas's statement of May 4 is reprinted in Shogan, *A Question of Judgment,* pp. 277–78.

28. Fred Graham, "Abe Fortas," in *Justices of the United State Supreme Court,* ed. Leon Friedman and Fred Israel (New York: Chelsea House in association with R. R. Bowker, 1969) 4:3026.

29. See, e.g., "Some in G.O.P. Ask Fortas to Resign—No Democrats in Congress Express Support for Him in Wolfson Fee Dispute," *New York Times,* May 6, 1969.

30. "A Shadow Over the Supreme Court," *Washington Post,* May 6, 1969.

31. Quoted in Shogan, *A Question of Judgment,* p. 240.

32. *Cong. Rec.,* 91st Cong., 1st sess., 115, pt. 9: 11419.

33. *Cong. Rec.,* 91st Cong., 1st sess., 115, pt. 9: 11260.

34. Wyzanski notes, n.d., Box 8, Graham Papers. "Mrs. Fortas, Also a Lawyer, Is Tax Expert," *New York Times,* May 16, 1969; and, e.g., "Douglas Foundation Casino Sale Noted," *Washington Evening Star,* May 10, 1969.

35. "Fortas's Old Firm Faces U.S. Inquiry," *New York Times,* May 7, 1969. "Quietly" quote in "Finding of Missing Data in Fortas Safe Probed," *Evening Star,* May 7, 1969. See also Vera Glaser, "Capital Newsmakers," *Washingtonian,* December 1968, p. 32.

36. Interviews with Carol Agger (May 1987), Paul Berger (May 1985), and Milton Freeman (Dec. 1983). See also Dennison, "Finding of Missing Data in Fortas Safe Probed": "Disclosure of the grand jury probe seemed likely to bring out in the open a growing debate here over whether the Nixon administration was reacting politically to the Fortases."

37. Patrick Buchanan to Richard Nixon, May 6, 1969, Nixon Presidential Papers Project, National Archives (hereafter, Nixon Project).

38. Shogan, *A Question of Judgment*, pp. 242–44.

39. Conversation with Jack Landau, Dec. 1983. For events recounted in the next several pages, see Shogan, *A Question of Judgment*, pp. 246–56; and Murphy, *Fortas*, pp. 560–69.

40. Murphy, *Fortas*, p. 561.

41. Henry E. Petersen, interview by Fred Graham, Dec. 24, 1969, Box 8, Graham Papers. According to John Ehrlichman, Mitchell believed the chief justice was a good candidate because Warren "had every reason to feel gratitude for the [gracious] manner in which his retirement was being handled by the President" (John Ehrlichman, *Witness to Power* [New York: Simon and Schuster, 1982], p. 116).

42. Quoted in Bernard Schwartz, *Super Chief: Earl Warren and His Supreme Court, A Judicial Biography* (New York: New York University Press, 1983), p. 762.

43. Quoted in Shogan, *A Question of Judgment*, p. 249.

44. Whitman Knapp to Judges of the Second Circuit, Aug. 5, 1975, FP. See also "Fee is Explained," *New York Times*, May 16, 1969: "The events today disclose that Chief Justice Warren did play a central role in the outcome [Fortas's resignation]. He was willing to meet with Mr. Mitchell to receive the information against Justice Fortas, and he notified the President soon after he learned of Justice Fortas's decision." As G. Edward White observed of Warren in another context: "Despite his calculated nonparticipation in politics while on the Court, he had remained acutely aware of the political implications of his actions." White, *Earl Warren* (New York: Oxford University Press, 1982), p. 312.

45. "Justice Abe Fortas on the Spot," *Newsweek*, May 19, 1969, p. 29. Copies were available on the weekend of May 10.

46. Shogan, *A Question of Judgment*, p. 252.

47. For Harlow, see Summary, Staff Meeting, May 13, 1969, Nixon Project. See, "Mitchell Said to Confer with Warren on Fortas," *New York Times*, May 11, 1969; and Fred Graham, "Mitchell Confirms that He Gave Warren 'Certain Information' about Fortas," ibid., May 13, 1969.

48. "Justice Department Reported Studying Fortas-Wolfson Tie," *New York Times*, May 9, 1969.

49. Quoted in Murphy, *Fortas*, p. 568.

50. Interview with Henry Petersen, Dec. 24, 1969; Graham conversation with Bill Lambert, Aug. 29, 1969, Box 8, Graham Papers.

51. "Fortas Tie to Wolfson Is Detailed," *Washington Post*, Jan. 23, 1977.

52. Shogan, *A Question of Judgment*, p. 263.

53. Undated notes, Nixon Project.

54. Alexander Butterfield to Herbert Klein (communicating the President's wish), May 15, 1969, ibid.

55. Shogan, *A Question of Judgment*, p. 268.

56. "Jurist under Pressure" *New York Times*, May 14, 1969.

57. Max Frankel to Fred Graham, n.d., Graham Papers, Box 8.

58. Fortas, "The Generations," May 8, 1969, FP. See "Fortas, In Talk, Avoids Fee Furor," *New York Times*, May 9, 1969. The article indicated that the crowd had warmly greeted Fortas.

59. Shogan, *A Question of Judgment*, p. 256.

60. "Fortas, In Talk, Avoids Fee Furor."

61. Fred Graham, "The Fortas Case," *New York Times*, May 11, 1969; Alan Barth, "'Thou Shalt Nots' for the Court," *Washington Post*, May 18, 1969.

62. Interviews with Eugene Bogan (May 1985), Barbara Winslow (May 1985), Carol Agger (May 1987), Mercedes Eichholz (May 1986), and Helen Muller (Jan. 1987).

63. "Fortas, In Talk, Avoids Fee Furor."

64. William Street "'No Interviews,'" *Memphis Commercial Appeal*, May 13, 1969.

65. Interviews with Winslow, Mercedes Eichholz (Oct. 1988), and Martha Field (Sept. 1985). For the Blacks, see Black and Black, *Mr. Justice and Mrs. Black*, p. 220.

66. As implied by Elizabeth Black in Black and Black, *Mr. Justice and Mrs. Black*, p. 220.

67. Ibid.

68. Interviews with Winslow and Agger.

69. "Mitchell Said to Confer with Warren on Fortas."

70. Porter, LBJOH, p. 37.

71. William O. Douglas, *The Court Years, 1939–1975: The Autobiography of William O. Douglas* (New York: Random House, 1980), p. 358.

72. James Simon, *Independent Journey: The Life of William O. Douglas* (New York: Harper and Row, 1980), p. 396.

73. Fortas recounted the conversation to Bruce Murphy.

74. Interview with Clark Clifford, July 1985.

75. Douglas, *The Court Years*, pp. 357–59; Black and Black, *Mr. Justice and Mrs. Black*, p. 220.

76. Interviews with William Brennan (Dec. 1985) and Potter Stewart (Sept. 1985). See also Douglas, *Court Years*, p. 359.

77. Interview with Winslow.

78. Fortas to Earl Warren, May 14, 1969.

79. Ibid.

80. "Fortas on His Resignation: 'There Wasn't Any Choice For A Man of Conscience.'"

81. Quoted in Murphy, *Fortas*, p. 572.

82. (Strom Thurmond Reports to the People), "Douglas Is Next," June 2, 1969, press release 15, no. 19, D110, Folder Supreme Court, Gerald R. Ford Papers, Gerald R. Ford Library.

83. Black and Black, *Mr. Justice and Mrs. Black*, p. 121.

84. Interview with Clifford.

85. Memorandum for Messrs. Tolson et al; for Congress, see *Cong. Rec.*, 91st Cong., 1st sess., 115, pt. 9: 12557 (remarks of Senator Williams).

86. "The Fortas Puzzle: What Was the Flaw?" *New York Times*, May 18, 1969.

87. Fred Graham to Fortas, June 19, 1969, Box 8, Graham Papers.

88. Conversation with Bill Lambert, Aug. 29, 1969, ibid.

89. Shogan, *A Question of Judgment*, p. 260; Earl Warren to Nixon, May 14, 1969, Nixon Project.

90. Interview with Lady Bird Johnson, April 1986.

91. Quoted in Shogan, *A Question of Judgment*, p. 260.

92. Murphy, *Fortas*, pp. 574–75.

93. Quoted in ibid., p. 1.

94. Quoted in ibid., p. 196.

95. Interview with Agger; interview with Harold Burson, May 1987.

96. See, e.g., "The Fortas Puzzle: What Was the Flaw?"; "Washington's Dinner Guests Are Served War, Want and Fortas," *New York Times*, May 12, 1969.

97. Remarks of Rex Lee at Memorial Service for Fortas, 102 S. Ct. 47 (1982).

98. Vincent Blasi, review, "'He Could Never Have Enough,'" *New York Times Book Review*, July 31, 1988, p. 27.

99. Interview with Howard Koven, July 1987.

100. Confidential interview 14.

101. Caroline Bird, *The Invisible Scar: The Great Depression, and What It Did to American Life, from Then until Now* (New York: David McKay, 1966).

102. Fortas made that comment to Mercedes Eichholz. Interview with Eichholz.

103. Eric Sevareid, television broadcast, "Cronkite News," May 15, 1969; interview with Sevareid, May 1985.

104. "Fortas on His Resignation: 'There Wasn't Any Choice For a Man of Conscience.'"
105. Robert Burt to Laura Kalman, May 1, 1989.

## 17. "SUDDENLY EVERYTHING SEEMS OLD-FASHIONED"

1. Liz Carpenter was told about this conversation by June White. It occurred between Agger and White's husband, William S. White, at a dinner party at which Carpenter was present (interview with Liz Carpenter, May 1986).
2. Interview with Mercedes Eichholz, May 1986.
3. Thus, for example, Fortas wrote Paul Berger, who was still under investigation by the Justice Department, to say he wanted to help in any way that he could, even to the point of spending hours in the library (interview with Paul Berger, May 1985).
4. Confidential interviews 42 and 7.
5. See Lesley Oelsner, "Panel Urges Strict Ethics Code for Judges," *New York Times*, June 8, 1972.
6. Interview with Eichholz, May 1986. See also Fortas to Marc Fasteau, May 23, 1969, FP: "My wife and I are going away for about two weeks to get some relief from press and photographers."
7. Interviews with Frances Arnold (July 1984); Eugene Rostow (July 1985); Thurman Arnold, Jr. (July 1985).
8. Thurman Arnold to Fortas, May 16, 1969, FP.
9. Confidential interviews 11, 17, and 37.
10. Fortas's surprise reported in interview with Victor Kramer, Dec. 1984.
11. Confidential interviews 15 and 17.
12. Confidential interviews 22 and 14.
13. Confidential interview 15.
14. Interview with Frances Arnold; Hugo L. Black and Elizabeth Black, *Mr. Justice and Mrs. Black: The Memoirs of Hugo L. Black and Elizabeth Black* (New York: Random House, 1986), p. 233; interview with Thurman Arnold, Jr.
15. Confidential interview 15. "I'm sure he [Porter] must have said a lot of things he didn't mean, or if he meant them, he wouldn't do," another partner added. According to this individual, Porter was "very upset about the whole business" and blamed himself for Fortas's problems (Confidential interview 22).
16. Fortas quote from Victor Navasky, "In Washington, You Just Don't Not Return a Call from Abe Fortas," *New York Times Magazine*, August 1, 1971, p. 33.
17. Fortas to Ramsey Clark, Feb. 13, 1974; Fortas to Jacob Javits, Feb. 13, 1974; both in FP.
18. See discussion below.
19. Confidential interviews 17 and 15.
20. Navasky, "In Washington, You Just Don't . . . ," p. 33.
21. "Abe Fortas Today: A Lawyer's Lawyer," *Washington Post*, Dec. 16, 1979 ("Many observers were surprised that she could remain at a firm that had given her husband such a slap in the face"); confidential interviews 9, 10, and 22 (speculating on why Agger had done so).
22. Cass Canfield to Fortas, June 13, 1969, FP; interview with Carol Agger, May 1987.
23. Fortas to Harry Walker, June 13, 1969, ibid.; Navasky, "In Washington, You Just Don't . . . ," p. 7.
24. J. Edgar Hoover to Fortas, Nov. 10, 1970; Fortas to Hoover, Nov. 12, 1970; both in FP.
25. "Book," ibid.
26. Comment, "The New Public Interest Lawyers," *Yale Law Journal* 79 (1970): 1107, 1139; Edgar S. and Jean Camper Cahn, "Power to the People or the Profession?—The Public Interest in Public Interest Law," ibid., p. 1048.

27. Comment, "The New Public Interest Lawyers," pp. 1007–09; Stephen Wexler, "Practicing Law for Poor People," ibid., passim; Cahn and Cahn, "Power to the People or the Profession?" pp. 1047–48 (see also pp. 1032–37 for a description of the advantages which could accrue from increasing law firms' public-interest work).

28. "Introduction to the Issue," ibid., p. 981.

29. Fortas, "Thurman Arnold and the Theatre of the Law," ibid., p. 1000.

30. Ibid., p. 995.

31. Ibid., pp. 1002, 1003.

32. Ibid., pp. 1002, 997.

33. "Fortas Deplores Court Disruption," *New York Times,* Oct. 4, 1970. Arnold would have been delighted with Fortas's memorial tribute. In April of 1969 Senator Ribicoff had sent Arnold a copy of a statement by Ralph Nader charging that the lawyers at Arnold & Porter were "eminent specialists in cutting down consumer programs in their incipiency or undermining them if they mature" (Abraham Ribicoff to Thurman Arnold, April 1, 1969, FP). Arnold responded sharply:

> Perhaps a rule that counsel should not make any representation on behalf of his client without the prior approval of Mr. Nader would satisfy him. The necessity of hearing representatives of both sides of a case, even if one of them happens to be General Motors, may slow down many of Mr. Nader's praiseworthy objectives. But it is the only course consistent with the constitutional idea that adverse interests are entitled to have their claims presented by counsel of their choices.
>
> Mr. Nader has every right to attack the claims and arguments of any group which he thinks opposes the consumers' interests. He has no right, however, to attack such a group for *presenting* its claims and arguments (however wrong they may be in his eyes) to the men who must make the decisions. That, of course, is what he is doing. . . . He is saying to your Committee that we should get rid of skilled advocates because they confuse the court (Thurman Arnold to Abraham Ribicoff, April 3, 1969, ibid).

34. Fortas, "Thurman Arnold and the Theatre of Law," p. 1003.

35. Interview with Charles Reich, Dec. 1985.

36. Navasky, "In Washington, You Just Don't Not . . . ," p. 33.

37. Reich quote in "Protest Has Value to New Yale Hero," *New York Times,* Oct. 16, 1970. See Fortas to Charles Reich, Oct. 22, 1970; Reich to Fortas, Oct. 26, 1976; Fortas to Paul Porter, Oct. 29, 1970; all in FP. If he had actually said that of the firm, Reich later commented, he would have deserved Fortas's condemnation (interview with Reich).

38. Interview with Harold Burson, May 1987.

39. Fortas to John Loeb, July 16, 1969, FP; interview with John Loeb, Dec. 1983; interview with Bella Linden, Sept. 1984.

40. Interview with Sheldon Karon, July 1987.

41. Interviews with C. Girard Davidson (July 1984), Leon Keyserling (July 1985), and Martin Riger (May 1987).

42. Robert Pack, *Edward Bennett Williams for the Defense* (New York: Harper and Row, 1983), p. 360; confidential interview 44.

43. William O. Douglas to Fred Rodell, Sept. 15, 1969, Fred Rodell Papers, Treasure Room Collection, Haverford College.

44. Interview with Howard Koven, July 1987.

45. Ibid.

46. Fortas to Rexford Tugwell, April 30, 1970, FP.

47. Interview with Koven.

48. Fortas to Lyndon Johnson, August 8, 1970, FP.

49. Specifically, his average annual income was $390,577. The least Fortas earned during one year in the 1974–1982 time period was $282,676 (1975). The most he earned was $521,534 (1979). During the first three months of 1982, he earned $205,093. I am indebted to Carol Agger for supplying me with a summary of Fortas's tax returns.

50. Interview with Koven.

51. See Casals file in FP.

52. Quote from interview with Koven.

53. "'But I'm afraid if anything came up outside of Texas, he'd feel at liberty to consult me,' says Fortas with a little laugh" (Navasky, "In Washington You Just Don't Not . . . ," p. 24).

54. Quote in Fortas to John Loeb; Fortas to Benjamin Sonnenberg; and Fortas to Edwin Weisl; all letters dated June 20, 1969, FP.

55. Interview with Koven.

56. See, e.g., Fortas to Johnson, Dec. 19, 1972, ibid.

57. Fortas to Johnson, July 30, 1971, ibid.

58. Fortas to Johnson, July 12, 1971, ibid. As it turned out, Rostow had to cancel the engagement.

59. David Wise to Robert Schulz, Jan. 17, 1972; Mary Rather to Fortas, Feb. 22, 1972; Fortas to Mary Rather, Feb. 28, 1972; all in FP.

60. Fortas to Joe Frantz, July 12, 1971, ibid.

61. Abe Fortas, "He Was America," *New York Times*, Jan. 25, 1973.

62. Johnson to Fortas, Dec. 28, 1972, FP.

63. Lady Bird Johnson to Fortas, Aug. 21, 1979; Fortas to Lady Bird Johnson, Aug. 31, 1979, ibid.

64. See "Benjamin Lach" file, FP.

65. Interview with Koven.

66. For Nixon meeting, see David Parker to Henry Kissinger and Dick Fairbanks, Feb. 20, 1973, Nixon Project, National Archives. For message to Carter, see Hubert Humphrey to Fortas, March 6, 1977; Fortas to Hubert Humphrey, March 14, 1977, both in FP.

67. Quote in interview with David Lloyd Kreeger (May 1985). Stevens himself put it less flamboyantly. "He's the only board member I've ever really missed," he said of Fortas (interview with Stevens, July 1985).

68. Interview with Eichholz.

69. See, e.g., Fortas to Ralph Becker, June 23, 1975, FP.

70. Draft Minutes of Executive Committee Meeting Held, June 4, 1979, ibid.

71. Leonard Garment, "Annals of Law: The Hill Case," *New Yorker*, April 17, 1989, p. 107.

72. Quoted in Navasky, "In Washington, You Just Don't Not . . . ," p. 26.

73. On the press, see, e.g., Joseph Goulden, *The Superlawyers: The Small and Powerful World of the Great Washington Law Firms* (New York: Weybright and Talley, 1972).

74. "Fortas Registers as Bank Lobbyist," *New York Times*, Aug. 6, 1970.

75. Interview with Karon.

76. Fortas to Victor Navasky, Aug. 8, 1970, FP.

77. Interview with Karon; Sheldon Karon to Laura Kalman, July 6, 1989.

78. Quoted in Garment, "Annals of Law," p. 109.

79. "Abe Fortas Today;" interview with Karon.

80. Interview with Koven.

81. Interview with Karon.

82. Harold Burson to Laura Kalman, May 6, 1987.

83. Interview with Burson.

84. Fortas quoted in Navasky, "In Washington You Just Don't Not Return a Call from Abe Fortas," p. 7.

85. Fortas to Isaac Stern, Nov. 9, 1976, ibid.

86. Interview with Karon; also see the letters between Fortas and Alexander Schneider in ibid.

87. Garment, "Annals of Law," pp. 110, 107.

88. He spoke with Peter Irons, for example, about the New Deal lawyers, and with Katie

Louchheim and Joel Seligman about the SEC. He talked with Robert Caro and Merle Miller about Lyndon Johnson, and with Bruce Murphy about his relationship with Johnson.

89. Fortas to Robert Shogan, May 17, 1971, FP.

90. Interview with Charlotte Woolard, May 1984.

91. For clients, see interview with Loeb. For students, see, e.g., the letters between Fortas and Holly Cox in FP.

92. See the numerous letters between Fortas and Van Buren from 1976 through 1978 in ibid; confidential interviews 9, 10, and 45.

93. Interview with Karon.

94. Interviews with Koven and with Margot Collins, July 1985.

95. Interview with Karon.

96. Interview with Harry Blackmun, Dec. 1983.

97. William O. Douglas to Fortas, Aug. 4, 1969, FP.

98. See James Simon, *Independent Journey: The Life of William O. Douglas* (New York: Harper and Row, 1980), p. 452.

99. Fortas, Book Review, *New York University Law Review* 49 (1974): 374–76; Fortas to Max Isenbergh, April 6, 1981, FP.

100. See William O. Douglas, *The Court Years, 1939–1975: The Autobiography of William O. Douglas* (New York: Random House, 1980); AF Draft, Aug. 29, 1977, FP; Warren Burger to Fortas, Oct. 2, 1980; William Rehnquist to Fortas, Sept. 19, 1980, both in ibid. Fortas did not retain a copy of his letter to Burger in his files, but Burger's and Rehnquist's letters to him give a sense of its contents.

101. Douglas to Fortas, October 15, 1979, FP.

102. Thus, for example, he was invited to a dinner for the Court that Earl Warren hosted in 1970, and he attended John Harlan's funeral with other members of the Court in 1971 (Earl Warren to Fortas, Feb. 12, 1970, ibid.; interview with Blackmun).

103. "Warren Assails Proposal to Screen High Court Cases," *New York Times,* May 2, 1973; Douglas to Fortas, Dec. 21, 1972, FP.

104. "Ill-advised" in Fortas to Eugene Gressman, Jan. 3, 1973, ibid; "the distress of new Justices" in Fortas to Henry Friendly, June 16, 1976, ibid.

105. Fortas to Warren Burger, Dec. 19, 1972, ibid.

106. Fortas to Friendly, June 16, 1976.

107. "Fortas Is Ranked as a 'Near Great,'" *New York Times,* Nov. 9, 1972.

108. Clint Murchison, Jr., to Fortas, Nov. 21, 1972; Fortas to Murchison, Dec. 4, 1972; both in FP.

109. Interview with Karon.

110. Louis Wolfson to Fortas, March 30, 1973; Fortas to Wolfson, April 5, 1973; both in FP.

111. Bob Woodward, "Fortas Tie to Wolfson Is Detailed," *Washington Post,* Jan. 23, 1977.

112. Bernard Fensterward, Jr., to Fortas, Jan. 27, 1977, FP.

113. See, e.g., "Fortas Tie to Wolfson Is Detailed"; "Fortas, While a Justice, Said to Have Offered Aid to Wolfson in S.E.C. Case," *New York Times,* Jan. 26, 1977.

114. Carol Agger to Mathilde Krim, Aug. 14, 1972, FP.

115. Fortas, "March to Decency," *New York Times,* June 8, 1972.

116. Fortas to Johnson, July 24, 1972, FP. "You are always just and clear and see things in perspective," Johnson replied. "And, I thank you too for your sweet thoughts of me that came through almost every line" (Johnson to Fortas, July 31, 1972, ibid).

117. Fortas to Wolfson, April 5, 1973.

118. Fortas to H. R. Haldeman, Aug. 31, 1972; Fortas to Richard Nixon, Sept. 15, 1972, FP.

119. "Justice Fortas: 'I Don't Believe Liberalism Is Dead'—but," *New York Times,* March 15, 1973.

120. Carl Albert to Fortas, Jan. 22, 1973, FP.

121. Fortas to Albert, Jan. 18, 1973, ibid.

122. Fortas to Alfred Friendly, Jr., March 26, 1974; Alfred Friendly, Jr., to Edmund Muskie, April 15, 1974, and April 17, 1974, all in ibid.

123. Fortas to Peter Lehner, Oct. 30, 1973, ibid. See also Fortas to Donald Riegle, Jr., June 20, 1974, ibid.

124. "Fortas Suggests a Bill to Give Immunity to Nixon If He Resigns," *New York Times*, Jan. 13, 1974.

125. Fortas, "The Constitution and the Presidency," April, 14, 1974 (Draft of speech for University of Washington lectures on jurisprudence), FP.

126. Fortas to Edith Green, March 20, 1974, ibid.

127. Draft article for *New York Times*, June 25, 1973, ibid.

128. See Fortas to Cyrus Eaton, June 27, 1973; Fortas to Edith Green, June 25, 1973; Fortas to William Hathaway, Aug. 1, 1974; Edith Green, form letter addressed to "The Honorable _____," July 19, 1973; Fortas to Edith Green, March 20, 1974; all in FP. See also Abe Fortas, "The Constitution and the Presidency," *Washington Law Review* 49 (1974): 987–1012 (based on a lecture delivered at the University of Washington).

129. See Edith Green to Fortas, March 13, 1974, FP.

130. Fortas to Green, March 20, 1974.

131. Interviews with Walter Slocombe (May 1985), Martha Field (Sept. 1985), and Carol Agger (May 1987). See also Richard Nixon, *RN: The Memoirs of Richard Nixon* (New York: Grossett & Dunlap, 1978), p. 420.

132. Garment, "Annals of Law," pp. 107–08. "The horror" is Fortas's term.

133. Interview with Koven.

134. Fortas, Draft, June 25, 1973, FP.

135. Abe Fortas, interview by William Gibbons and Patricia McAdams, Sept. 9, 1980.

136. Interview with Karon.

137. See Fortas, "The Case Against Capital Punishment," *New York Times Magazine*, January 23, 1977; Draft for remarks delivered at a meeting of the Association of the Bar of the City of New York, May 3, 1977, FP.

138. Quote from "Fortas Backs Reagan Plan to Trim Government," *Memphis Press-Scimitar*, May 2, 1981. "Fortas Wishes Reagan Well, But . . . ," ibid., May 6, 1981; Milton Britten to Fortas, May 6, 1981, FP.

139. Fortas to Thomas Eagleton, Jan. 20, 1982, FP.

140. Brief in Opposition to Petition for Certiorari, *Partido Nuevo Progresista* v. *Gerineldo Barreto Pérez and Partido Popular Democratico*, Supreme Court of the United States, No. 80-1540, April 8, 1981, FP. See Fortas to Inés Muñoz Marín, Jan. 30, 1981; Jaime Benítez, Jan. 30, 1981; both in FP; and interview with Rafael Hernández Colón (July 1985); and Fortas to Jaime Benítez, May 19, 1981, FP.

141. Interview with Hernández Colón; Fortas to Jaime Benítez, Oct. 30, 1981, FP.

142. Interview with Hernández Colón.

143. Fortas to Jaime Benítez, Jan. 5, 1982, FP.

144. Brief for Appellees, *Jesus Rivera Rodríguez* v. *Popular Democratic Party*, No. 81-328, Jan. 4, 1982, pp. 10, 35, FP.

145. *Fortson* v. *Morris*, 385 U.S. 231 (1966).

146. Brief for Appellees, *Rodríguez* v. *Popular Democratic Party*, pp. 20, 29.

147. 385 U.S. 242 (1966); "The Supreme Court, 1966 Term," *Harvard Law Review* 81 (1967): 149. Elizabeth Black, who was present at the Court the day Fortas announced his dissent in *Fortson* v. *Morris*, noted: "Abe was flushed with anger and stated his dissent with more heat than usual" (Black and Black, *Mr. Justice and Mrs. Black*, p. 157).

148. Bernard Schwartz, *Super Chief: Earl Warren and His Supreme Court, A Judicial Biography* (New York: New York University Press, 1983), p. 679.

149. Interview with Hernández Colón.

150. Interview with Jose Trías Monge, July 1985.

151. Conversation (July 1989) with Geoffrey Aronow, an associate at Hughes, Hubbard & Reed at the time the case was tried.

152. Interview with Hernández Colón.

153. See Jim Mann, "The Court Hears One of Its Own," *American Lawyer,* June 1982, p. 46; "Abe Fortas Returns to Court After Dozen Years' Absence," *Washington Post,* March 23, 1982.

154. Interview with Hernández Colón.

155. Interview with Koven.

156. Mann, "The Court Hears One Of Its Own," p. 46.

157. Interview with Blackmun.

158. Interview with Hernández Colón.

159. James Rowe to Carol Agger, April 8, 1982 (letter given me by Carol Agger).

160. *Rodríguez* v. *Popular Democratic Party,* 457 U.S. 1 (1982).

161. Interviews with Eichholz and Koven.

162. Fortas to Peter Lehner, April 5, 1982, FP.

163. "Requiem for a Friend," *Washington Post,* May 26, 1982.

164. Conversation with Mercedes Eichholz, Aug. 1988.

165. Interview with Lady Bird Johnson, April 1986.

# Index

AAA. *See* Agricultural Adjustment
   Administration
Abel, Bess, 229
Acheson, Dean, 403n5
ADA. *See* Americans for Democratic Action
*Adderly* v. *Florida*, 281
Agger, Carol, 19, 43–44, 48, 67, 100, 102,
   105, 106, 108, 112, 114, 161, 186, 187,
   192, 193, 194, 205, 233, 237, 296, 300,
   320, 345, 350, 353, 362, 382, 387, 400,
   411n96, 426n63; courtship and marriage of,
   44–45, 195–96; at Yale Law School, 53; and
   Fortas's discharge from Navy, 108–09; as
   friend to the Johnsons, 199–200; and Fortas's refusal to accept attorney general post,
   231–32; and Fortas's Supreme Court appointment, 242–43, 244, 245; as target in
   Fortas investigation, 366–67; and Fortas's
   resignation, 371, 372, 374, 378, 379; attitude of toward Nixon, 394
Agricultural Adjustment Act, 32, 409n53; constitutionality of, 35–41
Agricultural Adjustment Administration (AAA),
   26; Fortas as lawyer for, 27–34, 39–42; and
   peach marketing agreement, 34–39
Agriculture, Department of. *See* Agricultural
   Adjustment Administration
Akerman, Alexander, 39–41, 411n81
Albert, Carl, 395
Alcoholism: as legal issue, 257–60

*Alderman* v. *United States*, 256
Allen, George, 116
Allen, James, 28
Allott, Gordon, 351, 353–54
Alsop, Joseph, 56, 62, 428n133
American Amortization Company, 20–22
American Bar Association, 379
Americans for Democratic Action (ADA), 129,
   135, 208
American University: Fortas seminar at, 326–
   27, 351–52, 354, 355, 476n210
Anderson, Marian, 67
Andrews, Bert, 128, 134, 432n53
Angell, James Rowland, 51
Animal Welfare Bill, 219
Animal Welfare Institute, 177, 207
Anti-Semitism: as factor in law careers, 14–
   15, 45, 68–69; and Ibn Saud, 105, 109; and
   Fortas's nomination as chief justice, 346–47
Antitrust laws: during the New Deal, 29–30;
   and *FTC* v. *Dean Foods*, 267–68; and *U.S.*
   v. *Arnold, Schwinn and Company*, 270–71
Armour Meat Packing House, 20
Armstrong, Walter, 79
Arnold, Frances, 126, 381
Arnold, Thurman, Sr., 13–14, 18, 23, 50,
   114, 115, 116, 164, 165, 202, 260, 344,
   405n56, 431n28, 431n32, 439n104; and
   peach marketing agreement case, 36–38;
   enters private practice, 125, 126; and Peters

Arnold, Thurman, Sr. (continued)
case, 141–43, 433n95; and McCarran committee, 149–50, 435n144; as corporate attorney, 154; as Fortas's law partner, 184–86;
as Fortas's friend following resignation, 380;
death of, 381; Fortas's tribute to, 384–86,
482n33. *See also* Arnold & Porter; Arnold,
Fortas & Porter
Arnold, Thurman, Jr., 185, 381
Arnold, Fortas & Porter, 443n18; establishment of, 126; loyalty cases handled by, 129–
37, 150–51, 432n67; and court tests of
loyalty programs, 137–44; as counsel for
Dorothy Bailey, 138–41; as counsel for John
Peters, 141–43; as corporate law firm, 152–
58; interrelationships among partners in,
184–86; characterizations of, 186–88; treat-
ment of associates at, 188–91
Arnold & Fortas, 125, 126
Arnold & Porter, 384, 482n33; Justice Depart-
ment investigation of, 366–67; rejection of
Fortas by, 380–82
Arts: Fortas as advocate for, 220–21, 388–89
Ashmore, Harry, 464n15
Auchincloss, Louis, 408n14
Austern, Thomas, 34, 409n53
*Avery* v. *Midland County*, 261
Ayers, Eben, 428n141

Bailey, Dorothy, 138–42, 433n89
Baker, Bobby, 174, 221–22
Baker, Howard, 331
*Barenblatt* v. *United States*, 164
Barr, Joseph, 354
Barth, Alan, 347
Baruch, Bernard, 91
Battle, Lucius, 220
Bazelon, David, 161, 247–48
Ben-Gurion, David, 300–301, 465n36
Benítez, Jaime, 77, 170, 234, 235, 237, 238,
239, 288–89, 399, 452n40
Bentley, Elizabeth, 127
Berger, Paul, 367, 374, 481n3
*Berger* v. *New York*, 338
Berle, Adolf, 208, 246, 325, 451n166
Bernhard, Arnold, 386
Betancourt, Romulo, 234
*Betts* v. *Brady*, 180–83
Biddle, Francis, 103, 104, 202
Bittman, William, 363
Bituminous Coat Act, 69

Bituminous Coal Division, 30; Fortas as chief
counsel to, 68–70
Black, Elizabeth, 372, 381
Black, Fred, 313–16
Black, Hugo, 115, 140, 143, 164, 165, 183,
274, 275, 359, 372, 373, 399, 438n104,
457n44; and Johnson Senate race, 201–02;
and *Gault* case, 253–54; and *Powell* case,
258–59; on the right to privacy, 265–66; and
*Snyder* v. *Harris*, 272–73; and *Brown* v.
*Louisiana*, 280–81; and *Tinker* v. *Des Moines
School District*, 290; relationship of with
Fortas, 320–22, 349, 372, 469n13, 470n20
Blackmun, Harry, 392, 400
Blacks: and racial unrest during Johnson ad-
ministration, 307–09, 467n90
Blasi, Vincent, 377
Bloom, Esta Fortas, 7, 9
Bloom, Julius, 220
*Bloom* v. *Illinois*, 257
Blue Melody Boys, 9
Bogan, Eugene, 345–46, 353
Bone, Homer, 72, 73–74, 418n63
Bosch, Juan, 232, 234–40, 452nn40, 42, 43,
453nn49, 54, 57
Brandeis, Louis, 30, 36, 159
Brennan, William, 161, 253, 266, 281, 311,
313–14, 320, 343, 357, 373, 399, 400,
461n11, 461n26
Brown, Henry, 278
*Brown* v. *Louisiana*, 278–81, 321, 461n11
Broyhill, Joel Thomas, 394
Buchanan, Patrick, 367
Buckner, Emory, 25
Budenz, Louis, 147–48
Bundy, McGeorge, 233, 234, 239, 293, 294,
295, 312, 452n38
Bunker, Ellsworth, 239
Burger, Warren, 143, 392–93, 400
Burlew, E. K., 71
Burling, John, 92
Burson, Harold, 391
Burt, Robert, 378
Burton, Harold, 140, 142
Business Council, 299, 339, 448n105
Byrd, Harry, 333
Byrd, Robert, 329, 471n68

Caamaño Deñó, Francisco, 232, 234–39,
452nn40, 42
Caballero, Julio, 237–38

Cain, Harry P., 431n28
Calder, Alexander, 403n2
Califano, Joe, 302, 381
Calistan Packers: and peach marketing agreement, 36–39, 410nn67, 69
Caplin, Mortimer, 177, 389
*Cardona* v. *Power,* 260
Carmody, John, 67
Carnegie Hall, 388
Caro, Robert, 100, 484n88
Carpenter, Liz, 195, 225, 317, 481n1
Carter, Jimmy, 388
Carver, George, 304
Casals, Pablo, 176–77, 293, 387
Celler, Emanuel, 372
Chambers, Whittaker, 127
Chandler, Alfred, 444n21
Chandler Act of *1938,* 55
Chapman, Oscar, 92, 435n9
Chavez, Dennis, 104
Chavoor, Evelyn, 433n89
Christopher, Warren, 332–33, 335, 473n112
Citizens for Decent Literature, 342, 344
Civil Aeronautics Board, 389
Civil Rights Bill of *1957,* 203
Civil rights cases: Supreme Court ambivalence toward, 277–82
Civil rights law: Fortas as advocate of, 213
Clancy, James, 342–44
Clark, Charles E., 13, 24, 46, 50, 51
Clark, Ramsey, 164, 315, 316, 330–31, 360–61, 382, 471n73
Clark, Samuel O., 414n67
Clark, Tom, 115, 117, 129, 164, 427n104; and *FTC* v. *Dean Foods,* 267, 268, 269
Class action suits, 272–73
Clayton Act, 267
Cleland, John, 343
Clifford, Clark M., 192, 203, 206, 208, 217, 222, 225, 226, 351, 354, 373, 403n5, 437n73; as adviser to Johnson, 202, 205, 293, 295, 306, 317, 327–28, 464n13
Coal: regulation of, 68–70, 92–96
Coal Commission. *See* Bituminous Coal Division
Cohen, Benjamin, 100, 200, 245, 294, 403n5
Cohen, Manuel, 361, 369
Coit, Henry, 20, 21, 22
Columbia Power Administration, 74
Columbia Power Authority, 72
Columbia University, 283

Communism: fear of as basis for loyalty programs, 126–33; Fortas's firm's response to, 133–37, 432n67; as issue in Bailey case, 138–41; as issue in Peters case, 141–43; congressional investigations of, 144–51; as issue in Dominican Republic intervention, 232–33, 235–40; as issue in Fortas confirmation hearings, 248
Conceptualism: as theory of law, 15–17
*Concerning Dissent and Civil Disobedience* (Fortas), 283–84, 287, 288, 289, 463n62, 467n90
Condon, Edward, 144–45, 218
Consumer credit: as legal issue, 20–22
Continental Enterprises, 359, 363
Cooper, John, 355
Coplon, Judith, 127
Corbin, Arthur, 50–51
Corcoran, Thomas, 28, 100, 113, 162, 163, 200, 202, 203, 208, 403n5, 427n95, 428n133; encourages opportunities for Fortas, 114–16; and Pauley nomination, 117, 118, 119, 120; relationship of with Lyndon Johnson, 205–06
Countryman, Vern, 55
Covington, J. Harry, 34
*Cox* v. *Louisiana,* 278–79
Cravath, Paul, 157, 187
Crime: as issue during Johnson administration, 309–11
Cronyn, Hume, 167
Currie, Lauchlin, 435n144
Cutler, Lloyd, 52, 156

Davidson, C. Girard, 237, 386, 453n63
Davidson, T. Whitfield, 200, 201
Davies, Ralph, 110, 112
Davis, Chester, 408n23
Davis, Clifford, 426n76
Davis, David, 338
DeLoach, Cartha, 314–16, 360
Dempsey, Jack, 76
*The Desperate Hours* (Hayes), 262
Detroit, Mich., 307–09
Dewey, Thomas, 184
De Witt, John, 80, 420n29
Diamond, Norman, 68, 69, 70, 126, 187, 216
Diehl, Charles, 11, 12
Dirksen, Everett, 329, 330, 331, 332, 338–39, 349, 355, 356, 372
*Disobedience and Democracy* (Zinn), 292

Dixie Peaches, 9

Dodd, Bella, 148

Dominican Republic: U.S. intervention in, 232–40, 452nn34, 38, 39, 40, 42, 43, 453nn49, 54, 57

Donovan, Hedley, 477n11

Donovan, William J., 25

Dorsen, Norman, 254

Doskow, Ambrose, 27, 43, 44

Douglas, Helen Gahagan, 134, 433n89

Douglas, William O., 23, 45, 50, 66, 71, 75, 76, 100, 107, 109, 161, 164, 180, 183, 200, 202, 204, 209, 259, 260, 265, 280, 281, 311, 320, 324, 347, 359, 366, 386, 399, 403n5, 415n101, 439n104, 475n178; as Fortas's mentor, 18–20, 25, 51–52, 64, 76, 109, 116, 243–44, 385; and consumer credit study, 20, 21; at the SEC, 46–48; and Protective Committee Study, 53–61; and the Public Utilities Division, 61–64; on Peters case, 143; as advocate of Fortas's Supreme Court appointment, 243–44, 248; and Fortas's resignation, 373, 374

Downey, Sheridan, 78–79

Draft card burning, 282–84, 285, 461nn32, 35

Draft deferment: as issue for Fortas, 102–06

Dulles, John Foster, 56, 58, 89–90, 133

Dunn, Joseph, 69

Durham, Monte, 178–79

*Durham* v. *United States*, 178–80, 258

Durr, Clifford, 100, 135

Eastland, James, 248, 329, 330, 335, 338, 340, 346, 350

Eastman, Joseph, 94–96, 422n113

Eban, Abba, 465n44

Edgerton, Henry, 139

EEOC. *See* Equal Employment Opportunity Commission

Egypt. *See* Six-Day War

Ehrlichman, John, 346, 370

Eicher, Edward, 75

Eichholz, Mercedes, 19, 241, 242, 244, 245, 246–47, 296, 324, 372, 380, 389, 401

Eichholz, Robert, 296, 371, 464n17

Eisenhower, Dwight D., 142, 162, 174

Elliot, Alfred, 78–79

Elman, Mischa, 220

Emanuel, Victor, 62–63

Emerson, Thomas, 27, 43, 44, 136, 408n8

Endo, Mitsuye, 81

Engelhard, Pollak, Pitcher and Stern, 25

*Epperson* v. *Arkansas*, 273–76, 321

Equal Employment Opportunity Commission (EEOC), 210–11

Ervin, Sam, 328, 329, 395; as Fortas opponent, 338, 339, 340, 342, 343, 347

Evans, Courtney, 315

"Experimental Jurisprudence and the New Deal" (Frank), 29

Fahy, Charles, 81–82, 420n38

Fairman, Charles, 332

*Fanny Hill* (Cleland), 343

Farley, Jim, 32

Farm prices. *See* Agricultural Adjustment Administration

Federal Trade Commission (FTC), 156–57, 163–64; and Dean Foods case, 267–69

Federal Works Administration, 67

Federated Department Stores, 157–58, 163–64

Fernós Isern, Antonio, 170, 171, 173

Ferrer, José, 167, 183

Field, David Dudley, 164

Field, Martha, 372

Field, Stephen, 164–65

Figueras, José, 234

Finkelstein, Louis, 300

Finlay, Luke, 15, 50

Fish, Hamilton, Jr., 104

Flag burning, 284–86

Fly, James Lawrence, 37, 40, 41

Fong, Hiram, 247

Forage Foundation, 322

Forrestal, James, 77, 80, 88

Fortas, Abe: many facets of, 1–2, 191–92, 401; liberalism of, 2–3, 28–29, 217, 292; childhood of, 7–8; importance of music to, 8–9, 192–94, 391, 401; academic achievements of, 9–11, 12–13; extracurricular activities of, 11–12; admitted to law school, 13–14; as student at Yale Law School, 14–15; and legal realism, 15–18, 249, 271–76; as editor of *Yale Law Journal,* 17, 23, 24–25, 407n110; William O. Douglas as mentor to, 18–20, 25, 51–52, 64, 76, 109, 116, 243–44, 385; and consumer credit study, 20–22; fellow students' view of, 23–24; early career opportunities of, 25–26; at Agricultural Adjustment Administration, 27–31, 32–34; Jerome Frank as influence on, 31–32; and peach marketing agreement, 34–39; and citrus growers' case, 39–41; negotiating ability of, 42; as perceived by housemates, 42–43; marriage of to Carol Agger, 44–45; and decision to work for SEC, 45–48; loyalty of, 48, 121, 240; as Yale professor, 49–53; and Protective Committee Study, 53–61, 414n67; as perceived by subordinates at SEC, 60–61, 62–63; as assistant director of Public Utilities Division, 61–64; on staff at the Department of the Interior, 65–68; as general counsel to Public Works Administration, 67; as chief counsel to Bituminous Coal Division, 68–70; as perceived by subordinates at Interior, 70, 97–98, 100, 112–13; as director of Division of Power, 71–75; as mediator between Homer Bone and Harold Ickes, 73–74; considered for SEC commissionership, 75–76; named under secretary of Interior Department, 76, 77, 110; as social reformer, 78–83, 212–17; and California water resources, 78–79; as opponent of martial law in Hawaii, 79–80; as advocate for Japanese-Americans, 80–82, 419n29; and European Jewry, 83; international concerns of, 83–91; and reform program for Philippines, 84; and Puerto Rican issues, 84–87, 388, 421n66; and fight for U.N. trusteeships, 88–90, 421n80; leadership style of, 91–101; and coal miners' strike, 92–96; and Standard Oil contract, 97; as friend to Lyndon Johnson, 98, 100, 107, 161–62, 163, 196, 199–200, 202, 318, 387–88; and draft deferment issue, 102–06, 424n14; enlistment in Navy, 105–08, 425n50; indecision of after discharge, 108–10; return of to Interior, 110–13; considers resigning from Interior, 113–16; considered for judgeships, 115–16; and Pauley nomination, 117–21; begins private practice, 125, 126; as opponent of Truman loyalty program, 129–33; and strategy for loyalty cases, 133–37; seeks court test of loyalty boards, 138–44; responds to anticommunism in Congress, 144–51; as corporate attorney, 152–58; as loyal advocate for clients, 158–59; ideological autonomy of, 159–60; and government influence, 160–66, 168–69, 206–07; as counsel for Puerto Rico, 166–77, 207, 398–400, 439n120; as counsel for Animal Welfare Institute, 177; as counsel for Monte Durham, 178–80; as counsel for Clarence Gideon, 180–83; as partner with

Arnold and Porter, 184–86; role of in law firm, 187–88; relationship of with law firm associates, 188–91; attitude of toward religion, 194, 300; feelings of for children, 195; appeal of to women, 195–96; relationship of with wife, 195–96; as adviser to Congressman Lyndon Johnson, 199–202; personal relationship with Senator Johnson, 202–07; and Johnson's presidential aspirations, 207–09; as counsel to Johnson's associates, 209–10, 221–22; and Vice-President Johnson's role on the EEOC, 210–11; as adviser to President Johnson while in private practice, 212–17, 222–27, 228–30, 449n132; as Johnson's "handy man," 217–21; as advocate for the arts, 220–21, 388–89, 401; and Jenkins case, 224–27, 262, 450n147, 451n166; and requests for White House intercession, 229–30; refusal of to accept government position, 230–32; as Johnson's emissary in Dominican Republic crisis, 232–40, 452nn34, 38, 42, 453n49; as "C. J. Davidson," 237–39; Supreme Court appointment of, 241–48; concept of law of, 249–50, 276, 473n116; as advocate for juvenile offenders, 250–55, 456n9; as guardian of criminal rights, 255–57, 442n206; and alcoholism issue in *Powell* v. *Texas,* 257–60; as advocate for disenfranchised, 260–61; and right to privacy, 262–67; and reputation as champion of big business, 267–71, 333, 458n92; and civil rights cases, 260–61, 277–82; and draft-card burning, 282–84; and flag-desecration issue, 284–86; and *Tinker* v. *Des Moines School District,* 286–90; controversy surrounding symbolic speech opinions of, 291–92, 463n62; as Johnson's adviser on Vietnam, 293–300, 303–06, 464nn13, 14, 15, 466n67; concerns of for Israel, 300–302, 391; as Johnson's adviser on domestic issues, 306–10; and propriety of relationship with Johnson, 310–18, 337–40, 342, 354, 473n112; as Supreme Court justice, 319–20, 473n116; relationship of with Hugo Black, 320–22, 349, 372, 469n13, 470n20; financial concerns of, 322, 352–53, 376–77, 482n49; as consultant to Wolfson Foundation, 322–25, 360, 376–78, 393; as speaker on college campuses, 326; as leader of American University seminar, 326–27, 352; nominated as chief justice, 327–35, 475nn177, 178; appearance of before Judici-

Fortas, Abe (continued)
ary Committee, 335–42; obscenity rulings
of, 342–44; organized opposition to, 345–50;
further allegations against, 351–58; and
withdrawal of nomination, 355–58; and
problems arising from Wolfson connection,
360–65, 367–70, 373–78, 393–94; attempts
to force resignation of, 367–70; as speaker
on college campuses, 370–71, 382; resignation of, 372–76; and aftermath of resignation, 379–86; rejection of by law firm, 380–
82; return to private practice sought by,
385–86; as law partner with Howard Koven,
386–87; return of to private practice, 389–
92; relationship of with other justices after
resignation, 392, 484n102; reputation of as
justice, 393; feelings of toward Nixon, 394–
97; political concerns of, 397–98; death of,
401
Fortas, Carol Agger. *See* Agger, Carol
Fortas, Esta, 7, 9
Fortas, Joe, 7
Fortas, Mary, 8
Fortas, Meyer, 7, 8, 10
Fortas, Nelle, 7
Fortas, Rachel Berzansky, 7, 8, 10
Fortas, William (Woolfe), 7, 8, 9, 10
Fortas, Woolfe. *See* Fortas, William
Fortas & Koven, 387
*Fortson v. Morris,* 399
Frank, Florence, 245
Frank, Jerome, 17, 75, 101, 114, 245; as
counsel to the Agricultural Adjustment Ad-
ministration, 26, 28–34, 410n69; as admin-
istrator, 30–31; as influence on Fortas, 31–
32; and need for Fortas's assistance, 45, 46–
48; and Public Utilities Division, 62–64
Frank, John, 438n104
Frankel, Max, 370
Frankfurter, Felix, 27, 30, 34, 36, 140, 143,
244, 312–13, 403n5, 439n104, 469n5
Franklin, Benjamin, 356
Freedman, Walter, 415n101
Freeman, Milton, 60, 126, 137, 150, 151,
155, 430n20, 431n28
Freund, Paul, 392–93, 439n104
Freund Report, 393
Friant, Julien, 33
Friedman & Koven, 386, 387, 390
FTC. *See* Federal Trade Commission
Fuchs, Klaus, 127
Functionalism. *See* Legal realism

Galbraith, John Kenneth, 240, 350
Gardner, Warner, 80, 104, 106, 435n9
*Gardner v. Toilet Goods Association,* 269, 270
Garment, Leonard, 389, 391, 397
Garner, John Nance, 33
Gault, Gerald, 251–53, 456n9
Gellhorn, Walter, 103, 104, 106, 107
Gerbert, Elkin, 359–60, 364
Gesell, Gerhard, 19
Gideon, Clarence, 180–83
*Gideon's Trumpet* (Lewis), 183
Gilbert, Joseph, 178
*Ginsberg v. United States,* 343
Ginzburg, Ralph, 343
*Ginzburg v. United States,* 343, 344, 474n150
Goldberg, Arthur, 240–41, 245, 278–79, 313,
322, 356, 357
Goldman, Eric, 223–24, 450n156
Goldschmidt, Arthur ("Tex"), 73–74, 78, 79,
97–98, 100, 194, 199, 200, 229, 445n2
Goodwin, Richard, 220, 450n139
Gore, Albert, Sr., 98, 333
Graham, Fred, 375, 473n123
Gray, Horace, 332
Gray, Howard, 68, 70
Green, Edith, 396
Gregory, Dick, 462n41
*Gregory v. Chicago,* 462n41
Griffin, Robert, 331, 332, 333, 334, 337, 338,
350, 351, 355, 360, 366, 472n84
Griffiths, John, 252, 270, 271–72, 469n13
Griswold, Erwin, 160, 469n5
*Griswold v. Connecticut,* 261–62, 264–66
Gross, H. R., 372
Guzmán, Silvestre Antonio, 239

Haas, Saul, 73, 74, 105
Haldeman, H. R., 395
Hamilton, Walton, 18, 23, 50, 126, 188,
439n104
Hand, Augustus, 156
Hannegan, Robert, 114, 119, 120
Harlan, John, 142, 143, 182, 253, 274, 275,
285, 286, 320, 321, 349, 359, 484n102
Harlow, Bryce, 369
Harman, Avraham, 300, 301, 465nn36, 44
Harness, Forest Arthur, 104
Harper, Fowler, 110
*Harper v. Virginia Board of Elections,* 260
Harris, Edwin, 117
Harris, Seymour, 216
Hart, Philip, 339, 353, 355, 473n112

Hartman, Sigfried, 56, 57–58
Harvard Business School, 51, 413n13
*Harvard Law Review,* 268, 269, 280, 291
Harvard Law School: Fortas's application to, 13–14; advocacy of conceptualism at, 15–17
Hastie, William, 115
Hawaii, martial law in, 78, 79–80
Hayes, Joseph, 262
Healy, Robert, 62, 63, 64, 76
Heckscher, August, 325
Heinz, John, 160
Hellman, Lillian, 136
Henderson, Leon, 21, 66
Henkin, Louis, 291
Hernández Colón, Rafael, 399–400
Hickenlooper, Bourke, 146, 147–48
Hill, James, 262–64
Hill, Lister, 349
*Hillsborough Packing Company* v. *Henry Wallace,* 39–41
Hirshhorn, Joseph, 220, 380
Hiss, Alger, 127
Ho Chi Minh, 297, 464n15
Hoffa, Jimmy, 315, 469n123
Holtzoff, Alexander, 115, 139, 178
Hoover, J. Edgar, 313–16, 362–64, 382, 427n104, 478n15
Hopkins, Harry, 66
Horsky, Charles, 152, 162
House Committee on Un-American Activities (HUAC), 135, 144–45
Howrey, Edward, 156
HUAC. *See* House Committee on Un-American Activities
Hughes Aircraft, 390
Humane Slaughter Bill, 177, 207
Humphrey, Hubert, 208, 212, 307, 347, 388
*Hunter* v. *Erickson,* 470n20
Hussein, Ibn Talal, 300, 302

Ibn Saud, 105, 109
Ickes, Harold, 64, 77, 83, 85, 89, 99, 322, 416n5, 418n54, 421n66, 429n142; as Secretary of the Interior, 65–68; and Bituminous Coal Division, 68; and private utilities, 70–74; and differences with Homer Bone, 73–74; and consideration of Fortas for SEC, 75–76; and water resources issue, 79; and Japanese-American internment, 80; and coal miners' strike, 92–94, 96; as boss, 102, 106, 121; and Fortas draft deferment, 102–05, 424n14; anti-Semitism of, 103, 120,

424n14; and Fortas discharge, 107–08; and wish for Fortas's return, 108–10; and deteriorating relationship with Fortas, 110–13; and Fortas's resignation, 116; and opposition to Pauley nomination, 116–20
Ickes, Jane, 107, 416n5
Imbert Bareras, Antonio, 236
Impeachment: Fortas's alternative to, 396
Indigents: Fortas as advocate for, 180–83, 248
*In re Gault,* 251–53, 321, 456n9
Insanity: legal determination of, 178–80, 257–58
Interior, Department of: Ickes as secretary of, 65–68, 102; Bituminous Coal Division of, 68–69; and private utilities, 70–74; Fortas named under secretary of, 76; Bureau of Reclamation of, 79; and martial law in Hawaii, 79–80; and sovereignty issue in Pacific islands, 88–90; Fortas's style as under secretary of, 91–101; and coal regulation, 92–96, 111–12; Fortas's departure from, 102–08; Fortas's return to, 110–13; Fortas's resignation from, 113–16. *See also* Philippines; Puerto Rico; War Relocation Authority
Internal Revenue Service, 360, 361, 366, 367
Irons, Peter, 483n88
Israel: Fortas as friend to, 300–302, 391, 465nn36, 44
Istomin, Eugene, 379, 401
Istomin, Marta Casals, 176, 194

Jackson, Henry, 174
Jackson, Robert H., 140, 141, 142, 438n104
Janeway, Elliot, 100, 105, 108, 109, 112, 114
Japanese-Americans, internment of, 78, 80–82, 92
Javits, Jacob, 346, 382
Jenkins, Walter, 206, 207, 222; charged with disorderly conduct, 224–27, 450n147, 451n166
Jenner, Albert, 328
Johnson, Lady Bird, 161, 195, 199, 200, 201, 204, 205, 217, 222, 224, 231, 241, 244, 313, 334, 357, 388; and Fortas's resignation, 375–76; on Fortas memorial service, 401
Johnson, Lynda Bird, 161
Johnson, Lyndon, 117, 163, 196, 446n8, 448n104; as Fortas's friend, 98, 100, 107, 161–62, 199–200, 317, 484n116; as advocate for Puerto Rico, 168–69; and 1948 Senate election, 200–202, 446n8; Fortas as

Johnson, Lyndon (continued)
  adviser to, 200–202, 222–27, 228–30, 306–
  10, 387–88, 449n132, 483n53; Fortas's relationship with, 202–07, 317–18; presidential
  aspirations of, 208–09; efforts of on behalf
  of associates, 209–10, 221; and EEOC, 210–
  11; first speech to Congress as President,
  212–13; reform efforts of, 213–17; Fortas as
  "handy man" for, 217–21; relationship of
  with Kennedy family, 223, 306, 313–17; and
  Fortas's refusal to accept attorney general
  post, 230–32; and Dominican Republic
  crisis, 232–40, 452nn34, 38, 453n54; and
  Fortas's appointment as Supreme Court justice, 241–47; Fortas as adviser to during
  Vietnam war, 293–300, 303–06, 464nn13,
  15, 466n67; and Six-Day War, 301–02,
  466n57; and propriety of friendship with
  Fortas, 310–18, 337–40, 342, 354, 357; and
  Fortas-Thornberry nominations, 327–33,
  356–57, 471n54; as supporter of Fortas
  nomination for chief justice, 334–35, 349–
  50; reaction of to Fortas's resignation, 376,
  378
Johnson, Luci Baines, 330
*Johnson v. Avery,* 255
*Joint Anti-Fascist Refugee Committee v.
  McGrath,* 140–41
Jones, Jesse, 66
Judaism: significance of to Fortas, 8, 14, 82–
  83, 194, 300, 391, 401. *See also* Anti-
  Semitism
Judicial disqualification, 164–65, 438n104
Judiciary Committee (House): and Nixon im-
  peachment hearings, 395–96
Judiciary Committee (Senate): Fortas's ap-
  pearance before, 335–42, 357–58; obscenity
  cases as issue for, 342–45, 353; Fortas's
  refusal to reappear, 351; and Wolfson case,
  360
Jurisprudence: theories of, 15–18, 29. *See also*
  Legal realism
Justice Department: investigation of Wolfson,
  359–60; investigation of Fortas, 362–64,
  366–70
Juvenile offenders: Fortas as advocate for, 250–
  55, 456n9

Kaiser-Frazer Corporation, 155–56
Kalven, Harry, 278
Karon, Sheldon, 390–92
Katzenbach, Nicholas, 162–63, 184, 185, 216,

  217, 241, 247–48, 317, 356, 466n67; and
  Fred Black case, 313, 314, 315, 316, 317
Kennedy, John F., 145, 212–14, 294, 338;
  Fortas's attitude toward, 207–09, 212; and
  EEOC, 210; assassination of, 212, 217–18
Kennedy, Joseph P., 59, 208
Kennedy, Robert, 211, 223, 295, 306, 313,
  314–16
Kennedy Center, 221, 223, 388–89, 394, 401
Kenny, Robert, 109
Kent, Morris, 251
*Kent v. United States,* 251
Kerner Commission, 467n93
Keyserling, Leon, 27, 43, 386
Keyserling, Mary, 137, 449n133
Kiker, Douglas, 370
King, Martin Luther, Jr., 281, 282
Kintner, Robert, 56, 62, 415n81
*Kirkpatrick v. Preisler,* 261
Kleindienst, Richard, 363
Knox, Frank, 97, 107–08, 425n48
Kollek, Teddy, 300
Korth, Fred, 209–10
Koven, Howard, 386–88, 392, 400
Krash, Abe, 179, 182, 183, 188, 189, 212, 243
Kreeger, David Lloyd, 68–69, 70, 317
Kreuger and Toll Company, 56
Krock, Arthur, 119
Kroger Company, 176

Laboy, Luis, 218–19
Lambert, William, 360–65, 367, 369
Landau, Jack, 367
Landis, James, 32, 59, 74, 403n5
Langdell, Christopher Columbus, 15–17
Lattimore, Eleanor, 145–47
Lattimore, Owen, 145–50, 148–50, 162, 185,
  434nn114, 118
Law-Business program, 51–52, 413n13
Lawrence, Alexander, 330, 472n73
Lazarus, Fred, 157, 176, 211, 216, 246, 298,
  333
Lazarus, Irma, 229
Lazarus, Maurice, 157, 158, 216, 298, 326,
  333, 351, 452n34
Lazarus, Ralph, 158, 160, 164, 216, 299, 339,
  341
Lazarus, Simon, 228, 467n73
Lea, Clarence, 55
Leavy, Charles, 424n148
Lee, Higginson Corporation, 56–58
Legal realism: as theory of law, 15–18, 23; and

the New Deal, 29; in peach marketing agreement case, 37–38; as issue at Yale Law School, 49–50; and the Supreme Court, 249, 271–76

Lerner, Max, 23

Leventhal, Harold, 68, 70

Lever Brothers, 119, 155, 158, 176

Levitt, Daniel, 250, 325

Levy, Arnold, 68, 69,. 70

Levy, Gustave, 322, 326, 345, 351, 352

Lewis, Anthony, 183, 474n150

Lewis, John L., 68, 383, 426n87; and coal miners' strike, 92–93, 96; offended by Fortas statement, 111–12

*Life* magazine, 397; as defendant in *Time* v. *Hill*, 262–64, 266; and Fortas-Wolfson connection, 360–65

Lilienthal, David, 71, 72, 73

Lincoln, Abraham, 338

Ling, James P., 375

Linowitz, Sol, 325

Littell, Norman, 97

Llewellyn, Karl, 249, 455n1

Loeb, John, 161, 301, 302, 305, 326, 351, 386, 390, 466n47

Long, Russell, 329

Louchheim, Katie, 53, 483n88

Louisiana: breach of peace statutes in, 278–81

Lovett, Robert Morss, 97

*Loving* v. *Virginia,* 320

Loyalty boards, 127–33, 431n32; Arnold, Fortas & Porter's strategy for, 133–37; reviewed by courts, 138–43, 433n95

Luce, Henry, 83

Macaulay, Stewart, 159

McCarran, Pat, 148–50

McCarran Internal Security Act, 128

McCarthy, Joseph, 144–51, 306, 383, 434n118

McClellan, John, 329, 338, 341, 344–45, 353

McCloy, John, 77, 78, 80, 88, 91, 100, 112

McCollester, Parker, 160

McDougal, Myres, 50–51

McGovern, George, 394

McGowan, R. A., 87

McGrath, J. Howard, 139, 140–41

McKinney, Preston, 34–35

MacLean, Donald, 410n67

McLean, Evalyn Walsh, 204

McMurray, Howard, 100, 106

M'Naghten rule, 178–80, 258, 259

McNamara, Margy, 161

McNamara, Robert, 161, 295, 301, 304, 388, 452n38, 464n13

McPherson, Harry, 204, 205, 217, 221, 222, 307–08, 347, 355

McReynolds, James, 274

Macrory, Patrick, 158, 191, 192, 195, 246

Macy, John, 218

Magruder, Calvert, 172–73

*Mallory* v. *United States,* 310, 340

Manchester, William, 223

Mann, Tom, 239

Mansfield, Mike, 331–32, 354

Marcus, Stanley, 161, 176, 322

Marshall, J. Howard, 101

Marshall, Thurgood, 319, 356, 399, 400

Martin, John Bartlow, 235, 236, 453nn49, 57

Mary James, Sister, 229

Mathews, George, 62, 63, 64

Medina, Harold, 165

Meredith, James, 284–85

Merritt-Chapman & Scott, 359–60, 363

*Meyer* v. *Nebraska,* 274, 275

Meyers, Ernest, 23, 246

Miller, Jack, 343

Miller, Merle, 206, 484n88

Mimieux, Yvette, 317

Minton, Sherman, 142

*Miranda* v. *Arizona,* 255–56

Mitchell, John, 362, 363, 367–70, 479n44

Moore, Underhill, 17–18, 23, 411n96

*Mora* v. *Torres,* 172

Morgenthau, Henry, 66, 83, 114

Morgenthau, Robert, 359, 360

Morse, Wayne, 333, 386; and coal miners' strike, 93–96

Moscoso, Teodoro, 175–76, 219, 423n136

Moyers, Bill, 224

Muller, Helen, 193, 371

Muller, Theodor, 185, 193, 467n71

Muñoz Marín, Inés, 167, 254

Muñoz Marín, Luis, 85–86, 110, 218, 234, 237, 319, 333, 356, 358, 398; as governor of Puerto Rico, 166–76, 440n145

Murphy, Bruce, 484n88

Murray, James, 173

Muskie, Edmund, 395

Myer, Dillon, 80, 82, 83, 92

Nader, Ralph, 389, 482n33

Nasser, Gamal Abdel, 300

National Investors Company, 58

National Labor Relations Board, 216, 269–70
National Power Policy Committee (NPPC), 71
National Reclamation Act of 1902, 78
National Recovery Administration (NRA), 29, 30, 34, 35, 69
Navasky, Victor, 385, 389
Navy, U.S.: Fortas's enlistment in, 105–08, 425n50
Nelson, Richard, 229
Nelson, Robert, 444n21
New Deal: as influence on Fortas, 3, 27, 28, 32, 65, 130, 131, 270; and legal realism, 29
New Progressive Party (NPP), 398
*New Republic,* 78
*New York Times* v. *Sullivan,* 262
Nickerson, Albert, 339
Nitist Club, 12
Nixon, Richard M., 207, 210, 263, 331, 377–78, 388, 389, 433n89; as opponent of Fortas nomination as chief justice, 345–46, 475n177; and Fortas investigation, 362–63; attempts of to force Fortas's resignation, 366–70; Fortas's attitude toward, 382, 394–97; resignation of, 396–97
Norris, George, 73
Northeastern University, 370, 371
NPPC. *See* National Power Policy Committee
NRA. *See* National Recovery Administration

OAS. *See* Organization of American States
O'Brian, John Lord, 431n28
O'Brien, David, 282, 283, 461n35
O'Brien, Robert, 75
Obscenity cases: as issue in Fortas confirmation hearings, 342–45, 353
O'Dwyer, Paul, 347
Olds, Leland, 71, 72, 206
O'Mahoney, Joseph Christopher, 168
*Ordeal by Slander* (Lattimore), 150
Organization of American States (OAS), 232, 233, 452n39
Otis and Company, 155–56
Overholser, Winfred, 180

Pacific islands: and trusteeship issue, 88–90, 421n80
Page, Dorothy, 229
Parr, George, 159, 200, 209
Parvin Foundation, 324, 366, 374
Patterson, Cissy, 204
Paul, Randolph, 83, 106, 114, 160, 186
Pauley, Edwin: nominated as under secretary

of the Navy, 116–20, 428nn133, 141
PAW. *See* Petroleum Administration for War
Peach marketing agreement, 34–39
Pearson, Drew, 145, 146, 147
Peek, George, 31, 408n23
*Pentagon Papers, The,* 387–88
*People* v. *Stafford Packing Company,* 37
Percy, Charles, 389
Peres, Hardwig, 10, 13
Peres, Israel, 10, 13
Perlman, Philip B., 140
Peters, John, 141–43
Petersen, Henry, 367, 368, 369
Petroleum Administration for War (PAW), 101
Philippines: Fortas's concerns for, 84
Phillips, Cabell, 114
Pierce, Walter, 72, 73
Pierson, DeVier, 354
Piute Pete, 229
Pollak, Louis, 185, 275, 333–34
Pollak, Walter, 25
Poor Debtor Court (Boston), 21
Popular Democratic Party (PDP), 398
Porter, Paul, 118, 119, 120, 126, 131, 200, 201, 202, 216, 228, 241, 245, 326–27, 361, 374, 380, 381, 382, 431n27, 481n15; and Bailey case, 138–40; on government influence, 161; as Fortas's law partner, 184, 185, 186; and Fortas nomination as chief justice, 333, 334, 335, 345–57, 348, 350–53, 355; Justice Department investigation of, 366–67, 374. *See also* Arnold, Fortas & Porter; Arnold & Porter
Post, Troy, 229, 326, 351, 353
Pound, Ezra, 130
*Powell* v. *Texas,* 257–60, 321
Power, Division of, 71–74
Pressman, Lee, 30–31
Prichard, Edward, 115
Privacy, right to, 261–67
Procter and Gamble, 164
Progressive politicians: as force for reform, 2–3, 22–23, 250
Protective Committee Study, 53–61
Public Utilities Division, 61–64
Public Utilities Holding Company Act of 1935, 61–63
Public Works Administration (PWA), 67
Puerto Rico: Fortas's reform efforts on behalf of, 84–87, 98–99, 423n136; Fortas as advocate for, 153, 166–77, 218, 388, 398–400, 439n120; political status of, 169–75, 398–99, 440nn142, 145

PWA. *See* Public Works Administration

Quezon, Manuel, 84

Racial unrest, 277–82, 284–86, 307–09, 467nn90, 93
Rauh, Joseph, 136, 150, 153, 154, 206, 350, 365
Rayburn, Sam, 100
Reagan, Ronald, 345, 398
Reapportionment, 247, 260–61
Reconstruction Finance Corporation, 47
Reed, Stanley, 140, 142
Reedy, George, 205, 206, 222
Reich, Charles, 159, 189, 385, 386
Reis, Harold, 174
Reorganization Act of *1939*, 68
Reynolds, Donald, 222
*Reynolds* v. *Sims*, 260–61
Ribicoff, Abraham, 334–35, 482n33
Richardson, Seth, 138
Riger, Martin, 194, 386, 414n67
Ripley, Dillon, 220
Rittmaster, Alexander, 359, 360
Rivers, L. Mendel, 282
Robb, Charles ("Chuck"), 161
Robinson, Joe, 471n54
*Robinson* v. *California*, 257–59
Rodell, Fred, 474n150, 475n178
Rogers, William, 156, 165, 185
Romney, George, 307–09
Roosevelt, Eleanor, 89–90, 210
Roosevelt, Franklin D., 27, 33, 84, 212, 213, 214, 217, 383, 408n10; Ickes's relationship with, 66; and transfer of PWA functions, 67; considers Fortas for SEC commissionership, 75; appoints Fortas as under secretary of interior, 76; and Japanese-American internment, 82; and War Refugee Board, 83; and Puerto Rico issue, 86; and coal miners' strike, 93–96; and Fortas draft deferment, 104; on Fortas's departure from Interior, 106; and Fortas's return to Interior, 109–10; names Arnold to court of appeals, 125
Rose, Leonard, 401
Rosenberg, Ethel, 127
Rosenberg, Julius, 127
Rosenbloom, David, 257–58
Rosenman, Samuel, 66
Rostow, Eugene, 52, 69, 81, 312, 380, 463n62
Rostow, Walt, 388
Rostropovich, Mstislav, 401
Rovere, Richard, 139, 184

Rowe, Elizabeth, 200
Rowe, James, 168, 200, 202–03, 205, 207, 208, 403n5
Rusk, Dean, 295, 301, 312
Russell, Richard, 327–28, 329–30, 332, 356, 471n73, 472n84
Russell Sage Foundation, 325–26
Russia. *See* Soviet Union

S & W Straus, 54
Sabath, Adolf, 54, 55
St. Sure, Adolphus, 38
Salinger, Pierre, 220
Sánchez Vilella, Roberto, 167, 168, 169, 439n120
Sanders, Harold ("Barefoot"), 332, 350, 355
San Francisco Charter, 89, 90
*Schackman* v. *California*, 342–44, 353
Schlesinger, Arthur, 467n72
*Schmerber* v. *California*, 256
Schneider, Alexander, 193, 246, 317, 391
Schroetel, Stanley, 91
Schwinn Company, 270–71
Scorsese, Martin, 388
Securities and Exchange Commission (SEC), 30; Fortas's decision to work for, 46–48; Protective Committee Study for, 53–61; Public Utilities Division of, 61–64; Fortas considered for, 75–76; and Wolfson case, 322, 325, 359–60, 369, 393–94
Seib, Charles, 225–26, 227, 451n174
Seligman, Joel, 484n88
Sevareid, Eric, 130, 378, 401
Shaffer, Samuel, 349, 368–69
Shogan, Robert, 369, 370, 472n84
Shtokalo, I. Z., 172
Siddal, Robert B., 443n18
Sidey, Hugh, 464n13
Simon, James, 60
Simon, William, 153
Six-Day War, 300–302
Slattery, Harry, 76
Slocombe, Walter, 321
Smathers, George, 333, 335
Smigel, Erwin, 444n26
Smith, Beverly, 42, 43
Smith, Harold, 114
Smith, Paul, 326, 351, 353
Smith, Roy, 62–63, 64, 415n93
Smith Act, 129
Snyder, John, 429n141
*Snyder* v. *Harris*, 272–73
Sobeloff, Simon, 143

Sonnenberg, Benjamin, 326
Sorenson, Theodore, 212, 213, 214
South Side High School, 10
Southwestern College: Fortas as student at,
    10–13
Soviet Union: Fortas's concerns regarding, 90,
    295, 297
Speech, symbolic, 282–92, 461n32
Standard Oil, 97, 110
State Street Furniture v. Armour Company, 20,
    22
Stern, Isaac, 177, 192–93, 220, 245, 302,
    303, 317, 379, 390, 401, 450n141
Stettinius, Edward, 105, 425n34
Stevens, Roger, 220, 221, 223, 389, 401,
    483n67
Stevenson, Adlai, 162, 195, 240
Stevenson, Coke, 200
Stewart, Potter, 183, 254–55, 259, 271, 274,
    281, 311, 319, 320, 373, 469n13
Stimson, Henry, 33, 66, 77
Stolz, Colie, 9
Stone, Harlan Fiske, 165, 335, 420n38
Straus, Michael, 98, 112–13, 424n14
Street, Sidney, 284–86
Street v. New York, 284–86
Stromberg v. California, 279
Sturges, Wesley, 18, 26, 47, 50, 60
Subversive Activities Control Board, 330–31
Sullivan & Cromwell, 56, 58
Supreme Court, U.S.: Fortas as attorney be-
    fore, 157, 183, 392; Fortas appointed to,
    241–48; as interpreter of law, 249–50; and
    rights of juveniles, 250–55; and rights of
    criminals, 255–60; and right to vote, 260–
    61; and reapportionment, 260–61; and right
    to privacy, 261–67; and antitrust cases,
    267–71; legal realism of, 271–76; and civil
    rights protests, 277–82; and symbolic
    speech, 282–92; Fortas's feeling toward,
    319–20, 322, 473n116; Fortas nominated as
    chief justice of, 327–56; Black's concerns
    for, 359; Fortas's resignation from, 372–76;
    Freund Report for, 393
Supreme Court of Puerto Rico, 398
Symington, Stuart, 169, 207, 208–09, 333,
    473n97

Tatum v. United States, 178, 179
Taylor, Hobart, 210
Taylor, Paul, 78, 79, 218
Tennery, B. J., 326, 351, 352

Terminiello v. Chicago, 288
Tet offensive, 305
Theoharis, Athan, 313
Thomas, Norman, 12
Thornberry, Homer, 327–33, 335, 342, 355,
    356, 471n54
Thorpe, Elliot, 147–48
Throop, Allen, 52, 60
"Thurman Arnold and the Theatre of the
    Law" (Fortas), 384–85
Thurmond, Strom, 338, 340–41, 342–43,
    345, 352, 366
Tigar, Michael, 313–14
Time v. Hill, 262–67, 321, 362
Tinker v. Des Moines School District, 286–90,
    321
Title, legal concept of, 271
Tobey, Charles, 117, 118, 119
Tolson, Charles, 117, 118, 119
Tolson, Clyde, 314–16
Trampler, Walter, 193, 379, 401
Trías Monge, José, 167–68, 170, 171, 172–73,
    399, 440n142
Troutman, Robert, 211
Truman, Harry, 114, 338, 422n89; and Pauley
    nomination, 116–17; loyalty program of,
    126–33, 144
Trust Indenture Act of 1939, 55
Tugwell, Rexford G., 30, 31, 32–33, 77, 153,
    387, 411n96, 435nn8, 9; as governor of
    Puerto Rico, 85–86, 98–99
Twentieth Century Fund, 325
Tydings, Joseph, 143, 146–47, 148
Tydings, Millard E., 84

United Nations: Fortas's attitude toward, 87–
    90; Goldberg appointed ambassador to, 241
United Palestine Appeal, 83
United States v. Arnold, Schwinn and Company,
    270–71
United States v. O'Brien, 282–84, 461n32
United States v. Wade, 256
United States v. Yazell, 321
United Steel Workers of America v. R. H.
    Bouligny, 320
Untermeyer, Eugene, 56, 57
Untermeyer, Samuel, 56, 57
USSR. See Soviet Union
Utilities: regulation of, 61–64, 70–74

Vaca v. Sipes, 269–70
Valenti, Jack, 218, 221, 224, 230

Van Buren, Abigail, 391
Vance, Cyrus, 307
Vieth, G. Duane, 136, 156, 159, 162, 187
Vietnam war: protests against as Supreme Court issue, 282–84, 286–90; Fortas as Johnson's adviser on, 293–300, 303–06, 464nn13, 14, 15
Vinson, Fred, 140, 142, 338
Vote, right to: Fortas's opinions regarding, 260–61

Walker, Harry, 326
*Walker v. Birmingham,* 281
Wallace, Henry, 31, 39, 66, 240, 427n95
War Labor Board: and coal miners' strike, 93–96, 423n120
Warnke, Paul, 157, 437n73
War Refugee Board, 83
War Relocation Authority (WRA), 80–83, 92
Warren, Earl, 142, 143, 181, 253, 254, 263, 274, 280, 359, 373, 393, 399, 484n102; as chairman of commission on Kennedy assassination, 217–18; and *U.S. v. O'Brien,* 282–83, 461n35, 462n36; proposed resignation of, 327–28, 331, 332, 348, 356; Mitchell's meeting with, 367–68, 479n44
Warren Court, 340–41, 346, 348
Washington School of Psychiatry, 177
Watergate scandal, 395–97
Watson, Marvin, 313, 316
Wechsler, Herbert, 92
Weisl, Edwin, 317
Wessin y Wessin, Elias, 232, 236
West, Charles, 76
Westwood, Howard, 27
White, Byron, 259, 265, 314, 338

White, Edward, 332, 335
White, William S., 210, 481n1
Whitehair, Francis P., 39, 40, 410n73
Wickenden, Elizabeth, 200, 247
William Alanson White Foundation, 178
Williams, Edward Bennett, 222, 344, 363, 386
Williams, John, 366
Wilson, Will, 362, 363, 367, 369
Wilson, Woodrow, 19, 29, 333
Winslow, Barbara, 371, 372, 374
Wiprud, Arne, 125
Wiretapping, 256–57; as issue in Black case, 312–15
Wirtz, Alvin, 76, 200–201
Wise, David, 388
Wofford, Harris, 210
Wolfson, Louis, 322–25, 393–94; as factor in Fortas's resignation, 359–65, 367–70, 373–78, 477n9
Wolfson Family Foundation, 323–25, 360, 364, 365, 367, 368, 393
Woodward, Bob, 393–94
Wright, Charles Alan, 273
Wyzanksi, Charles, 366

*Yale Law Journal:* Fortas as editor of, 17, 23, 24–25, 407n110; consumer credit issue of, 21, 25; tribute to Thurman Arnold in, 384–85
Yale Law School: Fortas's admission to, 13–14; Fortas as student at, 14–20, 405n56; Fortas as professor at, 49–53

Zinn, Howard, 292